CW01664357

The sources of social power

VOLUME 3

Global empires and revolution, 1890–1945

Distinguishing four sources of power in human societies – ideological, economic, military, and political – this series traces their interrelations throughout history. This third volume of Michael Mann's analytical history of social power begins with nineteenth-century global empires and continues with a global history of the twentieth century up to 1945. Mann focuses on the interrelated development of capitalism, nation-states, and empires. Volume 3 discusses the "Great Divergence" between the fortunes of the West and the rest of the world; the self-destruction of European and Japanese power in two world wars; the Great Depression; the rise of American and Soviet power; the rivalry between capitalism, socialism, and fascism; and the triumph of a reformed and democratic capitalism.

Michael Mann is Distinguished Professor of Sociology at the University of California, Los Angeles. He is the author of *Power in the 21st Century: Conversations with John Hall* (2011), *Incoherent Empire* (2003), and *Fascists* (Cambridge 2004). His book *The Dark Side of Democracy* (Cambridge 2004) was awarded the Barrington Moore Award of the American Sociological Association for the best book in comparative and historical sociology in 2006.

The sources of social power

VOLUME 3

Global empires and revolution, 1890–1945

MICHAEL MANN
University of California, Los Angeles

CAMBRIDGE
UNIVERSITY PRESS

CAMBRIDGE UNIVERSITY PRESS
Cambridge, New York, Melbourne, Madrid, Cape Town,
Singapore, São Paulo, Delhi, Mexico City

Cambridge University Press
32 Avenue of the Americas, New York, NY 10013-2473, USA

www.cambridge.org
Information on this title: www.cambridge.org/9781107655478

© Michael Mann 2012

This publication is in copyright. Subject to statutory exception
and to the provisions of relevant collective licensing agreements,
no reproduction of any part may take place without the written
permission of Cambridge University Press.

First published 2012

Printed in the United States of America

A catalog record for this publication is available from the British Library.

Library of Congress Cataloging in Publication data
Mann, Michael, 1942–
The sources of social power / Michael Mann.
v. cm.
Contents: v. 1. A history of power from the beginning to AD 1760 – v. 2. The rise of classes and nation-states, 1760–1914 – v. 3. Global empires and revolution, 1890–1945 – v. 4. Globalizations, 1945–2011.
Includes bibliographical references and index.
ISBN 978-1-107-03117-3 (hardback : v. 1) – ISBN 978-1-107-63597-5 (pbk. : v. 1) –
ISBN 978-1-107-03118-0 (hardback : v. 2) – ISBN 978-1-107-67064-8 (pbk. : v. 2) –
ISBN 978-1-107-02865-4 (hardback : v. 3) – ISBN 978-1-107-65547-8 (pbk. : v. 3) –
ISBN 978-1-107-02867-8 (hardback : v. 4) – ISBN 978-1-107-61041-5 (pbk. : v. 4)
1. Social history. 2. Power (Social sciences) I. Title.
HN8.M28 2012
306.09–dc23 2012028452

ISBN 978-1-107-02865-4 Hardback
ISBN 978-1-107-65547-8 Paperback

Cambridge University Press has no responsibility for the persistence or accuracy of URLs for external or third-party Internet Web sites referred to in this publication and does not guarantee that any content on such Web sites is, or will remain, accurate or appropriate.

Contents

Preface

I embarked on this project in the early 1980s, intent on producing a single book on power relations in human societies. It was intended to contain a few empirical case studies that would accompany some theoretical reflections on power. However, the case studies grew and grew into a four-volume historical narrative of power relations. Volume 1, published in 1986, contained a history of power in human societies from the beginning to just before the Industrial Revolution. At that point, I intended to produce only a second volume that would bring the story up to the present time. That volume also grew uncontrollably, and indeed, when it was published in 1993, it only covered the most advanced countries of the world in the period 1760–1914. I have been at work on Volumes 3 and 4 since 1993 – although my work was interrupted by several forays that produced books on fascism, ethnic cleansing, and American foreign policy. In Volume 3, I decided I had to rectify an omission in Volume 2, the neglect of the global empires created by the most advanced countries. These are, of course, essential for an understanding of modern societies. Consequently, this present volume starts in the empires well before 1914 and finishes in 1945. This meant that a Volume 4 would be necessary, taking my narrative of power from 1945 to the present day. As I have been working on these two volumes alongside each other, Volume 4 will be published a few months after this one.

I hope the reader will excuse this story of much-delayed culmination. I am an incurable empiricist who must support every generalization made with a mass of supporting data. This has involved a great deal of research.

I would like to thank numerous people for the aid they have given me in writing this book. Above all, I want to thank John A. Hall, friend and ever-supportive critic of everything I write. Ralph Schroeder, too, has been a great help and critic. Bill Domhoff has been extraordinarily helpful for years in sharing his profound historical knowledge of American policy making. He has helped greatly with Chapter 8. Barry Eichengreen provided helpful comments on Chapter 7 and reassured me that I had roughly understood the work of economists on the Great Depression.

I have been a Professor at the University of California at Los Angeles throughout the writing of this book. I am grateful to the Department of Sociology for providing me with such a congenial and collegial academic home and to the Department and the University for its generosity in providing me with research funds and time off for writing. I have also been privileged to have taught many talented UCLA students. In my classes, we have often discussed topics contained in this volume, and included in the weekly reading have been several draft chapters of this volume. They may not realize how much their papers and the general class discussions have helped me improve my arguments.

I should also acknowledge the stimulation provided by the Sociology 237 seminar, begun by Ivan Szelenyi and continued by myself and my colleagues Rogers Brubaker, Andreas Wimmer, and CK Lee. Bob Brenner and Perry Anderson have been a constant source of stimulation in the seminar series of the Center for Social Theory and Comparative History, as have the distinguished scholars invited to the Center to present papers. Conveniently for me, these have touched upon most of the topics considered in this book, so they helped me understand them better. The reader will note the large number of works cited in my bibliography. Reading them would not have been possible without UCLA's wonderful University Research Library, now renamed the Charles E. Young Research Library.

Nicky Hart has been my main source of support for more than thirty years, and she and our children, Louise, Gareth, and Laura, have helped make my life worth living.

1 Introduction

The third volume of my history of power in human society concerns the period of history leading up to 1945. However, I cannot put a precise starting date on this period because two different timescales are involved. My second volume, on the advanced industrializing countries, ended in 1914, so here I resume their domestic stories in 1914, although I go back a little further in the cases of the United States and Japan. I am also concerned here with global empires, which I neglected in my second volume. This involves the second, much longer, timescale, starting well before 1914. We will also see that the years 1914–1945 must not be seen as a period quite apart, an island of chaos amid a sea of tranquility; its crises were the culmination of long-standing structural tendencies of modern Western civilization.

The main story in both periods is that globalizations were well under way. Note the plural: there was more than one process of globalization. As I have argued throughout my volumes, human societies form around four distinct power sources – ideological, economic, military and political – that have a relative degree of autonomy from each other (this is my IEMP model of power). So what is generally called globalization (singular) actually involved the plural extension of relations of ideological, economic, military, and political power across the world.

Around these sources congeal the major power organizations of human societies. In this period, the most fundamental were *capitalism*, *empires*, and *nation-states*. Modern globalization has involved three main institutional processes, the globalization of capitalism, the globalization of the nation-state, and the globalization of multiple empires (eventually replaced by just one empire, the American empire). All three – capitalism, nation-states and empires – interacted and were transformed. During this period, capitalism steamed ahead through what Schumpeter called *creative destruction*: empires rose and then were beginning to fall; the replacements would prove to be multiple nation-states, yielding uneven bundles of citizen rights to the masses. The big picture of this period in the advanced countries is that the masses were leaping onstage in the theater of power – concentrated in cities and factories, conscripted in mass armies, mobilized by demotic ideologies and mass parties. Yet this contrasted greatly with the colonies, where the masses were only just beginning to stir.

So although globalization proceeded apace, it was geographically and institutionally *polymorphous* – that is, it crystallized in different, competing forms.

Put most simply, the boundaries of the three networks of interaction – and those of the four sources of social power – differed. The global expansion of rivalrous empires did not unite the world but divided it into segments; the rivalry of nation-states fractured international regulation and led to terrible sundering wars. European civilization rose but then fell as a result of its own hubris. Hence, my title, *Global Empires and Revolution, 1890–1945* – plural and divisive, the core subject matter of this volume. After 1945, the empires were collapsing and most nation-states were turning swords into ploughshares, soldering the world back together again. Therefore, my fourth volume will be entitled *Globalizations* – still plural but tending toward greater integration of the globe.

Capitalism, empires, and nation-states also generated contending ideologies. Capitalism generated ideologies of class and class conflict, some of them revolutionary but most of them compromised by the winning by the people of civil, political, and social citizenships rights – as specified by T.H. Marshall in the 1940s – although women lagged well behind men in this achievement, as did some ethnic/racial groups. Citizenship strengthened nation-states, capitalism became ever-more global and transnational, and the contradiction between national and transnational relations intensified. Empires generated ideologies of imperialism, anti-imperialism, and racism. Nation-states generated ideologies of nationalism, some of which became extremely aggressive. The conflicts between some of these ideologies peaked in two world wars, after which their relations became less warlike, with most disputes resolvable by "soft" negotiation rather than by "hard" war. However, civil wars over who exactly constitutes "the nation" still dominated some swathes of the world. All these conflicts generated highly ideological global movements, in this period secular as well as religious. So globalization has never been a singular integrating process; instead, it has been a series of disparate and uneven outward thrusts into the world, generating some integration but also fractures and a series of ever-more global crises.

My second volume, dealing with the period from 1760 to 1914, focused on what I called the "leading edge of power," the capitalism and nation-states then found principally in Europe and North America. Here I continue my focus on the leading edge of power, which through this period comprised the United States, Western Europe, the Soviet Union, China, and Japan. Some of my chapters focus on a particular country or region; others are more broadly comparative. They blend historical narrative with theoretical concepts and explanations. I reintroduce empires into my narrative because they were the main vehicle through which the power of the West (later joined by Japan and the Soviet Union) extended globally. To better understand empires, I begin my empirical analysis by backtracking well before 1914 to discuss the development of three empires: British, Japanese, and American. The last one is still with us, the only global empire there has ever been.

To write a history of power in the modern world may seem absurdly ambitious. Societies are complex, and there is a massive oversupply of information about the period, outstripping anyone's capacity to absorb it. Flaubert observed that, "Writing history is like drinking an ocean and pissing a cupful." The techniques of historical sociology enable me to take a shortcut through identifying the main social-structural trends of societies, and this enables me to drink less but thicker liquid. What follows is not straightforward historical narrative. It mixes doses of narrative, which may appeal more to historians, with doses of theory and comparative analysis, which provide the staple of macro-sociology. I seek to explain the development, expansion, and variety of the fundamental power structures of the period: the triumph of capitalism and of the nation-state; the rise and fall of empires, fascism, state socialism, and all their ideologies; and the growing destructive capacity of warfare and economies. By half-closing our eyes, it is possible to construct an onward-and-upward evolutionary story of the twentieth century, and this is often done. Have not capitalism and nation-states brought increased life expectancy, literacy, and prosperity to much of the world, and are they not still doing so? Has not class conflict been successfully compromised by the institutions of citizenship? Has not war given way to peace for much of the world? Finally, have not capitalism and democracy seen off both state socialism and fascism and extended their penetration of the world? One might even be tempted by all this to devise a *nomological* (law-like) explanation of the period, providing laws of modern evolutionary development.

This is not possible for three reasons, however. First, the period from 1914 to 1945 was a very uneven experience even in the advanced countries. They twice fought terrible world wars, but they also made love between times; they experienced both reforms and revolutions, and one Great Depression disrupted what would otherwise have been a period of almost continuous economic progress. These were the three Great Disruptions of the period. Second, the previously presented trends are all rather Western-centric, because other parts of the world did not go through most of these sequences. Third, although the "West" and the "Rest" did exhibit structural tendencies, other major influences and outcomes were contingent, double-edged, and subject to reversal. The world did not form a single whole. Capitalism, nation-states, empires, wars, and ideologies had distinct logics of development, but each interacted with and was intermittently thrown off course by the others. Long-term structural tendencies interact with period-specific problems and human adaptability to generate new patterns of human behavior. Humans are not fully rational, steering their projects steadily in achievement of their goals. Their creativity, emotions, miscalculations, and misadventures often upset instrumental reasoning and broad secular tendencies.

Thus, processes of globalization have been punctuated by a series of unexpected world-changing crises – that is, events whose extreme urgency was self-evident at the time but that could not be solved through existing institutions. The most important crises discussed in this volume are World War I, the Great Depression, and World War II. My fourth volume will continue this theme by discussing Mutually Assured Destruction (MAD), the Great Neoliberal Recession of 2008, and Climate Change. These last three crises still hang over us.

We shall see that these structural crises had multiple causes and stages cascading on top of each other in unexpected and unfortunate ways. They were contingent because different causal chains, each one of which we can trace and explain quite well, came together in a way that we cannot explain in terms of either of them, yet which proved timely for the outcome. In these crisis cases, the timing was bad for the world. What we call a major crisis is not really a singular event, although it has a culminating peak, for it piled up together a series of smaller crises with different causes. Weaknesses of social structure that would otherwise have remained latent and relatively unimportant were found out as the cascade continued and crisis mounted. The cascade was by no means inevitable.

Indeed, such crises usually reveal human beings at their worst, unable to take what might seem with hindsight the actions necessary to avoid or solve them. All of these crises could have been avoided, although as the cascade continued, the necessary steps would have had to be more and more radical. They remind us of human fallibility and the ever-present possibility of regress or the shifting of the tracks of development. Consider the two world wars. They were catastrophic mistakes, bringing disaster to most of the combatants, yet they also changed the world. These changes were to a large extent contingent; they were by no means inevitable. Without World War I, I argue, there would be no Bolshevik Revolution and significant fascism, and without World War II, there would be no Chinese Revolution, Cold War, global American empire, and perhaps a lesser development of capitalism. I could continue with such counterfactuals – the trends that did not happen but might have happened in the absence of some more contingent major event. Although earlier centuries also contained crises of war and economic upheaval, they were less likely to have been so global in their implications. Perhaps also because we have more hindsight over earlier periods, we think we see more overall pattern and less contingency there. It probably did not seem that way to the actors involved.

Such singularities seem to make impossible the nomological quest for social-scientific laws and drive us toward the opposite pole of explanation, the role of the *ideographic*, the unique, in human affairs. Not only do times and places differ, but macro-processes like wars and economic booms and slumps have unique effects. Wars do have structural causes, usually plural, coming together in contingent but timely fashion. We can do quite well at explaining the different plural chains that did come together, but then we encounter human decision making, often of small groups of people. A small group of statesmen decided to go to war in 1914, whereas one man was decisive in precipitating World War II. Neither behaved very rationally, and emotions loomed large in their decisions. Yet these decisions were also set amid deeper causal chains of militarism, interimperial conflict, and rivalry between different ideologies and economic systems. So the first distinctive challenge in writing about this period is in assessing to what extent contemporary power relations are the product of the logic of development of macrostructures and to what extent these have been redirected by both timely conjunctures producing world-historical events and individuals in positions of great power.

Combining these tendencies might suggest a model of *punctuated equilibrium*, of social change, in which in normal times capitalism, nation-states, and others evolve or develop in path-dependent ways, slowly and according to their own logics and inbuilt potentialities. They are, however, disrupted by intermittent crises that force them down new tracks – a model summarized as "long stability-short rupture" by Streeck (2009). This model is explicitly used by economists in conceptualizing long-term economic development, but it is inadequate because the logics of development of capitalism, nation-states, and others differ from each other *orthogonally* – that is, in non-determinant ways. They also occupy different geographical spaces and embody different temporal rhythms of development, and yet they do infuse each other. The task of theorizing social change is considerably more complicated and more dynamic than most prior theories have assumed.

Assessing the impact of crises involves a certain amount of counterfactual speculation – what would have happened had no war or other antecedent condition occurred. Counterfactuals, however, are always implicit in causal arguments. If we say that A caused B, we are saying both that A and then B occurred (which is a factual statement) but also that without A occurring B would not have occurred (unless some alternative cause was also present). This is a counterfactual statement involving some broader implicit speculation; I will make counterfactual logic more explicit.

The second substantive challenge is to determine the most important social structures and processes of the period. For this, I deploy my IEMP model of the four sources of social power – ideological, economic, military, and political. I contend that broad explanations are not possible without considering all four.

The Sources of Social Power

Power is the capacity to get others to do things that they would otherwise not do. To achieve our goals – whatever they are – we enter into power relations involving both cooperation and conflict with other people, and these relations generate societies. The endeavor involves three modalities of power, also used in Volumes I and II.

(1) We may distinguish *distributive* from *collective* power – that is, power exercised *over* others, and power secured jointly *through* cooperation with others. Most actual power relations – say, between social classes or between a state and its citizens – involve both. Workers and employers may conflict with each other, but they also need to cooperate to secure their daily bread. Collective power is of special interest in the twentieth century, which saw a colossal increase in human ability to collectively extract more resources from nature. The increasing productivity of agriculture and industry enabled a fourfold world population growth, from 1.6 billion in 1900 to almost 7 billion in 2010, with the average person being taller, heavier, living twice as long, and becoming twice as likely to be literate. These increases are rightly regarded as tremendous human achievements. Yet ironically, the increased extraction of resources from nature has also had a dark side of environmental consequences, which might even threaten human life on Earth. What hubris that would be: our greatest triumph becomes our ultimate defeat!

(2) Power may be *authoritative* or *diffuse*. Authoritative power involves commands by an individual or collective actor and conscious obedience by subordinates. This is found most strongly in military and political power organizations, although leadership of a lesser sort exists in all power organizations. Diffused power, on the other hand, is not directly commanded, but spreads in a relatively spontaneous, unconscious, and decentered way. People are constrained to act in definite ways, but not by command. This is more typical of ideological and economic power relations, as for example in the spread of an ideology like socialism or economic markets. The constraints of markets are usually experienced as impersonal, even natural, and may become almost invisible as a power process.

(3) Power may be *extensive* or *intensive*. Extensive power organizes large numbers of people over far-flung territories. It is the most obvious aspect of globalization. Intensive power mobilizes a high level of commitment from participants. The greatest power flows from a combination of the two, persuading or coercing more people to do more things collectively.

The most effective exercise of power combines collective and distributive, extensive and intensive, authoritative and diffuse power. That is why a single power source – say, the economy or the military – cannot alone determine the overall structure of societies. It must be admixed with other power sources. I turn at the end of Volume IV to the fundamental theoretical issue of whether one power source could be considered ultimately primary over the others. I turn now to a fuller explanation of the four sources of power. I repeat, these are organizational means by which we can efficiently attain our varied goals, whatever these may be.

(1) *Ideological Power* derives from the human need to find ultimate meaning in life, to share norms and values, and to participate in aesthetic and ritual practices with others. We seem to not be able to do without religion or more secular "isms." I prefer the term "ideology" to the more amorphous word "culture." Religious meaning-systems will continue to figure in this volume, as will secular ideologies like patriarchy, liberalism, socialism, fascism, nationalism, racism, and environmentalism. The power of ideological movements

derives from our inability to attain certainty in our knowledge of the world. We fill in the gaps and uncertainties with beliefs that are not in themselves scientifically testable, but which embody our hopes and fears. No one can prove the existence of a god or the viability of a socialist or Islamist future. Ideologies become especially necessary in crises where the old institutionalized ideologies and practices no longer seem to work and alternatives offered have no track record. This is when we are most susceptible to the power of ideologists who offer us plausible but untested theories of the world.

In previous volumes, I distinguished between *transcendent* and *immanent ideologies*. Transcendent ideologies are the most ambitious. They break interstitially through existing institutions, attracting converts from many different power networks and creating their own networks, such as a new religion or fascism or green environmental movements, among many others. Immanent ideologies strengthen the emotional and moral solidarity of existing power networks. Some ideologies combine both. Racism transcends class divisions at the same time it is uniting the "white race," as we see in Chapter 2. Max Weber (in Gerth and Mills 1946: 280) described the great ideologies of the world with a metaphor drawn from the railroad. Ideas generating "world images," he said, were the switchmen (signalmen) of history, switching it onto a different track. This is true of transcendent and immanent ideologies.

In "The sources of social power revisited: a response to criticism" (2006: 346), I distinguished a third type, *institutionalized ideologies*, indicating only a minimal presence of autonomous ideological power. They are often hidden inside institutions, normally taken for granted or even only lurking in the subconscious. They are thus conservative, endorsing values, norms, and rituals that serve to preserve the present social order. They are found most often in very stable societies, like the West in the period from 1950 to 1980, whereas transcendent and immanent ideologies are responses to social instability and crisis. Patriarchy is a very good example of an institutionalized ideology, long taken for granted, long enduring even when under attack. This is what Marxists traditionally thought of as ideological power because they thought that social change was explained by the material level of society. This is not my view.

Powerful ideologies provide a bridge between reason, morality, and emotion. They make sense to their initiates, but they also require a leap of faith and an emotional commitment. There must be some plausibility, because an ideology would not spread otherwise, but the perception that it makes sense tugs at us morally and emotionally as well as scientifically. As Jack Snyder (2005) argues, this has the important consequence that groups infused with ideological fervor are more powerful than those who lack it. The main markers of the presence of an ideology are the claim to a total explanation of society and a better – often utopian – future as well as the conferring of qualities of good and evil on human actors and their practices. The combination enables both sacrifice and violence. The first two types of ideological power tend to be wielded by vanguard movements centered on younger generations, with charismatic leaders and resolute, passionate activists. I must confess to a certain degree of prejudice against the most powerful ideologies, preferring more pragmatic and compromising solutions to social problems.

Must science be considered a major ideology in modern civilization? Schroeder (2007, 2011) says not, but he argues that unlike all previous civilizations, a technology-driven rapid-discovery science now dominates all ideologies. Science, he correctly notes, is not about belief, but about certain knowledge whose findings can be replicated and refined through standardized technologies of research. Science, said Ernest Gellner, is quite distinctive from all previous forms of natural philosophy because it can actually transform the material world, and has spectacularly done so in a series of transformations of both the social and natural world, enormously enhancing the collective power of human beings, for good or ill. In this volume, I especially stress the transformations wrought by the second industrial revolution. Yet science also differs from true ideologies in its aspiration to be emotionless, and it is always subject to cold scientific refutation, unlike ideologies. Scientists themselves usually believe this, so, charlatans apart, they rarely try to command our obedience. Schroeder accepts that the relative autonomy of science also inhabits rather rarefied elite professions and research institutions with almost no capacity to mobilize social movements. The consequence, however, is that modern science and technology construct great techniques of power, but usually in the service of others. In its remarkable invention of nuclear power, for example, science has been subordinated to economic, political, and military power holders. That is why I cannot really accept Schroeder's notion that science is the third major *autonomous* structure of modern societies alongside his other two – market capitalism and the state. Science is actually distinct, anomalous, among forms of knowledge. It has had emergent properties in increasing the collective powers of human groups, but it has very little distributive power, for it places itself at the service of those who wield other sources of social power. That complicates my model of power, but then societies are always more complex than our theories.

Ideologies (and science) have a very diffuse and extensive geographical logic: they are not contained by military or economic networks of interaction because they may spread wherever human beings communicate with each other. This leads to the *revolutionary* or *liberating* qualities of ideology, the sense of freeing oneself from local power structures, more mundanely of freedom of thought. The diffuseness of ideology, however, also often gives it an open-endedness, as ideas and values from one local tradition or historical civilization mingle with those from others. This has become increasingly important in the process of globalization. Temporally, ideologies are also distinctive, in a way resembling punctuated equilibrium. An existing power structure generates its own ideology, which gradually becomes institutionalized as routine in the lives and beliefs of its inhabitants (although there are always dissident subcultures). When this seems no longer able to explain what is going on in the social environment, a period of ideological ferment may generate a new and powerful ideology whose adherents then change (or try to change) society fundamentally. Most people, however, cannot live intensely at the ideological level for very long, and this ideology settles down into being rather like its predecessors – an institutionalized justification for mundane and rather pragmatic behavior by social actors.

(2) *Economic Power* derives from the human need to extract, transform, distribute, and consume the produce of nature. Economic relations are powerful because they combine the intensive mobilization of labor with very extensive circuits of capital, trade, and production chains, providing a combination of intensive and extensive power and normally also of authoritative and diffused power. The first of each pair centers on production, the second on markets. Economic power relations are those that penetrate most routinely into most peoples' lives; most of us work for about one-third of every day. The social change economies bring is rarely swift or dramatic, unlike military power. It is slow, cumulative, and eventually profound.

The main organization of economic power in modern times has been industrial capitalism, whose global development is central to this volume. *Industrialization* refers to the growing division of labor and developing tools and techniques of industry. Capitalism has three main properties: (1) it endows private ownership of most economic resources on a few; (2) the bulk of workers are separated from ownership, in command only of their own labor skills, but formally free to sell their labor on open markets; (3) capitalism treats all the means of production, including labor, as commodities, tradable on markets, and this means that all four main forms of market – capital, labor, production, and consumption – are traded against each other in markets. Capitalism has been the most consistently dynamic power organization in recent times, responsible for most technological innovation and most environmental degradation. Its "forces of production," to use Marx's term, have developed enormously over this period. In broad terms, it is possible to identify distinct phases of their development. This period began with industrial capitalism, developed into *corporate* or *organized capitalism* in the early twentieth century, combining high productivity with rising but still quite low consumer demand, and substantially confined within national cages. Then during World War II, it became more Keynesian, combining high productivity with mass consumer demand, although still predominantly exercised within national cages and only coming to full fruition after that war (as we see in Volume IV).

This is what Schumpeter (1957) famously called "creative destruction," whereby growth occurs through the destruction of old industries and organizational forms and the creation of new ones. However, its temporal rhythms are not quite as sudden as this might suggest. What we think of as an economic invention is rarely a sudden breakthrough; it is a cumulative succession of many instances of tinkering. Geographically, capitalism also brought a diffuse and fairly steady process of market expansion across the globe. Its expansion has been complex, combining national, international, and transnational networks of interaction (terms explained later). Capitalism also combines intensive with extensive power, penetrating deeply into our lives and broadly across large social spaces. *Commodification* is the term for the gradual extension of market rationality into both public and private life. The commodification of everything is only an exaggeration of a real historical process that is still ongoing in capitalism.

Capitalism's "relations of production" (again Marx's term) centers on social *classes*, groups with a common relationship to economic power resources. Classes are highly important in all human societies, including our own. Sociologists used to spend much effort trying to define exactly which class occupations and households were part of. That was misplaced ingenuity, because occupations are extremely diverse and many people have what Wright (1985) termed "contradictory class locations" – for example, many possess high skills but no capital and only a little power in economic organizations; others possess high organizational power but no capital. So I will identify classes only in broad, commonsensical terms. Naturally, therefore, classes have very fuzzy boundaries. For classes to become real social actors, they require two properties identified by Marx: being a class "in itself," definable in terms of objective relations to the means of production, but also being a class "for itself," possessing a degree of collective organization. The identity of his capitalist class, owning the major means of production and generally exhibiting clear collective intent and effective organization to preserve its own privileges, poses little problem, although at the lower reaches of property-holding it blurs into what Marxists have called the petite bourgeoisie. At higher reaches, it blurs into a stratum of well-rewarded but usually capital-less managers and professionals. The peasantry is relatively unproblematic, but not so the working class. To the extent that it exists, it requires not only a solid core of subaltern workers, in the past manual (blue-collar) workers, but also the existence of a labor movement pressing for its interests. The strongest working-class movements managed to draw in peasants and lower white-collar workers, too. As for the middle class, that is even less precise, and middling persons have had very varied political stances and organizations (as I showed in the case of the nineteenth century in Volume II, Chapter 17). As in everyday usage, I will plural the term to "middle classes" when I am emphasizing diversity.

The role of classes has been uneven. Class conflict between workers and their employers and peasants and their landlords figured very largely across the period of this volume, sometimes inducing revolution, although more often capitalist reform. Then, as we see in Volume IV, working-class organization and all pressure from below declined in the North of the world over the last decades, and the capitalist class is now less challenged from below. This has become a more asymmetrical class structure, with capital possessing much more power than labor. In the South of the world, however, workers and peasants have been stirring recently and will probably rise to greater collective organization in the future.

Classes usually contain distinct fractions. I will distinguish finance capital as a distinct capitalist class fraction. The working and middle classes are more routinely fractionalized into sections and segments. *Sectional* collectivities appear when a skilled trade or a profession organizes collectively but for its own narrow interests, not for a class as a whole. Many labor unions and all professional associations organize on this basis. Classes and sectional actors organize *horizontally*, at their own level of stratification, separated hierarchically from others. Thus, capitalists are above workers, skilled are above unskilled workers, physicians are above nurses who are above hospital cleaners. *Segments*, however, are *vertically* organized, in industry typically comprising all the workers of a firm. Employers needing experienced workers with job-specific skills may offer them the "golden chains" of pensions or health care in order to retain them. This divides them from other workers in the same class or section elsewhere. So have nations that divide workers in different countries from each other. With globalization and national citizenship, national identity has fractured and weakened potential class action. The capitalist class often has dual identities, as both transnational and national. In contrast, American and Mexican workers could in principle be seen as part of a transnational working class, but American workers have been highly privileged by their nationality and regard this as much more important to them than any class solidarity with Mexicans. Indeed, in many ways Americans are "above" Mexicans, exploiting them in a quasi-class relationship (although labor unions would deny this). Classes, sections, and segments crosscut and weaken one another. The stronger are sections and segments, the weaker are class identities, and vice versa.

(3) *Military Power.* Since writing my previous volumes, I have tightened up the definition of military power to "the social organization of concentrated and lethal violence." "Concentrated" means mobilized and focused; "lethal" means deadly. Webster's Dictionary defines "violence" as "exertion of physical force so as to injure or abuse" or "intense, turbulent, or furious and often destructive action or force." These are the senses I wish to convey: military force is focused, physical, furious, and above all lethal. It kills. Military power holders say, "If you resist, you die." Since a lethal threat is terrifying, military power evokes distinctive psychological emotions and physiological symptoms of fear, as we confront the possibility of pain, dismemberment, or death.

Military power is most lethally wielded by the armed forces of states in interstate wars, and this has been especially true in this period. Here is an obvious overlap with political power, although militaries always remain separately organized, often as a distinct caste in society. Despotic political rulers become very wary of military autonomy, for they bring the threat of military coups. Where they distrust the military, they tend to build up armed police and security battalions as their own praetorian guard, offering armed protection against dissidents and the military alike – the guard therefore being a blend of military and political power. Stalin and Hitler did this, also purging their officer corps. Organized lethal violence also comes from non-state actors such as insurgents, paramilitaries, and gangs. In this volume, paramilitaries are found among revolutionary movements of the right and left. Of course, after World War II most warfare in the world has not been between states but between civil war factions, and these cause the majority of fatalities – military power is not only wielded by big battalions.

Military power is much less rule-bound than the other power sources. The rules of war are always precarious, as we recently saw on 9/11 and in Afghanistan, Iraq, and Guantanamo Bay. Internally, military power relations combine the apparent opposites of despotic hierarchy and collective comradeship, intense physical discipline, and esprit de corps, the combination meaning that soldiers will not respond with flight, the instrumentally rational thing to do when facing terror. Military power wielded over outsiders defined as enemies is the most despotic power imaginable. Militarism, however, pervades other organizations, too. For example, their militarism made the larger fascist movements more formidable than their socialist rivals.

Military power plays a more intermittent temporal role in human societies. It can endure in the form of stable military regimes, although otherwise it comes in sudden explosive bursts, terrifying and destructive – very rarely constructive. Yet it has been curiously invisible to most social scientists. It has been a necessary (if lamentable) task of my volumes to restore it to its central place in human societies. In the present volume, I shall argue that European history had for centuries been unusually militaristic, and that this militarism enabled the conquest of global empires and spread like a disease to Japan and the United States. Twentieth, and indeed twenty-first, century development owes much to military power relations.

(4) *Political Power* is the centralized and territorial regulation of social life. The basic function of government is the provision of order over this realm. Here I deviate not only from Max Weber – who located political power (or "parties") in any organization, not just states – but also from political scientists' notion of "governance" administered by diverse entities, including corporations, nongovernmental organization (NGOs), and social movements. I prefer to keep the term "political" for the state – including local and regional as well as national-level government. States, not NGOs or corporations, have the centralized territorial form that makes their rules authoritative over persons residing in their territories. I can resign membership of an NGO or a corporation and so flaunt its rules. I must obey the rules of the state in whose territory I reside or suffer punishment. Networks of political power are intensely,

routinely regulated and coordinated in a centralized and territorial fashion, so political power is more geographically bounded than the other three sources. States also normally cover smaller, tighter areas than ideologies, economies, or military striking power.

We may distinguish between the *despotic* and the *infrastructural* powers of the state (although the distinction could be applied to any power organization). Despotic power is the ability of state elites to make arbitrary decisions without consultation with the representatives of major civil society groups. Infrastructural power is the capacity of a state (whether despotic or democratic) to actually penetrate society and implement logistically political decisions throughout the realm. I made this distinction in "The autonomous power of the state: Its origins, mechanisms and results" (1988a), amending it somewhat in "Infrastructural power revisited" (2008), although in this volume I will amend it further, especially with regard to communist and fascist regimes. Infrastructural power enables states to diffuse their power through or penetrate their societies ("power through"); the exercise of despotic power is by a state that has a degree of authoritative "power over" society. So states may be strong in either of two quite different ways. They can command anything they like of their citizens (despotic power) or they can actually get decisions implemented across their territories (infrastructural power). We should not confuse the two. Clearly, democracies and despotisms have very different combinations of strengths, as we shall see in later chapters.

Punishment by the state is more bureaucratic than violent. Legal rituals and routines make most states' violence minimal. Regulation exercised from the center through territories, rather than either legitimacy (ideology) or violence (military), is the key function of the state. Its agencies pursue law and ritualized political deliberations in courts, assemblies, and ministries. True, behind law and coordination lies physical force, but this is only rarely mobilized into lethal action. Political force is evoked as a ritualized, machine-like, rule-governed, and nonviolent constraint. Law allocates punishment along agreed sliding scales. If found guilty of minor offences, we receive a probationary sentence or a financial penalty. For more serious offences punishment escalates, and we are coercively deprived of liberty in prison. Unless we resist, however, incarceration remains ritualized and nonviolent – we are led from the dock, handcuffed, and placed in a locked cell.

The most violent states discussed in this volume obviously blurred the divide between political and military power. Nazis and Stalinists killed large numbers of people whose only crime was to possess a supposed enemy identity as a Jew or kulak. Legal forms were phony. They tended not to rely on the armed forces, however, but on large formations of specially created armed security police. All of the power sources, however, sometimes blur into each other. Economic and political power blurred in the Soviet Union, as the state owned the means of production. In some states today, officials control much of the economy, operating it under corrupt capitalist principles, but these cases do not invalidate the distinction between political and economic power. Nor do very violent states negate the usefulness of dividing political from military power.

In this period, most of the leading states began as dual; they were becoming nation-states at home but had empires abroad. Then all empires except the American one collapsed, and the *nation-state* – a state ruling over geographically defined and bounded territories in the name of the people – became globalized as the hegemonic political ideal (although not necessarily as the reality) of the world. Through the nineteenth and twentieth centuries, the nation-state became more extensive over the world and more intensive for its citizens, caging their rights within its boundaries and laws. Sentiments of nationalism grew. As we shall see, aggressive nationalism was important, but appeared only intermittently, more a consequence than a cause of war (except in Nazi Germany and militarist Japan). Yet nationalism did have considerable emotional content and ritual reinforcement – a true ideology, at first transcendent, then immanent. As part of the growth of the nation-state, "subjects" were transformed into "citizens," enjoying equal civil, political, and social rights. Fukuyama argues that good government provides three things: public order, the rule of law, and accountable government (2011). Most modern governments had provided public order, and by the twentieth century, Western states provided the rule of law (if often race- and class-biased) plus accountability through elections (to some or most males). Civil and political rights were then extended to all, as liberal democracy spread across the advanced countries, but the addition of numerous social rights spread social liberalism or democracy, as well. The extension of such rights and of democracy more generally then spread somewhat unsteadily across the world.

In Volume II, Chapter 3, I discussed different theories of the modern state and concluded that class, elite, and pluralist theories were all too simple to encapsulate what states actually do. I argued that the modern state is *polymorphous*, crystallizing in different ways according to different political issues and according to the different interests of core constituencies lobbying on these issues. Almost all modern states have been, in matters of political economy, essentially capitalist. Structural Marxists and neoclassical economists believe this imposes limits on what states can do. Block has brought this rather abstract concept down to the level of social actors by observing that the cutting edge of this limit is *business confidence* – the fear by governments that business will only invest in a national economy if it has confidence in the general political/economic climate provided by the state. If it does not have confidence, then its capital will be invested abroad or not invested at all, either of which does economic damage and will reduce the legitimacy of the government. He notes, however, that government and business can be pressed toward some reform by pressure from below (1987: 59). In this book, I shall stress the actual variability of these supposed limits and the influence not only of class and other political struggle but also of indebtedness, and, especially in the case of investor confidence, that its limits may actually harm the general interests of capitalism.

Modern politics do of course crystallize importantly on capitalism and class struggle and its compromise. However, modern states also crystallize around military versus relatively pacific strategies, and these also impose limits: at one extreme, defeat or needless suffering in a war; at the other, the sense of national humiliation induced by the regime backing down against the aggression of others. Again, governments will lose legitimacy, endangering the survival of the regime. Many states also crystallize on religious versus secular issues, centralized versus decentralized, and so forth, each with distinctive constituencies of support, each imposing rough limits. We cannot reduce these to the capitalist crystallization (although some Marxists have attempted to do this), but they are not diametrically opposed to it, either. They are just different, and that makes for political complexity. They pull in different directions, and often lead to consequences intended by no interest group.

States also project military and political power externally, in what we call *geopolitics*. *Hard geopolitics* involve war, alliances, and deterrents to avoid war. *Soft geopolitics* involve interstate political agreements concerning nonlethal matters like law, the economy, health, education, the environment, and so forth. Especially since 1945, soft geopolitics have involved many intergovernmental organizations (IGOs), which write the fine print of international agreements, police conformity, and punish breaches with fines. This politicizes international space, submitting it to routinized political regulation. In contrast, hard geopolitics militarize it. Many theorists of globalization assume that it undermines nation-states, but they are largely wrong: Globalization has taken both a transnational and international form, the latter structured by the geopolitics of states and empires. Nation-states intensified their capture of their population, as subjects were transformed into citizens, with multiple rights within and very few outside the state's boundaries. Nationalism was the ideology generated by this capture.

The four power sources do have a degree of autonomy from each other, especially in modern societies. Economic outcomes are mainly the outcome of economic causes, ideologies are outgrowths of prior ideologies, and so forth, an autonomy emphasized by Schroeder (2011). Ultimately, to my mind, the four are *ideal types* – they rarely exist in the world in pure form; they occur in impure mixtures. All four are necessary to social existence and to each other. Any economic organization, for example, requires some of its members to share ideological values and norms. It also needs military defense and state regulation. Thus, ideological, military, and political organizations help structure economic ones and vice versa. The power sources generate overlapping, intersecting networks of relations with different socio-spatial boundaries and temporal dynamics – their interrelations produce unanticipated, emergent consequences for power actors. Societies are not composed of autonomous levels or subsystems of a given socio-spatial network of interaction. Each has different boundaries and develops according to its own core internal logic. In major transitions, however, the interrelationships and very identities of organizations such as economies or states, are metamorphosed. So my IEMP model is not a social system; rather, it forms an analytical point of entry for dealing with messy real societies. The four power sources offer distinct organizational networks and means to humans pursuing their goals. The means chosen, and in which combinations, depends on interaction between the power configurations historically given and institutionalized and those that emerge interstitially within and between them. This is the main mechanism of social change in human societies: preventing any single power elite from clinging indefinitely onto power. Institutionalized power relations are being constantly surprised by the emergence of new interstitial power configurations. The sources of social power and the organizations embodying them are *promiscuous* – they weave in and out of each other in a complex interplay between institutionalized and emergent, interstitial forces. I am unwilling to initially prioritize any one of them as ultimately primary in determining social change, although at the end of Volume IV I draw some conclusions on the question of ultimate primacy.

2 Globalization imperially fractured: The British Empire

Introduction: Types of empire

Empires have provided the most dominant type of rule across the large-scale societies of history. This is because social groups can attain many of their goals by expansion through force of arms. In a sense, empires need no further explanation. They help the more powerful groups achieve goals that humans generally desire, and so they have been ubiquitous through history – at least until war became too destructive to achieve such desired goals. Because Europeans were greatly increasing their powers in the early modern world, they naturally sought to conquer the world, as they were heavily armed and driven by both material and ideal interests. Imperialism has been a core feature of modernity.

Our modern English word "empire" derives from the Latin *imperium*, "the power wielded by a general commanding an army and a magistrate armed with the law" – that is, a combined political and military power. Modern usages add a geographical element – power exercised over peripheral regions by a core power. I define an empire as a centralized, hierarchical system of rule acquired and maintained by coercion through which a core territory dominates peripheral territories, serves as the intermediary for their main interactions, and channels resources from and between the peripheries.

Note, therefore, that empires blend political and military power at their cores. Empires initially grow through military power, deployed or threatened by the core, and force is then intermittently repeated whenever the periphery resists. Empires often claim that they are charities, selflessly bringing good to the world. They may indeed bring benefits to those they rule, but these are only possible by-products. If you want to help others, you do not march into their homes, kill many of their young men, rape many of their young women, and then impose an authoritarian political regime from which some benefit may later flow. The initial point of empire is to plunder the land, possessions, bodies, and souls of others precisely because one has the military power to do so. Acquiring empire is therefore essentially an expression of military authoritative power. It is commanded. The preconditions for empire are more varied; after conquest, empires may rule by wielding other sources of power – political, economic, and ideological – and indeed benefits may then flow. Modern empires are distinctive in containing a great deal of economic imperialism, because capitalism is much more effective at integrating the economies of core and periphery than previous modes of production were. Some make the plausible argument that today, capitalism has largely replaced military expansion as the way to profit and global integration, and I consider this in later chapters as well as in Volume IV.

Because empires vary, I distinguish several main types.

(1) *Direct Empire* occurs where conquered territories are incorporated into the realm of the core, as in the Roman Empire and the Chinese empires at their height. The sovereign of the core also becomes sovereign over the periphery. After military conquest, much political power is wielded, at first despotically. Once institutionalized, authoritative political power radiates outward from center to periphery, and more diffuse economic and ideological power follows it. Finally, the empire may do a disappearing act when the conquered peoples acquire a Roman or Han Chinese identity themselves and political power becomes less despotic and more infrastructural. Power may thus move successively through military to political to economic to ideological forms – the natural sequence among the most successful of empires. Most historic empires expanded over the territories of neighbors, the Russian Empire being the last of these. Most modern empires, however, spread overseas, and they are more difficult to integrate. Moreover, racism prevented these overseas empires from performing this disappearing act, for it prevented the conquered peoples from identifying themselves as British, Japanese, or American. In modern times, without large numbers of settlers, direct rule has been difficult to accomplish and expensive to maintain. So modern empires have turned to more offshore kinds of empire.

(2) *Indirect Empire* is a claim of political sovereignty by the imperial core, but with rulers in the periphery retaining some autonomy and in practice negotiating the rules of the game with the imperial authorities. There is continuing military intimidation, although not usually repeated conquest, and the imperial state rules more lightly, possessing lesser despotic and infrastructural power. As Lord Cromer said of the British, "We do not govern Egypt, we only govern the governors of Egypt" (Al-Sayyid, 1968: 68). Americans attempted this in the Philippines in 1898, but massive resistance forced a partial climbdown. The United States did not subsequently attempt indirect empire other than in temporary circumstances. In indirect empire, locals staff most of the army and administration and dominate provincial and local governments. The British would retain central political power and a military monopoly so that they could repress native revolts, but everyday rule required collaboration with native elites and some deference to their economies, polities, and cultures.

These first two types, unlike the others, involve territorially delimited occupation – *colonies*.

(3) *Informal Empire* occurs where peripheral rulers retain full formal sovereignty, but their autonomy is significantly constrained by intimidation from the imperial core, which combines varying degrees of military and economic power. This has become the predominant form in modern empires, as capitalism

can add considerable economic coercion. R. Robinson (1984: 48) explained this in the specific case of the British Empire as

> coercion or diplomacy exerted for purposes of imposing free trading conditions on a weaker society against its will; foreign loans, diplomatic and military support to weak states in return for economic concessions or political alliance; direct intervention or influence from the export-import sector in the domestic politics of weak states on behalf of foreign trading and strategic interests; and lastly, the case of foreign bankers and merchants annexing sectors of the domestic economy of a weak state.

Because uses of the term "informal empire" are often imprecise about the nature of coercion, I distinguish three subtypes, involving differing forms of coercion.

(3a) *Informal "Gunboat" Empire* is where military power is deployed in short, sharp interventions. The gunboat and its equivalents cannot conquer a country, but they can administer pain by shelling ports (more recently by bombing) and then landing troops for brief incursions. The European empires, Japan, and the United States all jointly administered such pain to China in the late nineteenth and early twentieth centuries. The resulting unequal treaties between them and China were routinely enforced through political controls over Chinese customs revenues and budgets, reinforced by military interventions where necessary. American "Dollar Diplomacy" at the beginning of the twentieth century was another example of direct military intimidation, but without colonies. These military and political interventions involve authoritative, commanded power.

(3b) *Informal Empire through Proxies* uses local proxies to do the coercion. In the 1930s, the United States shifted toward subcontracting coercion to local despots who supported U.S. foreign policy, giving them economic and military aid in return. Then, in the post–World War II period, the United States added covert military operations to aid its local clients, mainly through the newly formed Central Intelligence Agency (CIA). This is indirect military intimidation, in which the authoritative power is not directly commanded from the core.

(3c) *Economic Imperialism* replaces military coercion with economic coercion. In the second half of the nineteenth century, Britain saw that the logistics of launching gunboats across the globe was too daunting and turned toward purely economic coercion. In Argentina, for example, Britain used its domination of imports, exports, and investment to enforce free trade and strict payment of debts. The United States later expanded this, intervening inside peripheral economies through international banking organizations that it leads. In such "structural adjustment," the peripheral country is free to say no, but the deterrents are powerful – the denial of foreign investment and trade. Because there is little or no military force or indeed authoritative power of any sort, under my definition this is not strictly imperialism, yet the term "economic imperialism" is widely used and I will continue using it.

(4) *Hegemony* herein is used in the Gramscian sense of routinized leadership by a dominant power over others, which is regarded by the latter as being legitimate or at least normal. Hegemony is built into the everyday social practices of the periphery and so needs little overt coercion. Whereas in indirect and informal empires peripheral regimes feel constrained to serve the imperial master, under hegemony they defer voluntarily to the hegemony's rules of the game, which are seen as normal, natural. Hegemony involves more than Nye's notion of "soft power." He defines this as purely ideological, "the ability to get what you want through attraction rather than coercion or payments. It arises from the attractiveness of a country's culture, political ideals, and policies" (2004: x). Although there is undoubtedly an element of such "soft" ideological power in hegemony, I doubt whether Britain in the nineteenth century or the United States today could command other states merely by offering attractive values and policies. Sweden and Canada have not been able to do so. Britain and the United States have been different because some of their practices have been built diffusely into the everyday lives of others, compelling them to act in certain ways, as those of Sweden or Canada have not. In the nineteenth century, the rule of the pound sterling and today the rule of the U.S. dollar have involved economic seigniorage, whereby other countries buy pounds sterling or dollars at low rates of interest, benefiting the British or the Americans, respectively, more than themselves. This has been seen by foreigners as simply what one does with one's export surpluses. It is diffuse, not authoritative power; no one is directly commanded. Weaker states may also pay for a hegemonic state to establish military bases in their territories to defend them from others – as the Europeans have done by inviting in the United States.

These types involve descending levels of military and ascending levels of political, economic, and ideological power as we move from direct to indirect, through the informal subtypes of empire to hegemony. In fact, mere hegemony is not empire at all, as it is not experienced as coercion. Because these are ideal types, no actual empire fits neatly within any one of them. Indeed, empires typically combine several of these forms of domination.

How do we explain the spread of empires? Doyle (1986: 22–6) notes that the explanation must blend together forces from within the core power, forces from within the periphery, and forces from the overall international relations system. Empire does give an opportunity for its dominant groups to increase their rewards, whatever they may be – loot, steady profit, status, the conversion of souls, and so forth. However, we must go beyond metrocentric explanations based on the core, such as the Hobson/Lenin theory of imperialism, the "gentlemanly capitalism" thesis of Cain and Hopkins (1986), and the exceptionalism often deployed to analyze the American empire. Equally limited are pericentric explanations focused on the periphery, such as Gallagher and Robinson's (1953) explanation of informal empire in terms of instability in the periphery luring on imperial expansion and structural realist theories reducing empires to the systemic properties of international relations. Mixtures of all three are required.

Imperial beliefs are required, too. First comes a perception that one has preponderant power over the target region, with no great rival power blocking the way. This will enable seizure by force. Confidence in success is thus a precondition of imperial expansion, and military success is usually, albeit not always, its cutting edge. Historians debate the relative weight of three further motives: for economic gain, geopolitical strategic security, and an ideological sense of status or mission. One may gain economically, not through market exchange, but by seizing economic resources by military force. In Volume II (1993: 33), I distinguished two main conceptions of economic profit and interest. A diffuse market logic sees interests and profit served by activity within markets; an authoritative territorial logic sees them as secured by direct or indirect control of territory and its resources. The latter generates most imperialism, although there are also intermediate forms, such as mercantilism and informal empire. A similar distinction has been made recently between a "logic of capital" and a "logic of territory" by David Harvey (2003), although as a Marxist he tends to downplay the latter.

The motive of strategic security is usually seen by imperialists as defensive expansion against threats from other states or empires. The bigger the empire, the less secure it feels! H. James (2006: 101) believes strategic insecurity to be the major motive of empires, but I would rate it alongside the lure of profit through seizure. Ideological motives seem somewhat less dominant but come in two main types. The first involves a strong emotion to assert status dominance by force, which, judging from their monuments, seems to have driven forward many ancient rulers – as it did Napoleon or Hitler (for whom it was also a racial status). The elites of great empires often felt slights and rebellions as humiliations (often racial humiliation) to be revenged in spades (we will see examples of this from both the British and American empires). More oriented to values than to emotions is an ideological sense of mission. Empires always develop mission statements. The Romans said they brought order and justice to the conquered, the Spanish brought the word of God, the British free trade and prosperity, the French *la mission civilisatrice*, the Americans democracy and free enterprise. In fact, modern Western empires have also subscribed to a broader sense that they collectively were bringing civilization and Enlightenment values to the world, although this was also often inflected with racism. Mission statements typically strengthen after expansion has begun, for they offer more elevated motives than mere profit or insecurity; they deflect attention from the militarism of the project, and they are useful in giving a sense of moral uplift to the imperialists themselves. Once elevated, however, a mission may take on a life of its own and drive on further expansion. These motives involve military, economic, strategic/geopolitical, and ideological power sources – and of course, they are usually mixed together, if in different combinations.

These are the concepts I use in this volume to discuss all modern empires. I start with the extraordinary European expansion into the globe. I ask why the Europeans were so good at acquiring empires, whom they benefited, and why they collapsed so quickly. After a general introduction, I focus on the British Empire, the biggest of them all.

Why were the Europeans so good at imperialism?

Modern empires effected the greatest transformation when accompanied by settlers. Crosby's (1993) theory of "ecological imperialism" identifies four types of settler. First, the humans, the greatest predators, bent on ruthless conquest, stealing natives' land, goods, and trade, and often enslaving or massacring them and settling on their lands. Second, their domestic animals – pigs, cattle, horses, dogs – which came to dominate animal husbandry in the New World. Those animals that turned feral soon dominated its wildlife, too. Third, their weeds. European ploughs were often the first to turn over New World topsoils, and European weeds had evolved to thrive in their wake. Weed seedlings brought on boots and animal hides drove out indigenous plants. More than half of all weed species found today in the Americas and Australasia originated in Europe. Fourth, European disease microbes, against which many natives had no immunity. Ethnocide resulted – massive death-dealing, largely unintended. Humans, weeds, animals, and microbes together constituted a ferocious ecological imperialism that transformed the globe.

There was also a more beneficent side to such species empires. In the Columbian exchange, apples, bananas, peaches, pears, coffee, wheat, carrots, and turnips went west and maize, potatoes, sugar, tomatoes, squash, cocoa, pineapple, and tobacco came east to Europe (and Asia). More than square kilometers conquered, number of souls converted, or trade volumes achieved, these exchanges brought the greatest transformation of everyday material life since the original transition to agriculture. It diversified the human diet and was a significant factor in extending the human life span. It specifically aided the agricultural revolution in England, which was a crucial precondition for its industrial revolution. Those who point today to McDonaldization or the all-season supermarket as indicating food globalization highlight the trivial in comparison. The Europeans also changed the languages of continents, and their tri-continental Atlantic trade (manufactures, slaves, sugar/cotton), linking European ports with Africa and America, provided distinctively capitalist integration from the late seventeenth century onward, as the first Iberian imperial economies had not done. At first, penetration outside the Americas was confined to sea coasts and navigable rivers. Later, the powers unleashed by the Industrial Revolution enabled Europeans to extend empire over land, as well. By 1914, 400 years after Columbus, Europeans ruled most of the world.

This was the first phase of modern globalization, but it offered only a limited integration. The unique feature of this era of imperialism was the existence of multiple, rival empires – Spain, Portugal, Holland, Britain, France, Russia, Germany, Belgium, the United States, Japan, Italy. Each constituted a distinct global slice, the leading edge of *fractured globalization*. It also produced racial fracturing as the imperialists struggled to understand their evident power superiority. Although capitalist markets, production chains, and ideologies strained to break transnationally through political boundaries, there was no single global market, as can be seen from the fact that prices did not converge much before the end of the nineteenth century (O'Rourke & Williamson, 2002). Each empire granted monopoly licenses and pricing power to its own trading companies. Each power traded disproportionately within its own empire and sphere of interest, protected by mercantilist practices that were somewhere between market and territorial conceptions. Wallerstein's "capitalist world system," beginning in the sixteenth century and governed by singular principles, was potentiality, not actuality. What he called the "periphery" of the world system had only marginal contacts with what he defined as "core" and "semi-periphery." Much of the daily life in the nonwhite colonies remained largely unchanged by imperialism, because imperialism was spread so thinly. Most colonized peoples in the nineteenth century saw ruling elites as rarely as people in medieval Europe had. Empires were extensive but not intensive.

The Europeans did not conquer the whole world. The strongest civilizations and those at the edge of the European logistical reach adapted European practices and survived. Japan, China, the Ottoman Turks, and Persia held onto their core historical territories. Although India was conquered, its Hindu and Muslim cultures remained highly resilient, as did the Muslim Middle East. Only Japan managed to join the imperialist club.

The proximate cause of European success was superior military power, not a higher level of civilization, scientific revolutions, or capitalism. Its proficiency at war was already long-lived (Bayly, 2004: 62). Over the second millennium AD, Europeans were probably more warlike than the inhabitants of any other continent. Europeans were from Mars. Rough statistics of global wars are available from 1494, better ones from 1816. European wars dominated both periods (J.S. Levy, 1983; Gleditsch, 2004; Lemke, 2002). Although these data may undercount early nineteenth-century wars in Latin America and precolonial wars in Africa, a contrast with East Asia is on firmer ground. This region saw a 300-year period of peace between the 1590s and 1894, broken only by barbarian incursions into China and five fairly small two-state wars. During the preceding 200 years, China was only once at war, with Vietnam. In Japan, firearms were banned for two centuries from 1637 onward. In contrast, the European powers were involved in interstate wars in nearly 75 percent of the years between 1494 and 1975, and no twenty-five-year period was entirely free of war (J.S. Levy, 1983: 97). The Chinese system of exacting tribute from its neighbors helped maintain Asian peace and was more symbolic than material because China paid more than it received. It was hegemony, allowing much international trade, run especially by Chinese business clans, to flourish across Asia (Arrighi, 2007: 314–20; Andornino, 2006).

The Europeans did not rate highly the martial arts of their enemies. In Africa and the Americas, they respected the bravery of their enemies but believed they themselves were far more organized and better equipped – which they were, usually. In Asia, it was different, for they believed they were dealing with civilizations that had become soft and not very warlike. The British wrote with contempt of Indian warfare, in which negotiations and bribery decided the outcome of battles. In contrast, natives noted, Europeans went ruthlessly for the jugular. The eighteenth-century Chinese sage Cheng Tingzuo wrote, "Far-off Europe! ... Its people are known for their many-sided cleverness [and] excessive ingenuity. They have investigated to the utmost such cruel things as firearms." Fukuzawa Yukichi, a major theorist of the Meiji Restoration in Japan, lamented in 1875, "We have had too long a period of peace with no intercourse with outside. In the meantime, other countries, stimulated by occasional wars, have invented many new things such as steam trains, steam ships, big guns and small hand guns etc." An African complained, "White men [fight] dirty and, what is worse, to kill" (Elvin, 1996: 97; Etemad, 2007: 86).

The causal chain of European militarism stretches back a long way. War within Europe had long been profitable for its warriors. In the tenth century, Europe contained a core comprising the former lands of the Frankish Empire and a periphery composed of weaker states, tribes, and self-governing peasant communities. The rulers of the core then conquered, enserfed, and colonized peripheral peoples, offering land and other benefits to knights, soldiers, priests, farmers, artisans, and traders accompanying them. Among all classes, younger sons and illegitimate sons inherited little and had to find their own way in the world. They found the promise of land or trade in a newly settled area, lacking rigid status differences – a formidable inducement. Bartlett (1994) shows that for a period of about 400 years, up to 1350 AD, the more politically organized and militarized core swallowed up the periphery. As he notes, the correct term for cores conquering, colonizing, ruling, and "civilizing" their peripheries is *empire*. The Norman conquests and those of the Teutonic Knights in Lithuania fit especially well into my definition of empire.

For the core, war was profitable, and it also exported younger wellborn sons, militarily trained but without inheritances – the *juvenes* and *milites* who otherwise caused trouble at court. They could be sent off to conquer new lands, just as accompanying traders could conquer new markets and priests new souls. In this colonial expansion, the settlers often became autonomous, founding their own states in the periphery, as Visigothic and Frankish lords did in Spain and as Normans did in many places. The primary motive for expansion was economic but feudal: wellborn men lacking inheritance sought land and peasants from whom they could extract rent and labor services. Lust for land was the primary motive, then trade, and then the saving of souls. A warrior ideology, blessed by God and carrying high social status, also enabled young men to set off more easily on quests that carried significant risk of death. But because land came with peasants tied to it, this usually was not territory acquired at the expense of other people.

By 1350, the result of this first colonizing phase was a Europe filled with mostly small states. No one can accurately count them because there were so many gradations of sovereignty. Tilly (1990: 45) estimates between 80 and 500, depending on how we count! There followed a second, "state-swallowing phase," lasting several more centuries. Only twenty-five states were left by 1900, as minnow states got swallowed by bigger ones. In the east, the winners were the Romanov, Habsburg, and Ottoman monarchs, by whose names we conventionally call empires. In the west, the minnows were swallowed into what we call national states such as Spain, France, and England. However, they too were really imperial, as the Basques, Provencals, or Welsh could attest.

In this second phase, the main goal remained territory, although now through subordinating existing lords and serfs. The swallowers were more often states than the earlier loose associations of lords, although acting in association with moneylenders and merchants. These states very gradually tightened their hold on the population. War remained profitable for the bigger states, and a warrior ideology continued to help young men take risks in pursuit of profit. War was not profitable or rational for the smaller states, but they learned to anticipate defeat through marriage alliances with greater powers, which then peacefully absorbed them. Defunct states rarely have their chroniclers, and Europeans' collective memory of war was as glorious and profitable, so they kept waging it. Greater problems would come when they had swallowed the minnows. They would then turn against each other, as had happened earlier among the last surviving states in ancient Chinese history.

Before then, however, the Europeans launched their third phase of imperialism, this time across the globe. The Romanovs and Habsburgs struck out eastward across land, although the Habsburgs only constituted "empire light," a loose federation of peoples to some extent seeking common defense against more powerful neighbors. In contrast, Portugal, Spain, Holland, France, and Britain founded overseas empires. The causal chain of European militarism had entwined with the chain of naval technological innovation to generate transoceanic possibilities. This also came at a timely moment, when the major non-European empires were experiencing stagnation or decline. Thus, expansion could be successful. It was also assisted by settlers escaping from poverty or religious oppression. By the twentieth century, Europeans and their settlers seemed to dominate the earth, but in a fractured rivalry.

It had been a rather path-dependent millennium of military power. War had been key to life and death for the European state. If a state failed to improve its military power, it ceased to exist. Repeated war-making within the continent had gradually nurtured an intensive form of warfare whereby smallish armies and navies could pour intensive firepower onto the enemy. The coordination of disciplined infantry, cavalry, and artillery (initially archers, then cannon) created the battlefield impression of a war machine to their enemies. Technical improvements to guns on land and especially at sea came in rapid succession, and the cost of guns steadily declined. Between 1600 and 1750, the rate of successful fire per soldier in the French army jumped more than tenfold (J. Lynn, 1997: 457–72). Although firearms were invented by the Chinese, they had not proved effective against mobile nomadic cavalry, China's main enemy, and had been little developed. Japanese guns stagnated during the long peace of the Tokugawa period. In contrast, Europeans fought continuously and gained a lead in metallurgy, ballistics, and explosives. Chinese sources recognized that Europeans were ahead of them by the early 1500s (Chase, 2003: 142; cf Bryant, 2008). However, the guns of the Europeans were not at first technically superior to those of the three "gunpowder empires" facing them – Ottoman, Persian, and Mughal (and the post-Mughal states of India). The difference was more in training, discipline, and tactics; that is, military organization. The gunners of naval vessels and land batteries had been trained to deliver much more coordinated, continuous fire; the complex coordinating tactics of infantry, cavalry, and artillery had reached levels superior to their enemies, whose forces, often much larger, seemed like jostling crowds by comparison.

Naturally, this military superiority had preconditions among the other power sources, especially improved revenue-raising capacity by states and commercial companies. States began systematically taxing and conscripting their citizens, and this developed a more territorial sense of statehood as the required infrastructures expanded to fill each state's territory. In West Europe, states became more national. This dual fiscal-military Darwinian process left only the fittest military and political powers to confront overseas peoples. Small European forces could not easily overcome native armies operating over open lands to which horse archers or light cavalry might be more suited. Yet as European gunnery intensified its firepower, eventually no other military could withstand it in fixed battle. This was especially true at sea, which involves more confined, intensive warfare. Then the largely conjunctional harnessing of this intensive militarism to the economic power of industrial capitalism increased European power over land, too. However, it was not a very intensive power unless accompanied by European settlers. Intensive firepower by small armies made for battlefield victories, but it did not make for postconquest states able to maintain day-to-day control over the population.

There was almost seamless continuity between the second and third phases of imperialism for both Spain and England. In January 1492, Granada, the last

Moorish Kingdom of Spain, fell to Their Most Christian Majesties, Ferdinand and Isabella. Three months later, Christopher Columbus set sail for the Indies; in October, he found a continent blocking the way. Mexico and Peru were quickly conquered by conquistadores and clerics, younger sons again, mostly from the impoverished gentry of Extremadura and Andalucia. The main lures were still feudal –new realms for the king, land with dependent peasants for the conquistadores, high social status, and the Church's acquisition of souls. Pervading all was greed for the gold and silver of the Americas. Spanish imperialism predated capitalism.

Somewhat later, English conquests in Scotland and Ireland proved laboratories of overseas empire (Ohlmeyer, 2001: 146; cf Canny, 2001). The city of Londonderry in Northern Ireland was the model for overseas colonies, "planted" with Protestant settlers from London and Scotland settled to rule over and "civilize" the Catholics of the island. The titles of Lenman's two books, *England's Colonial Wars, 1550–1688* and *Britain's Colonial Wars, 1688–1783,* indicate that the first set of colonial wars was fought by the English within the British Isles; the second by the newly homogenized British in other continents. The stream of settlers increased, for Scots and Irish had stronger motivations to escape poverty and exploitation back home.

Overseas colonialism maintained some medieval traditions. Europe still exported the troublesome energy of younger sons, bastards, restless missionaries, farmers, and artisans risking lives to seek an upward mobility and social status denied back home. Europeans could only flourish in temperate zones, so imperial thrusts elsewhere involved trade more than settlement, leading to informal empire without colonies, a commercial-naval imperialism derived from Venice and Genoa and then Portugal, Holland, and England. In the process, it became merchant capitalism based on exploiting differences between prices in different parts of the world, often by monopoly. Two imperial trajectories were thus established, one centered on land war and directly ruled settler colonies, the other on navies to secure commercial monopolies and informal empire. Once the productivity of European settler farms and plantations generated profits recycled by the merchants to Europe (and Asia), the two became linked in a broader capitalist imperialism, outstripping the boundaries of any state. Traders often did not stay offshore long. Troubled, they said, by disorder among the natives and wanting to enforce monopolies, they sought control over the interior.

As imperialism expanded, it became both more capitalist and more statist. Military power was reinforced and rechanneled by economic and political power. European expansion was virtually inevitable given this brute degree of power superiority. Only a European war comparable to that of 1914–1918 or some great revival of a non-European empire might have stopped it, and neither was likely. Yet the different logics of state territorial conquest and diffuse market exploitation never fully merged. Europe was what I called in previous volumes a "multi-power actor civilization," with no single center of power and with formidable dynamism, for good or ill. This gave European imperialism a restless, uneven dynamic, pushed onward by states and private adventurers/capitalists/missionaries/settlers, with licensed trading-mercantilist companies representing the intersection of the two. Holding together such dispersed, dynamic territories in single empires would prove difficult. These empires were not long-lived.

Did the British empire do anyone any good?

I cannot deal with all these empires, so I focus on the biggest one. Britain won its first overseas colonies in the seventeenth century. More came in the mid-eighteenth century after victorious wars against France. After losing most of North America, Britain reoriented itself to Asia and then Africa, adding a final batch of League of Nations mandated territories after victory in World War I. Possessing superior naval power backed by efficient state tax-gathering at home, and inheriting traditions in which aggressive war was routine and normal, British elites could develop an empire, and did so. Britain also pioneered the agricultural and industrial revolutions that gave it a lead in domestic productivity, providing the economic power for its militarism. Britain was fortunate to be expanding at a timely world-historical moment, when there was both an exploitable balance of power within continental Europe and stagnation or decline among major states elsewhere. The cohesion of elites, institutionalized in the king in parliament – the product of a different causal chain – meant they could devise effective policies to exploit these contingencies.

All this enabled a small offshore island to go global, intensive power to go extensive. The lack of any one of these military, political, and economic power resources probably would have stymied global expansion; a stronger Asia might have restricted Europeans to more equal trade there. There was no overall vision of expansion, no inner logic of the development of a world system hegemon, but each generation of elites found new opportunities. The consequence was the Greenwich Meridian as the universal standard of time, the pound sterling as the world's reserve currency, and (boosted by the United States) English as the world's lingua franca. By 1920, this empire covered a quarter of the land surface of the Earth, the biggest – although in certain respects the thinnest – empire ever.

Whom did it benefit? It obviously brought profit to the merchants, manufacturers, investors, and settlers who survived the adventure – and many did not. Although often wrapped up in piety, the search for profit and upward mobility drove most of them onward, allied to an adrenalin-charged pursuit of adventure among young males, which enabled them to risk their lives. The British and Dutch, however, were probably the only European empires to have increased the wealth of the mother country, although they were later joined in profit by the Japanese. The other empires were costly, less clearly in their subjects' interests (P. O'Brien & Prados de la Escosura, 1998; Etemad, 2005). The lure of empire was usually delusional for the masses.

Did the conquered natives benefit from empire? The imperialists themselves said so, and so at first did Karl Marx. Lord Curzon, viceroy of India, declared, "The British Empire is under Providence the greatest instrument for good that the world has seen." Field Marshal Smuts, prime minister of South Africa, said it was "the widest system of organized human freedom which has ever existed in human history." For a long time, most British scholars concurred (as did French scholars regarding their empire). Marx, however, had changed his mind, and argued that British-free trade harmed the natives – they would have done better with protective tariffs, he said. In recent decades, empires have lost virtually all their allure. Postcolonial studies founded on the anger of the formerly colonized, abetted by the guilt of postimperialist countries, have turned highly negative. There have been official apologies delivered by the British, American, and French governments for the misdeeds of their long-dead predecessors – we are terribly sorry about genocide, slavery, and exploitation. Yet empire retains adventurous popular allure in the West, and best sellers remain pro-imperial.

Moreover, some scholars have recently urged the United States to take up Britain's imperial burden for the good of the world. In his books *Empire* (2002) and *Colossus* (2004), Niall Ferguson urged the United States to bring peace, representative government, and prosperity to the world. The British, he said, developed a liberal empire by pioneering "free trade, free capital movements and, with the abolition of slavery, free labor." They sunk "immense sums in developing a global network of modern communications" and promoted "the optimal allocation of labour, capital and goods in the world." They brought "a global peace unmatched before or since ... Western norms of law, order and governance," representative government, and "the idea of liberty" (2002: xx–xxv). Although Ferguson admits the British committed atrocities along the way, he dates these before 1850, and says they were fewer than in other empires. The clincher, he says, is that since the British left, former colonies have greatly deteriorated. He backs up these assertions with data on economic growth and representative government (which, as we shall see, are hardly impressive).

The economist Deepak Lal (2004) also advocates an imperialism of free trade, although he does not believe empires can impose their values or their institutions on alien cultures. It is counterproductive if they try, he says. Unusually for a neoliberal, he does not see free markets as natural, because they depend on order, and this comes from military pacification institutionalized into a rule of law that secures property rights, encourages property owners to invest, producers to exchange, and workers to choose their preferred employment. Empires throughout history provided such order, he says. The economic historian Harold James (2006) argues similarly, although he recognizes tension between freedom and order and empire. Lal says that the British Empire was the most effective of all because its capitalist and industrial revolution was backed by free trade, assisting the integration of the world economy, enabling countries such as India or Ghana to join it. He produced little data to support this, relying more on the general precepts of neoclassical economics. Are these panegyrics to the British Empire justified, or are the postcolonial denigrators to be believed?

British expansion and military power

I deal with the worst first. In the temperate zones, settlers wanted the land, but often not native labor, so they used their firepower to drive the natives off. This happened most brutally where the settlers were self-governing, and most of these colonies were British. The present-day continental United States contained somewhere between 4 and 9 million Native Americans at the initial point of contact. By 1900, in the U.S. Census only 237,000 were left, a loss rate of over 95 percent. Australia contained over 300,000 aborigines at the time of the First Fleet. In the census of 1921, there remained 72,000, a loss rate of 75 percent. Although disease was the biggest killer on both continents, the settlers rejoiced at the death-toll and supplemented it with rolling waves of genocide. The more representative the settler polities, the greater the killing – democratic genocide. The settlers were worse than the colonial authorities (Mann, 2005: Chap. 4). This was a perverted kind of globalization. Instead of integrating the world's peoples, it wiped them out and replaced them with Europeans. The Europeans would then use their skills to exploit the natural abundance of the land. This was true above all of those settlers who became Americans.

Compared to ethnocide and genocide, slavery seems mild. By the sixteenth century, it was dying out in Europe, but the economics of New World sugar, tobacco, and coffee revived it abroad. Modern slavery resulted from the conjuncture of modern agriculture, industry, and navies. It involved large, concentrated, and coercively disciplined labor forces in plantations and in factories processing agricultural products. Because it is difficult to enslave people in their own country (they can resist or escape), however, slaves were brought by European naval power from other continents and thus became racial, unlike almost all previous slavery. Africa knew slavery already, of course, and African elites had no taboo against enslaving those outside their kin networks. They were doing it under Arab leadership long before the Europeans arrived. Nor did they have taboos on women working, as Europeans did. So Africans could be employed to enslave other African women and men. This was not possible with Europeans. "The rise of slavery in the Americas," says Eltis (2000: 279), "was dependent on the nature of freedom in western Europe." It was soon led by the freest people of all – the British.

Approximately 12–13 million slaves were forcibly taken from Africa and transported to the New World. Two million died en route from overcrowding, poor nutrition, and cruel policing. By 1770, the British were carrying most slaves, and their plantations in the Caribbean and North America were the biggest employers of slaves, pioneering mass production geared to mass consumption. This was "the first, least-camouflaged expression of ... capitalist logic," and it enabled the colonial transition from the export of precious metals to agrarian capitalism (Blackburn, 1997: 554; Eltis, 2000: 37; D. Richardson, 2001). In the Americas, slavery was accompanied by semi-free bonded European labor. Wallerstein (1974) showed that this conjunction of free labor in the core and coerced labor in the periphery was a structural feature of colonial capitalism, an innovation over older empires. However, I must add that the majority of the native population, although exploited, were not coerced in this way. Slavery and plantations embodying tight disciplining of labor were islands of coercion amid more numerous peasant proprietors and other largely autonomous households. They felt coercion less directly and less frequently. The political equivalent was the duality that emerged between the national citizen in the motherland and the imperial subject abroad. Obviously, this was not free trade, and equally obviously, slavery did not benefit the slaves; they would rather have stayed poor but free in Africa. So far, the British Empire was all negative for these natives.

At the end of the eighteenth century, however, radicals and Evangelicals brought ideological reform campaigns in Britain. One was against government corruption, especially outrageous in India. This movement was successful, and from then on British colonial administration proved relatively uncorrupt (as Ferguson says). More spectacular was the second campaign, which permanently abolished slavery in the British Empire in two stages, in 1807 and 1833. In the political campaign for abolition, Christian belief in the equality of souls seemed to have overcome economic power interests, for the slave trade was still profitable and abolition produced the collapse of the sugar industry in the British West Indies. Drescher (2002: 232) says it was "the most expensive international policy based on moral action in modern history." Yet, British capitalism remained invested in the slave trade and now switched to using foreign ships. Profit is less susceptible to moral rhetoric than are politics – another indication of the dual nature of this statist/capitalist empire. Nonetheless, no subsequent movement, British or other, was ever again to achieve a comparable gain for native peoples (B. Porter, 2001: 219–20). The biggest benefit of empire had come quite early – before 1850 – was less liberal than evangelical, and was undercut by capitalist cunning.

Trade was better than slavery, but it was unequal. British colonial trade centered on the triangular exchange of manufactured goods from England, slaves from Africa, and plantation produce from the Americas. Then the East India Company took over in Asia. One company official remarked of Indians,

"The Natives are a quiet and timid people not addicted to war . . . the Revenue may be collected from them with very great facility" (Lenman, 2001b: 110). The imperial economy now centered on the exchange of manufactured goods from the core for materials from mines, agriculture, and simpler manufactures from the periphery. In time, the value of manufactured exports from core to periphery greatly exceeded the value of imported materials from the periphery, and the balance was made up by "invisibles," finance, shipping, and other transport plus professional and government services.

Unequal exchange endured. In the Roman Empire and Chinese empire, provinces had become more equal with time, as the core invested in the periphery and Roman and Chinese settlers intermarried with natives. These empires brought benefits to conquered natives, who were assimilated into the imperial identity. However, the Europeans did not assimilate the natives. The export of raw materials from the colonies was encouraged by zero tariffs, even sometimes by export subsidies, but the Europeans forced them out of higher-profit sectors like manufacturing, shipping, and international trade, seeking monopolies for themselves. So the North American colonies were allowed to produce crude pig iron, but not steel. This forcing out was clearest in India. Over thirty years, the East India Company forced down the price of cloth finished by Indian weavers by building up the power of Indian merchant-intermediaries. These were guaranteed credit and the backing of East India Company soldiers to impose better terms of exchange, suppress collective action by the weavers, and enforce an eventual clothing monopoly for the company. The producing weavers were proletarianized, and any merchant who did not comply was driven out. The weavers probably enjoyed a higher standard of living than their British counterparts in the eighteenth century, but empire then reversed this. The mere threat of military power was generally enough to secure contracts and monopolies, without its actual use (Parthasarathi, 2001). These markets were backed by authoritative control of territory, an entwining of the two logics distinguished earlier. This undermined what had been a large and vibrant Indian textile industry. India was "plundered" (Ray, 2001: 514–6). Francis Xavier, Jesuit proselytizer of the East Indies, declared that "empire" was "to conjugate the verb to rob, in all its moods and tenses" (Appleby, 2001: 97–8). Colonial wars were expected to pay for themselves out of the spoils (P. Marshall, 2001: 5). Some natives did benefit – such as the Indian merchant-intermediaries – but they did so at the expense of the majority.

We should not exaggerate the significance of empire back home. Its profits were not enormous, providing just above 1 percent of British annual gross domestic product (GDP), only a tenth of Britain's trade with Europe. Of two main contributions, the first came through the Columbian exchange of crops, which played a part in the English eighteenth-century agricultural revolution, which could feed population growth and release labor to the towns. The second contribution came in the 1770s when the profits of slavery provided somewhere between 21 percent and 55 percent of total British investment capital at a critical moment for the industrial revolution, and when its sugar mills and labor-control methods influenced the emerging factory system in Britain. The mills and plantations in the colonies offered more intensive forms of control over labor that soon spread to the working class (more rarely to the peasantry) in the mother country. However, the empire was more of a boost to an economy already booming than a major cause of the industrial revolution itself (O'Brien, 2004; Blackburn, 1997; Schwartz, 2004; Inikori, 2002, disagrees). Later, India and the white Dominions became more important economically, but British economic growth was not fundamentally the product of empire.

Ideological mission statements were not as prominent as in the Spanish empire, yet the British (and Dutch) did claim to export freedom. Their rule was "commercial, Protestant and maritime," all qualities supposedly embodying freedom as opposed to the despotism of continental Europe and Asia (Armitage, 2000: 173, 193). Expansion was led by freelance adventurers – entrepreneurs, soldiers-for-hire, missionaries, even scientists – raising their own funds, backed by businessmen, churches, and scientific societies. Private armed trading companies usually preceded formal colonial rule among the British, French, and Dutch. The Enlightenment helped legitimate it, for the "productive" Europeans were "improving" and "ameliorating" the earth's resources, but "the Profligate Native" was wasting them and deserved to be brought under forcible tutelage (Drayton, 2000: 90, 229–34). Ironically, in the late twentieth century, this ideology went into reverse, as the green movement in the West praised natives for having lived at one with nature, whereas Westerners had pillaged and ruined it.

The British usually behaved correctly when signing treaties with native leaders. Yet the small print, by stages, pushed them out of their land and trade. When they resisted and killed British citizens, this was decried as an outrageous primitive atrocity inflicted by racial inferiors. This emotional response brought terrible retribution. Whitehall would have preferred not to get involved, wanting companies and colonies to pay their own way and not cause trouble. Nonetheless, officials knew their ultimate duty was to protect British citizens. If they did not, the outrage back home might force them out of office. This was empire as catchup, as the authorities struggled to catchup with events precipitated on the ground by bands of armed settlers and merchants. More territories were acquired and the empire became bigger and more direct, almost inexorably, but without an overall vision (B. Porter, 2004: chaps. 1–3; Burroughs, 2001: 170–2; Galbraith, 1963).

From the mid-nineteenth century, Britain shifted toward free trade. Its technological lead meant its goods needed no tariff protection. British liberals remained in denial about "empire" (as Americans are today), arguing that the Royal Navy was simply freeing up markets (B. Porter, 2005: chap. 5). Informal empire, "the imperialism of free trade," now became more extensive than the colonial empire (Gallagher & Robinson, 1953). Some markets were opened up with gunboats, as in China and Siam, and then very low tariffs were enforced. Otherwise, little force was needed because under free trade, the British got most of the trade, anyway. The British Empire was lightening as it widened and became more capitalistic.

Europeans, Americans, and Japanese acquired more colonies in the "New Imperialism," a burst of expansion from the late 1870s to World War I. Because Marxism and the social sciences were now flourishing, this drew explanations that remain influential even today. The liberal journalist John A. Hobson (1902) said the New Imperialism arose from the need to invest surplus domestic capital abroad. He produced tables showing a big increase in British foreign trade and investment during this period. Lenin extended Hobson, claiming, "The more capitalism is developed, the more the need for raw materials ... the more bitter competition becomes, the more feverishly the hunt for raw materials proceeds throughout the whole world. The more desperate becomes the struggle for the acquisition of colonies." Indeed, he said, overaccumulation of capital in the advanced countries produced a surplus that could only be invested in overseas empires (1939: 82). Lenin, Hilferding, and others detected economic concentration and monopoly in the advanced countries, and argued that monopolies at home needed protected territorial markets abroad – colonies. These three tendencies of capitalism were believed to intensify interimperial rivalry, fracturing capitalism and leading to great wars. They recognized that imperialism predated capitalism, but said capitalism gave it a new bite.

However, Hobson, Hilferding, and Lenin were wrong. First, there was cooperation in the international economic system. Britain no longer had a manufacturing lead, but it had the world's reserve currency and the biggest banking system. Foreign banks almost all had branches in London in order to clear trade-related payments. They parked their profits in London banks in the form of low-interest short-term deposits called commercialized bills of exchange. By 1908, the parked funds of foreign and colonial banks were somewhere between one-third and one-half of total bank funds in Britain. The British banks used these funds to make longer-term, higher-interest loans to peripheral countries, as the United States does today. Both made financial arbitrage profits out of borrowing low and lending high (Schwartz, 2004: 118–19). This was an agreed practice among the powers (as it is today) because having a secure reserve currency and financial institutions in the imperial core was advantageous to all – as long as British (and American) credibility remained higher than any alternative. So the world of capitalist finance did not favor increasing imperial rivalry. When that did materialize, it came from different sources.

Moreover, the vast bulk of trade and finance flowed among the advanced capitalist countries, with only a sliver involving the colonies, and neither Hobson nor Lenin realized that only a fraction of British colonial trade and capital went to nonwhite colonies. The vast bulk went to the white settler colonies in Australasia, South Africa, and Canada; whites were trading among themselves. In any case, the increase in overseas investment mainly resulted from compounding and reinvesting overseas profits and an increase in the value of foreign assets already held. It was not surplus capital from the core.

An alternative explanation, advanced by conservatives as well as Marxists, was *social imperialism*: expansion abroad might divert class conflict at home. Some politicians suggested this, and it sometimes seemed to work, but not in Britain. The working class remained largely uninterested in empire and the flow of British settlers was declining (B. Porter, 2005: chaps. 6, 9). Some of these economic arguments make some sense for particular empires, such as Japan (see Chapter 4). However, they are not a good explanation of the New Imperialism in general or of British imperialism in particular.

Explanations focused on economic relations in the core are too parochial; we must also think globally. First, the disparity in military power between empires and natives was increasing. In the late nineteenth century, the steamship, Maxim gun, and quinine (offering protection against tropical diseases) made possible the conquest of larger swathes of lands by smaller militaries (Headrick, 1981; Fieldhouse, 1973). Etemad (2007: chap. 3) says quinine is overrated, agrees with the impact of the Maxim gun after 1880, but sees the decisive enduring advantage of the Europeans as their ability to train large numbers of natives to do their killing for them. When this happened, imperialism's intensive firepower could really go inland. Second, great power rivalry was intensified by the sense that a finite globe was filling up, so it was necessary to grab territories now, before it was full. In the 1880s, German and Belgian imperialism suddenly appeared in East Africa and French imperialism revived; in the 1890s, Japan, Italy, and the United States sought colonies, as well. This was a strategic motive – if we don't grab colonies, our enemies will. There were economic motives, too. Capitalists hoped to make a killing, sometime in the future. Africa just might possess untold riches, and Asia did have immense markets. In a formal sense this was globalization, if still fractured, because almost the whole globe was formally colonized, even if imperial rule over the hinterlands was often very tenuous.

Yet empire rarely dominated politics back home. Colonies remained a low priority in Westminster. Major politicians avoided the colonial offices as career breakers, and debates about empire reliably emptied the Commons. Imperialists – a diverse group of overseas business interests, adventurers, missionaries, and other ideologists – wanted more resources than the politicians would finance. The British governments asked realist questions: How much would an expedition cost? Was it worth it? These questions enjoined caution and relative lightness of rule once a conquest was made. However, major colonial rebellions when British people were killed brought righteous vengeance. Even so, British defeats in Afghanistan only led to temporary reprisals and eventual withdrawal. (Sound familiar?) Expansionary ideals and outraged pride were subordinated to the strategic goal of limiting Russian influence in Afghanistan, cheaply. Only the determined Boer rebellion in South Africa produced an election fought on imperial issues. Then after World War I, governments were desperate for economies, and they sought them in the colonies (Kirk-Greene, 2000; B. Porter, 2005: 105–8; Fieldhouse, 1999: 73–6). British and European issues remained much more important than empire. The imperialist crystallization of the British state remained a lesser one at home.

Lenin believed the scramble for Africa and World War I were linked, but the powers managed to diplomatically regulate the scramble. In 1885, they signed the Treaty of Berlin, which allowed a power to claim African territories if it could effectively patrol their borders. So they all pushed far inland with small forces, making for an entirely nominal presence. They did not dispute a rival's claim to a real presence, however, because their own claims were equally dubious. There were on-the-spot solutions to dangerous confrontations. Take the "Fashoda Incident." On the news that a French force was marching across Africa to the headwaters of the Nile, the British government sent out its own expedition, having previously refused all demands to annex the Sudan. The French force marched a vast distance to reach the town of Fashoda, on the Nile, reaching it at the same time as a British naval force. There was an uneasy pause as they faced one another, and then the French backed off, as the British had gunboats and they did not. Now the British did annex the Sudan. Two empires had managed to regulate their rivalry – at the expense of the periphery. Crises of imperial rivalry loomed perennially, but they were settled diplomatically. As we see in Chapters 5 and 14, Europe's death-throe wars of 1914 and 1939 were not precipitated by imperial rivalry overseas. What finished them off was their rivalry in Europe. Lenin was wrong.

As the twentieth century dawned, the British government was still playing catchup with the adventurers. Men like Stanley, Rhodes, Goldie, and Lugard sought monopoly licenses from the British government for their companies. The king of the Belgians formed his own private company, the most exploitative of all. The adventurers carried guns on their shoulders and blank treaty forms in their pockets. African rulers were persuaded or forced to sign away rights to land or trade. The chiefs assumed gain would follow an alliance with the British; instead, the company sought harsher terms of trade. Then native rulers or traders resisted, and disorder ensued. In temperate zones of Africa, armed settlers entered in numbers unanticipated by the chiefs, seizing their land. African disunity combined with military disparity to ensure a British victory if it came to a fight (Vandervort, 1998; Wesseling, 1989).

As in most empires, mission statements loomed larger as the empire was consolidated because they gave a higher moral tone to expansion. Few people like to think of themselves as being simply rapacious. This was a "civilizing mission" given a racial slant because it was conducted by the "Anglo-Saxon

Race," spreading "Commerce, Civilization and Christianity" – nineteenth-century signifiers of freedom. Violence was unavoidable, it was said, because the natives were at "endless war" with each other, unable to provide order. Although economic profit lured on the adventurers, the state would also step in for strategic reasons if rival empires were glimpsed on the horizon, almost regardless of the chances of profit (Pakenham, 1991: xxiv; Reid, 2007; Gallagher & Robinson, 1953; Fieldhouse, 1973: chap. 13). Motives became increasingly mixed.

Violence remained perennial on the expanding frontiers of empire. Southern African settlers were milder than settlers in North America because they wanted the natives as laborers, yet atrocities still resulted. In Natal in 1874–1875, settlers and British troops massacred the Hlubi and Putini men, women, and children. Natal's Zulus suffered the same fate in 1906. In the 1860s and 1870s, gunboats made annual punitive expeditions up the Niger River, razing villages and killing men, women, and children wherever opposition to British traders was raised. George Goldie's National African Company acquired a Royal Charter in 1879 to enforce "free trade" up the river. In reality, this meant suppressing African traders. The Brassmen, hitherto effective traders, were faced with starvation. In 1895, they retaliated and killed some company employees. There was outrage in Britain, and Goldie asked the British government to "exterminate" them. King Koko and his chiefs, fearing the worst, wrote a letter of apology to the Prince of Wales, saying they were "now *very sorry indeed, particularly* in the *killing* and *eating* of parts of its employees" (their own emphasis). The apology was backed by sympathetic British liberal pressure groups, and little repression ensued, but the company soon resumed its practices and the Brassmen starved. In 1895, Rhodesia was settled by treating everything in the realm of Chief Lobengula – land, cattle, possessions – as loot to be divided between Rhodes' commercial company and other white armed bands. Anyone who resisted died. Between 1870 and 1902, Britain acquired fifteen new colonies and protectorates in Africa by force or the threat of force (Pakenham, 1991; Headrick, 1981: 73–4). Settlers were still seizing land in Kenya in the 1940s.

From 1871 to 1914, the British fought about thirty colonial wars (not counting perennial violence along the northwest frontier of India). Between them, the British, French, and Dutch fought at least 100. In Kenya alone, the British fought one battle per year over a twenty-year period (Wesseling, 1989: 8–11; Wesseling, 2005). European losses in these colonial wars amounted to 280,000–300,000; the conquered peoples lost around 50–60 million, of whom 90 percent were civilians (Etemad, 2007: chaps. 4, 5). This refutes *democratic peace theory*, the supposed tendency of democracies not to make war with each other. Most native polities were direct democracies, in which the community participated in decisions about peace or war and men did not have to fight against their will. Because the British, French, and Dutch governments were broadly representative (for men), democracies were fighting each other with great regularity.

The wars were getting bloodier, perhaps more than prior wars among Africans. The colonists claimed natives were "savage," "bloodthirsty," and war-prone, despite the fact that although Ethiopian and Zulu Empires and the Sokoto Caliphate had intermittently used "scorched earth" tactics, most African chiefs, in a context where they could rarely utterly defeat their rivals, preferred diplomacy and ritualized low-level conflict to all-out war (R. Smith, 1989; Reid, 2007). One difference between Africa and Europe was that labor was scarce in Africa, not land. Most African rulers saw little point in expanding their territories. War as profit did not mean capturing territory but capturing slaves to use or sell. Africans perceived the violence of the British as beyond the goal of capturing people. Europeans urged that the Africans be "soundly beaten," as that was the only way to make them amenable to colonial rule (Vandervort, 1998: 2, 185–205, 219). Colonel Callwell's best-selling military manual, "Small Wars" (1906 edition: 40, 148), declared that in fighting natives who avoided pitched battles, a war of attrition must attack what the enemy "prizes most," destroying crops and villages and running off cattle. "Uncivilized races attribute leniency to timidity. A system adapted to … [Europe] is out of place among fanatics and savages, who must be thoroughly brought to book and cowed or they will rise again." Was this liberal empire?

Britain always contained anti-imperialist pressure groups. Even Prime Minister Gladstone appeared to be anti-imperial in his famous speech of 1879 upholding the right of Zulus and Afghans to defend themselves:

> If they resisted, would not you have done the same? And when, going forth from their villages they had resisted, what you find is this, that those who went forth were slain, and that the village was burned … the women and the children were driven forth to perish in the snows of winter. … To think that the name of England, under no political necessity, but for a war as frivolous as ever was waged in the history of man, should be associated with consequences such as these? Remember the rights of the savage, as we call him. Remember that the happiness of his humble home, remember that the sanctity of life in the hill villages of Afghanistan among the winter snows, is as inviolable in the eye of Almighty God as can be your own.

Gladstone is still relevant to Afghanistan today! Ironically, however, under his administration the British conquered more territory than they had under the pro-imperial Disraeli! In the United States, the liberal President Woodrow Wilson was later caught in a similar contradiction, sending in the marines more often than his supposedly more imperialist predecessors. Unfortunately, liberalism did not yet have much effect on imperial outcomes, although it did generate opposition along the way.

Violence continued after World War I in Iraq, handed to the British as a Mandate by the League of Nations. In Kenya, it continued into the 1950s, led by settlers still expropriating land (G. Kershaw, 1997: 85–9). When the Mau Mau revolted in 1950, the response was ferocious. About 20,000 Kenyans died in combat and more than 1,000 were executed after cursory trials in kangaroo courts – more than the French executed in Algeria. Many more died in British detention camps. The Mau Mau killed thirty-two European settlers in all – a typical imperial disproportion. These atrocities, occurring not in the 1850s but in the 1950s, should dispel notions that the empire became necessarily liberal through time. Among the tortured was Husein Onyango Obama, President Obama's grandfather. He had his testicles squeezed between metal rods, leaving him with lifelong bitterness toward Britain (*The Observer*, 14 December, 2008).

Here is one policeman's memory of interrogating Mickeys, British slang for the Mau Mau:

> They wouldn't say a thing, of course, and one of them, a tall coal-black bastard, kept grinning at me, real insolent. I slapped him hard, but he kept right on grinning at me, so I kicked him in the balls as hard as I could. He went down in a heap but when he finally got up on his feet he grinned at me again and I snapped, I really did. I stuck my revolver right in his grinning mouth and I said something, I don't remember what, and I pulled the trigger. His brains went all over the side of the police station. The other two Mickeys were standing there looking blank. I said to them that if they didn't tell me where to find the rest of the gang I'd kill them too. They didn't say a word so I shot them both. One wasn't dead so I shot him in the ear. When the sub-inspector drove up, I told him that the Mickeys tried to escape. He didn't believe me but all he said was "bury them and see the wall is cleared up." (quoted by D. Anderson, 2004: 300; cf Elkins, 2005).

Once colonies were conquered and pacified, violence lessened because there were not enough Brits to maintain it. Without a mass of settlers, there was a retreat from direct to indirect rule through native elites, although the native regiments offered the colonialists some degree of countervailing power. A combination of force and conciliation with elites resulted in stability and peace. This was the greatest achievement of the British Empire – a small country ruling a vast empire with a tiny permanent civil service, backed by local elites and large native-troop levies. This was not yet the age of nationalism across most of the world. Local elites would side with the empire if they thought it could suppress any rebellion; ordinary natives would fight for the empire if it paid them. In most atrocities mentioned above, most of the troops were natives. There were always winners and losers among natives, especially under indirect rule.

Informal empire spread over the independent states of the semi-periphery, where neither direct nor indirect rule were possible, but where Britain possessed influence. In Latin America, this originated in British naval support for their rebellions against the Spanish Empire. The economies of the countries Britain aided then became owned by City of London corporations. Investment in Argentina was the highest, but the country was too big and far away for gunboat diplomacy to be effective. So Britain resorted to the economic coercion of structural adjustment programs. Argentina contributed 10 percent of Britain's imports and exports around 1900, but Britain contributed 50 percent of Argentina's and most of its investment capital. Argentina had tried but failed to raise more in New York, Paris, and Berlin. Thus, Britain could pressure Argentine governments into pro-British policies. Pressure was especially effective after Peru was sanctioned in 1876 for defaulting on British loans (I. McLean, 1995; M. Lynn, 2001; Cain & Hopkins, 2002: 244–73; Darwin, 2009: chap. 3). Informal empire was tougher in China, Siam, the Ottoman Empire, and Egypt, where free trade, monopolies, and debt rescheduling were backed by persistent gunboat diplomacy. It involved some occupation of ports, but for the most part imperialism remained offshore.

This empire varied greatly through time and space. When it was liberalizing into informal empire in earlier zones of expansion, bloody conquest and direct empire dominated new colonies. Although Ferguson and Lal provided too rigid a dichotomy of pre-1850 versus post-1850, there was a tendency toward more pacific rule, but its timing varied between regions, as they were conquered at different times. I now examine the three more peaceful sources of power: economic, political, and ideological.

Economic power relations: A global economy?

The British Empire was global, yet it was only a segment of the world, and it was turning inward on itself as the twentieth century dawned. Darwin (2009) notes three main zones of high profit: the settler white Dominions; the commercial, informal empire of the City of London; and Greater India, which provided bullion, markets, and military manpower. Ferguson (2004) presents statistics purporting to show considerable economic growth in the empire in the late nineteenth and early twentieth centuries. Yet, bizarrely, his data are almost all from the white Dominions – Australia, New Zealand, Canada, and South Africa – which had the highest growth rates in the world at that time. He adds figures showing that 40 percent of total British foreign investments went to the colonies (2004: 191). However, more than 70 percent of this went to Canada, Australia, and New Zealand. South and Central America, ruled by people of European stock, were "neo-Europes." Only about 10 percent of total British foreign investment went to Asia and Africa, although the British were investing far more overseas than any other European power. The French and Germans were aiding the development of Eastern Europe more than their overseas empires; the Americans were trading most with Canada and Britain.

It is often said that Britain reoriented itself away from Europe and into its empire in the late nineteenth century, "a consolation prize for a failure to do well in a more global setting" when faced with other rising powers, says H. James (2006: 102). The retreat was narrower than this, however, into a white Anglophone macro-region comprising the Dominions, and the United States absorbing 60 percent of all British foreign investment (Davis & Huttenback,

1987: 37–9, 56–7; Simon, 1968; Clemens & Williamson, 2004). The solidarity of the Anglo-Saxons was to be fully revealed in the world wars. The period before 1914 is often asserted to have been the most global phase of capitalist development, as the ratio of foreign trade to world production was at its highest. This is also misleading, because the trend was fractured. These trends indicate instead two things: a more integrated North Atlantic economy and the global diffusion of the white race.

In the white Dominions, and to a lesser extent in the neo-Europes of Latin America, exterminating the natives and then throwing off the imperial yoke produced the best economic outcome for the settlers, if not for the natives. This was a contradiction of the overseas empires. Their control over colonies was initially greatest where there was support from white settlers, but the settlers decided they could get on better without the imperial power.

European and American countries did benefit economically from British leadership. Although they were sovereign states running their own economies, they also benefited from the free import of British capital and skilled labor. There was easy technology transfer; foreigners copied and improved on British production methods. However, following the prescriptions of Friedrich List and Alexander Hamilton rather than Adam Smith, they protected their infant industries, and after mid-century, they had become competitive with Britain and could lower their tariffs. After 1870, they adopted the norms of the gold standard and kept their currencies at the current parity of exchange for gold, as set by the British Treasury. This enabled lower-cost borrowing and greater inward investment. Starting in the 1870s, most European countries, Japan, and the Dominions adhered to the gold standard. The United States and Italy usually did so, returning at current parity if they temporarily left it. Other southern European countries could not manage this, but they shadowed the gold standard, whereas South Americans often had to suspend convertibility and devalue (Bordo & Rockoff, 1996; Obstfeld & Taylor, 2004). There was a hierarchy of states; those at the top were white. Except for Japan, the gold standard was also a white standard.

O'Rourke & Williamson (2002) reveal some convergence of commodity prices across developed economies at the end of the nineteenth century, a better measure of an integrated transnational economy than the trade/GDP ratio normally used. Yet it was more trans-Atlantic than global, serving to further integrate Europe, North America, the Antipodes, and southern cone of Latin America, and was buttressed by massive European migration across the Atlantic. Whereas classical economic theory would suggest that capital flows to places with labor surpluses, here white capital followed white labor; race overruled economic theory. For much of the world, the nineteenth-century transport revolution was a mixed blessing. It increased the price of primary products relative to manufactured goods, improving the terms of trade for peripheral countries and encouraging them to shift toward export-oriented agriculture. This tended to deindustrialize the more advanced countries, especially India. Thus, rates of growth in per capita income on the periphery began to lag further behind, and global income disparity widened (J. Williamson, 2006).

Britain's colonies did share in the boom of 1860–1914, when territories belonging to an empire had almost double the international trade of the few independent countries (Mitchener & Weidenmier, 2008),[1] although most profitable industry and trade were owned by citizens from the homeland, and most profits were repatriated. Some colonies were deindustrialized, more reliant on exporting raw materials and foodstuffs. These were increasingly available from richer countries, too, usually in higher-tech versions – beet for sugar cane, refined foods, chemicals for natural dyes, synthetics for natural fibers, and so forth – so this lowered the prices of poor countries' goods relative to rich ones (P. O'Brien, 2004). Milanovic, Lindert, and Williamson (2011) have used Gini coefficients to calculate what they call *exploitation rates*, the proportion of the surplus accruing to the elite beyond that necessary to keep the population alive. In a sample of thirty preindustrial societies, six had a rate of exploitation of 100 percent; that is, the elites took all of the surplus. These were all colonies, of various empires, but included India and Kenya. The other three colonial cases in their sample, British Bihar and two measures for Java in the Dutch empire, had a rate of around 70 percent. It seems that surplus generated within colonies went to white elites and a few local collaborators. The incomes of the colonial elites would place them in the top 0.1 percent of the world population even today! Going by these measures, the *raison d'etre* of colonial empires was exploitation.

The most striking feature of the age of empire was the emergence of the greatest global inequality the world has ever seen, "the great divergence." The white race industrialized and other races did not – except for the Japanese. Mass living standards and life expectancy improved substantially in the imperial homelands, but only very slightly in most native colonies. This was offset by population growth, so that the number of people living in poverty actually increased (van Zanden et al., 2011). Starting about 1860, trade between the homelands and their empires – except for the white Dominions and Indian bullion – contributed proportionately much less to homeland economies than they had earlier. The colonies were too poor to buy the products of the Second Industrial Revolution, and the advanced world turned more into itself (Etemad, 2005: 293). Unequal development then persisted in the period 1914–1950. In this period, the white race globalized and other races were substantially excluded. Economic globalization was not just fractured between empires, it was also racially segregated.

[1] Michener assures me that the British colonies did better, even if he excludes the white Dominions.

The jewel in the crown: Economic power relations in India

India was the most valuable colony, taking a quarter of British exports and most of the British investment going to Asia and Africa. It allowed Britain to run the gold standard; its million-plus army defended the empire. Its GDP grew from 1880 to 1920 by less than 1 percent per annum, then it leveled off; in the 1930s, it declined (Roy, 2000: 218–23; cf Tomlinson, 1993). In the 100 years before independence in 1947, development averaged 0.2 percent per year – at a time when Britain itself experienced growth almost ten times that rate. Life expectancy probably showed no improvement either, unlike Britain (International Labor Office, 1938). This was not due to population growth wiping out economic gains, as population growth was lower than in Britain itself. British medical policy in India was also minimal. Whenever more ambitious medical improvement policies went against the grain of local practices, the British backed off. Thus, concludes Arnold (1993), few Indian bodies were colonized.

India was an enormous country, and it didn't contain many British. In 1931, only 90,000 Brits were economically active, two-thirds of them in the army or police. Two thousand British administrators governed almost 300 million Indians; it was remarkable they could govern at all. We must not exaggerate their role, for good or ill. Was it their fault the country remained mired in poverty, illiteracy, and mortality? The British were not the prime movers in the economy, and could not abolish barriers to development created by local social structures (Tirthankar Roy, 2000: 262; cf 1999: 59). British policy only had marginal effects, but was it marginally helpful or marginally harmful?

Dadabhai Naoroji was president of the newly formed Indian National Congress. In his famous economic balance sheet of British rule (1887: 131–6), he appealed to the better nature of the British. Praising their efforts, he asked only that they live up to their promises. However, his criticisms were pointed and correct. He saw British economic policy as geared to keeping the country open for British exports, which had a competitive edge over Asian goods. Free trade meant Britain could export manufactured goods to India and take raw materials in exchange. This harmed Indian artisanal industries unable to compete with British manufactures (Roy, 1999; Washbrook, 2001; Parthasarathi, 2001; Roy, 2000: 128; Roy, 1999). Textiles struggled back to relative prosperity by the 1870s, but the value of its exports was much lower than raw materials and agricultural produce (B. Porter, 2004: 53). Indian expertise in shipbuilding, mining, and metals, seen as strategic industries, was suppressed, and railway equipment was imported from England (Arnold, 2000: chap. 4). The suppression was accomplished not by military force but by manipulating the terms of trade; exploitation was indirect.

There was some improvement in the twentieth century. Indian nationalists organized boycotts of foreign goods, pressuring the British into infant industry protection. In 1896, Indian mills had supplied only 8 percent of Indian cloth; by 1913, they supplied 20 percent, and by 1945, 76 percent (Maddison, 2007: 128). The British, however, had their own reasons for the shift. World War I increased the strategic significance of India and the need for defense and other public expenditures. They did not want to increase land taxes because this would have alienated the landowners they depended on to rule locally. So they shifted to taxing imports to get revenue from tariffs, and this also kept out German and Japanese goods. Industries such as textiles, iron and steel, sugar, and paper received protection as average tariff rates rose from 5 percent in 1900 to 25 percent by 1930. They also wanted to save India-related sterling expenditures, so Indian needs were increasingly supplied within India and not from Britain. Starting in about 1934, industry grew, and was then boosted by World War II. India had shifted toward dirigisme even before independence, which did benefit Indians (Kohli, 2004: 253–4).

British fiscal policy, Naoroji noted, was to siphon off export receipts to London. India had a large export surplus with other countries, but a large deficit with Britain. Because the currency of the whole empire was sterling, Indian profits of about 1 percent of Indian national income and perhaps 20 percent of India's net savings returned to Britain (Maddison, 2007: 121). This met 30–40 percent of Britain's deficit with other industrialized countries, enabling Britain to balance its external account, remain on the gold standard, and provide the world's reserve currency (S.B. Saul, 1960: chap. 8). This policy was deflationary, because of low tariffs, high exchange rates (to encourage imports), and massive military budgets. India was the keystone of imperial defense, providing most of the Empire's battle-ready troops deployed throughout the world (Darwin, 2009: chap. 5). Without moving India's wealth and soldiers abroad, the Empire could not have survived.

Naoroji, however, accepted that there were also benefits of British rule. Starting in 1900, spending on railways and ports usually exceeded direct defense spending, although it was used to move troops around and channel goods to and from Britain. Irrigation projects were mostly in the Punjab, the main military recruiting ground and settlement area for military veterans. Tomlinson (1993: 148–9) says, "Administrative concerns took precedence over development initiatives … the advances that were made in India … were largely achieved in spite of the inertia created by an administration that ruled in economic matters by a mixture of benign and malign neglect" (cf Misra, 2003; Subrahmanyam, 2004; Roy, 2000: 243, 252–7, 273). These investments were less than the amounts being siphoned back to Britain, although railways did help integrate the economy, as did imperial weights and measures, currency, and contract law. The average height of Indians increased very slightly under the British, an indication of slightly improved health, although height increased much more after Indian independence (Brennan et al., 1997). Integration became a disadvantage in 1929, when India felt the effects of the

Great Depression (Tomlinson, 1993: 69–70), but as Lal argues, overall, integration is better than exclusion.

Most Indian elites did quite well. Indeed, the British shared exploitation with them. After the British destroyed the post-Mughal states, they reduced land taxes, which benefited landowners. Inequality in the villages widened and landless laborers grew in numbers. Property owners also benefited from expanded trade and education (Maddison, 2007: 120ff). Literacy rates doubled in the twentieth century, although from such a low level that it benefitted a relatively small sub-elite. About 5 percent were literate in 1911, 11 percent in 1947. By the time of independence, most civil servants at all levels were Indians – and English-speaking, as English had been the only language of instruction in higher education since 1835. English became the linguistic unifier of the elite in a multilingual subcontinent. It was to prove a Trojan horse, generating a nationalism expressed in English.

On the debit side, mass famines increased during British rule. The famine of 1876–1878 killed around 6–8 million persons, the two famines of 1896–1897 and 1899–1900 nearly 20 million. Cornelius Walford (1878–79; cf Digby, 1901) noted that throughout, grain was still being exported to London. Famines are partly natural, partly social, as Mike Davis shows for India (2000:110–11, 158–9, 172–3). Taxes increased peasant vulnerability to drought. Whereas precolonial authorities adjusted revenue demands to harvests, the British had inflexible taxes derived from a bureaucratic state at home, and they firmly adhered to utilitarianism and free trade. The Famine Commission's Report of 1878 stated, "The doctrine that in time of famine the poor are entitled to demand relief ... would probably lead to the doctrine that they are entitled to such relief at all times ... which we cannot contemplate without serious apprehension." Viceroy Lytton warned his staff to resist "humanitarian hysterics," ordering "no interference of any kind on the part of Government with the object of reducing the price of food." Viceroy Lord Curzon declared, "Any government which imperiled the financial position of India in the interests of prodigal philanthropy would be open to serious criticism; but any Government which by indiscriminate alms-giving weakened the fibre and demoralized the self-reliance of the population, would be guilty of a public crime" (M. Davis, 2000: 31–3, 162).

Laissez-faire ensured that even during famines grain surpluses were exported to England. British consumers, unlike Indians, could afford to pay the higher prices that shortages generated. Indian requests for tax relief were denied. M. Davis (2000: 22) concludes, "Imperial policies toward starving 'subjects' were the moral equivalent of bombs dropped from 18,000 feet." He asks, "How do we weigh smug claims about the life-saving benefits of steam transportation and modern grain markets when so many millions, especially in British India, died alongside railroad tracks or on the steps of grain depots?" Markets and railroads extracted food more efficiently from the famished areas, pulled by greater purchasing power elsewhere. Ironically, the populations of these famished areas would have been better off without railroads; then they could have consumed their own produce. As in the Irish famine, government said it must not interfere with the natural workings of markets, which supposedly brought the greatest efficiency for the greatest number.

Lakshmi Iyer (2004) devised an ingenious test of government in India. After the 1858 reforms, Britain directly ruled about half the land area and three-quarters of the population. The rest was ruled indirectly, through Indian princes, who ran their own budgets. Although the British ruled over the more prosperous agricultural areas, they developed fewer public goods – schools, health clinics, and communications infrastructures – and native rulers raised higher taxes than the British. The difference might result from the land quality, so Iyer separated out princely territories that lapsed into British rule when the prince died without an heir. This was a random process from the point of view of economic development. The lapsed regions also had fewer public goods. Thus, Indians had fewer public goods under British rule than under native princes.

After the initial phase of imperial plunder, the British Empire had no massive impact either way on the Indian economy, except during famines. Some policies were harmful; some were beneficial. Overall, a little economic development occurred, but elites rather than the masses benefited. We cannot know what India's fate might have been without the British. Had it maintained its independence, its economic fate might have been worse – such as China's – or it might have been better – such as Japan's – had it been able to enter the world economy on its own terms. At the point of British conquest, post-Mughal India was somewhere between these two – neither stagnant nor very dynamic. It was a former great civilization in decline, showing limited signs of recovery. After all, it had been the buoyancy of Indian manufacturing and trade that attracted European intervention; India had supplied a quarter of the world's textiles. Some of the post-Mughal native states – such as Mysore and the Maratha – were modernizing, property law was evolving, and Indian science was slowly developing (Bayly, 1996: 21–38; Arnold, 2000: 1–18; Maddison, 2007: 130, is less optimistic). All of this was aborted under colonialism. The contrast with India after independence is striking: The average rate of GDP growth in British India was 0.1 percent, compared to the growth rate of 1.7 percent in India after independence. Easterlin (2000: table 1) declares 1945 the turning point for India. Although no decisive answer is possible, the most plausible British-free counterfactual scenario is slightly better economic development.

There were some colonial success stories. Malaya boomed on the basis of transplanted rubber trees, nicely timed to meet growing demand for tires. Although most plantations were British owned, with profits repatriated to Britain, there were spin-offs for the locals. By 1929, British Malaya had the highest per capita GDP in Asia, and it provided employment for thousands of migrants from India and China (Drabble, 2000: 113). West African farmers benefited from cocoa transplanted from America. In Ghana, African peasants and traders developed a booming industry with the aid of improved transport infrastructures. Indeed, transplants were probably the most beneficial product of imperialism, yielding foodstuffs and medicines for the world. Kew Gardens rather than Whitehall was the most benign patron of British imperialism, although this may have been due more to the British passions for gardening than to imperialism itself (Drayton, 2000).

Most colonies depended on exports from a single agricultural crop or extractive industry, rendering them vulnerable to fluctuating commodity prices. This fostered *gate-keeper states*, in which colonial capitals were port cities levying taxes on imports and exports and issuing licenses, the conduit between the valuable economic enclaves and the imperial core. The mines and plantations sent their goods directly abroad, with minimal spin-off for the local economy, and other inland territories lay outside the government's logistical reach (Cooper, 2002: chap. 1). Alongside India, only white-dominated South Africa was bequeathed infrastructures that integrated the country. Although tropical exports grew by more than 3 percent from 1883 to 1913, this did not impact the lives of most producers because most farms were European-owned (Reynolds, 1985). West African export marketing boards in the late empire did rechannel excise taxes into development projects, but settler agriculture eroded forests and common grazing lands. The world's croplands grew 70 percent between 1850 and 1920. The result was underemployed rural labor, which held down the level of wages (Tomlinson, 1999: 64–8). There was little economic development for Africans until the 1940s.

Africa was colonized later than India, when the British were, in principle, committed to development. African colonies were poor, however, and provided little profit; the authorities would not lavish resources on them. In 1903, the Colonial and Sudan Offices in London had a combined staff of just more than 200, few of whom had ever been to the colonies. In Africa, 1,200 colonial civil servants were spread over fifteen colonies; they could only govern by accommodating native elites. As attempts to impose private-property relations generally caused discontent, the British backed off, except where natives were expropriated for the benefit of European farms or mines. As in French and Belgian colonies, they sometimes imposed forced labor, as land was plentiful but labor scarce. Enclaves of British ownership of high-value resources were set amid broader territories where the British (or French) merely divided and ruled. They had special difficulty in penetrating Islamic civil society in the north of the continent. Most colonialisms lightened through time once the colonial power and its settlers had expropriated much of the valuable land, and once they learned the economies of rule through native elites. The worst atrocities generally came early – the Spanish in the Caribbean, the British in North America – although they happened among the latecomer empires, too – the

Belgian King Leopold's mines in the Congo, the Germans in Southwest Africa, the Italians in Ethiopia.

Overall, there was limited economic development in Africa (Maddison, 2007: 228). Etemad (2007) suggests that after catastrophic population declines in colonial conquest periods, the population more than recovered, suggesting real economic growth that a higher birthrate then undermined. I condemn the economic record of colonies in the conquest stage of empire; thereafter, it became more ambiguous, although there was variation between colonies as well as between those who became favored clients of the imperial power and those who did not. Colonialism certainly cannot be blamed for the whole extent of the great divergence. There was imperial exploitation, as we have seen, but the main reason for the great and growing economic difference between the West and the Rest lay in differences between the internal conditions of the mother countries and the colonies. The West industrialized; the Rest did not – except for Japan and its colonies.

Political power relations in the colonies

The big picture in political power relations was again a contrast, this one between the emergence of civil and political citizenship in the imperial core and the white settler colonies versus subjection in the colonial periphery – between nation-state and empire. Lal and Ferguson say the British Empire provided "good government," in the sense of being relatively efficient, low cost, and uncorrupt. Ferguson, however, also stressed its encouragement of representative government, and this is dubious except for the white Dominions (Ward, 1976). No other colony developed even a restricted franchise at even the local level until after World War I. In Asia, a few appointed (not elected) native members sat on governors' councils, but without any say in military or foreign policy. This double standard between settlers and natives provoked perennial backlash, and the British realized they must rule less directly – with the help of native elites – after the Indian Mutiny in 1857 and again half a century later in Africa (Louis, 2001: vii-ix; Crowder, 1968). They chose elites whom they believed to be traditional rulers, yet British support actually made kings, chiefs, and high castes stronger than they had been previously (Mamdani, 1996). This was movement away from representative government, an alliance between British and native upper classes to head off potential nationalist opposition.

Like all imperialists, the British claimed empire was for the benefit of the natives. This involved Lamarckian notions of social evolution, whereby the "environment" of British rule would uplift the natives. Colonies were held in "trust," "to protect and improve the coloured races." British leaders were divided over how much improvement was possible. Thomas Macaulay declared in the House of Commons, "The public mind of India having become instructed in European knowledge ... may, in some future age, demand European institutions." When an Indian parliament was eventually established, he said, it would be "the proudest day in English history." William Wilberforce (leader of the antislavery movement) envisaged the "gradual introduction of our own principles and opinions; of our laws, institutions and manners; above all, as the source of every other improvement, of our religion, and ... morals." Of course, Britain itself did not yet have responsible, representative government (B. Porter, 2004: 32–3; B. Porter 2006: 52; A. Porter, 2001).

British living standards rose starting in the 1870s, and life expectancy shot up as the twentieth century arrived. British men now acquired political citizenship, lessening the flow of settlers. Moreover, "civilizing" the empire no longer meant integrating natives into a given social order, as it had for the Roman Empire. Even at the end of the eighteenth century, differences in GNP per capita, living standards, and mortality rates across the world had not been significant, but they were by the beginning of the twentieth century. In the 1880s, there was an outpouring of imperialist sentiment that development was the white man's burden. This would not threaten the core's superiority over the natives, because the core was developing much faster. Now a lesser-trusteeship notion appeared: the British Empire would tow the native populations along behind it in a continuing process of unequal economic and political development.

As the British franchise broadened, both pro-imperial and anti-imperial movements tried to raise popular consciousness of empire. The working class was not much affected by the propaganda, but the middle classes adopted a positive attitude toward the empire, seeing it as a philanthropic enterprise, such as helping the poor at home. Imperialism was patriarchal, raising a "family" of child-like colonial nations to eventual adulthood. British liberalism promised self-determination upon adulthood – but not just yet. Nonetheless, the classic texts of liberalism and socialism – of John Locke, John Stuart Mill, and Karl Marx – were written in universal terms, without being restricted to advanced civilizations. Reading them might bolster the confidence of literate nationalists in the legitimacy of their cause.

Pressure came from the natives, especially in India. Reform battles in the 1880s secured entry of Indians into the lower provincial civil service (Sinha, 1995: 100–1). The newly formed Indian National Congress and the Muslim League both demanded political representation. Instead, Viceroy Lord Curzon promoted the "traditional" authority of "Indian gentlemen of the highest birth and position," at the expense of Congress nationalists, a class strategy to undermine nationalism. He also tried to divide-and-rule between Hindus and Muslims, but the election of a Liberal government in Britain in 1906 brought some movement, adding a few elected members on a restricted franchise into provincial legislative councils (Dilks, 1969: 239; R. Moore, 2001: 435–45; cf B. Porter, 2004: 211–16; Darwin, 2009: chap. 5).

Africa was more varied, but further back in its development. The Sudan Political Service ruled much of Africa, and remained 100 percent British until 1952 (Kirk-Greene, 2000: 248–9). In 1923, the governor of Nigeria declared, "In a country such as Nigeria, which in too many areas has not yet emerged from barbarism, a strong, and within limits, an autocratic government is essential." (Wheare, 1950: 42). Lord Lugard, the theorist of indirect rule in Africa, said:

> The ideal of government can only be realised by the methods of evolution which have produced the democracy of Europe and America, -viz., by representative institutions in which the comparatively small educated class shall be recognised as the natural spokesmen for the many.... The verdict of students of history and sociology of different nationalities ... is ... unanimous – that the era of complete independence is not as yet visible on the horizon of time. (1922: 193–7)

In 1938, Colonial Secretary Malcolm Macdonald said, "It may take generations, or even centuries for the people in some parts of the Colonial Empire to achieve self-government. But it is a major part of our policy, even among the most backward peoples of Africa, to teach them and to encourage them always to be able to stand a little more on their own feet" (Marx, 2002: 151). These men had a different time frame than the "backward peoples" themselves.

Some officials were skeptical. Sir Alfred Lyall, a senior official in India, saw the writing on the wall as early as 1882, saying, "I know of no instance in history of a nation being educated by another nation into self-government and independence; every nation has fought its way up in the world as the English have done" (B. Porter, 2006: 53). Nationalists increasingly demanded some self-government. India saw cycles of agitation, strikes, riots, then repression, then more riots, and finally concessions. In 1913, the Congress and Muslim League both demanded full self-government. World War I boosted the legitimacy of their demands, as hundreds of thousands of Indians fought for the Empire in Europe and Africa. After mass demonstrations, in 1919 the number of elected members of provincial councils was increased, and some provincial ministries were placed under their control. General Dyer's bloody suppression of demonstrators at Amritsar in 1919 was counterproductive, helping the Congress and Muslim League recruit mass support. The proportion of Indians in the imperial civil service rose from 5 percent in 1915 to 10 percent in 1920 because of wartime shortages of British men. With very little British immigration after the war, the proportion continued rising, reaching 42 percent in 1939 (Kirk-Greene, 2000: 248–9), strengthening nationalists more than the gentry. In 1935 (again in response to riots), the British proposed representative and responsible government at the local level. Nationalists rejected this, demanding complete independence. Many British Labour politicians supported independence; most Conservatives thought the Empire would last a long time yet. Curzon, however, came sadly to doubt this: "There is slowly growing up a sort of national feeling" that "can be never wholly reconciled to an alien government. The forces and tendencies at work are on the whole fissiparous, not unifying." He pinned his hopes on "perpetually building bridges over that racial chasm that yawns eternally in our midst," but he sometimes wondered how long it could all last (Dilks, 1969: 95, 105).

Hinduism and Islam helped resistance. Even early resistance by Mughal gentry and merchants had involved some sense of patriotic defense of an Indian state under alien occupation. Some rudimentary sense of nationalism made sense to dominated people, and assisted the rise of a single Hindu religion/culture from out of a plethora of cults and sects. It asserted a spiritual superiority over the materially superior British (Bayly, 1996: 345–52; Bayly 2004: chap. 6; Chatterjee, 1993: 121; Ray, 2003). This occidentalism fed Gandhian nationalism at the same time the new Indian middle class, educated in British schools, developed a more secular ideology of modernization and reform. Across the Asian colonies, conservative cultural reactions shifted into a nationalism claiming to be more modern than the British (Gelber, 2001: 152–61).

Development, although limited and unequal, increased the size of the nationalist middle class. Ironically, imperial success produced its own gravediggers. By the interwar period, Gandhi, and the Congress and Muslim League led mass movements. Their unity depended less on an actual Indian nation (for Indians were divided along religious, caste, ethnic, and class lines) than on common experience of repression and racism – as in most colonies.

Ideological power relations in the colonies

The big nineteenth-century ideological trend was a surge in racism. In earlier periods, successful empires culturally assimilated their conquered peoples, helped by the fact that they expanded over neighbors who were not very different from themselves. Russians were still doing this in the nineteenth century, so they assimilated the most conquered natives. The Western Europeans, however, went overseas – halfway across the world – to encounter seemingly "alien" people physically different from themselves. They struggled to understand these alien qualities, of which skin tone was the most obvious. They distinguished them by race, although not initially in a biological sense, as their religion taught them that all were descended from Adam and Eve. Theirs was at first a classification in terms of power. The weakest races were "savages," the strongest were "civilized," although most of these were considered "decadent." Explanations for backwardness emphasized geographical and social factors such as climate, terrain, bad government, and ignorance of religion. Christians, however, said that even the most backward had reason and souls; they were "of our same blood," although they needed to be shown the light. Most initially believed race differences didn't have to be permanent, an ideology that offered some encouragement for universal globalization, as did Enlightenment values. Montesquieu used an intelligent Persian ambassador and Voltaire an intelligent Huron Indian to cast a critical, often amused eye on their own French society. As Katzenstein (2010) reminds us, civilizations are not singular but plural, and somewhat open-ended. The combination of racism, imperialism, orientalism, Christianity, and Enlightenment ideas could lead in different directions.

The Spanish converted and married among Aztec and Inca elites. At first, cohabitation and intermarriage were also common among British settler populations, but slavery encouraged racism. Notions of a white race seem to have first appeared among American planters wishing to distinguish themselves from slave "blacks" and to justify their exploitation (T. Allen, 1997). Such racism was not yet apparent in Asia, where Europeans respected the civilizations confronting them. Intermarriage, cohabitation, and concubinage were common. In 1780, one-third of British men in India who left wills included bequests to Indian wives or companions or the offspring of such liaisons (Dalrymple, 2002: 34). Yet in the 1780s, the East India Company shifted policy to discourage mixed marriages and removed sons of mixed-blood marriages from its employ, having previously given them preferential treatment. There was a further jump in racism in India in the 1830s. Blood and civilization were now "much the same thing ... the calibration of blood became of vital significance for the colonial order" (Bayly, 1996: 219; Sen, 2002: 143; Collingham, 2001). Cohabitation and concubinage were now considered immoral, and marriage outside of the Christian community was deplored. Racial segmentation lowered barriers among Europeans, as they were all white. Class divisions among colonists were now less important than in the mother country. The British also brought notions of improvement, both material and moral. Eighteenth-century Britain was rapidly improving, and by contrast, Hindu and Muslim societies seemed static or decadent; Indians were denounced as incorrigibly idle and corrupt.

In Britain, racism was not yet as strong. In "the final debates over British emancipation in the House of Commons in 1833, not a single MP argued for, or from, any racial incapacity of Africans" (Drescher, 2002: 81). In India, racism was undercut by the need for indirect rule. Macaulay said, "We must do our best to form a class who may be interpreters between us and the millions whom we govern, a class of persons Indian in blood and colour, but English in taste, in opinions, words and intellect" (Young, 1957: 729). They educated the sons of the gentry, Brahmins, and other notables in English, and adapted their own class distinctions to the traditional statuses of Indian society. Indian elites seemed civilized; Indian peasants did not. British class and Indian caste merged, as princes, Brahmins, and Muslim notables became the "gentry leaders of a caste-based society" (Cannadine, 2001: chap. 4). Although differences among natives seemed less in Africa, the British used them, too. Princes, high-caste families, chiefs, and other notables were accorded power, uniforms, honors, medals, and titles. Indirect rule mediated race with class, restraining racism in the public sphere.

However, the British cultivated two rival native elites, traditional notables and a newly educated middle class – lawyers, professionals, administrators – confined to lower administration, and treated worse. The Africans' discontent translated into a populist nationalism, appealing to the people as a whole, ignoring class divisions among the natives. The British affected to despise them. Whereas they saw the "gentry" as "natural leaders," civilized, martial, and manly, they called the civil servants *babus*, a derogatory term meaning "soft, effeminate," and mocked them for speaking overcorrect, stilted English. African hereditary chiefs were preferred to "mission boys." In the Sudan, the latter were called "Effendis," aping European ways, and "boys," working under British "men" who were actually younger than they were. In Iraq, the British preferred the "untainted gentry," tribal sheikhs, over "unreliable" urban nationalist lawyers and politicians (Burroughs, 2001: 181–2; Cell, 2001: 243; Sharkey, 2003; Dodge, 2003: chaps. 4, 5). This was indirect rule degenerating into divide-and-rule, class against nation.

Racism continued to dominate the private sphere in India. The intimate lives of the British and natives remained separate; caste and religious barriers reinforced this. Hindu notions of purity centered on who could marry and dine with whom; there could be no contact with the unclean. Women reinforced private segregation, for this was their sphere. Higher-status Hindu and Muslim women drew back from the public sphere, a place of daily humiliation by Europeans, into a private realm they could control, and which they said embodied their spiritual superiority to Westerners (Chatterjee, 1993: 122–30). The British injected "bodily closure" into their dress and comportment, abandoning loose Indian garments in favor of the uniformed, buttoned-up, top-hatted sahib and his crinolined, corseted memsahib. Comfort was subordinated to stiff formality as an "affective wall" was built between the body and environment (Collingham, 2001). Natives were not allowed in social clubs, and European women were discouraged from doing social or charitable work among the poor, as many had back home. Intermarriage became rarer; by 1900, it was taboo for British men to associate with Indian women. In Africa, the British (and French) passed laws against intermarriage. Few British in India or Africa (except for settler zones) conceived of their stay as permanent; if they could afford it, they educated their children in British schools. Their comings and goings between core and periphery made them cultural hybrids, "suffering for Empire," fearful their children would pick up Indian ways. The insecurities of a small white community set among 300 million Hindus and Muslims did not favor good relations (Procida, 2002: 97–100, 195–8; Buettner, 2004).

In the late nineteenth century, biological racialism increased. "Racial degeneration" seemed to explain stagnant and backward societies. Careless sexuality and interbreeding had to be avoided, and patriarchal models were added. Civilized races that were militarily inferior to the Europeans were "effeminate," the more backward were "child-like." Sir Lepel Griffin, a senior British official in India, merged racism and patriarchy in splendid fashion, declaring:

> The characteristics of women which disqualify them for public life and its responsibilities are inherent in their sex and are worthy of honor, for to be womanly is the highest praise for a woman, as to be masculine is her worst reproach, but when men, as the Bengalis are disqualified for political enfranchisement by the possession of essentially feminine characteristics, they must expect to be held in such contempt by stronger and braver races, who have fought for such liberties as they have won or retained (Sinha, 1995; cf Sen, 2002; Stoler, 2002: 78).

Patriarchal racism tended to convert indirect rule into segregated apartheid. African natives were seen as more primitive, but they were becoming Christians, so social Darwinism could never quite triumph over Lamarckian and Christian notions of improvement. Through Christianizing and development, racial differences could in theory be transcended. Missionary schools also provided literacy, perhaps the major benefit of empire. Missionaries had much less success among Muslims, Hindus, and Buddhists. Had the Romans conquered a major people who possessed a rival salvation religion, they might have had difficulties, too. They had enough trouble with a minor sect, the Jews.

Intimate racism made it difficult for natives to identify with the imperialists. Many were attracted to British civilization, but were repelled socially and racially by whites. Some were loyal because they depended on the British for their privileges. Yet racism experienced intimately and in public by the new middle class prevented the British Empire and the French empire from taking the Roman or Han Chinese route to cultural assimilation. Although economic, political, and military power relations all helped form racism, the primary influence came from ideology, the search by the British for an explanation of civilization differences as filtered through current British ideologies. The greatest significance of racism was its effect, for it is the last ideology that imperialists should embrace! The inability of the colonized to feel British or be accepted as British (or French) was to doom the project of a cross-ethnic class alliance, especially when economic development and political representation began to move forward, as this expanded middle-class nationalism. European imperialism contained a terminal contradiction: Although the ideology of racism might increase the cohesion of the white colonists, this was outweighed by the loss of legitimacy it brought to the natives. Racism was imperial suicide.

Overall, empire did not benefit the natives. The commanding heights of military, political, and economic power were held by Europeans, buttressed by an increasingly racist ideology, greater in the private than the public realm. Not surprisingly, natives resented this and then resisted. Overall, I end up closer to postcolonial negativism than proimperialist enthusiasm. New colonies were acquired with blood and iron. After pacification, the costs for the natives declined, although the benefits were rarely striking. The world should thank Britain for its agricultural and industrial revolutions, science, and botany rather than its empire. Although its empire was relatively mild compared to others, the world would have been better off without it. The world remained fractured rather than moving toward a single world system; transcontinental integration was largely reserved for the white people of the world.

The weakening of empires

It took 400 years for the British Empire to expand to its fullest, but only 40 years to collapse. European dominance was brief; overseas empires were difficult to integrate, white settlers demanded representative governments, and racism prevented assimilation elsewhere. The two world wars were the final assassins. India sent 1.2 million soldiers to help the British in the first war, and 2 million in the second. Military participation generated similar political demands as in Britain itself. In response, self-government reforms were implicitly promised for war's end. One Indian nationalist exulted prematurely that the first war "has brought forward history fifty years." In 1917, Sir Edwin Montagu, the Liberal secretary of state for India, seeking to "arrest the further defection of moderate opinion," promised "responsible government" (B. Porter, 2004: 232–4). War's end also provided emboldened demobilized soldiers who joined teachers, lawyers, trade unionists, and civil servants to form nationalist movements in the colonies. The rise of Japan emboldened resistance among Asian people. In 1917, President Wilson thrilled them all when he declared the United States entered the war to ensure that "every people has a right to choose the sovereignty under which they shall live." That same year, the anticolonial Bolsheviks seized power in Russia, inspiring other radical nationalists across the world.

World War I brought defeat for Germany, which now lost its fairly small empire. It brought victory for the British and French, and they faced down the turbulent aftermath in their much larger empires with a mixture of repression and pragmatic adjustment to local elites. Rule was lighter still in American colonies. Japan was also victorious in the war, and it pressed ahead with a more directly ruled empire, which I discuss in Chapters 4 and 12. The payoff to natives in the European empires, however, was minimal, except for whites in the Dominions and Ireland. The postwar settlement brought further betrayal, as some colonies of losing powers were transferred to the winners. Woodrow Wilson could not get a statement supporting self-determination into the League of Nations Charter, and Japan was unable to get anyone, including Wilson, to agree to a racial-equality clause –that threatened both empires and

Wilson's own Democratic Party. The great powers conspired to keep imperialism afloat.

Nationalists in the colonies mostly felt betrayed by the war's aftermath. There were not many of them, but empires were creating their own gravediggers. As natives became more educated and urban, they imbibed more of the official ideology of empires, in the British case liberalism and in the French case secular republicanism. The contrast between these ideologies and the real-world exploitation and racism of the empires was jarring, and conducive to resistance.

Air power proved a cheap, effective tool of repression while keeping one's own casualties to a minimum. Iraqi rebel villages were bombed and sprayed with mustard gas when Britain faced an Arab-Kurdish revolt in 1920. It was devastating, forcing the capitulation of most village leaders. When news eventually got out of the bombing casualties, Colonial Secretary Winston Churchill was defiant, declaring, "I do not understand this squeamishness about the use of gas. I am strongly in favor of using poisoned gas against uncivilised tribes [to] spread a lively terror." Air power was seen by the British as "an explicitly moral instrument of social control" against the "semi-civilized." It presaged *risk-transfer militarism,* transferring risk from one's own forces to the soldiers and civilians of the enemy. When the bombing stopped, however, the British had to resort to indirect divide-and-rule, just like the Ottoman Empire before it and the Americans recently. The British turned to the Hashemite Faisal – a spare king from Syria in exile – installed him, and relied on a blend of his urban Sunni support and tribal sheikhs to rule over Shi'a, Kurdish, and Sunni peasants (Dodge, 2003: chap. 7). This was sowing the seeds of later ethnic/religious oppression, brought to fruition by Saddam Hussein and the Americans.

Yet a general sense had emerged in the West that empires might soon be obsolete. Values deriving initially from the Enlightenment and the American and French Revolutions were being reinterpreted globally in the light of imperial and racial oppression. Even in the mother countries of empires, this was causing ideological unease. In the interwar period, only Japan and Italy were still acquiring colonies, and there was widespread denunciation of their atrocities – although these were no worse than those of earlier empires. Liberals and socialists increasingly considered empire acceptable only if it was relatively peaceful and led to development. Ideals of civilizing and assimilating native peoples were spreading. Assimilation ideals spread at the beginning of the twentieth century among French imperial administrators, but this would have created more African French people than the population of France. This was obviously unacceptable to the French, so assimilation was targeted to only an educated or *métis* minority. The broader policy changed toward *association*, the French term for indirect rule. In Muslim regions, the French empire relied on some emirs, brotherhoods, and sects to repress others – divide-and-rule (Betts, 1961; Conklin, 1998; D. Robinson, 2000). In the 1920s, French and

British colonial officials lobbied for more development funds, but the governments said they could not spare the cash. Rhetoric came more easily, and the British Empire was now declared to be a “Commonwealth” embodying “liberty, tolerance and progress” (B. Porter, 2005: 312). Empire now had to be nice, a tough requirement. Ultimately, racially boosted nationalism would triumph. In 1939, it seemed that it might still take a long time to throw off the imperial yoke, but then came World War II – and it was all over.

3 America and its empire in the Progressive Era, 1890–1930

When the United States came to dominate the world after World War II, its institutions became of global significance, so I pay a great deal of attention in this volume to them. The United States today is the most capitalistic of powers, and the only remaining imperial power, and both have major global reverberations. The most common trope deployed to explain this is *American exceptionalism*, the claim that the United States has long been utterly different from any other country. We shall see in later chapters that this has been greatly exaggerated, except in one respect – race. Overall, however, the trope works better today than it did in the past. In this chapter, I examine the United States both at home and abroad, at home dealing with a distinctive progressive reform movement even when it was joining the Western imperialist club – a very mixed story.

Americans do not like being called imperialist. Did not the Founding Fathers and the Constitution light the lamp of liberty for the world? Did not the United States lead the fight against fascism, communism, and other empires? The United States is said to have inspired freedom, not empire, its involvements abroad helping other peoples attain liberty, too – "Wilsonian interventionism," not imperialism. Americans are in denial about empire because the United States began by conquering an empire within its own continent, then within its own hemisphere, and finally acquired near-global domination. After the continental phase, three outward imperial surges occurred, one after 1898, a second after 1945, and a third, failed one, came at the turn of the twenty-first century. In this chapter, I focus on the 1898 surge. I exclude American involvement in East Asia, which will come in chapters focussed on China and Japan. American involvement in World War I is discussed in Chapter 5.

Imperialism phase 1: Continental empire, 1783–1883

In this first phase, white Americans conquered and settled what is now known as the continental United States. Because the states are now integrated as one country, this is not thought of as imperialism. Indeed, at the end of the nineteenth century, the word "empire" was reserved for overseas conquests. Yet the continental American phase was actually the most vicious one, for it dispossessed and killed more than 95 percent of the 4–9 million native inhabitants. They mostly died from disease, although this was viewed with callous indifference interspersed with bursts of deliberate killing. The pace of ethnocide and genocide quickened when the United States attained independence from Britain and California and the Southwest were wrested from Spain and Mexico. This quickening also happened in Australia and to a lesser extent in Canada, New Zealand, and South Africa when white settlers achieved self-government. Settlers almost everywhere were more lethal than colonial or church authorities were – the more the de facto self-government by settlers the greater the killings by settlers. I documented all of this in *The Dark Side of Democracy: Explaining Ethnic Cleansing* (2005: chap. 4). For the United States, this phase was normal settler colonialism – seizing the land without the natives. There was nothing Wilsonian or humanitarian about it, nor many Enlightenment values, but it was also not exceptional, except in scale. The settlers also imported slaves from Africa; after slavery was abolished in the British Empire in 1833, the United States became the main home of slavery (apart from Africa itself). Thus was generated a racial hierarchy: civilized whites on top, then decadent Latinos, then primitive African Americans, then savage Native Americans. This had consequences for phase two of U.S. imperialism, where similar racial groups were encountered in the hemisphere.

By 1883, the Pacific was reached and the territorial frontier closed, finishing the first imperial phase. No major powers threatened the United States. The British Empire was the biggest rival in the hemisphere, but it was friendly and shared an Anglo-Saxon identity. America's Monroe Doctrine of 1823, warning other powers against interference in the hemisphere, was only enforceable with the help of the Royal Navy. The United States was not yet expansionist abroad. Congress would not vote taxes for wars, and apart from the enormous blip of the Civil War, the army was small, adequate only for intimidating Indians, Mexicans, and striking workers. In 1881, the navy comprised only fifty ships, mostly obsolete. The State Department was focused on commerce, carried mainly by foreign ships. Maybe American imperialism was over – this was the nineteenth-century equivalent of the European Union, nice but harmless.

During this period, from the 1880s to World War I, the trope of American exceptionalism has focused on two supposed domestic differences from European countries: an absence of socialism and a weak state. Werner Sombart's book *Why Is There No Socialism in the United States?* (1976) was the classic expression of the first one. Sombart contrasted America with Germany, his homeland. There was little socialism in America and plenty in Germany, but Germany – not the United States – was the exception. No other country at that time had such a large Marxist movement. Countries like Sweden, Denmark, and Austria later developed milder Marxian parties, but these are not the appropriate comparison. Because the United States was initially settled mainly by people from the British Isles, we would expect more cultural and institutional similarities with the British and Irish than with Germans or Scandinavians. We might expect greater similarities with Canada, Australia, and New Zealand, also Anglophone and settler societies. Yet none of the Anglophones have seen much socialism, and their labor movements have all explicitly rejected Marxism (Bosch, 1997, McKibbin, 1984). The United States has not been exceptional in lacking socialism, provided we compare it to similar countries. Yet we can rephrase Sombart's question, because the United States has sometimes differed from the other Anglos. These countries developed *Lib-Lab* politics, merging an older liberal tradition with an emerging labor movement. For Britain, Australia, and New Zealand, Lib-Lab policies were carried by nonsocialist Labour parties powerful enough to form governments. Canada and Ireland have had only small Labour parties achieving bit-player status in coalition governments. The United States, however, has never had a serious labor party at all. In this sense, it has been the most extreme of the Anglos. The appropriate exceptional question would be "Why no lib-lab tradition?" – except that this emerged in the New Deal.

Has the United States been exceptional in having a weak state? Happily, like the other Anglos, it has been weak in terms of *despotic power*, the ability of a ruler to issue commands without routine consultation with subjects/citizens. The American Constitution had designed institutions expressly to prevent the emergence of either a monarch/dictator or mob rule. It separated and divided powers between the federal, state, and local government; the executive, legislative, and judicial branches; within the executive between elected and appointed officials; and within the legislature between Senate and House of Representatives. The extent of separation of powers is indeed exceptional among modern states.

However, the United State's *infrastructural power*, its ability to penetrate its territories and get commands executed, has not been low, although it was federally dispersed. We can crudely measure this in terms of the proportion of GNP consumed by government at all levels – federal, state, and local. Under this measure, nineteenth-century U.S. government lagged well behind the major European countries because of the small size of its military. If we count only civilian government expenditure, it was only slightly smaller – all American governments consumed 7 percent of GNP compared to 8 percent in Great Britain, 9 percent in France, and 10 percent in Germany (Mann, 1993: Tables 11.3–11.4). In terms of infrastructural power, its strength was enough for its purposes (Novak, 2008), and Leviathan was stirring.

The Second Industrial Revolution

Given its size, abundance of natural resources, temperate climate, and settlement by Europeans, the United States was always likely to become a great economic power. It was bigger than all the other powers, a resource-stuffed continent of fertile soils and minerals, located thousands of miles away from any predator. From early on, Americans ate better and were healthier, taller, and longer-lived than Europeans, making it the world's most tempting destination for migrants.

They came in the millions, first from the British Isles and Northwest Europe, then from the rest of Europe, Latin America, and Asia. The migrants were younger, more educated, and more enterprising than those left behind. There were whole industrious communities fleeing persecution – Puritans, Jews, and the middle-class losers of twentieth-century revolutions in Cuba, Iran, and Vietnam. The core promise of this New World was a freedom that combined religious tolerance, political liberties, and economic enterprise. The association of civil and political freedom with capitalism has continued to appeal to new waves of migrants and to be characteristic of American ideology.

All that was required for such human capital to flourish amid such natural abundance was government able to assist the exploitation of natural and human resources, develop good communications over such an underpopulated continent, and keep immigration open. Labor shortages could then be obviated by using abundant natural resources plus imported capital to mechanize and raise labor productivity. Reliance on labor-saving, capital-intensive, and resource-intensive technology has been the American way. The shortage of skilled labor spurred on standardization of industrial techniques such as transferable parts, which then enabled the transfer of technology across industries and mass production based on deskilling labor. Government geological services exposed the natural resources and government had the power to donate supposedly virgin lands for exploitation. Capital came mostly from Britain, because the rate of return was high and the British were kith and kin. The United States came to have a unique advantage in the industrial era as the greatest plunderer of the resources of nature, developing manufactures whose waste was then emitted back into a nature conceived of as a bottomless sinkhole. America was extremely wasteful throughout the production chain in its use of natural resources. (Abramowitz & David, 2001: 42–4). This used to be seen as a sign of American virtue; now it is seen as a vice. By 1910, however, the United States was the most populous and greatest industrial nation. It was not inevitable that it would become a great military power; that was more conjuncture.

The federal government subsidized and regulated communications infrastructures such as the post office, telegraph, and telephone (John, 1997); the states and local authorities sponsored and donated land for railroads and canals. This was not laissez-faire; there were no immigration restrictions until 1882. Afterward, despite the constraints associated with Ellis Island, Asian Exclusion Acts, and the Southwest border, immigration policy mostly remained open. Human capital was cultivated through education and public health measures. By 1890, the United States was in the top tier of countries in educational spending and the proportion of children receiving primary and secondary education (Lindert, 2004: chap. 5). Land grants were used from 1862 onward to establish universities that would "teach such branches of learning as are related to agriculture and the mechanic arts." All government employment, including state and local government, ranked third in proportionate size among fourteen countries – the biggest was the United Kingdom, followed by the Netherlands (Tanzi & Schuknecht, 2000: 25–6).

Rapid nineteenth-century urbanization in the United States, as in other industrializing countries, had produced an increase in mortality rates, mainly through communicative diseases. In the 1890s, city governments improved the protection, filtration, and chlorination of water supplies; installed separated sewage systems; improved hygiene in hospitals; and standardized milk pasteurization and safe meat. This accounted for about half of the reduction in mortality in cities occurring from the last third of the nineteenth century to World War II. The second industrial revolution provided the other half by improving purchasing power and diets. The consequence was a healthier and taller population, able to work harder and think better (Floud et al, 2011). In terms of development, says Novak (2008: 758), "The trail of the state is over all." Government infrastructural power penetrated all corners of this continent-sized country. It was not an infrastructurally weak state, although its federal level was small. As its global rivals were far-flung overseas empires more difficult to integrate, American infrastructural political power over its entire domains was actually greater.

In the 1870s came a second industrial revolution, based on technological innovations coming fully on-stream at the beginning of the twentieth century. It centered on new hi-tech industries – chemicals, iron and steel, and mining – all utilizing electricity and internal combustion engines, two "general purpose technologies" diffusing across the economy. There was half a century of sustained scientific and technological discoveries that dominated the twentieth century (Smil, 2005), beginning the age of what Collins (1994) has called "high consensus rapid-discovery science." These discoveries, when made into working technologies, changed both capitalism and the world. This is why Schroeder (2011) wants to make science and technology the third part of his triad of modern institutions, alongside market capitalism and the state. Most discoveries were not made by the tinkering artisans and gentlemen scientists of the first industrial revolution. Science now had some institutional autonomy in universities and other lab settings, and its research findings were submitted to peer review by other scientists. Yet technological and commercial exploitation mostly came from the new research departments of big capitalist corporations and wealthy backers hoping to found such corporations, assisted by national patent systems granting property rights to the inventors. Amid fierce international competition, every little refinement of technique was backed by a patent, capturing scientific and technological innovation for private ownership, the consequence of new patent laws.

The Second Industrial Revolution was responsible for Schumpeter's insight that capitalism's unique gift was to generate "creative destruction." For him, the "creation" came from "competition from the new commodity, the new technology, the new source of supply, the new organization … competition which commands a decisive cost or quality advantage and which strikes not at the margins of the profits and the outputs of the existing firms but at their foundations and their very lives." He neglected only the degree of state involvement in some of the new technology (especially railroads) plus the extension of patent rights, which made investment in new technologies more predictably profitable. The "destruction" came as the new means of production tore apart current market positions, condemning existing inventories, ideas, technologies, skills, and business models. Thus, capitalism "incessantly revolutionizes the economic structure *from within*, incessantly destroying the old one, incessantly creating a new one. This process of Creative Destruction is the essential fact about capitalism. It is what capitalism consists in and what every capitalist concern has got to live in" (Schumpeter, 1942: 82–5).

It was actually capitalism's second great phase of creative destruction. The first one, in the late eighteenth and early nineteenth centuries, had created both an agricultural and industrial revolution, in the process destroying much of the agricultural labor force. The second one centered on corporate capitalism, mostly coal-burning, generating mass industrial production and rising productivity in both agriculture and industry that were diffusing through the advanced countries in the new century. The productivity of agriculture continued upward, generating better diets with higher calorific intake for both men and women. Yet at the same time, it neither increased real wages much nor greatly boosted mass consumer demand. Capitalism was excellent for diets, less so for wages. Nevertheless, whatever its imperfections and fluctuations, capitalism was pioneering an unprecedented level of economic development.

I list some of the major patented discoveries. Von Liebig's use of inorganic materials to provide plant nutrient led to the fixation of nitrogen, synthetic nitrogens, and ammonium sulfates. These new fertilizers boosted agricultural productivity, perhaps averting a Malthusian crisis in the early twentieth century; otherwise, population might have increased beyond agriculture's capacity to feed it. Instead, foodstuffs were cheapened and calorific intake, life expectancy, and the flow of workers from agriculture to industry all increased. Synthetic chemistry also changed war, generating mass production of explosives and poison gas. These discoveries indicate the central place of the chemical industry in this phase of capitalist development. The internal combustion engine, diesel engine, and electrical power boosted mechanical engineering, making cars, trucks, and tanks possible. They enhanced the transport of commodities, developing markets over wider geographical terrains. They also enhanced the killing powers of states, a significant feature of the twentieth century. Incandescent and then neon lights, reinforced concrete, wireless telegraphy and the telephone, aluminium and then stainless steel, X-rays, radioactivity, the synthesis of aspirin, and air conditioning all moved rapidly from inventions to usable, commercial technologies, generating a massive increase in collective economic power (Smil, 2005) – and profits for those who invested in them.

The science came from many countries, but the United States and Germany led in bringing it to the market. Germany invented the research university and the United States led in electricity-powered workbenches and assembly lines and motorized transport, all powerful tools for intensifying production and markets. The United States had the advantages of a bigger domestic market and the most natural resources, especially coal, which before World War I provided about 90 percent of the fuel for industry across the world. In fact, it remained the biggest source of energy throughout this period, although the use of natural gas, hydroelectric power, and especially oil grew after the war. The American lead was not in corporate size, as Europe had corporations of almost equal size (Hannah, nd). It lay more in greater productivity, born of resource-intensive technologies, and improvements in human health. Floud and his collaborators (2011) stress a virtuous circle: healthier workers could not only work harder, they could also think better, increasing the rate of technological change, which in turn improved wealth and diet, enabling people to work even more productively. This was occurring in most advanced countries, but the United States had the lead and kept it through the first half of the twentieth century.

All of this also enlarged the scale of organization of both capital and labor; it intensified the links between industrial and financial capital. In 1915, Hilferding called this "Organized Capitalism"; Chandler (1977) called it the replacement of the "invisible hand" of the market by the "visible hand" of the corporation housing mass production and coordinating different branches – research and development, production, sales, and so forth. This growth in scale was to continue until the 1970s in the advanced economies. Its effect was to "massify" the workforce in large units of production and control them by tighter bureaucratic hierarchy. Independent artisans lost much of their autonomy when converted into skilled and semiskilled employees of the corporation. They resisted, of course, fueling the growth of labor unions, just as tightening nation-states fueled the growth of socialist and lib-lab resistance.

Corporations are bureaucratic and hierarchical with rule by fiat from above at each level of their organization charts. In that sense they are like any despotic regime, yet the relations between corporations remained largely governed by the market, continuing the "disembedding" of market capitalism from traditional community constraints. Polanyi (1957) thought this was only a phase until the 1940s, when communities reacted against the harshness of markets and "re-embedded" them. Schroeder (2011) disagrees, arguing that markets have retained and even extended their power. In this volume, I will chart Polanyi's counterattack, leaving the question of how successful and permanent it was to Volume IV.

The Second Industrial Revolution made America into the biggest national economy, although it was not globally dominant. Its markets were principally domestic, protected by high tariffs. Although its finance capitalism was growing, it was still an offshore destination for British capital, and a part of the North Atlantic segment of the world economy.

The state also grew, continuing to do so into the 1970s. Economic "catch up" depended on imitating or adapting new technologies and organizations, and states were well-suited to coordinating intelligence-gathering, capital-gathering, and infrastructural development. "Late development" was thus more statist than the industrial pioneers, as we will see in the case of Japan. The relative strength and precise mix of corporations and states – of economic and political power – varied across both time and place, and variations in their interactions helped structure not only economic power relations but also domestic politics and geopolitics.

U.S. corporations were very strong politically, their dominance expressed in an alliance between Northeastern manufacturing business and the Republican Party, both committed to the gold standard and high tariffs, flanked by a Supreme Court vigilant in protecting national market integration, with a free trade-favouring South left in the cold (Bensel, 2000). This gave Northern capitalists the ability to outflank the collective organization of workers. Rapid industrialization and growing corporate power, however, increased inequality, urbanization, and immigration, which were increasingly defined as social problems. From the right, the Reverend Josiah Strong thundered against seven great "perils" assailing the country – immigration, Catholicism, poor public education, Mormonism, alcoholism, socialism, disparities of wealth, and urbanization (Blum, 2005: 217). From the center and left came critiques of corporate power from the Progressive Movement.

The Progressives: Modernization versus redistribution

Movements to reform and regulate capitalism appeared in all the advanced countries at this time. The United States movement called itself Progressive, responding to a widespread perception that a new urban-industrial, corporate, and multiethnic society was emerging that was incompatible with traditional institutions. It was, said Woodrow Wilson, "a new world, struggling under old laws." Progressive conveyed two main meanings. One was to *modernize* existing institutions, to make them more efficient at generating economic growth and social order in new conditions. This was intrinsically neither of the right nor the left, and so drew support from across the political spectrum. British liberalism and French republicanism had some of the same qualities. The other was more radical: to restrain capitalism and *redistribute* power away from corporations to less privileged Americans, to restore the greater equality of power and wealth and the greater autonomy of ordinary people believed (correctly) to have existed in the past. I will assess the weights of these two strands of progressivism.

The modernizing wing favored enhancing the capacity and efficiency of government, still dominated by patronage-driven parties (especially at the local and state levels) and the law courts. Government was dominated by the 40 states and 6,000 local political entities, often run by city "machines" or rural notable cliques. Modernizers said the federal government needed enlarging and all governments needed protecting from patronage and corruption. This tended toward a statist ideology favoring rational regulation of society by the state. Richard Ely said, "We regard the state as an agency whose positive assistance is one of the indispensable conditions of human progress" (Jacoby, 2004: 5). The size of the federal government did increase, although only proportionately to the size of the economy, and a more uniform tax system emerged (Campbell, 1995: 34). The Pendleton Act of 1882 began a slow bureaucratization that reduced the "spoils" system. Many Americans, however, especially Democrats and southerners, blocked further reform, fearing "big government" (Mann, 1993: 365–7, 393, 470–1; R. Harrison, 2004: 265–70; Orloff, 1988: 45–52). The radicals favored more accountability, not more rule by bureaucrats and corporations. They secured the direct election of senators, the revival of citizen referenda in about twenty states by 1920, and primary elections in sixteen states. They hoped these would restrict the power of corporate and government elites, but elites adapted by bringing financial resources to bear on the referenda to get the results they wanted, as they still do today (Goebel, 2002: 154–6, 194–6). The radicals wanted legislative supremacy and more explicit statutes so the administration and courts would have less discretion in interpreting them. They largely failed; the courts continued to interpret the law with a conservative, pro-business bias (Sanders, 1999: 388–9).

The radicals also attacked concentrations of economic power, arguing that grants, licenses, and contracts from government brought a conspiracy among railroads, banks, and trusts to exploit the people and destroy small business. Their antitrust laws, however, perversely encouraged legal full company mergers that increased corporate concentration (W. Roy, 1997). Riding on a wave of protest, and bringing the populist movement within the Democratic Party, William Jennings Bryan broke with the Party's traditional distrust of government to demand regulation of the evil trusts. He lost the election of 1900, but his victorious Republican opponent, Theodore Roosevelt, stole some of his antitrust program. City and housing planning reforms ensured cleaner water, sewerage, and hospitals, but radicals were often frustrated by the judiciary's devotion to private property rights. When the courts blocked plans for municipal control of railroads, however, radicals established railway commissions, enabling public monitoring of rates and services. This method of control extended to public utilities (Rodgers, 1998: 160–207; R. Harrison, 1998). This was a success; although limited to the sphere of public services, it had great implications for the health and productivity of the population.

Even some corporate leaders recognized the need for regulation to protect legitimate business from illegitimate business, to increase market predictability, and to build politics around the more rational economic order they said the corporation embodied. They also hoped mild reform would take the sting out of more radical schemes. The Sherman and Clayton Acts restricted the power of trusts, although not by as much as the radicals had wanted; the courts pleased business in granting corporate assets the same rights of protection as private property. The period entrenched what is called corporate or managerial liberalism (Weinstein, 1968: ix–x; Sklar, 1988; Dawley, 1991: 64; Kolko, 1963: 3, 284). Some progressive intellectuals had initially supported radical demands made by workers and small farmers, but they then downplayed this "to establish a new kind of nonpolitical expert administration ... [which].... would create an efficient modern state that ... would insulate the government from the pressures of democratic politics," an "administered corporate democracy." They also denounced radicals and socialists preaching utopias to the workers (N. Cohen, 2002: 15, 113, 255–6; Fink, 1997: chap. 2). The redistribution of power was subordinated to an efficient bureaucratic and corporate order (Wiebe, 1967: 132, 145–6, 166, 295). Wealth inequalities rose in the first decade of the twentieth century to the highest level during that century. At the same time, American government subsidies and transfers to the poor were the stingiest (alongside Japan) in a sample of seven countries (Lindert, 1998; James & Thomas, 2000; Tanzi & Schuknecht, 2000: 31). There was reform, but it was dominated by the modernizers, not the radicals. Capitalist power was somewhat regulated, but not reduced.

The South tended to split on these issues, for although it remained segregationist, jealous of states' rights, and morally conservative, it also contained many agrarian populists. Farmers, still 37 percent of the population in 1900, were enraged by monopolistic railroads, banks and trusts, and tariffs that exploited them to the benefit of industry. They had not wanted to create a larger, more regulating state, yet this was the unintended outcome of their struggle to protect themselves from the great trusts (Sanders, 1999: 1, 29, 388–9). Their greatest influence came when senators and congressmen from the southern and western periphery could unite with Republican dissidents from the Midwest and border states – plus the few Democrats who were responsive to labor unions – to overcome the northern corporate core of the Republican Party, in power in Washington from 1896 to 1912. After that date, they strengthened railroad regulation, secured at least some antitrust legislation, and played a role in the creation of a Federal Reserve System of banking in 1913. Twelve new regional banks controlled money and credit flows and acted as lenders of last resort in any banking panics, coordinated by a Federal Reserve Board in Washington (Sanders, 1999: 77–8). These measures benefitted not only corporate modernizers but also small business and farmers who were vulnerable to railroad charges and banking crises. Yet political economy continued to privilege industry over agriculture, and farmers could not prevent the long-term decline of their sector. Farmers' incomes fell until World War II.

In Sweden and Denmark, redistributive reforms were secured by a labor-farmer alliance, but the American labor-farmer alliance was only tenuous. Sanders says labor unions were only a "rather uncreative and undemanding appendage" of the alliance, fighting for their own sectional interests. American Federation of Labor unions (AFL) largely ignored federal politics because they identified the state with repression, as did the syndicalist "Wobblies." Thus, labor issues were marginal to progressive programs (Bensel, 2000: 143–56; R. Harrison, 1997, 2004 (double check from 2005): chap. 4; Lichtenstein, 2002: chap. 1). Dawley says, "the social-justice planks in the Progressive platform incorporated watered-down socialist demands on wages, hours and working conditions.... By diverting socialist ideas into safe channels, and then posing as the only alternative to cataclysm, progressives succeeded in outflanking socialists" (1991: 134–6). Few of these social-justice planks were implemented.

Skocpol (2003) showed that American mass voluntary associations thrived from the late nineteenth to the mid-twentieth century. This included fraternal societies such as the Masons; religious societies such as the Women's Christian Temperance Union; veterans' organizations such as the American Legion and the Grand Army of the Republic; education pressure groups such as the PTA; farmer organizations such as the Grange and the American Farm Bureau Federation; business groups; and unions. The AFL was the biggest organization of all. Local associations sent delegates to regional or state associations, which then elected delegates to a national body. Skills learned within the association were wielded lobbying politicians. Many of the largest associations brought together people from different occupational and income levels, encouraging a sense of national fellowship in a common citizenship. Through these means, ordinary people wielded political power.

Although some ordinary people did wield power, judging from results, it seems business did best, temperance did quite well, most of the others sought more specialized interests to varied effect, and unions did poorly. In a study of California, Wisconsin, and Washington, Clemens (1997) notes some of the conditions for effectiveness. Pressure-group politics built up most successfully from the local level in states with weak political parties and mixed economies, she says. She focuses on three associations: the Farmers Alliance and the General Confederation of Women's Clubs both claimed 1 million members, and the AFL claimed 1.5 million. They did achieve some piecemeal reforms at the state level once they abandoned radical rhetoric and organized as state federations. For unions, the main issues were workers compensation, mothers' and old-age pensions, unemployment insurance, and health insurance. Many labor-sponsored bills were introduced in state legislatures, and a few passed, later becoming models for New Deal reforms (cf Orloff, 1988: 55–7). Farmer cooperative federations were effective where they worked closely with state agricultural agencies; women's clubs were effective where they could work with state educational agencies. Of course, Clemens picked states that did see reform; most states did not or saw quite different reforms. Across the Bible Belt states, voluntary associations pressed most for moral conservatism, including repressive sexual laws, segregation, and creationism. Voluntary associations were media for pressing their members' agendas, but those agendas were extraordinarily varied.

Radicals' main problem was business dominance. Business welcomed government spending on highways and schools because this brought construction contracts, lower transaction costs, and a more skilled workforce. State and local government spending on these items increased ten-fold between 1902 and 1927. Business, however, flatly opposed redistributive welfare programs, and it could threaten a progressive state with an *investment strike* – business could relocate to wherever costs were lowest and unions weakest. Much of the textile industry now moved from north to south. State and local government expenditure on welfare did increase fourfold over those years, but this was less than the overall growth in the economy. Welfare spending remained only 9 percent of highway spending and 6 percent of spending on education (Hacker & Pierson, 2002: 293–4). In most areas, social citizenship remained largely stalled. This was capitalism largely unfettered by the state. The cause of labor lagged.

Labor movement but no working class

The Second Industrial Revolution inevitably brought collective resistance from workers. My second volume (1993: 635–59) noted that before World War I, American workers were just as aggressive in pressing their interests as workers in other countries (cf Voss, 1994). Among six leading countries, only British workers were more likely to join unions than Americans, but the American strike rate was the highest of the six. It was only in the 1920s that American union and strike rates began to seriously lag behind most other industrial countries, but labor needed allies. Depending on farmers was not a long-term solution because agriculture was favoring large consolidated farms and small farmers and laborers were being forced off the land. Feminists were few in number; agitation among African Americans, Mexicans, or Asians alienated most whites; and workers were on their own.

In Volume II, Chapter 3, I outlined a polymorphous theory of the state, arguing that states "crystallize" in different forms, according to the issue areas and balance of social forces involved. One of the major crystallizations of the modern state is as capitalist, generating the politics of class struggle, as Marxists argue. However, modern states have also crystallized in other forms, some of which have undercut working-class formation. I now discuss seven supposed weaknesses of labor (identified by Lipset & Marks, 2000) from this perspective, drawing parallels with the most comparable cases, the other Anglophone countries.

(1) American labor faced superior military power. The strike rate was high because employers would not settle disputes peacefully and had access to military power. I showed in Volume II that before World War I, many more American workers were killed in labor disputes than Europeans, except for Russians. This violence flowed from repression mounted by police, private employer paramilitaries such as Pinkertons, the National Guard, and even by the regular army (Archer, 2007: chap. 5). Few workers saw this as a despotically weak state!

The United States state had crystallized as militaristic at home in order to repress Native Americans and police slavery and Mexicans. Military power was now used mostly against workers, less against craft unions fighting for sectional interests than against general industrial unions and socialist-led demonstrations and strikes. These were seen as especially dangerous because they raised the specter of working-class solidarity, whereas craft unions did not. Thus, the broader "new unions" that made their appearance in both Britain and Australia in the 1890s were much weaker in the United States (Archer, 2007: 31–9). Fear of repression steered the AFL to confine its organizing to skilled workers who could use their power in the labor market to force employers to negotiate. Sectional, not class unionism dominated until the New Deal, and this was partly due to military power. When Tsarist Russia deployed far more repression, however, this encouraged workers toward revolutionary socialism. Why did this not happen in the United States? Employers must have possessed other advantages, as well.

(2) Employer violence could be portrayed as legitimate law enforcement. As is often remarked, this state crystallized as one of "courts and parties," and the courts remained antiunion, upholding employers' absolute property rights. The United States had all three of Fukuyama's criteria for good government, including the rule of law – but whose law was it? Orren (1993) says labor law was even infused by "feudal" laws governing "master-servant" relations. Judges administered statutes imported from Britain that treated workers as the property of their employers. One judge said the law recognized only "the superiority and power" of the master, and the "duty, subjection, and ... allegiance" of the worker. Vagrancy statutes forced able-bodied males into the workplace, and the "entire" contract kept them there: a worker hired for a period of time was not entitled to any of his wages until he completed the entire term of his contract. Some courts also required workers seeking employment to obtain a testimonial letter from their previous employer. Because employers were under no legal obligation to provide such letters, the courts could stop workers from moving. Freedom was for employers, not workers (Glenn, 2002: 86–8; Burns, 2009). In this respect, America was feudal not Europe, lagging in civil citizen rights.

Roy and Parker-Gwin (1999) identify the main thrust of employer powers as the legal protection of employer collaboration through the recognition of corporations, mergers, and trade associations but nonrecognition of workers' collective actions, which were seen as infringements of individual liberties and property rights. Collective action was often defined as a "criminal conspiracy." Courts struck down laws passed by pro-union states against *yellow-dog contracts* that banned workers from joining unions. Some courts recognized that workers could band together to bargain over wages, but rarely about anything else. On maximum working hours, the courts might paternalistically protect workers whom the judges considered vulnerable – such as children, women, and sometimes men in dangerous work like mining – but not men in "normal" occupations. Between 1873 and 1937, the protection of women was at first stronger at the state level, but then federal courts joined in; all courts became more protective of children in the early twentieth century (Novkov, 2001). In contrast, the refusal to assist male workers lasted until the New Deal.

By this period in Australia, conspiracy charges against unions were no longer upheld, and at the end of the century came the progressive labor arbitration system discussed in Chapter 9 (Archer, 2007: 95–8). The collective rights of British unions were legally recognized in 1875, and the state largely withdrew from labor relations, giving unions full bargaining freedoms. In Germany, France, and other countries the state took a more active role, but although officials usually sided with employers in labor disputes, they were also conscious of their duty to preserve public order. If they felt employer intransigence was the major threat to public order, they put pressure on employers to compromise. This rarely happened in the United States, because the preservation of capitalist property rights was considered synonymous with order.

(3) The law helped isolate unions ideologically more than in European countries. Capitalism came embedded in a broader ideology of individual rights of both person and property, and some violence by the state or employers was considered legitimate to preserve property rights. This gave unions legitimacy problems among Americans if they broke the law (Lipset & Marks, 2000: 237–60; LaFeber, 1994; Rosenberg. 1982: 48). We later see that Japanese workers faced comparable military, political, and ideological obstacles, so the United States was not entirely exceptional in these respects.

(4) The U.S. labor force was divided by race, ethnicity, and religion, and this was largely exceptional. Where black and white workers toiled in the same company or industry, employers could exploit the racial gulf. The Pullman Car Company divided and ruled, pitting already prejudiced workers against each other. Race was to undercut class at Pullman for almost a century (Hirsch, 2003), although racism often reinforced the sense of solidarity of white workers. Yet ethnic diversity was as important in the Australian labor force and did not hinder class solidarity there. It was religion – Protestant or Catholic – that most divided American (as opposed to Australian or British) workers, says

Archer. Nonetheless, the Republican Party took a chance in appealing to workers across religious lines, and was rewarded with a large working-class vote from 1896 onward. Unions could also have done this, he argues, but did not (2007: chap. 2). To keep the South low wage and nonunionized, Southern elites claimed organized labor wanted to weaken the white race. In this period, the South was proportionately bigger than it is today – seventeen states had educational segregation until 1954. One big reason labor was nationally weak was because race trumped class over a third of the country.

(5) The success of American economic development is sometimes said to have explained U.S. labor weakness – prosperity made workers happy. The United States, however, was not exceptional in this respect. Australian workers were even more prosperous and ate better than Americans, yet they formed powerful unions and a Labour Party (Archer, 2007: 23–30). America's crucial economic difference was in being continental, with divisions between "a northern, advanced and developing industrial core, a rapidly settling western frontier, and a relatively stagnating southern periphery" (Bensel, 2000: 99). Each contained distinctive class conflicts making national class solidarity unlikely: capitalists against workers in the Northeast, farmers against creditors in the West, smallholders and sharecroppers against planter-merchants in the South. Northern industry dominated the major federal issues of political economy, tariffs, taxes, debts, and gold (Bensel, 2000: 175–8). Parts of the West were economically interdependent with the North, but the South felt exploited by the North, especially by its high tariff policy.

(6) This state had crystallized as a quasi-democracy accountable to white males. Workers were not excluded from political citizenship. In Germany and Russia, the political exclusion of all workers papered over workers' sectional, segmental, regional, ethnic, or religious differences. My Volume II showed that political exclusion, more than economic exploitation, was the main driving force toward the formation of working-class consciousness in Europe. This driver was absent in the United States, but it was also absent in Australia and New Zealand and largely absent in Britain. What distinctively disadvantaged U.S. labor was not citizenship but the party system.

(7) British, Australian, and New Zealand economies and politics tended to generate a national party division between liberals and conservatives. Labor then inserted itself within liberalism and grew to dominate it, generating lib-lab politics. Regional differences were sometimes important, but did not much detract from this national struggle. In the United States, however, as political economy took a regional form, the political parties crystallized as regional. The Republican Party represented northern industry above all, but starting in 1896 it also represented the sectoral interests of northern industrial workers. The Democratic Party represented most clearly the South and agriculture. Both parties represented distinct regions, sectors, and ethnicities and organized patronage machines around such identities. Whatever the experience of

class exploitation at the workplace, it was less easy to translate class conflict into politics. Only small third parties like the Greenbacks and Populists mobilized on a class basis, among small farmers and farm laborers and seeking worker support with pro-labor platforms. Region and economic sector trumped class and prevented a broad farm-labor alliance, and in the South race trumped everything.

Both major parties got some worker support. Southern workers and non-southern immigrant workers plus most subsistence farmers supported the Democrats. African Americans, Appalachian subsistence farmers, and native-born northern workers voted Republican. However, workers were not influential in either party. Northern corporations dominated the Republicans; smaller business dominated the southern Democrats. Workers might resist their employers in the workplace, but could not do so in elections. It wasn't a question of an absence of socialism but of any national political influence – in a polity that paradoxically enfranchised workers. From 1896 to 1912, the Republicans dominated the White House and Congress, becoming more like a standard big-business conservative party, but the Democrats did not offer a lib-lab alternative. The regional crystallization of politics was decisive in isolating unions from a broader class base and from dominant ideologies, thus making military repression of them easier.

(8) Some scholars stress political institutions. Electorally, they stress the obstacles confronting a third party in a first-past-the-post system. Yet Britain, Australia, and New Zealand had the same electoral system and their labor movements first won mining and industrial constituencies and then moved on. Presidential elections have only one national constituency. Here, a vote for a third-party labor candidate hurt any center candidate, helping a conservative win. The American electoral system could yield third-party congressmen and even a few senators, but not easily a president. This was a factor, yet hardly a decisive one. Presidents had to respect the power of the South, whatever their own views on race. The reason they did not equally respect the power of labor was that other crystallizations weakened that power. U.S. federalism is another important political institution; it is also often seen as an obstacle to labor. Labor issues were the concern of the federal government only if they involved interstate commerce, and most were matters for the states. Some say unions were hampered by having to fight the same battles over and over, state by state. However, federalism might equally help labor make initial gains in sympathetic industrial states containing many union members, and then take its strategies forward into more difficult states. Federalism also gave each state an incentive to lower its labor costs to attract business investment, generating a race to the bottom (Robertson, 2000). This was not decisive in Australia, also with a federal system. There, labor parties formed state by state and then merged into a national Labour party (Archer, 2007: 84–6). These two procedural aspects of democracy were not insuperable obstacles.

Some of these eight causes weakened the power of labor in the United States compared to other industrializing countries. In this male democracy, the regional crystallization (also racial in the South) most influenced political alignments and most weakened the prospects for a worker-farmer alliance such as emerged in Scandinavia and Australia. The Democrats generally expressed rural radicalism in the West and the South, although in the South they embodied racist and antiunion sentiments. Northern business controlled the ruling Republican Party, although industrial workers were its clients. The political system was an obstacle to labor organization giving employers control of the courts and military power. This did not deter all unionism, but it did deter established craft unions from forming broader industrial unions or political parties in alliance with less skilled workers. If they attempted to expand among less skilled workers, drawing on class ideology, this provoked repression. Gompers, president of the AFL, drew the pragmatic conclusion that it was better to eschew class-based unions and labor parties and organize on the basis of craft monopolies. The AFL unions were also mostly Protestant, making them less appealing to Catholics. There were unions, but there was not an organized working class. This does offer some support for the "exceptional" trope.

My Volume II stressed crucial contingent events, especially the two AFL national conferences of 1892 and 1893, at which Gompers thwarted an attempt from industrial unions to form a Labor Party by rigging the ballot procedures. Had this dubious election gone otherwise, perhaps a Labor Party might have stolen a large slice of the Republican and Democratic votes and a three-party system might have emerged. Voss (1994) sees an earlier window of opportunity, in the 1880s when the Knights of Labor briefly bridged the gap between crafts trades and industrial unions, but then were beaten back, she says, by repression coming from united employers backed by governments. Robertson (2000) suggests a third, later window, just after 1900 when the great corporate merger movement led to an "Open Shop War," which the AFL unions lost. All three class challenges to the status quo lost, probably less contingency than a pattern. American unions shared only a little in the union growth of the period, and unlike European and other Anglophone countries, workers did not strike deals with liberals that took the country down lib-lab or socialist paths. Lib-lab causes were beginning to lag in the Progressive Era. Overall, this made the United States extreme, although not completely exceptional.

Redistributions achieved:Education, gender

Two main redistributive reforms were accomplished during this period, neither being primarily class issues. One concerned gender: securing the vote for white women in 1920 doubled the numbers of those entitled to political citizenship. The United States was not in the first group of states to enfranchise women (New Zealand in 1893, Australia in 1902, Finland in 1906, and Norway in 1913), but the second burst (1918–1920), when fifteen countries enfranchised women. The second achievement concerned education: the United States remained among the leading countries in overall educational spending and the proportion of boys and girls educated at primary and secondary levels. The United States had developed mass public primary schools in advance of European countries (Lindert, 2004: chap. 5). In the early twentieth century, the United States also expanded secondary schooling. Between 1910 and 1940, the proportion of young people graduating from high school rose from 9 percent to just more than 50 percent.

Early democratization is often seen as a major cause of American educational progress (Skocpol, 1992: 88–92), although authoritarian Prussia was also a leader in education. American women were being educated long before they got the vote. More important was local control over education plus either Protestantism, religious diversity, or a strong secularist movement, which generated better education (Lindert, 2004: 104–10). American schooling was controlled locally, as in the other Anglo-white settler colonies, which were also in the vanguard of educational reform. In these countries, local communities were choosing to tax themselves in order to benefit their children, an investment very close to home. The more homogenous and stable the local community, the earlier the decision to expand elementary and high schools, and districts with more schooling had more equality and were more ethnically homogenous (Goldin & Katz, 1999, 2003). Schools have always been central both to the life of local communities and to the sense of nationhood in the United States. The children of a nation of immigrants, in a continent-sized country, received their education in a resolutely English-speaking system, where they learned that they lived in the freest country on earth. As in other countries, the teaching of history was conceived as a way of teaching national virtue. The major educational debates of this period concerned religion: whether the schools should continue to convey essentially Protestant themes or whether Catholic immigration had made this undesirable.

Girls were educated less than boys – as in the other leading countries – but they were not usually educated in the same schools as boys (Goldin & Katz, 2003). Patriarchy was a little weaker in the United States, as it was in the other white settler colonies. This is generally attributed to *frontier life* – a lack of established institutions, to the need for the whole of a settler household to contribute to production, and to a shortage of women, which increased the power of women in the household. Discrimination was more marked in the labor market, although female employment doubled between 1880 and 1900, and rose a further 50 percent by 1920. Wage differentials between men and women were static, a minor achievement in an era where overall income inequalities were widening.

No country saw great increases in other social citizen rights at this time. No country thought it was moving toward a welfare state until after World War I, but American men were lagging. Among the fifteen most industrialized countries before the New Deal, the United States ranked between ninth and fifteenth on the adoption, diffusion, and making binding of five different welfare programs for men – fifteen measures of welfare altogether (Hicks et al, 1995: 337; cf Tanzi & Schuknecht, 2000; Hicks, 1999; Rodgers, 1998: 28–30; Keller, 1994: 178–82).[1] Unusually, women did a little better than men in welfare programs before the New Deal. Little was achieved by either sex at the federal level; at the state level, men also achieved little. There was more chance of passing pro-union legislation in western states – which had little industry – than in the northern industrial states (Hacker & Pierson, 2002: 289–90, 294–5). Before 1923, no states passed laws regulating men's maximum hours or minimum wages, but maximum hours laws for women had passed in forty-one states and minimum wage laws in fifteen. There was no unemployment insurance until the New Deal. Workmen's compensation for injuries received at work was in place in forty-two states by 1920, mostly a response to working-class juries awarding bigger damages to workers than the new compensation laws provided (Bellamy, 1997). Only six states passed laws establishing old-age pensions for men. In contrast, forty states paid pensions to poor single mothers caring for young children, by 1930 forty-six paid pensions. The United States led in granting benefits to single unwed mothers; in Britain, unwed mothers could not draw any benefits until after 1945 – immorality was not to be encouraged (C. Gordon, 1994:44; Kiernan et al, 1998: 6; Gauthier, 1998: tables 3.1 and 3.2).

Women were doing better than men because they bore and reared children. Motherhood was politically valued because the children were the future of the race (Mink, 1995). The 1908 Muller versus Oregon Supreme Court judgment established the legality of maximum hours for women, declaring "the physical well-being of woman becomes an object of public interest and care in order to preserve the strength and vigor of the race." Skocpol (1992) calls this the "maternalist" route to social citizen rights. Along the second employment route, minimum wages were a genuine achievement, although limiting hours was considered to be protective of the "weaker sex." Mines and factories were provided harsh labor conditions, and the gentler sex needed some protection from them. Of course, white women were considered more deserving of protection than black, Asian, or Mexican women (Glenn, 2002: 83–6). Such protections, however, also reduced labor market competition for the principal breadwinner: the man.

[1] The exception was the Civil War pensions granted to veterans and their widows and dependents. At their height, they were more than a third of all U.S. federal spending, received by 1 million veterans or dependents (Skocpol, 1992). France had lesser military pensions, and Germany and Austria-Hungary granted military veterans government employment after their service. U.S. pensions came when the federal government had a big budget surplus due to high tariff revenues, and they rose and fell with the tariff (Hacker & Pierson, 2002: 288–9).

Maternalist arguments pressed by women's clubs and female social workers claimed the poor health of military recruits in World War I resulted from inferior mothering (although European soldiers thought the Americans looked supremely healthy). In 1920, women got a federal Women's Bureau, followed the next year by a Children's Bureau and an act empowering the first major federal health care program. These "new government functions were normatively justified as a universalization of mother love," says Skocpol (1992: 522). She believes middle-class women's movements were decisive in achieving the programs, but, as with the vote, women were beating against a door that was already ajar. For the vote, the ideology of liberal individualism was exploitable by feminists; welfare reforms and patriarchal and religious ideologies favored them. Women also led the temperance movement, the most successful social movement of the era in the United States and probably anywhere. It secured the destruction of red light districts in the 1910s and Prohibition in 1918. It saw drink as a male vice leading to the maltreatment of women and children. Male-only recreation was the problem, companionate marriage the solution. Men were the weak sex, but women could morally strengthen them. Alas, Prohibition proved a failure; men were incorrigibly weak and sinful.

Maternalist programs were not costly and business was not hostile, not even to women's hours and wages legislation, after business lobbyists had watered down the bills (Hacker & Pierson, 2002: 291–2) There were few recipients, payments were low, and intrusive restrictions were placed on eligibility "to superintend and discipline as well as support its recipients" (C. Gordon, 1994: 45). Skocpol says this was potentially en route to a maternalist welfare state, which never quite materialized (1992: 526). Although these programs were stingy, they were the first recognition that the federal government should assume a welfare responsibility for the poor. So far, the United States was no laggard, and it was sometimes a leader in gender redistribution. It was more consistently a leader in educational reform. These areas of successful reform did not constitute a direct threat to capitalist power. They were orthogonal to it, a distinct political crystallization.

Racial regress

The United States was exceptional among advanced countries in the presence of a large oppressed minority race within the nation. Although Brazil did not fully abolish slavery until two decades after the United States, the racial component of its slavery had never been as pronounced as it was in the United States. As a result, after emancipation in Brazil, former slaves were incorporated into society more than in the United States. Although skin color persistently correlated with class in Brazil, it had not set black Brazilians apart as a separate caste. Australian aborigines and New Zealand Maoris did form substantial racially defined minorities in their countries, but they differed in that aborigines mostly lived apart from white society, and Maoris had more power.

During an era labeled Progressive, there was no racial progress – in fact, quite the reverse. Native Americans had mostly been killed, and the survivors were marginal to national life. African Americans were different. Most lived in the South, where, although essential to the regional economy, they became more segregated, economically exploited, and excluded from civil and political citizenship. Most blacks (and some poor whites) were disenfranchised and intimidated in the backlash against Reconstruction. In Virginia, the turnout for the potential electorate had decreased by half over two decades, to only 28 percent by 1904 (Dawley, 1991: 161). No African American would have agreed that this was either a weak or democratic state.

Most "progressives" were indifferent to the condition of African Americans, even seeing segregation as supported by new racial science. The Supreme Court decision in Plessy versus Ferguson 1896 that public segregation was legal was "an instance of Progressive jurisprudence in its reliance on up-to-date social theory and its readiness to accept state regulation" (Keller, 1994: 252). The Court consistently undermined the rights of African Americans supposedly established after the Civil War in Amendments 13, 14, and 15 of the Constitution, abolishing slavery, guaranteeing due process, equal protection, and the right to vote (Burns, 2009). States rights were reasserted, mainly to protect the South's low-wage racial economy, and between 1890 and 1920 Southern Jim Crow laws and lynchings and northern white race riots all increased (Belknap, 1995: 5–9; Dawley, 1991: 240–1). Such racism was to strongly impact American imperialism. The only racial progress came inside segregated black communities, where literacy and schooling expanded. Less than 10 percent of southern blacks were literate in 1865, but 55 percent were in 1890 (Blum, 2005: 82–3). Black churches acquired organizing space free from white harassment, a black middle class arose to service its own community, and there were persistent attempts at resistance (Glenn, 2002: 109–43). It would take a long time for these seedlings to flower as successful rebellion.

There was also nativist backlash against immigrants. Restrictions imposed on Chinese and Japanese immigrants culminated in 1924 in the Asian Exclusion Act (with negative consequence in foreign policy, as we see in Chapter 4). As migration from overseas declined, Mexicans were substituted for other workers. In agriculture, race entwined with labor forms such as contract labor, debt peonage, convict labor, and anti-vagrancy laws to prevent millions of workers from acquiring citizen rights (Glenn, 2002: 186–92, 156–8). Well-meaning maternalist programs saw social workers imposing "racial liberation" on women, getting them to adopt the mothering and nutritional practices of the Anglo middle class. "Still eating spaghetti, not yet Americanized," wrote one social worker of an Italian family. Another noted Jewish food was "generally overseasoned, over rich, over sharp, or overconcentrated." A pamphlet advised replacing Mexican food with sandwiches of lettuce or graham crackers (Mink, 1995: 90–1). The move toward a nation united by its junk food had begun.

We should not unduly reproach the United States for its racism. It was not exceptional for the period, provided we include other countries' overseas colonies. Britain, France, Germany, Belgium, and Japan in this period were acquiring new colonies and denying rights to populations considered racially inferior. The liberation of these peoples from colonialism came at about the same time African Americans got their civil rights, and black people in both the United States and the colonies explicitly drew the parallel. Europeans and Americans shared the legacy of slavery; the only difference was that Americans inherited it in their domestic power arrangements.

Overall, the progressives helped modernize economic and political power and make gender and educational improvements. They made business more honest and open, but they failed to redistribute much power. Government infrastructural power was harnessed to big business. America became dominated by the corporations, banks, and trusts and aided by federal and state bureaucracies, all relatively uninterested in workers or farmers, and with zero interest in Native Americans, African Americans, and Asians. Education surged forward, women made giant political strides, some poor mothers received some slight help, and unions slowly expanded. These reforms, however, were not usually achieved through class action, and they left economic conservatism dominant in the North and racial conservatism dominant in the South. Populists were fading, and unions remained apolitical. There was almost no socialism, and lib-labs were making little headway. The United States was not yet exceptional, but in this period it was one of the more extreme advanced countries. In particular, workers were organizationally outflanked by a more collectively organized capitalism. Japan was the most comparable case.

The conservative 1920s

America experienced an unusual Great War. Although 2 million American soldiers were mobilized and 1 million reached the front, they only fought for 17 months. Their losses were 116,000 compared to more than 1 million each among other combatants. Mass mobilization warfare had certain regularities. Because the United States was on the winning side, the war legitimated existing power structures. As its war did not last long, American anger at the incompetence of the ruling regime or unequal sacrifices did not have time to surface, unlike all of the other participants. As no significant sacrifices were made by the American people, no promises had been made of a better life afterward. Because the United States experienced only a year one of war, it felt only the first surge of patriotism, rallying round the flag and the troops, attacking those lacking patriotic fervor for war. As a result, this war reinforced existing power distributions.

This was bad news for socialists, syndicalists, and radical populists, who just before the war had been showing signs of life (as in most countries). Many opposed the war as having nothing to do with the American people or its values. They were right, but their only reward was persecution. A patriotic surge supported the wartime persecution of pacifists and the left (Lipset & Marks, 2000: 237–9). To general approval, the socialist Eugene Debs was sentenced to ten years in prison for making an antiwar speech. He had managed to win 6 percent of the vote in the 1912 presidential election, but in 1920, campaigning from prison, his vote fell to 3.4 percent. Socialism was harmed by the war. Nor was it helped by the emergence of Bolshevism in Russia. Although, as elsewhere, the war produced more state regulation of the economy, this was temporary (although some of it was revived in the New Deal). Schemes of state-led reforms influential before the war were discredited, as most were German-derived (Rodgers, 1998: chaps. 6, 7).

During the war, the federal government cooperated with unions in return for no-strike pledges. This helped the normal postwar surge of unions and strikes, but in the United States, this faded more rapidly and completely than elsewhere, assisted by repression. An unrestrained open-shop era re-emerged (Haydu, 1997). Helped by anarchist bombings, President Harding encouraged the most lethal of America's "Red Scares." In the Palmer Raids, 10,000 leftists were arrested, many were beaten and imprisoned, and those who were foreign-born were deported. The AFL unions, mainly craft-based and sectionalist, were lumped together with socialists and "wobbly" syndicalists into a single "Red Menace." The American Legion and the Ku Klux Klan led mobs to break up union meetings, destroy union offices, and even perpetrate lynchings.

There was much violence in the 1922 railroad strike. Wartime regulation had boosted railroad union membership to 400,000, and 80 percent of the workers laid down their tools in response to postwar privatization and deregulation plans. Employers refused to recognize the unions, and imported strikebreakers escorted by company police, local and state militia, and finally federal marshals. After violent confrontations, President Harding felt compelled to intervene. He first sought compromise, but most employers would not yield. The attorney general then persuaded him that the solution was a blanket antitrust injunction against the strike, backed by federal force. This finally broke union resistance. The more fortunate railroad workers were allowed back on the job, but on employers' terms, including being forced to join company unions and sign yellow-dog contracts. This naked class struggle was won by the bosses (Davis, 1997).

Although unions were stagnant in many countries in the 1920s, the U.S. labor movement was in serious decline. Union density fell from 17 percent in 1920 to only 7 percent in 1933. Only Japan (a much less industrial country) now had fewer members. Unions survived only in the older craft trades, and were largely absent from growth industries like chemicals, steel, automobiles, and rubber products. Socialist party membership fell fourfold between 1920 and 1921, from 109,000 to 27,000. It halved again the following year, never to recover, and the socialist vote fell to insignificance by 1924.

Repression had widespread support, because its targets were depicted in the media as extremely violent and even as traitors to the nation. Socialists and communists were denounced as "aliens," and restricting immigration was considered necessary to stop the flow of un-American ideas. The Ku Klux Klan acquired a national mission: to preserve the White Protestant Ascendancy against blacks, Catholics, Jews, and "foreign Bolsheviks." Half a million women joined a KKK women's movement in the early 1920s, and the Klan became "integrated into the normal everyday life of white Protestants" (Blee, 1991: 2–3). Reaction also helped derail feminist hopes of passing an Equal Rights Amendment. Conservative Republicans dominated the 1920s.

Yet economic growth resumed; the war had been profitable for the United States. With Britain and Germany heavily indebted to American banks, it was now the world's leading economic power. Growth resumed as corporations took advantage of their new global dominance. The annual growth rate of real GNP during the 1920s was more than 4 percent; manufacturing productivity rose more than 5 percent (Abramowitz & David, 2001). Business concentration increased: by 1930, 100 corporations controlled almost half the economy. The electrified workbench, the internal combustion engine, and the assembly line were general-purpose technologies increasing productivity (David & Wright, 1999; Abramowitz & David, 2001; R. Gordon, 2005). The automobile assembly line became the symbol of modernity. Nine million motor vehicles were on the road in 1916, 27 million in 1930, and at a much lower cost to the consumer. Steel, glass, rubber, and oil industries grew. Suburban growth was stimulated by the automobile, and this stimulated construction. Field (2011) says poor planning, inefficient land use, and naive investment bubbles led to overdevelopment with poor infrastructures and uneconomical subdivisions. However, electricity reached 60 percent of homes, producing a minor boom in household appliances. Textiles expanded through ready-made clothes, and chain stores and catalogs helped the growth of a middle-class consumer society. Newspapers and magazines were financed by mass advertising; radio, motion pictures, and recorded music took off; and Hollywood replaced France as the home of movies. The nation became more economically integrated, and economists responded with theories of the national, nationally caged, economy (Barber, 1985).

Racist legislation dried up immigration, and an unemployment rate of only 4–6 percent over the decade motivated some corporations to retain their skilled workers by offering them the golden chains of welfare benefits plus promotion through internal labor markets (Berkowitz & McQuaid, 1992: chap. 3; Cohen, 1990). "Welfare capitalism" segmented the labor force, undermining potential class solidarity. Labor shortages stimulated mass migration of African

Americans to the North, where they got higher wages but housing segregation – ambiguous integration into mainstream America.

In the 1920s, per capita personal income probably rose slightly (Costa, 2000: 22). David & Wright (1999; cf Smiley, 2000) say real wages rose, but R. Gordon (2005) says the share of labor in national income remained static. Although income data is ambiguous, what isn't ambiguous is that average life expectancy at birth and the average height of native-born men rose in the 1920s, both signs of better nutrition over a longer period of time (Steckel, 2002). Inequality declined during World War I, but rose afterwards. By the late 1920s, income and wealth inequality was higher than in any decade of the twentieth century (Wolff & Marley, 1989; Piketty & Saez, 2003).

Economically, agriculture did the worst. The incomes of farm laborers and small farmers fell markedly, along with agricultural prices. In response, they often overworked the soil. Many abandoned their farms and migrated, weakening rural populism. The cities remained multiethnic, but ethnic conflict among whites declined. The national Ku Klux Klan collapsed, and it became largely a southern force (Blee, 1991: 175–6). Democrats freed themselves from the chains of Prohibition dividing Protestant from Catholic workers. The two major parties were becoming more like the parties of other industrial countries, with the Republicans the party of business, the Democrats the party of the popular classes – except for the South (Craig, 1992; Dawley, 1991: 213–4). There was now potential for a lib-lab alliance, although the real thing still did not emerge. The Democratic leadership remained conservative and it did not look like they were returning to power soon. America had shifted rightward, reinforcing most of its prior conservative tendencies and the impression of American exceptionalism.

The much-trumpeted new consumer society was not a universal addition to citizenship, as it was not shared by all. American society as depicted by Hollywood was privileged and foreigners envied it. American workers envied it, as well. Half of Americans lived at or very close to subsistence level and still borrowed through pawnbrokers and local loan sharks. The burgeoning credit industry was persuading middle-class families that home mortgages were not irresponsible debt but a sign of respectable independence, but workers still rented their homes (Calder, 1999). Underconsumptionists argued that consumption was depressed by poor purchasing power among the masses. The rich had the money to invest, but the mass of workers had less to spend. This was blocking any general transition of capitalism from great productivity to great consumer demand, as it was in other advanced economies, too. Only the middle and upper classes were benefitting, and this brought the danger of overcapacity and a stock market boom with shaky fundamentals. In 1929, this brought on the Great Depression, a global crisis that was to cause a great surge in suppressed labor discontent and bring the United States back into the global mainstream of domestic politics. Movement into the mainstream occurred earlier in geopolitics.

Imperialism phase 2: Hemispheric empire 1898–1930s

At the very end of the century, the United States suddenly moved into the club of overseas imperialists, expanding into Central America, the Caribbean, Pacific islands, and China. Overseas imperialism had been slow in coming. Although the Monroe Doctrine of 1823 had made an early claim for hemispheric dominance, it could only become reality when Britain and its navy turned away to focus on Asia and Africa; the United States filled its own continent; the second industrial revolution made the United States a major economic power; and the United States acquired a substantial navy. All this was in place by the 1890s, meaning that now the United States could seek profit, supposed security, and geopolitical status by imperialism abroad. It promptly did so, like the other latecomers of the time – Germany, Japan, and Italy. Nothing exceptional here.

U.S. policy had been to pursue a minimal informal imperialism aimed at preventing others from closing markets to American goods. To assist this, they grabbed coaling and naval stations across the Pacific as well as islands rich in guano for fertilizer. In 1890, U.S. Navy Captain Alfred Mahan published his influential *The Influence of Sea Power on History*, arguing that a modern economy depended on international trade, which needed protection by a blue-water fleet. As the federal government now had a large budget surplus, it was spent on building ships. American elites were drawn by the ideology of an Anglo-Saxon mission to the world. Naval policy shifted away from merchantmen, cruisers, and coastal-defense vessels and toward battleships, and by 1898 the United States had the world's third-largest navy. It was easy for the leading industrial country to develop a battleship fleet. The army was only 25,000 strong, but land war was not contemplated.

There were also new strategic considerations. The New Imperialism was filling up the globe, and the United States joined in the scramble for East Asia, unwilling to be left out. Signs of European activity within the American hemisphere made U.S. diplomats nervous. France was planning a Panama Canal, German investments were growing, and European governments were sending gunboats to recover debts from governments in the region. There was consensus in Washington that this outside interference must stop. In 1895, the United States moved its ships to enforce a solution to a boundary dispute between Venezuela and British Guiana. Britain was minimally consulted, Venezuela not at all. Secretary of State Olney exulted at this success, declaring, "Today the United States is practically sovereign on this continent and its fiat is law" (LaFeber, 1993: 2142–83; Ninkovich, 2001: 12–13). By 1898, President McKinley had also resolved to take over the Panama Canal project from the floundering French and to set up a U.S.-controlled Canal Zone, a shell state carved out of Colombia or Nicaragua. The United States, was seeking to buy, not seize, the territory, as it had bought Louisiana and Alaska earlier.

At home, the second industrial revolution brought increasing conflict between employers and labor unions and tensions generated by mass ethnic immigration. *Social imperialism*, developing empire abroad to help alleviate class and ethnic struggles at home, seemed a solution to some (Weinstein, 1968). Progressives advocated addressing conflict by increasing workers rights and stimulating mass consumer demand; conservatives rejected the loss of employer freedoms and the higher wages that this implied. However, empire had little backing from below, primarily because there was no settler lobby. Americans were still focused on upward mobility at home. As the United States remained a net importer of capital, there was no surplus of U.S. capital seeking new outlets – the Hobson/Lenin argument for imperialism did not apply. Because the Depression of 1893–1897 was attributed to saturated domestic markets, some industrialists did favor capturing markets abroad to absorb surplus production.

In 1895, economic recovery was initially led by export, and for the first time the main exports were manufactured rather than farm goods. They were exchanged for Latin American and Caribbean raw materials and agricultural produce that the United States itself could not produce, such as sugar, coffee, and bananas. That trade was dominated by large corporations involved in mining and plantations for sugar, tobacco, coffee, and tropical fruits, and was serviced by American-owned railroads and ports. The banana producers amalgamated in 1899 into the giant United Fruit Company (UFCO). Sugar corporations coupled refining in the United States with intensive plantation production in the Spanish Caribbean. By 1895, U.S. business had invested $50 million in the Spanish colony of Cuba, and trade between the United States and Cuba was now bigger than Cuban-Spanish trade (Ayala, 1999; Perez, 1990; Schoonover, 1991: 170). Although these corporations comprised only a small part of the American economy, they comprised most of the Americans interested in policy toward the region. An imperial lobby was forming, and it saw the remaining Spanish Empire in the Americas as there for the taking.

This was potential economic imperialism, led by corporations and banks, not the ad hoc networks of adventurers and armed trading companies, as in the British Empire. Some say this lobby caused the war of 1898 against Spain (LaFeber, 1993: chaps. 4, 5; P. Smith, 2000: 27–9; Schoonover, 1991, 2003). Mead (2001) sees it as a "Hamiltonian" government-business collaboration to expand a dynamic national economy. Industrialists like Andrew Carnegie and John D. Rockefeller pushed for this. Although most businessmen and most presidents cared little about foreign policy, McKinley's election in 1896 brought in a pro-business Republican president committed to an active search for foreign markets, backed by an expanded fleet (LaFeber, 1993: 330–3). McKinley could also see a strategic opportunity to remove Spain from the hemisphere. The United States had to prevent other empires from grabbing the Spanish colonies. So they decided to grab them first.

However, any policy would have to carry a Congress reluctant to spend money on foreign ventures; some business with interests in the region still favored propping up the Spanish Empire. Foreign policy remained low on Congressional priorities; even business requests for a better consular service abroad were mired in partisan infighting (Pletcher, 1998: 4, 26–45). Trubowitz (1998: 31–95) believes, however, that Congress was shifting. Voting records through the 1890s reveal a foreign policy cleavage between North and South. Northern Congressmen favored tariffs to protect domestic industry, plus naval expansion (shipbuilding was in the Northeast) and informal imperialism to pry open markets in the Americas and Asia. Southerners favored free trade because they depended on cheap agricultural exports, and their main trading partner was Britain, who they feared would be alarmed by naval expansion. Westerners were more oriented to domestic markets, but could provide swing votes in return for support on domestic issues they considered vital. The Northerners were more willing to trade votes. The populists, traditional opponents of imperialism, concentrated in the South and West, now split. Thus, an imperial crystallization was gathering steam in Congress, but this was representative government with competitive elections and a vigorous yellow press, in which they reached the mass public through appeals to interests wrapped up in ideals. In the last chapter, I noted that in Britain the emergence of broad manhood suffrage put pressure on politicians to make empire seem legitimate. Similarly, any American empire must be portrayed as having done good for the people as well as having served big business interests, which were suspect to many Americans in the Progressive era.

Some argue that a growing sense of an American mission to the world was the main cause of this burst of imperialism (Ninkovich, 2001). Many Americans then, as now, believed that they were the freest people on earth, and this carried a sense of responsibility to the world. Was this responsibility as example or mission? The example was embodied in John Winthrop's famous 1630 description of Americans erecting "a City upon a Hill, the eyes of all people are upon us." There was a national consensus around setting such an example, but this might lead to isolationism rather than empire. The second sense was of an imperial mission carrying the American example to the world, redeeming it through humanitarian intervention. Theodore Roosevelt declared that Americans would be remembered for their imperial virtues, just like the Romans. "All the great masterful races have been fighting races, and the minute a race loses the hard fighting virtues ... no matter how skilled in commerce and finance, in science or art, it has lost its right to stand as the equal of the best." (Auchincloss, 2001: 4). Senator Henry Cabot Lodge boasted, "We have a record of conquest, colonization and expansion unequalled by any people in the Nineteenth Century. We are not about to be curbed now" (Schoultz, 1998: 135). He added that American imperialism would spread "freedom," not the "crass materialism" of the British and French. Some added social Darwinism: it was the duty of the white race to "uplift the darker races." Others demanded that those suffering under the Spanish yoke be liberated. This had broad appeal, especially among populists, who would otherwise reject a foreign policy driven by business and strategic elites.

Anti-imperialists declared that freedom could not be carried at gunpoint, and that imperialism was a betrayal of American constitutional freedoms. Others reached anti-imperialism by way of racism: intervention abroad risked "racial pollution." Nativists in California saw Asians as the main source of racial contamination; southern Democrats feared Latinos and Negroes of the Caribbean. William Jennings Bryan, the defeated Democrat candidate in 1900, yoked together very different arguments against empire, declaring "the Filipinos cannot be citizens without endangering our civilization; they cannot be subjects without imperiling our form of government" (Schoultz, 1998: 142). Here, constitutional rights and racism were unusually conjoined to oppose imperialism. Imperialists and anti-imperialists came from both left and right.

The debate was evenly balanced, which raises a counterfactual question: what if the United States had stayed out of foreign ventures? Then the Spanish colonies would have achieved their independence later and the United States might have continued isolationism until World War I, and even stayed out of that war. The world would have been greatly changed, but this war was precipitated less from events in the United States than in Cuba. A bloody insurrection began there in 1895. Spain responded with repression, including the invention of the "concentration camp." In the United States, advocates of "Cuba Libre" urged that American constitutional traditions required assisting freedom fighters. Interventionists only triumphed, however, when the U.S. battleship *Maine* – sent in 1898 into Havana harbor to show the flag – blew up and sank, killing more than 200 American servicemen. This was popularly attributed to the dastardly Spanish, although it was more likely an accident. Emotions took over and Congress pressured President McKinley to declare war, although he may have favored intervention. The military assured him of victory, and rebels were abundant in both Cuba and the Philippines. The sinking of the *Maine* – clearly a contingent event – might have been a timely pretext, for by now war was overdetermined (Offner, 1992: ix & 225; cf Peceny, 1999: 56–65).

The Spanish-American War lasted only three months. There were swift American victories, including the destruction of the wooden Spanish fleets not just in the Caribbean but across the Pacific, as well. A "splendid little war," said Secretary of State Hay, but the acquisition of occupied Spanish colonies had not been thought through, and McKinley and his advisors had no clear idea of what to do with them. In a sense, this was accidental empire. During the continental expansion, the Supreme Court had decided that "the constitution followed the flag" (not for Indians, of course, but they were dead). So annexation should have given constitutional rights to the former Spanish subjects.

McKinley, however, did not want to admit into "a share in this government of a motley million and a half of Spaniards, Cubans, and Negroes, to whom our religion, manners, political traditions and habits, and modes of thought are, to tell the honest truth, about as familiar as they are to the King of Dahomey" (Schoultz, 1998: 142). Because the word "colony" was not acceptable, Cuba, Puerto Rico, and the Philippines plus some small Pacific islands were euphemistically termed by the Supreme Court "non-incorporated territories" in order to prevent natives from being citizens. In reality, these were colonies.

The Cuban colony

Cuba was strategic, only ninety miles from Florida and – together with Puerto Rico – it controlled access to the Caribbean and Central America. So the United States occupied it (Boot, 2002: 134–5). The administration now sought to control the Cuban aftermath. U.S. forces did not consult the Cuban rebels about the conduct of the war, they cut them right out of the Spanish surrender, and they refused to recognize the rebel Republic. The United States decided that *libre* meant "remove the Spanish from the hemisphere and protect U.S. business freedoms from the insurgents." In his war message to Congress, McKinley said he would "place hostile constraints on both parties in Cuba" (LaFeber, 1994 :202; Perez, 1983: 178; Perez, 1998: 19, 79–80; Offner, 1992: 194, 222). The insurgents seemed dangerous, especially former sugar and tobacco workers. The U.S. Consul described them as men "unused to either civilization or Christianity.... The Negro element, together with adventurers from abroad ... [is] seeking power or gain." McKinley's minister to Spain said a "protectorate over Cuba seems to me very like the assumption of responsible care of a madhouse" (Schoultz, 1998:136).

When the United States suppressed a popular rebel movement, the occupation was not welcomed. American clients were mainly elites, described as "the business class fully capable of good judgement," "the decent element," "the intelligent and educated," "property-holders," "white men, and of good family and position. Among the principal military officers there are only three of negro blood." Governor-General Wood was pleased to note that in the assembly, elected on a restricted franchise, "whites so greatly outnumber blacks." Yet he changed his mind, saying, "I should say that we have about ten absolutely first class men and about fifteen men of doubtful qualifications and character and about six of the worst rascals and fakirs in Cuba." Senator Platt remarked, "In many respects they are like children" (Schoultz, 1998: 144–8, 202). Governor-General Wood and Secretary Root said it would take decades of American tutelage to reach not self-government but "annexation by acclamation." General Shafter exclaimed, "Self-government? Why these people are no more fit for self-government than gunpowder is for hell!" (Healy, 1963: 36, 91–6, 148; cf Hunt, 1987)

In 1903, the Platt Amendment was written into the Cuban constitution, requiring Cuba to "maintain a low public debt; refrain from signing any treaty impairing its obligation to the United States; to grant to the United States the right of intervention to protect life, liberty, and property; validate the acts of the military government; and, if requested, provide long-term naval leases." (Langley, 1980: 21). This was extremely constrained sovereignty. The U.S. military administration remained on the island for twenty years, supervising the Cuban client government. The naval base at Guantanamo Bay, acquired then, still proves useful for dubious imperial roles today.

American corporations now took over the sugar industry, as they did in Puerto Rico – also occupied in 1898 – and the Dominican Republic, after an eight-year U.S. occupation began in 1916. The islands were safe for American corporations to control inputs and gain leverage over competitors, coupling production with low labor costs. There was economic growth, but the peasants did not benefit. Railroads were extended, but as usual in colonies, they took the production of foreign-owned companies to the ports and out of the country. Most of the lines did not run outside of the sugar season, and there were no backward links or multiplier effects on the economy. This was economic growth but not development (Ayala, 1999; Zanetti & Garcia, 1998). Yet this was after the abolition of slavery, so employees of U.S. corporations were spared the worst forms of colonial exploitation. Indeed, they were usually paid more than workers in other island sectors.

U.S. military power was repeatedly flourished. If Cuban elections went the "wrong way" or a client government became unpopular, U.S. troops intervened. The U.S. ambassador explained the policy: "Make 'em vote and live by their decisions." If there was trouble, "We'll go in and make 'em vote again" (P. Smith, 2000: 52). The United States was fairly democratic at home, but its rule in Cuba was despotic.

The Filipino colony

President McKinley had not initially thought of annexing the Philippines, but said his conscience had triumphed after several sleepless nights:

> I went down on my knees and prayed to Almighty God for light and guidance.... one night it came to me ... there was nothing left for us to do but take them all, and educate the Filipinos and uplift them and civilize them and Christianize them and by God's grace do the best we could by them, as our fellow men for whom Christ died.... And the next morning I sent for the chief engineer of the War Department (our map-maker), and I told him to put the Philippines on the map of the United States" (Schoultz, 1998: 89).

He appeared not to know that the vast majority of Filipinos were Christians.

At first things did not go well. Again, the new government was formed without consulting the insurgent allies. They resisted, and a three-year colonial war killed between 200,000 and 400,000 Filipinos, many in U.S. concentration camps adapted from the Spanish. Rebel areas were denied food, creating what one U.S. officer called a "howling wilderness." More than 4,000 American soldiers died, mostly from disease. Had McKinley known all this in advance, he might not have claimed the islands. The occupation generated the first major anti-imperialist movement in the United States, with Mark Twain its most famous spokesman. A professor of Sociology at Yale University, William Graham Sumner (1899) described the war as "the Conquest of the United States by Spain." He meant that in acquiring colonies, the United States had been conquered by Spanish imperialist values, the concentration camps being an example.

The Americans then sensibly lowered their mission sights. They learned what British and French imperialists had earlier learned: repression would work only when harnessed to a deal struck with local elites – indirect empire. Ethnic minorities were armed to fight the Tagalogs who dominated the insurgency. Upper-class Tagalogs then lay down their arms rather than losing their properties. With few Americans choosing to staff the imperial Mission or set up businesses there, the Filipino *caciques* – the richest sixty families with vast patronage networks – learned to exploit their indispensability. The families were also needed to vote taxes because the U.S. Congress refused to vote funds for the colony. This was different from Puerto Rico, says Go (2008), where local elites' economic power was severely disrupted by the American presence (and a terrible hurricane), forcing them into political changes including acceptance of the American multiparty system, which was absent in the Philippines. Although the Americans complained perennially about the corruption of the elite's patron-client relations, whenever they suggested reform, the families conjured up the specter of revolution and the United States backed down. The main impact of the American administration was that the elite, *illustrados* ("enlightened"), extended their networks of control from local to national politics and to the new institutions introduced by the Americans such as a reformed and expanded school system (Hidalgo, 2002; Go, 2003, 2008: 254; Boudreau, 2003; Ninkovich, 2001: 54–9). As usual, empire was empowering traditional elites, but without American colonists, white racism was comparatively unimportant and took a Lamarckian form. American tutelage, based on study of British imperial institutions, would lift up the natives to a state of civilization (Go, 2011). Congress was also influenced by anti-imperialists, who were growing in strength after World War I, and by American farmers competing with Filipino goods. As neither real democracy nor large profit could be attained, there was less point in keeping the islands, and this was reinforced when the navy decided in 1908 that the U.S. bases were too exposed and far from the United States (Pomeroy, 1974: 158–9). The events of 1941 proved this.

By 1912, Filipinos controlled their own government except for defense and schools. The gilding on the top of the expanded education system was provided by the 100 Filipino *pensionados* per year sent to U.S. colleges, mostly the children of the elite; by 1920, school enrolment neared 1 million (Calata, 2002; Ninkovich, 2001: 60–72). The United States had rapidly moved from direct to indirect rule to substantial self-government, much more rapidly than happened in any British colony. In 1934, the United States began a ten-year preparation for Filipino independence, the first imperial power to make such a move (Villacorte, 2002; Roces, 2002). Only Japanese aggression delayed full independence to after 1945. This was a genuine achievement of American imperialism, although it was really the Filipino elite that obtained self-government.

American racism merged with patriarchy had a silver lining. "Child-like" natives could be tutored and brought to "maturity," quite rapidly in the case of the Philippines and Puerto Rico. It was our duty to uplift the darker races, who were "emotional, irrational, irresponsible, unbusinesslike, unstable, childlike," "little brown brothers," "lacking manliness, effeminate." Latinos and Filipinos came below whites but above Negroes in the race hierarchy, and savages lived in the backwoods. All had been "debased" by Spanish rule, but with tutelage, all except savages and Muslims might govern themselves. Actually, as Go (2011) notes, it was only because the Philippines had already reached quite a high level of civilization that tutelage could work, and work quicker than in most British colonies (cf Go, 2004; Rosenberg, 1999: 31–5; Hunt, 1987: chap. 3; P. Smith, 2000: 48–9). Popular cartoons showed a very large Columbia or Uncle Sam or a GI giving a helping hand or showing a light or a path to small, childlike Filipinos or Latinos. Some depicted parental chastisement, such as the forcible bathing of a bawling black Cuban by U.S. General Wood or Columbia cutting off a Chinaman's pigtail (symbol of a reactionary society) with scissors whose blades were labeled "20th century progress" – racism and Enlightenment values admixed in the customary imperial way. Yet children and little brothers eventually become adults; races were not seen as permanently inferior.

The 1904 St. Louis World Fair included a live colonial exhibit from the Philippines, including 1,000 "savages" and "Non Christian tribes," arranged by level of civilization. The lowest were the savage Igorots – headhunters, dog eaters, nearly naked – they were the biggest crowd pullers. The most civilized were U.S.-trained Filipino soldiers, demonstrating the American ability to civilize. By the 1930s, Americans assumed the task had been largely accomplished. There was now no need for colonies, even virtual ones, and the model in Asia was that the United States would now stay offshore, enforcing American interests – mainly the free trade of the "open door" – through informal empire, without any territorial encroachments.

Why colonies were temporary

Just before 1900, the United States had for both economic and strategic reasons embarked on an easy war that rather unexpectedly brought colonies. It then backed away from direct or indirect empire to envisage only temporary colonies and then moved further to only informal empire, for reasons that were rooted more in the conditions of the time than in an inherent American aversion to empire (cf Go, 2011). There were six main reasons for this removal.

(1) The United States had been initially burned in Cuba, the Philippines and Puerto Rico. The easy part was defeating the Spanish; the hard part was ruling without settlers and having alienated local elites. This should sound familiar because the recent occupation of Iraq had the same combination. The local allies turned against U.S. occupation, the ideal mission was abandoned, sites were lowered. The United States stayed in Cuba twenty years, in the Philippines for forty years, and is still in Puerto Rico, but it did not want more of these experiences.

(2) The United States sent out almost no settlers. In Africa, the British Empire was still being prodded into acquiring new colonies by British settlers and adventurers on the ground. The settler lobby was also strong in the empire of Japan. Settlers were still entering, the United States, however, not leaving. The exception was Hawaii, where an incoming population of American planters ensured that Hawaii did become an American colony, controlled by them. After World War II, there was a happy ending: it became assimilated as a state of the Union. Social imperialism needed backing from below, but this was lacking in the United States. There was no great popular lobby for colonies.

(3) The Europeans were mid-way through the scramble for Africa, provoked by fear of other powers grabbing territory first. No rival was seriously scrambling for the Americas. Germany or Japan might be tempted into the Philippines, so the British urged the United States to stay there. The maximum threat in the American hemisphere was a foreign gunboat or two, and the United States could scare them away by cheaper informal means, which the British also preferred in this hemisphere.

(4) After three centuries of European expansion, Britain and France had already experienced colonizing institutions – a colonial civil service, trading companies with monopoly licenses, and colonial armies and navies. These carried on doing what they were trained to do. Latecomers Germany and Japan had militarism and state-assisted companies, and Japan also sent out settlers. Latecomer United States did not have such institutions, except for a navy that was more suited to informal empire than colonies. Compared to the other empires, the United States lacked colonial institutions, expertise, and personnel.

(5) This was the beginning of the age of nationalism, when educated propertied elites on the periphery were articulating ideologies involving anti-imperial and racial adaptations of a constitutional revolution, diffusing globally. It was more difficult to establish colonies. European empires had conquered countries earlier, before modern nationalist movements had arisen. Now, however, rebels had more ideological power. In 1898, an Italian army was defeated at the battle

of Adowa by an Ethiopian monarch mobilizing a Christian nationalism nurtured by struggles against Muslim neighbors. From 1899 to 1902, the British in South Africa were shocked by a rebellion of the Boers, settlers of Dutch stock with their own national culture. Like the British in South Africa, however, the Americans learned to deal with nationalist rebels by yielding them more self-government – they yielded privileged Filipino elites "cacique democracy" (B. Anderson, 1988). They were willing to share power with the United States to preserve their property rights, but the United States failed to achieve this elsewhere, and sought less colonial modes of control.

(6) This period saw the rise of corporate capitalism, where large agro-business and banking trusts were seeking to extract monopoly concessions abroad. Latin American countries already had Western-style states guaranteeing property rights and issuing monopoly licenses. Many regimes were corrupt and conflict-ridden, but coercively reforming rather than destroying them was the simpler tactic for foreign corporations. The way to greater profit in the hemisphere was not to colonize but to coerce offshore with gunboats. The British were already doing this in the hemisphere, and for the Americans informal empire was the obvious solution. Americans chose the form of imperialism to which they were best suited. It was more capitalist than statist, and the statism was then administered in lighter doses.

Informal empire with gunboats

The United States did not draw the lesson that it should abandon imperialism; it simply changed imperialist forms. Between 1899 and 1930, the United States launched thirty-one punitive military interventions, one a year. In Asia, the United States remained a junior partner to the Europeans. Its open-door policy, proclaimed by Secretary Hay in China in 1899–1900, was an imperial latecomers insistence on entry to Chinese markets on the same unequal terms as the Europeans enjoyed. In 1900, the United States contributed 5,000 troops to the joint imperial force that put down the Boxer Rebellion, and this got them into the unequal treaties club, just as it did Japan, with its 8,000 troops. The main market the war kept open was the supply of opium to China, which the Boxer rebels and the Chinese imperial government had tried to close. The United States was thus a party to one of the great stains of modern imperialism, although only as junior partner to the British, who supplied the opium. The open door only opened one way, because until the 1930s American markets remained highly protected (Eckes, 1995).

Twenty-eight of the 31 interventions were in Central America and the Caribbean. The countries of the region had few wars, but uneven development meant that in most countries a few enclave economies were able to export agricultural goods or raw materials, and the bulk of the country remained desperately poor. Inequality worsened by the reinforcement of class and ethnic and racial differences. There was intense political struggle between conservative, liberal, and nationalist prescriptions for reform. The consequence was political instability and coups, for which Americans were rarely responsible (Mares, 2001). Yet foreign business intensified inequality and frustrated national development, as its profits came from monopoly concessions in mining and agrobusiness enclaves, with little relationship to the rest of the economy. The main native beneficiaries were the landowners and merchants who were clients of foreign business plus workers in the enclaves who did better than workers elsewhere (Bucheli, 2005: chap. 6; Dosal, 1993). Most profits were repatriated abroad, and there were few backward linkages. Again, this was growth without development. A study of the coffee, henequen, and oil industries between 1850 and 1929 concludes that American companies adversely affected the economic development of most of Latin America (Topik & Wells, 1998).

The key problem was monopoly concessions to foreign business, doled out by a corrupt but compliant oligarchy headed by *caudillos* whose role was to keep order and repress popular protest. This aborted a truly constitutional order and national economic development in Cuba, the Dominican Republic, Guatemala, and Nicaragua (Leonard, 1991: 95; Whitney, 2001: 1–9, 18–20; Hall, 2000; Dosal, 1993: 1, 75–94, 119–40). They were intermittently challenged by liberals and radicals mobilizing under the banner of nationalism, but American business tended to oppose these, alarmed by anything carrying the "perilous potential of revolutions" (Hunt, 1987: 105). Jittery U.S. businesses inveigled the U.S. government into a pattern of intervention that deployed economic pressures to destabilize the liberals and military intervention to destroy the radicals (Paige, 1997: 45–6; Mahoney, 2001: 19–23). This was government catch-up after provocations by corporations.

After armed intervention, the United States might then take over the customs houses and state budgets to ensure "sound finances," a more direct and coercive form of today's structural adjustment programs. Theodore Roosevelt started it, drawing on British policy in Egypt (Rosenberg, 1999: 41–52). Under President Taft, it became known as "dollar diplomacy." American "money doctors," brought U.S. banking loans to stabilize the local currency, denominate it in dollars, move the gold reserves to New York, reschedule the debts, and supervise its budget and the collection of customs revenues (Paige, 1997, 79–80, 162–8, 178; Mahoney, 2001: 190). The doctors sought sound finances, ensuring repayment of foreign debts at source, making the country attractive for foreign investment. It also extended the dollar zone, a discrete trimming of the global rule of British sterling.

Dollar diplomacy came embedded in a business version of a civilizing mission. In Veeser's (2002) account of Venezuela, no one mentioned democracy. Instead, they said they were spreading the rationality and inevitability of free markets, which would then encourage "sane and progressive" government (opposition was "insane" or "irrational"). The racial and patriarchal ideologies of imperialism were given a business twist: the "maturity" and "manhood" of the white race had developed "self-control, mastery and the ability to plan for the future.... Three centuries of Spanish rule had developed children, not independent self-reliant men," Edwin Kemmerer of Princeton University declared to an outraged audience of Filipino students at Cornell University. Yet his sentiments were those not just of bankers but also of "small-town Main Streets, mid-level managers and aspiring professionals," says Rosenberg (1999: 33–9). Dollar diplomacy was a form of unequal treaty, benefiting U.S. business and foreign bondholders most, then the local clients, and very little the local society. Unlike modern structural adjustment programs, however, it was not hegemonic and required repeated military interventions. It was dollar-plus-gunboat diplomacy, a political crystallization with a main constituency among those U.S. corporations with interests in the region.

This could not solve the underlying local problems. The long-run effect of U.S. interventions probably compounded local instability, although they had not created it. The marines stayed for anywhere between three months and twenty-five years (in Nicaragua) without the United States ever claiming sovereignty – with Panama a half-exception because of the unique importance of the canal. Intervention was followed by an expansion of U.S. agro-business trusts locally, as Ayala (1999) shows in the Caribbean sugar industry. The supposedly liberal Woodrow Wilson sent the marines in more than the self-proclaimed imperialist Theodore Roosevelt, and this returned the Democrats to imperialism. The policy was now bipartisan, although it rarely evoked much popular attention.

From 1900 until the mid-1930s, U.S. administrations sometimes claimed they intervened to restore democracy. The gunboats furthered freedom, self-determination, and free self-government, but whenever there was a whiff of social revolution (i.e., redistribution) or liberal or populist movements appeared to threaten U.S. business interests, the United States overthrew them with short, sharp military intervention (Schoonover, 1991: 173; Leonard, 1991: 79–81; Whitney, 2001: 138–9). Profit, followed at a distance by strategic security, was the dominant motive aroused by the imperial state crystallization. In Cuba, Governor-General Wood said, "When people ask me what I mean by stable government, I tell them 'money at six per cent'" (Ninkovich, 2001: 102). Venezuelan President Juan Vicente Gomez became a loyal ally of the United States. In return, the United States turned a blind eye to the brutalities of his twenty-seven-year dictatorship, calling him a "democratic Caesar" (Ewell, 1996: 107). Caudillos learned to manipulate democratic rhetoric, denouncing their local enemies as dictators or revolutionaries. By the end of this period, ruthless tyrants ruled over countries where the United States had most insisted on democracy earlier (Drake, 1991: 33). Max Boot, always seeking to find good in American empire, concedes that this democratizing project failed, but says this was because, "Dictatorship was indigenous; democracy was a foreign transplant that did not take, in part because America did not stick around for long enough to cultivate it" (2002: 251). Yet on balance, American interventions exacerbated social conflict and took constitutional government out of reach (cf P. Smith, 2000: 63).

It was not rational: a policy encouraging national economic development with a measure of redistribution would have aided local stability and economic growth, boosting U.S. trade and American corporate profits. Costa Rica was the local proof that such an alternative strategy would have been beneficial for both parties. The more independence a Latin American country had from the United States, the more economic growth it achieved, as in the British Empire. However, the lobbying of corporations benefitting from monopoly concessions blocked this. American imperialism in the hemisphere was unusually corporate. For most Americans, empire was not on their radar screen; nor was it for most American business. The few corporations with monopoly concessions in extractive and transport industries or with plantations in the region differed. Because there was no major counter-interest group, these corporations had a malign hold over American imperialism. In the first half of the twentieth century, countries further away from the United States were better able to control and protect their economies, and their economies grew faster than the nearby countries in which the United States intervened heavily. That steers us toward regarding this imperialism as exploitative.

Policy goals were also filtered, and worsened through a racist ideological lens derived back home, the most direct impact of domestic onto foreign power relations. Races were arranged into a civilizational hierarchy: whites above mestizos above blacks above indigenous populations. The British were experienced in indirect empire, doing deals with native elites, identifying big class and cultural differences among natives. As we saw in the last chapter, their racism surged freely through colonial private life, but public policy was more pragmatic, as reflected in the rather bland British official documents of the time. State Department papers differed. One briefing paper read, "Political stability in these countries more or less in direct proportion to percentage of pure white inhabitants." The Brazilian desk briefed the secretary of state that the mestizos were "self-centered, lovers of pleasure and power," and Negroes were "almost wholly illiterate and of childlike ignorance." The Mexican desk said Mexico was "governed by an Indian race of low civilization, and it would be a fundamental error to deal with such a government as with that of highly civilized white races, or to expect justice by the mere force of logic when justice conflicts with national aspirations." The U.S. ambassador agreed, saying, "There is very little white blood in the cabinet." He then went through its members individually, identifying them as "Indian," "Jew," "pure blooded Indian and very cruel," and so forth (Schoultz, 1998: 278–9; Hunt, 1987). The people were "dagos," "niggers," or "savages." The whites had been "degraded" by centuries of Spanish "decadence" and "race mixing."

Roosevelt called Colombians "contemptible little creatures," "jack rabbits," "foolish and homicidal corruptionists," "of fatuous weakness, of dismal ignorance, cruelty, treachery, greed and utter vanity." Marine General Smedley Butler called Nicaraguans "the most useless lot of vermine I have struck yet." A senior U.S. army officer said, "The Haitians are, as you know, a very hysterical people." The entire hemisphere contained 15 million "slightly Catholicized savages," "beggars sitting idly on a pile of gold," "a continent almost literally going to waste." These were stronger prejudices than British imperialists now expressed. The strength of these prejudices was contributed by American racism at home, and it increased the chances of military intervention.

Venom was directed at anyone who opposed the United States. Nicaraguan President Zelaya was described by Roosevelt as an "unspeakable carrion," Venezuelan President Castro as "an unspeakably villainous little monkey" (Schoultz, 1998: 210, 243, 254; Ewell, 1996: 98–9, 109; Auchincloss, 2001: 57; McBeth, 2001). Friendlier Latino elites (always whites) were "the better sort," "the commercial element," "of good family and position." They were, however, greatly outnumbered by "desperately selfish, irresponsible political brigands ... little better than savages." "The peasants ... have the mentality of a child of not more than seven years of age," they are "irrational," "inefficient bandits," "acting without settled principle," "whose appetite for rapine, blood, and revolution, can never be satisfied" (Schoultz, 1998: 76, 148, 164, 172, 179, 183, 210; Park, 1995: 23–4, 33, 44, 78–90). These quotes were from American diplomats, soldiers, and businessmen. With such stereotyping, American policy could hardly be realist, based merely on economic or geopolitical interest. It seemed obvious that these people were incapable of good government. Imperialism protected American business interests filtered through racist ideology.

It was nonetheless imperialism light. The United States used only enough force to help American corporations control the export and financial sectors; the American public showed little interest. This was essentially private diplomacy, costing little, but after World War I, more Americans opposed imperialism, and the gunboat empire visibly faltered. The marines went in and usually soon left. The installed and supposedly client regimes, however, often subverted U.S. prescriptions, whether out of nationalism or corruption. Resistance against U.S. forces became more persistent as anti-imperial ideals spread (LaFeber, 1984: 16–18, 302, 361; Leonard, 1991: 60–8). In the 1920s, even the bankers decided gunboat diplomacy was not yielding results. In 1928, Herbert Hoover and his Democrat challenger Al Smith both campaigned on a softer foreign policy.

The United States had already found a new tactic – training indigenous militaries to suppress opposition. From their ranks came client dictators who would keep order with indirect American military and economic assistance. The United States now wholly abandoned any democratizing mission. "He may be a son-of-a-bitch but he's our son-of-a-bitch" is the remark conventionally attributed to Cordell Hull, FDR's secretary of state, describing Rafael Trujillo, dictator of the Dominican Republic. It was also applicable to Anastasio Somoza Garcia in Nicaragua, Juan Vicente Gomez followed by Marcos Perez Jimenez in Venezuela, Fulgencia Batista in Cuba, and Francois ("Papa Doc") Duvalier in Haiti. A long period of proxy informal imperialism began. There have been many more sons of bitches since then.

By 1935, Marine General Butler, retired, had acquired a new perspective on his career, which he expressed in *Common Sense* magazine:

> I spent 33 years and four months in active military service and during that period I spent most of my time as a high class thug for Big Business, for Wall Street and the bankers. In short, I was a racketeer, a gangster for capitalism. I helped make Mexico and especially Tampico safe for American oil interests in 1914. I helped make Haiti and Cuba a decent place for the National City Bank boys to collect revenues in. I helped in the raping of half a dozen Central American republics for the benefit of Wall Street. I helped purify Nicaragua for the International Banking House of Brown Brothers in 1902–1912. I brought light to the Dominican Republic for the American sugar interests in 1916. I helped make Honduras right for the American fruit companies in 1903. In China in 1927 I helped see to it that Standard Oil went on its way unmolested. Looking back on it, I might have given Al Capone a few hints. The best he could do was to operate his racket in three districts. I operated on three continents. (Schmidt, 1998: 231)

Yet the gangster wasn't too violent. The enormous imbalance in power between the United States and the countries of the region meant that interventions did not result in massive fatalities. The United States made four brief forays into Mexico and realized it was too big to control, so smaller countries took the brunt; neither their governments nor their rebels could mount sustained military resistance to U.S. forces, except in peripheral jungle and upland areas. As most atrocities committed by all empires came in response to resistance, there were relatively few American atrocities.

The United States also found local clients without difficulty. Not princes, chiefs, or imams, as in the British or French Empires, but Filipino cacique families owning plantations and businesses, and Latin American landowners and businessmen oriented to export production. This was a *comprador bourgeoisie* of lawyers, financial advisers, merchants, and politicians capable of diffusing nationalist resistance. Class undercut nation. Many realists also saw little point in opposing the United States because rebellion would probably not succeed. In Honduras (seven small interventions), the Liberals eventually abandoned their earlier development program and encouraged an enclave economy allowing U.S. entrepreneurs to dominate (Mahoney, 2001: 176–8). The American empire was to adhere to this class model of informal rule throughout the twentieth century.

By the late 1930s, the U.S. goal was to keep Nazi Germany out of the hemisphere. However, despite the ideological lure of fascism, the sons of bitches knew on which side their bread was buttered. During World War II, only Argentina did not support the United States. Indirect coercion through proxies did not unduly strain finances or manpower or alarm the American public. American corporations made profits, and so did the local *comprador* class. Roosevelt named this his Good Neighbor Policy, but it was mostly a change of means. The United States conceded advantages that had become obsolete and retained those necessary to its economic and strategic interests (Gellman, 1979, 1995; cf Roorda, 1998: 22–30; B. Wood, 1961; Mares, 2001: 68). The policy gave the dictators breathing space to pursue their own interests, and some began national development projects that Dollar Diplomacy had discouraged earlier (they later developed into import substitution industrialization [ISI] programs). During the New Deal, the United States seemed to favor a reformed capitalism, encouraging Latin Americans to believe the United States might soon encourage economic reform in the hemisphere. Unfortunately, World War II interrupted this prospect, and the moment was gone.

American policy toward the hemisphere remained constant over the twentieth century. It was in place before the Bolshevik Revolution, and the existence of the Soviet Union made little difference. America did do empire, especially in its own hemisphere, although mainly through milder imperial forms. It was pragmatic in the sense that the United States learned from its early unsuccessful burst of colonialism to lighten and make rule less direct, and American rule was lighter than that of other empires. This may be as good as modern imperialism got, but it was not entirely pragmatic. Options for the United States were narrowed, however, by the mixture of intense racism and fear of anarchism; less a fear that leftists might actually achieve revolution than that their agitation would produce only chaos (Hunt, 1987: chaps. 3, 4). Liberals were opposed because they might open the floodgates to chaos. The tragedy of U.S. policy was that it made chaos more likely, because it intensified inequality, corruption, despotism – and thus, resistance. This was because it was not purely materialist or instrumentally rational; it was strongly emotional, the beginnings of paranoid anticommunism.

Conclusion

In this chapter, we have seen the inexorable progress of the United States toward becoming the principal economic world power, although this power was not yet projected globally. Its domestic bias, produced by numerous forces, was toward capitalism. It disfavored not only labor but also racial and ethnic minorities, although it disfavored women less than most countries. Like all countries, the United States was unique, although the pro-capitalist bias was beginning to seem somewhat exceptional, as the customary trope has often asserted. However, this was not to last much longer. In foreign policy, the United States had moved more contingently toward adding yet another imperial segment to the world, although by the end of the period it was backing away from this role. The two trends add up to an American historical development that, in its totality, was rather complex, buffeted back and forth by a plurality of power sources and crystallizations. Like all empires, it differed from others, but it was not exceptional.

4 Asian empires: Fallen dragon, rising sun

Introduction: The Western Threat

This volume deals with the rise and fall of European power in the world. The successors were to be the United States, the USSR and, eventually, East Asia, so I devote various chapters to all three. This chapter deals with East Asia in the period up to about 1930. I chart the rise of Japan, the one country to resist Western imperialism, industrialize, and develop an empire of its own. It did so largely at the expense of the world's oldest surviving empire, China. I take China-Japan relations forward to about 1930, just before Japan unleashed the aggressive militarism that was to cause its own downfall and assist the eventual dominance of East Asia by Chinese communism.

East Asia was at the outer logistical limits of the Western powers. They could not colonize either China or Japan, and had to remain content with an informal empire with gunboats. China and Japan were advanced civilizations endowed with a cultural solidarity out of which modern nationalism could rise, enabling them to resist, adapt, and devise their own national versions of modernity. However, this was a much longer process for China. In this period, I will contrast divided Chinese elites – unable to consistently pursue the reforms necessary to modernize or turn back foreign imperialism – with more cohesive Japanese elites – able to reform at home and emulate Western imperialism abroad.

Over more than a millennium – from its unification in 221 BC to AD 1911 – Chinese empires dominated much of Asia. They had sponsored economic development, commercialization, and some proto-industrialization. The upper classes had lived well, and the rest had lived well enough for China to generate large population growth. It was not surprising that the emperor considered himself the Son of Heaven, and his realm the "Middle Kingdom," superior to all others, capable of dominating the known world. Yet in the early fifteenth century, China had backed away from a global realm, burning the last of seven fleets that had reached Africa half a century before the Europeans arrived there. Instead, it chose to focus its resources on defending the northern frontiers. China continued to exact homage and tribute from other Asian states and occasionally launched punitive military expeditions in Turkestan and Tibet. Yet in early modern times, Chinese domination had mostly consisted of peaceful hegemony, with few wars (Fairbank, 1968, Andornino, 2006). It was partly due to Chinese restraint that the islands of Japan were able to enjoy a millennium of independence and growth of their civilization. .No: stet Networks of artisanal production and trade also flowered across Asia to produce the world's most developed international economy in the early modern period.

Yet in the eighteenth century, the Europeans developed mercantile and industrial capitalism and arrived in Asia as well-armed imperialists. By the early nineteenth century, East Asia was feeling significant British pressure. A Chinese Empire that was already in decline was losing authority in its tributary states, and its population growth was outstripping productivity. Warships provided British sticks, while opium exports from India provided addictive carrots undermining Chinese imperial power. The Qing Emperor and his court tried to ban opium imports but lacked the infrastructural power to implement the ban. By the 1830s, British merchants were flooding the Chinese market each year with 30,000 chests, each containing 150 pounds of opium extract.

In 1840, zealous Chinese officials destroyed opium stocks in British warehouses and arrested two drunken British sailors; the British sent in warships. In the First Opium War, British military superiority produced a rapid victory and the Son of Heaven was forced to sign humiliating treaties, ceding Hong Kong, providing five "open ports" to the British, forbidding Chinese courts to try British citizens, and forcing China to pay an indemnity for starting the war. The opium trade was ratcheted up, as was the export of bonded Chinese labor to the European empires in Asia. Further Chinese resistance generated a second Opium War in 1856–1860 with the same outcome. The ensuing treaties freed the opium trade from regulation, and freed Christians to propagate their faith across China. Within a few years, other Western imperialists also secured unequal treaties with China. These typically restricted the Chinese (and other Asian countries) to imposing very low tariffs (below 5 percent) on imported goods at the same time most Western markets remained far more protected.

Yet China was too big and populous to be conquered, and the imperial authorities and Chinese elites still provided enough extensive infrastructures to keep the Westerners confined within the coastal provinces. Western imperialists could neither colonize China nor effectively deploy their normal divide-and-rule tactics, finding enough dissident native elites who would assist them in overthrowing the rulers. China would remain independent.

The Chinese official who had led resistance against British opium urged the empire to resist better by adopting Western organization and technology. Such ideas spread and officials and intellectuals debated reforms, Western writings were translated, and there were some gestures at institutional reform. The court embraced a cautious "Self-Strengthening Movement" trying to adapt Western science and technology to existing Chinese institutions. County-level administration, however, was controlled by local gentry landowners who also served as the local officials, and most of them were not keen on change. The imperial state had fewer resources than Japan's state – taxes comprised only 5–10 percent of the harvest, compared with 30–40 percent in Japan (Esherick,

1995: 57) – and Chinese local officials took a larger informal cut. The different balance of central-local state relations was the crucial reason for Chinese weakness and Japanese strength. Yet as Western capitalism entered China, many landowners moved to the cities to take advantage of its opportunities, which weakened their control over the peasantry. Attempts to raise taxes or rents met with more local resistance (Bernhardt, 1992). Local militias defended the village against the government, and local banditry increased. Government and elites alike were losing some of their despotic power.

Dutch and Russian attempts to open up Japan had failed, but caused much debate in Japan over whether resistance should strengthen indigenous traditions or adapt Western ways (Hane, 1992: 58–64). The foreign threat was renewed in 1853, when four American warships anchored at Edo (Tokyo) Bay. Commodore Perry reported: "Steam was got up and the anchors were weighed that the ships might be moved to a position where their guns would command the place of reception." He noted with scorn that the Japanese sailing ships were becalmed, unable to move up the river mouth. He sent in a landing party and commented:

> The whole number of Americans, including sailors, marines, musicians, and officers, amounted to nearly three hundred … composed of very vigorous, able-bodied men, who contrasted strongly with the smaller and more effeminate-looking Japanese. These latter had mustered in great force [but].… The loose order of this Japanese army did not betoken any very great degree of discipline.… Their arms were swords, spears, and matchlocks … they presented at least a showy cavalcade (Hawks, 2005: 247–50).

The Americans were underestimating Japanese strength, but the Japanese were also overestimating the Americans. They did not know that Perry's "black ships" comprised one-quarter of the entire U.S. Navy, but they did know about China's unequal treaties, so they perceived an imminent threat requiring both reform and diplomacy. The last Tokugawa Shogun declared, "A country's very existence depends on the observance of treaties.… If we alone, at such a time, cling to outworn customs and refrain from international relations of a kind common to all countries, our action will be in conflict with the natural order of things" (Auslin, 2004: 142). Unequal treaties followed. Japan had to open its ports, ensure rights of extraterritoriality for foreign residents, grant most favored nation clauses, and accept fixed low tariffs on trade with the West. The imperial encounter had begun for both Asian powers.

The rising sun

At the time of Commodore Perry, Japan was ruled in the name of an emperor by a shogun, flanked by 250 feudal lords (*daimyo*), initially with strong local roots. As daimyo powers weakened in the late Tokugawa period, those of local communities strengthened, at the same time – unlike China –becoming more interconnected. This became "a decentralized yet hierarchically integrated" state and market system, with much capacity for collective organization (Ikegami, 1997: 133, 171, 235). In 1864, Japanese forces successfully withstood British gunboat diplomacy, inflicting some loss of life on the British (Auslin, 2004: chap. 4). With the humiliation of China in view, however, more Japanese were urging that survival required not only adapting Western power techniques but also changing Japanese institutions.

In an ensuing power struggle between conservatives and reformers, the conservatives could not agree among themselves on a coherent policy, so the reformers won out (Hane, 1992: chap. 4). Between 1866 and 1868, they deposed the shogun, put down rebellions, and inaugurated the reforms known as the Meiji Restoration. This formally restored rule from the shogun to Emperor Meiji and handed real power to an oligarchy of samurai from Satsuma and Choshu Provinces in alliance with lower-level nobles from the old court at Kyoto. They aimed at increasing Japan's economic and military power together to achieve what they called a "wealthy country, strong military" capable of matching the West. The oligarchs accordingly took the dramatic step of abolishing all feudal and class privileges and restrictions on participation in economic life. The daimyo domains were abolished, and 420,000 samurai had their annual stipends commuted into state salaries, pensions, and government bonds. This was a determinedly radical and nationalist program pushed by a coherent court elite.

It was not entirely a revolution from above. Although the new Meiji central state pressured local communities toward reforms, it could not compel them. So an alliance developed between the state on the one hand and local merchants, manufacturers, and richer peasants on the other, all favoring economic and political modernizations from which they might jointly benefit, ranging themselves against an old feudal order most personified by the mass of samurai. Reform was not plain sailing. The state's shift to fixed money taxes forced many small peasants to raise cash by selling land, so they became tenants or laborers. The state sometimes printed money to finance reform, leading to rampant inflation followed by constriction of the money supply. This intensified resistance, first from the samurai – who were crushed in 1877–1878 – and then from poorer peasants – who suffered in the depression of the 1880s. Peasant discontent remained, because like most industrializing states, this one subsidized industry by taxing agriculture. As Barrington Moore (1967) noted, this was an instance of "labor repressive" agriculture, although as severe as in communist industrialization projects. However, peasant resistance actually helped the reformers because frightened local leaders asked the state to bring its conscript army in to restore order, thus surrendering military power and political autonomy to the central state. The cohesion of state and local elites was ensured, and they retained despotic power.

Japanese statism was built on a centralized militarism with no parallel in China, but it had not come ready-made from a Japanese culture of obedience to hierarchy, nor had it been simply imposed by the Meiji oligarchs. It was achieved gradually, over a couple of decades, but only after intense conflict. The reforms were designed not only to modernize but also to protect local elites so that they could hold onto power whatever the dislocations modernization brought. The object was to devise a system to tap the energy of the Japanese people without letting them share power. The ideal was a state ruling in the name of the people, mobilizing nationalism, but without the people's participation ruling – a despotic nation-state.

The Meiji oligarchs could build on four strengths of the country. First, ecology produced much denser population concentrations, enabling more national mobilization than China. Second, late Togukawa Japan already had more commercial and cultural integration than China; the urban-rural gulf was not as great. Third, unlike Chinese political elites, the Meiji oligarchs managed to remain united and secured some control of the localities as well as the center; reform could be implemented. A fourth strength lay in Japan's geopolitical situation, which was more benign than China's. This allowed its elites to squabble and reform for three decades without serious foreign intervention. The white empires were at the limits of their logistical reach and at this period focused on elsewhere. The United States was distracted by its own Civil War and Reconstruction, and Britain and Russia were now more interested in China than Japan. This timely contingency meant that the Unequal Treaties imposed on Japan proved less disruptive to Japan's economy than those imposed on China. The Japanese believed this was only a breathing space before the Western powers struck again.

During this vital breathing space, lasting into the twentieth century, Japan sent diplomatic missions to the West. The most famous one, the Iwakura Mission of 1872–1873, had a dual purpose (Nish, 1998). The first was to revise the unequal treaties, but no country they visited was prepared to do this. The second was to find out about Western institutions, science, and technology and to suggest how Japan might adapt those that seemed useful. This was much more successful. Their main point of reference was now the West, not China or East Asia, as it had been in the past. There was little antiwhite racism, for they had too much to learn from the alien *gaijin*. They referred to the West as "civilization and enlightenment" and determined to force through a late development program adapted from the latest Western models.

The Meiji reforms covered all four sources of social power. In political power, they introduced a German-style state in the sense that a strong bureaucracy shared power with a parliament. To this they added the distinctive Japanese focal point of the divine emperor, the *tenno*, in whose person sovereignty rested. The Meiji Constitution, enduring until the middle of the twentieth century, began with the words, "The Empire of Japan shall be reigned over and governed by a line of Emperors unbroken for ages eternal." The constitution reserved military, police, public welfare, constitutional revision, and emergency powers for the Emperor, although in other spheres he had to get approval for his actions from the parliament or diet (the lower legislative house), although this could be retroactive. Ideologically, the emperor's legitimacy was buttressed by values of religiously sanctioned authority, loyalty, and family piety. The emperor system, the *tennosei*, rested on duties toward one's own father. The *kokutai*, the principles governing the national polity, embodied the notion of political harmony and loyalty to the nation and state, personified by the emperor, who was – literally – its father.

Yet the oligarchs were hardly likely to hand over their powers to an emperor who so far had only been a figurehead. In practice, the tennosei worked differently. The oligarchs disliked what they saw of republicanism and individualism in France and America, and they fashioned a state in which elites could continue to rule through collective institutions embodying patriarchy, duty, and loyalty. As in Germany, the executive and legislature both possessed power. The diet had mainly budgetary powers and (unlike Germany) often rejected the prime minister's budget. It was checked by an aristocratic upper house, the House of Peers. Yet the prime minister and his cabinet might not come from either house; they were appointed individually by the emperor, on the advice of his counselors. There was no cabinet responsibility, and each major political institution – parliament, bureaucracy, army, navy, prime minister, individual ministers – was separated from the others. They formally communicated with each other only through the emperor, who had, in principle, the power to make executive decisions, especially in matters of war and peace. Access to the emperor was thus crucial to the exercise of power, the way to get policy announced and implemented. Some senior cabinet members of high social status had personal access to the emperor, and so did the members of an influential Privy Council composed of oligarchs, most of whom were not ministers. So also did the highest military officers. Policy was made within these circles, but it was unclear who was actually responsible – except, finally, the emperor. Different elite factions could "capture" the person of the emperor and claim to speak in his name. Thus, a constitution of such ambiguity could be turned in different directions.

Bix (2001) notes that the tennosei system allowed the emperor to play a major role in either formulating policy or failing to correct those who claimed to be speaking in his name. The system worked mainly through the pervasive social network ties of the oligarchs, and through shared values and norms biased toward community, hierarchy, and duty rather than individualism, equality, and rights. As Woodiwiss (1992: chaps. 1, 2) notes, the new Meiji legal code did confer rights on individuals, but circumscribed most of them by the need for public order as defined by state agencies. This was probably the most conservative element of the constitution, limiting civil citizen rights. Capitalist freedom of property was not absolutely guaranteed, nor was workers' rights to organize. This was rule by the law more than the rule of law, and not only the judiciary administered the law but the police and military, too (Hane, 1992: 95–7, 128–30). All of this was distinctively Japanese, different from Western modernizers.

Yet this idealized despotism was never fully realized, and politics became riven by a contradiction between the conservative oligarchs and the technocratic and class forces set in motion by their rapid industrialization. The oligarchs could not control these forces, and indeed did not want to block them. They believed political parties were socially divisive and claimed rule was better by "transcendent cabinets" able to transcend party or factional interests. Starting about 1895, however, they were forced to strike deals with political parties forming in the diet, mainly representing middle-class groups. These secured a gradual broadening of the suffrage from only about 1 percent of the adult population in 1910. Universal male suffrage passed the Lower House in 1911, but was rejected by the House of Peers. In the 1920s, the diet parties began to get the upper hand, passing universal male suffrage in 1825, with the prime minister being a party leader for the first time. For a time, liberal parties gained at the expense of conservative ones at the same time labor organizing grew. As Japan industrialized, ownership of heavy industry and finance also became more concentrated, and the heads of its conglomerate corporations, the *zaibatsu*, acquired power, mostly exercised through informal political advisory roles and the financing of political parties. Their influence was shadowy but large, especially in domestic legislation. By the mid- to late 1920s, Japan seemed to be moving toward a blend of democracy and capitalism recognizably in the same family as Western regimes, although still containing distinctively Japanese characteristics.

However, Japan's civil citizenship remained more restricted, partly because the military wielded more autonomous power. The official justification was that this was necessary as the bulwark against foreign militarism. The constitution gave it "the right of autonomous command" so that the high command reported directly to the emperor, not to the prime minister or cabinet. Military officers do not always favor war, but they do seek to expand military budgets, status, and autonomy. Battles over budgets united officers divided on strategic issues. With their direct connection to the tennosei, Japanese officers believed that the armed forces embodied the spirit of the kokutai, which was essentially harmonious. Dissent must be repressed; thus, the army played a more autonomous and reactionary role within Japanese domestic politics than was the norm in Western countries, suppressing the left and opposing parliamentary institutions as divisive and corrupt.

Militarism was key but new, despite the fact that Japan had been feudal for centuries, replete with sword-wielding samurai. Yet it had been at peace, and the samurai had been tamed as "vassal-bureaucrats," their martial culture turned away from warfare into a ritualized "proceduralization of honor." They carried swords in the street but did not use them. During the turbulent

Restoration, the oligarchs found that mixed samurai-farmer militias fought better than purely samurai forces, hence the formation of a peasant conscript army officered by former samurai. It took time for peasants to learn the discipline and obedience for which Japanese forces later became famous. Samurai culture turned toward military service to the nation and emperor (Ikegami, 1997; A. Gordon, 2003: 66–7). Schumpeter's view of imperialism as generated by older, traditional social structures has even less relevance to Japan than other powers discussed so far. Its militaristic imperialism was brand-new, generated by Japan's precarious geopolitical position, and the internal organization of its armed forces was consciously modeled on the West, especially on the French army and the British navy.

The Meiji reformers also had considerable economic success. They could build on late Tokugawa developments because by the mid-nineteenth century, commercial markets of a capitalist type were more evenly developed than across China, and they had broadly diffused proto-industrial production. Thomas Smith (1988: 43–4) says that most Japanese farm families had over a generation's experience of working part-time in nonagricultural occupations. Handicrafts and artisan skills were widespread, especially in textiles. Sugihara (2000, 2004) suggests that the proto-industrialization embedded in Japan's household agriculture developed a labor-intensive form of industrial development, first in textiles then in other industries – quite different, he says, from the capital-intensive development of the West. Whereas land and capital were scarce, labor was cheap and skilled. Female labor was heavily exploited, and literacy was high for an agrarian society – about 40 percent male and 10 percent female literacy, well above Chinese levels (Ikegami, 2004: 214–6, 300–2). This was a low-wage, high-productive economy – unusual for a developing country. Ikegami says the Tokugawa period saw a "network revolution," a combination of a somewhat decentralized polity, a commercializing economy, a diffusing artistic performance culture, and spreading commercial publishing networks. This produced a "civil society," in which the upper and middling layers of Tokugawa society shared a "proto-modern" sense of culture, comprising "tacit modes of communication and a Japanese national identity," riven by status differences but generating social solidarity through rituals of status interaction. This, she says, provided the ideological underpinnings of Japan's modernization (2004: 10, 221).

The state then assisted investment-led growth by abolishing feudal and class privileges, and the new land tax of 1873 gave it a predictable annual revenue enabling public investment. Merchant capitalism was already dynamic, but now Japan acquired Western industrial capitalism, science, and technology (Lockwood, 1954: 35). There was, nonetheless, suspicion of foreign investment, believed to be the way Britain and France had begun to capture colonies (A. Gordon, 2003: 71). A very large 30–40 percent of overall capital formation came from the state itself, building infrastructures and model factories and quietly subsidizing infant industries, as the unequal treaties prohibited protection through high tariffs. The remaining investment came from rural agricultural elites and merchants moving into coal and textile production, deploying steam and then electric power acquired from the West. The Japanese learned fast: British firms built the first railway line in the country in 1874; eight years later, Japanese engineers built a line of similar length over more difficult terrain, without foreign help (T. Smith, 1988: 45).

More rapid industrialization began after about 1885, and until 1913 GNP rose by somewhere between 2.6 percent and 3.6 percent per year, higher than had occurred in the West (Crawcour, 1998: 391). Government-subsidized economies of scale then generated the famous zaibatsu conglomerate firms, at first financial cliques, then after 1900 adding industrial conglomerates. Heavy industry was subsidized and capital and technical assistance was offered to export industries. Wars in 1894 and 1904 led to further state subsidies to war-related industries. Government expenditures on goods and service rose to 10 percent of GNP in the 1880s, higher than in Western countries. The crucial role of government intervention, says Crawcour (1997a: 446), was that government could induce the coordinated start up of, say, an ironworks, a coal mine, and a rail line – interdependent activities which, if all were built together, could make each one profitable. The market alone could not do this, because private investors would be unwilling to finance any one of these activities on its own. As Japan was a late developer, it could look abroad (and to people such as those British railroad engineers working in Japan) for the requisite models of how to industrialize, then the state could nudge private capitalists toward implementing them. As remained the case in East Asia throughout the twentieth century, this was a state-coordinated more than a state-planned industrial economy. Beginning now and continuing right through the century, Japan was very successful in promoting economic development.

Development was also capitalist, and state direction seen as a temporary aid. Once industrialization got going, the government would supposedly retreat from economic life, although it never quite did. Light industries were entirely private. Japan had been shifted by the Great Powers to near-free trade by 1868, and because the markets of China and the British Empire were open (and Britain welcomed Japanese development as a counterweight to Russia), Japan exported across Asia, especially textiles. Japan was unusual in that its heavy industries (initially importing its machinery from the West) produced for domestic consumption; its balance of payments were maintained by light-industry exports, produced by a low-paid but productive female labor force that could outcompete Western manufactures. The size of Asian markets enabled Japanese exports to become huge and generate the capital to purchase Western technology. That, says Sugihara, was the key to the distinctive East Asian labor-intensive form of industrialization.

World War I (whose causes had nothing to do with Japan) then generated an economic boom for the country. Japan entered the war on the Entente side, but was only militarily active (and successful) during its first weeks. It soon found it could satisfy world demand for nonmilitary goods that combatant powers were no longer supplying themselves. The war years saw growth of almost 9 percent per annum, and Japan paid off most of its foreign debts. Up to now, agriculture had probably shared in the upswings, although it was overtaxed. Postwar difficulties followed boom, however, and growth was sluggish during the 1920s. Agriculture did worst because of global overproduction and cheap imports from Japan's first colonies. There were major rice riots in 1918, followed by the devastating Kobe earthquake of 1923. There was recovery until the Great Depression in 1930 and 1931, although Japan recovered quickly. Overall, these were good decades. Between 1913 and 1938, Japan's average annual growth rate was 3.9 percent, much higher than any other country – only Norway reached even 3 percent. The birth rate increased steadily until about 1923, but increased life expectancy ensured that population growth continued thereafter (Mosk, 2001; Minami, 1994; Pratt, 1999; Tsutsui, 1998; Crawcour, 1997a, 1997b; T. Nakamura, 1998: table 2; Maddison 2007: table 4). Although not as developed as the Western powers, Japan had substantially industrialized, and every year saw it further outstrip China.

A national system of compulsory elementary education and an expanding secondary and tertiary education developed alongside expansion of private commercial publishing of newspapers, pamphlets, and books. However, Japanese ideological solidarity was hindered by its written script, kanji, which was far too complex to be used as a universal script. This was a principal issue of debate among the reformers: liberals wanted major simplifications; more conservative reformers resisted. Proposals to shift from kanji to the simpler systems of kana or romaji failed, but kanji itself was simplified. Now children learned to write in the colloquial form of the language instead of the range of historical and classical styles used previously. This was probably a cultural barrier to the masses coming onstage in the theater of power. Nonetheless, by the first decade of the twentieth century, Japan was publishing more titles than any other country except Germany, and twice that of the Americans (Gluck, 1985:12). Both public and private media propagated the notions of the tennosei and kokutai, blending the new with the traditional: emperor worship, nationalism, the centrality of the armed forces and the empire, harnessed to the old virtues of the agrarian village community, the family, and the spirit of Bushido and Shinto Confucianism. Nationalism was inculcated through schools, the armed forces, military drilling in schools, the Imperial Military Reserve Association, and many propaganda campaigns. A cynic remarked that the Japanese had to "eat for the nation, wash our faces for the nation, go to the toilet for the nation" (A. Gordon, 2003: 137). The close connection between education and the military would push Japanese nationalism more easily toward aggression.

The extent to which Japanese of different classes and regions internalized the official values is difficult to assess. It varied, of course, by how much people thought they were benefitting from this social order. Although there was economic growth unparalleled anywhere in the world, there were also the normal capitalist cycles exacerbated by an increasingly global economy, in this period especially caused by agricultural overproduction. Massive migration from the countryside caused dislocation, and so did wars. So to debates about state-building and nation-building were added the "social problems of modernity" (Gluck, 1985: 27–8). Liberalism, socialism, and feminism appeared, although there was a more social, less individualistic sense of morality than in the West and less glorification of the acquisition of wealth. Morality, nonetheless, contained a tension between egalitarian common values like equal citizenship and opportunity versus hierarchy, filial obedience, obedience to rank, bureaucratic, and military expertise, and loyalty to the emperor (Gluck, 1985: chap. VIII). Alternative paths of development remained.

The emergence of japanese imperialism

By 1900, Japan was emulating Western imperialism. Many view Japanese imperialism as derived from a highly militarized economy and state, but this had not been true initially. When it came, it owed much to contingent factors: Japan's lack of domestic raw materials for industrialization, its relatively restricted domestic market, and its high population density (all the opposite of the United States) pressured toward some form of expansion abroad. As Japan industrialized, it had to import an increasing proportion of its resources – far more than the other powers – and it had to pay for them by increasing exports. When the Japanese economy began to grow and its population transition began, population overcrowding also seemed imminent. So Japan's modernizers agreed that the country must secure more access to raw materials and export markets, and send more settlers abroad. This made imperialism more likely.

What form would imperialism take? Japanese elites expected to expand outward, much as Western nations had, deploying a range of policies from trade treaties opening up foreign markets to the acquisition of colonies. Up until the 1890s, the dominant Japanese policy was informal imperialism – opening up markets, if necessary by intimidation, to give Japan the same unequal rights that the Western powers already enjoyed in the region. However, the Western powers were reluctant to lift the unequal treaties they had imposed on Japan let alone allow Japan equal access to Chinese markets. Britain, France, and the Netherlands already had substantial colonies in Asia. The French were colonizing Vietnam, and Russia was moving into North China and Korea, building railroads connected to its own Far Eastern territories. The United States, France, Germany, and Britain were moving beyond the Chinese treaty ports into territorial spheres of influence in the interior, building railroads, mines, and factories and leasing large tracts of land complete with extraterritorial judicial and police rights. They were seeking control over markets through informal imperialism backed by military intervention. Many Asians believed this was a step toward an eventual partitioning of coastal China into colonies or protectorates.

In this world, commented one Japanese statesman, "the strong ate the meat of the weak." In weakening China, the Japanese resident minister remarked, "When there is a fire in the jeweller's shop, the neighbours cannot be expected to refrain from helping themselves" (Tarling, 2001: 25). If a resource-poor country like Japan got shut out from such opportunities, it might then be forced into similar submission. Thus, it made no sense for Japan to pursue merely an open market policy, especially when it labored under unequal treaties. Some form of expansive imperialism was the obvious model of development for Japan – just like its rivals. Japan was not joining just the industrial age but the age of imperialism, as well.

Imperial expansion was possible and perhaps not too costly, for in Northeast Asia, China's tributary states could be picked off. Two targets were especially tempting: Korea was a weak state; Taiwan was almost stateless. Both were tributaries of China, which now had only a wavering influence on Korea and almost none on Taiwan. Japan was in the opposite geopolitical situation to the United States, threatened by foreign imperialism. It steered toward its own imperialism to avoid the visible fate of a weakening China, and expansion was the best form of defense. Thus, Japanese imperialism is easier to understand (and perhaps forgive) than American expansion of this period. Nor were Westerners surprised by Japanese imperialism; they recognized it as their own practice. Only its success astonished them.

Military expenditures grew from 15 percent of government outlays in the late 1880s to an average of 34 percent between 1891 and 1900, and to 48 percent between 1901 and 1910 (Crawcour, 1997a: 445). The policies of the Meiji oligarchs, reinforced by urbanization, industrialization, emperor worship, a national army, and a national education system, had generate a popular kokutai nationalism the oligarchs saw as a useful internal weapon against domestic conflicts. This tempted them toward *social imperialism*, mobilizing the masses from above, deflecting domestic tensions through a quest for collective survival and expansion against foreign threats.

In Korea and Taiwan, security concerns were initially primary. These territories were seen as key to the building of a defensive perimeter surrounding the home islands. There were also minerals in Korea, but both Korea and Taiwan sent mainly agricultural produce to Japan in exchange for settlers and manufactured products from Japan. The two gradually became dependent economies. In the interwar period, 70–90 percent of their trade was with Japan, and by 1935 the colonies took nearly a quarter of Japan's exports when the minerals of Manchuria and the markets of China were added. Whether any of these territories ever justified the outlays that went on acquiring them is another matter, as their contribution to the Japanese economy was never enormous (Lockwood, 1954: 52). That was a more general problem of empires at this time, for few were making a net profit. It was not simply an instrumentally rational drive for economic profit that drove imperialism forward. The emotional desire for glory, security-laden fear of rivals, local weakness, and opportunity egged on by particular interest groups – some of them economically motivated, others seeing it as a domestic power-enhancing strategy – plus the lure of plausible future profits tempted them onward, one step at a time – as they did Japan.

Beginning in 1876, Japan could impose unequal treaties on Korea. In 1894, the failure to cope with a domestic rebellion in Korea exposed the weakness of the monarchy. When China sent in a small army to restore order, the Japanese government used this as a pretext for war. Japan comprehensively won the short war because of better-trained officers that acted as a cohesive force, unlike the squabbling Chinese forces – a reflection of the broader differences among elites in the two Asian powers. Japan was careful to show restraint elsewhere so as not to alienate Westerners. In any case, Britain was friendly, because it wanted Japan to balance against the more feared Russia. Britain was the first to repeal the unequal treaties with Japan in 1894, and the other powers followed by 1899. As a result of the war, Japan acquired a freer hand in Korea without colonizing it. Japan also received a financial indemnity from China, became a party to its unequal treaties, and annexed the nominally Chinese island of Taiwan, apparently with little forethought, simply because it had become available at very little cost.

These were the fruits of a successful short war. Japan was now moving from fear of the imperialism of others to recognition of its own imperial opportunities. By now, "Japanese decision makers suffered less from paranoia than euphoria" (Dickinson, 1999: 256). The United States delightedly seized comparable opportunities elsewhere in the world three years later. War was also a part of the international economy: Japan was paying for its wars by borrowing on the London market, and that is where it invested its Chinese indemnity. Imperialism was a legitimate form of international investment, and British financiers were investing in Japanese imperialism (Metzler, 2006: chap. 2). Globalization was continuing its complex rise, with increasingly caged nation-states pursuing fractured imperialism amid a broader economy that had distinctly transnational tendencies. That Japan was becoming a normal, predatory power was bad news for China.

Enfeebled dragon

For the Chinese dragon, the defeat of 1895 was devastating. Chinese pretensions to superiority in Asia were revealed as hollow. The Japanese had taken away two tributary territories with little difficulty. There was a sense of crisis at the Qing court; self-strengthening reforms had failed to deal with rising pressures. Chinese institutions needed changing, said the anti-court and anti-Manchu (the Qing dynasty was originally from Manchuria) constitutionalist movement. This centered on students and intellectuals, especially those educated abroad, plus reform-minded officials and military officers. However, their nationalism had little resonance among the landlord-official class dominating the provinces. Political divisions within Chinese elites widened, especially in the aftermath of the failed Boxer uprising against the foreign imperialists in 1904. The court promised a constitution but failed to deliver.

The result was the 1911 Revolution, a political not social revolution (Skocpol, 1979), confined to overthrowing the emperor and his court. Peasants – the majority of the population – were not involved. This was a gentry and urban middle-class movement with ideals based on Sun Yat-sen's famous "Three Principles of the People" – nationalism, democracy, and people's livelihood. "Nationalism" meant overthrowing the "foreign" Qing dynasty and expelling the foreign imperialists. "Democracy" meant introducing an elected republican form of government, although with a property franchise and without parliamentary sovereignty, for Sun believed modernization required an authoritarian center. "People's livelihood" involved some land reform under the slogan of "land to the tiller," and some state capitalism. Sun later developed a rather Leninist-model political party to achieve these goals, with a small vanguard of professional revolutionaries supported by a larger number of dues-paying members, organized in cells, obeying the party leader. The Soviet Comintern was impressed, and instructed the tiny Chinese Communist Party (CCP) to assist Sun (Dreyer, 1995: 120–1). Sun's party had little social base, however, because China lacked much of a bourgeoisie – or indeed a working class – and the majority of peasants showed little interest. Without a mass base, the new Republic of China was an attempt at reform by elites influenced by diverse liberal, socialist, and nationalist currents of thought operating in a rather disorderly environment. They faced an uphill struggle.

In 1912, the last emperor – the boy Pu yi – was forced to abdicate. Sun had to yield the presidency of the new republic to Yuan Shikai, a reforming warlord and commander in chief of the army. There were violent disputes among the various military and political factions of the new regime, one of which was the newly formed Kuomintang Party, the KMT (GMD in some transliterations from the Chinese). The incompleteness of the revolution had further weakened the authority of the state over the provinces. Landlord-official elites were holding power locally, and many were hostile to the new government. The stronger ones controlled their own region as warlords. As Skocpol (1979: 238–42) emphasizes, this was different from the prerevolutionary situation of France and Russia. In China, the landlord class had kept most of its local power, but was being cut adrift from the central state. It might keep down its own local peasants, but if peasant *jacqueries* did start, it would not be easy to call on the central state for help. China was fragmenting because of a lack of solidarity between the state and its natural agents of support in the provinces. This was the decisive difference from Japan. There was no equivalent of the Meiji Restoration, no union of reforming Chinese oligarchs.

As the new republic struggled to impose itself over the regional warlords, Japan took advantage of World War I to join the Entente side and seize German possessions in China. It then increased pressure on China, seeking to make President Yuan Shikai a Japanese client. He resisted the pressure, and in 1915 boldly declared himself the new emperor of China. This appalled his republican allies, and he was forced to abdicate the next year. By 1917, China had half-disintegrated into shifting alliances of regional warlords, none able to control more than a slice of the country. In an "age of the warlords" lasting from 1917 to 1927, peasant self-defense movements like the Red Spears expanded to defend their local communities against the Japanese, bandits, warlords, communists, or the republic itself (Perry, 1984: 439–41).

In the more advanced coastal cities, where some industry and commerce had appeared, constitutional aspirations lived on. In 1919, student demonstrations against the Beijing warlord government and Japanese interference erupted, sparking off a so-called Awakening among the urban classes. The momentum of this nationalist May Fourth Movement enabled Sun Yat-sen to establish a KMT formally Nationalist government in Nanking in alliance with the communist party. After Sun's death in 1925, General Chiang Kai-shek took over the KMT leadership. He faced warlords and fascists on his right and communists and KMT radicals on his left. By 1931, however, he had reconstituted a republican government in Nanking with control over much of Eastern and central China. He had contained the KMT left wing, massacred the communists, and secured the submission of many warlords, but this brought radicals and warlords inside his regime, reducing its cohesion. In Jiangsu province, for example, the left-KMT continued to control local party institutions, conducting anti-Japanese boycotts, attacking merchants as tools of imperialism, and destroying temples in anti-superstition campaigns. Factional clashes continued well into the 1930s, sometimes erupting into armed conflict (Geisert, 2001). Before 1937, Chiang's KMT regime made some progress (discussed later), but politically and militarily, the Chinese dragon remained enfeebled, no longer a predator but more a tempting prey.

China was tempting because its coastal economy was showing signs of life. The economy remained largely agrarian, commercialized long ago but without much recent development. It was dominated by small landowner peasants, about half of whom owned their own plots and half of whom rented. Its backwardness means we have few reliable aggregate data and overall estimates differ widely. Rawski's (1989) statistics suggest a healthy per capita economic growth of just more than 1 percent per year in the years between 1914 and 1937 – not growth at Japanese levels but better than British India. Brandt (1989) also sees commercialization leading to growth in agricultural production and real wages. Perkins (1975) saw some aggregate GNP growth in the period, although wiped out by population growth. Philip Huang (1985, 1990), discussing impoverished areas in North China and the richer delta region around Shanghai, detects only *involutionary growth*: peasant households had to work harder in order to stay exactly where they were. Although these disputes have not been settled, there was probably some economic growth during this period (Ma, 2006: 10; Richardson, 1999: 81–2), even though most Chinese were living at around subsistence level. There were marked regional differences and not much national economic integration, but the Great Depression did not hit China badly; it was protected by its backwardness, lack of national integration, and low volume of foreign trade. It was also on a silver not gold standard. Industry probably grew right through the Depression. Military disruptions, not economic, were the biggest problem of the period (Wright, 1991, 2000; Chang, 1969: 60–1; Myers, 1989).

Two regions definitely saw growth and modernization: Manchuria and parts of North China had extractive and heavy industries; a booming commercial-manufacturing sector grew around the treaty ports, especially Shanghai. The Shanghai region contributed about 7 percent of China's GDP (Ma, 2006: 9; Perkins, 1975: 119). These areas saw improved transport infrastructures, significant foreign and later Chinese investment, and more secure property rights. Manufacturing industry grew at around 10 percent per year between 1912 and 1936 (Chang, 1969: 71). The treaty-ports system now provided substantial economic spin-offs. In world systems analysis, China is seen to have experienced dependent development, as a peripheral economy dependent on the Western capitalist core. Yet Chinese commercialization was centuries old and largely independent of the West, and Manchuria and the treaty ports were becoming less dependent (Bergère, 1989: 4; Ma, 2006; Brandt 1989).

However, the division between Manchuria and the treaty ports versus the rural bulk became ever clearer in subsequent political and military developments. The China seen by foreigners was the coast and Manchuria, both with tempting pickings. Given the normal ideology of imperialism, foreigners believed they could substantially develop the country and enjoy profit for themselves. They saw potential Chinese markets as enormous. China's tragedy was that its areas of economic modernization, from which any national strength might be derived, were also its areas of greatest strategic vulnerability. Although the British and Americans were now turning away from colonies – seeking more informal methods of expansion in China – the Japanese were having good experiences with colonies – and, along with the Russians, they were nearby.

Japan: Colonial sunshine

Japanese imperialism was superior to other imperialism in one important respect: economic growth. In Taiwan, forty-plus years of direct Japanese colonial rule brought annual average GDP growth between 1913 and 1941 somewhere between 4 percent and 4.5 percent. This laid the groundwork for Taiwan's post-1950 economic miracle (Kim & Park, 2005; Maddison, 2007: table 4). The height of Taiwanese men increased up to about 1930, after which it leveled off until after World War II. This is a sign that health had improved (Olds, 2003; Morgan and Liu, 2007). Korea was bigger, with an existing state and a more cohesive culture. The Japanese at first sought to rule Korea indirectly, through the Korean monarchy and elites. Yet they could not find a reliable Korean client regime, and conflict with Russia over the Korean peninsula was growing. In 1898, the other powers had forced Japan to cede the Kwantung Peninsula in Manchuria (taken from China in 1895) to Russia. Japan and Russia now had competing railroad-building projects in these areas. Britain remained more concerned about Russia, and signed a naval treaty with Japan in 1902. Because the United States and France took their lead in the area from Britain, Japan would not face interference from the Western powers. Japan was now the strongest foreign power in Korea, but remained frustrated by Russian meddling in a country it viewed as "the keystone of national defense" (Duus, 1995: 175–84).

The military was initially reluctant to confront Russia, yet reasoned that Russia would be stretched logistically by a major war on the Pacific until it finished building all its projected railroads and ports. At that point, the balance of power might shift toward Russia, so Japan decided to strike Russian forces pre-emptively in 1905 – quite similar to Germany's pre-emptive strike on Russia in 1914. No one else intervened, and the London *Times* approved of the surprise attack (Lone, 2000: 100–5). The West did not expect a decisive result, but to general surprise, the Japanese triumphed. The main Russian fleet sailed thousands of miles from the Black Sea to arrive in the Sea of Japan. There, in the battle of Tsushima, it sailed too close to Japanese coastal batteries and fatally underestimated Japanese naval skills, suffering "an annihilation with scarcely a parallel in the history of modern sea-warfare" (Dickinson, 1999: 256; Evans & Peattie, 1997: 124). The Russian army did better in Siberia and Manchuria, where both armies took heavy losses, although superior Japanese organization gradually prevailed. Several common stereotypes of the Japanese were false during this period. Although the mass media in Japan propagandized aggressive, glorious nationalism, their news reels depicting the suffering of the soldiers appalled many Japanese. Analysis of soldiers' diaries shows that Japanese soldiers were not, at this stage, fighting fanatically for nation and emperor. They feared death and were thinking of their villages and loved ones. They also treated enemy prisoners well. Army service did make many soldiers realize for the first time that they were Japanese, as opposed to Russian, Chinese, or Korean (Shimazu, 2009). They internalized banal nationalism, and enemy nations were shooting at them, but there was not yet much aggressive nationalism.

Russia, beset by the 1905 Revolution at home, needed its army for domestic purposes. It wanted the war ended quickly, so made major concessions. The Treaty of Portsmouth (New Hampshire) gave Japan unchallenged indirect rule in Korea and on the Kwantung Peninsula in Manchuria. The rest of Chinese Manchuria was in practice controlled by the Japanese military and local warlords. It was the first war victory for centuries inflicted by non-Europeans over a major European power. Not only Japan celebrated, but many of the oppressed peoples of the world, as well.

So far, Japanese expansion resembled Western expansion, although by virtue of being forcibly opened up and then facing a lack of natural resources Japan was pushed faster into imperialism. Although the war with Russia had been pre-emptive, so had Prussia's nineteenth-century wars and the U.S. wars of 1898. Japanese elites saw the war with Russia as Japan's first great mission. By the death of Emperor Meiji in 1912, the government said Japan was receiving respect from "countries that turn toward Japan as the sunflower toward the sun" (Gluck, 1985: 90, 216–7).

The next imperial escalation occurred in 1910, when Japan increased its troop strength in Korea and quietly annexed it. This step was unprovoked, for with Russia defeated and still recovering from revolutionary turmoil, there was no threat to Japan. All Japanese political factions believed in expansion in Korea. Moderates hoped to do this by helping Korean reformers achieve public order and sound finances, but the Korean reformers – harassed domestically by both monarchists and anti-Japanese nationalists – failed to make much headway. The Japanese felt themselves sucked into more direct rule in order to establish order, although their presence guaranteed disorder. One destabilizing factor was the presence by 1910 of 170,000 Japanese settlers demanding more security, supported by hard-line nationalists and conservative oligarchs back home. Although Japan was going through an industrial revolution, it was to take the best part of a century (just as for the British) for this new wealth to filter down to ordinary Japanese people, especially if they were peasant farmers. For them, the lure of settler colonies was strong. Social imperialism whipping up aggressive nationalism had a social base. The Western powers protested the Japanese annexation, but Japan responded that it had resulted from the inadequacies of informal imperialism. Although annexation was supposed to decrease Japanese insecurities, it increased them by elevating anti-Japanese sentiments among its rivals. The armed forces now demanded and got higher military budgets for imperial defense. Thus was Japanese militarism racheting up, although still without any master plan (Duus, 1995; Lone, 2000: chaps. 8–10).

Japanese elites devised the usual imperial Mission statement, claiming Koreans were incapable of modernizing themselves, were "uncivilized" and "backward," living in "filth, squalor and indolence," their politics dominated by "passivity, corruption and toadyism." This should sound familiar from my chapters on the British Empire and American empire. Yet there was enough shared ethnic heritage and cultural affinity between the two Asian countries to make the "uplift" of Koreans seem possible. The Japanese attempted cultural assimilation: if Koreans and others could be induced or forced to speak Japanese and use Japanese cultural concepts (for example in choosing their names), they could become more or less Japanese. Above all, the widespread assertion that Koreans, Taiwanese, and others were "neighbors" – perhaps from the same original ancestry – meant that Japanese colonialism was not actually as racist as European and American colonialism of the time (Duus, 1995: 203, 399–423; Eiji, 2002).

However, the Japanese did not treat natives benignly. As Korea was in the neighborhood, Japan could move in a large army, its raw materials and consumer markets could be integrated with Japan, and there were many willing Japanese settlers. The protectorate ruthlessly repressed Korean resistance, and settlers were given conqueror's privileges, purchasing farms at knock-down prices and dominating the profitable government and business sectors. Duus (1995: 431) says the key Japanese colonial actors "were not powerful metropolitan business interests but restless, ambitious, frugal elements from the middle and lower strata of Japanese society." Trade with Korea was not enormous, yet the Japanese handling it made big profits (Duus, 1995: 284–8). Thus, settler and business interests encouraged a form of social imperialism in Japan that was more populist than the big business-dominated social imperialism envisaged by Hilferding.

Japan did succeed in modernizing Korea. Apart from its tiny Micronesian possessions, the Japanese Empire was much more compact and closer to the mother country than the colonial possessions of other empires, and the population of Japan itself was uniquely (alongside the United States) greater than that of all its colonies combined. There was no fear of competition or of being swamped, and no desire to exclude the colonial peoples from the economic benefits of empire. Agrarian and industrial technology transferred freely to the colonies. In Taiwan, development was led by the colonial government much more than by private enterprise (Peattie, 1988: 254–5). Railroads and roads integrated the peninsula, built for military purposes but providing economic spin-offs. By 1945, little Korea had half as many miles of modern roads as the whole of China. The education system expanded many times over. The decay of the country's ancient irrigation systems was reversed, and fertiliser factories were built. Japanese investment rose first in agriculture, then in industry. Manufacturing rose from 6 percent of GDP in 1911 to an astonishing 28 percent in 1940 – far outstripping China or India or anywhere else in Asia apart from Japan itself. During the first two decades of the protectorate, Korea was seen as a rice basket for Japan, but after about 1933, its industries were an advanced supply base in a military-industrial complex stretching from Japan to Manchuria. Annual GDP growth rate between 1911 and 1939 was around 4 percent, the same as Taiwan and Japan itself. Korea was the only colony of any empire to undergo much industrialization (Kim & Park, 2005, 2008; Eckert, 1996; Chou, 1996; Cha, 2000; Ho, 1984; Maddison, 2007: table 4). As in Taiwan, the Japanese laid the basis for the post-World War II economic miracle. Average Korean life expectancy also rose, from 26 to 42 years over the life of the colony, demonstrating that economic growth translated into a better material life for most Koreans. This first wave of Japanese imperialism did not contribute to the global Great Divergence, and it served to integrate rather than fracture parts of East Asia.

These achievements, however, were matched by a dark side. Business was largely taken over by the Japanese, forced labor was widespread, repression of resistance was savage, and there were forcible attempts to suppress the Korean language, family names, and culture. Adopting Japanese family names meant rejecting the whole patrilineal tenor of Korean family culture in favor of the Japanese *ie*, which is more like a household (Chou, 1996, Eiji, 2002: 334–5). Japanese colonies also ended up suffering terribly in the later stages of the Pacific War, during which many thousand Korean women suffered the mass rapes of the "comfort women" system.

For these colonies, any answer to the question, "Did the Japanese Empire do anyone any good?" must differ from the one given for the British Empire. For the British, in Chapter 2, I attempted to balance marginal benefits against marginal costs. Japanese costs and benefits were both much bigger, making overall judgment difficult. It depends on how one evaluates economic well-being against brutal repression; most Koreans believe that the latter outweighs the former. They remember only the harm the Japanese did them, although the Taiwanese are more generous toward their former conquerors. Korean scholars have also recently acknowledged the long-term economic benefits of Japanese rule (Shin et al., 2006). Yet the many thousand Japanese settlers who got the wealth and upward mobility denied to them in the more closed society of Japan did best. This was important in building popular support for an empire of the rising sun.

The Japanese debate over imperialism

Imperialism was a firmly entrenched political crystallization. Few Japanese doubted its utility, and the disputes concerned what kind of imperialism it should be (A. Gordon, 2003: 74, 122–3). Direct territorial imperialism was the eventual path chosen, but this was not preordained. After the 1905 war with Russia, there was no serious threat to national security. The imperial powers all had their spheres of influence: Russia in Northern Manchuria; Japan in parts of Southern Manchuria, Korea, and Taiwan; the United States in the Philippines; France in Indochina; Britain in the Yangtze Valley, South China, and South Asia; Germany in the Shantung Peninsula and scattered Pacific Islands. Together, they participated in China's international concessions. Might this be an acceptable balance of power? Could Japan now settle for what it had, plus a gradual expansion of informal imperialism and increasing participation in international markets?

Asia was being filled up by empires, and the threat of war would become greater if the other powers viewed Japan less as balancing against Russia than as potentially dominating the region. After 1905, the Japanese military and civilian establishment initially doubted the wisdom of using force to further the Japanese sphere of influence in Northeast China. A less risky alternative would be to guarantee the neutrality of the region through international agreements giving market access to all foreigners. This would avoid Russia seeking revenge once it did revive, and it would lessen military expenditures, too. However, World War I and the Bolshevik Revolution upset this balance of power. Germany was put out of the picture by its defeat, the Russians were again weakened, and France and Britain needed time to recover. There seemed a window of expansion for Japan. It had made easy gains in the first year of the war, acquiring the German colonies of Shantung and Tsingtao plus Micronesian islands. Shantung was a possible jumping-off place for expansion in either Manchuria or North China. Japan had followed up these acquisitions in 1915 by making "Twenty One Demands" on China, which included recognition of Japanese rights in Shantung and railway building in China. To both Chinese nationalists and other powers these demands seemed to presage further Japanese expansion.

By the 1920s, Japan had colonial empire in Taiwan and Korea; informal empire in further parts of Manchuria and China; and substantially free trade with the rest of Asia, the British Empire, and the United States. There was consensus that Japan must defend its "line of sovereignty," Japan plus its colonies, at the same time protecting a broader "line of interest." Because Japanese international trade was still expanding, the positioning of this line of interest was unclear. Expansion might be by extending international markets; extending informal imperialism through spheres of influence in Manchuria, parts of North China, and Fukien (the Chinese province opposite Taiwan); or extending the line of sovereignty, acquiring more colonies.

Japanese historians distinguish liberals from nationalists or militarists in debates over foreign policy. None of the main factions were liberal in the Western sense of favoring only open markets, but neither was the West itself. In a world of empires, most Japanese liberals did not want to alienate the other powers, but they might radicalize if they thought militarism could work at low cost. These debates pitted those favoring informal empire against those favoring colonies or protectorates. Debates over Korea and Manchuria revealed this – whether to expand by armed force or by negotiating further concessions from the Chinese and Manchurians, and whether to stop for at the Great Wall for now or go beyond it. The foreign service tended to favor the first set of options and the army the second (Duus, 1995; Matsusaka 2001; Brooks, 2000).

The 1920s seemed to favor the liberals. World War I saw the triumph of the liberal powers, the creation of the League of Nations, and the Washington Naval Treaties of 1922 (Dickinson, 1999: 151, 242–56). The treaties limited the size of navies, including Japan's, but ended British dominance in Asia and permitted Japan the possibility of playing off the United States against Britain. The United States was now Japan's largest trading partner and supplier of foreign capital, and most politicians favored a cautious policy of market expansion plus informal empire in China, not more colonies. Shidehara Kijuro, the dominant foreign minister of the 1920s, favored expansion but preferably in cooperation with other powers. Any expansion would be at the expense of China, but many Japanese held out hopes of Chinese consent for an Asian revival led by Japan. They believed the Chinese might welcome Japanese tutelage. Yet growing Chinese nationalism made this delusory. Japan was expanding too late in world-historical time. This was still the age of empires, but the more civilized parts of the empires were being increasingly confronted by nationalism – as the British were finding in India and the Japanese were about to in China.

The KMT government sought to abrogate China's unequal treaties. Shidehara, supported by Japanese consular officials in China and most big business, was prepared to bend to British and American pressure to renegotiate the treaties, provided China pay its debts to Japan. Other Japanese politicians, supported by Japanese business interests in China, resisted, and conservatives feared a republican virus might spread from China to Japan. Fear of leftism united most elites (Hata, 1988: 282–6), but militarism was not very popular. Once wars ended, politicians sought to reduce the military budget with popular support, because this meant lower taxes. As military budgets were reduced momentum swung toward the moderates, and the more Japan industrialized, the more dependent it became on international markets. Most economists counseled conformity to the rules of the international economy. As the markets Japan most depended on were those of the British Empire and the United States, it would not be a good idea to alienate these two powers.

As the economic debate tilted, it brought adherence to liberal economic doctrines: classical economics, open markets, the gold standard, deflationary policies, and an accompanying moral rhetoric of thrift. Japan was not on the gold standard in the 1920s, and liberals urged its reinstatement. This was opposed on both the left and right by those favoring a more statist and nationalist path of development. Conservatives wanted to preserve their own power within the Meiji Constitution through the bureaucracy and the House of Peers. Empire, arms, and authoritarianism were seen by conservatives as the core of the Japanese kokutai, and liberal admirers of Anglo-Saxon civilization favored parliamentary politics at home and informal empire abroad. So-called Germans, favoring the former route, were drawn more from oligarchs; the army officer corps and state bureaucrats, "Anglo-Saxons," were more influential among the political parties and the civilian middle class.

The middling levels of the officer corps were the most extreme, and they were beginning to show some independence from the high command. They were imbued with self-confidence born from recent military achievements. They saw Japan leading a glorious pan-Asian resistance to the West (a two-level nationalism) through either "total war" or "the Imperial Way." The Imperial Way became important later, and is discussed in Chapter 13. The total-war faction was led by Lieutenant-Colonel Kanji Ishiwara, an influential military theorist who saw in history cycles of short, sharp, and decisive battlefield encounters followed by "wars by annihilation or exhaustion" fought by whole peoples to the death. Japan's previous wars had been of the short, decisive type, requiring organization, attacking élan, and high morale. The rise of the modern industrial state, however, was making short, decisive war obsolete. A period of wars of annihilation would now follow, leading to a final encounter between the United States – leading the West – and Japan – leading Asia. He wrote, "The last war in human history is approaching . . . 'titanic world conflict, unprecedented in human history' – which will be the gateway to a golden age of human culture, a synthesis of east and West, the last and highest stage of human civilization" (Peattie, 1975: 29, 57–63). His world-historical vision was of a final, glorious Japanese triumph.

The total-war faction concluded that Japan must build up material resources for this future war by expanding in Manchuria and China to build a self-sufficient industrial power base on the Asian mainland, preferably with Chinese cooperation. Nationalist economists like Takahashi Korekyo said the way to make Japan a great power was to work with China to create "one unit. . . . harmoniously joining Japan's financial power and China's natural resources, Japan's industrial abilities and China's labor power" (Metzler, 2006: 128). Ishiwara proposed that in Manchuria the Japanese run heavy and high-tech industry, the Chinese run small business, and Koreans would do the paddy farming (Peattie, 1975: 100). What Japan should do if the Chinese and Koreans turned down such an offer he didn't say. Economic policy should be geared to long-term military build up, not the short-term profits of bankers or zaibatsu. Serving officers should also venture into the political realm to influence policy. Total-war policy was to acquire resource-rich colonies, build up a military-industrial complex in Japan, and strengthen the military role in politics, although preferably without military adventurism that might alienate the other powers. War with them might eventually come, but as Navy Minister Kato said, "Unless we have the money, we cannot make war" (Iriye, 1997: 50–62).

Those favoring colonies or protectorates argued that Japan had the military power to expand into the vacuum left by China's decline. This was the Japanese neighborhood, and the other powers were far away, except for a Russia weakened by revolution. Military actions had already been successful, increasing the attraction of further interventions. Decadent, corrupt, divided China would be easy, and piecemeal conquest through short, sharp battlefield encounters against the warlords was deemed possible. An expanding Japanese sphere of influence in Northeast China would secure its economic resources. A short war would give a breathing space and bring long-term resource benefits. Japan could not stand still, especially in Manchuria. Its influence there must grow or it would be forced out. Such arguments dominated army-planning circles (Peattie, 1975: 96–8; Barnhart, 1987; Jordan, 1987).

There were domestic pressures, too. The earlier victories had given aggressive nationalism a somewhat popular base, and conservative oligarchs and bureaucrats favored social imperialism as a way of hanging onto power and defeating "subversive elements." The Soviet Union was building up its forces in the north; leftist KMT elements were active in coastal China. Conservatives feared that the lure of a republic might spread from China to Japan, so they and the army played up the threat of Bolshevism and Soviet expansionism. Settler and business interests in China were promising riches for everyone, and there were popular demands to subsidize settlers. Although population experts doubted settler colonies were viable and favored assisted migration into South America, there was much media agitation for government-aided migration into Asia (Wilson, 1995: 253–5; L. Young, 1998). This coalition also mobilized an attractive mission statement of defense of the Asian race against the West (Iriye, 1997: 13–26). Media exaggerations of the welcome available to Japanese settlers in Korea and Taiwan contrasted strongly with the news from the United States, where racist laws against Chinese and Japanese immigrants culminated in the Federal Oriental Exclusion Act of 1924, banning all Japanese immigration into the United States. Japanese opinion was shocked by the "yellow peril" scare in the West (Iriye, 1997: 26–8). Japan had failed to get an antiracist clause added into the League of Nations Charter, as the other great powers either had racist empires or were internally racist. Western "liberalism" seemed hypocritical.

The choice between these geopolitical options was not decided by some rational perception of Japan's objective interests, but by the balance of distributive power within Japan itself. After World War I, this initially tilted leftward. There were tensions between conservative oligarchs and the new technocratic bureaucrats and urban professionals. The government operated a cheap food policy, aided by food imports from the colonies, which depressed prices for peasant farmers, fueling rural protests and riots. Workers were also agitating for greater rights, including the franchise, boosted by the Bolshevik Revolution and by popular demands for reducing the military budget. Under threat, some oligarchs believed compromise was necessary. To strengthen Japan, the masses must be brought inside the political nation, with the diet acting as a safety valve for popular unrest. The oligarchs continued to lose ground as political parties began to dominate the lower house of parliament during the Taisho Democracy period of the 1920s. Universal male suffrage was introduced in 1925, and civil citizenship rights also increased (Benson & Matsumura, 2001: 21–38; Nish, 2002).

However, liberalism was undercut in three ways. First, the franchise over-represented rural areas (as it still does today), and the countryside was more easily controlled by patron-client networks – peasants were represented by landed notables, not peasants. Second, manhood suffrage was accompanied by a Peace Preservation Law that restricted civil citizenship. This rule of class-biased law banned groups seeking to alter the form of government or abolish private property and permitted the police to repress socialist and communist parties and trade unions and interfere in elections on public order grounds. Third, most of the middle class, now enfranchised and controlling their own liberal parties in urban areas, abandoned their brief alliance with the masses below. Conservative and liberal parties – controlled by the upper class, supported by the middle class – contended for power, with leftists, workers, and peasants largely excluded. Citizenship rights stalled, leaving most Japanese half-subjects, half-citizens.

The tilting of distributive power back toward conservatives and imperialism did not result from the needs of Japanese capitalism – it would have benefitted from a more liberal route. The argument of the nineteenth-century liberal John Hobson that imperialism was driven by excess capital seeking overseas profit cannot be applied to Japan, which was a substantial importer of capital until World War I and never had much surplus capital. Nor could Lenin's notion of super-profits being extracted from colonies apply, as very little private Japanese or foreign capital investment went to the colonies. Private capital almost all went to Japan itself, because this was more profitable (Lockwood, 1954: 35). Nor does Lenin's stress on the power of finance capital monopolies work for Japan, and more recent notions of a dominant military-industrial complex consisting of the zaibatsu conglomerates and the armed forces only became important late on in the process – when it brought disaster to Japan. Until the 1930s, the zaibatsu were focused more on banking and trade than on heavy industry, and big business was not much involved with Japan's colonial enterprises, in which smaller business predominated (there were exceptions, such as Mitsui, active in China). Indeed, big business remained ambivalent about imperialism until the late 1930s. Although business supplied the military, it depended heavily upon Anglo-American imports. Major business leaders supported Shidehara. Things changed in the late 1930s when the economy as a whole came to resemble a gigantic military-industrial complex, with the "new zaibatsu" at its core. Big business had not precipitated that shift, although it did participate in the corporatist compromises struck between all these groups in the period 1937–1938 (T. Nakamura, 1998; Berger, 1977: 85, 225, 333–4, 345–6; J. Snyder, 1991: 134). Corporate capitalism did not directly drive the Japanese Empire forward, although it urged the suppression of leftist and working-class groups that opposed imperialism.

The weakness of the peasantry and the working class also weakened the anti-imperialist camp. The tennosei played its part in this, generating an ideological bias toward social harmony, duty, obedience, and patriarchy over conflict and class. This did not stop workers and peasants striking or even rioting in support of their grievances, but it did encourage them to seek redress by petitioning for respect, dignity, and the right to benevolence within the system; that is, to seek class-collaborative solutions rather than class conflict (T. Smith, 1988: chap. 10). This was also the bias of the legal code, especially the various Peace Preservation and Police Laws from 1900 onward enjoining conciliation through public authorities rather than conflict between independent employer and worker organizations. The legal code did not tolerate the role of "outsiders" (i.e., national unions) in trade disputes, and this had the effect of damping down class consciousness (Woodiwiss, 1992: 58–66).

Thus, national unions remained undeveloped. Apolitical worker organizations had been inherited from earlier periods. Japan had developed "traveling" skilled workers such as journeymen in the West, although without the artisanal organizations that in the West had then provided the first, craft-based, national unions. When Japanese factories developed, they confined worker organization within the individual enterprise. Workers agitated shop floor by shop floor, not nationally. There were several attempts to found national unions, but the main thrust of collective action lay within the firm. Japan adapted the usual variety of workers' movements – anarcho-syndicalist, communist, socialist, social-democratic, and conservative-corporatism unionism – but all existed simultaneously in the different firms and cities of Japan, without any national resolution of their varying goals and tactics. Factionalism weakened their ability to build upon the periods in which membership and strike activity expanded, during 1917–1919 and to a lesser extent in 1930–1931 (A. Gordon, 1985: 416–25, 251; 1991: 203).

Japan also developed a dual economy. The heavy industry sector – chemicals, iron and steel, and machinery – was capital-intensive, mainly supplying Japan's own needs. It required high-skilled workers who would adapt to technological change and not be disruptive. It could afford to pay its mainly male workers to achieve this, and developed seniority pay and some welfare capitalism in order to retain experienced workers (Taira, 1988: 618–9; A. Gordon, 1985). The much bigger secondary sector consisted of small enterprises in light industry and agriculture exporting their products. Labor-intensive, they paid low wages. Textile factories were the most numerous, staffed mainly by young women supplied on contract by their families or villages until they could get married. They were paid only 50–70 percent of men's wages for longer hours, but saw themselves as temporary workers. They were poor material for unions, although they became more active during the 1920s. However, Japan was still a country of small enterprises. Until 1930, only 40 percent of workers were in establishments of five or more persons, and about half of these were young women. Women formed a larger proportion of the manufacturing workforce than in any other country, being an actual majority in the 1920s, although not in the 1930s. Almost 40 percent of Japan's farm families were involved in silkworm breeding, and their daughters went into the mills to spin it (Taira, 1988: 619–21; A. Gordon, 1991: 36–7, 64, 75–8, 185; Gordon, 2003: 100–5; Metzler, 2006: 226). There was sectoral inequality and widening gulfs between agricultural and manufacturing wages and the primary and secondary sectors. This made it difficult to generate general worker unions or worker-peasant movements. Class identity was weak.

Peasants joined the left in the conflict-ridden period 1917 to 1925. The Meiji reforms had included little land reform, and commercialization impoverished many of the tenant farmers who worked almost half of Japan's arable land. The more commercialized areas saw the most conflict, and following the Rice Riots of 1918, tenant-farming unions flourished. Peasants continued to express grievances, but rarely in class terms. They wanted membership in the existing rural community, but on fairer terms. The authorities, briefly panicked by the conflict years, took steps to enmesh them in state-run mediation and cooperative organizations (Taira, 1988: 578–89). Because their sons formed most of Japan's soldiers, rural households depended at least in part on military wages. They were also led to believe they could be freed from poverty by migration as settlers to the colonies. This combination meant that right-wing militarism came to have more resonance in many rural areas than socialism. The Japanese rural population never again developed the links to the urban working class, radicalism, or anti-imperialism such as those that appeared in the late nineteenth and early twentieth centuries in countries such as France, Spain, or the United States.

I have analyzed workers' movements as a contest between three types of organization: class, sector, and segment. The more workers were riven by sectoral differences between industries and segmental differences between employers the less the chances for general working-class organization and mass socialist movements. The urban working class was divided between heavy and light industry and segmentalism within heavy industry. As in the United States, its employers hoped to pre-empt the need for unions. All this weakened both working-class movements and liberals. In these respects, Japan in 1929 resembled the United States. Neither was exceptional, both had gone through a period of reaction, but this was not yet set in stone. It was to require the more contingent events of the Great Depression and war in China to push Japan further into military imperialism abroad and a quasi-fascist despotism at home, at a time when the United States turned leftward and away from imperialism. In Asia, the years 1930 and 1931 were to prove crucial, as we see in Chapter 12.

Conclusion to Chapters 2–4: Three empires

Over the last three chapters, I have analyzed three empires whose mother countries were in three different continents. More broadly, empire had become entirely normal for any rising industrial power, just as it was for the older powers. Japan, the United States, Germany, Italy, and Belgium were all latecomers to empire. Although they all had different ways to industrialize, involving distinct blends of corporations and states, there was one best way to acquire empire: build up armed forces modeled on those of the established imperialists. Whereas Japan's domestic modernization had very distinctive forms, the armed forces with which it fought wars and captured colonies were almost identical to Western forces. Rival empires and militarism originally devised by Europeans had diffused to non-European powers and then dominated almost the whole world.

However, whereas the American turn to overseas imperialism (like the German, Italian, and Belgian) came after debates confined within elites with only moments of popular resonance, the Japanese turn was more broadly supported. The main reason for the difference was that whereas the United States was unthreatened from outside and its empire was the choice of a few people amid general indifference, many Japanese believed they had little choice. Expansion abroad, they believed, was the only possible defense against foreign imperialism. The alternative was to be squeezed between Russia, Britain, and the United States. As the decline of Spain in the American hemisphere, the decline of China seemed to offer pickings in the neighborhood. After initial all-out war in 1898, Spain had been expelled from its colonies and the Americans had found a lighter informal imperialism appropriate to a country that lacked overseas settlers, whose state lacked imperial competence, and whose mass public was uninterested in empire. In contrast, in the 1920s, Chinese decline remained tempting, there were 1 million Japanese settlers abroad, and early Japanese experiments with colonies had been very successful, unlike those of the Americans. The relatively liberal 1920s at home and abroad temporarily restrained further Japanese adventures, but by the end of the 1920s, this had stalled. The biggest difference between the two countries was the greater power and popularity of the military within Japan. This would prove the tipping force toward more imperialism, with no parallel in either the United States or Britain, when the Great Depression struck. Without that global crisis, it might not have tipped at all.

The British Empire was the most complex. Its capitalism was the most transnational, so its expansion perennially exceeded its current imperial domains.

This resulted in two distinct processes. First, the state was mostly playing catch-up, struggling to rule domains that had first been won by independent adventurers, trading companies, and settlers. Second, British economic and financial expansion outstripped its imperial control, forming the embryo of what was to become after 1945 a more universal, transnational form of globalization. In the two relative latecomers, the United States and Japan, the second industrial revolution saw two different and more organized forms of capitalism. In the United States this was mainly corporate but not statist, although it was inward-looking and protectionist. At the beginning of the new century there was a burst of imperial expansion, although this did not have great domestic support and was soon lightened. Both British and American imperialism were relatively pragmatic, except for shared racism and American nascent anticommunism. In Japan, corporate capitalism was more state-coordinated, with power of policy initiation increasingly tilting toward the state. This generated a military-led direct form of imperialism abroad, pursuing a more emotional, glory-seeking path. This was widely argued as vital to maintain Japanese prosperity, but it would eventually destroy it.

Rivalrous empires fractured the globe in new ways. It was not only that each empire set up barriers against outsiders, for there were other more complex fault lines. British and American expansion were part of an increasingly interdependent North Atlantic economy – which is sometimes taken for globalization tout court – but it wasn't, as it principally set up a new macro-regional fault line. Racism did this on a more expansive scale as the solidarity of the white race increased. Adding complexity, these two countries, plus the British white settler colonies, sometimes narrowed this down to the Anglo-Saxon race. There was a countertrend at first among the mother countries toward more of a sense of nationhood. Nonetheless, economic expansion might be viewed as a way station toward a more universal, transnational globalization, especially because finance capital was diffusing more freely across national boundaries. Yet the Great Divergence was also widening the economic difference between the motherlands of empire and their colonies plus independent poor countries. I have argued that imperial exploitation contributed relatively little to the divergence, however. It was principally caused by a simple difference within countries: those in the West industrialized, the Rest did not. The Japanese empire differed, for there was no trend toward greater economic divergence between Japan and its colonies. They all had similar rates of growth and their economies were becoming more integrated. However, other forms of Japanese exploitation and the Japanese near-racial sense of their superiority over other Asians prevented much integration in other power relations. The globe was still seriously fractured. The year 1914 was to reveal this in spades.

5 Half-global crisis: World War I

During the first half of the twentieth century, the world was deeply fractured by two great wars. Indeed, it is conventional to treat the period 1914–1945 as a complete contrast to the periods preceding and following it, a period in which conflict and chaos reigned. No one would dispute the fracturing that occurred in this period, but I have already emphasized fractures that were in place well before the war. We will see how the Great War mainly intensified these.

After a century of only small wars in Europe, the Great War struck the continent like a cataclysm. Its epicenter may have been Europe, but it reverberated across most continents to become nearly global. I discussed its causes at greater length in Chapter 21 of Volume II, although I now add more of an emphasis on the European warrior culture (discussed in Chapter 2) that had spread aggressive imperialism within the continent and overseas. In the nineteenth century, wars had receded in Europe as their increasing devastation became apparent and the Great Powers formed alliances intended to deter them. By 1914, the two main alliances ranged Germany, Austria-Hungary, and Italy against Russia, France, and Britain, with the Ottoman Empire unaligned. The balance of power had entered diplomatic discourse as something that could prevent war. Yet war was still the default mode of diplomacy, militaries continued to modernize, and the continent's young men were conscripted and trained as reserve troops – all well before this war. Only Britain, with a capital-intensive rather than labor-intensive military, lacked conscription. Children (boys and girls) read stories of romantic and heroic imperial adventure and socialized into a militaristic culture. Europeans were still from Mars. Europe was what in previous volumes I called a multi-power-actor civilization, composed of many distinct, competitive actors emerging from all four sources of power and all thoroughly decentralized. There I praised the dynamism of this configuration in generating the "European Miracle" of unprecedented economic growth. There is no necessary reason why multistate systems should generate much war, but when they come enveloped in a culture of militarism, as Europe did, it is likely to generate endless war and competitive imperialism.

Yet although this war was mostly fought between countries with empires, squabbles over their colonial possessions or international trade did not cause it. Colonies now seemed less essential to commercial profit, as the recent African scramble had produced disappointing results. Because the white race had a common interest in keeping down the natives, many also reasoned correctly that war among whites could only destabilize all the empires (Strachan,

2001: 495–6). It was in fact mainly a European war, fought for dominance in that continent. There was little military action in Asia and none in Latin America. Japanese participation in the war did not last long. Instead, the precipitating conflicts in 1914 lay as usual within Europe itself. War came in the traditional form of attacks by two Great Powers – Austria-Hungary and Germany – on two small ones – Serbia and Belgium – to whose aid came major protecting powers. This revealed the essential path dependence of military imperialism within Europe over an entire millennium.

On the other hand, the outbreak of war in Europe was also rather contingent, for it came after a dizzying sequence of events that might easily have gone otherwise. On June 28, 1914, a young Serb nationalist, Gavrilo Princip, was emerging from a delicatessen in Sarajevo, then part of the Austro-Hungarian Empire. He had sought sustenance after he and his friends had botched an assassination attempt on the Archduke Franz Ferdinand, heir to the Habsburg throne, who was visiting the city. To Gavrilo's great surprise, he suddenly saw the Archduke's open car reversing toward him; it had lost its way. A confused chauffeur was about to cause the Great War! Seizing his chance, Gavrilo ran alongside the car, pulling out his pistol. The police had no time to react. He fired two shots at point-blank range at the Archduke and his wife, Duchess Sophie; they were both dead within half an hour. The conspirators were rounded up. They were shown to have connections within the Serbian government – the head of Serbian military intelligence had supplied their weapons, and Serbian cabinet members knew of the plot yet had done nothing to stop it.[1]

Serbia had recently wrested Macedonia and Kosovo from the Ottoman Empire, and was intent on expanding amid the remaining Serb communities of the region, presently ruled by Austria-Hungary. Ironically, the dead Archduke had been a moderate voice urging negotiations with Serbia. His death strengthened the Austrian war party, which convinced most of the court that they had to punish Serb nationalists or face other assertive nationalists seeking to dismember the multiethnic empire. The court, hamstrung by bickering between Vienna and Budapest over military budgets, also believed that war might be the only way to get the military modernized. The monarchy was reassured when the German government offered it unconditional support on July 5–6. After much debate in Vienna, for the elderly Emperor Franz-Josef was a cautious man, Austria delivered the Serb government a stiff ultimatum on July 23, demanding an independent commission of enquiry into the assassination. Serbia replied evasively, and began to mobilize its armed forces. So on July 28, Austria mobilized its forces and declared war on Serbia – although Field Marshal Conrad said his forces would not be able to actually strike until August

[1] The paragraphs that follow rely on my Volume II, Chapter 21, supplemented especially by Williamson & May (2007).

15. There was time enough to stop the slide to war, and this was as of yet only a regional conflict.

Yet Russia was Serbia's Great Power protector, and its regime hoped that if it mobilized, this would deter Austria from war, restore the prestige of the Romanov dynasty, and defuse internal strife. On July 28, the tsar ordered a partial mobilization, only against Austria. This was supposed to avoid war, but the Austrians immediately counter-mobilized against Russia as well as Serbia. The tsar's high command then informed him that only a general mobilization, against Germany as well, was technically possible. The next day, they talked the tsar into ordering this general mobilization. It began a month after the original assassination and only a week after the Austrian ultimatum to Serbia. Coincidentally, French President Poincaré and his foreign minister were visiting St. Petersburg at the time. They did not try to restrain their Russian ally. The French leaders still hoped their alliances with Russia and Britain would deter Germany, and reasoned that it was no bad thing for Russia to threaten Germany.

Throughout the crisis, German leaders seemed immune to threats, prepared to risk general war in support of Austria. In Berlin, the Russian general mobilization was seen as threatening, although the high command knew from intelligence reports that it was probably not. It pretended to feel threatened because it wanted war, and was prepared to take on both France and Russia, sequentially rather than both together, hopefully. Thus, the German government responded with its own mobilization in the west as well as the east. To the apparent surprise of most of the German cabinet, this included seizing railheads and fortified positions in Belgium and Luxemburg, foreign countries whose neutrality France and Britain guaranteed. This was a provocative move, especially as under the Schlieffen Plan German mobilization, seeking to expose the flank of the French armies, had intended to attack through Belgium into northern France. Then the Germans would turn east toward Paris to deliver a decisive blow that would quickly knock France out of the war. Alternatively, if the French counterattacked northward, the Germans might envelop their flank in Belgium. In either case, Germany would then turn to the Eastern Front and deal with Russia, seen as its more dangerous enemy. The assumption, shared by other militaries, was that military technology and organization had developed to a point where offense would dominate defense, and a swift enveloping attack might bring victory.[2] How wrong they were!

The willingness of German leaders to countenance a possible two-front war may seem surprising, but they expected a swift offense would avoid that. Additionally, the kaiser and some others did not expect Britain to fight, despite

[2] Some doubt whether Germany was committed to the Schlieffen Plan, or indeed whether such a firm plan really existed. Yet in 1914, the German army did try to implement a more flexible version of the supposed plan. See Zuber, 2002; Strachan, 2001: 163–84.

its alliance with France and guarantee of Belgian neutrality. Britain's government had refused to promise France help, and had failed to deliver Germany a war ultimatum over Belgium. Its deeply split ruling Liberal Party only had a small parliamentary majority. In the cabinet, those opposing threatening a war outnumbered those favoring it (essentially only Foreign Secretary Grey, Navy Minister Churchill, and Prime Minister Asquith). This was the only government in which pacifists significantly opposed militarists. Although these were of lesser political stature within the cabinet, the leadership feared that its voters would desert in droves if the government adopted too bellicose a stance. This was a limit placed on the military crystallization of the state. The threat of civil war in Ireland, which it still ruled, was also a more pressing concern for the British government. Most politicians rate domestic issues higher than foreign ones, and this was the case here. So the British failed to deter Germany.

In private, the leaders of the two major British parties and the foreign office professionals agreed they could not tolerate the Germans reaching Channel ports. For centuries, the British had based their policy on sustaining a balance of power within the continent of Europe. Allies had always been essential because within Europe Britain was only one among several Great Powers. Its European alliances had enabled the steady expansion of the British Empire elsewhere into a position of dominance over large segments of the world. Therefore, German domination of Europe, and more specifically of North Sea ports, was not acceptable to professional geopoliticans. Britain imported most of its food, and if the power of the Royal Navy was challenged, said Kipling, there might be "no coffee or bacon for breakfast." Yet the leaders also believed the British people would not accept such cold-blooded geopolitical motives for war. Thus, they preferred to wait until "little Belgium" was attacked, when they could whip up moral outrage and bring more support for war among Liberal voters – their way around the pacific limits they had imposed on the government. It also proved convenient that German forces entering Belgium committed widely publicized atrocities. For, as we saw in Chapter 2, the British Empire believed itself to be a charitable organization to protect the less fortunate peoples of the world. In reality, British leaders fought the First World War, as they were to fight the Second World War, to defend the power of their imperial state, not the independence of Belgium (or, in 1939, Poland).

Many German leaders thought Britain would probably fight if France were attacked, but they knew the British had evaded making any promises, and most had not realized that their own mobilization plans involved the invasion of Belgium. When this dawned on them at the end of July, they did not pull back because they felt this would bring a loss of prestige, because they underestimated Britain's strength, and some of them actually wanted war. Many Germans had convinced themselves that the British were more capitalist than martial. Foolishly believing in British liberal cant, they saw the British as "traders," not "heroes" in Werner Sombart's famous formulation. The British lacked martial "spirit" and a sense of "honor," they said. Whenever the British fought, it was for mere profit, and it was difficult to see profit in this coming war. Thus, they would not fight or they would not fight well. The generals, who were important in German decision making, were correct in not rating the British army highly, but British militarism was not readily visible to Europe, as it was mainly naval and global. Not Europeans but far-away natives felt its sharp end – although they could turn it swiftly toward a very damaging naval blockade of Germany. Even Germans who did appreciate this mostly saw the British Empire as brittle, and hoped the war might encourage its natives to revolt. They also saw that Britain had entered a period of relative decline (Strachan, 2001: 1128–30). This may have been becoming true, but they were jumping the gun. British decline was only just beginning, and it would have been better for Germany to wait another ten years before mounting such a challenge, because by then they would have achieved economic hegemony within Europe anyway (Offer, 1989). Human fallibility was an important cause of this war.

Therefore, World War I started in the first week of August, as the statesmen all declared war on each other. Their declaration was the consequence of a fluky assassination followed by a series of decisions by the Great Powers to support their lesser allies. Some autonomy of military planning from civilian control and an inability to predict the decisions of other governments or predict the nature of the coming military campaign – which did not privilege offense over defense – further aggravated the situation. A Balkan crisis had become a crisis involving three great monarchies, then all the powers, and then a quasi-world war. This was not inevitable; it was a piling up of pressures, a concatenation of different causal chains, some of which were rooted quite deeply in power structures and others were more contingent. Weaknesses were exposed that might otherwise have remained latent, yet which reinforced the drift to war – such as the split among British liberals or the autonomy of some militaries. The impact they had on each other was mostly rather contingent, but their combined effect was to increase the likelihood of war. This was intensified by ideological passivity, as the apparently acceptable default military mode of diplomacy set in, combined with fear of humiliation if they backed down. The limits imposed by the military crystallization of the state favored war not peace. Boosted by social Darwinian pseudo-scientific theory, they saw war as inevitable, even necessary. The fittest would drive out the backward and declining (they all considered themselves the fittest, of course). Some also thought war-inspired patriotism could provide relief from domestic class or ethnic conflict, and some thought this war could not last long. The combination made statesmen believe that the worst thing to do in a militaristic, multipower civilization was to back down.

The statesmen did not identify national interests in particularly material terms. Although a few territories were in dispute, these were not initially the primary issues at stake for most powers, except for the Serbian-Austrian dispute. Only after the war began were rival war claims to territory, industry, and trade formulated. Before then, the statesmen were primarily fighting for status, in Max Weber's sense of the term. Although they did assume that victory would bring material gain, they had not submitted this to rigorous examination. What is more striking is their shared emphasis on honor, glory, status, credibility, and shame, fear of being seen as weak and thus ridiculed – the emotional insecurities of little boys fighting on the playground. Conceptions of being a man were involved. All the decision makers were, of course, men. Offer (1995: 234) says, "The commencement of the First World War was a chain of insults that no leader in a position of public visibility could afford to ignore." Among the statesmen, status and masculinity concerns were both national and personal. They were national because backing down or failing to honor promises to allies were felt to lower the status of one's state; they were personal because the statesmen could not face their own humiliation if they backed down. Of course, they themselves were conveniently too old to fight.

Concerns about status were also embedded in broader ideological conceptions. These were mostly national states becoming nation-states, claiming to embody some universal values, usually values of the Enlightenment. To themselves, France represented liberty, Britain democracy, Germany a higher culture, and Russia and Austria – being multiethnic and dynastic – embodied tradition and order. These qualities supposedly suffused each national community. To back down was to lessen the sway of those universal values in the world. As a cause of war, ideological power was important at the emotional, national, and universal level – and remains so today.

However (again, as today), a genuine sense of honor was everywhere blended with manipulation. War had to be seen as defensive and therefore honorable, so they dissembled to achieve this impression. German leaders used Russian mobilization to claim the moral high ground, just as the British used the invasion of little Belgium. This ideological embedding of European militarism – its default status, martial/little boy emotions, manipulations – is what I wish to add to the more detailed analysis of the slide to war that I gave at the end of my second volume. Alas, Ferguson (1999: 1–30) is not correct in saying that European militarism was in decline. This remained a militaristic continent, although demonstrating the pathos as well as the power of militarism, and now existing with pathetically few material interests at stake.

However, three of the Great Powers were undoubtedly more provocative than the others. The Habsburg court saw this as survival time. If they did not stand up to the Serbs, they believed their dynastic empire might collapse. Their overwhelming motive was strategic insecurity. Russians and Germans had more mixed security motives. On the one hand, the Russian government had recently claimed a pan-Slav mantle and believed it could not now avoid helping the Serbs without significant loss of prestige, which in turn might threaten the survival of the Romanov dynasty. On the other hand, some Russian leaders saw territorial opportunity: now was the time to expand at the expense of the Habsburgs, to reach the Straits of Constantinople (a long-desired goal), although this was blended with a desire to restore Russian pride after the mauling received at the hands of Japan in 1905. The provocative climate among German elites was double-edged. There was the geopolitical insecurity of a centrally located power "surrounded" by enemies, feeling it must strike out against them in self-defense. Yet there was confidence in the prowess of Germany's armed forces. Historians vary in the weight they give to these two sentiments. Ferguson (1999:149–54) and Strachan (2001: 1–35) see German leaders as nervous and insecure, striking out as gamblers, risking an immediate attack on Russia, before current Russian modernization plans had come to fruition, trapped between the need to attack Russia and France right away and the need to wait before attacking Britain. Yet Hewitson's (2004) evidence reveals most German leaders at ease with diplomatic brinkmanship, seeing war as the normal default mode of national growth, confident that the German army would bring victory. Whichever the dominant emotion, they shared the need to fight, now.

These three regimes were despotic, Russia most so, Germany least. The three dynasties and their courts feared a modernism that was not congenial to their style of rule. A war might prolong their rule; after all, what was the point of dynasties if they could not fight and win war? War had always been the route to dynastic glory, a decidedly noninstrumental goal. The only German peculiarity was that its militarism had recently been very successful, giving its leaders more confidence in aggression. It was risky, but it might work. For the other two sets of elites, it was ideological folly. Uncomfortable with capitalist and democratic modernity, these old regimes decided to stick with what they knew well: militarism. Had the Habsburg, Romanov, or German governments been dominated by industrialists, financiers, or other civilians, it is unlikely they would have gone to war. Russia was half-way through a military modernization program; Austria-Hungary was in no condition to fight a major war; and the German rate of economic expansion meant that in another decade or so Germany would have dominated Europe and secured its place in the sun peacefully. However, broad-based civilian elites were not in control in these three regimes. Nor were the people, who remained largely passive and possessed little knowledge of what was threatened in their name.

Did democracy make a difference? France was a masculine electoral democracy, Britain was substantially so, and they were not the aggressors. However, democracy was still quite thin. Except where workers were urbanized, industrialized, and "massified," most people still deferred to their "betters" and were politically quite passive, especially in foreign policy. In any case, it is difficult to tell whether democracy made for this difference in Britain and France, as they were also satiated powers, satisfied with the empires they already had. Both can be faulted for not having produced bolder and more coordinated diplomacy to avert war. However, democracy contributed to the British failure, for the Liberal leaders deferred to the strong streak of pacifism in its party and what it believed was the predominant antiwar sentiment of the people. They preferred to wait until poor little Belgium was attacked. Braver leaders might have bitten the domestic political bullet – if only to preserve their imperial powers, they should have made clear to Germany earlier their position on Belgium and France. Alternatively, they might have been more understanding of Germany's desire to possess geopolitical power commensurate with its economic power. Ferguson (1999: 168–73) observes that at this stage Germany had limited war aims on the continent, which did not greatly threaten British power.[3] It only enlarged its war aims later, after the war was well underway. Could the British not accept that France had declined and that Germany would now be the dominant power on the western half of the land continent of Europe? Could Britain not live with that?

France's President Poincaré dithered, for he was in a difficult situation. Fearing German aggression, he spent his years in office strengthening the French military and firming up the British and Russian alliances. This included getting his generals to abandon possible pre-emptive strikes into Belgium. These had made military sense because France had a bigger field army, whereas Germany would have to take time to call up its reservists. However, this plan alienated the British, and was shelved. Yet his main failure was in Russia during the July crisis, when he failed to restrain the Russians. Indeed, against the advice of his foreign minister, Viviani, he gave them an unconditional pledge of loyalty. He could have done better, but the responsibility of the British and French regimes was much less. In August, France had to fight, as it was invaded; there was popular consensus over that. Britain fought because its statesmen felt German warships in Belgian ports were unacceptable, and gilded with stories of German atrocities in Belgium, the people mostly accepted that. Both countries had global empires, but their homelands now seemed vulnerable.

Other peripheral states joined in more instrumentally. The Ottoman Empire declared for the Central Powers in 1914 because Germany offered it more aid, and Russia was its most threatening enemy; Japan declared for the Entente in 1914 because it could easily seize nearby German colonies; bribed with Austrian territories, Italy deserted the Triple Alliance and joined the Entente in 1915. These were very materialistic motives – provided their side won! The little Balkan states broke both ways, and America and China joined the Entente late, only in 1917, and for very mixed motives.

Through all of this variety, one irrationality shines through, as it does through most wars. Almost all states going to war breeze confidence of victory, but how can this be when there are always at least as many losers as winners?

[3] Having berated Ferguson in Chapter 2 for his views of the British Empire, it is a pleasure to cite repeatedly and positively his excellent book on World War I.

This war was also likely to carry immense costs, and the number of genuine winners might be very small. In the event, only the United States and Japan could be said to have had "good" wars, worth the (relatively little) effort they put into it. The overconfidence elsewhere had much to do with the insulation of leaders (and peoples, as we see later) inside their national cages. There they imbibed a collective enthusiasm for war, largely unaware of the enemy's identical enthusiasm.

Once war was declared, military power took over. The fighting spread, becoming severe around the outer edges of Europe, on the Eastern Front, in the Balkans, and on the Caucasian front between Russia and Turkey. Because the main combatants had colonies, it also became an interimperial war, with fighting scattered through the world's colonies. The war was half-global. Britain and France drew on substantial resources from their colonies and dominions. Britain's Indian army had 1.2 million men, the largest volunteer force in the world – 60 percent were Punjabis. Britain's white Dominions provided a further 1.2 million men to the war. Two million Africans fought or labored for the European powers, and at least 250,000 of them died in Africa (not counting the death-toll of the pandemics that swept in at the end of the war). Fighting spread across all of Africa except for Liberia, Ethiopia, and the small colonies of Spain and Italy, although it was on a small scale because of enormous logistical difficulties. An Indian Army corps traveled across the world to stiffen British troops on the Western Front, and African and other colonial troops, totaling more than 600,000 men, replaced the huge French losses. The French General Mangin was renowned for racist respect for his Senegalese troops: he believed they were more impervious to pain than Frenchmen. Bizarrely, Japanese fought Germans in Micronesia, and Australians and New Zealanders fought against Turks at the entrance to the Black Sea. The Germans called it a World War, and it half-deserves that title; the British and French called it the Great War, and it was certainly that. It can now be seen as a deadly way station on the route to a less fractured, more universal process of globalization – although few saw that in advance, and in itself it was a terrible fracturing of European civilization.

War broke out within Europe, however, and focused there, not in the colonies, so it was essentially a European rather than a global war. After the British won the naval battle of the Falkland Islands in December 1914, even the so-called world fleets of Britain and Germany were largely confined to the North Atlantic and adjacent sea-lanes. The war concerned "survival" in Europe, especially for the Habsburgs, Romanovs, Ottomans, Serbia, and Belgium, to a lesser extent for France, and even Britons and Germans persuaded themselves of a threat to their survival. The Greater Powers fought for geopolitical status filtered through the dual ideological notion of security and honor, which prevented anyone backing down. If one accepts that the only war that makes sense is one fought with a good chance of material or strategic gain, this war was not sensible. Few wars are.

The fact that it was not a very materialistic war means it was not fundamentally about capitalism. None of the powers threatened capitalism, and there were few warmongering capitalists beforehand. World systems theorists say the war was about hegemony – a rising Germany seeking to wrest hegemony in the world system from a declining Britain. By now, as we see in Chapter 7, the role of sterling as the reserve currency was only possible thanks to the active cooperation of the Bundesbank and other major central banks. British-German trade was also increasing, and their economies were becoming more interdependent. Indeed, in general the nineteenth century Atlantic economy was greatly expanded in the decades before the war. This was the period when the ratio of international trade to world GDP grew to its highest level before the 1990s (Chase-Dunn et al., 2000). Much of the growth, especially in investment patterns, was substantially transnational. The economy was globalizing in quite cooperative ways. Moreover, Britain had never really been a hegemon, and German leaders did not want to be one. They wished merely to weaken Britain, France, and Russia, and take their rightful place among them in the sun in a multipower system. The other powers resisted, of course, as they would have done in any of the last eight centuries. Economic and military power relations were going down different tracks, the former increasingly cooperative the latter more fractured, descending into a war that would obviously greatly harm the economy.

Capitalists' main preoccupation is to make profits, preferably secure rather than risky profits. Capitalists rarely involve themselves much in foreign politics, although they do show a keen interest, and intensively lobby the state on domestic issues directly relevant to their profit rate – such as taxation, subsidies, wage rates, labor unions, and so forth. For their part, politicians want to remain in power, and they normally recognize that the health of the national capitalist economy is essential to that. So we might expect to find a normal congruence of interests between states and capitalists, although leftist governments will cause capitalists concern. On the basis of this reciprocity, a functional Marxist theory of the state has arisen, asserting that modern states pursue the interests of capital in general, embodying "capitalist rationality" (Zeitlin, 1980: 25), and this will be so of even nominally leftist governments (Offe & Ronge, 1974; Block, 1987, Zeitlin, 1980). I reject such functionalism, although I do concede some truth in their empirical assertions when political decision making crystallizes on economic issues, especially domestic ones. However, as I argued in Chapter 3 of Volume II, states are polymorphous, crystallizing in different forms, pressured by different constituencies, over different policy arenas. Capitalists generally have little interest in religion, morality, gender, or family issues, on terrorism or most (although not all) wars, and the state will not usually embody capitalist rationality on any of these issues. So although most business in all countries did not want war in 1914, they did not lobby much for peace, nor did they follow the diplomatic and military intricacies narrated above that brought this war on.

Ferguson (1999: 33) is correct in declaring, "The Marxist interpretation of the war's origins can therefore be consigned to the rubbish bin of history." The war was not about profit or wages because peace was, and was considered to be, better for both. If, nonetheless, it was about hegemony, it was an irrational way to seek it. Indeed, war was to bring revolutions against capitalism, and many suspected this beforehand. As the world's stock markets proved, capitalists were not party to the gathering storm. Not until the last week of July, after the Austrian ultimatum to Serbia, did stock prices begin to fall; once war started, the markets had to be closed to prevent collapse (Ferguson, 2006: 84–91). Of course, once engaged in war, capitalists figured out how to make money from it – capitalists can make money from anything. When Germany began to make territorial demands on resource-rich parts of Belgium and France and on British and French colonies, German heavy industrialists eagerly latched onto them. However, neither industry nor capital started the war. It was started by ideologically inflected, status-obsessed statesmen wielding geopolitical reasons that did not make all that much sense.

Nor did the people or their supposed nationalism start it. Although by now most people had a routine, banal sense of their own nationality, few were aggressive nationalists, and most just believed what their betters told them. Nationalism was not the problem. Organized labor, most peasants, and even most of the middle class were not warmongers (apart from that middle-class fraction I labeled nation-statist in Volume II). The nationalist and imperialist pressure groups that organized pro-war demonstrations were outnumbered before the war by larger antiwar protests. The people, however, were largely irrelevant to decision making. This was a war decided on by political and military elites, although they should have been the ones most knowledgeable and likely to have misgivings about what was to come. In this respect, it is not clear that any of these powers were democracies (quite apart from the limitations of their contemporary franchises) because the most important and most devastating political decisions for a century were not made through any process of consultation with the masses. This remains entirely normal in "democracies" in the sphere of foreign policy.

Yet once declared, the war – like almost all modern wars – was at first quite well supported across the classes and political spectrum (Strachan, 2001: chap. 2; Audoin-Rouzeau & Becker, 2002: chap 4.). The statesmen could lightly tug at the strings of national identities and hierarchical loyalties that were already well-established. In my second volume, I argued that they had been established by the gradual extension of power infrastructures across the territories of states. Economies, working conditions, health, education infrastructures, and military conscription were increasingly nationally regulated by the state. People were factually implicated in the nation-state as a circumscribed network of social interaction. This led to a somewhat latent sense of national identity well described by Billig's (1995) term "banal nationalism." This involved a secure national identity, intermittently renewed by what he calls "flagging" in everyday life of symbols of national identity. The flag was not so much fervently waved as just hanging there on buildings; language, cuisine, music, and distinctive landscapes all evoked national identity. We must be careful, however, not to project sentiments of today backward in time. In 1914, most of these sentiments were filtered through social structures that remained hierarchical. The people deferred to local notables, young men deferred to their elders and betters, and women deferred to men. Women loyally supported the war, apart from some radical feminists who were greatly outnumbered by women urging men to "be a man" and enlist – and handing out white feathers as a symbol of cowardice to those who didn't. Although all the key decision makers were men, in this era it might not have changed much if half had been women. Above the level of ordinary people stood the political parties, most of them still hierarchical patron-client networks. These were half-citizens, half-subjects.

Such banal but hierarchical nationalism briefly became "hot," which in this context meant enthusiastic and confident in the justice of the national cause and the likely outcome, as well as willingness to fight. Although some statesmen were gloomy on the onset of war – such as British Foreign Secretary Grey's famous remark, "The lights are going out all over Europe" – there wasn't much fear expressed in the popular press or street demonstrations after the war began. Isolated in their nation-states, experiencing a brief rally around the flag, most people bizarrely perceived this as a defensive war, fought in defense of their version of civilization against others' barbarism. Those who believed in God thought he was on their side. They thought it would be easy – as in the adventure stories they had read. Thus, they cheerfully, irrationally expected to win the war quickly. The troops left home shouting, "Back by Christmas!"

We have the benefit of hindsight. We know that the only soldiers who did return by Christmas were mangled and maimed – for the dead were buried in the field. During this war, just more than 60 million men were mobilized into the armed forces. The dead in action numbered 9.2 million, more than 15 million were wounded, and almost 8 million were listed as either prisoners of war (POWs) or missing. Most of the missing were men whose remains were too mangled to be identified – this was so of more than half the Frenchmen who died defending their country. Half of all the troops were therefore termed "casualties." The small Balkan countries suffered the highest proportion killed – Serbia lost 37 percent of its soldier; between 15 percent and 20 percent of German, Austrian, Russian, and French troops were killed; and between 10 percent and 15 percent of British Empire, Italian, and Ottoman troops died. Infantry losses were highest, because more of them served at the front. The French lost one in three infantry officers, one in four privates. Nine hundred French soldiers and 1,300 Germans died every day, and the mayhem lasted four full years. The First World War was probably the costliest in combatants' lives, the most destructive of the terrain over which it was fought, and most wasteful of armaments. It was fought between the largest armies ever maneuvered, requiring the greatest logistical organization of supplies ever assembled.

Military power has its own techniques, social organization, and logic of development, but it is a logic like no other, because in war nothing is inevitable. Military power has an inherently contingent streak. Had things gone according to plan on the Western Front, Germany would have won the war quickly, and they might indeed have done so. German leaders had staked all on a short war and expected that offense would triumph over defense. It did not; defense triumphed. Millions of men could be efficiently delivered to the railheads, but to advance further involved men and horses walking slowly beside trucks along clogged roads under artillery bombardment. Supply and coordination problems undid the Germans. Belgians tore up the rail lines, there were not enough roads in Northern France, and German trucks kept breaking down. Remarkably, Kluck's 1st German Army did still arrive en masse at the Marne in August, as per plan. It had moved 14.4 miles every day for 3 weeks, accompanied by 84,000 horses requiring 2 million pounds of fodder a day – a remarkable military feat. However, they arrived tired and without much artillery – in no condition to overcome French forces. Over the next month, on the River Marne German troops were again and again repulsed by Joffre's French forces – with 250,000 casualties, a mass slaughter for Germany. This gave time for the British to deliver their force to France. There followed a race to the sea as both sides attempted to outflank the other westward. Here the decisive battle was in October–November at Ypres in Belgium, the only major Belgian city still held by the Entente. Although this encounter destroyed much of the British Expeditionary Force, it also stopped the German advance dead. German myth remembered the battle as the Kindermort or death of the children, the raw recruits into the reserve battalions who composed most of the German forces there. The possibilities of a short war ended with the stalling of the German advance on two sectors of the Western Front.

The war proceeded as a meat grinder on a Western Front stretching 475 miles from the Swiss border to the North Sea, 10,000 soldiers per mile. A mature level of industrialization meant that the Germans, British, and French could keep millions of men in the field all year round, under arms, fed, clothed, and free from serious diseases (a novelty in the history of warfare). The Germans clearly had the edge for the next two years, but even they hadn't figured out how to take and hold territory amid a battlefield technology dominated by artillery and the machine gun, then more suited to defense. Massed infantry could make the initial breakthrough, although at great cost of lives. Then, however, the defenders could bring up reserves by rail to the rear of the breach faster than the attackers could walk there. The counterattack in large numbers followed – pushing the front back to around the initial front line where the resupply ratio began to reverse itself. All the main combatants poured money into the science and technology of killing people, rewarded with remarkably quick development of submarines, fighter planes, tanks, and shells. The most lethal development on the battlefield came in the shape of the artillery shell, mainly shrapnel, aimed not at strategic communications and hardware (as in World War II) but at destroying the enemy infantry. Artillery fire had probably caused the majority of casualties since the era of muskets. Now the figure rose to more than two-thirds (Collins, 2008: 58).

It meant enormous sacrifice of life to take small pieces of ground. Field Marshal von Falkenhayn had earlier advised the kaiser to negotiate peace, but as commander of German forces on the Western Front, he became ironically embroiled in what he called "a war of attrition" to kill as many French as he could around Verdun in February 1916. This, he believed, could bring France to the negotiating table. After 10 months, his attrition had cost 550,000 French and 434,000 German casualties, but it did not take Verdun nor bring the French to negotiate. It was this grim, determined French defense – under the slogan "Les Boches ne passeront pas" (the Huns shall not pass) – that provided the military key to the war in the West. This was a complete contrast with the opening of World War II.

Then, partly to draw German resources away from this sector, a force two-thirds British, one-third French counterattacked over a twelve-mile stretch of the Somme River. Entente forces attacked simultaneously in Galicia on the Eastern Front and in Italy. The five-month Battle of the Somme cost 1.1 million casualties. On July 1 (the first day), despite lobbing 3 million shells at the Germans, the British army took its heaviest ever one-day losses – 57,000, including 19,000 dead. It was also the heaviest one-day loss by any army in either world war, perhaps in any battle ever (unless one believes the figures given in ancient Chinese annals). At the end of the Battle of the Somme, the British had recovered their territorial losses. They had advanced three kilometers, a death rate of two men per centimeter! However, their determination also had a bigger consequence. The German high command now decided it could not win what it called a "war of machines" on land and turned to submarine warfare at sea, a fateful decision.

The Eastern Front contained more open spaces, fewer trenches, and more movement. The Germans placed one-third of their forces here and made big initial territorial conquests against Russian forces, as did the Russians against the Austrians and Turks. Here, however, local communications systems were primitive, making further coordinated advances and artillery assaults difficult. The Austrians counterattacked, taking Russian territory. The dead kept mounting in the east, too, but there was a decisive outcome. Russian forces collapsed under the strain, revolution broke out, and the Bolsheviks sued for terms (see Chapter 6).

On the Western Front, attrition did not favor Germany in the long run. Once checked, the Central Powers were at an increasing quantitative disadvantage in economic power resources. They were overweighted two-to-one in population, GDP, naval ships, and troop numbers. They were strangled of their foreign trade by a British naval blockade, and they found it increasingly difficult to supply their troops and civilian populations. Their GNP was declining, Britain's was increasing, and France's began recovering from late 1915. On the Western Front, Germany was confronted by France – with a bigger army – and Britain – wealthier, with more global resources, capable of taxing more efficiently, borrowing at lower rates of interest, and providing supplies (especially coal) and financial subsidies to its French ally (Broadberry & Harrison, 2005; Ferguson, 1999: chap. 5; Offer, 1989). Once this discrepancy became clear, no new combatant sided with the Central Powers rather than the Entente. As an alliance, the Central Powers were weaker than the Entente, and became ever more so.

Germany had offsetting military strength, with the best-trained soldiers (all regulars or reservists) and lower-level officers able to take flexible decisions according to local conditions. The German army was more streamlined, with a higher proportion of front-line troops, and almost invariably inflicting more casualties and capturing more prisoners than their enemies. Ferguson (1999: 300, 336) says that between August 1914 and June 1918, every month the Germans killed or captured more Entente soldiers than they lost themselves. He estimates it cost the Entente $36,485 to kill an enemy soldier, whereas it cost the Central Powers only $11,345 to kill an Entente soldier, a striking disproportion. Early on, a German knockout blow on the Western Front was always possible, yet the French managed to roll with the punches and the British managed to mount a much bigger commitment on land than they had ever envisaged. Then, as the coordination and technology of the French and British forces improved, a German knockout blow became less probable. The Germans made one last great push on the Western Front in early 1918, and British leaders worried that a decisive breakthrough might be coming, yet underneath it all economic power was slowly overcoming military power to prevent a German victory.

Stalemate was also helped by the fact that neither of the two greatest powers could deliver the other the knockout punch: the British (even together with the French) could not defeat the German army on the Western front, and the resources of the British Empire were too formidable elsewhere across the globe. First Sea Lord Admiral Fisher saw the British naval blockade of Germany as part of a "federation of all who speak the English tongue." Offer (1989) concurs: "The real assets for British security were the bonds and resources of the English-speaking world." That was correct, except that many of Britain's colonial troops could not speak English. The colonies and the white Dominions virtually doubled Britain's economic resources and provided another 50 percent to its military manpower.

Britain's sharp edge was the Royal Navy. Despite doing quite well in its sally out into the North Sea at the Battle of Jutland in May 1916, the German

High Fleet retreated back into its bases for the rest of the war. There were indeed German ships in Belgian ports, as in British nightmares, but were confined there by the Dover Patrol, and Germany could not break out of the continent. Submarine warfare was an effective German reaction to its inferior naval strength, another German gamble on a short war, seeking to decimate British destroyers and merchant ships, but it was not very effective in this war, and in the long run it produced blowback. A submarine had only two choices: to either sink a merchant ship or let it pass. The submarine could not surface to discover the ship's nationality or cargo without losing its great advantage – invisibility. Thus, German submarines kept sinking the ships of neutral countries, including those of the United States – a risky proposition. For their part, the British blockaded Germany, mopped up most of its colonies in Africa, eventually in 1918 defeated the Ottoman Empire in the Middle East, and offered enough support and subsidies on the Western Front to French forces to enable them to survive the German attack. That, however, was the limit of British capacity. It needed the entrance of the United States into the war to produce a decisive victory.

Russian forces did eventually disintegrate in revolution, enabling Germany to win the war in the east and to begin to transfer some troops westward in late 1917. By then, German submarine warfare coupled with American global ambition had brought the United States into the war. German offensives in the spring of 1918 gained ground, but as usual, they overextended their front line, and Entente forces drove them back again. In the summer, the Entente was making gains, and its new tanks and airplanes were taking a toll. With the failure of the last desperate German assaults on the Marne from July 15 to August 5, 1918, the reality sunk in – more than 1 million American troops had arrived in France (although they were ill-prepared and poorly-led). America's entry also signaled unlimited financial loans to its allies. Woodrow Wilson had campaigned in the United States on the slogan "He kept us out of the war." This great liberal rather revealingly told Lansing, his secretary of state, that neutrality was essential because, "White civilization and its domination over the world rested largely on our ability to keep this country intact." However, a combination of his desire to be the arbiter of Europe and the country's growing economic bonds with Britain then made him want to join in. Manipulating the threat of submarine warfare, he brought his country into the war. The German generals now told their leaders they could not continue to fight.

Without the United States' entry, Germany would probably have continued fighting, and a more equal peace might have been negotiated – and that would have been a better outcome for the world. With America in the war, however, there was no alternative but German surrender. The British and French also knew they should make peace, as the longer war endured the greater American power over them would be. There had been two main possible counterfactual outcomes of the war. First, Germany might have achieved its early knockout blow in France, forced the British out of France, and then turned to Russia. With success there, the British would probably have come to terms and accepted German predominance on the continent. Second, had Germany not escalated its submarine warfare, it might have kept America out of the war. Then there could have been a negotiated peace when the Germans, French, and British all realized victory was not possible. Either eventuality would likely have avoided a Nazi rise to power, World War II, and much else besides. Once neither of these counterfactuals emerged, however, the disparity in economic power between the two blocs determined the final result: the gamble on a short war had failed.

Why did the Soldiers Fight?

This may have been a war precipitated by elites, but it was fought by the masses. How and why did soldiers and civilians sustain such military power? The war impacted the warriors most. Why did they fight and why did they continue fighting, as they faced enormous risks?

To some extent in this martial civilization, it was routine. Countries had persistently made war; it was normal, and it was normal for young men to obey orders and go off to fight. A mixture of enthusiasm and disciplined routine began this war. Trained reservists used to military discipline could quickly enlarge professional armies. Their ranks were supplemented during the first year or two by volunteers, a product of the initial nationalist war enthusiasm. The number of German volunteers rose to 308,000 by the beginning of 1915. At first, the British, without many reservists, relied almost entirely on untrained volunteers, getting as many as they could handle – a remarkable 2.4 million in the first eighteen months of the war. High unemployment helped the first wave at the beginning of the war, but the biggest wave came in early September, when it was becoming clear the war would not be just a walk in the park (A. Gregory, 2003: 79–80). Volunteering then began to decline, and conscription was introduced everywhere. Britain lagged, only introducing it in 1916. No country had difficulty in enforcing conscription to raise the required numbers of soldiers. Only a few minority populations seemed reluctant – such as Irish Catholics and French-Canadians. There were five main reasons for compliance.

(1) Young men were enveloped by a militaristic culture that depicted wars as normal, honorable, heroic, and glorious. The stories read by British schoolboys were about the glory of empire and navy – and the heroes with whom the reader could identify always survived, to be garlanded with glory. Forty-one percent of British boys belonged to organizations such as the Boy Scouts or the Boys' Brigade. Britain, like Europe as a whole, was used to military drills.

(2) Adventurous motives kicked in, in the form of desire for escape from the drudgery of mundane working or middle-class life, and a quest for adventure

among young males. They did not envisage adventure as bringing death; it did not bring death in adventure comics and books.

(3) Recruits signed up believing this was a legitimate war of self-defense. This is what their governments, local notables, and the mass media told them, and they had no alternative sources of information on foreign countries. Other countries had attacked them or were "strangling" them (the German version) and God was on their side. After the war started, they perceived it as the defense of civilization against barbarism, helped along by publicity of enemy atrocities. Germans were enraged by the *francs tireurs* – the French and Belgian guerrillas killing their soldiers out of battle – then by the British blockade that starved them. German atrocities in Belgium and Northern France enraged the British and French. Although soldiers' insecurities and propaganda exaggerated atrocities, nonetheless, some were real.

(4) Recruitment was local. Volunteers signed on in local units, for example in the British "Pals' battalions," and their commitment was to people they knew and notables they deferred. They were honored and partly financed by their local community. Peer-group pressure to enlist urged not being a shirker. To be a man was an important emotional drive, especially as reflected in the eyes of women, reinforced by their white feathers. This was local rather than national reinforcement.

(5) Steady pay was a factor at first, and it continued among the poor, as the war soon brought full employment (Silbey, 2005: 81, 123; Winter, 1986: 29–33).

Although some of these motives were expressed in nationalistic terms, their substance had been present among recruits to European armies over most of the previous millennium: a militaristic culture; supposedly barbaric enemies; local community pressures enforced by respected local notables; masculinity; adventure; steady pay; and encouragement from social hierarchies.

They were not initially afraid, for they expected to win quickly. Once at the front, however, war was not at all like the adventure stories. Death came raining down, but rarely through heroic personal combat. It came normally from long-range artillery fire. It was unbearable to cower down before it in trenches or areas near the rear with almost wholly unpredictable chances of dying. Officers were convinced that the experience shattered most of their men and that only about 10 percent of their soldiers had the "offensive spirit" to attack the enemy at all. Killing was very hard to do, apart from those who manned the artillery batteries (Bourke, 1999: chap. 2, 73). The armies maintained their cohesion nonetheless. At the front, the intimacy of the soldiers' living conditions and their extreme shared experience and interdependence helped reinforce comradeship. A man on his own was a dead man; his unit was a support group, sometimes even a surrogate family. Again, there was a combination of comradeship and hierarchy, the traditional dual organization of military power. Unfortunately, there was no systematic research on this until the classic World War II *American Soldier* studies. Volume II of that project revealed that most American infantrymen said that their primary motivation during combat derived from the strong emotional ties that developed within the unit rather than any more general social commitment to either the army as a whole or to national ideology (Stouffer et al., 1949).[4] This was probably also the case in World War I, say Smith, Audoin-Rouzeau, and Becker (2003: 98–100), although they also detect some nationalization occurring among French troops. Because local dialects blocked communication, a common "trench slang" appeared. Army meals forced a common "French" diet on men whose prior cuisines had been regional. French soldiers imbibed more French national culture as the war progressed.

The intensification of national cages charted in Volume II meant that soldiers had a banal sense of national identity, seeing themselves as straightforwardly German, French, British, and so forth. Nonwhite colonial troops, however, did not. Anzacs discovered through their conflicts with martinet British officers that they also were not British. Almost all bought into the notion that this was a defensive war, so national identity became patriotic defense.

This was obviously so for French soldiers. Audoin-Rouzeau & Becker (2002: chap. 5) argue that most French soldiers believed they fought in a just cause, defending civilization against barbarism. They believed God had blessed their cause. Other French historians are skeptical, doubting that ideological commitment was very relevant to soldiers' experiences in the trenches. Maurin suggests that by 1916, the *poilus* ("hairy ones") had forgotten why they were fighting. They fought because they were told to and because this resonated amid the disciplining hierarchies to which they were accustomed: class, state, school and Church (1982: 599–637). Smith et al. (2003: 101–12) detect French patriotism of a more grounded, "banal" type. The poilus felt they had to expel the Boches from France, and being mostly peasants, they appreciated that this required digging trenches every meter of the way. The defense of the soil of France was not an abstract concept for them. They also believed they were defending their families and communities and creating a "New France" for their children. They also demonstrated cultural traditionalism. During leisure hours, they carved and molded wood, metal, and other substances into figurines and bas-reliefs, "conservative and conventional idioms rooted in prewar conformities." Bullets and twisted metal became crucifixes and sculptures of the Sacred Heart, and landscapes and they painted female nudes exactly like those in popular newspapers. Patriotism was revealed more in practice and discipline imposed by routinized authority structures than in abstract rhetoric.

British troops appear closer to Maurin's model. Their defense of Britain was not so direct, for they were fighting abroad. Their sense of being British included a measure of patriotism, but they also complied because they were used to obeying their social superiors. They exhibited deference to officers provided the officers treated their own authority as normal and did not

[4] As we will see in Chapter 14, this may not have been true of all World War II armies. Despite similar conclusions (influenced by the *American Soldier* research) of Shils and Janowitz (1948) on the German Wehrmacht, more recent research has suggested that large numbers of German soldiers were strongly motivated by Nazi ideology.

condescend to them (Bond, 2002). These were all still hierarchical societies, now buttressed by strict military discipline. Austria-Hungary had probably the least popular commitment to the regime. By 1917, the politically conscious among the minority nationalities knew they would be better off in defeat than victory, yet they fought almost to the end; it was difficult to do otherwise. All the hierarchies were in place, and people did what they were told because that was how the world worked.

One important source of legitimacy for the authority structure was they were not asking the men to do anything that the officers – or at least the visible junior officers – were not. Officers led by example, and their casualty rates were higher than their men's were. In Britain, the lower middle class, in commercial and clerical jobs, were more likely to sign up to fight than workers were. Because they were also healthier and more likely to pass the medical and thus be assigned front-line tasks, they were more likely to die. Recent Oxford and Cambridge students, the elite of the junior officer corps, were the most likely of all to die, as were the graduates of St. Cyr and the École Normale Superieure, some of whose cohorts suffered a 50 percent casualty rate (Winter, 1986; Smith et al., 2003: 69). As the carnage continued, all armies had to expand their officer corps, and more were promoted from the ranks. Combat became a more class-leveling experience, enhancing the sense of comradeship. The major inequity was urban-rural: industrial workers, especially skilled workers, were often in protected occupations and were less likely to be conscripted and killed than peasants and farm laborers, whose families could work the farms while their men fought. This inequity was widely resented in rural areas, undercutting potential postwar class unity between workers and peasants. In these ways, potential class discontent was avoided. All of this was later to fuel fascism.

Naturally, soldiers' motivations varied. Most tried to keep their heads down, a few were superpatriots, a few viscerally hated the enemy, some remained excited by high-octane masculine adventure, and some just liked killing people (Ferguson, 1999: 357–66; Bourke, 1999). However, the notion of the pursuit of glory did not last long in the trenches. The soldiers' postwar reluctance to talk about their war experiences involved consciousness that their behavior – sometimes cruel, sometimes cowardly, most often prudent – had not been consistent with supposed warrior ideals. Authoritative answers are not possible, however, and scholars of violence in general are divided: some believe that human beings dislike violence, especially killing, and are very poor at it (Collins, 2008); others believe they adore it. Whatever the "natural" human dispositions, human societies develop elaborate social organizations and legitimacy routines that make killing on a mass scale a whole lot easier (Malesevic, 2010) – especially in traditionally warlike Europe.

At the front, there was more resignation than enthusiasm. Death or injury were substantial risks; more than half of the French soldiers were wounded twice or more. Most men were intermittently terrified and enduringly emotionally damaged. Alcohol and tobacco helped, although psychiatric medicine was rudimentary and there was no real diagnosis of suffering soldiers. The British and Americans recognized "shell-shock," the French *commotion* ("concussion") or *obusite* ("shellitis") (Audoin-Rouzeau & Becker, 2002: 25), but the military and medical authorities often assumed these were covers for shirking. In World War II, "combat exhaustion" was thought to render most American soldiers ineffective after 140–180 days, and 1 in 10 American soldiers were hospitalized for mental disturbances. In the Great War, soldiers served continuously for much longer periods. Keegan says this war revealed a psychological threshold among soldiers above which they would not willingly engage in further offensives, and that all the main armies had reached this threshold by the summer of 1918, except for the recently arrived Americans, who were therefore able to decide the issue (1978: 335; 1999: 331, 338, 348–50, 401). Demonstrations of nationalism or patriotism seemed in bad taste in such an environment and were discouraged by the soldiers.

Most of the rural Bavarians studied by Ziemann (2007) served in fairly quiet zones. Their letters home revealed them as reluctant warriors, not nationalists, in favor of peace from 1917 onward. Class consciousness was strong, because the soldiers saw their officers as abusive, arrogant Prussians. They were held in place by harsh discipline, alleviated by privileged leaves to return to their farms at times of seasonal pressure.

Despite the horrors of the trenches, discipline and comradeship meant compliance with orders. Surrendering was dangerous because the enemy response was unpredictable. In the heat of battle, many who threw down their arms were killed by their captors, specialized "trench-cleaners" consumed with rage at the deaths of their friends or fearful that escorting prisoners back through no-man's land was too dangerous (Audoin-Rouzeau & Becker, 2002: 40). Surrendering was safer in large numbers, and this only happened at the end of the war. Russians were surrendering massively in 1917, and from August 1918 German surrenders on the Western Front rose almost fourfold (Ferguson, 2006: 131).

Deserting was risky, too: you might be caught and summarily shot. The rate of French desertions was only 1 percent (Maurin, 1982: 522). It was higher in Italy and Russia, but not considered a serious problem by the high commands (Wildman, 1980: 203–45; Ferro, 1972). It was probably highest in the Ottoman armies, where the authorities lacked the infrastructures to catch them. Turkish and Kurdish soldiers might melt away if they were stationed near their homes, but at the front survival was seen as staying within the command structure rather than stepping outside of it. Front-line troops were better supplied with food, alcohol, and tobacco than were civilians. In the winter of 1917–1918, mass meetings of British soldiers protested that although they risked their lives for their country, their wives and children were not fed properly back home.

Officers gradually realized that morale was higher if soldiers got rest, leisure, and leave. A secure material routine reinforced the sense of unit loyalty that developed across most armies. It was the only available protective environment, enveloping the soldier (Keegan, 1978: 274–8, 314–7). It was a true cage (making me realize that the caging metaphor I use for nation-state is only a limited tendency), in which the well-fed animals felt more secure inside than outside, and where they couldn't see far outside the cage in any case. Maurin's French veterans say they knew virtually nothing of the overall conduct of the war beyond what they read in newspapers brought in from the rear (1982: 581–97). Middlebrook's (1972) British veterans of the Somme saw only a few yards in each direction, and their eyewitness accounts add up to a chaotic, incomprehensible battle. New recruits at the front were better informed and more nationalistic, as there was far more propaganda back home than at the front. The soldiers' communications and logistics were controlled by the chain of command. That, rather than an independent ideological commitment, is why most soldiers fought to the end.

Thus, there were few mutinies, at least until the final weeks of the war. In the British, German, Ottoman, and American armies there were almost no mutinies. The most serious incident in the British army was behind the lines at Etaples in the Pas de Calais, directed not against the generals but against abusive military police and non-commissioned officers (NCOs). Australian troops stood up for themselves, although some of their protests were defined by British officers as mutinies. Slightly more than 3,000 British soldiers were sentenced to death for desertion, cowardice, mutiny, or other offences, although only 346 sentences were carried out. However, this was more than the French total of executions and seven times the German figure – although the Italians shot more than twice this number (Ferguson, 1999: 346). These were all small numbers given the size of the armies.

Rather more serious-seeming were the big French mutinies of June–December 1917. They have attracted considerable attention – culminating in William Faulkner's powerful allegorical novel, *A Fable* (1954; for scholarly works, see Pedroncini, 1967, Smith et al., 2003: 117–31). Between 25,000 and 40,000 soldiers, in a rippling movement across one sector of the front, refused to obey orders to implement the aggressive infantry strategy of Marshal Nivelle. In April 1917, he had commenced an intense artillery concentration on a narrow corridor, the infamous Chemin de Dames, that was intended to result in the elusive breakthrough when the infantry charged. All it had actually produced were devastating French losses, so for several weeks the poilus refused to charge against the German lines, demanding better food and shelter and peace (but not surrender). They did not attack their officers, they yielded no ground to the enemy, and they said that if the Germans attacked they would fight back. Virtually no revolutionary propaganda was found among affected regiments, and they were isolated from leftist militants in the rear. Even communications between mutinous units were poor. It was more a wave of wildcat strikes than a mutiny.

Ironically, the wave occurred just after General Nivelle had been replaced by Pétain, who believed frontal attacks cost too many lives. He was switching to the expenditure of machines rather than lives, and he improved soldiers' conditions. Like Pétain, the soldiers sought a change in policy and did not see themselves as stepping outside legitimate channels of protest. Smith et al. suggest they were part of the shift leftward of the French war effort, personified in the capital by the coming to power of Clemenceau, and at the front by Pétain's strategy of *tenir* ("holding on"), which replaced Nivelle's *grignotage* ("advancing through 'nibbling'"). Pétain did address the soldiers' grievances, although forty-nine ringleaders were shot as a warning to future mutineers (Pedroncini, 1967: 194, 215). Despite such incidents, and enormous losses, the French armies held on. By the end of the war, they were in better shape than earlier, and probably in better shape than the Germans.

After the battle of Caporetto, Italian soldiers fled in disarray before the advancing Austrians, but this was a military rout, the result of an incompetent and disintegrating command structure. The Italian army was the least experienced in previous wars. It had expected easy pickings from the imminent collapse of Austria-Hungary, but even in decline, the Habsburgs led a professional army. As in France, the appointment of a more competent and caring commander solved the Italian problem, and enticed most of the "detached" troops to return to the colors. Ottoman soldiers endured two routs, the first when their commander in chief Enver Pasha led them too hastily into a frontal attack on Russian entrenched positions at the beginning of the war in 1914; the second rout at the hands of the British in September 1918 at Megiddo in Palestine. In between times, despite enduring worse conditions than any other armies, they regrouped and fought hard, earning the respect of their adversaries.

As the war progressed, the Austro-Hungarians' ability to resist Russian forces weakened. They collapsed before Brusilov's offensive in 1916, and the Germans had to help. The Austrians now operated autonomously only against Italian and Balkan foes; they were then reprieved by the Russian Revolution. Yet weakness stemmed mostly from poor organization and equipment. In common with Russia, the high command had difficulty amidst primitive communications fighting a two-front war (only the Germans managed this competently), and the officer corps was soon decimated, contending with the centrifugal tendencies of a multinational, multilingual empire. Hungarians largely fought their own war, independently of the Austrian high command. Mutinies were rare in the Austrian and Hungarian core regiments. Even in regiments composed of national minorities – who by 1917 clearly wanted to leave the Dual Monarchy – there were only a few serious incidents, beginning in May 1918, and not on the scale of the French mutinies (Zeman, 1961: 140–6, 218–9; Rothenberg, 1977: 78–84). Falkenhayn and Ludendorff stiffened minority regiments by either integrating them with German units or introducing German officers and NCOs. Prussian sergeant majors persuaded Czechs, Ruthenes, Croats, and others to fight for the Habsburg overlord, even to the end (Stone, 1975: 254–5, 262–3, 272–3). A Czech Legion was formed from POWs held by the Russians to fight against its former overlords, but with this exception the multinational army wavered more because of its weak command structure and poor provisioning than because of unwillingness to fight.

The navies of the two Central Powers did experience mutinies in 1918. The German mutinies resulted from lack of fighting – the fleet had been trapped by the British in and around their ports for two years. There was a mutiny in Austrian naval units at the Gulf of Kotor in February 1918, demanding better conditions and an end to the war. There was a brief skirmish before loyal units suppressed them. Four sailors were executed, and nothing further untoward happened. German and Austrian army mutinies at the end of the war tended to occur among rear echelons rather than at the front (Carsten, 1977: 21). Nevertheless, neither Central Power failed on any occasion to find rear troops willing to implement martial law on civilians – until it became known that the high commands no longer wanted to prosecute the war.

Then everything changed. Now everyday decisions had to be made autonomously by groups of officers and men. Released from hierarchical constraints, they were free as individuals and small groups to make decisions. Would the logistical routine of moving supplies and men continue tomorrow? Should the soldiers sit where they were, inactive and confined to barracks and positions? Was there any point in fighting, when surrender was imminent? Most Austrian soldiers now decided to stop fighting. The German revolution started when Kiel sailors refused under these circumstances to sail out against the British. More generally, officers, soldiers, and sailors now discussed what they should do. Outcomes varied: some obeyed orders, some mutinied, most sat still. Only the first outcome would maintain the regime, as revolts had started and regimes needed troops to suppress them. Once command disruption meant discussion and choice, there would not be enough routinized obedience outside the officer corps itself. As long as army units were engaged in combat, the command structure only rarely allowed what we might imagine to be a mass of soldiers to communicate with one another.

Defeat came with unexpected speed to Germany and Austria-Hungary. When the German Spring and the Austrian June offensives petered out, Ludendorff realized his armies could not hold on for long against the arriving waves of Americans. On August 14, he communicated this to the two monarchs. Weeks later, they were suing for terms. Armistices were signed in early November; in October, the new Habsburg Emperor Charles had virtually abdicated when he granted the right of minorities to form their own states. Once regime organization disintegrated in defeat, soldiers and workers rose up in revolt. In the end, compliance and legitimacy had been less ideologically than organizationally based, and now the organization of discipline collapsed. I deal with these revolutions in Chapter 6.

Total war

By 1916, a few were calling it "total war." The term indicates the mobilization and targeting of national economies and populations. It exaggerates, of course, because the fronts were fairly static, there was little bombing of civilians, and pain was very unevenly distributed across the combatant nations. Yet it does convey the sense that mobilization involved not merely armed forces and their logistics but also much of the economy and civilian life. It was a type of warfare made possible by an industrial, scientific-technological economy coordinated by a modern state. I noted in Volume II, Chapter 1, that nineteenth-century improvements in infrastructural logistics had enabled far greater centralized organization of power resources. Western states had not sought (nor would they have been permitted) to wield even a fraction of these potential powers. Now, however, the deployment of armies of millions armed to the teeth and of navies consisting of many hundreds of technologically complex ships required massive state intervention in the economy. Governments made rapid demographic calculations about the supply of young men to replace the casualties, and the demand for labor of the military, industry, and agriculture. The exercise made them aware of labor shortages, as at the beginning they had all made the mistake of taking too many workers out of necessary industries into the armed forces. To compensate, they sought to increase the supply of female and adolescent labor, and they counted on women to run the farms while their men fought. Governments also attempted to control wages and prices, to mediate between capital and labor, and to plan the volume of armaments, textiles, food, and other goods produced. As the combatant governments still would not negotiate – which would now have been the sensible thing to do – they all intensified their efforts, especially in 1916 when several old regimes were shunted aside. The assumption of power by Lloyd-George in Britain, Clemenceau in France, and generals Hindenburg and Ludendorff in Germany meant commitment to total war. The cage trapped civilians as well as soldiers, if not to the same extent. The war, although half-global, intensified nation-states in the more advanced parts of the world.

The effects on states were dramatic. The jump in the proportion of GDP going to military purposes in wartime resembled the pattern I noted in Volumes I and II throughout recorded history. It rocketed in World War I to hitherto unknown proportions – to 59 percent in Germany, 54 percent in France, and 37 percent in Britain during the highest year (either 1917 or 1918). More backward powers could not manage a level of extraction this high. Russia and Austria-Hungary could only manage a third, and the Ottoman Empire probably only a fifth (Broadberry & Harrison, 2005: 14–15). Much of the activity of private industry and, to a lesser extent, agriculture was now subordinated to the needs of war. Production committees, organized by the state, decided what to produce across a whole range of industries. Total war was state-centric.

Nonetheless, these remained capitalist economies. In all countries except Russia, the crucial production committees were staffed jointly by industrialists and financiers working alongside ministers, civil servants, and generals. In Germany, the high command formally dominated the committees, but in practice the generals had to negotiate with the industrialists and they often failed to control them (Feldman, 1966). British ministers and civil servants negotiated with businessmen and excluded the military (Burk, 1982). In France, all three – ministries, high command, and industrialists – were brought into the central wartime planning organizations, although outside of Paris businessmen enjoyed much autonomy (Smith et al., 2003: 61–4). In the United States, businessmen predominated (Koistinen, 1967), as they mostly did in Italy (Sarti, 1971: 10). Autocratic Russia deviated. When patriotic industrialists set up voluntary War Industries Committees, they were largely ignored. The regime did not intend to share power, even with capitalists (Siegelbaum, 1983: 118–9, 156–8; Gatrell, 2005). Most businessmen had secure national identities, so they became quite patriotic and believed in the war effort, and relations with government were generally quite amicable. Because businessmen had the autonomy to allocate work and investment among themselves, however, the result was cartelization, price-fixing, and high profits. As the state's demand was insatiable, profits kept flowing; patriotism was good for business. Capitalism had not caused the war, but it took command of its economic infrastructure.

War was more total in some countries than others: Japan only fought for the first few months of the war; the United States was only a combatant for the last fifteen months. Both of these countries profited from war, exporting to the Entente countries goods they no longer produced themselves. The United States had been in recession in 1914, but by 1918 its GDP had risen 13 percent (Rockoff, 2005). Italy joined only in 1915, and its south was not greatly affected. If we can believe the figures, the Italian GDP rose 15 percent by 1918 (Galassi & Harrison, 2005). At the other extreme, Belgium and parts of the Ukraine and Belarus were "totalized," occupied and pitilessly exploited by German armies (Horne & Kramer, 2001: Zuckerman, 2004; Liulevicius, 2000).

The combatants also varied in the extent that war could be adapted into their economies. Britain was the most economically advanced of the initial combatants, and it also ruled the waves. Thus, it remained the freest to trade and make financial transactions internationally. As we saw in Chapter 2, the Anglo-Saxons also ruled the international economy. The British state's coordination of the war economy was ad hoc, a set of piecemeal reactions to demands and bottlenecks as they arose, because the adaptability of its market economy did much of the heavy lifting for war. Although the British people did make sacrifices for the war, Britain was not attacked, and it experienced GDP growth of about 15 percent between 1914 and 1918 (Broadberry & Howlett, 2005). As there was full employment and government rationing of what were adequate food supplies, this also translated into improvements in mass living standards. Winter (1986, 1997) calculates that differences in life expectancy between the classes narrowed in wartime Britain, and overall life expectancy improved – despite the slaughter of young men in Flanders. For the rest, war was quite good for them, and redistribution occurred without the need for directly redistributive policies.

France benefitted from the British and American connection, able to borrow and receive raw materials from both. The British and French could also combine their purchasing arrangements from the rest of the world. France possessed a rather decentralized capitalist economy – an advantage in an invaded country – and could bounce back from a difficult 1914 and 1915, involving the loss of its productive northern territories, to a level of recovery that avoided great suffering. Outside of Paris, industrialists, led by the biggest firm in each industry, were given their head to organize their own armaments production – and profits. Because their production boomed and provided full employment, however, and rural France outside of the north also did quite well, most French civilians did not suffer much in the war (Godfrey, 1987; Hautcoeur, 2005; Smith et al., 2003: 60–8). Thus, two-thirds of the original Entente took total war in stride.

It was different in Russia, as it was for the Central Powers. The war totaled their economies. Germany channeled more of its economy into war needs than any other country, and most consistently privileged its military over civilians. It also suffered under an effective British blockade isolating it from the international economy. Despite looting the resources of conquered Eastern European regions – or whatever was left after the retreating Russians laid waste to the countryside – its national income declined by a third during the war. By 1918, coal production was 83 percent and iron and steel 53 percent of what they had been in 1913. For the poorer urban population, the major problem was getting food. Although Germany had advanced industries, its agriculture was not modern, being divided between large-scale estates and small peasant farming. It was difficult to get landowners or peasants to release their surpluses at prices the urban working or lower middle classes could afford, rather than to the more profitable black market, which in Germany became very big, although it did not in Britain or France. In Berlin – especially if we allow for the black market – inflation rocketed; this did not happen in either London or Paris (Manning, 1997: 258–60; Ritschl, 2005). The difficulties were even greater in Austria-Hungary, also blockaded, with less industry and poor coordination between its provinces. Output declined, agricultural districts hoarded food, and the urban population starved. Although the state started the war absorbing more than 30 percent of GDP, the collapsing economy meant the government could extract less and less from it (Schultze, 2005).

The Ottomans ruled over an agrarian economy, and lacked the infrastructural power to extract more resources. They could only finance their war with enormous deficits (Pamuk, 2005) and by seizing the assets of the massacred Armenian population. This backward empire could not really reach up to total war – except for its genocide against the Armenians (Mann, 2005: Chaps. 4–5). In withstanding all Entente attempts to take the Dardanelles, however, which controlled access to the Black Sea, it made sure that Russia remained blockaded, unable to receive supplies year-round from its allies. This added to Russia's economic woes caused by major losses of territory, peasant hoarding, and chronic transport difficulties, which I will detail in the next chapter. As we see there, the Russian crisis was of an order of magnitude greater than that in other countries.

Some say democracy coped better with total war. Feldman (1966) says that although Germany's military machine was more efficient, its authoritarian government was incompetent: democracies were better at organizing industry for total war and distributing food and other materials to soldiers and civilians. Neiberg (2005:7) agrees, saying that Britain, France, and the United States won the war because they "depended less on the authority of antiquated monarchical systems" (cf Winter, 1997: 10–11, Offer, 1989). Others disagree: Ferguson (1999: 257–81) remarks shrewdly that if the Entente was more efficient as well as having much greater resources, the war would have been over much quicker. There were Entente as well as Central Power blunders – for example, the huge, purpose-built but useless French arsenal at Roanne, and British shell shortages. Adamthwaite (1995: 25ff) says French diplomacy was dominated by "muddle and confusion," its tax revenue system was inadequate, and its financial practices antiquated. The rise of real wages in Britain may indicate an inability to pour surpluses back into the war effort. Some have seen the German food distribution system as producing rotting surpluses in military warehouses as the towns went short, with too many under-coordinated agencies failing to achieve equitable distribution of goods and services (Bonzon & Davis, 1997; Winter, 1997: 21–2). Yet others say the opposite: Allen (2003) praises the German food-delivery administration. He says it took care to consult with civil society groups, including the socialists. Despite the deficiencies of the rationing system, most Berliners preferred it to the black market. So who was more efficient?

For Germany and Austria, additional difficulties were presented by the blockade, backwardness of agriculture, and a war fought against the odds that had to privilege the military and war industries over civilians and other industries. For the government to cope with this and be seen to be distributing food adequately, stopping a burgeoning black market, was virtually impossible. The incompetence was in declaring war in the first place, not in its prosecution when things got difficult. Without some more precise comparative measures, we cannot rank the countries in effectiveness, except that Russia would be at the bottom and Britain at the top – not coincidentally, the least and the most economically advanced countries. If democracy did make a difference, it was at the margin. The essential difference was level of economic development. The disparity in economic resources between the two sides, exacerbated by Britain's military ability to blockade the Central Powers, put pressures on their war administrations that Britain, France, and the United States did not have to face. Less democracy than bigger economic resources constituted the crucial difference.

The impact on civilians: Support for the war

We cannot be precise about public opinion, because there were no national elections or opinion polls but plenty of censorship. If discontent was expressed, the government suppressed it. The establishment was generally loyal, and most political parties and pressure groups supported the war. There was some early positive enthusiasm for war, especially among the middle and upper classes, but there was also anxiety and alarm. In Britain, letters to newspapers expressed varied sentiments: Welsh writers often lacked enthusiasm, and many English correspondents said they would have preferred neutrality to war. They also expressed more hostility to Russia and Serbia than to Germany. The supposedly "massive" pro-war demonstration on the August 3 bank holiday on the eve of war turns out to have been only between 6,000 and 10,000 strong, in a city of almost 7 million. "War enthusiasm" in Britain in August 1914 was just a myth (Gregory, 2003). Mueller (2003: 66) says that British and German people felt simultaneously "fear and enthusiasm, panic and war-readiness." Everywhere, war was most commonly seen as a necessary evil (Ferguson, 1999: chap. 7). Nationalism was there, but it was not turned into hatred of the national enemy or very aggressive.

Becker (1985: 324) says that the French Union Sacrée had a narrow basis: France had been the target of foreign aggression and needed to be defended; beyond that, politics remained divisive. Different political tendencies gave their own interpretations of the war. Socialists managed to weasel their way around their pacifist tendencies by declaring that they were not fighting against the German people, only against its reactionary leaders and capitalist class. Becker (1977) examined French childrens' essays and found big regional differences and more support for the war in urban than rural areas. Popular support grew, however, as the war began and President Poincaré convinced the public that Germany was the aggressor. Then propaganda kicked in, mostly transmitted through voluntary patriotism and self-censorship of the editors and journalists themselves, who wrote of unbroken military success laced with heroism. Eventually, the French public learned to decode the real meaning of reports such as, "Our brave young lads are far from beaten. They laugh, joke and beg to be allowed back to the firing line." This meant a defeat – all these victories yet the front line did not move! Yet what was the alternative? Almost everyone wanted peace, and leftists, strikers, and others intermittently demanded it, but German leaders were not offering peace, and the one element of the Union Sacrée that survived was the idea that peace must not be bought at the price of defeat (Becker, 1985: 325, quote from 38).

Many Germans later remembered the August Experience of 1914 as a moment of intense national solidarity, the final accomplishment of German unification. Yet Verhey (2000; cf Ziemann, 2007) shows this was also a myth. There was much government propaganda; those who did approve of the war had license to publicize their views, but dissenters were censored. There was a carnival atmosphere in cities that lasted about six weeks, and then faded. Urbanites were more warlike than villagers; workers and peasants were more pacific than the bourgeoisie and the educated. The real enthusiasts were young, middle-class urban males. What benefits Germans expected from the war differed according to their class and their politics. Conservatives hoped the war would suppress class struggle and bring a patriotic rallying around the flag and the regime. Liberals and socialists hoped the war would bring more progressive benefits to the people, especially once it was recognized that this was total war involving major sacrifice from the masses. Germans hoped subjects would become citizens; the French hoped for a new France; and the British a land fit for heroes. They were all hoping to make a fuller transition from subject to citizen. The right of the German Social Democratic Party and perhaps most of its working-class supporters had no difficulty combining socialism and patriotism. The Socialist Center would have opposed the war had not they feared that this would give the government grounds to suppress the party. Only far leftists voiced outright opposition, although their deputies still voted for bills to finance the war. It was difficult to oppose the war without embracing unpopular defeatism, as the enemy was not seeking peace. Only in Russia, Italy, and the United States did substantial socialist groups stick by their principles and denounce the war. Practical politics generally triumphed lamentably over principles.

Most people endorsed their leaders' call to arms. Few had international experience that might have led to firm alternative views. In that absence, defense of little Belgium, democracy (Britain), the Republic (France), our rightful place in the sun, our spiritual idealism (Germany), or even of the monarchy (Austria-Hungary) could initially justify much. Negative views of the enemy as criminals or aliens grew. The French were seen as decadent, materialistic, and corrupt; Germans were regimented and hostile to liberty; Britons were rapaciously capitalistic; Russians were Asiatic, corrupt, living under despotism, with a primitive religion. The Russian specter was especially useful in Germany because it could rally round Catholics as well as Protestants, liberals and socialists as well as conservatives; Britain's alliance with Russia was seen as a betrayal of western civilization (Hewitson, 2004: chap. 3; Nolan,

2005: 2–6, 47–8; Mueller, 2003; Verhey, 2000:118, 131). Nationalism had not been responsible for the war; aggressive nationalism was the consequence of the war.

Audoin-Rouzeau and Becker (2002: chap. 5) note that the war was seen as a "crusade," a "struggle between civilisation and barbarity," everywhere the enemy was believed to be committing atrocities against civilians – murders, rapes, mutilations, and deportations. The scale of death was not just the product of technology; it needed murderous men, as well. There were racial stereotypes of the enemy: French troops claimed Germans smelled bad and gave racial-science explanations of this; Germans denounced the racial treason of the British and French, whose nonwhite colonial troops in Europe they accused of cannibalism. Isabel Hull (2005) says that the German military had already devised an "institutional culture" of a "war of annihilation," swift, decisive, ruthless, savage in destroying the enemy, in order to compensate for its lack of numbers and vulnerability to two-front warfare. Yet Russian and Balkan armies seem to have been equally terrible toward civilians, and all armies raped women and shot prisoners. The British blockade could be seen as the greatest atrocity: it lasted beyond the war's end, until June 1919, and is estimated to have killed more than half a million civilians. This was a brutal war.

The first string of victories brought more enthusiasm in Germany, visible through flag flying in working-class neighborhoods. However, the war's stalemate then dissipated this. Germans who still favored the war shifted from open demonstrations of enthusiasm to grim determination to just keep going. After the German surrender, the military tried to shift the blame to German civilians, who it claimed had failed to maintain this determination – the stab-in-the-back myth.

The impact on civilians: Suffering and class conflict

As the war continued, it bit deeper in the more "totaled" countries. Vienna had the biggest problems, as Hungary and other regions stopped sending it food. The government might impose price controls on food, but the farmers could sell at higher prices to merchants who used the black market to sell to the wealthier. Food queues were long and ubiquitous. As shortages increased, so did desperation, black markets, criminality, and recriminations among neighbors. "In this war the enemy was not Russia, France or Britain, but one's neighbours and colleagues," says Maureen Healy (2004). Vienna's ethnic tensions were exacerbated by the gradual breakdown of essential services. Ethnic stereotypes of the "profiteering Jew" and the "Russophile Czech" grew, making enemies out of much of the Viennese population. Young men who did not enlist but stayed in the city were attacked as "shirking Jews" or "conspiring Czechs." Under the pressures, even the family weakened. Fatherly authority ceased to define manhood or legitimate the monarchy; masculinity existed only at the front.

Women had to keep the family together, yet were still denied legitimacy as family heads. Healy concludes that Viennese society had collapsed under the pressure before the war ended.

Whereas British men consumed around 3,400 calories throughout the war, German men's intake fell to less than half this amount, with women's intake even lower. Belinda Davis (2000) describes food protests occurring in Berlin from early 1915, culminating in October, as enraged women stormed markets for scraps of potatoes or bread. British blockade, mass conscription, confiscations of livestock, brittle transport and storage systems, and failure to regulate prices all combined to generate serious urban food crises. The British blockade came into full force in March 1915: the collapse of animal feed and fertilizer imports was particularly damaging, contributing to a fall in Germany's agricultural production of at least 40 percent (Offer, 1989). Beginning in 1916, Berlin's mortality rates began to rise dramatically, generating an enduring demographic crisis absent from London and Paris, which saw more temporary crises – London in 1915, Paris in 1917 (Winter, 1997: chap. 16). The German authorities tried hard to respond with improvements in food distribution. Keith Allen (2003) says that an impressive array of municipal authorities and voluntary organizations provided midday meals and ensured bread supplies in Berlin. There were also attempts to extend welfare state provision for the family, with a Family Aid scheme and increasing attempts by local authorities to pay unemployment benefits (Daniel, 1997: 176–81). All this brought the regime some extension of legitimacy.

Things got worse as the war wore on, however. Rations got smaller: the regime could not persuade or coerce farmers and merchants to supply food at affordable prices rather than at higher prices on the black market. This brought inflation and sliding regime legitimacy from 1916 onward. Police reports singled out working-class women as showing most discontent, for they could not be easily sanctioned (by being sent to the front, for example) and they were responsible for the difficult task of putting food on the family table. They staged numerous demonstrations. Food shortages undercut attempts to get more women into the war industries, as did the conservative attitudes of German employers. What was the point of a low wage if there was nothing to buy with it? Better to put one's efforts into illegal means of getting food (Daniel, 1997: 196). The result was a labor shortage as well as a food shortage. Swelling discontent also meant that the authorities felt forced to extend their propaganda and surveillance apparatuses. Discontent was not necessarily leftist. There were calls for a "food dictator" with the power to force "internal enemies," such as farmers and merchants, into more patriotic behavior, and there was little class solidarity between workers and peasants (Moeller, 1986). Germans and Austrians both voiced anti-Semitic stereotypes of the food hoarder (K. Davis, 2003: 132–5; Daniel: 1997: 253). Populism could veer left or right.

These difficulties led to more solidarity, at least among the urban populace. Suffering breached class distinctions, with lower middle-class people experiencing shortages alongside workers. Keith Davis (2000: chap. 3) reports much middle-class sympathy for the protests of "women of lesser means." Jeffrey Smith (2007) sees a growing "nationalist vernacular," a patriotic populism emerging in opposition to the Wilhelmine regime, initially led by the middle class but then uniting Germans across class lines, shattering the status- and class-ridden world of the monarchy. Nationalism was capable of metamorphosis. This transformed ideology achieved a kind of success with the establishment of the dictatorship of Hindenburg and Ludendorff in late 1916, making the kaiser irrelevant, and the replacement of Bethmann-Hollweg as chancellor by Michaelis, credited with improving food distribution. This was a top-down attempt to displace populist discontent, and it partially worked. Populism was not yet opposed to class rule. Yet Smith sees the revolution of November 1918 (discussed in the next chapter) not as a disjuncture caused by a suddenly lost war but as a steadier intensification of this rising nationalist vernacular – although women did experience discontinuity, having been politically active during the war but marginalized when political parties and unions returned at war's end.

War-industry wages held up better. Governments ensured that skill differentials narrowed, and women's wages came closer to men's as they entered heavier, better-paid industries and male wages fell. However, subsistence became harder in most places. The housing stock deteriorated under pressure from refugees from war zones and movement into war industries. Inflation rose faster than wages, and mass living standards in Russia and the Central Powers declined beginning in early 1916, then more rapidly in 1917 as blockades bit. In France, full employment and overtime tended to compensate for the decline in real wages, the families of soldiers received welfare benefits, and the peasant economy did well as prices rose. French capitalists made big profits, although workers and peasants were able to screw back a basic adequacy of living standards. Becker (1985) presents French official surveys showing civilians managed to avoid real economic hardship. Ordinary British people did better, and Americans prospered with full employment, national self-sufficiency, and the export of goods and credit to the Entente. The Central Powers suffered once the British blockade became effective. Russia suffered once the Turkish-German blockade was effective and its distribution system became overloaded by the demands of moving food to the towns, raw materials to the manufacturing centers, soldiers to the front, and refugees out of the war zones (for France, see Smith et al., 2003; Gallie, 1983: 231; for Russia, Gatrell, 2005; Ferro, 1972: 19–22; Hasegawa, 1981: 84–6; for Germany, Moore, 1978: 282–4; Feldman, 1966: 472; Daniel, 1997: chap. 3; for Britain, Routh, 1980: 136–46; I. McLean, 1983: 168; for a comparison between Germany, Britain, and the United States, see Bry, 1960: 191–214, 306–9; for comparisons between Paris, London, and Berlin, see Winter & Robert, 1997).

Work conditions worsened as people labored harder for longer hours. Women worked particularly hard, brought into industry and agriculture to replace departing soldiers, and still providing domestic labor, and in the worse-off countries scavenging for food. Women also knew they would be kicked out of industry once the war ended. Work discipline became more authoritarian. Greater coercive powers were lodged with employers, backed by ministries and military authorities. Emergency measures restricted health and safety codes, especially for women and adolescents. Labor market and trade union freedoms were mostly suspended. Foreign workers, common in Germany and France, were badly treated.

In Germany, whether the war exacerbated class inequality has been much debated. Kocka (1984: chap. 2) asserted that it did, but has been challenged by Ritschl (2005), who shows that although the share of wages fell in armaments, it rose in some other industries. Because there was full employment and rentiers and those living off wealth suffered through declining share and especially bond values, overall in Germany, as in other countries, inequalities narrowed (Manning, 1997). Many believed that profits in industry and agriculture were enormous, pursued to the detriment of the war effort. Rationing was introduced, but was perceived as unfair when distribution systems broke down and black markets for the wealthier flourished (Feldman, 1966: 63–4, 157, 469–70, 480–4). German farmers were adept at pushing up prices by withholding food supplies from the towns. As war bit hard into living standards and reduced caloric intake, workers' ability to work productively declined. Indeed, the better health of workers in the Entente countries must have been an advantage in industrial productivity and war-making capacity. In the cities, some Germans could not find enough food and others consumed conspicuously. The experience brought closer the living standards of workers and the lower middle classes. Capital and labor seemed revealed as two great polarized camps, as the Communist Manifesto had predicted but peacetime had not confirmed. Nationalism had seemed to trump class consciousness in 1914 and 1915, but then this shifted toward uneasy cohabitation between the two. Discontented groups often led by leftists were developing a more populist version of nationalism, wresting possession of it from the upper classes. This was not class trumping nation but class capturing nation, bending it toward more progressive purposes. Only in Russia did this fully occur, although we can detect it as a tendency almost everywhere.

In Germany, however, it touched the countryside less, as peasants could better survive, even benefit from, food shortages. Class relations were more transparently coercive. Employers could call on the state to suppress dissent over issues such as arbitrary dismissal, transfer, downgrading skills, and bonuses for overtime, shifts, and arduous and dangerous work (very contentious in armaments). This created the impression of an all-powerful, integrated ruling class and state elite. Once the war ended, it might weaken capital's ability to organizationally outflank worker and peasant movements, for then both sides would be organized at the national level. Before the war, capital had also possessed considerable transnational organization. The war, for a time, ended this. Capital was becoming trapped in the terrain of the state.

Also contributing to malaise were the emotional constrictions of war – food shortages, the lack of variety in consumption and leisure, interruptions in life projects, the absence of young men. Yet deprivations, inequalities, and coercion did not lead to overt class conflict during the war – except for Russia. There was more trouble in neutral countries, suffering lesser economic hardship, no violent deaths, and little emotional deprivation. Strike rates did begin to rise in the combatant countries for which we have data during the last two years of war, but they were nowhere near back to prewar levels, and they were not rising as fast as in neutral countries such as Norway, Sweden, and Spain (Meaker, 1974: 30–9, 76–95, 141–5). Although deprivation and postwar turbulence were linked, the timing of disturbances was only erratically related to cost of living movements, and the revolutionary core proved to be relatively well-off industries such as metalworking (Cronin, 1983: 30; Feldman, 1977; Meaker, 1974: 38–9).

However, the co-opted party and union leaders could no longer organize much discontent. They could transmit grievances through the state administration, and concessions were made to them to help bolster their authority over the workers. Thus, class dissent through conventional channels had been "organized out," and it was slowly finding new shop-floor organizational forms to express itself. Whatever workers felt about the war, they cooperated. To step outside of cooperation risked officially organized community censure, then repression. Demonstrations and strikes in support of grievances related to work or food shortages were risky. Organizers were often radicals, but they wanted it to seem that antiwar or political sentiments emerged spontaneously from the crowd. If their hand was detected, they would be arrested and conscripted or tried.

Where skilled-trade shop stewards were strong, employers had to conciliate on the shop floor, especially in metalworking and ammunition industries. They were pressed by labor shortages and a desperate need for production: unorganized workers might leave for other employment; organized workers might quietly resist. As long as the stewards kept resistance contained within the plant conciliation might occur, aided by the military or ministry authorities. When employers resisted this, government sometimes tried to pressure them, although not with great success (Kocka, 1984: chap. 4). If workers tried public protest, the government might dismiss, conscript, or try them for sedition. When Karl Liebknecht, the left-wing socialist, voted in December 1914 in the Reichstag against war credits (the only deputy to do so), he was conscripted and sent to the front. British unions were stronger. When Lloyd-George tried to remedy labor shortages by bringing unskilled "dilutees" into skilled jobs, he later commented ruefully, "The actual arrangements for the introduction of diluted labour had to be made separately in each workshop, by agreement with the skilled workers there." The British wartime strike rate was much higher than the German (Ritschl, 2005: 55–7). French unions were weaker: the unions were excluded from government and employer negotiations until late on in the war. If skilled men were returned from military service because industry needed them, they remained under military discipline and their employer could send them back to the front for insubordination, inconceivable in Britain. French conditions then improved as socialist armaments minister Albert Thomas made collective bargaining compulsory and introduced minimum wages. Russian conditions were harsher: workers raising grievances were often threatened with conscription, usually carried out in the case of strikers. Everywhere on the shop floor, workers quietly extended their informal powers, if ultimately contained by union and socialist party leaders and government controls (Smith et. al., 2003; Godfrey, 1987; Becker, 1985: chap. 17; Gallie, 1983: 232–4; Pedersen, 1993, chap. 2, esp. 84–6; Hasegawa, 1981: 86–9; I. McLean, 1983: 73–5, 83–5, 91, 120, 138; Feldman, 1966: 116–37, 373–85, 396, 418–20; Broue, 2005: 53).

Because this was, from about 1916, a people's war, it was demanded and hoped that popular sacrifice would be rewarded with more political and social citizen rights afterward. Nationalism turned progressive. The war was supposedly not one regime against another, but the entire nation defending its security and its values. The biggest political shift came in Britain. About 60 percent of men already had the vote, but in March 1917, all British men (but not women) were granted the vote. In Germany and Austria, this was the first occasion on which socialists had ever been consulted about major policy matters, and the Prussian class franchise was abolished in 1917, although it remained in the other Länder, and the German Reichstag did not get full sovereign powers. Some monarchical despotism remained. In the economic realm, rationing, minimum wages, and regulated prices seemed a possible prologue to social citizenship in Marshall's sense. The coming to power of Lloyd-George and Clemenceau and even the military dictatorship in Germany seemed implicit recognition of the shift.

During the war, more citizen rights were promised, but only vaguely. Lloyd-George promised a "land fit for heroes" – afterward. Austro-Hungarian nationalist movements assumed that they would receive more self-government after the war in return for their sacrifices. The overseas peoples of the empire were also infected by citizenship aspirations. Definite political promises were made in British policy toward the Arabs who revolted against the Ottoman Empire: they would get their own state if they made common cause with British troops against the Empire. Most of them complied. Alas, Perfidious Albion only made them part of the British Empire. Indians and other advanced nationalist movements in the British Empire and French empire made the same assumption and expected more self-government, although there were no definite promises. Again, they were to be deceived. Popular expectations were not raised right across the globe, but in many places within it. This was dangerous for existing regimes – especially if they lost the war. The losers did not have much overseas empire, however, so the dams burst in Europe. The two Russian revolutions of February and October–November 1917 burst first, emboldening militants globally, but in January 1918, it appeared as if revolution itself might spread elsewhere in Europe. I deal with this in Chapter 6.

Conclusion: A pointless Great War

When it was finally over, the three dynastic empires that had started the war were all destroyed, and so was the Ottoman Empire. Nation-states, many of them embodying greater citizen rights, were established almost everywhere around Europe, but the overseas empires remained. British and French power were formally restored, although irreparably damaged, and only Americans and Japanese profited much. The United States had passed from being a major debtor to being the world's banker, owed massive sums by all the European powers. Japan had acquired German colonies in the Far East, jumping-off posts for later expansion in China and across the Pacific. Europe had been deeply fractured by the Great European War after its statesmen had made a series of ghastly errors for which their continent would pay dearly. Power would now begin to shift toward other continents, as more peaceful processes of globalization continued for a time. To understand why they started the war, we must place ourselves back in a culture in which war was considered normal and legitimate, in which states were believed to have survival and security interests that ordinary male citizens were expected to defend with their lives, and in which all obeyed authority figures regardless of how stupid these were – unto death. Such was the Europe of 1914. Aggressive nationalism mainly emerged as a consequence of the war, not its cause. It was then transmuted into a populist nationalism, full of discontents about power inequalities in the conduct of the war, and longing for the war to be ended. The war helped the masses leap onstage.

It was certainly not a rational war, although it had been generated by the culture and institutions of a militarism originally rationalistic and that were still treated as such. Nor were the ensuing peace treaties rationally oriented to achieve both of their principal aims, to break German power and yet find an enduring peace settlement. The war has long been seen in a negative light, as purposeless, led by incompetents – "lions led by donkeys," as the British described their military. Recent historians have sought to rehabilitate the reputation of politicians and generals, and claim that for Britain and France at least, the war was worth fighting (Bond, 2002). I am skeptical. We should condemn these statesmen, including British and even French ones, for their impatience with diplomacy, their folly in leading Europe into war, and then, when it stalemated, their failure again to use diplomacy to negotiate a compromise peace. From their point of view, their pursuit of a combination of strategic security and status – prestige both personal and national – might have seemed rational, but it was callous folly. We should regard their policies as irrational and inhumane. We should condemn the generals who continued sacrificing their soldiers to their meat-grinding gods. Neither the statesmen nor the generals were on the front line, risking their own lives. In modern warfare, elites fight for their own honor with the lives of others; spectator-sport militarism is easy to do. We should take one principal lesson from this war: we should never allow the militaristic culture of that civilization to be made legitimate again so that mass slaughter might be regarded as once again either worthy or necessary.

Rudyard Kipling wrote a moving couplet on the death of his son at the battle of Loos in 1915, the day after his eighteenth birthday:

> If any question why we died
> Tell them, because our fathers lied.
> ("Epitaphs of War 1914–1918," *The Years Between*, 1919)

That was uncomfortably close to the truth. The fathers should have known better. The war had been set in motion by statesmen honoring a war fought by others as the default mode of diplomacy among states. This was the Achilles heel of this multipower-actor civilization, which would soon bring it crashing down to the ground. Yet the war did have a silver lining: it weakened rule by the elders and betters. It was fought, provisioned, and suffered by the masses, who as a consequence were now brought thoroughly onto the stage of citizenship and power in postwar Europe.

Its result – who won, who lost – was not in the end accidental. Although other outcomes might have come out of the first year or two of war, as it ground on it became more likely that the bigger battalions of Western democratic capitalism would win, a victory for their strength more than their virtue. Even if not quite a world or total war, European militarism had shaken the foundations of European society, causing its decline if not yet its collapse. Europe's two greatest empires, Britain and France, had just survived, although the war helped the passing of power to others. It had destroyed despotic monarchy across most of the continent, although other traditional institutions tried to pretend that nothing much had changed. Yet all were being vigorously challenged, as the on-stage masses listened to new ideologies emerging out of war and postwar sufferings. Whether the masses experienced victory or defeat, their participation and sufferings were now to change the world and their own aspirations for the future – as we already saw in Chapter 2 in the case of Indians. Nowhere was this clearer than in Russia.

6 Explaining revolutions: Phase 1, proletarian revolutions, 1917–1923

Introduction: Theories of revolution

On the surface, the twentieth century seems dominated by evolutionary change, as there was considerable material progress through the century. The power structures present at the beginning of the century then diffused globally – capitalism, the nation-state, and (less thoroughly) democracy – but the process did not seem so evolutionary at the time. Two revolutions dominated the first half of the century, launched by the Bolsheviks and Chinese Communists. They inspired further revolutions and counterrevolutions across the globe – including Fascism and the scorched-earth counterinsurgency strategy of the United States. This became a period of rival ideologies sweeping across the globe. The last quarter of the century was then dominated by the unraveling of these revolutions, and (less completely) by the triumph of one ideology.

These were broad trends, transnational, even global. They might be viewed as a *punctuated equilibrium*, general tendencies being suddenly rechanneled by wars and revolutions. Yet with the collapse of the multinational European empires, trends and disruptions were also partially caged by nation-states, each of which experienced war and revolution (or reform) differently, according to the balance of forces in each one of them. This necessitates a nationalist approach that analyzes each major country separately, and also recognizing the transnational diffusion of revolutionary and counterrevolutionary waves across the globe. I discuss the revolutionary and counterrevolutionary waves spreading from Russia into central Europe in this chapter. I discuss the Chinese revolution in Chapter 13, and I discuss the wave it induced in Volume IV, which will also include my final explanation of modern revolutions.

Most definitions of revolution combine the overturning of both political and social or economic relations. I extend this usage, defining revolution as a popular insurgent movement radically and violently overturning at least three of the four sources of social power. The term "revolution" is sometimes defined as a transformation of political power relations alone, as Tilly (1993) does. Thus, he finds no less than 709 cases in Europe alone between 1492 and 1992. I call almost all of these political revolutions, preferring to limit the term "revolution" to the few more transformative cases. Let me note that hitherto, political revolutions had been dominant. In the modern period, these had mostly taken a constitutional form, separating legislative and executive authority according to rules laid down in constitutions or common law. These political revolutions had come in waves ever since the American and French Revolutions, although they had been acquiring more reformist social content through the nineteenth century. The last wave of constitutional political revolutions had come just before World War I, lasting from the failed revolution in 1905 in Russia to the Young Turk seizure of power in the Ottoman Empire in 1908 to the Mexican Revolution of 1910 and the Chinese Revolution of 1911. In all of these, the ideal was overwhelmingly political and not economic. The Bolshevik Revolution fundamentally changed this, and the waves that emanated from it dominated the rest of the twentieth century.

Revolutions are not easy to explain because they are somewhat contingent and unpredictable. When crowds riot in the streets and insurgents arm themselves, the outcome is inherently uncertain. Quality of decision making and leadership obviously matter. Fierce repression or judicious reform might nip the insurgency in the bud so that some potential cases of revolution never come to our attention. Urban revolutions generally start as purely political revolutions and then unsteadily escalate, although most political revolutions do not escalate further. Rural revolutions tend to have more social content and use violence earlier. All this makes explaining revolution more difficult.

Marxism has dominated both revolutions and revolutionary theory in the twentieth century. In this sense, it became, alongside liberal constitutionalism, the first truly global ideology, its adherents believing that its models applied to the globe, leading eventually to a global society. It can be thought of as a secular form of Salvationism, and it gave its cadres ideological power comparable to that of the salvation religions. Noting the contingency of revolutionary disturbances, Marxists have explained them overall in terms of their master-concept, class struggle. Marxism sees revolutions from the English Civil War to the French Revolution as struggles between old feudal classes and the rising bourgeoisie. The first Russian Revolution of February–March 1917 was seen as a short-lived triumph of the bourgeoisie, the Bolshevik Revolution of October–November 1917 was the triumph of the working class, and the Chinese Revolution was the triumph of the peasantry. Marxian interpretations have then supplemented this basic model with analysis of other social groups as well as of organization and leadership on both sides of the barricades. Barrington Moore (1967), clearly influenced by Marxism, offered an analysis in terms of the power relations between social classes and the state. Marxian theories are of the long run, seeing revolution as a consequence of very long-run structural tendencies. However, major Marxian contributions to theory have come from revolutionaries, such as Lenin, Trotsky, Mao, and Che Guevara, and they have added short-term tactics to structural causes.

Lenin's 1920 summary of revolutionary causes in Russia can be our starting point:

> It is not enough for revolution that the exploited and oppressed masses should understand the impossibility of living in the old way and demand changes, it is essential for revolution

> that the exploiters should not be able to live and rule in the old way. Only when the *'lower classes' do not want* the old way, and when the 'upper classes' *cannot carry on in the old way* – only then can revolution triumph (1947 edition: II, 621, his emphasis).

Note his equal emphasis on both main classes: a lower class seeking to overthrow the old order, and an upper class whose resistance becomes enfeebled. It takes at least two to make a revolution.

A second line of theory runs from structural-functionalism, emphasizing social strains, disequilibria, and dissensus as causes of revolution. These conditions, however, are not easy to operationalize, and are much more widespread than revolutions, which are quite rare. This is also a problem for theories focused on relative deprivation felt by either dissident elites or the masses. The J-curve model of relative deprivation has the advantage of being testable, for it suggests that revolutions occur during an economic downturn period following a long period of growth – aspirations rise and are then dashed, making people more discontented. Yet, sometimes this does happen before a revolution and sometimes it does not. It needs stretching to fit either Russia or China, the two main revolutions of the period, because an economic downturn is not the best way to describe two countries devastated by mass mobilization warfare, and China's revolutionary process lasted a full twenty years. These theories suggest that revolutions occur when people are dissatisfied, yet most people adjust to exploitation, however bad it may be, if they feel there is little they can do to improve their lot. Revolutions come when dissatisfied people believe that the ruling regime has weakened to such a point that they can challenge it. The second cause adduced by Lenin acts back upon his first cause.

Recent scholarship has followed Lenin's lead in focusing at least as much on how ruling regimes weaken as on insurgent movements from below. Theda Skocpol began this shift. She explained the French, Russian, and 1911 Chinese Revolutions in terms of geopolitical pressures on states interacting with class conflicts. Thus, she argued, modern revolutions were caused by "(1) state organizations susceptible to administrative and military collapse when subjected to intensified pressures coming from more developed countries abroad, and (2) agrarian socio-political structures that facilitated widespread peasant revolts against landlords" (1979: 154). She saw both of these as necessary causes of revolution, and that combined, they are a sufficient cause. When both are present, revolution necessarily results. She argued that her three states were all fighting costly, losing wars that weakened and divided them, making them vulnerable. This is now generally accepted, but she says that the insurrectionary movement came from agrarian class conflicts and specifically from discontented peasants. This involved her study of three main variables: "the degree and kinds of solidarity of peasant communities … the degree of peasant autonomy from direct day-to-day supervision and control by landlords and their agents …[and] the relaxation of state coercive sanctions against peasant revolts" (1979: 115, 154). This makes sense, but wasn't there another important actor? Was there no bourgeoisie in the case of France, no proletariat in the case of Russia?

Others have added to her approach. Goldfrank (1979: 148, 161) identified four necessary and cumulatively sufficient causes of revolution. Two affected the rulers, two the insurgents: (1) a tolerant or permissive world context where foreign powers will not intervene or will aid the rebels; (2) a consequent political crisis paralyzing the administrative and coercive capacity of the state; (3) widespread rural rebellion; and (4) dissident elite movements in the urban sector. The first three interacted to produce a revolutionary situation; the fourth emerged to effect political and social transformation after the military superiority of the revolutionaries was clear. This last phrase seems to me to suggest a fifth necessary condition, military power superiority. Goldstone (2001) distinguishes three essential conditions for regime survival: (1) whether it has the resources necessary to undertake effectively or with justice the tasks required of it; (2) whether elites are united rather than divided or polarized; (3) and whether opposition elites can link up with protest by popular forces below. Foran (2005), writing about twentieth-century revolutions, identifies five conditions favorable to revolution: (1) dependent economic development; (2) an economic downturn; (3) a repressive, exclusionary, and personalist state; (4) a strong political culture of opposition; and (5) a "world-systemic opening."

These perspectives overlap, emphasizing political divisions within the old regime, generated mainly by external geopolitical pressures. On the insurgents' side, it is necessary that both rural and urban popular classes want major changes and can link up with opposition elites who will head the movement. A few writers have placed the role of the state above all other causes, saying that a state highly repressive but narrowly based (i.e., factionalized), exclusionary, or personalist or a patrimonial state without strong roots in civil society are the most vulnerable. They say that if only class conflict mattered, workers and peasants would attack capitalists and landlords, not the state. For a political outcome, we need political causes (Goodwin 2001; cf Goldstone, 2004). There is some sense in all of these perspectives.

I will not depart greatly from them, although I frame causes in terms of the four sources of social power, all of which assist or hinder revolution. I note also that a state trying to cope with insurgents might be weakened in two different ways: it might be factionalized, unable to present a united front to the insurgents, or it might lack basic infrastructural powers to impose its will across the country. I also stress military causes more. In twentieth-century waves of revolution and attempted revolution, class struggle was important, but so was the ideological cohesion of the opponents, the strength and stance of the existing state, and the balance of military power between the state and other states and between the contending domestic movements. I stress the role of peasants, workers, and soldiers: these were all industrializing countries, which were at least half (sometimes much more than half) agricultural, hence the importance of workers and peasants. Mass mobilization warfare also had a profound effect on the possibility of revolution in the twentieth century. Most revolutions – and all the major ones – came in the course of wars or their denouement, but for revolution, power must be seized violently. The balance of military and paramilitary power within society ultimately determines whether a revolution is successful or not, or whether indeed it deters militants from even contemplating revolution.

My methodology also departs somewhat from conventional models. I follow Foran in comparing revolutions to "non-revolution," in which an attempted revolution failed. However, a nationalist comparative method dominates, taking each national revolution as an independent case and then seeking common causal factors across them all. This method has its strengths, but revolutions have rarely been independent cases. Almost all modern revolutions were led by people who became Marxists, orienting themselves to a theory of history they believed had global application. They had a utopian goal, although this did not prevent them adapting or changing the theory in the light of their own experiences. There was a learning process leading toward new tactics, as there also was among counterinsurgencies. Revolutions interacted with each other through space and time. Moreover, the comparative method is too egalitarian. Two revolutions were far more important than all of the others put together: the Bolshevik and Chinese Communist revolutions immediately sparked off a wave of further attempted revolutions in their macro-regions as well as influencing the world. It is likely that without one or both of them, most other revolutions would not have occurred. Nor was revolutionary time linear; revolutions came in two waves initiated by these two revolutions, and they came during and immediately after the two great wars of the century. So to understand twentieth-century revolutions, we must focus first on the two great ones whose significance dwarfs all others. We must analyze them in their temporal and spatial context, and we must give military power relations a bigger role than do any of the scholars referred to previously in this chapter. The end of World War I saw revolution spread from Russia to central and Eastern Europe, yet these other revolutions all failed. I seek here to explain why.

Reform and revolution in the early twentieth century

The key issue for relatively advanced countries in the first half of the twentieth century was how to satisfy the aspirations of the popular classes – peasants, workers, and the lower middle class – for full citizenship in the nation-state. This concerned all of T. H. Marshall's three forms of citizen rights, discussed at greater length in Chapter 9: civil, political, and social. Participation might have been sought through revolution, although that was rather rare. Far more common was citizenship attained through reform, in which dominant classes and elites were pressured into widening the suffrage, recognizing civil rights and labor unions, and offering welfare to provide a guaranteed standard of living for all within a reformed capitalism. Reform was the norm, not revolution, as we see in Chapter 9.

What paths were taken immediately before the Great War broke out? As I discussed this at length in Chapters 17–20 of Volume II, I here briefly review the background. The second industrial revolution brought bigger corporations and factories, especially in iron, steel, metal manufacturing, chemicals, and mining as well as more urbanization, state bureaucratization, and expanding militaries. The labor force was being homogenized as employees, and its organizational vanguard were skilled factory workers living in working-class districts of cities (and more rural mining communities). Subjected to and resenting much more hierarchical control than in the past, these workers revolted. In all industrializing countries, labor unions were stirring. However, as I argued in Volume II (repeated in Chapter 3), workers might have formed three different types of movements: (1) class organizations that sought to represent the interests of workers as a whole and that marched under Socialist or syndicalist banners; (2) sectional organizations that represented only a particular type of occupation (usually skilled); or (3) segmental organizations that organized on the basis of their present place of employment, on which they greatly depended because their skills and rewards were not easily transferable elsewhere. The second industrial revolution was concentrating the labor force; an employers' offensive was aiming to de-skill sectionally organized craft workers, forcing them into the growing ranks of the semiskilled. This produced more class-based union growth, involving a surge of strikes, socialism, and syndicalism just before the outbreak of the war; labor unrest was on the rise before the war (Silver, 2003: 125–8).

This was not yet a massive threat. By 1914, no labor movement organized half the labor force. Australia had 31 percent unionization, Britain and Denmark 23 percent, Germany 17 percent, then other countries tailed back to the United States with only 10 percent. In the more concentrated metals, mining, chemical, and textile industries unions were stronger, and class consciousness was growing. Yet most unions were led by craft workers whose sectionalism remained strong. New, larger corporations also required skills particular to each firm or sector, in which management and workers had a higher level of mutual dependence. This induced segmental unionism, organized at the level of the firm. Some were company unions – in the United States contemptuously called yellow-dog unions – but others showed independent syndicalist tendencies. Both sectional and segmental unionism tended to undercut class solidarity among workers, and in practice, most labor movements contained elements of all three. I also argued that political exclusion most tilted the balance toward class organization and revolutionary sentiments. If all workers were excluded from political citizenship, this could override sectional and segmental differences to generate avowedly class movements, sometimes espousing revolutionary sentiments – although their actual everyday practices might be more reformist.

Socialist and labor parties were also on the increase everywhere except the United States. Their vote in elections was rising most rapidly just before the war. The German Socialist Party (SPD) easily led the way, by 1912 becoming the largest single party, with 35 percent of the vote. No other socialist or labor party had as much as 25 percent. Because workers often associated the state with repression, they often distrusted national politics. Nonetheless, both unions and socialism or anarcho-syndicalism were growing, increasingly worrying the old regimes of the world, the more alert of which were beginning to devise strategies besides repression that might woo workers away from extremism (see Chapter 9).

Each country blended these tendencies in distinctive ways. As we saw in Chapter 3, the United States had long enjoyed white male democracy, with political exclusion of only African Americans and women. Yet political elites and dominant classes yielded up little economic reform, and employers and government turned more frequently to repression than in other countries, except for tsarist Russia. The United States was an odd combination of democracy and repression, leaving labor more frustrated than socialist. By now, Great Britain and its former white settler colonies had enfranchised most men, and unions and Labour parties were free to organize. Class organizations existed but espoused little socialism. The Anglophone countries offered variants of a lib-lab path to reform. More socialistic variants of this path were found across Scandinavia and in the Netherlands, Belgium, and France. Northwest Europe already seemed to be heading toward the reformism of liberal democracy, free trade unions, and the first stirrings of welfare reform. Spain and Italy were more mixed: although they had parliaments and elections with a wide male franchise, these were corrupt and controlled by local notables. *Caciquismo* was the Spanish term for this top-down form of corrupt class control; *trasformiso* was the Italian word for the executive's ability to bribe parties into forming a compliant set of ministers. Workers could form unions and parties, but their practical exclusion from political citizenship drove them leftward toward socialism and syndicalism. Both countries contained substantial agrarian discontent in some regions. They also had powerful, conservative Catholic Churches. There was some prospect for revolutionary confrontations in both cases.

The German and Austro-Hungarian Empires retained more despotic institutions. They had parliaments with universal male suffrage, but voting was class weighted and the emperor, not parliament, was sovereign. Unions were permitted, but their freedom of assembly and to strike were curtailed by ritual forms that disciplined workers without much resort to violence. The combination created large socialist parties, excluded from participation in government, ostensibly committed to revolution, but moderate in their actual practices. Moreover, the regime and many local authorities were sponsoring welfare reforms to head off socialism and divide the working class.

The most extreme case was tsarist Russia. Despite rapid industrialization that produced the largest factories in the world, the regime refused to yield democratic or economic reform and allowed workers few collective rights. Wholesale exclusion predictably generated revolutionary consciousness among workers, peasants, and even the middle classes. When minimal reform produced more demands from below, repression followed. When Russia was defeated by Japan in the war of 1905, there was an upsurge of revolutionary violence. Although it was repressed, Russia under the last tsar seemed headed less toward reform than another attempt at revolution.

Finally, as noted in Chapter 19 of Volume II, agrarian class relations were varied. By 1910, only Britain had decimated its agrarian population. Only four countries – Britain, Belgium, Australia, and Switzerland – had more employed in manufacturing than in agriculture. The United States still had 32 percent in agriculture, Germany had 37 percent, France 41 percent, and Russia and Austria-Hungary just more than 55 percent (Bairoch, 1982: table A2). These were really dual agrarian-industrial societies. In France, Spain, Italy, and the United States, some peasant regions were radical, others conservative; in Germany and Austria-Hungary, they tended more to conservatism. Russia contained most agrarian discontent, as the abortive revolution of 1905 had revealed.

Before the war, Russia had the most exclusionary regime and then experienced the only successful revolution; Germany and Austria-Hungary practiced somewhat lesser exclusion and then saw failed revolutions; the others, with more inclusion, saw reform. This ordering might suggest that war might not have been a necessary part of the explanation of revolution. Maybe the same outcomes would have occurred even had there been no war. As we saw in previous chapters, the war was not the product of such class relations – it was largely attributable to the traditional militarism of the European powers. Whether class relations would change as a result of the war obviously depended on two major axes of military participation. First, some countries were only marginally involved in the war, such as Japan and the United States. It was unlikely the war would much affect them. Some were totaled by the war – Russia, Germany, and Austria. Second, there were winners and losers. Winning might be expected to legitimize existing power relations, subject only to reforms flowing from a people's war. Losing might have the opposite, delegitimizing, consequence.

The Bolshevik Revolution

Russia was exceptional in two ways: it had the only successful revolution, but also the only case in which revolution broke out during the war and not after it. Revolutionary disturbances among workers, peasants, soldiers, and urban crowds began in late January 1917, and lasted throughout that year. The Romanov dynasty was overthrown in early March, and a Provisional Government came briefly into power in a would-be constitutional political revolution that also brought some ideological transformation. However, there was no economic transformation while the Russian military was still fighting desperately against the Germans. Then in October, the Bolsheviks overthrew the Provisional Government. By the end of 1921, the Bolsheviks had cemented their power, rejected constitutionalism, and were transforming political, economic, and ideological power relations. They had replaced capitalism with state ownership; religion, monarchism, conservatism, and liberalism with an official ideology of Marxism-Leninism; and despotic monarchy, not with a constitutional socialist democracy, but with a despotic party state. Coming as a result of mass popular insurgency, it was clearly a revolution. Indeed, it remains the only accomplished revolution in the history of Western capitalism.

As I indicated, Russia was already in trouble before World War I. Reformers had sometimes succeeded in extracting concessions from the Romanov court – setting up a parliament with restricted franchise (the Duma), setting up conciliation procedures with labor, and so forth. Each time, however, ensuing popular pressure for more concessions alarmed the conservatives who ultimately had the upper hand at court. Nicholas II really did believe in his divine right to rule. The court was driven more by ideology than by the instrumental rationality of how to survive through compromise. Repression and withdrawal of concessions followed. This revealed a somewhat divided state, yet because the reactionaries always won out and liberals and constitutionalists had little power, this was not fatal to the relative coherence of the regime. Yet vacillation ending in repression built up discontent among the people – not to the point where Lenin's two conditions were actually met, but to the point where waves of demonstrations and strikes persuaded conservatives at court to urge Russia's entry into war in 1914 (among other reasons) in order to swamp discontent with a tidal wave of patriotism.

Russia's small revolutionary parties had little initial influence on a popular movement demanding constitutional reform, not revolution. The core of three main socialist factions – Mensheviks, Bolsheviks, and Socialist Revolutionaries or SRs (who were more moderate than their title suggests) – were formed by students, teachers, and some workers (or peasants, in the case of the SRs) relatively well-educated, intellectually minded, trying hard without much success to establish a mass base. Lenin's early theory of a small secretive vanguard party was in reality making the most of a bad job. The Bolshevik Party claimed it had 23,000 members at the beginning of 1917; the real figure must have been much less.

I have analyzed the backgrounds of the top sixty-eight Bolsheviks in 1917, the members of the party's central committees and the Bolsheviks on the

Military-Revolutionary Committee of the Soviets. Of the sixty-one whose parental backgrounds are known, only nineteen were worker or peasant. Only two were women, one of them being Krupskaya, Lenin's wife. Later on two more were added, one of them being Trotsky's wife. The top Bolsheviks were highly educated: only nine left after elementary schooling (out of the sixty-six whose education is known). They were the intelligentsia attracted to general ideologies, but more dropped out of university or technical institute than graduated (nineteen to seventeen), a sign of their disaffection with intellectual orthodoxies. Of the sixty-six whose own occupations are known, fourteen had started as workers, ten had middle-class careers, and six had always combined one or the other with revolutionary activity. This left thirty-six (55 percent) who in adulthood were professional revolutionaries, without any other occupation. The average age at which all sixty-eight had first acquired a police file had been only seventeen (the range being from age thirteen to twenty-seven). Their average age by 1917 was obviously older, at thirty-four years. As Riga (2009) shows on a larger population of leading Bolsheviks, they were also disproportionately Jewish or from Russia's ethnic minorities, with distinctive grounds for alienation from Russian society. This was a *groupuscule* of marginals, going nowhere fast. Persecution had tended to make them more cohesive and committed to a long-term theory of history (for the short-term looked pretty bad). Their utopian, salvationist creed could only become relevant if Russia fell apart. Although many people expected some kind of revolutionary crisis to break out in Russia, almost no one – including Lenin – expected it would lead to a socialist revolution.

Then came the war, like a thunderclap. Russians now experienced the same cycle of popular sentiments as people in the other powers, but speeded up. Patriotic enthusiasm burst out, but barely survived Russia's catastrophic defeats in East Prussia in the first months of the war. Poland was lost, and still the Germans pressed forward (Jahn, 1995). Russian losses were enormous – almost 4 million dead by late 1915. Strikes disappeared as the war began, but only until a strike-wave of July 1915, which came much earlier than in other combatant countries. Repression damped this down. K. Murphy (2005: 225) notes that in a giant Moscow metalworks, arrests by the tsarist security police were far greater than Bolsheviks were to launch in the 1920s. Repression dispersed the revolutionary militants but did not stem worker unrest. A second strike-wave came in the autumn of 1916. In November 1916, moderates in the state Duma warned Tsar Nicholas disaster was coming unless he moved toward constitutional rule. In response, he dissolved the Duma and postponed elections for a year. Like Louis XVI before him, the tsar's reactionary obstinacy was probably a necessary condition for what followed. In response, in early 1917, came a full-scale insurgency while Russian armies were still fully engaged in the war.

It started with a strike-wave in January and February. St. Petersburg was brought to a halt by strikes, demonstrations, and bread riots; Moscow followed.

Women were prominent in a major demonstration on International Women's Day and in bread riots and other demonstrations. The crowds demanded bread, peace, and reform and denounced the tsar personally. They were seemingly without overall leadership. The Duma moderates now asked the tsar to abdicate, hoping to replace him with a more reform-minded royal. He again ignored them, and on February 25th asked the St. Petersburg-region military commander to use all necessary force to suppress the insurgency. The general tried to comply, but his troops mutinied on the 27th, most of the soldiers joining the demonstrators. Then the mutiny spread to Moscow. From then on, the revolutionaries possessed weapons and trained soldiers. An emperor without troops is an emperor without clothes; this was the end for Nicholas.

The tsar's cabinet submitted its resignation on the 27th and suggested a military dictatorship, but the generals backed away from a proposal that had no historical precedent in the country. On March 2, the court, ministers, and high command abandoned the tsar, and next day they abandoned attempts to find another tsar from the Romanov family. This was not, as in France in 1789, the maturing of long-simmering factionalism within the state. The few Duma liberals had been unable to do anything beyond protest verbally. This political revolution had come suddenly, unexpectedly from below, although this gave liberal moderates an opportunity. A minority of the Duma proclaimed a Provisional Government headed by Prince Lvov. As the popular mood shifted leftward, the SR Kerensky, a centrist, succeeded Lvov as head of the government. He promised new elections with universal suffrage. This was the last attempt at a purely political revolution seeking constitutional government.

The seeds of further revolution were planted at the same time. Russia remained a predominantly agrarian economy, but its industry was unusually concentrated and modern. Around Moscow and St. Petersburg (now Petrograd), there were giant factories and major working-class communities, as there were in mining districts. This made for a strong working class in these key areas, not heavily dependent on the labor unions, as amid repression they were ineffectual, but generating many unofficial movements. The bosses were also weakened, because so many of the factories and mines were foreign owned. As Trotsky (1957) noted, these two factors made for an unusual degree of class conflict in the main urban-industrial areas. Workers now set up the Petrograd Soviet of Workers' Deputies, based on the workers' councils set up in many Russian cities during the failed 1905 revolution. The strikers elected deputies to represent them, and were joined by representatives of the soldiers and socialist parties, mainly Mensheviks and SRs. The Soviet's first decree was to set up soldiers' soviets (governmental councils) in all military units, but at this stage the Soviet was not aspiring to be a government, it merely sought to put pressure on the Provisional Government. These were still social democrats, not revolutionaries.

In February, the army's refusal to repress the demonstrators had been key; the officers were divided. Some doubted the autocracy's ability to govern in the twentieth century. The armed forces had been modernized, and by 1911 only half the army officers were noble (down from three-quarters in 1895) and only 9 percent of major generals or higher had possessed land or a house in 1903. The armed forces were modernizing, but the regime was not. Disaffection then rose during the war, when the regime's infrastructures proved incapable of supplying the army with enough shells. The officers would have preferred a constitutional monarchy, but a liberal republic would do if it could guarantee order and military supplies. Faced with a choice between the Duma and reaction, they preferred the Duma. This was especially so in the lower officer corps, for the high casualty rate among officers had necessitated promotions of men from lower backgrounds.

Few officers cared much about politics. They wanted above all to fight the war, and within days of the outbreak of rioting in 1917, most of them saw that their men would not continue fighting for the tsar. Within another month or two, they were even accepting a role for soldier soviets, risking sharing command with people they regarded as agitators. They were forced to accept this to preserve some authority over the troops. Some were coerced by their men, but most sought to find any authority structure that could shift supplies, get the men to defend their positions, mount artillery barrages, and even occasionally attack the enemy. Hence, monarchists' strident recriminations after the revolution: the armed forces had betrayed the old regime (Hasegawa, 1981: 459–507; Wildman, 1980; Mawdsley, 1978; N. Saul, 1978). The officers confirmed Lenin's statement: they "could not carry on in the old way." Yet this had resulted mainly from Lenin's other cause: the soldiers, the armed part of the lower classes, did not want to carry on in the old way. Although there was already ruling class unease, the old regime only became helpless when faced by the refusal of the masses to comply. It could not then guarantee order, the primary requirement of good government. This was a revolution from below against a regime whose infrastructural power, devastated by the war, weakened its repressive power.

True, the regime's ability to alienate intelligentsia and modernizers had divided sections of the ruling class (Haimson, 1964). However, this was not very visible outside the court and administration. In any case, the disputes at court between mildly liberal persons and hard-liners generally ended with the triumph of the latter. Factionalism among the ruling class was not a major problem in Russia. Instead, the collapse of the regime's infrastructural power due to the war was its Achilles heel.

Two major divisions that, as we shall see, split apart the potential revolutionaries in Germany, Austria, and Hungary were of lesser significance in Russia. The first concerns the peasantry, the second the working class, and both spilled over into the broader rural and urban populations. As I noted, these were agrarian-industrial societies. Although agriculture was deeply touched by the development of capitalism, the class grievances it generated differed, and the war had added conflicts over bread between the urban and rural populations. In Russia at the beginning of the twentieth century, massive discontent was surfacing simultaneously in both sectors. Trotsky (1957: chap. 1) explained the Russian revolutions in terms of "combined and uneven development." Severe class conflicts that in other countries appeared separately in time here appeared together: landlords against peasants, the final crisis of feudalism, seen by Trotsky as having occurred earlier in other countries, coincided in Russia with capitalists against workers, the crisis of capitalism.

The level of turbulence among Russian peasants was higher than in other countries. From the emancipation of the serfs in 1861 to the implementation of Stolypin's reforms after 1907, Russian agriculture underwent a much more rapid agricultural transformation than that of other major powers. This process had created more exploitative absentee rentier landlords, and weakened their power in the countryside; the peasant directly working the land had more autonomy there. This led also to the emergence of stronger peasant village communities. Peasants now had both the grievances and the power to revolt. They did so in 1905, but the failure of that revolution convinced the Bolsheviks and many of the Menshiviks in the cities and the Socialist Revolutionaries in the countryside that class struggle was not just a metaphor (as it was for most Marxists at the time): they would actually have to fight and militarize in order to achieve victory. That revolution and the Spring of 1917 revealed that if tsarist authority wavered, masses of peasants would refuse to pay rents, attack manors, and seize and redistribute land belonging to the nobility, rich peasants, and other private owners who had received common lands under the Stolypin reforms (Gill, 1979: 1–17, 38–46; Skocpol, 1979). Lenin said the seizures revealed class struggle between landowners and rich and poorer peasants, in which socialists must ally with poor peasants. Yet in 1917, the peasants did not move until after the fall of the monarchy, in February. They were not the initiators of action.

Nor was there any intrinsic economic connection between the discontents of peasants and industrial workers. Political parties had failed to devise a coherent program of reform appealing to both. The SRs expressed rural discontent, but their urban resonance declined. Conversely, in the towns and industry, Menshevik and Bolshevik Socialists became prominent but had little resonance in the countryside. During 1917, the Bolsheviks did devise an ad hoc program to appeal to peasants, but this opportunism contradicted their Marxist theory. Although they had proposed the collectivization of industry and the nationalization of land, in August 1917, after urgings from Stalin and others, Lenin changed tack and offered to give land to the individual peasant – or rather peasants could keep the land they had already seized! The revolts of workers and peasants occurred almost simultaneously, and were aimed at the same ruling class. Yet their demands differed, and their concurrence was not governed by the same economic forces. For a revolution to occur, other links between the urban and rural sectors were needed.

The first link was that many workers were themselves ex-peasants because of the unusual rapidity of industrial development in Russia, which the war intensified. In St. Petersburg, the number of factory workers grew from 73,000 in 1890 to 243,000 in 1914 to 393,000 in 1917 (S. Smith, 1983: 5–36). Most of the new unskilled and semiskilled industrial workers were peasant migrants to the cities, although most leaders were urban-born, better educated, and more skilled. A similar pattern of migration was visible in Spain at this time, with the same result: greater contacts and mutual influences between urban and rural movements, with both Socialists and anarcho-syndicalists active in both sectors. The relative contributions of ex-peasants and urban-born workers to the revolution remains controversial, but significant numbers of each were involved in strikes and demonstrations. The soviets, workers' councils, although famously associated with the industrial proletariat, derived from the peasant village tradition of electing the headman (Bonnell, 1983: 433–4; Mandel, 1983; S. Smith, 1983: 57).

Second were the links unwittingly provided by the state. State intervention in class relations was greater than elsewhere, and the war intensified this. The state was now responsible for delivering supplies to the troops and cities and looking after the millions of refugees displaced by its own scorched-earth military tactics when they retreated. Under the pressure, the primitive transport system virtually collapsed. The tsarist state could draw on modernized industries at one end of the chain and modernizing armies at the other, but lacked the infrastructures to efficiently connect the two. This was the major reason its armies fared so poorly. The loss of Poland, Galicia, and much of the Ukraine meant Russia's national income dropped by about a third, industrial production halved, and food production declined. When supplies began to fail, the regime fell back on what it knew best – coercion. It attempted to force peasants to deliver their food surpluses to the army and towns. However, the central state met resistance from local administrative authorities trying to prevent grain surpluses from leaving their own areas. Peasants preferred to sell their produce on the black market, whose prices were higher than the officially sanctioned prices. The Provisional Government established after the February revolution had no better luck contending with the problem. As power at the center weakened, nationalists in peripheral regions began to make demands for greater autonomy for national minorities. Many of them allied first with the constitutionalists and then with the Marxists. They became particularly overrepresented among the Bolsheviks. Civil disorder grew.

The war greatly intensified disaffection and links among rural and urban masses. Military defeats, economic crisis, bread shortages, and swarms of refugees affected most of European Russia, rupturing class differences, throwing workers, peasants, and the middle class together into a popular mass – a people, increasingly believing itself ruled by incompetents. The tsar was derided as an old woman, an idiot, and a drunk for his failure to properly conduct the war. Patriotism switched from attachments to the tsar, flag, and empire to comrades and the people, a quite different sense of nationhood. Popular sentiment then became firmly antiwar. Some victories against the Austrians helped, and victories against the Germans might have saved the regime, but they were unlikely to come. Anger became the dominant popular sentiment directed first at the tsar and then at elites and the bourgeoisie, seen as alien "others" lying outside the nation, threatening Russia's renewal, not deserving to share in its fruits (Gatrell, 2005; McAuley, 1991; Jahn, 1995: 91–7; Gill, 1979: 170–87; Steinberg, 2001: introduction). The court, industrialists, creditors, landowners, and the black market were distinct exploiters, but the state was embedded in them all, and this fused diverse protests together. Workers, peasants, and even much of the ordinary middle class came to see each other as allies, and to see salvation in transformation.

The third and probably most important link was that conscripted peasants and workers served together in the war, and they were armed! Sixty percent of soldiers and junior officers were peasants; a third of naval ratings were factory workers, and a quarter were peasants. Heavy losses meant that more of them were promoted into the lower officer corps (Mawdsley, 1978: 6–7, 157–9; Wildman, 1980: 98–101). The sailors murmured for different reasons, after two years of inactivity on disease-ridden ships, locked up by winter ice, and the superiority of the German fleet in the Baltic, unable to break the German-Ottoman lock on the western Black Sea. Military conscription was particularly important for peasants. As Shanin (1971: 259) observes, "The modern conscript army is one of the few nationwide organizations in which the peasantry actively participates. The segmentation of the peasantry is thereby broken." Ex-soldiers had long provided the core of most peasant rebellions. Mutiny during active service had not been common, but in this war the soldiers had endured more than two years of being used as cannon fodder, thrown straight at the Germans to make up for Russian inferiority in artillery. They lacked food, shoes, shells, and even sometimes guns. Then they were sent to the front with no weapons, and told to grab those of fallen comrades. The German army made mincemeat of them. Russian soldiers killed in the war may have been around 2 million, but 5 million also became prisoners of war. Such staggering losses led to mutinies, fraternization with the enemy, and desertions. Armed deserters were prominent in the peasant land seizures of mid-1917. As Skocpol says, "Much of the intravillage politics of rural Russia in 1917 took the form of younger men, with guns and ideas brought home from the wartime military experience, challenging the authority and caution of older traditional leaders of the *mir*, who were also often heads of patriarchal families." She adds, "The result was almost certainly to push the land revolution to its conclusion sooner and more violently." (1979: 138). Yet the peasants did not move until after urban insurgency had brought the regime to its knees. In an overwhelmingly agrarian society, peasant insurgency was a necessary condition of the revolution's success, but peasants did not initiate it.

Serious army mutinies had begun in 1916. Unlike French mutinies described in the previous chapter, Russian generals did not have the option of remedying their soldiers' grievances by shifting to artillery bombardments, for they lacked the shells. As discontent became politicized, inactive fleets and rear garrisons took the lead. Sailors and soldiers stationed with the Baltic Fleet and in the capital's garrisons (330,000 strong) joined the urban insurrections as soon as they began. Not a single regiment would move to suppress them, despite repeated orders. This was decisive; the state no longer had a monopoly of military power. Throughout 1917, insurgency came from soldiers as well as workers, and they successively transferred their loyalties from the tsar to the Provisional Government, to the Soviets, and then to the Bolsheviks within the Soviets (Rabinowitch, 2004: chap. 8; Wildman, 1980: 375). Peasants and workers had compatible goals but could not easily act together until they were uniformed comrades. Military power had shifted from the regime to the insurgents, so a successful revolution was possible.

There had also been a trial run of revolution in 1905, also precipitated by an unsuccessful war. Peasant land seizures had coincided with worker protest and their common sufferings as soldiers and sailors in an incompetently run war. Defeat by Japan had led to the forming of soldier-worker Soviets in the Far Eastern provinces, and to separate worker and peasant protests (with virtually no soldier participation) in the more crucial west provinces. The regime had first responded with offers of reform, but when feeling secure in 1907 it turned to repression. This had been a short war, without prolonged food crises or much solidarity between soldiers, workers, peasants, and urban populations. Because of it, militants learned to distrust compromises offered by the regime.

This union between workers, peasants, and soldiers proved unique across Europe. The position of peasants differed widely among countries, but they rarely turned their discontents against the state or capitalism. Spain was the main exception. There, strikes and urban demonstrations also occurred over the same broad period as peasant unrest. As in Russia, there were few intrinsic connections between the discontents of workers and peasants. In Spain, they both rose up in insurrection, but separately. Their insurrections were within months of each other: socialist workers rose in August 1917; anarcho-syndicalist peasants in the summer of 1918; syndicalist workers in March 1919. Yet the time lag was enough for a Spanish army under normal military discipline to suppress each in turn. Meaker (1974: 1, 63) attributes the failure of the revolutionary left in Spain to disunity between peasants and workers and between Marxists and anarcho-syndicalists, both divisions being reinforced by geography. Spain, however, was neutral in the world war, and its state provided no common cause to discontented workers and peasants and no mass of discontented soldiers. Without the unity provided them by tsarist incompetence in war, the fate of revolution in Russia may have been a rather more violent version of events in Spain.

Furthermore, splits between reformers and revolutionaries were not very evident on the shop floor. Although the political parties squabbled, few worker militants were following their disputes. Workers were autonomously radicalizing, and this was most evident in state-run enterprises, employing a third of St. Petersburg factory workers (S. Smith, 1983: 10). Tsarism's willingness to back employers with force even against moderate worker demands had given worker reformists little encouragement. It is difficult to be a reformist when no one offers you any reforms. A few liberal Russian employers persuaded a few worker representatives to sit on war industries committees, but these were so harried by regime hostility and labor's own suspicions that they were ineffectual (Siegelbaum, 1983: 159–82).

Common experience of exclusion and repression pushed skilled and unskilled workers alike toward more radical sentiments and violence. By 1914, St. Petersburg workers in big metalworking plants were responding more to the language of class than to sectional trade unionism. Workers in construction, transport, communications, and services were also beginning to form unions. The demands of war expanded metal and chemical manufacturing as well as the numbers of less skilled, ex-peasant, young, and female workers. Craft workers still provided union leadership; unskilled workers, ex-peasants, and women provided rank-and-file members and crowds. Women were underrepresented in worker agitation but overrepresented in bread demonstrations. In industries without craft traditions, protests were less organized, less political, but sometimes more explosive. The combination encouraged class identity and more turbulent protest movements (Hogan, 1993; McKean, 1990; S. Smith, 1983: 190–208, 253; Bonnell, 1983; Mandel, 1983; K. Murphy, 2005: chap. 1).

By the beginning of 1917, Marxist factions were still squabbling on the sidelines. There was just as little cohesion among revolutionaries as among the tsarist regime, in real trouble and among the emerging Provisional Government. Although Bolsheviks were influential in a few sectors, no single political faction could organize on a citywide basis let alone Russia-wide basis, so events in 1917 began with fluid and fairly spontaneous worker and urban movements. A "revolutionary sub-elite" of young, educated, city-born metalworkers made most of the running on their own, demanding workers control through soviets. They remained suspicious of the sectarianism of Lenin and other exiled leaders. Although Lenin returned to Russia in April, he remained on the sidelines a little longer (McKean, 1990).

The collapse of the tsarist supply system starved the cities and undermined those who supported the war effort – Conservatives, Kadets, and the Mensheviks and SRs who had joined the Provisional Government. Most of the people who were vocal favored a non-monarchical government that could give them bread, land (in the case of peasants), and, above all, peace. Perhaps the parties of the Provisional Government might have generated a democratic constitution resembling that of the Weimar Republic. The Provisional Government decreed some civil liberties and promised elections, but most of its members feared a democracy that might be peasant controlled, likely to ratify land seizures, cancel foreign debts, and make peace. Had the Provisional Government held elections, the SRs, dominant among the peasant majority, would probably have won, and the chances of this loose, decentralized, and somewhat incoherent party maintaining a stable government were not great.

The Provisional Government refused to make a separate peace with the Central Powers. In June, it chose instead to launch an offensive against the Germans. This failed miserably, and wasted more Russian lives. Had the Russian government been able to hold on to become one of the war's victors, its legitimacy would have increased (Service, 1997: 52–3). In 1917, however, as casualties mounted, defeat loomed. The Bolsheviks plausibly denounced the Provisional Government as warmongering imperialists. The government declared that it would be responsible, respect its treaty obligations, and continue the war. Had it made peace, there was a good chance it would have averted the Bolshevik Revolution. In reality, it remained dominated by its conservative wing, some of whom still expected an eventual victory that might even gain Constantinople, a traditional goal of imperial Russian expansion. Max Weber, a German patriot, assessed the chances of Russia leaving the war. He concluded it would not, as most of the Duma and administration remained "extremely imperialist." This, he argued, was for domestic purposes: the war kept the peasants subordinated in the army, and the war was the way to get loans from international capitalism that feared the cancelation of Russian debts. He thought that the radicals in the Provisional Government were the losers in this, going along with "imperialist demonstrations" that would "in the long run, dig their own graves" (M. Weber, 1995: 264–5).

This was true, except that Weber did not see that the Provisional Government was digging its own grave. More suicidal spadework came as it delayed land and other reforms until after the election of a Constituent Assembly. It hoped this assembly would not approve them, but to be on the safe side announced that it could not hold an election during the war. The SRs, hitherto active in the factories, now faded there. In contrast, the Bolsheviks and their allies among the Left SRs and the Menshevik-Internationalists denounced the war and urged its immediate end. By now, the Petrograd Soviet had mushroomed into a national movement headed by the All-Russian Central Executive Committee of Soviets. The Bolsheviks were quite separate from this, but now allied with it, urging "All Power to the Soviets." They demanded ratification of all peasant land seizures and urged all this happen right away, before any elections. Their most famous slogan was simply "Bread, Land and Peace!"

The ensuing shift toward the Bolsheviks is simple to explain: they offered what most people wanted. During 1917, public opinion and militancy swung by stages toward them. Many factories already had soviets attempting to maintain the production that could pay workers' wages. Beginning in April, the Bolsheviks had sponsored militias to provide local order, and these became the "Red Guards." Most workers saw the soviets and the Red Guards not as revolutionary (whatever that meant) but as protecting their own livelihood. There was a large gap between all these concrete aspirations – for peace, land, bread, control of the factories, and law and order – and Marxist utopias of a classless, conflict-free society without patriarchy, which the Bolsheviks also preached. Their ideology of salvation was more important within the ranks of the Bolsheviks than in their relations with the masses. Their theory of history made them believe that history was on their side, a very powerful ideological boost to them. Yet the orthodox theory had taught them that the bourgeois revolution was necessary before their own, so they had to ally with bourgeois liberals. However, they believed that the underlying historical process could be speeded up (Marx himself had indicated that), so they regarded pragmatic alliances with other groups as short-term necessities. They sometimes pretended to be reformists, and they talked about the people rather than the proletariat in order to harness the new populist nationalism war had created. However, they had their eyes firmly fixed on a proletarian revolution, and there was little danger that they might settle back into permanent reformism. Revolutionary ideology actually helped them be opportunistic in the meantime. This duality remained after they seized power, for it gave them the overall direction of the extraordinary revolutionary transformation they would attempt and proved useful as a means of short-term deviations from that direction.

Yet in practical terms, many workers were already acting like revolutionaries, whatever their beliefs. By creating soviets and Red Guards, they were expropriating capitalist property and supplanting the state's monopoly over the means of violence. The Provisional Government lacked its own means of mass mobilization and had to turn to the generals to suppress the soviets. The most significant coup attempt was that of General Kornilov, but when he called on regiments to attack the revolutionary headquarters, the soldiers would not follow their officers. Railway and other transport workers would not let them move, anyway. Most of the organized workers and soldiers – not just Bolsheviks – then identified these military moves, some of which were supported by the Provisional Government, as counterrevolutionary: the bourgeoisie was seeking to repress the proletariat. This Marxian analysis was essentially correct, and it made quite incredible the long-term strategy of waiting for the bourgeoisie. The Bolsheviks clearly had to make a strategic shift. After all, their power was rising. By the autumn of 1917, they were winning most of the elections to the factory soviets and the national Soviet. They now had 100,000 members (Rabinowitch, 2004; Mandel, 1983; McKean, 1990; Suny,

1998: 54; Wade, 2000; Figes, 1997: 331; Kenez, 2006: 27–8; Melancon, 1997; K. Murphy, 2005: 53–62).

The Bolsheviks lost some popularity in the "July Days" when they failed to support a rising by Petrograd soldiers and workers, believing it to be premature. There was much debate afterward as to whether they had acted wisely. They recovered some popularity by helping stop Kornilov's coup. Then they offered reconciliation to the Mensheviks and SRs in September, asking them only to break with the Kadets and other bourgeois parties. When there was no response, the Bolsheviks seized power without them – perhaps what Lenin had been aiming for all along. With the help of a fairly small number of revolutionary soldiers, they launched their coup in October, months after power on the ground in the major cities had been acquired by workers and soldiers. It was fairly bloodless, which was essentially what Marx and the first generations of subsequent Marxists had expected. Although Marx wrote of a violent seizure of power to be followed by the armed people standing vigilant over the dictatorship of the proletariat, this involved crowds storming and protecting buildings, only some of them armed with lethal weaponry. In 1917, attempts at rightist coups were not directly thwarted by revolutionary military force; rather, the coup soldiers melted away before they reached their destination. Few subsequent revolutions were to be like this, and the Bolsheviks soon discovered they needed more military force to defend their revolution.

Neither the Bolsheviks nor Lenin possessed the extraordinary powers of perspicacity and manipulation sometimes attributed to them (Pipes, 1990; J. Dunn, 1972: 42). If anything they were hesitant, following on behind the workers – that is what Trotsky said. Lenin did eventually perceive the window of opportunity, and he used his personal charisma and organizational shrewdness to persuade the more cautious majority of the party. Orthodox theory plus decades of persecution and isolation had induced a fear of striking too soon. Lenin's main contribution to the revolution was to overcome this fear. Lenin, Trotsky, and then other Bolsheviks were fairly responsive, listening with well-developed antennae to popular demands, then acting on them. Rabinowitch exaggerates in saying that at this stage Bolshevism had an "essentially open and mass character," but it was not the tight vanguard party laid down fifteen years earlier in Lenin's *What is to be Done?*, nor the dictatorship it was soon to become. Its line was simply popular. In Guzhon, the largest metal factory in Moscow, Murphy says there were only nine Bolsheviks in April 1917, and their numbers rose little during the year; the metalworkers union there supported the Bolshevik line, and it had 3,000 members by September, with 500–800 attending regular factory meetings. They resisted regime attempts to close the factory by occupying it themselves: Bolsheviks in practice, not principle. In rural areas, the Left SRs made much of the running, more radical than their leaders in the capitals. Around the Russian periphery, minority nationalists seeking regional autonomy led the way. In all three respects, the watching Bolsheviks came to the realization that their orthodoxy of distinct stages of revolution, commanding a waiting game, could be bypassed. The masses were ready. All three of these movements contributed to the revolution, but its outcome was decided by fairly small numbers of people in the two capitals (Rabinowitch, 2004: 311; 169–73, 308–9; Wade, 1984; 2000: 207–8; Suny, 1998: 50–52; Figes, 1997: 471; K. Murphy, 2005; Raleigh, 2003; S. Smith, 1983; Mandel, 1983; McKean, 1990; Anweiler, 1974).

Unlike many recent theorists, I have identified the popular classes – not just the working class – as the main movers of revolution. Workers, peasants, urban crowds – all including many women – and especially soldiers and lower officers brought the regime to its knees, allowed liberal constitutionalists their failed moment of destiny, and urged the Bolsheviks on to their revolution. Outside of the officer corps, divisions within the regime played a relatively minor role until the point when it became clear that the old regime might not survive popular insurgency. This is quite close to Marx's vision of a proletarian class revolution. I do not support Goldfrank's or Goldstone's emphasis on dissidence and factionalism among urban elites. Tsarism was quickly succeeded by the Provisional Government; neither of them was greatly riven by internal factionalism – with the crucial exception of the military. It was their inability to produce policies that the masses could accept that undid them both.

Nor do I accept Skocpol's emphasis on peasants to the exclusion of workers. True, so much peasant discontent followed by the seizure of so much land meant that peasants would not aid repression of the revolutionaries in the cities. This was indeed a necessary condition for a successful revolution. However, this revolution was accomplished by the seizure of state power, above all in the two capital cities, and that was the work of industrial and other urban workers, urban intellectuals, and army and navy contingents that were not mostly formed of peasants. The war immobilized the bulk of the armed forces, which meant that only relatively few armed soldiers were necessary to storm the Winter Palace. The great mass of disaffected peasant soldiers made their way back to their homes, many of them leading local insurgencies. It was to be different in China, where both the cities and state power were seized by a peasant army. In Russia, the peasants made their own insurrection in the countryside, and stayed there. In fact, the seizure of state power in the cities was also a necessary condition for the success of the peasant insurgencies. Without it, the armed forces of an intact state would have crushed the peasants, as was the fate of almost all peasant insurrections in history. Although the immobilization and then the support of peasant soldiers were necessary to the success of the revolution, workers, worker soldiers, and their leaders were the main movers.

Military power in the shape of unrelenting pressure on Russian soil was the major factor propelling mass popular discontent toward support for a movement potentially capable of achieving a revolution. This is closer to Skocpol than to Marx, for military causes were foreign to his thinking. Goldfrank's explanation of revolution in terms of a permissive international context or one supportive of the rebels or Foran's stress on the world system are also along the right lines, but they are too anodyne to capture the causal power of the ferocious war and devastation launched by the German Empire on Russian soil. Yet Goldstone's argument that a dissident elite must be capable of linking up with the popular insurgency certainly fits. That is what the war enabled the Bolsheviks to do.

Without this sequence, the likeliest outcome would have been chaos and disintegration in the Russian Empire – just as was soon to happen to the Austro-Hungarian and Ottoman Empires. There could not have been a different revolutionary transformation, because no other political grouping could mobilize the popular force to achieve one. There was little chance of an enduring bourgeois revolution, as the Provisional Government that was its only possible vehicle lacked mass mobilizing power and depended on reactionary army officers for its survival (Hobsbawm, 1994: 58, 64–5). The only minimally plausible alternative strategy for avoiding revolution might have been a firmer alliance between all the liberal and socialist factions of the Provisional Government plus the more cautious Bolsheviks and some of the worker soviets. Could this have produced a viable regime steering toward a form of social democracy? It would have required enormous sacrifices by the more conservative factions of the government, accepting the overthrow of property rights in the countryside and the factories alike, and risking elections that had a very good chance of throwing them out of power. They were not prepared for such sacrifices. It was at this point that the cohesion of the two sides switched, the Provisional Government became more factionalized and the party discipline of the Bolsheviks held down their potential factionalism.

My emphasis on the war means I reject an explanation stressing systemic social or economic contradictions, long-term structural causes, unlike Marx, Barrington Moore, and the Russian scholar Haimson (1964). Haimson argued that the prewar upsurge in labor violence, polarization between workers and other classes, and deepening divisions within the regime would have brought revolution to Russia even without the war. Peasants were already highly discontented, the officer corps and other would-be reformers were wondering if tsarism was appropriate to modernity, the tsarist regime was inadvertently creating worker revolutionaries by suppressing sectional trade unionists and political reformists, and the regime was dithering over reforms and then repressing them. I agree that long-term structural tendencies of the Russian regime and capitalism would have produced an attempt at revolution without the war, but I doubt there could have been a successful revolution – which is the only one that counts. Although we should not underestimate the stupidity of the Romanovs, revolution was not possible by parliamentary dissidents and workers alone. How would they have joined with peasants without the war? Even if they could have joined with other groups, there remained military power: how to avoid repression if the regime has the guns? When ordered to fire into demonstrating workers, soldiers almost always do so, whatever their social backgrounds, because they are under strict military discipline. For them, military power trumps class identity. In Russia, however, this discipline crumbled under extreme war pressures. I doubt that the royal court would have been so stupid as to allow its divisions to prevent this happening in peacetime.

The war intensified, made transparent, and piled on top of each other diverse prewar weaknesses of the tsarist regime to create a revolutionary cascade. The union of workers, peasants, and soldiers was very unusual, sustained through state oppression combined with incompetence at mass mobilization warfare. This allowed the Bolsheviks to attack the regime with increasingly plausible invocations of exploitation. Curiously, the Bolsheviks, as Marxists, saw the real enemy as capitalism; few Russians felt likewise. They wanted above all to overthrow tsarism, but the war induced them to overthrow capitalism, too.

Yet ideological power also mattered in the final stages of this revolution, especially within the Bolshevik movement itself. Its secular salvationism promised a worldly utopia in this world on the basis of social (class) solidarity and greatly reinforced its sense of disciplined comradeship and that history was on its side. The power of the goal meant that they were less fussy about the means. Thus, the ideology presented to the masses was simple, populist, unorthodox, and opportunistic. By addressing a strong appeal to peasants, they filled up a hole in traditional Marxism, but promising them their own plot of land deviated from their revolutionary program of collectivism.

Lenin had assumed before coming to power that if the Bolsheviks took advantage of the radicalism of the factories and streets, support for a socialist revolution would come. Yet as workers, peasants, and soldiers showed themselves to have very varied politics, the Bolsheviks saw more direction from above was required to be on course for salvation. Once they seized state power in October, they reimposed hierarchical controls, including one-man management and labor discipline, and they incorporated soviets and unions into their own state. Once the outlines of this dictatorship became clear, many workers turned against them (S. Smith, 1983: 260–5). Yet the Bolsheviks now had the military power to repress dissent. Military power was as decisive in maintaining the revolution as in making it. That revolutionary soldiers had kept their guns and distributed some to sympathetic workers had enabled revolution. Now the Bolsheviks held onto weapons through the Red Guards and other formations. This gave them power they held onto through the civil war that followed. The military march toward one-party despotism had begun, perverting the direction of their route. The combination meant that after the revolution, and after a short period of pragmatic relaxation, they would return more to their original ideological orthodoxy, but it would be salvation through force.

Without this disastrous war followed by the emergence of an organized revolutionary party combining a salvation ideology with acute antennae for popular sentiment, the revolution would not have succeeded. Some subsequent Marxists also emphasize the war, but explain it in terms of capitalist imperialism, which we saw in the last chapter was false. Instead, European militarism had made war the default mode of diplomacy. Lenin repeatedly remarked that Russia was the weakest link in the capitalist chain. In military terms, it certainly was. Skocpol and others rightly emphasize the causal power of internationally induced political crises, but Russia in 1917 was not a case of a budget crisis induced by too much war. This is too bland to convey the catastrophe of total war, invasion, starving towns, and mobbing refugees. Military power was primary in tipping over class conflicts into revolution. The war was primary in producing the downward political cascade that increased the factionalism of the Provisional Government, but then the ideological solidarity of the Bolsheviks made the revolution successful.

This revolution involved the conjunction of two distinct causal chains: one led from an authoritarian monarchy propping up a highly concentrated capitalism by force, generating discontented lower classes; the other led from European militarism into mass mobilization warfare and Russia military disaster. The first gave the working class and peasantry the desire for revolution; the second gave them the unity and power to accomplish it. The growth of the Bolshevik Party was a product of the first chain while its politics took advantage of the second one. Party members had an ideological confidence in eventual victory and a strong party discipline originally acquired in conditions of clandestinity. This helped keep Bolshevik cohesion amid the downward spiral of the country, and it aided the strategy of capturing populist nationalism in order to achieve class revolution. After the revolution, their ideological power and discipline became decisive in structuring the form of state socialist society.

Without the war, workers and peasants might still have risen up, but separate risings would have been put down separately, as in Spain. Even if the two risings had been conjoined, the military power of the regime would not have been neutralized. With rare exceptions (such as Iran in 1979), this has only happened in twentieth-century societies through defeat in war. Without the war, the Russian future did not promise much benefit for the masses – at best an authoritarian regime backing up an exploitative capitalism, at worst disintegration and chaos. Without the war, the Bolsheviks' two successes – capturing and holding power and preserving Russia as a Great Power – would not then have had massive impact on the world. The military power relations of World War I created the Soviet Union – and were also ultimately responsible for the Terror, one-half of the defeat of Fascism, a nuclear arms race, a Cold War, and so forth.

War and European labor movements

The Bolshevik Revolution influenced the world: sometimes it encouraged workers and peasants to greater resistance; sometimes it inflamed counterrevolutionaries. However, serious attempts at revolution were made only within Russia's own macro-region, in central and Eastern Europe. Splits between reformists and revolutionaries occurred in all European labor movements, reinforced by sectional differences between craft and unskilled workers and segmental differences between industries. When employers conciliated reformers or were pushed to do so by their states, this undermined the left, which needed working class unity to achieve revolution; reformists did not need unity beyond the level of individual employers to achieve their goals. The immediate prewar period had seen more militancy and convergence toward craft socialism in industry, leftist reformism in politics, and solidaristic working-class urban communities. The war then added further tensions.

(1) As in Russia, armaments and heavy metalworking industries grew and became the vanguard of the labor movement. Although war production threatened craft control of mechanization with the introduction of more semiskilled workers and coercive discipline, craftsmen remained privileged in terms of wages, shop-floor control, and exemptions from conscription. Between them and the main expanding mass of workers – unskilled, often female, often rural migrants – there was less solidarity than in Russia. Starting about 1916, militancy increased, led by metalworkers, but it still embodied a contradiction between socialism and sectionalism.

(2) Unlike Russia, European labor leaders were incorporated into the regime as the war brought the first substantial dose of *corporatism*, class relations mediated through tripartite institutions of state representatives, employers, and workers. Socialist/Labour Party and union leaders were brought into cabinets in Britain and France; in Germany, Austria, Hungary, and Italy they were consulted about legislation for the first time. In return, they voted war credits, enjoined patriotism on their rank and file, and sought no-strike pledges from them. In Germany, the SPD right fully endorsed the war and government plans to annex foreign territory; its center looked both ways, supporting the war at the same time it lobbied ineffectually for peace negotiations. Nationalism trumped class consciousness for varied reasons, some of them instrumental. Unionists were put onto boards supervising labor relations and industry production. They raised workers' grievances with government and employers and policed no-strike laws and new labor codes. In return, employers got industrial peace and stability plus high and often guaranteed profits. At the national level, employer and union organizations both increased their activities. In Germany, this introduced cooperation between Socialist and non-Socialist unions as well as the first employers' Industrial Council (Feldman, 1966: 119).

Incorporation then extended down union hierarchies. The German Auxiliary Service Law of December 1916 introduced compulsory civilian mobilization, abolishing workers' freedom to change jobs. In return, committees included union representatives in all registered enterprises of more than fifty employees. Similar trade-offs occurred in the Austrian complaints commission of March 1917 and the Italian committees of industrial mobilization of August 1915. Union and party officials, sometimes still calling themselves revolutionary Socialists, were incorporating, showing the old regime how responsible they could be. This involved suppressing rank-and-file discontents that conflicted with the agreed codes.

(3) Under this system, rank-and-file militants lost formal organizing powers and lacked the dilemmas of responsibility that accompanied them. Strikes and antigovernment demonstrations were banned and restrictions were placed upon plant and local bargaining. Informally, shop stewards representing craft workers in essential war industries retained illegal powers at the shop-floor level and could establish networks of like-minded militants across the major industrial cities. However, they could not trust the open political party structures of the SPD or the antiwar leftist Independent Social Democratic Party (USPD). If exposed, they would be conscripted or jailed.

In peacetime, the dilemma between reform and revolution had confronted most working-class movements. Now war incorporated the leadership, and rank-and-file militants were free to indulge in radical rhetoric but constrained to act in secrecy. Their "revolutionary shop stewards movement" lacked the organization that the reformist national leadership had built-up over a thirty-year period (Sirianni, 1980). Sometimes national leaders helped repress leftist strikes (Feldman, 1966: 128–9). Their reformist leanings intensified, because they could get concessions by participating in capitalist states, although they were less able to mobilize agitation to pressure reform. Minority leftist leaders remaining outside the corporatist structures – usually because of opposition to the war – became more radical and hostile toward reformists, especially where their own persecution worsened. They built-up networks of protest against the war and the regime, but were deprived by persecution of extensive organizational channels among workers. Shop-floor militants centered in metalworking trades formed a revolutionary shop steward movement; they controlled the factories and often opposed national union leadership, but had little organization beyond the factory (for Britain, see J. Hinton 1973; I. McLean, 1983). The mass of workers were undergoing sacrifices, and saw systematic injustices in the conduct of the war. Yet they were ambivalent toward all three sets of available leaders. The consequence everywhere, in the advanced countries and the colonial and semicolonial world as well, was a postwar explosion of labor unrest (Silver, 2003: 125–9). The Bolshevik Revolution emboldened radicals and frightened conservatives everywhere, but both tried to learn from Russia. The consequence was attempted but failed revolutions, but only in its own macro-region and only among the defeated powers.

Germany: Failed revolution, precarious reform[1]

In defeat, the German Reich collapsed. In the last two weeks of war, naval and army units mutinied. On October 28, 1918, sailors at Kiel refused to put to sea; on November 3, they seized their base and marched on nearby towns. That sparked workers, soldiers, and other urban demonstrators to seize local administrations and factories across Germany. They met little initial resistance. Most insurgents wanted a new government, distrustful of one composed of old regime notables. The latter, vividly fearing a repeat of the Bolshevik Revolution, started negotiations with the leaders of the majority reformist faction of the Social Democratic Party (SPD) to forestall the ultraleftist Karl Liebknecht and revolutionary shop stewards from proclaiming a "Bolshevik" government. The SPD lacked the cohesion of the Bolsheviks. Although they all claimed to be Marxists, the reformists had developed an evolutionary Marxist theory: that socialism would eventually come after a long process of escalating but negotiated reforms. Pragmatism was not just for the short-term, as among the Bolsheviks; it would be for a considerable period. This was hardly salvationism. The kaiser abdicated on November 9. There were riots, and perhaps twelve people were killed that day, but the transfer of power was peaceful. Prince Max of Baden, the last imperial chancellor, formally handed over his powers to SPD Chairman Friedrich Ebert, a former leatherworker. Two days later, Germany surrendered.

Political order in prewar Wilhelmine Germany had rested on cooperation between the monarchy and the Conservative Parties, usually with the conditional support of the National Liberal Party and\or the Catholic Center Party. In the first postwar elections, however, the decline of the Conservatives and National Liberals and the sudden surge of the Social Democrats transformed parliamentary politics (Childers, 1983: 15–49). The Catholic Center Party held onto its vote and committed itself for the first time to universal suffrage and cooperation with the Social Democrats. The shift of the Catholic Church from reaction to democracy was a significant change in Germany. As a ruling regime, the old order of monarch, landowners, officers, industrialists, and conservative political notables seemed finished.

Workers' representatives overwhelmingly sought revolution not reform, but aggressively. They extended wartime workers' committees coordinating food distribution, housing allocation, and relief for veterans and their dependents. These became workers' councils, paralleled by soldiers' councils. Most councils were coping with chaos in the factory, the street, and the community,

[1] For 1918–1919, I relied most on Broue, 2005: part 1; B. Moore, 1978: 275–397. On the SPD, see Broue, Breitman, 1981; Hunt, 1970; on the USPD, see D. Morgan, 1975; on the KPD, see Fowkes, 1984; Broue, 2005: part 2. For comparisons with other countries, see Carsten, 1972; essays in Bertrand, 1977; Cronin and Sirianni, 1983.

not pursuing a political strategy. Yet they included the Revolutionary Shop Stewards of Berlin, who had been preparing a coup when Ebert's installation as chancellor forestalled them. Nobody could be certain of the workers' and soldiers' councils intentions, and many among the old regime and the bourgeoisie feared that Bolshevism would deprive them of their power and property; one may be terrified of a major threat even if it has a low probability of occurring. Momentarily lacking coercive powers, the propertied classes were prepared to compromise to avert disaster.

This suited the SPD majority faction for whom the prewar contradiction between Marxist rhetoric and moderate electoralism now intensified. Some had voted for war credits out of nationalist enthusiasm, believing they could be Socialists and patriots. Most of the SPD had voted for the war, however, believing that otherwise the government would repress them. They had then compromised with the old regime to keep their organizations intact for postwar usage. During the war, they were incorporated into government agencies – unlike their counterparts in Russia. In the aftermath of war, the SPD leaders seized their opportunity. After consulting the Catholic Center Party, the radical liberals, and the USPD (which had split off in 1917 in opposition to the war), the SPD established a provisional government and set in motion procedures for a republican constitution and universal suffrage elections, giving women the vote and ending weighted class voting among men. This was a political revolution, from a semi-authoritarian monarchy to a parliamentary republic.

Big employers had taken initiatives as soon as they realized the monarchy would fall. A few had learned compromise from wartime cooperation with unions, but fear of Bolshevism was their biggest motivation, so the rhetoric and actions of the revolutionary Socialists were very useful to the reformists. This was the indirect, top-down route to greater social citizenship I will stress in Chapter 9. Employers said they would recognize unions as the representatives of labor, establish factory workers committees, and institute labor exchanges and mediation committees on the basis of equal representation. In return, they asked the unions to agree to "the maintenance of the economy," meaning the maintenance of capitalism and managerial powers. Two weeks later, employer representatives conceded an eight-hour day, collective wage agreements, and the end to subsidies to "yellow unions." These were traded for the right of management to run their own businesses. The employers "bought time for capitalism" (Balderston, 2002: 8). The concessions constituted most of the prewar labor movement's program, and the unions accepted the deal. Both sides wanted to get industry working again (Feldman, 1966: 521–31).

A liberal democracy, an SPD government, and some social democratic policies had been established within a month, a considerable reformist achievement by both sides of the class struggle. As no serious resistance had been met, none of the old institutions except the monarchy had been destroyed. The SPD leaders now combined public negotiations with those to its left – the councils, shop stewards movement, and USPD – over how much socialism should be injected into the new Republic, and private conversations with old regime notables. On November 10, Chancellor Ebert and the USPD agreed on the composition of the Provisional Government. They would have equal representation on the Council of Peoples' Representatives, supervised by an Executive Council picked by workers' and soldiers' councils – revealing how strong the left was now assumed to be. However, on returning to his palace Ebert, in the traditional telling of the story, was called to the telephone to speak with Ludendorff's successor, General Groener, the principal negotiator with labor during the war. Groener later recollected that their conversation went along these lines: "The officer corps could only cooperate with a government which undertook the struggle against Bolshevism.... Ebert had made up his mind on this.... We made an alliance against Bolshevism.... There existed no other party which had enough influence upon the masses to enable the re-establishment of a governmental power with the help of the army" (Broue, 2005: 169; B. Moore, 1978: 293–4; Ryder, 1967: 149–64).

Thus, capitalism, landownership, the army, and the civil service were preserved in exchange for a political democracy, welfare reforms, and industrial conciliation. The SPD leadership was for reform anyway, but its contacts with the old regime constrained its freedom of leftward manoeuver. The decisive power arena lay inside the military. The soldiers' councils wanted the armed forces to be more democratic, with no brutal discipline, and with elected officers sharing administration with elected committees. They declared themselves ready to fight to achieve these goals, and they could have overpowered the Freikorps and other bands of rightist veterans now roaming the country. Who would control the official army of 100,000 men permitted by the Versailles Peace Treaty remained unclear. If Ebert had been more radical, he would have asked the high command to hand over its powers to him while he organized its successor. He also failed to reform the higher civil service or the judiciary, which remained a reactionary force, often disallowing Weimar social rights legislation during the 1920s (Mommsen, 1996). The SPD understood economic power, saw political power as parties and elections, and neglected the bureaucracy, judiciary, and military. Reform did not extend to these spheres – a highly imperfect revolution even of politics. Ebert saw the soldiers' councils not as an ally, but as a threat. Revolution was not what the majority SDP leaders had in mind; they needed the army and judiciary to protect themselves from both right and left.

The left, despairing of the SPD leaders, debated whether it could mount its own revolution without them. The antiwar stance of the ultraleft Socialists, the USPD, and some of the workers' and soldiers' councils won increasing support through 1918 – probably more than did their socialism. They were strong in a few cities, including Berlin, but they lacked national organization. To compensate, they proclaimed socialism to be a *movement*, an organic emergence in the working class rather than an organization coming to the working class from an outside vanguard party. This was Rosa Luxemburg's line, expressed in her famous anti-Lenin pamphlets, *The Mass Strike* (1906) and *Organizational Problems of Social Democracy* (1904). The left advocated mass strikes as the road to revolution, and it supported the workers' councils. However, although leftists opposed the SPD sellout, they could not agree on an alternative strategy. When Ebert had acted, they dithered, splintered, and failed to wield the powers that their agreement with Ebert seemed to have given them. Dithering was understandable, given their situation – fervent revolutionaries, but with little mass support.

As the workers' councils extended their powers over factory-street-community politics, their diversity grew. The revolutionary shop stewards from metalworking crafts and heavy industries had been least incorporated into the state in wartime, and they were experienced in factory and local agitation, but they lacked regional or national organization. Along with the USPD left, they formed the Spartacist faction, demanding workers control of production. They saw workers' councils as the key institution of the coming socialist society, as soviets were viewed by their counterparts in Austria, Hungary, Italy, and Russia. The Spartacists were important in Berlin, but not nationally. They viewed the events of late 1918 through a Bolshevik lens: the first political revolution had established a bourgeois democracy, and this would be shortly overthrown by a second, proletarian revolution – as in Russia. Unfortunately, their theory did not correspond to power realities. There was no mass support for a second revolution; most workers supported the majority SPD in the national election of January 1919. They wanted order, a rebuilt economy, and satisfaction of labor's traditional demands for maximum hours, minimum wages, unemployment and disability insurance, and organizing rights. The majority SPD was working hard to achieve these, but in the election, the SPD was dismayed to find that the bourgeois parties had revived to near their prewar strength. The politics of worker activism had dominated the last few months, and the SPD had forgotten that electoral politics gave expression to the rural areas, the middle class, and the churches. They counseled workers not to demand more, and most workers agreed.

Then the left split. The ultras had the support of few soldiers' councils, and they did not seek to ally with them once they realized most were not revolutionaries. They lacked a theory of military power. Focused on the struggle of industrial workers at the point of production, they saw the enemy as the capitalist class. Their theory of the state saw it as capitalism's regulator and repressor. They did not appreciate the polymorphous nature of the state or the autonomy of the military. Although it was obvious that states and capitalism were tottering because of military collapse not capitalist crisis, it was theorized that revolution was much less a military than economic process. If the Reichswehr remained intact, however, and if the soldiers' councils were allowed to disappear through demobilization, the revolution was over. In fact, the game was over quickly, as Chancellor Ebert came to terms with the high command, and the left did not build its own army. The troops were demobilized and off home they went, leaving their arms behind them. The soldiers' councils melted away.

So by the time of the first national delegate conference of councils in December 1918, few soldiers' representatives remained, and the conference was dominated by the SPD. The SPD never became a monolithic organization, and leftists remained free to express their views and pass resolutions at congresses (Harsch, 1993). Power sharing through the Executive Council seems never to have occurred, and the USPD remained regionally fragmented, exerting leftist pressure but not articulating a clear program. Without national organization, the remaining workers' councils were isolated cells of a future socialist utopia, not a method of revolutionary government (Mayer, 1977).

Some Spartacists decided nonetheless to go for broke and launch the second revolution. They believed they had to do it early, before the new regime was institutionalized and the soldiers disappeared home. There were only a few hundred Spartacists, compared to the 25,000 Bolsheviks in Russia in 1917. A mass of workers was ready to strike or demonstrate, but not to engage in armed struggle. During the brief Spartacist insurrection of January 1919, led (against their better judgment) by Karl Liebknecht and Rosa Luxemburg, the USPD dithered and offered little support. Most workers' councils sided with the SPD leadership, throwing protective cordons around public buildings. The SPD government allowed officers from loyal army units to deal with the rising. They mutilated and then killed Liebknecht and Luxemburg, and dispersed other leftists (Broue, 2005: chap. 12). It was a bloody fiasco, not to be romanticized; it was foolish, and only damaged progressive causes.

Angered by the SPD betrayal of revolution, surviving ultraleftists maintained their optimism that worker discontent could be translated into revolution. They moved into the Communist Party, the KPD, founded just before the Spartacist coup, and now displacing the USPD as the main far-left party. The SPD was above all an electoral organization, aware of the middle-class and women's votes it had created through universal suffrage. The leadership did not want Bolshevism to scare them away, and believed most women would vote for the center and right. In the first election of January 1919, the SPD received more votes than ever – 38 percent – but had to form a coalition government with the Catholic Center and liberals. It was prepared to alienate the left in order to conciliate the center; this electoral strategy was broadly successful. By 1924, 46 percent of its votes were coming from women, a proportion it held onto until the end; until 1930, between 30 percent and 40 percent of its vote was nonmanual (Hunt, 1970: 111–48).

SPD repression of the ultras stabilized the state, reassured the middle class, and preserved democracy. It also alienated the left, and some workers went over to the USPD, then the KPD. In the Republic's second election in 1920, the SPD vote dropped to 22 percent; the USPD rose from 8 percent to 18 percent. The SPD recovered to remain electorally superior, but to govern it needed bourgeois support. In 1919 and 1920, strikes became bigger and more political, especially in the industrial Ruhr, not hitherto a major center of revolution (Tampke, 1978; Geary, 1981; B. Moore, 1978: 227–353). This led to the Ruhr insurrection of 1923 under KPD leadership, which Broue (2005: 709) calls "an unprecedented pre-revolutionary situation … the German October," as inflation and unemployment had leveled class differences. The so-called Red Army in the Ruhr may have comprised more than 50,000 workers (B. Moore, 1978: 328). Coordination, however, was minimal, most workers would not fight, and nobody had armed them. Trotsky, who also thought this was a revolutionary situation, lamented the military incompetence of the KPD (Broue, 2005: 900). Half-baked revolutionary projects, suppressed by a state that was partly SPD, made for a blood feud between Socialists and Communists, which ten years later was to undermine the chances of a united left standing up to the Nazis.

It was too late: the point of maximum political opportunity (the Spartacist rising) had occurred at least a year before the point of maximum working-class disillusion with SPD reformism. The Republic and capitalism were now semi-institutionalized, and so was the split in the labor movement. A highly organized Socialist Party and the principal union federation were defending a bourgeois Republic as the avenue to social reforms, and potentially – it claimed – to "evolutionary socialism." Broue (2005: 168) concludes that fundamental differences from Russia prevented a German revolution: the German bourgeoisie remained strong, he says, because it had two additional instruments at its disposal, the support of a mass Socialist Party and an office corps "of rare quality." However, this also presupposed a divided working class, which was not the case in Russia, but the bourgeoisie was not as united as Broue suggests. Much of it had not wanted to compromise with the SPD in the postwar crisis, and when the danger from the left subsided in the mid-1920s, this faction reasserted itself and was on the road to Fascism. Liberals, Catholics, and industrialists had shown tactical acumen during the postwar crisis, making sacrifices for survival. They were important in avoiding the fate of their counterparts in Russia. They averted revolution.

The failure of this revolution was in a sense overdetermined. There were four main causes, any one of which might make a successful revolution unlikely. First was a major split within the working class movement, contrasting greatly with the Bolsheviks. Because its reformist wing was able to seize power and successfully make reforms, it was far more popular among workers than the revolutionary wing. Second, once the monarchy was disposed of, dominant classes remained united and (in the first crucial period) pragmatic. They would compromise with the reformist socialists, and so survive – later they would renege on this deal. This was similar to the Bolshevik strategy. Third, there was no tradition of peasant revolts, nor much indication of discontent among the rural population. No alliance between the urban-industrial militants and peasants was possible, although this cause was less important than in the other countries, as Germany was much more industrial and less agrarian than the other countries. Fourth and crucially, was the absence of an army in revolt. A few leftists were armed, but so were the Freikorps paramilitaries and units of an army whose autonomy Chancellor Ebert had guaranteed. That meant that the revolutionaries could not reach the first stage of a revolution, the successful occupation of the capital city and its government buildings. This fourth factor was a consequence of a different war outcome to Russia – defeat accompanied by demobilization. It was this plus the divisions among the Socialists that played the largest part in the defeat of revolution in Germany.

(2) Austria: Failed revolution, urban reform[2]

Austro-Hungarian defeat brought disintegration of the monarchy into national states and revolutionary turbulence in the two former capitals, Vienna and Budapest. Vienna now became the capital of a small country called Austria, populated overwhelmingly by Germans. Its two bourgeois parties, the Christian Socials and the smaller German Nationals, had a record of opposition to the Habsburg regime, so were not as implicated in its military defeat as their conservative counterparts in Germany. They dominated the countryside and the middle classes. The large Socialist Party (the SPO) was strong in Vienna and among the working class in the cities. By 1921, the socialist unions had recruited 59 percent of the nonagricultural labor force, a very high proportion for the time. In the urban-industrial sector, Austrian socialism was hegemonic. It also managed to remain relatively united through the turbulence of war and its aftermath. As elsewhere, the second industrial revolution and the war had encouraged a revolutionary shop stewards' movement and a Left Socialist faction, but these opted for influence within the Austrian Socialist Party rather than for adventurism outside. Unlike Germany, the Socialists did not have to face many disruptive ultras or Communists competing on their left flank. This was a more genuinely Marxist party than its German counterpart, and its major theorist, Otto Bauer, was more leftist than his German counterparts. It kept its cohesion and some of its ideological power – aggressive reformism was thought to promise a very different future – but there was a rough national balance of power between left and right. Neither could overpower the other. Until 1920, they worked warily together to establish a democratic republic.

The Socialists had one advantage over their comrades elsewhere. When the Habsburg multinational army disintegrated, most of its officers promptly

[2] I have relied in this section upon Carsten, 1972,; Gulick, 1948; essays in Rabinbach, 1985; and Zeman, 1961:134–8.

departed to their own national states. Thus, in Vienna the military command structure largely disappeared, leaving the soldiers' councils as the principal military units remaining in the cities. The SPO seized its opportunity, leading the restructuring of the armed forces as well as the civil service. The Socialists also formed a well-drilled paramilitary, the Schutzbund, to defend their own core constituencies. In the cities, this meant an ability to withstand attempts at communist coups in April and June 1919 using their own resources. Conversely, the rural areas were securely controlled by the right and its Heimwehr ("Home Guard") paramilitaries, formed out of rightist veterans.

Bauer tried to pioneer a third way between capitalism and socialism with the aim of creating enduring embryo socialist institutions and culture within the shell of a capitalist society. This was exemplified by "Red Vienna," in which an aggressive reformism was pushed across workplace, community, and electoral politics through education and social welfare programs, community building programs, and rent subsidies for the poor. It achieved significant economic redistribution within Vienna, although this also alienated much of the capital's middle class (Jill Lewis, 1983). It had a degree of ideological commitment rooted in the community, yet it was largely confined within the capital city, in a country that was not as urban or as industrial as Germany. Electorally, the SPO could not quite match the combined middle-class and rural vote, so after 1920 it remained in opposition. One consequence of this was that the official armed forces of the country became controlled by the right.

Bauer believed these limitations resulted from the balance of class power in the country. In the short run, he saw conservatism as too strong to be pushed back throughout the whole country. Thus, the Socialists should convert their core constituencies into defensible fortresses. The party's Linz program of 1927 was unusual for a Social Democratic party, stating openly that military force might be needed at some point in the future to protect itself from a bourgeois assault. In the long run, said the party leadership, the party could demonstrate the superiority of its municipal socialism, institutions, and culture to a majority of Austrians. Through education and enlightenment (*Bildung*), socialism could triumph (Rabinbach, 1985). However, Bauer's balance of power meant that the party – like other Socialist parties of the period – lacked an agrarian organizing strategy. It was believed that the example of Vienna would attract the peasantry, not direct rural mobilization.

Despite the normal decline of union membership in the 1920s, Austrian unions still had 34 percent of the nonagricultural labor force in 1931, the Socialist vote remained stable, and for a decade the city was militarily protected by the Schutzbund. The Socialists eventually succumbed to the stronger military forces of the army and the Heimwehr militia, controlled by rural and middle-class conservatism. In the end, the party leadership's pessimism overwhelmed it. It would not use the Schutzbund to defend itself against an increasingly authoritarian even fascist right, resisting the urgings of its leftists and youth movement to fight until it was too late. Instead, it tried to make compromises with the right, yielding democratic institutions to corporatism in the vain hope that Austria would survive with some of its democracy and municipal socialism intact. Later, in exile, Bauer rued his mistake: the party leadership, he reflected, should have called a general strike, mobilized the Schutzbund, and fought against the fascists in March 1933. There was then a chance of victory, but the party tamely submitted, leaving only a few of its more spirited militants to attempt an unofficial uprising, which was suppressed. The uprising occurred in Linz, Hitler's hometown (Mann, 2004: 232). After 1933, with Fascism ascendant and Hitler casting covetous eyes on the country, it would be difficult for Austrians to pursue their own path. Hitler obliterated the Socialists in 1938.

Yet this had been a near miss, although for an aggressive reformism, not a Bolshevik-style revolution. Let me review the same four factors as in Germany. First, unlike Germany, there were no important divisions within the left, although it was aiming not at revolution but at the first reformist stages of what its theorists believed or hoped would lead to a gradual and evolutionary transformation of society. Second, as in Germany, once the monarchy was disposed of, the dominant classes and the Church remained united, producing something of a stalemate in class conflict. Third, as in Germany, the countryside was conservative, generally supporting the Church and dominant classes, producing something of a stalemate between left and right. Because Austria was more rural than Germany, this tilted the overall balance of power somewhat rightward. Fourth, given the disintegration of the old imperial army, there was also something of a stalemate between leftist and rightist militias, but the emergence of both Austro-Fascism and Nazism saw a right more determined in its use of paramilitary force than the softer left. Revolution in the Bolshevik sense was never on the cards, but the stalemate was relatively overdetermined, and the eventual outcome was the triumph of the fascist Will.

(3) Hungary: Revolution and counter revolution[3]

Hungarian elites had dominated the southeastern half of the Habsburg Dual Monarchy. Defeat was experienced, as in Austria. Bourgeois parties were not compromised by participation in the old regime, and with Socialists, they formed a transitional coalition government. The army disintegrated, leaving soldiers' councils as the intact military units in the capital. Hungary suffered further defeats in fighting neighboring small states backed by the Entente, which proposed stripping Hungary of half its prewar territories. Hungarians expected the liberal-led government of Count Karolyi to talk the Entente out of

[3] This section draws on Carsten, 1972: 238–46, Tokes, 1967; Janos & Slottman, 1971; Eckelt, 1971, and Vermes, 1971.

this, but Karolyi failed, and continued a losing war on the borders. The regime lost authority, and Budapest was ruled mainly through workers' and soldiers' councils, its army unable to accomplish an honorable peace. This had resemblances to Russia.

The labor movement split into three main factions. A Socialist Party had been thrust from prewar insignificance in an economically backward country into ministerial positions. Never having been incorporated into political or economic power relations (unlike the German Socialists), it lacked reformist practice and was relatively open to leftism. One faction split-off to form a Communist Party, and Hungarian prisoners of war and exiles converted to Bolshevism in Russia. They returned in November 1918 under the skilled leadership of Bela Kun as a compact party and paramilitary. Expanding war industries had generated a revolutionary shop stewards movement in Budapest among skilled metalworkers. Together with soldiers' councils, they controlled the factories and streets. Kun's Communists proved dynamic, and they managed to recruit many Socialist Party leftists as members or sympathizers. The two parties were beginning to overlap. Kun and other leading Communists were then imprisoned by the coalition government. Events looked as if they might follow the German pattern: factionalism, Socialist Party sellout, confused action in the streets, and leftist adventurism.

Karolyi now dismissed the ineffectual government and invited Socialists to form a new one. Unbeknownst to him, Socialists and Communists were in the process of merging into a single Hungarian Socialist Party, and what he actually got was a government dominated by Communists astutely led by Bela Kun. Responding to pressure from the Budapest streets and believing Kun's statement that a Russian army was coming to the rescue, in March 1919 the Socialists proclaimed a Hungarian Soviet Republic, with Kun as Foreign Minister but the real leader behind the scenes. The new regime promptly dismissed Karolyi from his position as president. Kun's promise to restore Hungary's prewar boundaries, making Hungary a federation of self-governing ethnicities, brought him popularity and the support of some patriotic officers. The bourgeois parties fled into the countryside, where they joined forces with landowners and made overtures to invading Slovak, Serb, and Romanian armies.

The revolution might seem to have been on the road to success, and for four months the regime survived, its factionalism papered over by the need for defense. A Red Army was hastily assembled and thrown successfully against Slovak forces, but the regime was starved of resources, and did not help its cause with an agrarian collectivization program when the peasants wanted their own land. The countryside was further alienated by the regime's ideological commitment to total transformation. This notably included an antireligious campaign – better to focus on the Church's vast landholdings – and by roving paramilitaries practicing red terror against those who opposed them. This was the most agrarian country of the central European cases. There was some peasant discontent; a worker-peasant alliance was a possibility, but was squandered by the Marxian productivist orthodoxy of the revolutionary regime (Tokes, 1967: 185–8, 193, 195; Eckelt, 1971:82–7). This revolution also attempted major ideological and cultural reforms – its minister of education was the Marxist intellectual Georg Lukacs. The Salvationist creed was there, but it was trapped in Budapest, and the soviet could not even resupply armies facing superior forces in the countryside. The regime counted on help from Russia or revolutions in neighboring countries, but neither happened. The Bolsheviks in Russia were too enmeshed in civil war, and other revolutions had faded. On August 2, 1919, the Soviet collapsed when an advancing Romanian army defeated the Red Army. After a short phase of conciliatory government, White repression then began in earnest. Wielding ferocious anti-"Judeo-Bolshevik" rhetoric (for twenty of Kun's twenty-six ministers and vice ministers were Jews), the white terror killed ten times as many as the Reds had been able to. It was all over for the Socialists. Most insurgents paid with their lives – although Bela Kun paid later, at the hands of Stalin.

There were few problems on the left regarding factionalism and lack of ideological cohesion. The Communists did hew to salvationist Marxism, like the Bolsheviks, but this alienated most of the population outside of Budapest, including peasants – the crucial swing vote. Second, the enemy was also united, boosted by fear of Bolshevism given an ideological backbone by the Church. Third, although the Hungarian armies had collapsed at war's end, and the initial balance of military power between the two sides was only slightly tilted toward the right, the intervention of foreign counterrevolutionary forces was decisive. This was a revolution against the odds. The fundamental weakness was in dealing with the peasantry. The avenging rural-based armies trampled over socialism's urban enclaves. In Hungary, the relationship between defeat in war and failed revolution was carried to a more dramatic denouement.

A brief note on Italy

Finally, Italy is a "halfway" case in both war and revolution, and this supports my general model. It was nominally victorious in the war, yet its armies were actually worsted by Austrian forces. Because Italy fought on the victors' side, its government and army remained intact. There were no soldiers' councils, only deserters and embittered veterans. Insurrectionist rhetoric emerged on both the left and the right, but without an enfeebled old regime. It also experienced half-revolution: there were mass strikes and factory occupations, but no leftists attempted to seize the state. The occupations did not spread outside of the working class core, and the movement fizzled out. The ex-Socialist Mussolini – who did have a political strategy, an armed paramilitary, and the sympathy of many army officers, state officials, and capitalists – watched the failure with interest. Militarily, the left was weaker than either the forces of the state or the fascist paramilitaries, and this was the decisive factor in the outcome. The state learned from the failure of the tsarist and Provisional governments in Russia, and the fascists adapted their mode of organization from the Bolsheviks. Italian Socialists were not yet doomed – the decisive actions of fascists were required for that – but their situation was unenviable (Lyttleton, 1977; Williams, 1975).

Conclusion

This chapter has examined revolution and attempted revolution in the period 1917–1923. In these cases, we saw that nationalism had not simply trumped class consciousness. Revolutionaries did best when they could claim leadership of the people, blending nationalism into a class model of society. We also saw hints of this in the reformist labor movements discussed in this chapter, but their blending mainly came later, as we see in Chapter 9. In fact, where class conflict remained most suppressed, in the United States, nationalism was actually quite weak. Class and nation continued to rise together.

Revolutionary turbulence was almost everywhere the consequence of defeat in World War I. Italy, not quite defeated, saw the least turbulence among these countries. Spain, a neutral country, was an exception. Was the connection between war defeat and revolutionary turbulence correlation or cause, or was it spurious, produced by some other underlying cause? The defeated powers were already less democratic. Did this hasten military defeat, and also make them more vulnerable to insurgents? In the last chapter, I rejected the connection between democracy and war outcome, but there is a weaker version of the argument. Three states were potentially weaker in defeat than the other states. In Russia, Germany, and Austria-Hungary, the army was central to the regime. The monarchs, their kinsmen, and their appointees were the government and the high command, and their courts and governments were dominated by military uniforms. If their armies failed, so did monarchical government. There was no such identity in Britain, France, Italy, or the United States. Political leaders could be changed without damaging the legitimacy of the whole state. Although despotic political regimes might stand or fall by the result of the war, parliamentary democracies could replace one ruling party with another.

The extent of collaboration between capital and the state in repressing worker and peasant protest also varied. At one extreme was Russia, where the heavy hand of the state dominated capital-labor relations. Then came Germany, followed by Austria-Hungary, then Italy and France, and then Britain. The United States was more complex, with repression of labor, but wielded less by the federal government than by state governments and law courts. If the Russian state failed in war, however, Russian business would have fewer autonomous power resources to deal with radical workers than business in a defeated Germany or Austria would, would have fewer autonomous resources than Italy and

France, and so forth. Capitalism was more vulnerable in some regimes than others. Germany, Austria, and Russia did not lose the war because they were not democracies, but once they had lost it, they were in more danger from revolution. This might be an economic as well as political revolution, aimed at the capitalist class as well as the state, for during the war the two had become transparently connected in exploiting the masses.

Only Russia saw a successful revolution. In Germany, Austria, and Hungary, defeat plus the Bolshevik Revolution created attempted revolutions that failed. In Italy, a bad war produced less revolutionary turbulence. Defeat had destroyed much of the organization of the state, caused capitalism to totter, and emboldened a socialist movement mobilizing workers, but not enough for a revolution to succeed. Invasion and defeat in both world wars led to successful revolutions (in Russia and China); major wartime sacrifice followed by defeat or great dislocation but without foreign occupation brought a short period of revolutionary turbulence and a failed revolution. As we see in Chapter 9, where wartime sacrifice was followed by victory, capitalism and old regimes reformed, modernized, and strengthened democratic citizenship. The victors saw no outbreaks of revolutionary turbulence, although they all experienced strike-waves aimed at extracting reforms from the state and employers. This also happened in most neutral countries. All the neutral Scandinavians experienced events similar to the reformist struggles in Britain and France. The extreme was Sweden in 1917, when garrison regiments marched side by side with protesting workers, but they did not carry weapons, the demonstrations passed off peacefully, and their main result was the founding of a legal Left Socialist political party.

Revolutionary turbulence was greater after the First World War than the Second. In the first, the major defeated states were not occupied or controlled by the victors. German and Austro-Hungarian armies surrendered standing almost everywhere on foreign soil. Only token victor forces entered their territories. The Ottoman Empire did have some of its territories occupied and dismembered, although Turkish forces remained in control of the Anatolian heartland, which proved less conducive to revolution than internal reform. In 1945, however, the victors took over the territory of the defeated powers, including Japan, to ensure satisfactory new regimes. The victors made sure that reform triumphed over revolution. Several countries experienced a more complex sequence of regime collaboration with the Axis Powers, the defeat of its forces, and then "liberation" by partly indigenous, partly foreign forces. These were partially free to form their own regimes, so three of them saw some limited turbulence: Belgium in 1945, France at the end of 1947, and Italy in 1949. In Greece, a two-stage civil war (December 1944–January 1945 and 1946–1949) was fought between a conservative government backed by Britain and the United States and the Greek Communist Party. Without the use of American and British power, these cases would have been more insurrectionary, and Greece might have fallen to the Communists. We see that mass-mobilization wars have always had important effects on class relations, but the effect has varied between the victors, the vanquished, and the neutrals, and according to local balances of class power, including, in the more revolutionary cases, the balance of military power.

In Germany, Austria, Hungary, and Italy after the first war, revolution failed because conditions present in Russia were more marginal there. These concerned the three groups who provided the revolutionary momentum in Russia – soldiers, peasants, and workers – ranged against the dominant classes and elites. There were several causes of success or failure. First, in all cases, the industrial working class and its often intellectual leadership led revolutionary and reformist struggles; the dominant classes formed the core of resistance. Second, the ideological and political cohesion of the left was weak. Factionalism on the left loomed largest in Germany and Italy, and spread right down to the shop floor. In Germany, the reformist SPD was willing to turn to rightist militias to suppress its own left, as Kerensky and his moderate socialist allies in Russia had been willing to do. However, the SPD, unlike Kerensky, had considerable support among workers for this. In Italy, a faction of the Socialist Party and syndicalists split off to form fascist parties. Third, apart from Russia and Hungary, the left was dominated by reformists, not revolutionaries. A firm will boosted by commitment to Marxism's salvationist creed was evident in Russia and Hungary, but only the Bolsheviks combined this with a short-term pragmatism attuned to the unpredictable flow of events. Fourth, the cohesion and infrastructural power of the ruling class was also important. The ruling regime in Russia was not very factionalized until the combination of the war and a developing revolutionary process broke it apart. Much more important here was the havoc the war played with the regime's infrastructural powers: it could not feed the towns or supply the army. The reverse was true in other countries, where the disruption of infrastructural powers at war's end and the disintegration of monarchies allowed the expression of mass discontent, but the ruling class swiftly recovered its cohesion, perceiving that what happened in Russia might happen again. From the global flow of class struggle, both sides learned lessons, but capitalism was safe and moderate Socialists helped save it.

Fifth and sixth, I have emphasized the role of soldiers and peasants. For soldiers, the difference from Russia was crucial. Russian soldiers rebelled during the war, kept their arms, and contributed them to the revolution. Elsewhere, soldiers' actions took place at war's end, just before or during demobilization. Victory felt good, defeat did not, but demobilization defused collective action and gave individual soldiers a better option – return home, leaving their weapons behind. Militias did form, but more on the political right than the left. Where Socialists did form militias, in Austria and later in Germany, they were still reluctant to kill people. Except for Hungary, Socialists were too nice for their own good – the opposite of Fascists, who eventually proved too bad for their own good. Officer corps and rightist militias suppressed the revolutions.

In fact, not even in Russia had the Socialists initiated revolutionary violence, for they rode to power on the backs of insurrectionary soldiers. Although Marxism used a violent-sounding rhetoric of class struggle and revolution, it did not yet have an actual military theory, a curious oversight for a revolutionary movement. The theory came to fruition with Trotsky during the Russian Civil War and Mao after the Shanghai disaster.

For peasants, conditions also differed. Agrarian transformations had begun earlier and were now institutionalized. Nowhere were peasants as available to the left as in Russia, and conflict was as likely as solidarity between rural and urban populations. Slower industrialization and urbanization had resulted in a more hereditary proletariat and greater ideological differences between town and country. During the war, food shortages worsened urban-rural conflict. Peasants favored high fixed prices for their goods or the black market; city dwellers wanted strict price controls and rationing. Peasant soldiers resented industrial workers' exemptions from fighting, so when revolutionary turbulence broke out across central Europe, peasants rarely participated. In these countries, half or more of the population and more than half of the army was drawn from the countryside. Conservatives held onto their rural power bases, and overcame urban insurgents. At one extreme, in Hungary, lack of peasant support was probably a sufficient cause of failure, as this was the most rural case. In industrial Germany, peasant support might conceivably have been dispensed with. Perhaps a determined revolutionary leadership might have bought off the peasantry, as in Russia, but this strategy had only occurred to the Bolsheviks after the peasants were already seizing land. The socialist parties of central Europe were industrially oriented. Peasants intruded into their consciousness mainly as soldiers, the likely instrument of their oppression. They were right – but they helped make it so.

These failed revolutions show that even when the working class' powers were boosted by defeat in war, they were not destined to achieve revolution. That was not merely the result of the general developmental logic of capitalism. The success of the Bolshevik Revolution was due to the sudden intervention of military and political power relations, but it deluded leftists elsewhere into exaggerating their own revolutionary chances. These would have been better had they mobilized support among exploited rural strata, although this was admittedly difficult. However, without peasant support and with worker divisions, with fewer arms in the hands of the revolutionaries than of the militaristic right, defeat was certain. This would then lead to further defeat as one-half of Europe pioneered new forms of despotic rightism, notably Fascism. There, apart from Russia, not revolution but counterrevolution was ascending. Across the world, the ideological alternatives had greatly widened: socialism, liberalism, and fascist-leaning authoritarianism all provided supposedly attainable utopias. Globalization was gradually becoming less fractured – more universal – but it was also polymorphous.

7 A half-global crisis: Explaining the Great Depression

Introduction

The Great Depression was the second major dislocation to hit the world in the twentieth century. The crisis, like the Great War before it, was half-global, although this one was substantially transnational, crashing through state and imperial borders, for most of a decade wreaking havoc in half the world's economies. In this chapter, we see a negative, disintegrating globalization.

States responded by attempting to withdraw a little from the global economy, intensifying nation-state cages. Because its epicenter was in what was now the biggest national economy – the United States – I focus most there. Compared to all other capitalist recessions, the Great Depression was off the scale in its depth and longevity, and was perceived at the time to be a crisis of capitalism itself. The left was encouraged, mistakenly seeing it as beginning of capitalism's death-throes, but the sense of crisis was also widespread among capitalism's greatest supporters – investors and entrepreneurs, conservative politicians and economists. They called for a major effort to save capitalism, and eventually, after a series of political compromises between right and left, capitalism was saved, but by being changed for the better into a more regulated, social democratic or lib-lab version of capitalism embodying social citizenship for all.

Because the Depression was an economic phenomenon, we should expect its major causes to lie in antecedent economic power relations. Most economists go much further, seeing economies as largely closed systems driven by rational actors who generate markets in which laws of scarcity, supply, and demand move continually toward equilibrium, punctuated by business cycles. Keynesians qualify this by seeing no necessary short-term drive to equilibrium, although they think that in the long run equilibrium will be re-established. Marxian economists contest all equilibrium, replacing it with the functional alternative of systemic contradictions. None of this is foolish. Indeed, when economists apply their systemic models to real-world economies, they make predictions about the short-term that often have a success rate of well more than 50 percent – which is above the level other social sciences attain. Economists have indeed developed a fairly good understanding of short-term business cycles.

Unfortunately for them, the development of the modern economy has included bursts of growth and crisis that were far from being normal cycles.

There had been a serious Depression in the 1870s, now another in 1929, then a Great Boom after World War II, and finally a Great Recession beginning in 2008. These were not mere cycles; they were too big and impacted by structural changes in the economy, although in different ways. Thus, they present two major problems for conventional economic theories: one emanating mainly from within economic power relations, the other from outside.

The internal problem is the sheer complexity of economies. For goods to be produced, sold, and consumed – that is, for markets to function – many phases of human activity are involved. Most economists (and most Marxists) believe there is some discoverable, determinate set of relations between these phases. The ideal of their endeavors is the creation of a mathematical equation combining all of them, but the interrelations may not be determinate. In theory, supply should equal demand, but think of all the phases and actors involved in the great chain between them – investors, inventors, workers, employers, consumers, savers, plus all the lobbyists and social movements and governments. These are all related to each other in the economy, but imperfectly so. They comprise a long causal chain, each part linked to a distinct causal side-chain, and these might be out of sync with each other. At normal moments of time, most of these links are sufficiently coordinated to generate a functioning capitalist economy, functioning imperfectly but well enough to produce a rough equilibrium and economic growth. When one phase of the economy is not working well, this is normally called a crisis, for example of the overaccumulation of capital or inadequate demand. Any contributing factor can be either too great or too small for smooth functioning. We are familiar in the post–World War II world with the difficulties of balancing supply and demand so that the economy steers between a profit squeeze for capitalists and underconsumption by workers. Similarly, lagging technological innovation may lead to industrial stagnation, or it may be too rapid, leading to the replacement of labor-intensive industries by capital-intensive industries, increasing unemployment and lowering consumer demand. A well-functioning capitalist economy might be seen as a process of steering down the middle in each phase of activity, avoiding too much or too little. The process is far from being a recipe for continuing equilibrium.

Economists' models can cope with a crisis specific to any single phase, and they can even suggest a solution – or at least a sticking-plaster solution – but a much bigger structural crisis should not be seen as being either merely a bigger specific crisis or a single systemic crisis. Instead, it is a concatenation of more contingent multiple crises, rippling outward as more unexpected weaknesses are "found out" in other phases, creating as it were a "perfect storm" of capitalism. A crisis in agricultural production may find out unsuspected weakness in rural banking; rapid technological innovation may lead to overinvestment, which finds out stock market weaknesses; a debt crisis infecting banking sectors in various countries may find out weaknesses in the European Union; and so forth. I will argue in this chapter that the Great Depression was such a concatenation of crises. Note, however, that if the opposite is the case, if all aspects are in sync, as they were after World War II, extraordinary growth may follow.

The external problem is recognized by economists, many of whom accept that they have not done very well at developing a theory of secular economic growth or decline. They recognize that extra market forces such as institutions, culture, and technology play major roles in economic growth and decline, but they only study them in perfunctory ways. In truth, sociologists do not offer much help, for we lack an agreed model of culture, institutional development, and technological innovation. Yet I do have such a model; I see them as driven by the sources of social power, but with emergent capacities of their own to power social and economic development. The institutions that matter most in modern societies are economic (markets, property, and corporations), military (armed forces and paramilitaries), and political (states), with geopolitics playing a mixed political and military role. In my model, culture – for which I prefer the term "ideology" – is largely generated by the interrelations of economic, military, and political power, although an internal logic of ideology itself is a drive to discover ultimate meaning in the world. However, when crisis strikes and existing power relations seem unable to find adequate solutions, new ideologies emerge, and some of them become powerful, changing power configurations, including the economy. My view of technology is that it is consistently steered toward the attainment or retention of distributive power by economic, military, political, and (occasionally) ideological power actors, but it has emergent collective powers.

This may sound rather abstract, although it clearly involves a multicausal explanation of structural economic crises. More specifically, this chapter presents a multifactor explanation of the Great Depression, seeing it as a concatenation of several distinct economic crises piling on top of each other, exacerbated by a burst of technological innovation and policy mistakes that were not accidental but powered by class and geopolitical ideologies.

The impact of World War I

The Great War cast a long and rather global shadow. To its participants, it had brought economic dislocation and rocketing military expenditure. In the UK and Germany, the rise was tenfold; in the United States, thirteenfold (although from a much lower base). The reverse happened when peace came: by 1920, military spending was back down to near prewar levels. Economists call the wartime rise a misallocation of funds, and note the difficulties of restoring allocations to equilibrium afterward, which is a punctuated equilibrium model. Most of these problems, however, seemed played out by the mid-1920s, except for a few countries. Most of Britain's foreign portfolio had been sold off to

America in order to pay for the war. It never got it back, and its general power declined. The dismantling of Austria-Hungary and the banning of postwar cooperation between Germany, Austria, and Hungary caused economic problems for these countries that only Hitler was to settle. Neutrals who had done well out of the war, such as Japan and countries exporting agricultural products, suffered difficulties as the combatant economies resumed normal production and needed less of their exports.

Yet none of this can be said to have actually caused the Depression. Similar disruptions, plus more physical destruction of resources, came from World War II, and this led not to global Depression but global Boom. By the mid-1920s, most of the world had seemingly recovered from this war and was experiencing mild growth. Normalcy seemed restored just before the Depression hit. Nor did the major problems of World War I adversely affect the United States, which had benefitted economically from the war yet now led the Depression. However, the war did have indirect effects on the Depression, because it impacted geopolitics, the condition of agriculture, and class conflict, and these in turn impacted directly on the Depression and helped diffuse it across the world. As the world remained divided into nation-states, however, some with empires, these effects differed according to the standing of each state/empire in the international order, the weight of agriculture in its national economy, and the power of its contending classes. Not all was transnational. I turn first to geopolitics.

Postwar geopolitics: Hegemony and the gold standard

Many describe the prewar economic order as embodying British economic *hegemony*, that is, Britain provided public goods and set the rules of the international economy. They diagnose the interwar problem as the lack of a single hegemonic power able to provide public goods or new rules for the international economy. Kindleberger (1986: 289) famously asserted, "From 1919 to 1929 Britain could not, and the United States would not, act in the capacity of world leader." Although he did not use the word "hegemon," he originated what is known as "hegemonic stability" theory, which is accepted by many economists as well as by world systems sociologists. They see British hegemony as having provided both public goods and order before World War I, and American hegemony as providing them after World War II. Because the interwar period lacked a single hegemon, it also lacked stability, as – it is said – the international economy cannot be run by a committee (Arrighi, 1994; Arrighi & Silver, 1999). This is a Hobbesian theory of order: we need a sovereign to impose rules upon us; otherwise, social life is nasty, brutish, and short.

Yet Britain had not been hegemonic before the war; its power within Europe had always been limited and dependent on alliance with other Great Powers. It had the largest imperial segment across the world and the biggest navy, but these were only quantitative differences. True, the pound sterling, tied to gold, was still the linchpin of world finances, but the British were no longer powerful enough to run the system by themselves. Adjustments to the Bank of England's bank rate did not, unaided, provide economic stability. By the turn of the century, the gold standard was maintained by international cooperation between the central banks and treasuries of Britain, France, Germany, and Russia. When the international economy was running smoothly, the British Treasury could nudge it along. When crisis struck, the others had to step in to help. It had been an informal committee of the Great Powers, helping Britain steer the world through financial crises. Eichengreen concludes, "What rendered the commitment to the gold standard credible … was that the commitment was international, not merely national. That commitment was activated through international cooperation" (1992: 31; cf Clavin, 2000: 44). Economic equilibrium was not a purely economic phenomenon; it was actually assisted by geopolitics.

The system allowed for some flexibility according to a country's economic power and stability. There existed several tiers of countries according to whether they adhered faithfully to the gold standard (such as Britain or France), whether they might leave it in a crisis but return at parity afterward (such as the US or Italy), or whether they could not adhere at all (such as most Latin American countries). Each tier got something akin to today's credit ratings (Bordo & Rockoff, 1996). The British led the gold standard, coordinating a coalition of powers recognizing the mutuality of their interests. This made it work quite well. Indeed, as I described in Volume II, international bankers had tried quite hard to avoid war. When the Great War came, it was not their fault.

The gold standard ended during the war, when everyone except the United States withdrew their currencies from gold, and free-floating currencies followed. For a time after the war, international financial instability paralleled domestic turmoil. Almost all currencies rapidly depreciated against the dollar, which diffused inflation globally. The war also destroyed British financial leadership. Britain had taken out a large mortgage to win the war, and was indebted to American financiers. Most of Europe was indebted to American and British banks. Wall Street was replacing the City of London as the world's major money market, but international institutions did not yet reflect this. The postwar world was not one of a balance of power but of a destabilized power structure.

Governments did then begin returning one by one to gold. When Britain returned sterling to gold in 1925, the gold standard was effectively renewed. It now lacked a leader, although the weight of the American economy and gold reserves dominated in reality. It wasn't the classic gold standard system of the prewar period. It comprised voluntary ad hoc cooperation among central banks trying to maintain a disparate set of gold parities, and few countries restored full convertibility. There was Anglo-American collaboration (especially between Montagu Norman and Benjamin Strong, the effective leaders of their central banks), but calls for permanent institutions of coordination were ignored. There was a period of relative stability, and almost all politicians, bankers, businessmen, and economists believed that the revived gold standard would maintain it. Economic performance did improve between 1925 and 1929 (Aldcroft, 2002).

The gold standard did not only involve technical matters. Convertibility to gold put an upper limit on the paper currency governments could print, and thus prevented inflation and budget deficits, which were considered irresponsible. Unlike in recent years, there was no general practice of modest inflation in order to promote growth. Credible commitment to a gold standard required that a country maintain fiscal soundness to investors so that its monetary authority could ensure long-run price stability and convertibility, with enough gold reserves to guarantee the currency. Given current ideological assumptions, these conditions should have been in place before returning to gold, but they rarely were (Hamilton, 1988). A shortage of gold did not help. Moreover, most governments returned their currencies to their prewar parity level as a crude signal of credibility, which they said was necessary for national honor, so nationalist ideology also played a role (Eichengreen, 1992: 163; Nakamura, 1988: 464). A country demonstrated its power by overvaluing its currency; credibility was for the investors, who had the ability to start a run on currencies. "Business confidence," which Block notes is generally the principal limit placed on state autonomy, was in this decade principally that of finance capital. The transnational power of financial speculators, so evident today, is in fact not new, nor is the tension between national and transnational aspects of capitalism. In the interwar period, however, investors were mainly drawn from "old regime" landed and propertied families, the dominant class from the late nineteenth century to the Great Depression.

The chosen level for returning to the gold standard bore little relevance to current economic health. Most currencies were overvalued (Britain, Italy, Japan, and the Scandinavian countries), although two important ones were undervalued (France and the United States). Gold supplies and currencies were poorly calibrated: 40 percent of the world's gold reserves had been sucked into the United States, and French undervaluation eventually sucked in a further 30 percent. They hoarded, "sterilized," their gold rather than use it productively, making it unavailable for other countries. From the point of view of the world economy, this was a serious mistake, ideologically driven amid geopolitical rivalry. It created inadequate gold reserves elsewhere, making investors uneasy. Decisions were made by financial authorities within each nation-state separately; no one assumed responsibility for the international order (Moure, 2002: 262–3). American isolationism was to play an especially damaging role. So national caging was the first problem for the gold standard. This was becoming a global economy, but there was neither a hegemon nor a committee in charge of it. That was a weakness of the interwar economy, but it need not have been too costly. Yet it was to be found out by an economic crisis.

The deflationary bias meant that countries with overvalued currencies felt compelled to pursue tight monetary policy to stem gold outflows and stock market speculation. They deliberately depressed their economies, instead of the needed monetary and fiscal expansion, maintaining their gold payments, signaling soundness to investors. Governments with undervalued currencies might have reflated, but there were no penalties if they did not, and the United States and France never reflated enough to improve the world economy. Instead, there was obsessive balancing of budgets (Bernanke & James, 1991; Clavin, 2000: 55; Temin, 1989: 19–25). This was another weakness, but again not necessarily a major one.

It did had implications for class conflict, which had been intensified in the aftermath of World War I and the Bolshevik Revolution. Political economy had been designed to please investors, not the masses. Finance ministers and central bankers were themselves drawn from the investing classes. The end of World War I saw a surge in democracy and popular class consciousness. Workers, small farmers, and others saw that the deflationary class bias of the gold standard hurt them. Mild inflation helps workers and small farmers, deflation hurts them, as it does economic sectors that are indebted or need loans to finance activity. Deflation lowers their commodity prices and increases the real value of their debts, but deflation helps most of the middle and upper classes, especially those on fixed incomes and rentiers whose assets appreciate in real terms (Clavin, 2000: 58–9).

This conflict of class interests remained important in domestic politics through the 1920s. It was not a fundamental weakness because it was eased by conservatives' ability to mobilize traditional institutions of deference and clientelism to secure many working-class and lower middle-class votes. The first postwar years saw a leftist offensive, as described in Chapters 6 and 9. To placate newly organized workers, wages rose sharply. Yet because other classes resisted actual redistribution, the result was inflation, especially in countries with strong labor movements, such as Germany. Inflation hurt most people, and increased support for conservatives committed to deflation. Their governments then hit workers hard, increasing unemployment and lowering wages. Deflating governments knew they were intensifying class conflict, and they sometimes modified policies to help particular groups whose power they feared, but the drift was clearly regressive.

In France, a leftist Cartel des Gauches came into power and proposed wealth and capital taxes to reduce the deficit. This provoked capital flight, increasing the fiscal crisis. Investors were covertly backed by France's central bank, willing to risk monetary collapse to bring down the left. Enough centrists were persuaded to desert the Cartel to cause its fall and bring in a more conservative regime under Poincaré. Parliament then gave him the power to resolve the budget without requiring a parliamentary vote. He abandoned attempts to soak the rich, introducing tight budgetary policy that stemmed the capital flight (Moure, 2002: chaps. 4, 5, p. 261; Eichengreen, 1992: 172–83). These struggles revealed the superior political power of transnational business confidence over nationally caged organized labor, if backed by major national parties and much of the middle class. The power of finance capital is older than most contemporary commentators think, as world systems theorists have also perceived.

Faced with similar class power, a minority Labour government in Britain also fell. Sterling was overvalued by about 10 percent, so industrialists had to cut their costs by 5–10 percent to remain competitive. They took it mainly from their wage bills, but this intensified industrial conflict. (Clavin, 2000: 50–1). Keynes understood the class implications of Conservative Chancellor Winston Churchill's return to the gold standard, denouncing it as a "deliberate intensification of unemployment" in order to lower the level of wages. He predicted it would bring increasing social conflict and even threaten democracy (Skidelsky, 1983: 203). In the General Strike of 1926, Churchill again played the class warrior but won. The unions were defeated after a long and bitter strike. Keynes was wrong; democracy continued, if on a more rightward path.

In Germany, deflation and the return to gold also enabled employers to increase working hours and reduce real wages at the same time taxation became more regressive. The early gains made by workers in the Weimar Republic were reversed. In almost all countries, the costs of deflation were imposed primarily on workers and farmers (Polanyi, 1957: 229–33; Alesina & Drazen 1991: 1173–4). This was especially clear in the United States, where working-class organization was negligible. Governments continued to prioritize the value of their currencies, to keep the "confidence" of transnational investors, backed by a more combative middle class. Leftist resistance was overridden, and politics in the mid-1920s shifted rightward. This carried an economic downside, however, for it lowered mass consumption and the potential for growth. The old regime was hanging on, but this was another weakness that might be found out in an actual crisis.

The gold standard also faced increasing nationalism directed abroad, although it was not very aggressive nationalism, as almost everyone had had enough of war. Before the war, geopolitical rivalries had been more insulated from international finance. Now the peace treaties forced Germany and Austria-Hungary to pay large reparations to France and Britain. Keynes saw that reparations were a nonproductive form of redistribution, bringing economic difficulties. Although the United States was more understanding than Britain and France about reparations, it insisted on the repayment of its own loans. Germany, initially in desperate economic straits, could pay reparations only with the aid of large American private loans to rebuild its economy. Dollars made it possible for foreign nations to repay reparations and loans, yet the United States, beset by domestic political pressures, maintained an average tariff rate of 33 percent, which made it difficult for foreigners to export sufficient goods into the United States to pay for their American loans. As one banker put it, "The debts of the outside world to us are ropes about the necks of our debtors, by means of which we pull them towards us. Our trade restrictions are pitchforks pressed against their bodies, by means of which we hold them off" (Clavin, 2000: 87). A dependency theory applied to the globe! The technological dynamism of the U.S. economy led to greater worker productivity and overcapacity, further lowering the prices of U.S. goods. Clearly, any reduction in U.S. loans would pull the plug out from the system. The United States did continue lending, but did not adjust domestic policies in return for comparable adjustments abroad. There was too little geopolitical cooperation (Moure, 2002; Clavin, 2000; Eichengreen, 1992: 209–10). Kindleberger was right in his negative pronouncement about the interwar period: there was no stable international regime, but fundamentally, because World War I had not solved geopolitical rivalries. Globally, this was a dual transnational-international economy without effective institutions of order. It was not that the world needed a hegemon to achieve order; it was that this particular multipower system could not provide it in a crisis, unlike its prewar counterpart.

In 1923, the German government announced it could not make the due reparations. In retaliation, the French and Belgian governments sent in troops to occupy the Rhineland. Germany, with only the tiny army decreed by the Treaty of Versailles, could not resist, but the outraged local population went on a sit-down strike, supported by loans from the Reichsbank, which caused hyperinflation and put Germany even further away from paying back either reparations or loans. The French could not fund their budget from reparations payments, as they had hoped. Instead, they had to raise taxes, which provoked class conflict. The U.S. government refused to alleviate the crisis by reducing the size of European debts, but instead offered private American loans that only increased debt. The United States did step in with the Dawes Plan to reschedule German reparations. That might have worked, but by 1928 crisis was stirring elsewhere, and this would seriously undermine international cooperation.

A committee might have run a gold standard, as before the war, but not amid these geopolitical conflicts. The United States might have assumed economic hegemony in principle, but not in practice, because most Americans believed in the primacy of domestic politics. Congress had to approve economic policy, but was parochial, unwilling to see a potential long-term benefit to its own districts or states from a healthy international economy. Woodrow Wilson had failed to talk Americans into the League of Nations. Americans were not much interested in international cooperation, let alone hegemony. Neither a committee of powers nor the United States was capable of leading the world economy. That was not necessarily disastrous, but it would become problematic if another crisis struck.

From recession to Great Depression

A recession now began across numerous countries. It hit Australia and the Dutch East Indies in 1927, Germany and Brazil in 1928, and in early 1929 Argentina, Canada, and Poland – all before the U.S. crash. Apart from Germany, the early sufferers were agricultural countries, and agriculture was the initial precipitator of crisis. Agriculture was easily the most important world industry. World War I had offered export opportunities to farmers in noncombatant countries, but at war's end there was agricultural recovery in the combatant and blockaded countries, and combined with continued technological development in agriculture, this produced overproduction and falling prices and incomes. Most peasants across the world sold their produce to merchants who sold it to the cities and for export. The peasants needed cash to pay their taxes, but when prices fell, peasants in the colonies and independent states such as China were caught in a scissors between their own declining revenues and the demands of landlords and tax officials. They turned to moneylenders, but were then in danger of losing their land to them. Although the attention of economists has focused on finance and industry in the Depression, the world's peasants were worst hit (Rothermund, 1996). Even in advanced countries such as the United States or France, close to 30 percent of the population still worked in agriculture. Their lowered demand was a major global deflationary force in the Depression – as it had been in the last Great Depression of the 1870s.

The recession then grew most in the United States and other advanced countries. Some American industries were already doing poorly before it struck. Mining, lumber, and textiles had been troubled through most of the decade; construction took a downturn after 1925. One factor in most countries was demographic. Because of war deaths, and in the United States declining immigration, fewer households formed, reducing demand, especially for housing. The index of general industrial production then turned down in the first half of 1929, before the stock market crash, indicating problems in the real economy. Excessive fixed investment, followed by overcapacity and a rapid drop in investment, was causing deflation and helped spark off recession. Those who were in debt amid price deflation or reduced demand for their product risked defaulting on their loans. They cut current spending to keep up their payments, further lowering demand. Businesses began to fail as construction and factory orders plunged. This is the "debt-deflation" view of the Depression, held, among others, by present Federal Chairman Bernanke (2000). Ironically, in 2008 he had to deal with a similar sequence of events.

This was unexpectedly exacerbated by a stock market bubble resulting from a different causal chain. In 1928 and 1929, the index of stock prices suddenly grew much more rapidly than the index of dividends, a sign of stock market overheating. In mid-1929, the composite stock price index of closed-end mutual funds proved overvalued by around 30 percent, also a sign of investor overconfidence (White, 1990; De Long & Shleifer, 1991; Rappoport & White, 1993, 1994). These indicated a credit-fueled bubble that partially concealed the recession underway. It is not easy to explain such an overvalued stock market, but credit was too easy and profits were high, so stock values and profits continued upward and investors assumed this would continue. This was a period of celebration and pride in America at the rate of technological innovation in the country, adding to the overly bullish stock market. The combination of the two problems – technology-driven overinvestment (especially in factory electrification) and low consumption – was unsustainable, creating a substantial excess capacity of anywhere between 14 percent and 31 percent by 1929 (Beaudreau, 1996).

What was needed for the creation part of Schumpeter's process of creative destruction was growth in new industries such as automobiles and household electric consumer durables, but consumer demand was too low to support the necessary expansion. When wages were rising much less than productivity or profits, overcapacity and overinvestment burst the stock market bubble. Rising inequality did not help demand either, because the rich spend a lower proportion of their income on consumption than the middle and working classes. Credit institutions for these people were barely developed, so could not help boost demand artificially (although our experience of the 1990s and 2000s does not suggest that this would be a satisfactory solution!).

President Hoover, his advisors, and the Fed recognized that the speculation was excessive. Unfortunately, the dominant faction believed in "liquidation." They expected the market to ultimately self-adjust – we might call them neoliberals in today's parlance. The role of government, they believed, was merely to help the market liquidate bad money, inefficient producers, foolish investors, and overpaid workers. The laws of capitalism were tough, but it was believed they worked! So in January 1928, the Fed began to deflate to put pressure on the markets, reducing the money supply and raising the discount rate a full one and a half points to 5 percent (Hamilton, 1987). It also discouraged lending collateralized with equities. The Fed had successfully fought two small recessions in the 1920s with deflation (at the expense of workers), and saw this one as another opportunity to liquidate, engineering a decline in stock market values, a rise in unemployment, and a lowering of wages. To most officials and economists, this was the cure. It was endorsed by economists as diverse as Schumpeter, Hayek, and Robbins. They viewed recessions as an inevitable shaking out of inefficiencies – the necessary downside of Schumpeter's view of capitalism as creative destruction. Indeed, Schumpeter argued that the choice was between recession now and a worse recession down the line if government attempted to boost the economy.

They were wrong. Unfortunately, deflation worked all too well, as the economy had already turned down, and the combination turned the bursting of the bubble into the "crash" of October 29, 1929, a day in which American common stocks lost 10 percent of their value. A large aggregate negative-demand shock came soon after the crash (Cecchetti & Karras, 1994). The unemployed and those who feared unemployment were drastically cutting their spending on consumer durables. Consumption collapsed in 1930, deepening the recession (Romer, 1990, 1993: 29; Temin 1976: 65; 1981; R. Gordon 2005). Those with capital now had incentives not to invest; amid deflation, their money was growing in value if they simply kept hold of it. This furthered the decline in industrial production, increasing overcapacity and long inventories. The profit motive, the key to capitalism, was turning perverse. The sum of individual capitalist preferences might be the collective ill. George Orwell illustrates the collective insanity of the Depression in this scene from his *The Road to Wigan Pier*: "Several hundred men risk their lives and several hundred women scrabble in the mud for hours … searching eagerly for tiny chips of coal" to heat their homes. For them, this arduously gained "free" coal was "more important almost than food." Standing idle nearby was the machinery they had previously used to mine more coal in five minutes than they could now gather in a day.

In late 1930, the first of four banking panics swept the United States. Seven hundred and forty-four banks failed, mainly in rural areas, the consequence of the agricultural depression. As interest rates rose, farmers' debts reached insupportable levels, and with more small banks than other countries, U.S. banking in rural areas was vulnerable. Because there was no deposit insurance, savers might lose everything, so they panicked and withdrew their funds. A second wave of bank failures hit from June to December 1931. No less than 9,000 banks failed during the 1930s. Surviving banks became more cautious in their lending, and built-up their capital stocks rather than make loans, adding deflationary pressure and accelerating the downward spiral of the money supply. With prices falling 10 percent annually, investors' best strategy was not to invest but to wait until next year, when their dollar would be worth 10 percent more. The government responded to falling revenues by cutting expenditures, adding further deflationary pressures. A change came when Roosevelt declared a "banking holiday" of one week in March 1933. While the banks were closed, an army of inspectors went through them, separating the solvent from the insolvent. This at least restored confidence in the banking sector. Regulation of them followed with the FDIC in January 1934.

By 1930, this was something much worse than a mere cyclical recession, especially in the United States. The median decline in output for the fifteen countries that began their decline before 1931 was 9 percent, but in the United States it was 21 percent. The consumer price index fell 2.6 percent, the supply of currency in circulation and bank reserves fell 2.8 percent, and the real interest rate rose to more than 11 percent, the highest since the recession of 1920–1921 (Hamilton, 1987). Between 1929 and 1933, U.S. real GNP fell by 30 percent, official unemployment rose from 4 percent to 25 percent – although the real rate was nearer 33 percent – and real gross domestic private investment fell by a mind-boggling 85 percent. As we have seen, this had not been a single great crisis, but a series of shocks that had piled onto each other, finding out weaknesses in the economy and government policy.

Yet the Depression struck unevenly across the world. It struck Western Europe and the Anglophone countries hard. Canada, the United States, and Germany suffered the most, although Belgium, France, Italy, Britain, and some Latin American countries also reeled. Even in these two macro-regions, however, the United States and Canada lost six times as much per capita income as Britain did, and three times as much as France. The Depression barely affected other large swathes of the world. China was only slightly affected, and the Soviet Union, Japan and its colonies Korea and Taiwan, and Eastern Europe continued to grow right through the Depression. Moreover, a number of advanced countries got out of it quite quickly by leaving the gold standard and reflating their economies. The United States could have done the same, and in fact later did begin to do so, but American overconfidence in 1937 produced another recession, and only the enhanced industrial demand of World War II enabled a full recovery. These international and macro-regional differences make me wonder whether the term "Great Depression" might actually be rather ethnocentric. Unusually, whites suffered the most. I don't think the label the "Great White Depression" will catch on, although it would have some accuracy, but not all whites suffered; some newer industries flourished, and their wages often went up. Indeed, beneath all the surface froth of economic cycles, the health of the people in advanced countries, as measured by increasing height, continued to improve (Floud et al., 2011). It was a half-global, half-crisis of capitalism.

Economists debate the causes

In the United States, the cascade of crises was truly dismal. Through the whole sequence of disparate shocks, the Fed continued with its tight money policies, which continued to make things worse (Romer, 1993). It let the banks fail. Monetarists have focused on these mistaken Fed policies. Milton Friedman & Anna Schwartz (1963: 396) say flatly, "Monetary forces were the primary cause of the Great Depression." Yet their method cannot support such a strong statement, because they only discuss monetary factors; theirs is a monetary narrative more than an explanation. They narrate how in the mid-1920s the Fed allowed the money supply to expand too quickly, and then spent the rest of the decade trying to rein it in, continuing to do this through the teeth of a recession. From a peak in August 1929 to a trough in March 1933, the stock of money fell by more than a third. They relabel the Depression the "Great Contraction" – a falling of income, prices, and employment caused by the choking effects of an inept policy of restricting the money supply. If the Fed had taken proper action and issued more money, by providing emergency funding to banks in trouble or buying government bonds on the open market to inject more liquidity after banks fell, this "would have eased the severity of the contraction and very likely would have brought it to an end at a much earlier date" (1963: 300–1).

The first of these statements seems true; the second is more debatable. The tight money policies maintained until 1933 did deepen the crisis. Because the United States had so much of the world's gold, monetary expansion might not have affected the convertibility of its currency and could have been deployed against the recession. Bordo et al. (1999) argue that the Fed could have countered speculative attacks with major open-market purchases. Then, they say, banking panics would not have followed, and recession might not have deepened into Depression. Of course, the officials would have had to get the sums and the timing just right, which is easy only with hindsight.

In analyzing why monetary policy was so inept, Friedman & Schwartz can only suggest an improbable "great man" theory. If Benjamin Strong, governor of the Federal Reserve Bank of New York for fourteen years, had not died in 1928 but remained as the dominant figure in the Fed, the Great Contraction might not have happened. They say, "The detailed story of every banking crisis in our history shows how much depends on the presence of one or more outstanding individuals willing to assume responsibility and leadership. It was a defeat of the financial system that was susceptible to crises resolvable only with such leadership" (1963: 418). This is not very plausible; it is unlikely Strong would have behaved differently had he been in charge in 1929, as he accepted liquidationist wisdom (Temin, 1989: 34, Eichengreen, 1992: 252). Virtually all officials did; they had used these policies before, and they had seemingly worked. They thought they had good reasons for their policies, and these were deeply rooted in the wisdom and society of their time. Why they all thought that way is something we must seek to explain.

Several economists have attempted to determine the relative weights of the disparate causes enumerated above. Cecchetti & Karras conclude that the shocks and contraction in the money supply contributed about equally to the initial downturn, and were then followed in late 1931 by a supply-side collapse. Until 1931, monetary factors may have been secondary; before then, nonmonetary factors accounted for around three-quarters of the decline in nominal incomes (Gordon & Wilcox, 1981: 67, 71; Gordon & Veitch, 1986; R. Gordon, 2005: 25–8). Fackler (1998) evaluates three alternative mechanisms by which recession became depression: a decline in the money stock (as Friedman & Schwartz argue), consumption decline (Temin's explanation), and the debt-deflation or credit view (Bernanke, 2000: chap. 2). His results suggest all three were involved, piling on top of one another (cf Brunner, 1981).

Friedman and Schwartz (1963: 359) correctly add that America's problems were transmitted to the world through the gold standard. Its fixed exchange rates, when the United States and France were hoarding gold, transmitted the impact of falling prices and profits in the United States to other economies. U.S. international loans immediately declined, which especially hit agrarian countries and reduced foreigners' ability to export. They felt they had to restrict credit and raise their interest rates, which meant they were also deflating amidst a recession. Had politicians loosened monetary and fiscal policy, this would have threatened their ability to exchange gold at its contractual rate. Governments felt their hands were tied as their economies collapsed, unless they abandoned their currency's link to gold (Eichengreen, 1992: 12–13, 216–22, 392; Bernanke, 2000: chap. 1). As Keynes said, "gold fetters" constrained national economies, extending the deflationary impact of Fed policies across the world.

There was a nationalist remedy: each nation should abandon the standard and then reflate, as Keynes argued. Indeed, those who left it quickest and then reflated did best. Smaller economies tended to leave first: Australia left in 1929, followed by Norway, Sweden, Denmark, Finland, New Zealand, Canada, Japan, some Latin American countries, and one big one – the UK – in 1931 (Bernanke & James, 1991). Those that then immediately devalued their currencies recovered quicker from the Depression, because this released the deflationary constraints and boosted their exports. Nationalism worked, diminishing globalization! As we see in Chapter 13, in Japan, Finance Minister Takahashi took the yen off gold, lowered interest and exchange rates, and increased fiscal spending, accomplishing the quickest recovery of all. Spain, which had never gone onto the gold standard and had little foreign trade, did not experience a depression at all. The benefits of leaving lessened as more countries went off the standard. Three major powers – Germany, the United States, and France – stayed in longer, with the aid of strict exchange controls. Between 1930 and 1933, German Chancellor Bruning pursued a terrible deflationary strategy, attempting to balance the books through austerity, at the same time staying on the gold standard. In Germany, crises cascaded onward.

Competitive devaluations do no general good. If a country devalues, its exports become cheaper and, in principle, it might be able to export its way out of recession. The effect, however, is lost if its trading partners do the same. In the 1930s, twenty countries devalued their currencies by more than 10 percent and several did it more than five times, so almost no country gained competitiveness, except briefly. Nor could countries export their way out of depression, as international demand was so depressed. Trade declined by a third during the Depression, an indication of declining globalization. It was helpful that one country after another moved to loosen monetary policy once it no longer worried about defending the exchange rate. This monetary stimulus was felt globally, and it helped initiate and sustain recovery. Because it also tended to redistribute from capital to labor, debts to bondholders depreciated in value. Of course, it would have been better if countries had coordinated stimulating monetary policies – avoiding wild fluctuations of exchange rates – but as there were no institutions to do this, nationally caged solutions were tried. Those in trouble felt they had no choice but to pursue unilateral policies, and monetary easing through competitive devaluation was better than no easing at all.

Many economists favor a two-factor monetary explanation of the Depression: Fed monetary mistakes plus the gold standard (Eichengreen, 1992; Bordo et al., 1998; Bernanke, 2000: chap. 1; Smiley, 2002; H. James, 2001; Clavin, 2000). Both involved regulatory mechanisms that failed. For neoliberals, this proves that government should not try to interfere with the market. The implication is that there was nothing structural amiss that lighter, more dexterous official policies could not have fixed. These are all highly technical matters, straining the limits of my expertise, but the discussion seems much too narrow. We must surely put the Fed, gold standard, and indeed all financial factors alongside what was happening in the world of production. Although current theories of economic growth emphasize institutions and technology, these approaches to the Depression barely mention either, except for financial institutions. Yet recession had started in production, not in the stock market, banks, or the Fed. Cole et al. (2005) show that monetary and deflationary shocks only contributed about one-third of the downturn across the seventeen countries they studied over the years 1929 to 1933. Productivity shocks contributed two-thirds. So let me shift to production.

Bernstein (1987) sees the financial crisis as exacerbating a production problem unevenly distributed across industries. He focuses on the impact of shocks from 1928 to 1932 on a national economy in transition, from an era dominated by the second industrial revolution, centered on industries such as textiles, iron and steel, transportation equipment, and mining. These had provided most of the value added in the economy before World War I, although as I have emphasized, this was still an economy of quite low consumer demand. However, the United States was now moving toward an economy that after World War II would be dominated by industries oriented more toward mass-consumption goods and services, such as appliances, automobiles, aircraft, petroleum, tobacco, chemicals, and processed foods plus services such as trade, transportation, finance, and government. The problem was that in the interwar period, the former set of industries still dominated the overall economy, providing most of America's industrial employment; yet these industries were no longer dynamic. They were mature and relatively concentrated, their era of technological dynamism lying behind them. Thus, they were no longer so attractive to investors. The newer industries were the reverse: expanding, highly competitive, and technologically dynamic. They did attract investment, indeed, high-technology stocks were the core of the stock market bubble. Its collapse was, in a sense, the product of too-rapid technological innovation. The rate of investment in this sector was to recover quite quickly after the Depression, but they were still relatively small, unable to absorb all the capital sloshing around.

Field (2011) says that despite appearances, right through the Depression decade the productivity of the economy was actually growing through new industries and products. By 1941, there was almost 40 percent more output than in 1929, with almost no increase in labor hours or input of private capital. The increasing output per hour was mainly the result of technological and organizational advances. There was a big increase in research and development (R&D) investment despite the drop in demand and decline in other forms of investment. New products were aided both by spillover from the New Deal road-building program and, says Field, from creative entrepreneurial responses to adversity. These benefits mostly came through the later New Deal period; in the Depression itself, the new products were not yet of sufficient weight in the economy to boost aggregate national investment, employment, and demand to healthy levels. These new industries depended more on consumer demand, and this had grown only slowly in the 1920s because of a relatively skewed distribution of income toward the rich. They were then hit by the post-1929 failure in effective demand. Although they did grow, their growth was retarded by low aggregate demand. Creative destruction may involve wading through a period of destruction before creation really flowers. Capitalism is not an equilibrium system. Creation of a type that can guarantee full employment is not a necessary tendency of capitalism – as we are seeing again today. After the Great Depression, it required World War II to generate that general growth that gave the new industries sufficient weight in the economy to spearhead future growth based on both growing productivity and mass consumer demand.

The notion of an economy in transition from the heavy industries of the second industrial revolution to consumer-oriented manufacturing helps explain why the Depression was initiated by the overaccumulation of capital, why it was a one-off occurrence, and also why it lasted so long in the United States. Even Keynesian policies of pump priming operated at the aggregate level were not the most appropriate policy response, for they boosted new and old industries alike. More selective industrial policies, distinguishing between the needs of different industries, would have been better, although once again, hindsight helps! During the New Deal, one of Roosevelt's close advisors, Rexford Tugwell, advocated such a strategy. Bernstein suggests that had he been heeded, a swifter recovery might have been forthcoming. Tugwell, however, was on the left of the New Dealers, not in command of policy, and as in most periods, government tended to get captured by politically entrenched old industries rather than technologically dynamic new ones. Roosevelt's National Recovery Administration was to set price codes for each industry, which perversely aided stagnant industries most.

Szostak focuses on technological innovation. Because technology had been the dominant engine of American growth, its misfires were also important. He explains the onset and longevity of the Depression in terms of uneven technological development. The three key-growth industrial sectors of the

1920s – automobiles, electrical supply, and radio – had saturated their markets by the time of the Depression, and had pioneered labor-saving process innovations. "Electrification, assembly lines and continuous processing induced the largest decadal increase in labor productivity the country had ever seen in the 1920s." Had these industries also spawned many new products in the interwar period, economic stability might have resulted. All three, however, saw a lag until products could be put into mass production phase. By 1929, automobiles were "a spent force," and the modern aircraft (the Douglas DC-3 of 1935) was not yet in production. Radio had saturated its market, and television was not yet on stream. Continuous process technology was generating breakthroughs in plastics, synthetic fibers, and pharmaceuticals such as sulfonamides and vitamins, but these involved more complex technologies that took decades (and war) to develop. They only hit mass markets after World War II (1995: 112–3).

In the 1920s, these dynamic industries increased productivity not employment, and they did not require much investment. The numbers of workers in manufacturing remained constant in the 1920s, although output increased by 64 percent. The main technological breakthroughs were shedding not creating employment (Szostak, 1995: 6, 103). Szostak estimates that industries using these technologies led the way in creating unemployment during the Depression. After considering other industries and adding on multiplier effects, he estimates total additional unemployment from these sources at 13 million – the unemployment rate at the trough of the depression (1995: 295). He briefly considers other countries, and finds their experience consistent with his argument. Agrarian societies, lacking such technologies, recovered quickly from the Depression. Britain had similar problems to the United States, but because it had lagged in innovation in the 1920s, it could recapture ground now and recover more swiftly from the Depression (1995: chap. 13).

Duménil & Lévy (1995) add managerial innovations. Labor productivity rose in firms and industries where it was coupled with modern corporate management systems – including electrified assembly lines – and streamlined purchasing, sales and research, and development processes. Like Beaudreau, they say this resulted in overcapacity. The 1920s had already seen a high annual failure rate among firms, of 1.05 percent. The modernizers were usually able to weather the Depression, but much of the capital stock tied up in traditional industries and firms was obsolescent. Between 1930 and 1932, the annual failure rate of firms rose to 1.35 percent, but many surviving firms also had to close some establishments. Half the establishments in the auto industry closed down, although the larger plants generally survived. There was not only lower capacity utilization but also outright destruction of productive capacity, which added to the impact of the contraction. This then worsened the investment crisis, as many dynamic firms did not need new funds, and investors would not lend to stagnant firms.

As the recession deepened and widened, governments and bankers recognized the need for more international economic cooperation. It was not beyond the wit of the bankers to iron out the technical problems of the gold standard, and they scurried around to consult each other. It helped that whatever their nationality, they were drawn from the same social class, "the most exclusive club in the world." They were at ease in each other's company, and they rarely needed interpreters. These highly cultured men – they were all men, of course – spoke English or French. Marx might have called them an executive committee for managing the common affairs of finance capital, and they certainly amounted to a small transnational capitalist class existing long before sociologists identified such a beast. However, they were mostly imprisoned by their orthodoxy, and although legally autonomous, with almost no government regulation of their activities, in practice they lacked the necessary political support from governments and parties to make international cooperation stick.

As we saw, geopolitics had strained international political economy from 1918 onward, especially through the mechanisms of reparations and war debts. By the time of the Depression, nationalism was strengthening. German, Austrian, and Hungarian nationalists still demanded an end to reparations, but they became more concerned with the return of their lost territories, taken from them by the Peace Treaties of Versailles and Trianon. In the wake of nationalism came a straining toward economic autarchy. It became more tempting for each state to cut and run. Some sensibly ran from the gold standard, but in the Depression, governments also began to impose tariffs and quotas on imports to protect their foreign-exchange reserves and domestic producers. The United States led the way with the Smoot-Hawley tariffs of 1930. Originating in pre-Depression promises by President Hoover to farmers, the bill escalated as business-oriented Republicans in the House of Representatives stampeded to raise tariffs on the products of their local industries. If tariffs lessened foreign competition in the domestic market, they thought it would lessen overcapacity. It was a deceptively easy solution to a recession, but it threatened long-term interests because other countries would retaliate and international trade might become depressed. On the one hand, economic health was threatened by the transnational power of finance capital; on the other hand, it was threatened by too much economic nationalism. Institutions for restraining both had yet to be devised; that had to wait until after World War II. For the present, economies stagnated, global economic integration stalled, and states discovered new economic roles.

Hoover had his doubts about tariffs, 1,000 American economists petitioned against it, and the Senate was reluctant to sign. Yet the worsening of the Depression persuaded those wavering to pass it. The new tariffs were nominally much higher, and they sent a signal to other countries to retaliate (Temin, 1989: 46). Canada, the United States' largest trading partner, promptly did so. The British turned to *imperial preferences*, tariffs to protect the whole Empire (for the first time in 100 years), and others followed. Global imports and exports declined and the payment of international debts was impeded, because countries were less able to export to the United States. The Europeans began to default and collapse into full-scale Depression (Eichengreen, 1992: 222–3).

At crucial moments international agreements proved out of reach, so the crisis deepened. Relations soured as Depression entwined with reparations and territorial revisionism. The German government had to share control of its own currency with the Bank of International Settlements, which led to constant wrangles. The French government of Pierre Laval, keen to demonstrate nationalism to the French electorate, insisted that the price of rescuing the first big bank to fail, the Austrian Kredit-Anstalt in May 1931, was that Austria weaken its ties with Germany and renounce a prospective customs union between the two countries. The Austrian government refused for long enough for the relief operation to collapse. The Austrian economy collapsed, as well, causing some German banks to totter, starting banking panic across Europe (Eichengreen, 1992: 264–80). Other emergency loans were too little, too late. This was the reverse of the pre–World War I situation, where geopolitical order had failed but financial order had worked. Now, no one wanted to go to war, so they fought with their checkbooks.

To explain the Great Depression, we must thus incorporate problems in production as well as in the monetary system, and in geopolitics as well as politics. The Depression came as a recession found out a series of weaknesses in production, finance, government, and geopolitics. The structural problems were greater in America than elsewhere, as, paradoxically, this was the most dynamic economy, transitioning from the second industrial revolution with a high degree of technological innovation that could not yet yield full employment of labor or capital. However, global agricultural depression, the international repercussions of the gold standard, the ideological attachment to deflation, and geopolitical tensions quickly spread the problems half-globally through both transnational and international processes. Several weaknesses piled on top of each other, deepening the recession. Absent any one of them, and the Depression might not have been Great. Absent perhaps two or three of them, and it would not have been a Depression at all, but something closer to a cyclical recession. As for solutions, at one extreme the monetarist explanation has the seeming allure of a quick-fix solution, whereas at the other end problems of uneven development would seem fairly obdurate. To correct underconsumption would also need radical social change, but ideology also mattered.

Ideological power: Contemporary theories of the depression

It seems remarkable how so many continued to believe for so long in the gold standard. Most American officials and economists believed in liquidating speculative excesses and defending gold reserves, as it would signal private actors to cause markets to self-correct. President Hoover had been commerce secretary before he became president, and saw the Depression as a global phenomenon rooted in German reparations. He strove hard for international collaboration, but growing economic nationalism stymied him. He tried voluntary initiatives to induce cooperation between economic interest groups, especially to increase investment, but by the summer of 1931, his state-nudged voluntarism was clearly not working. The market was not self-adjusting, yet Hoover would not resort to compulsory measures and sought to balance the budget to keep interest rates down, encourage investment, and maintain the gold standard (Barber, 1985; Kennedy, 1999). So in June 1932, he made a big mistake: he pushed through a compliant Congress the largest percentage tax increase in American peacetime history, a disastrous act in a Depression. The next month, the Fed also halted its expansionary open-market operations. Both the officials and politicians were floundering.

It was the same in other advanced countries. Bank officials managed currencies tied to gold and deflated to prevent capital flight. Even after countries left the gold standard, most did not immediately pursue expansionist policies. Most economists opposed expansion, including Schumpeter, Robbins, Hayek, and the Austrian School (DeLong, 1990). Only a few dissented, such as Hawtrey, Fisher, and Keynes. Eichengreen and Temin (1997) observe that the consensus was based on more than just technical or instrumental reason; it was also a mentality. Aldcroft (2002) calls it "received dogma – almost a religion." It was in my terms an ideology, comprising adherence to norms and values as well as beliefs about the facts. To adhere to the gold standard was to demonstrate the virtues of thrift, discipline, and responsibility. Gold was "moral, principled and civilized, managed money was the opposite," agree Eichengreen and Temin. They quote U.S. Treasury Secretary Mellon's famous call to morality: "Liquidate labor, liquidate stocks, liquidate the farmers, liquidate real estate … purge the rottenness out of the system …[so that] … people will work harder, live a more moral life." They also quote Hoover's later lament that the gold standard was "little short of a sacred formula," although he said he defended it as the only alternative to "collectivism," revealing class ideology, too. A common theme was that businessmen were more moral than workers. The jobless, claimed the president of the National Association of Manufacturers, "do not … practice the habit of thrift and conservation … they gamble away their savings" (Leuchtenburg, 1963: 21). In classical economic theory, however, it was easy to blame the workers, for the solution to recession was to lower wages. Thus, many drew the conclusion that minimum wages, fixed wage contracts, and trade unions should be abolished – class warriors, but only for the general good!

Morality was preached in other countries, too. In Japan, between 1928 and early 1930, the government had deflated the economy so that Japan could go onto the gold standard. It distributed a tract to every household urging retrenchment. This "moral education general mobilization" included poems, songs, and movies aimed especially at women, considered the main spenders. Here are a couple of stanzas and the chorus from a song (reproduced by Metzler, 2006: 204–5) that became a hit as the theme song of the movie "Number-one Woman":

> Even the blooming flower must close,
> isn't it so?
> Now its time to close the open purse
> (that's right, absolutely).
>
> [Chorus]
> It's the time, it's the season,
> all together, hand in hand (yes!),
> Let's retrench, let's retrench.
>
> You give up salt, I'll give up tea
> isn't it so?
> Lifting the gold embargo
> (that's right, absolutely),
> until the joyful lifting of the gold embargo.

There is no record of Finance Minister Inoue or anyone running the Japanese government giving up salt or tea.

The moral rhetoric of thrift, probity, discipline, and rectitude was applied not just to the gold standard but to submission to market forces more generally. In his study of France, Moure says veneration of the gold standard was a part of "rigid conceptions of economic orthodoxy," requiring "the discipline of work and economy" from all. It was a "natural system," which only "currency cranks" challenged (2002: 2, 51, 270–1). Faith in neoclassical dogma pursued deflation into the teeth of a Depression.

The importance of morality to "the spirit of capitalism" was famously emphasized by Max Weber (2002). He traced it back to the "elective affinity" between Calvinism and capitalism in the English-speaking world of the seventeenth and eighteenth centuries. Those virtues of thrift, probity, and rectitude are considered essentially Puritan. So was the notion of moral discipline that capitalism needed to instill in its workers (Gorski, 2003). By the early twentieth century, however, these virtues were not merely Protestant, but also infused with a sense of moral outrage at the "socialistic" demands of workers. Classical economics saw the level of employment determined only by the price of labor. Thus, economists urged that workers restrain and discipline themselves. Governments and the press urged workers take wage cuts for the good of the country. If they refused, there followed lamentations that the working class could not defer gratification. The virtues identified by Eichengreen and Temin were applied as one pole of a class antinomy, counterposing "our" virtues to the lack of discipline, thrift, and even civilization among the working class. Venom was directed especially against socialists speaking in the name of workers, offering delusory utopias of wealth and luxury for all. Behind both the technical theory and the moral rhetoric was the defense of privilege, property, and the right to have servants – that was, after all, the essence of civilization as these men understood it. It also went beyond the bounds of mere material interest. The combination of theory, morality, and interest into an intensely felt ideology was the reason repression of the working class and socialism was so ferocious in the United States, where the real threat of socialism was almost nonexistent (as we saw in Chapter 3). This was an old regime trying to surmount visible signs of crumbling by bathing itself in virtue, and in practice relying on repression – including the economic repression offered by deflation. It appeared to have weathered the postwar surge in working-class consciousness, and was hanging onto the gold standard because that was seen as the linchpin of its own civilization.

When the Depression arrived, the old regime perceived any loosening of monetary and fiscal policy as threatening the ability of a government to maintain its obligation to exchange gold at its contractual rate. To weaken in this way would communicate a lack of responsibility to "the markets," reducing investors' confidence in a government and its currency. This would generate capital flight. The power of investors and speculators to punish at the slightest sign of deviation reinforced commitment to the gold standard. This class pressure presupposed the gold standard, but they were not collectively organized. It was more like the behavior of a stampeding herd of cattle, acting as fear of losses struck contagiously among them.

Britain was the first major country to leave the gold standard, in September 1931, forced off by massive speculative capital outflows involving the loss of half of Britain's gold reserves (Eichengreen, 1996). This had a big effect in other gold-bloc British-influenced countries, places where British power remained strong such as Denmark and Japan (see Chapter 13). The United States was the main defender of the gold standard, and after the British left, its support became even more crucial because the standard was clearly in difficulty. The dollar was speculatively attacked; the Fed now felt it had no choice but to raise interest rates to stem the outflow of gold (Eichengreen, 1992: 293–8). Any suspicion that a government might abandon gold prompted investors to change local money into gold or a convertible currency. Deposit withdrawals spread panic and squeezed lending. This ultimately forced all governments off gold, but later than they should have done. Officials were in a genuine dilemma, asked to achieve contradictory goals of ending the Depression and protecting the standard. The first presupposed easier credit, the second tighter credit; the first would please the populace, the latter would please finance capital. They held loyally onto the latter, to the gold standard and deflation, because they believed this was the right and proper thing to do, because they feared the power of finance capital, and because they were from that very same class. There are lessons here for today.

There was opposition to this orthodoxy, rooted in changes in class structure and a growth of notions of social citizenship. Eichengreen and Temin (1997) suggest that extensions of democracy after World War I made governments more responsive to the demands of working-class voters for a greater share in the profits of capitalism. Governments were forced to trade off the traditional goal of exchange rate stability for newer goals such as keeping employment and wages up, as they had not in the prewar period. They instance the British rate of exchange, which was too high relative to the level of prices and wages left by wartime inflation. Either Britain's prices and wages should fall in order to make British goods competitive on world markets or the exchange rate with gold should be devalued to reduce the cost of British exports. Yet, they say, British trade unions had become too strong to accept cuts in wages, and the government would not devalue the pound. This produced something of a stalemate, which they see as helping push Britain into recession before the Depression struck. The argument also applies to France and Germany. Investors were jittery from the fear that governments would not prioritize their interests as automatically as they had before the war.

Yet in the 1920s, working-class power was limited to harrying around the fringes of economic policy. As we saw in earlier chapters, workers and peasants rarely cooperated, and this greatly weakened the left at a period when both classes were suffering. There was little chance of a leftist seizure of power in Europe after the initial postwar leftist surge had petered out. Deflationary policies ruled everywhere. Eichengreen and Temin are right to see growing democratic resistance in Europe to deflationary policies during the 1920s, but it remained on the shop floor and in the left wing of parties who were mostly out of power. It became entrenched in the left of the British Labour Party and the French Socialist Party (both briefly sharing power in the mid-1920s), in the left of the SPD and SPO, which were losing strength in the Weimar and Austrian Republics, and then in opposition Communist and Fascist Parties. Perhaps the entry of the lower classes into democracy made governments waver. Yet they ultimately put the orthodoxy of finance capital above workers and peasants. The French left were defeated by 1926. In Germany, Bruening and his authoritarian successors Papen and von Schleicher went down fighting for deflationary policies. Between 1930 and 1932, they decreed a 10 percent cut in prices, 10 percent to 15 percent cuts in wages, and a reduction of public spending by a third. The opposition to this included the Nazis. Once they came to power, it was the end for deflation. There was a similar outcome in militarist Japan.

In Britain, a minority Labour government came to power after the election of 1929, but was promptly plunged into Depression. Needing Liberal Party support, Labour defended the gold standard and sought to balance the budget, yet was providing relief for the unemployed under a program it had implemented itself. As unemployment shot up, the costs of unemployment assistance unbalanced the budget, triggering a confidence crisis in the markets and a run on the pound. This was class struggle, counterposing the power of transnational finance capital to that of nationally organized labor, but it was also a struggle over Labour's soul. Pressure from capital and the Liberals made the Labour government agree to change direction and deflate, but beset by left opposition within, the government broke up in disarray and resigned in August 1931. A few Labour leaders joined the so-called National (in reality, Conservative-dominated) government, but the official Labour Party went into opposition until World War II. Had a Conservative government been in power in 1929, it would have faced the same problem of escalating unemployment benefits. It would have presumably slashed them, and Labour might have then benefitted electorally, as the Social Democrats in Sweden and the Democrats in the United States did. These came into power with economic theories and policies that did not privilege capital, and they worked. A period of class bickering and policy drift, as occurred in Britain, France, and Germany, was obviously no solution, but nor was economic orthodoxy – and it was far more responsible for bringing on the Depression.

There were alternative theories to the orthodoxy of self-adjusting markets, liquidation, and deflation. In the United States, "structuralist" or "new" economists were more sensitive to the emergence of a more nationally integrated economy. They rejected the notion of a transnational market governed by immutable economic laws. They believed "informed manipulation" of fiscal and monetary policy could counter "fluctuations in aggregate economic activity." They had brought a mild nationalism into economics, arguing that a new and better economy could be developed domestically, nudged along by the federal government. It was possible to have "capitalism in one country" of a more popular kind. The notion of a more popular capitalism initially attracted both Republicans and Democrats. President Hoover recruited structuralists to study unemployment, and they anticipated Keynes in suggesting that countercyclical public spending could help ease recession and unemployment, although they differed in the extent of public spending envisaged (Barber, 1985; Bernstein, 2002: chap. 2).

The "institutionalists" were former progressives, and they remained strong in a few universities, especially Wisconsin and Columbia. Unlike neoclassicists, they did not believe that the economy could be separated from its social purposes. Students at Wisconsin were taught more about labor relations, unions, and welfare than about supply and demand. Institutionalists had a sense of mission: to improve the lot of workers in line with social justice and to boost consumption, which they saw as the way to economic growth. John Commons, the leading figure at Wisconsin, later remarked, "I was trying to save capitalism by making it good." In his view (typical of Progressives' faith in science and reason), "reasonable" employers and unions would jointly save capitalism, the one rejecting the invisible hand, the other rejecting socialism. Unions would help capitalists promote macroeconomic stability, offsetting underconsumption tendencies in the economy. Institutionalists sympathized with labor but were financed by corporate liberals, especially the National Civic Federation and Rockefeller family trusts. Men such as Commons, Slichter, and Douglas advocated countercyclical macroeconomic policies to smooth out business cycles of boom and bust (Kaufman, 2003, 2006; Rutherford, 2006).

Almost no one other than socialists eager to predict the end of capitalism suspected that the recession of 1929 would deepen and deepen. The dismal science failed to understand just how dismal things could get. "Underconsumptionists," however, were well-prepared to respond once depression began. They argued that the economy was consistently producing more than it could consume, as most consumers were so poor. Rising inequality was largely to blame, they said. Profits could not be used productively and underconsumption had already generated overcapacity, so profits went to feed the stock market bubble of 1928–1929. They also identified longer-term problems. Under pressure from the pro-business Coolidge administration and business interests, they said, the Fed kept the discount rate low in the 1920s. This had encouraged high, and eventually excessive, investment in manufacturing plants. The policy meant that business profited at the expense of workers and farmers. Popular economists such as Stuart Chase and George Soule observed that whereas wages had grown around 1 percent a year, profits had risen 9 percent in the period 1923–1928. This, said Soule, caused "a fatal lack of balance between industrial production and popular purchasing power" (Dawley, 1991: 337–8). During the first Roosevelt administration, New Deal economists were to give underconsumption theory a more theoretical veneer (Moulton, 1935).

Marxists went further, alleging that the main contradiction of capitalism was between the forces of production (technology, skills) and the class relations of production. When technological overcapacity choked off profits, a crisis of accumulation resulted. This affected both main social classes, although workers suffered more. They were largely right. Then, they predicted, would come the revolution. This was obviously wrong. Although there were not many Marxists in America, this theory did resonate popularly, inspiring hope among radical workers and some fear among insecure capitalists. Combined, these sentiments were enough to persuade others into class compromise, as we see in the next chapter.

Today, underconsumption theory has been largely rejected. Keynes showed that reduced consumer demand need not cause a recession, as private investment in factories, machinery, and housing or government purchases or an export surplus might all boost aggregate demand instead. The proportion of consumption in national income did not significantly change in the 1920s (Temin, 1976: 32), although if we accept Beaudreau's argument that technological innovations had massively increased productivity, the United States would have needed an increase in consumer spending, government spending, or exports for that increased production capacity to be used. The increased infrastructural spending of the New Deal was to attempt this.

At the time, most people seemed to have believed in underconsumption theory, especially farmers, who still constituted 23 percent of the U.S. labor force. We saw in Chapter 3 that American political economy had long favored northern manufacturing industry, at their expense. A brief respite had come in World War I, but then amid global overproduction prices fell, farmers' debts increased, and deflationary policies worsened their indebtedness. Industrial workers were mostly treading water in the 1920s, and their suffering only really began with the Depression. Unemployment, depressed consumption, and rising indebtedness were also major problems for small businesses. Economics were disputed in quasi-class terms, because it was not only a question of the best national policy – collective power – but also of distributive power – who benefitted and who lost.

When the recession worsened, underconsumptionists had their answer ready: monetary expansion plus federal pump priming to boost consumption. Redistribute purchasing power while maintaining industrial production, but reinflate prices and wages to force most of the inflationary increase in purchasing power into consumer's pockets. Then consumers would spend and profits, employment, and wages would all rise, so capitalists would also benefit – trickle-up economics! As there were already more than enough factories, government should finance large construction projects. When orthodox liquidationism failed to solve the crisis over a full three years of Hoover's term, underconsumptionism seemed plausible and useful in alleviating the class conflict rising through the Depression. In practical (although not theoretical) terms, in the short-run it was similar to Keynesian prescriptions.

Hoover could not go this far. "The sole function of government," he said, "is to bring about a condition of affairs favorable to the beneficial development of private enterprise." Roosevelt agreed, until he was elected, but afterward he and the Democrats turned toward the Wisconsin School. It provided the most influential approach in America at the time, because its ideas made sense to those politicians more responsive to the discontent of workers and farmers than to the anxieties of investors. In a democracy, they had the advantage of numbers.

Economic theories become important insofar as they can mobilize the commitments of power actors. Their truth content is contested and limited, but this can matter less than their plausibility as ideologies in explaining everyday experience. Laissez-faire plus deflation made sense to old regime experience, but when this got into difficulties, it made less sense to the popular classes, who then cast around for alternative ideologies. The Depression brought explanations into head-on collision, with varying outcomes. In the United States, there was a compromise, but one in which structuralists and underconsumptionists made headway, before giving way at the end of the 1930s to a half-Keynesian alternative.

These American approaches were simpler versions of the theories of the Stockholm School of economists in Sweden and Keynes in England. Keynes aimed to solve depressions and boost employment without sacrificing capitalist democracy, as fascism and state socialism were doing. In his *The General Theory of Employment Interest and Money*, published in 1936, Keynes argued against the general equilibrium theory that markets would necessarily self-correct. An economy might remain mired in recession for a long time. Wages, he agreed with the classical economists, were key. To get out of a recession through market forces, real wages would have to go down. However, Keynes noted that only nominal wages were set through negotiations over minimum wages, wage contracts, union power, and so forth. Classical economists attacked all of these as obstacles to flexible labor markets; Keynes saw this as both morally undesirable and ignoring power realities. Workers would certainly resist nominal wage reductions, unless they saw an equivalent fall in prices, but employment could only be boosted if real wages (workers' purchasing power) declined, and for this nominal wages would have to fall more than prices. This would also reduce consumer demand, worsening the recession. This would then reduce business revenues and expected profits. Investment in new plants and equipment would be riskier. If wages and prices were falling, those with money would expect them to fall further. The economy could spiral downward as those with money would not spend but wait as falling prices made their money more valuable. Classical orthodoxy assumed that if consumption fell, the rate of interest would fall, which would lead to increased investment, and demand would remain constant – the self-correcting market.

Yet, said Keynes, this ignores the profit motive that always operates in conditions of uncertainty. Expectations and confidence are crucial: businessmen only invest if they are confident of making a profit. If the fall in consumption seems likely to be long-term, they will expect lower future sales. So their liquidity preference in this situation is not to invest but to hold onto their wealth. The resulting "investment strike" converts a recession into a serious slump. This explains why capitalism could remain in far from optimum condition for long periods of time. However, added Keynes, government can step in. It might first cut taxes and let businesses and consumers keep more of their income, and so spend it, increasing aggregate effective demand. The weakness of this, however, was that they might not spend it but save it or pay off their debts with it. That would not increase effective demand. Second, it might intervene more directly by increasing government spending, because then all of the increase would be spent. This would boost effective demand. It would also involve running up modest deficits, but these would be more than paid off by a multiplier effect in terms of employment and tax revenue generated by more economic activity. Keynes knew there were risks in this, and I must emphasize that he only advocated such policies as short-term responses to recessions. If there was full employment, it would not work, but his discovery of effective demand was both novel and politically useful. It was to be the new centerpiece of policy in a period of increased regulation, to keep market forces from reinforcing perverse tendencies of capitalism. It was good for both capitalists and workers (Keynes, 1973: 249–50, chap. 19; Ingham, 2009: 43–50). As Polanyi (1957) noted, the 1930s saw the harbingers of a structural shift. Increased government intervention inside national markets, and increased nationalism abroad by abandoning the gold standard and introducing competitive devaluations and tariffs, effectively ended nineteenth-century liberal civilization. Because he saw the nineteenth century's "disembedded" liberal economy as a historical exception, he thought it had gone forever. We see today that this was wrong, although a period of increased state regulation of markets did follow immediately after he wrote.

Most economists now agree about the importance of perceptions of uncertainty in investment and consumption during recessions. Many also agree with Keynes' solution: if private actors fail to create aggregate demand during a recession, the government can resolve "the ignition problem," boosting aggregate demand by increasing its own expenditures and financing employment-creating projects, even at the cost of deficit financing. Limited public-sector borrowing would not increase interest rates excessively. Although the concept of the multiplier effect has been challenged, recent research has shown that in recessions it does operate, almost at the level predicted by Keynes (Auerbach & Gorodnichenko, 2011). Thus, government budget balances should be assessed in relation to the level of demand in the economy and not to rules of good housekeeping set within the private sector. If there is a budget deficit and large-scale unemployment, the deficit should be increased not reduced. Government can increase the stability of the economy by fiscal as well as monetary means. If only most politicians in the Anglophone countries understood this today!

Keynes offered theoretical justification for what some actors had intuitively grasped anyway. It was similar to what the Stockholm School of economists advocated and the Swedish Social Democratic government began to implement after their access to power in 1932. Keynes had to wait until Roosevelt's second tem before his ideas became part of American economic policy, but his policies continued to work for decades, although compromised by being harnessed to classical economic ideas. In rejecting the timelessness of general equilibrium theory, Keynes was introducing into economics real human beings, their perceptions, their institutions, and their power relations, preventing any eternal economic laws. This was also evident in his view of finance capital, which I discuss in Volume IV.

Conclusion

There is a spatial tension within capitalism. Although capital is in principle transnational and global – recognizing no national boundaries, moving wherever it sees profit – in the real world, it is constrained by the existence of national and imperial boundaries and their distinctive configurations of ideological, military, and political power relations. A major problem for capitalism in this period was that economic policy was conducted at the national level, but the most important sources of destabilization were transnational, and international regulation had collapsed as a result of the Great War. Geopolitical tensions and confrontations continued after the war. Politically, the early 1920s saw the continuing rule of the old regime, recovering from postwar scares and determined to preserve its economic dominance, but now challenged by movement toward democracy. The masses were making greater social citizenship demands, but they could not yet achieve them. Ideologically, the 1920s saw a rise in both class consciousness and nationalism. In this context, governments could not cope with a financial crisis spreading like a virus across state boundaries that reflected underlying structural weaknesses of an economy in transition. The Great Depression was a part of increasing economic globalization. It was a globalizing phenomenon, but one that produced not more global integration but disintegration. States taking more activist roles then reined this in.

Keynes, Roosevelt, and the Wisconsin School all declared that their mission was to save capitalism. Keynes and Roosevelt were patrician liberals in the early twentieth-century sense, with sympathy for and a sense of responsibility toward the working class. The Wisconsin School, from humbler social backgrounds, had more direct relations with workers and their representatives. They all believed that a more humane, peaceful, stable, and efficient society of democratic capitalism could be created provided it embodied a measure of economic security for all, a degree of social citizenship, which they believed must involve some class redistribution effected through state intervention. The state should mediate the rising class struggle of the period, representing neither capital nor labor but seeking conciliation between them.

There was more than one way of coping. The British muddled through, off the gold standard, ignoring Keynes in favor of Tory corporatism, and erecting tariffs around its empire – all of which did make for a mild improvement. The French procrastinated, divided, remaining on gold and making little recovery. The most successful democratic solutions were provided by the Keynesian-Swedish-American family of lib-lab reformers, using state intervention geared to growth and mild redistribution. To restore order to the economy, workers almost everywhere were given a little more social citizenship, generating a more efficient and humane economy, quite beyond what mere monetary expansion or exchange-rate flexibility could provide. It also slightly tightened the nation-state, although to varying degrees across the countries.

There were despotic solutions, as well. Fascism triumphed in Germany, Austria, and Italy, as did despotic rightism across one-half of Europe. These were ways of bringing the people onstage, although in nonspeaking roles. In Romania, Manoilescu developed a corporatist economic program, bringing nondemocratic solutions to economic difficulties. The despotic regimes shared a commitment to state intervention to solve economic problems with the democracies (although this does not mean that they were "socialist," as

Temin [1989], says). In early 1932, the Nazi Party proposed credit-financed job creation, and fought the election the next year on this platform. It proved popular. When Hitler came to power later in the year, he used force to bring Germany quickly out of recession through high military expenditure, depressing wages, eliminating independent labor unions, and increasing employment. This was the dose also imposed on the Japanese, with marked success (Temin, 1989: 29–31, 61–73, 100–3; Metzler, 2006, chap. 11). Neither regime had to combat a strong laissez-faire tradition, and they could draw on more statist traditions of political economy, but this now carried a terrible dark side. The New Deal, Swedish Social Democracy, Soviet Five-Year Plan, Fascism, Nazism, and Japanese militarism were, as Silver (2003: 143) puts it, "different ways of jumping off the disintegrating world market into the life raft of the national economy." Of these, social democracy or a blend of structuralism, underconsumptionism, Keynes, and Roosevelt were about as good as it got – but all policy packages that were successful put a brake on economic globalization and rebuilt economies more within national cages. When combined with inadequate national and international controls, economic globalization had caused the Great Depression, and the solution was to strengthen nation-state cages. Unfortunately, the cages most strengthened caused a world war.

Many economists like to portray the Great Depression as an aberration, an extraordinary occurrence that blew capitalism right out of its normal mild cycles as a result of either gross human incompetence or the intervention of noneconomic influences. It certainly was extreme, and as usual in human affairs, incompetence loomed large. However, it also embodied normal capitalist mechanisms. Excluding Fed mistakes, the Depression saw market mechanisms working quite well in the sense that negative information was efficiently transmitted to the principal actors, causing them to take actions that perversely intensified recession into Depression. Sacrificing most other goals to retain business confidence – this time of speculators – is also normal in capitalist states. Capitalism turns malign from time to time, because the sum of individual rational pursuit of profit as expressed on markets does not always generate the collective good.

We have seen that a cascade of shocks piled on top of each other led from a recession to the Great Depression. Most national economies of the 1920s were never very buoyant, but in the mid-1920s came a global agricultural recession caused by overproduction, which in turn was caused by a mixture of the legacy of World War I and technological innovations leading to higher productivity. In the United States, a downturn in construction and manufacturing began in 1928. This might be seen as a normal business cycle, but unfortunately, it coincided with a stock market bubble due to investors overconfident in the capacity of rapid technological progress to generate profit. Overinvestment and depressed production generated overcapacity, bankruptcies, bank failures, and rocketing unemployment. Credit dried up. The government and the

Fed responded mistakenly by deflating and restricting the money supply, as the dominant economic ideology dictated. It held that self-regulating market forces would re-establish equilibrium and the role of government should only help the market's liquidation of stock values, bad businesses, excess workers, and high wages. Then self-regulating market forces would re-establish equilibrium. As we saw, this was also the class ideology of the old regime, but it turned a worsening recession into the Great Depression. America's problems were then transmitted to an already-faltering international economy by finding out the weaknesses of the gold standard. Its fixed exchange rates transmitted the impact of falling prices and profits in the United States to other economies. U.S. international loans declined, reducing foreigners' ability to export. They felt they had to restrict credit and raise their interest rates, which meant they were also deflating amidst a recession.

The Depression only seriously damaged half the world – the white world – and in much of it, Depression did not long continue. Countries applied national economic remedies – coming off the gold standard, raising tariffs, and reflating toward full employment. Nation-states were recovering and even intensifying their powers, finding new roles and new ways of combating the transnational pressures of capitalism. Polanyi (1957) framed this in terms of the double movement of capitalism; on the one hand the perpetual expansion of supposedly self-regulating market relations, on the other the defensive reactions of society to protect itself from the consequences of the operation of that market. That is social self-protection, which he saw as the decisive feature of the new civilization arising. This model works quite well at a general level in this case – although it could not explain why some went to fascism, others to social democracy, and why it needed a world war to complete the movement to self-protection. Polanyi was too economistic.

To explain all of this, I have broadened analysis focusing on financial markets and fiscal and monetary policy to cover technological and industrial structures, class structure and ideology, and geopolitical rivalry and nationalism. This brings in the sources of social power more generally. Four major structural transformations in power relations were then underway. First, agriculture – the traditional mainstay of economies – was declining, depressed because of global overproduction – perhaps the first truly universal dose of globalization in the twentieth century. Its travails contributed to the first stage of the Depression. Second, industry was transitioning through rapid technological change from the heavy industries of the second industrial revolution to lighter consumer-oriented manufacturing, but the combination could not yet bear the weight of a full-employment economy. The old industries were no longer expanding, and the new ones were still small. Creative destruction was occurring, but too slowly. Third, the old regime class – still controlling the advanced world's finances – was seeking to hang onto its traditional dominance by speculative pressure on states and ideological adherence to liquidationism and the gold standard; this took half the global economy over the edge. Conversely, the expanding working and lower middle classes seeking more social citizenship did not have the power to challenge this orthodoxy until the Depression was well underway. Fourth, there was a transition in geoeconomic power away from British hegemony blended with coordination among the major national economies, but as yet there was neither another hegemony nor stable international cooperation, as the powers were geopolitically divided by conflicts arising from the peace treaties ending World War I.

In all these disparate fields of social life, weaknesses that might never have been exposed were found out as a recession spread and deepened into a Great Depression. This was not a single crisis of a whole system, driven by the inner logic of development of capitalism, whether this might be a striving toward equilibrium and growth (as in neoclassical economics) or toward systemic contradictions (as in Marxism). Rather, it was a rolling concatenation of more specific crises exposed one after another, all becoming connected – but partly contingently so – as the four great transformations – with their own causal chains – collided. This was a structural but not systemic crisis. It was not quite global because its disasters were largely confined to the advanced countries and the white race – justified payback, the others might say, for the evils of white empires!

It will be felt by many economists that this is not much of an explanation, as the various causal chains are just piled on top of each other, without numerical weights and not convertible into mathematical equations applicable in all times and places. However, that is how it seems to have happened in reality. Lawrence Summers (1986), a prominent economist often tempted by neoliberalism, observes, "Economists are much better at analyzing the optimal response of a single economic agent to changing economic conditions than they are at analyzing the equilibria that will result when diverse agents interact." How much truer this is when we analyze the conditions that result in disequilibria!

I also see support for this approach in what happened during and immediately after World War II – for the Great Depression was no more extraordinary than the equally unprecedented Great Boom that then began. As we see in Volume IV, this represented the coming to maturity of all four of these transitions: massive migration out of agriculture providing the labor for expanding urban-industrial sectors; an era of consumer industry expansion beginning in response to high demand; universal social citizenship emerging through welfare benefits, progressive taxes, and policy commitment to full employment; and the United States, undoubtedly a hegemonic power, supplying workable rules for the international economy. The combination would amount to a more universal form of globalization. The comparison reveals that economies are always entwined with the other sources of social power, in good times as well as bad.

8 The new deal: America shifts left

Introduction: The left into power

This chapter analyzes the response to the Great Depression at its epicenter. It also serves as a case study of the rise of social citizenship across the north of the world, analyzed more generally in the next chapter. During the 1930s, the United States granted increased social-citizenship rights boosting employment, welfare policies, union rights, and progressive taxation. The United States had hitherto lagged in these respects; now it played catch-up in devising a normal lib-lab welfare regime. It was no longer very different to other advanced countries, only exceptional in the timing of its catch-up. In this chapter, I discuss its extent, causes, and immediate effects. The causes are simple: above all, the need to play catch-up was caused by the Great Depression. As we saw in the previous chapter, this hit the United States hard. World War I had only produced a slightly conservative response in the United States, unlike most countries, but the Depression substituted for it as a radicalizing influence.

The second cause – and together these two offer a virtually sufficient explanation – was political. Depression had an almost uniform political effect across the world. Regimes in power at its beginning were discredited and fell, whether they were of the left or the right. In Sweden and Denmark, Conservative governments fell, and a Social Democrat-Agrarian Party alliance used Keynesian policies to affect recovery – and entrench the Social Democrats as the normal party of government for most of the century. In Canada, a Conservative government proposed progressive reforms, but nonetheless elections swept it out of office, and its Liberal successor inherited its reform policies. In Britain, the Labour government split, fell, and remained out of office until 1945. The Australian Labour government also fell, also delaying reform, but in New Zealand, the opposite happened: the Conservatives fell and Labour passed reforms. These were all institutionalized democracies; governments were replaced peacefully through the electoral process. The great virtue of institutionalized liberal democracy and political citizenship was that it was self-sustaining. Newly minted democracies and semi-democracies were more vulnerable. Governments held responsible for the Depression lost elections, but also often suffered coups. In Japan, a centrist government fell, and its rightist successor brought recovery by leaving the gold standard and embracing authoritarian militarism. In Germany, the Depression helped discredit all democratic politicians and then some authoritarians too, until the Nazis acquired power and brought economic recovery and much else besides. These were varied outcomes. Despite leftist hopes that this was the final crisis of capitalism, it wasn't. Nor did the Depression globally benefit the left. Capitalism survived everywhere, if reformed in different ways.

The United States was one of the countries where the Depression discredited conservatives – both the Republicans, who had been in power for a decade, and conservative Democrats, who had been in charge of their party since the mid-1920s. The fixed four-year terms of the American political system ensured that the Republicans had three years of failing to cope with the Depression. Then came Roosevelt's double victory in 1932, over Al Smith at the Democratic Convention and Hoover at the general election (Craig, 1992: chap. 11). The Democrats controlled the presidency, the Senate, and the House. A group of Progressive Republicans also favored reforms. Business and the Republicans had lost leverage, seeming to have failed the people. Because business had little ability to invest, any threat of an investment strike to discipline the administration or the more radical states would have been hollow. In the 1934 and 1936 elections, Democrats picked up more seats in the House and Senate. An electoral reversal came in 1938, but from 1934 to 1938, a liberal party ruled the United States for the first time – although conservative Southern Democrats still controlled important committees. There would still be back-room deals and backsliding, but most Democrats and their new officials and advisors – an assorted gaggle of experts, quacks, and hacks – aided by a few progressive Republicans favored more intervention, spending, and social citizenship.

On the campaign trail, Roosevelt had pledged radical changes through "Three R's – relief, recovery and reform." He declared, "I pledge you, I pledge myself, to a new deal for the American people." The New Deal fits perfectly into Polanyi's notion of society's self-protection against the damaging consequences of markets, but Roosevelt remained vague on what his New Deal might consist of. The party platform of 1932 had not even mentioned labor, and although he promised to increase aid to the unemployed, at the same time he would slash government spending – at one point, he claimed, by 25 percent. The "foundation of permanent economic recovery," he said, would be "a complete and honest balancing of the budget" (Leuchtenburg, 1963: 10–12; Barber, 1996: 19). However, his rhetoric was hardly honest.

In the First New Deal phase, during his first 100 days, came a flurry of legislation aimed principally at relief for both capital and labor. It included: help for banks, many of which had collapsed or were teetering; the Securities Exchange Commission regulated securities and banks and the Federal Bank Deposit Insurance Corporation (FDIC) provided insurance for them; a Civilian Conservation Corps Act set up work camps for 250,000 young men; a federal relief agency distributed $500 million to states and localities; the Agricultural Adjustment Act (AAA) set up a federal agency to subsidize farmers to keep up prices and incomes and cut production; a federal Tennessee Valley Authority built dams and power plants to generate employment and regional development; the U.S. Employment Service was established; there was assistance to the construction and home loans industry; a National Industrial Recovery Act (NIRA) set up an administration (the NRA) to devise codes of fair competition for each industry to regulate prices and incomes, with labor participation; and the gold standard was abandoned.

Then from 1935 came the more radical Second New Deal. Some of the previously described measures were strengthened: the Reconstruction Finance Corporation was expanded into a major bank. The Works Progress Administration (WPA) was established in 1935 as an enlarged agency to provide work for the unemployed. However, the Social Security Act of 1935 established wholly new national welfare programs based on insurance for unemployment relief and old-age pensions, providing federal grants to the states for direct assistance to the elderly, handicapped, and single-parent poor. The Wagner Act of 1935 finally accorded labor unions similar organizing rights to those of other democratic countries, also imposing similar regulation upon them, through a National Labor Relations Board (NRLB). Although the National Recovery Administration was declared unconstitutional by the Supreme Court, other agencies continued to regulate industries such as railroads and public utilities. In 1938 came a second Agricultural Adjustment Act (to replace the first one, also struck down by the Supreme Court) and a Housing Act to fund low-cost housing and mortgages. The Fair Labor Standards Act (FLSA) abolished child labor and set maximum hours and minimum wages for most industries involved in interstate commerce (it was later extended to other workers, too).

This five-year burst was a Progressives' cornucopia, an update of programs the progressives had failed to implement. Kennedy sees three themes: a basic level of security for Americans through public works and state regulation; the Keynesian belief that the private sector alone could not generate sufficient investment and employment to sustain a modern economy; and the nationalist assumption "that the United States was an economically self-sufficient nation" – the defensive response to the globalization of capitalism (Kennedy, 1999: 374–5). Without the Depression discrediting conservatism, no comparable shift would have occurred. No doubt the state would have gotten bigger more gradually, or perhaps World War II (if that happened without a Depression) would have provided its stimulus. For the first time in the United States, there was a straining toward a lib-lab regime, a blend of liberal and non-socialist labor ideals, as in the other Anglophone countries. Suddenly, European reformers were looking at the United States more than vice versa (Rodgers, 1998: 409–12), a dramatic reversal. It seemed to presage a major turning point in American power relations, further evidence that an enduring exceptionalism cannot explain American development.

In his comparative study of social welfare programs, Hicks (1999: chap. 3) notes that the second phase of welfare expansion, in the 1930s and 1940s, came mostly from the initiatives of social democratic or labor parties (sometimes in alliance with progressive liberals or Catholics), although in Canada and the United States it came from a secular liberal party. Nonetheless, the North American package of income maintenance, progressive taxation, and macroeconomic and industrial regulation at the national level was very similar to the agenda achieved elsewhere by Social Democrats. These occasionally claimed adherence to Marxist ideology; American liberals shuddered at the thought. However, policies were similar: the United States was no longer laggard.

Arguments have always raged over the New Deal. Economists argue over how much growth it brought. Historians argue about everything. Sociologists have divided over causation. Did the New Deal result from state autonomy or class struggle, and should we favor "top-down" explanations, stressing elites or capitalist class fractions, or "bottom-up" ones, stressing popular forces (Manza, 2000).

Five Sociological theories

We can identify five main approaches, deriving from the theories of the state I distinguished in Volume II, Chapter 3. The first is *pluralism*, liberal democracy's official view of itself. This sees rule by the people mediated by plural parties and interest groups whose power countervails one another. Indeed, Roosevelt acquired, maintained, and ultimately lost reforming power through fairly free elections and parliamentary struggles among parties and factions. Although American democracy did not operate as ideally as pluralists might wish, there is a place for an imperfect pluralism account of the New Deal.

State autonomy theory generates the second and third approaches, both ways of asserting the primacy of political power. Some emphasize the autonomy of *state elites*, arguing that experts at both the federal and individual state level, acting through think tanks and administrative agencies, had a substantial impact on New Deal policies where these agencies possessed a high infrastructural capacity to devise and implement coherent policies across the country. Reforms were implemented where experts and state capacities were strong and failed where they were weak. They stress the role of social scientists, especially economists, social workers, and agronomists. Theda Skocpol and her collaborators emphasized experts in their earlier work (Skocpol, 1980; Skocpol & Amenta, 1985; Skocpol & Ikenberry, 1983; Orloff, 1988). These scholars read like American Progressives, seeing modernization achieved by reason, carried by scientific professionals, coordinated by effective government.

I am skeptical of the power of elites and experts in liberal democratic states. Although in this volume I emphasize autonomous elites in fascist and communist regimes, liberal democracies try to prevent such autonomy, and no democratic constitution tries harder than the American. True, Roosevelt was an effective politician who consciously exploited his popularity in order to increase the power of the presidency (Campbell, 1995: 103–4). In this period, executive power did increase, but it might be circular to explain this in terms of expert power. Perhaps the voters, politicians, and powerful economic interest groups wanted bureaucratic power to increase to combat the Depression, and the New Deal might end if they tired of the experts and bureaucrats. I will find much evidence for this.

The Constitution as later institutionalized had set up one very powerful and autonomous state elite of experts, but it was charged with restraining executive power. These experts were recruited only from within their own rather caste-like profession, they had great expertise in an arcane and sacred body of knowledge, and they were appointed for life: the justices of the Supreme Court. The justices were mostly conservatives. They did play a major role in the New Deal – mainly by trying to stop it, by blocking New Deal legislation that seemed to enhance the powers of the federal government over the states. They also declared unconstitutional laws giving the experts of administrative agencies powers that should properly belong to the legislature. The justices felt they should be the only powerful experts within the state! The most powerful state elite hindered rather than helped the New Deal.

Experts also have both employers and social identities. They are hired, so have limited autonomy from their employer. Lawyers and businessmen (together with their policy advisors) formed most of the administration's own experts, followed at some distance by social workers and social scientists. Businessmen might be treated more in terms of their class identity, although the corporate liberals among them rejected some of the conservatism of their class. Social workers' identities tended to be liberal, such as Harry Hopkins or Frances Perkins. The lawyers were more mixed; they were not narrow specialists, for they read widely and imbibed the general economic and social thought of the times (Schwarz, 1993). A mass of young lawyers was brought in to draft proposed legislation and staff the new federal agencies. Bernstein (2002: 64) says FDR "created more opportunities for attorneys in the federal service than almost all other professional and academic fields combined." Most were young Ivy League graduates, often from liberal Jewish or Catholic backgrounds, but after a period of public service two-thirds of them returned to private practice, mostly with law firms in New York or Washington, handling the affairs of large corporations. A minority worked for unions, became law professors, or stayed in government service (Irons, 1982: 3–10, 299). As Domhoff (1990: 92) observes, these experts do not seem quite as autonomous as Skocpol and others suggest.

The second line of argument coming from state autonomy theorists suggests that state *institutions* play a considerable part in structuring outcomes. This they term an "institutional-political process" or "institutional politics" (Orloff, 1988: 40; Amenta & Halfmann, 2000). The dependent variable to be explained in this case is government policies. If we want to explain economic outcomes, we should generally turn first to economic causes, for military outcomes to military causes, for ideological outcomes to ideological causes, and for political outcomes to political causes. Sometimes the main line of causation will run along a different path, and may involve other sources of social power. We should expect New Deal policies, however, to be greatly influenced by political power relations, which in the United States means the federal and party systems, patronage politics, the distinctive power of the South on Capitol Hill, and elections – although most of these institutions are also stressed by pluralists. Institutionalists have also emphasized *path dependency*: new political developments are partially structured down paths set by old institutions, introducing more conservative trajectories. As we are here seeking to explain quite radical changes, path dependency must have been limited.

The fourth and fifth approaches comprise what political scientists call "power resource theory," and what used to be called class theory. Some emphasize *class struggle*, generally workers and small farmers against capitalists. They tend to see the New Deal as wrested from unwilling dominant classes by pressure from below; buttressed by liberal, radical, and socialist ideologies; they see its limitations exposed where the balance of class power tilted toward capital. They see workers, farmers, and others forcing concessions in a situation in which the final outcome was decided by class struggle (Goldfield, 1989; Piven & Cloward, 1977).

The second class theory sees the New Deal as involving struggle among *class fractions* (or segments) of the main classes. The organized working class was divided between craft unions and industrial unions. Within a generally conservative capitalist class, lay a corporate liberal or corporate moderate fraction, heir to the modernizing wing of the Progressive movement discussed in Chapter 3. They were willing to make concessions to popular forces in order to save capitalism and ally temporarily with responsible fractions of labor to thwart both radicals and conservatives, who they viewed as too shortsighted to see that capitalism needed modernizing. There is no consensus over which industries and sectors such corporate liberals inhabited (Domhoff, 1990, 1996; Domhoff & Webber, 2011; Swenson, 2002; Quadagno, 1984; C. Gordon, 1994; Tomlins, 1985; Jenkins & Brents, 1989). The strength of the two class approaches is that the Depression was a crisis of capitalism and did unleash popular unrest, which then generated debates among elites about how to maintain their own power. As the New Deal mostly involved economic policy, we would expect economic power actors to be significant in both pushing and opposing it – although we should resist an economic determinism that sees economic forces and classes as automatically translated into policy-making.

The approaches share some arguments in common. Recognizing the force of electoral pressures, each claims them as part of its own model. Pluralists see elections as the core process; for state autonomy theorists they reveal the importance of political institutions, especially parties; and for class theorists, electoral pressures reflect class conflict. All also recognize the role of the Southern states in strengthening conservatism, state autonomy theorists attributing this mainly to Congressional institutions; class theorists to the low wage; segregated labor markets to plantation agriculture and racial capitalism. Pluralists acknowledge that the South is an exception to their model. I touch upon all the approaches in my narrative of the New Deal, and confront them directly in my conclusion.

New Deal goals: Recovery, Regulation, Relief – and Reelection

The New Deal's first "R" was *Recovery* – attempting to undo the causes of the Depression as they were understood at the time. Because the Depression had thrown economists for a loop, Roosevelt's advisors were divided over how to recover. Arguments continued throughout the 1930s between budget-balancers, monetarists urging increasing the money supply, and structuralists urging increasing consumption. When some added sustained use of public spending, they became quasi-Keynesians. They said the administration should keep up prices and incomes and adjust structural imbalances in the economy, especially those between urban and rural sectors. It should provide more money for relief; subsidize farmers, the unemployed, and the poor; and make loans to homeowners and small businessmen who formed most of the electorate that had just voted in the Democrats. Most of the businessmen, the Wall Street crowd, and the Treasury group around Secretary Henry Morgenthau, plus most economists, said the administration should attempt to do all of this while keeping business confidence high and conforming to the market by keeping interest rates low and balancing the budget (Brown, 1999: 32–9; Barber, 1996; Olson, 1988; Kennedy, 1999: chap. 5).

It could not all be done at once. As an antidote to the Depression, the New Deal seemed action-packed, but its economics were cautious. American politicians were not ready for Keynesianism, and Roosevelt abhorred deficit financing. He also faced a Congress divided over whether to spend more. He hoped (as Hoover had) that private investors would restore economic stability, and he focused initially on maintaining prices. Roosevelt's best decisions were probably to leave the gold standard and engage in monetary expansion. The consequent moderate inflation was good for the economy – as was the case in the first post–World War II decades. There was economic growth after the disaster. A strong recovery began in 1933, interrupted by a short recession in 1937. Real GDP went up 90 percent between 1933 and 1941. Field (2011) says this was due partly to processes of "creative destruction" occurring as new industries and products came onstream, such as the DC-3 aircraft, refrigerators, improved automobiles, and nylon stockings – although most of these came onstream at the end of the decade. He adds that public works programs, especially the extensive road building of the New Deal, considerably increased efficiency and made trucking a boom industry. Financial institutions were modernized and regulated to make them more secure. The Glass-Steagall Banking Act of 1933 separated investment banks from commercial banks, securing depositors' funds against losses incurred by speculative ventures. It was reinforced by the Federal Bank Deposit Insurance Corporation (FBDIC, later FDIC), which guaranteed individual bank deposits up to $5,000, as well as by requiring transparent business operations regulated by the Securities Exchange Commission. Together, these ended American banking crises in the twentieth century, a major improvement. The ending of Glass-Steagall in 1999 helped bring on another capitalist crisis. At the other extreme, the NRA is seen as an inefficient price-fixing cartel, keeping prices and wages high, in accordance with underconsumption theory, but depressing output and consumption, the opposite of its goal. Even most New Dealers became unhappy with it. However, the NRA did establish national maximum hours and minimum wages, and ended child labor and the sweatshop. It was more effective in redistributing than in increasing the nation's collective power (Leuchtenburg, 1963: 69; Brinkley, 1996: 46–7).

The public viewed Recovery mostly as job creation, focused on improving the nation's infrastructures and environment. The Civilian Conservation Corps provided jobs and improved the environment. More than 200 million trees were planted, which helped stabilize soil erosion. As the Corps developed, environmentalists criticized it for focusing exclusively on resource production, the planting of too-few species, and on recreational needs, instead of creating and maintaining more complex ecosystems and protecting wilderness from overuse. The debate energized the environmental movement and propelled the United States into the forefront of green debates over the next decades (Mäher, 2008). Direct spending on these programs was quite small in relation to the overall size of the economy, so the pump-priming function was not great. There were spin-offs, however, in increasing productivity in transport, public utilities, and wholesale and retail distribution, and these sectors helped make up for uneven manufacturing productivity during the 1930s.

Overall, this was half a cure, producing half a recovery. It was better than Hoover had done, better than France did, but not as good as some other countries. Japan and Germany ran bigger budget deficits and recovered better, but the activism and popularity of the New Deal gave consumers, companies, and investors confidence that recovery was possible. It also provided many state institutions that later encouraged sustained economic growth (Romer, 1992; Steindl, 2005; Temin, 1989: chap. 3; Field, 2006).

How much of this half-recovery was due to the Roosevelt administration? Those who believe states can help economic recovery stress the impact of some of the reforms. Those who believe that capitalist economies work best when left alone credit recovery to capitalists and failures to the government (Smiley, 2002; Shlaes, 2008). Yet even Smiley concedes structural unevenness, and he agrees that dynamic industries contributed too small and stagnant industries too large a share of overall GNP. He agrees that throughout the 1930s, the main problem was that private investment remained too low, which he attributes to businessmen's fear of government intervention (2002: 126–32). Yet he produces no evidence for this, and it is unlikely, as the administration did not intervene much in private business nor did it impose major taxes on business. It was more likely due to inadequate market opportunities for substantial profit. The dynamic industries got investment, but they were small. The big stagnant industries were not attractive to investors, but this means that the selectivity of government intervention necessary to boost investment was much greater than politicians could accept. Bernstein sees Rexford Tugwell as the principal exponent of the selective investment strategy within the administration. The NRA and the undistributed profits tax of 1936 were Tugwell-inspired measures aimed at sectoral imbalances (1987: 190–2, 196–203). Yet both were repealed after two years.

Some success was evident. In Roosevelt's time in office, unemployment fell every year except during the recession of 1937–1938, partly due to the work relief programs. Real GDP grew at an annual rate of about 9 percent during his first term, and after 1938 by around 11 percent. The 1937 recession was popularly called the "Roosevelt recession" because it was widely attributed to a reduction of government spending combined with the impact of new taxes required by the new Social Security Act, which reduced private spending. This boosted Keynesian solutions, and Roosevelt responded with deficit spending. Yet this only reached $3 million, about 3 percent of national output – compared, for example, to President Obama's deficit spending of early 2009, which amounted to 10 percent of output. Treasury and Wall Street budget-balancers remained powerful, and no institutions of government could pump prime at will, so each bout of further spending required laborious struggles in Congress (Brinkley, 1996: chaps. 4, 5). This was too daunting, so policy oscillated. Even in 1940, 15 percent of Americans were still unemployed. Only World War II brought massive deficit spending (amounting to 30 percent of GDP in 1943), full employment, and Recovery.

Regulation: here the New Dealers could borrow from institutions introduced temporarily in World War I (Leuchtenberg, 1963; Rodgers, 1998: 415). Helped by subsequent wars, hot and cold, this surge in federal spending and regulation proved long-lasting, a permanent break with the past. Bordo et al. (1998; cf Campbell, 1995: 34) provide a time series for total government purchases of goods and services as a share of GNP. It was flat at around 8 percent in the

1920s, but from 1933 rose quickly to a new plateau of 14–15 percent until United States entry into World War II, when it again rose sharply. Federal government expenses rose even more sharply, from less than 4 percent of GNP to 9 percent in 1936. As Higgs (1987) observes, the Depression generated the first great upward "ratchet effect" of the American state (and World War II generated the second).

State growth was fitted into new macroeconomic theories. Roosevelt could take his pick among economic advisors who were structuralists, reflationists, inflationists, monetarists, planners, underconsumptionists, and deficit spenders. Yet he lacked interest in theories, and he was a man of politics more than policies (Domhoff & Webber, 2011: 3–5). A fiscal conservative and never a Keynesian, he came to favor a structuralist solution, but a cheap one (Barber, 1996). He expected relief programs not deficit spending would bring economic recovery. His trusted advisors were divided: conservative pro-business types such as Budget Director Douglas were backed by most Southern Democrats and Republicans; others wanted major reforms, but couldn't agree on which ones. Frankfurter, Corcoran, and Cohen thought the way to recovery was to restore capitalism by reviving competitive markets, opposing the "curse of bigness" with regulation to curb Wall Street and the corporations. This liberal interventionism was laced with progressive antitrust sentiments, but in order to restore free markets. This faction recruited hundreds of "legal realists" imbued with an ethic of public service, to staff a swathe of New Deal agencies and fight against Wall Street's best. Berle, Tugwell, Eccles, and Hopkins were social liberals, accepting economic concentration as an irreversible feature of a modern industrial economy, but seeking a dose of state capitalism to control it through planning, expanding public credit, and stimulating incomes, an implicitly Keynesian argument. They had outside support from labor and farmer organizations and liberals in Congress (Schwarz, 1993).

In 1933, the Frankfurter group accepted the need for central planning agencies such as the NRA and the Agricultural Adjustment Administration; the planners accepted the need for banking reform and securities regulation to make financial markets freer. The emphasis shifted from ad hoc central planning in 1933–1935 to the Keynesian deficit spending plus antimonopoly policy to fight the recession of 1937, and finally to war mobilization that brought more Keynesian central planning. Because the experts got their power from the center, they tended to favor federal not state administration of programs, although they had to abandon this if confronted by Congress or the Supreme Court. The simplest way of dealing with the factions was to let each have its own agencies and Roosevelt keep overall political control.

One very big agency was the Reconstruction Finance Corporation (RFC), introduced by Hoover but now empowered to make direct loans to businesses, insurance companies, farm cooperatives, school districts, and New Deal agencies. It became the largest investor in the economy. Being the major creditor of numerous banks, savings banks, building and loan associations, and railroads meant it could control the flow of capital and the level of dividends and corporate salaries. This was state planning on a large scale, although it had nothing to do with socialism. Its boss, Jesse Jones, a Texas lumber and banking billionaire, was pro-business if anti–Wall Street (Olson, 1988). His RFC rescued the banks and the credit system, although its loans to industry achieved little. Jones was too much the businessman to accept the state capitalism advocated by Tugwell and Berle. He wanted the RFC to revive private commercial lending, not replace it. The RFC and other public works agencies launched major economic development projects in the South and Southwest aimed at reducing regional inequality and generating a more integrated national economy. They were quite effective in this, although it was military expenditures during and after Wold War II that cemented the achievement (Schwarz, 1993; J. Smith, 2006). This was regulation on behalf of capitalism not redistributive reform, except that it was committed to a high-wage, high-consumption economy. These agencies were mostly run by lawyers and corporate businessmen.

Regulation in agriculture differed; state autonomy and class theorists debate why. Finegold & Skocpol (1984, 1995) contrast the success of the AAA with the failure of the NRA, geared to industrial regulation. Both were set up to reduce output and increase prices. Finegold & Skocpol say the greater success of the farm policy was primarily due to state capacity. The AAA, they say, was embedded inside an already-effective state bureaucracy – the U.S. Department of Agriculture (USDA) – with agents reaching down into the farms, drawing on a community of agronomist experts trained in the land-grant colleges, and consulting for the USDA (they might have added that farming matters also came before a congressional committee sympathetic to farmers' problems). They argue that the NRA lacked these attributes. In the absence of any prior existing bureaucracy, its administration was handed over to businessmen who sought to advantage their own firms. This was inevitable, as the federal government still lacked much bureaucratic capacity in business matters. However, it was really the sheer size of the NRA's task that was so daunting. More than 550 price code authorities and 2 million businesses were involved. They also set price codes too high, which produced a storm of criticism by consumers, government purchasers, and labor. Without economic growth, this was bad for the economy (Domhoff, 1996: 109–11). The sheer ambition of the project was probably more important than bureaucratic incapacity in defeating the NRA. No other country tried to get out of the Depression by enforcing price codes over the whole economy. The U.S. state did lack bureaucratic capacity for this task, but so would any state of the time.

There was a more obvious reason for the success of the agricultural program. If you offer money to farmers and in return ask them to work less, they will cooperate. The farmer "swapped some of his freedom for higher profits," says Hayes (2001: 135). Farm laborers lost out because they were largely unorganized, without unions. Large farmers did better than small ones, but the AAA especially harmed African-American farmers, also unorganized (Hayes, 2001: 132, 158). Robert Harrison says this was "radical intervention in the market for essentially conservative principles" (1997: 191). The legislation originated in the think tanks of corporate liberals, and government experts only entered into the discussions later. The bureaucracy once established to administer it was not autonomous, as it was mainly staffed by businessmen and large farmers (Domhoff & Webber, 2011: chap. 3; Domhoff, 1996: chap. 3). As the AAA proceeded, it increasingly favored richer farmers, as it has done ever since (Finegold & Skocpol acknowledge this). In one respect, the New Deal was the end of the road for progressives. Having been the core radicals in the Progressive Era, small farmers were relegated to the margins of American politics. Agricultural intervention was driven more by class interests than state elites, although in this sector class struggle was fading.

It was different in industries where class struggle and conflict among class fractions was more overt. The NRA was undermined by rivalry among employers, exacerbated class conflict with unions, and gave money to no one. Although in principle it entrenched the powers of unions, in practice most businessmen refused to cooperate with them, which intensified class conflict. When combined with unending disputes between all the parties over the codes, this made the agency unworkable (Domhoff, 1996: chap. 4). Here, a state capacity explanation seems less powerful than a simple class and sectoral one: farmers were bribed, farm laborers were unorganized, and industrialists and their workers were factionalized. In fact, so far, state capacity does not seem to be the cause of most New Deal programs. Obviously, experts worked on the details of programs, and when it came to the regulation of finance this was a very technical matter in which they did have much influence. In general, however, they were hemmed in by politicians who had rather conservative economic views and mass pressure demanding more radical change.

The New Deal figured in most Americans' lives as *Relief*. Public works programs linked together counter-Depression measures with redistribution to the poor and unemployed. In 1933, spending on the Public Works Administration was bigger than total government revenues, being almost 6 percent of GDP (J. Smith, 2006: 2). Amenta (1998: 5, 142–8) shows that by 1938, the United States was suddenly leading the world in social spending. It consumed 6.3 percent of GDP and 29 percent of all government spending, compared to 5.6 percent of GDP and 18.7 percent of government spending in Nazi Germany, 5 percent of GDP and 17.5 percent of government spending in Britain, and 3.2 percent of GDP and 17.8 percent of government spending in Sweden. Most U.S. spending was on relief. The WPA alone consumed 55 percent of social spending and employed 2.1 million adult workers, plus 1 million in youth employment programs. It had been given priority over the Social Security Act in going through Congress, and was visible throughout the nation. It remains visible today in the form of highways, schools, dams, hospitals, and public funding for the arts. It changed the landscape of America. Relief amounted to more than 70 percent of social spending, dwarfing the 16 percent on welfare based on the insurance principle. Thus, the United States "lead" might be only temporary. If the unemployment rate came down, so would this social spending. We should not draw too many conclusions from Amenta's figures.

Whether Relief programs were redistributive depended on how they were financed. Most payment came from more national debt, against the initial promises of the administration. It was being pushed half-wittingly toward Keynesian economics. The contradiction between balancing the budget and sustaining incomes was resolved by prioritizing the latter, broadened into a program of stimulating demand by deficit spending. These policies were a little redistributive; they were generally popular. During the election of 1936, the Republicans charged correctly that Roosevelt had broken his initial pledge to balance the budget. Yet this seemed to matter less to voters than that he was doing something about their plight.

There was a fourth "R" – *Reelection*. Electoral concerns are never secondary for politicians, especially one as shrewd as Roosevelt. Although on the crest of an electoral wave, he still worried. First came business, who he did not wish to alienate. Most businessmen supported the counter-Depression legislation of the first New Deal, but they turned against the more reform-oriented legislation of its second phase and supported the Republican opposition. About 80 percent of the corporate executives studied by Webber gave money to the Republicans in 1936. The only significant exceptions were Jewish and Southern businessmen, who contributed more to the Democrats; Catholic businessmen were divided in their loyalties. Yet as most big business was northern and Protestant, it was fairly solidly Republican (Webber, 2000; Manza, 2000). Roosevelt's tactic was to push forward bills he knew business would oppose, but then compromise in the redrafting process. The Supreme Court was also opposed, and this produced more trimming of original bills, especially reducing the degree of federal as opposed to state-level activism. The justices of the Supreme Court formed the most powerful state elite of the period, and being conservative, they blocked some programs. However, the New Deal went forward despite their distaste for it. They ultimately had only limited power.

In a liberal democracy, political parties become extremely important. In the United States, what seemed to be a two-party system actually contained three parties: Republicans, Democrats, and Southern Democrats. The Southern Democrats were powerful on Capitol Hill because (as detailed in Chapter 3) rural districts were electorally overrepresented, Southern elections were essentially uncontested, and the seniority and committee system on the Hill privileged those who kept getting reelected. Except between 1934 and 1938, Southern Democrats were dominant in the legislative process on the Hill, able to fight federally administered regulation and welfare programs if these seemed to benefit African Americans or raise wages. The planter-merchant elites ruling the Southern Democratic Party had disenfranchised blacks and many poor whites, retained their local repressive powers, and were committed to their racially segregated, low-wage economy, supported by a broader white racism. Their institutional power rested ultimately on their secure hold on racial capitalism in the South.

Neither of the two parties was cohesive. In the progressive period, the parties had been regional and sectoral, and although class voting was now increasing, it did not wipe out these rival bases of interest. The Republicans remained split between Northeastern business and Western agriculture, with a Midwestern Progressive faction closer to Roosevelt than to other Republicans. Their choice of the moderate Alf Landon from Kansas as their 1936 presidential candidate was an attempt to paper over their divisions. The Democrats were not cohesive, either. The New Deal pushed by urban Democrats met Congressional opposition from Southern, Western, Midwestern, and even New England rural Democrats. A handful of conservative Democrats usually joined the Republicans in voting against New Deal programs. Conservatives might vote against public works but for farm subsidies, denounce budget deficits but refuse to pass tax laws (Weed, 1994; Patterson, 1967; Kennedy, 1999: 338–9).

Above all, they could be bought. Roosevelt offered a deal to every group whose vote was targeted by his electoral advisors. The big spending programs offered federal dollars to states and local governments. Their distribution was geared more to the electoral importance of a state than to its level of poverty or unemployment. A disproportionate share of federal spending went to those states that had swung to Roosevelt in 1932 – and not to the poorest states (Couch & Shughart, 1998). Overall, the New Deal helped the poor in proportion to their electoral utility, a somewhat corrupted form of pluralism.

The modern regulatory state Roosevelt urged was contradicted by the particularistic patronage machines he utilized. The machines offered support provided they could manage the administration of programs, which Roosevelt often conceded (Mayhew, 1986: 292–4; Shefter, 1994). Southern legislators were happy with programs administered by states or local governments, as this would boost their own patronage. They welcomed local relief and infrastructural improvements. Hayes (2001: 185) says the new Deal saved South Carolina from economic collapse. In fact, much of the New Deal could not have been passed without the support of Southern Senators and Congressmen – liberals and racists united! However, they were against redistributive reforms and federal control being implemented in the South. Although there was popular support for these across the South, the region's politicians ignored this and were responsive instead to the landlord, planter, manufacturing elite. Their initial enthusiasm for the New Deal then waned and turned into opposition in 1938 (Hayes, 2001: chap. 9; Korstad, 2003). Polls showed that most Southerners supported New Deal programs, yet most of the people could not vote, deprived by the poll tax and other restrictive practices (Sullivan, 1996: 61–2). This was not pluralism but domination by a regional ruling class. These peculiar political institutions offered some support to political institutionalist arguments, although they ultimately largely rested on class interests in a low-wage racial economy.

The deals were ubiquitous, preventing a fully bureaucratic state or universal welfare system from emerging (Amenta, 1998). Almost every bill was subject to wrangling and vote-buying, in which the trend was toward the watering down of initially sweeping legislation. Yet the constant struggle between the federal and state governments and the president and congress did yield a more centralizing state. The proliferation of intergovernmental grants from federal to state and local reduced the independence of the different tiers of government, and required them to cooperate more with each other than in the past. It was fiscal centralization and administrative decentralization. The New Deal increased the share of federal in total spending by 9 percent, although all levels of government grew (Wallis & Oates, 1998: 170). It was not as centralized or bureaucratic a government as in Britain, France, or Japan, but it was more than the "Broker State … intervening in an ad hoc and piecemeal fashion on behalf of favored groups and sectors" identified by Finegold & Skocpol (1995: 20).

Reelection worked brilliantly: in 1936, Roosevelt's vote went up to 61 percent, the Democrats picked up seven Senate seats, and (including a handful of third-party allies) a further fifteen seats in Congress. There was little party discipline, but for four years, Roosevelt had a majority on the Hill and could pass legislation without needing the votes of the Southern Democrats. Only in the midterm election of 1938, after the second recession, did they lose this – losing seventy-one House seats and seven in the Senate. In 1940, Roosevelt's own vote and that of his party stabilized. The Democrats were in the White House for two decades.

Reform: Class Struggle and Political Opportunity

Did the Reform programs of the New Deal result from bottom-up popular pressure or top-down pressure arising out of a changing political opportunity structure among state elites and/or fractions of capital? I start with pressure from below. High unemployment is usually bad for labor unions, for the unemployed lose contact with unions and the employed know their bargaining power is weak and do not want to provoke their employer. This time, two factors favored a more vigorous response. First, in the Depression, employment, production, and demand all fell so much that most of the country was affected, and could sympathize with the unemployed. That sympathy is necessary for people to approve of programs to help the disadvantaged. Second, the shift to the Roosevelt administration and many Democratic administrations at the state and city level meant little state repression. Employers lacked the extra weapon we saw them reliant on in Chapter 3.

Millions of Americans were looking for work, alternating hope, despair, and anger. Shantytowns, bread lines, and soup kitchens proliferated. With help from socialists and communists, they formed councils, demonstrated, marched, and petitioned city halls. They received sympathy, not least from the shopkeepers and others whose livelihoods depended on their consumption. Housing evictions were resisted by tenants and their neighbors. If the police did disperse protesters with beatings and shootings, massive demonstrations ensued (Cohen, 1990: 262–6; Valocchi, 1990). There was a surge in popular leftism that lasted through 1935, a break out from the isolated labor movement of the Progressive Era that touched many middle-class groups, as well.

A Farmers Holiday Association caused trouble across rural areas. A "Bonus Army" of mostly unemployed military veterans marched to Washington in 1932, protesting they had never received the promised bonus for fighting in World War I. Hoover used troops to disperse them. When they returned to haunt Roosevelt in 1933, he preferred to send Eleanor to talk to them, and he even acceded to some of their demands. Starting in 1935, the Townsend Movement, organized by a retired physician from California, mobilized millions of followers to demand an old-age pension of $200 a month for the over 65s. Father Charles Coughlin stirred up a populist following directed against the rich and powerful, which then veered rightward to become America's largest fascist-tinged movement. Although these were not explicitly class movements, they did stir up anger against the rich and privileged.

Strikes rose from 1931, with spurts in 1933–1934 and 1937 (Jenkins & Brents, 1989: 896). More workers joined industrial unions, demanded legislation to legalize them, and sought national bargaining over wages and conditions. Ethnic differences among white workers were declining. Between 1933 and 1935, more strikes than ever before or since demanded union representation or more shop-floor control (Wallace et al., 1988: 13). Even the South did not escape the ferment: a 1934 strike affected textile mills across Alabama, Georgia, and the Carolinas; 200,000 workers walked out (Irons, 2000). Some American Federation of Labor (AFL) unions were also recruiting and striking outside their traditional crafts, but most employers were not disposed to yield, and their counterattacks took their toll. The AFL leadership also remained skeptical about industrial and political unionism, still preferring to rely on craft controls to push employers to negotiate, but this provoked rebellion. Led by John L. Lewis, head of the Mineworkers, most industrial unions broke away in 1936 to form their own Congress of Industrial Unions (CIO). Breakaways were sparked by agitation from below (Goldfield, 1989; Kerbo & Shaffer, 1986; Piven & Cloward, 1977: 48–60; Stepan-Norris & Zeitlin, 2003). Unionization increased from 10 percent to 25 percent of workers over the decade. Labor protests were much more widespread and effective than anyone alive could remember. The Depression of the 1890s had seen major strikes, and there had also been some in 1919, but on both occasions, striking workers had been isolated. Now protesters and strikers had national sympathy. Politicians grew reluctant to try such repression against the people.

The political opportunity structure was widening. Workers were shoving against a door creaking open. The Norris-LaGuardia Act, passed in 1932, banned court restraining orders and injunctions in cases arising out of labor disputes as well as yellow dog contracts for all workers. As the arsenal of repression weakened, more workers dared organize. They were also disillusioned with the near-collapse of private forms of welfare such as community credit associations and welfare capitalism. Demands for public welfare programs surged (Cohen, 1990: 218–49).

Workers were expecting the incoming Roosevelt administration to be sympathetic to their demands, and were quickly rewarded by the NIRA set up in June 1933 whose Section 7a gave workers the right "to organize and bargain collectively through representatives of their own choosing, and shall be free from interference, restraint, or coercion by employers." A National Labor Board (NLB) was set up to help settle strikes, although it had little enforcement machinery. Workers thought NIRA would set them free; unionization rates shot up within months (Piven & Cloward, 1977: 110; Irons, 2000: 77; O'Brien, 1998; Wallace et al., 1988: 5–7). Workers were encouraged to stand up and fight in organizations broader than just craft unions, and from 1935, the CIO was building up industrial unions from the work gang upward, fashioning relatively democratic organizations. The midterm elections of 1934 again strengthened the left. Although the NIRA collapsed, the epochal Wagner Act followed in 1935. This interaction between unionization and legislation from a sympathetic government was the first clear sign of a lib-lab alliance. There was no labor party, but a large part of the Democratic Party was now prolabor.

Roosevelt, aware that business opposed most of his legislation, knew he could ride the leftward shift. He also feared the Depression might generate a third party, an explicit party of labor. If the Democrats failed to combat the Depression, these would be ideal times for a third party. If it won a substantial number of votes, it would likely take votes from the Democrats and conceivably deliver an election to the Republicans. There were already leftist farm labor or labor parties in Minnesota, Wisconsin, and New York, and Roosevelt took care to consult them and deliver federal aid programs to the cities they controlled. In 1935, the populist Democratic Senator Huey Long of Louisiana threatened to run the following year as a "Share-Our-Wealth" candidate. A private poll commissioned by the Democrats said he might get 3–4 million votes, and deliver some states to the Republicans. A Progressive Republican ticket headed by Robert LaFollette might also join in, and it was unclear from whom he might take votes. About one in five or six Americans said they would join a new progressive party if one were available. His private poll predicted Roosevelt would still win easily, but few politicians take chances about elections. They aim to win as big as possible, just in case things go awry in the meantime.

Because Roosevelt believed business would oppose him no matter what, he decided to reciprocate their antagonism as an electoral weapon. He increased antibusiness rhetoric, calling big businessmen "economic royalists" and threatened to "equalize the distribution of wealth" and "throw to the wolves the forty-six men who are reported to have incomes in excess of one million dollars a year." Harry Hopkins, a radical New Dealer, exulted, "Boys, this is our hour. We've got to get everything we want – a works program, social security, wages and hours, everything – now or never" (Kennedy, 1999: 266–87; Leuchtenburg, 1963: 117). They got a big electoral victory, and they got programs. The Revenue Act of 1935 raised income and dividend taxes for the wealthy, together with a more progressive inheritance tax and bigger corporation taxes. This was to inaugurate a forty-year period of progressive taxes in America. Huey Long justly complained that Roosevelt was stealing his program (Amenta et al., 1994; Kennedy, 1999: 238–42, 275–6). Yet beset by hostility from businessmen, conservative Democrats, and Republicans, the bill was so watered down in Congress that the overall effect on income redistribution was small, except that it took substantial sums from the small number of millionaires.

Roosevelt did have a bigger political strategy in mind. He was always ambivalent about Southern support. He declared the South to be "the Nation's No. 1 economic problem," a low-wage, low-consumption region acting as a drag on the high-wage, high-consumption American economy he wanted. Along with many economists at the time, he thought this was an important cause of the Depression itself (Sullivan, 1996: 65). He doubted whether many reforms could come from a region controlled by a ruling class that excluded blacks and poor whites from the vote and used racism to keep wages low and the economy backward. Tactically, he tried to buy off their potential opposition to his programs with concessions. He also continued the 1920s strategy of rebuilding the party on a northern urban basis, using patronage and programs to secure the support of the northern city machines, leaving the Progressive Republicans to woo agriculture, and appealing to labor with anti–big-business rhetoric (Kennedy, 1999: chap. 9). Schlesinger (1960: 592) says that as the 1936 campaign developed:

> The Democratic party seemed more and more submerged in the New Deal coalition. The most active campaigners in addition to Roosevelt – Ickes, Wallace, Hugh Johnson – were men identified with the New Deal, not with the professional Democratic organization. Loyalty to the cause superseded loyalty to the party as the criterion for administration support.... It was evident that the basis of the campaign would be the mobilization beyond the Democratic party of all the elements in the New Deal coalition – liberals, labor, farmers, women, minorities.

This was a lib-lab strategy. Had it worked it would have confirmed his party as social democratic in all but name.

During the 1930s, far more Americans, especially workers – and particularly foreign-born workers – turned out to vote. They increasingly voted Democrat, wooed by the New Deal and the Roosevelts; they were less likely to vote by ethnicity and religion. Ethnicity was weakening, as a higher proportion of workers were born in the United States, and as nationalizing mass media, especially radio, spread. The nation was solidifying. First-time voters were more likely to vote Democrat – the poor and the youngest age cohort – but class was also solidifying. By 1936, workers were over twice as likely to vote Democrat as were voters from the upper middle class. Historically voting overwhelmingly Republican (the party of Lincoln), even African Americans shifted to splitting their votes between the parties (B. Anderson, 1979; Cohen, 1990: 253–61; Kleppner, 1982: 55–111; Manza, 2000). All of these were mainly urban trends – the countryside saw less change. Several New Deal programs targeted the middle class: the FDIC guaranteed all bank deposits up to $5,000 and the housing acts, and the Federal Housing Administration (FHA) gave favorable terms for refinancing mortgages. It was a popular more than a class strategy, but it had most success among workers.

In 1937, the sociologist Arthur Kornhauser interviewed hundreds of Chicagoans. Almost all thought wealthy businessmen had too much power, and three-quarters thought that working people were not treated fairly. Around three-quarters of manual workers interviewed voted for Roosevelt, supported the New Deal, and wanted the government to redistribute wealth. Between one-half and two-thirds of office workers did so as well. The workers blamed their employers and the capitalist system for the Depression, but did not favor government ownership. They favored a fairer system with some redistribution of wealth and privilege, insisted on their rights to organize, and saw themselves as equal contributors to the nation, entitled to full social citizenship – a new sense of moral and material entitlement (Kornhauser, 1940: 237; Zieger, 1995: 43–4; Cohen, 1990: 276, 282–5, 362–5; Gerstle, 1989; Lipset, 1983: 274–9).

The electoral pressure was for an expansion of government regulatory agencies. Thus, the main causal arrow went from popular pressure, mostly expressed through the electoral system, to the hiring of experts by all sides – business needed to bend its interests toward the fine print of legislation it recognized as being inevitable. Then the experts, their bosses, and Congress all wrestled over the exact content of programs. The democratic process involved much more than just class, but its sharp edge was the demonstrations, strikes, and unionization. There was such close interaction between class struggle and political opportunity that it is not easy to privilege one over the other. However, in the 1930s, America was suddenly becoming more similar to Europe, moving a little closer to the politics of "the democratic class struggle," a phrase coined by Dewey Anderson and popularized by Lipset. I focus on the two major redistributive bills.

The Wagner Act and labor unions

The AFL was a marginal player here. It had unsuccessfully opposed the appointment of Frances Perkins as secretary of labor (she was the first woman in any U.S. cabinet). It had pushed unsuccessfully for a thirty-hour bill, its preferred alternative to the NIRA. It played little role in either the Wagner or Social Security Acts, and later it opposed the minimum-wage provisions of the FLSA Act of 1938 (Manza, 2000; Lichtenstein, 2002: 63–71). Sidney Hillman of the Amalgamated Clothing Workers and John L. Lewis of the United Mine Workers, both CIO unions, had played a role in the NIRA, and Hillman was the only labor leader in a senior administration position. Both were important in pushing for the Wagner Act. Roosevelt himself had not been very interested in labor legislation, and only backed the Wagner Act at the last minute. Business hostility to labor legislation prevented the kind of compromise he had favored; he now had to choose class sides. Feeling betrayed by business hostility, and sensing more votes in it, he turned leftward and supported the Act.

Labor's influence was mostly indirect – on the streets and picket lines and through Congressmen and Senators from urban and industrial districts and states. Section 7a of the NIRA had already attempted to bring unions into consultative machinery, but employers had rarely recognized them, and then the Supreme Court disallowed the whole venture. There would obviously be a second attempt, given mounting conflict in society. In this context, the experts of the Wisconsin School of institutional economists, discussed in the last chapter, could come into their own. They believed that union leaders could play an important regulatory role by disciplining their members. Responsible unions could help overcome the plague of unruly militancy, which in counterpoint to employer aggression was creating industrial chaos. Together, responsible, reasonable corporate and labor leaders could help regulate the economy. As so many involved in the New Deal, John Commons and his followers wanted to save capitalism – by giving more power to organized labor.

Amenta (1998) studied the New Deal in four states – Virginia, Illinois, Wisconsin, and California. There he found the strength of support for New Deal programs varied according to the degree of democracy (it was low where blacks and many poor whites could not vote, and quite low where patronage machines dominated), the presence of liberal or left politicians, and the strength of labor and other reformist social movements. Amenta says this is a "political institutional" argument, although he also notes considerable class pressures. Unlike other countries, leftist politicians were rarely drawn from labor backgrounds, and they almost never endorsed socialist views, but they witnessed the growing discontent and disorder in their own districts and they wanted reforms to end them. They knew that most protesters and most AFL and CIO leaders were not extremists, and they wanted reforms to help them make legitimate gains and restore order among their followers.

The Act is popularly named after its sponsor – Senator Robert Wagner of New York – one of the leading New Dealers, with close ties to New York unions and corporate liberals. He had chaired the first attempt at a National Labor Board in 1933–1934, and in March 1935 he warned of a "rising tide of industrial discontent." Senator Robert LaFollette Jr., from Wisconsin – also a long-time champion of labor – and a Progressive Republican, predicted "open industrial warfare" if the demands of labor were not addressed. Representative William Connery of Massachusetts – representing an industrial district – a long-time sponsor of labor bills and Chairman of the House Labor Committee, foresaw "the gates of hell opened." Representative Martin Sweeney of industrial Cleveland predicted "an epidemic of strikes that has never before been witnessed in this country" (Goldfield, 1989: 1273–5). They were asking legislators less sympathetic to labor to save capitalism. They believed big business was now spoiling for a fight, and wanted to head them off, but Roosevelt was unwilling to use repression to solve rising conflict. Wagner's first bill was defeated. Roosevelt, not very interested in the project, got two of his top lawyers to draft a milder law, giving unions limited rights without enforcement powers. This passed in 1934, and was strengthened by a second act in 1935. Both owed something to this strike wave, but probably more to the midterm elections, which had returned more liberal Democrats, more progressive Republicans, and more radical third-party representatives. Public opinion was shifting leftward.

The Wagner Act gave more rights to unions by outlawing unfair labor practices by employers, allowing voters free majority votes over who should represent them. It protected the right to strike, imposed a duty on both sides to bargain in good faith, and set up a National Labor Relations Board (NLRB) to oversee compliance. It was a big gain for labor. The Act's preamble restated underconsumptionism: it would help promote economic recovery by raising wages and consumption. It used the language of the rights of the individual worker, not collective union rights, maintaining the impression of continuity with the Railroad and Norris-La Guardia Acts, which many Republicans supported (Fraser, 1989: 69; O'Brien, 1998: chap. 8). These were devices to secure votes from the political center. Southern Democrats supported the bill once Wagner accepted that it would not apply to agriculture or domestic service, the South's major industries. Thus, virtually all the Democrats and the Progressive Republicans supported the act; it was opposed by almost the whole of big business This was the only major piece of legislation to which business moderates contributed little (Domhoff & Webber, 2011: chap. 4; Swenson, 2002: 213–9). It resulted from the height of American-style class struggle, when lib-labs could overrule American business.

Most of business continued to resist the Wagner Act, as they had Section 7a. They still refused to recognize unions, and in the South, they were mostly successful. Southern textile workers had been greatly encouraged by the establishment of the NRA, but disillusioned by it in practice (Schlesinger, 1960: 424; Irons, 2000: 77; cf Hayes, 2001: 205; Korstad, 2003). In desperation, the textile workers launched a mass strike, but the union had little money and few staff; workers were repressed by employers' private armies, sheriff's deputies, and state militias, numbering 15,000 in the Carolinas alone. Seven strikers were killed in the worst incident. Georgia Governor Talmadge initially refused to send in his state troopers, but he did so when Georgia's textile manufacturers offered him $20,000 in campaign contributions. The strikers pleaded for northern unions and Labor Secretary Frances Perkins to intervene. The northern unions had their hands full elsewhere, and Perkins said it was "an unfortunate situation" but dared not intervene, as the administration needed Southern Democrats to pass its legislation.

Southern workers were just as keen as northern workers to join labor unions, and they might have overcome the resistance of their employers, but they were politically and militarily weak. Employers controlled the Southern Democratic Party, and most workers were prevented from even voting (Irons, 2000: chaps. 9, 10, pgs. 164–75; Hayes, 2001: chap. 7). After the firing of militants and the deployment of paramilitary repression, the local elites played the race card, thus dividing labor (Sullivan, 1996; Korstad, 2003). In the South, the New Deal failed to shift the balance of class and race power; it was different in some northern states. Lib-lab local and state officials had been brought into power by the elections of 1932, 1934, and 1936. The governors of Michigan and Pennsylvania refused to send the police in to break up strikes – repression might put them all out of office given the changed popular climate.

The Wagner Act promised reform in the name of both social justice and orderly regulation. Wagner's former staff members remembered the bill as being more conservative than radical, and they remember Wagner justifying it by saying it was as much as he could get. They said that he was influenced by the writings of Sidney and Beatrice Webb, leading members of the British Fabian Society, the major intellectual adjunct of the Labour Party. He also perceived that the United States was lagging behind Europe in labor relations, and needed more social justice and a more regulatory state (St. Antoine, 1998). Wagner was also conscious of the need to satisfy the Supreme Court. Lichtenstein (1992) says the Act was a "clear concession to the disruptive militancy of the era, but one that also sought to channel worker protest into predictable patterns under a system of state regulation." Responsible union leaders would control their members.

This motive was prominent among reformers in all countries. As elsewhere, labor's rise depended on its own power to create trouble and the belief of moderates from other classes that labor agitation could be steered into more orderly channels that would preserve capitalism from disorder or revolution. Whether unions would be able to press onward for further gains or would predominantly exercise a control function over workers was still open, as it was in other countries. Some Marxian writers emphasize the control functions of the Wagner Act, and of the New Deal as a whole. Tomlins says the "state offered workers and their organizations ... no more than the opportunity to participate in their own subordination" (1985: 327–8). However, he is arguing teleologically, reading back into the 1930s tendencies that appeared later. At the time, most observers stressed the forward march of labor. Unions had soared from organizing 10 percent to almost 25 percent of American workers in only a decade. A surge of militancy in industrial unions had lost them the support of corporate liberals (Domhoff, 1990: 82–9), but it did not seem to matter. In 1937–1938 CIO unions threatened U.S. Steel into a deal and took on and defeated the might of General Motors and Goodyear Rubber in union recognition strikes. Unions were here to stay.

The main causes of the Wagner Act were mass worker agitation backed by prolabor legislators, who in turn were responsive to constituents shifting leftward. This was popular struggle overcoming employer resistance, although a further necessary condition was the buying off of Southerners on Capitol Hill (Domhoff, 1990: 97–100). It was not state autonomy; it was more a Congressional than an administration-bureaucratic initiative. Of course, Senators and Congressmen in the most liberal states did have expert lawyers and institutional economists helping draft the legislation to recognize and regulate the labor unions. Yet the Wagner Act resulted predominantly from the democratic translation of the class struggle.

The Social Security Act and the welfare state

The Social Security Act (SSA) was Reform, irrelevant for Relief or Recovery. The first benefits were not paid out until 1941. It was more popular than the Wagner Act, and its appeal was cross-class. It was also more complex and technical, and its several components appealed to different constituencies. Unemployment insurance had a labor constituency, but was also the pet project of Roosevelt. Congress showed more interest than the President did in the old-age pensions component. The Aid for Dependent Children invoked feminist interest linked to administrative agencies, with less interest shown by the President or Congress. The President was deeply supportive of the overall act, although he made clear that the bill should not push federal programs over states rights and that it should be self-financing. He hated the dole, insisted on any program being fiscally sound, and opposed paying for it out of general revenue rather than from earmarked insurance contributions (Witte, 1962; cf Orloff, 1988: 69–76; Kennedy, 1999: 266–9). The models for the legislation also differed. The Wagner Act was based on prior U.S. state and federal legislation and bills that had failed to pass, with only limited borrowing from European precedents. The Social Security Act had few American public policy precedents, but there was experience in the private sector among insurance companies and welfare capitalists to add to European models. Welfare benefits also involved technical actuarial and financial knowledge, so experts were more important, drawn from both the private and public sector.

The act was popular: in December 1935, a Gallup poll asked, "Are you in favor of government old-age pensions for the needy?" Eighty-nine percent replied yes; the Depression created a national demand for security. The insurance principle was already established in private schemes, but many of these were under pressure from the Depression. Railroad workers had already received a retirement program through Congress in 1933–1934, and the corporate liberals of the Industrial Relations Counselors (IRC, a Rockefeller-funded private think tank) had made it actuarially sound, having realized that a government program could be sounder than private schemes. This widened support (Domhoff & Webber, 2011: chap. 5). The Depression had also increased the resonance of public assistance for the genuinely needy (i.e., grants without any prior insurance by the recipients). Roosevelt believed the insurance principle would be widely accepted, and assistance to the needy fitted his own patrician sense of responsibility for the less fortunate. Other politicians perceived the popularity of the social security concept and few wanted to be seen voting against it. The administration scared those wavering with the more radical programs suggested by the left (Witte, 1962: 103). The SSA passed both houses by nine-to-one majorities.

A small group of corporate liberals wanted to insert existing private schemes of insurance into a more secure, federally guaranteed system (Berkowitz & McQuaid, 1992: 109–14; Jacoby, 1997; Jenkins & Brents, 1989; Domhoff; 1990, 1996: chap. 5, forthcoming; C. Gordon, 1994; Swenson, 2002). Following efficiency wage theory in less competitive markets, they reasoned that paying good wages and providing long-term benefits helped them attract and retain skilled workers and segment the labor market. Yet they saw by mid-1934 that their schemes needed federal government support. Corporate liberals such as Gerard Swope of General Electric, Walter Teagle of Standard Oil of New Jersey, and Marion Folsom of Eastman Kodak initially approved of the New Deal, and they and other corporate executives had top positions on the influential Business Advisory Council and Committee on Economic Security. They believed the Social Security Act would alleviate competition from low-wage, low-benefit employers whose labor costs it would push up. If the firm remained central to the insurance principles of social security, the new system might also help keep unions out of their plants (Swenson, 2002; Berkowitz & McQuaid, 1992: chaps. 5, 6; Jacoby, 1997: 206–7). The IRC played a major role in discussions and drafts of the SSA. Two of the four men who wrote the old-age provisions were members of the IRC, and a third was an actuary for a life insurance company. For unemployment insurance, the IRC was placed on the payroll of the Committee on Economic Security. Thus, corporate liberals were important in the passage of SSA (Domhoff 1996: 117–76).

They were a minority in their class, however; most business was opposed to Social Security. Yet by 1935, even the conservative peak-business associations – the National Association of Manufacturers and the American Chamber of Commerce – knew that social security's time had come, made inevitable by the Depression's political landslide. So they spoke in general terms in favor of Social Security – although not in favor of the terms of whatever version of the bill was being floated that week. They fought tooth and nail on the details while professing to support the principle, but they knew in the end that it was a strategic necessity to accept one version or another (Hacker & Pierson, 2002: 299–301). Swenson (2002) disagrees, but his evidence for wider support from business comes mostly from after it saw the act working.

In the end, it was a compromise. The more radical Townsend, Share the Wealth, and Farm Labor Party bills contained universal guaranteed payments and federal control. They faced too much opposition to pass, but were useful in allowing less ambitious alternative schemes to provide some universalism and federalism. Frances Perkins said that without the Townsend Plan, old-age insurance might not have passed (Orloff, 1988: 67). The administration knew that too much federal control might be overturned by the Supreme Court, and would meet opposition in a Congress mindful of state rights. The Southern Democrats announced they would not accept federal interference, so Roosevelt and Perkins told the drafters to work within the limits of a shared federal-state program, leaving most matters of taxes, benefits, and eligibility to the states and excluding agriculture and domestic service. This bought Southern support, giving passage to the bill, but it excluded three-fifths of African-American workers (Witte, 1962; Schlabach, 1969: 114–26; Nelson, 1969: 206–7; Davies & Derthick, 1997; Kennedy, 1999: 257–73).

The AFL had shifted to support Social Security in 1932, and pushed hard for it. It wanted unemployment insurance paid by employers alone, but benefits were actually paid through a payroll tax levied on both employers and employees. However, low-paid workers got more in benefits than they paid in contributions. The New Dealers thought it politically useful to have workers make contributions because that would make it more difficult for conservatives to dismantle it later. The initial benefit level was set quite high so that older workers would be induced to retire, cutting the unemployment rate. Labor had to concede local discretion in paying out unemployment assistance to the needy poor (Witte, 1962; D. Nelson, 1969: chap. 9). Business and insurance companies wanted to preserve private and corporate welfare schemes intact. They succeeded, but without the right to opt out of the state system altogether. The program was paid for in a complex way, reflecting a compromise between universalism, employer interests, and states' rights. John Commons' pupils at

Wisconsin (such as Witte) and other economists were important in the initial drafting of the SSA. Although their initial preferences were for a more universal European system, they bent to pressure and added provisions derived from their experience of private-sector schemes. They were experts, they did have an impact on the legislation, and had their initial design survived into the act, they would have exercised considerable autonomy. However, pressure from Congress, corporations, and the insurance industry slashed their proposals and curtailed their autonomy.

In the end, said Frances Perkins, the bill was "the only plan that could have been put through Congress." The final compromise embodied in the act was probably closer to the corporate liberals than any other group (Kennedy, 1999: 270; Domhoff, 1990: 56–60, 1996: chap. 5; Domhoff & Webber, 2011: chap. 5; Rodgers, 1998: 444–5). The most dominant power actor over its own turf was the American Medical Association, whose hostility, backed by the insurance industry – both with reputed expertise – forced Roosevelt to remove any reference to medical insurance from the bill (Witte, 1962: 173–88; Orloff, 1988 75–6). This was the only case where virtually all the "experts" were on one side of an issue – the conservative side. As with the Supreme Court, the most powerful experts tried to block the New Deal.

Nonetheless, the SSA contained a national and compulsory old-age insurance system as well as largely compulsory, federally regulated state programs of old-age assistance, unemployment insurance, and aid to dependent children. Much of it was paid for by payroll taxes on employers and federal matching grants for state programs. In terms of anything that had gone before, it was radical. It was also redistributive and would likely become more so as eligibility among Americans gradually increased. Indeed, its actuarial basis changed in 1939, when Social Security stopped being fully funded by the recipients own contributions. In order to pay present retirees now, it became instead a pay-as-you-go program, transferring money in the form of Social Security taxes from workers to retirees as well as to their spouses and widows. This has remained a redistributive welfare state program, so despite the intervention of corporate liberals, Southerners, and others and the complexity of the power plays involved in the drafting process – all of which were important – the act did reflect some of the populist pressures the Great Depression and liberals' electoral victories had brought about.

New Deal limitations: Gender, race, dualism

The Social Security Act had blind spots, as did much of the New Deal. Neither women nor ethnic/racial minorities gained much. Women now voted, although not in such numbers as men did, but most women's organizations wanted reforms, so Roosevelt had to do something for women to preserve that part of his grand coalition. Yet welfare programs only conferred much benefit on women if they were members of households conforming to the patriarchal male-breadwinner model. There they benefitted because their husbands, fathers, and sons benefitted, but there was no progress for women as workers in their own right or as single mothers. Although there was little conscious discrimination against women, the programs provided benefits to preserve male workers' dignity and status as the provider for the household; women did not figure in the debates over insurance for old age. Rather, the pension was the way for men to support their families after they retired. Through widows' pensions, men could support their families even after they died (Kessler-Harris, 2001)! Women were mainly indirect members of the nation, onstage in the theatre of power but in nonspeaking roles.

Aid to Dependent Children (ADC) was provided to single mothers in households lacking the male breadwinner; this program slipped through without much fuss. Several states and many cities already had such programs, means-tested and only for the "needy." That made it easier for female and liberal experts on the committee to push ADC through (Witte, 1962: 162–5). C. Gordon (1994: 284–99) says it was a great step for women, yet was also deeply sexist. This was a recognition that women's "employment" might be as caregivers, although only if there were children but no man in the household. Unlike programs aimed at men, it also involved moral supervision by officials, who favored respectable widows over unwed mothers. The exclusion of agriculture and domestic service from the SSA also underprivileged women. Predominantly female occupations such as domestic servant, waitress, beautician, and retail worker were also omitted from the minimum wage and maximum hours standards of the FLSA. Turning much of the administration of New Deal laws over to the states and local government led to lower provision of benefits, and also made recipients – especially women – vulnerable to local officials' surveillance of their lives and supposed morals. This was also a problem for ethnic and racial minorities, of course (Mettler, 1999). The WPA did provide women with jobs, but they received less pay than men, and they suffered from the provision that only one family member could take WPA work (Amenta, 1998: 155–7).

The women's movement did not fight very hard for more. It was not a mass movement, and many feminists focused on the problems of white, middle-class women such as themselves, with little understanding of the problems of poor and low-paid women workers. Others were still operating within a maternalist discourse, and saw poor standards of motherhood and immorality, not material deprivation, as responsible for their problems. Of course, the New Deal did benefit most women, because most were living in male-breadwinner households (C. Gordon, 1994: 67, 195, 212–3, 258; O'Connor, 2001; Mink, 1995). However, the feminist momentum detectable in the period before the Great Depression seemed to be petering out. The gaping hole in the New Deal was the absence of programs for maternity benefits and family allowances, now figuring in the manifestos of some leftist parties – and legislated where these parties ruled (Hicks, 1999: 51). It is unclear why the momentum had ceased.

The impact on ethnic minorities was more mixed. The New Deal helped assimilate European immigrants into the nations, whereas the Depression had led to mass and sometimes forced emigration of Mexican workers. Then, once the agricultural labor force was perceived as white, sympathy to its plight grew. Federal programs and investigations into their exploitation began, although no legislation was passed until 1940, when conservatives and farm lobbies added hostile amendments that hit the agricultural unions and foreign workers hard. Thus, Mexican immigrants did not much benefit from the New Deal (Guerin-Gonzales, 1994).

In contrast, Native Americans benefitted from public works programs targeted specifically at them, and from the Indian Reorganization Act of 1934, which ended the sale of tribal lands and restored ownership of unallocated lands to Native American groups, enabling them to become "nations" once again. Yet the expansion of the welfare state into Native American lands turned their governments into the disbursers of federal assistance, which improved welfare but tended to limit the autonomy of each Native American community. Subsequent Native American writers have not seen this as an unalloyed gain. Both of these effects emerged from New Dealers' commitment to reform, but through federal authority, which in this case was unchallenged by either business or the South. They did not care one way or the other about Native Americans.

African Americans benefitted a little, mostly from relief programs. Blacks were overrepresented in the WPA, and received higher wages than they would earn in the open labor market, but they got the dirty jobs (Amenta, 1998: 158; Cohen, 1990: 279–81). Many of the New Dealers were antiracist, and the NAACP and antilynching movements strengthened among African Americans (Hayes, 2001: 170–5). Yet few blacks were covered by a Social Security Act that excluded agriculture and domestic service, and there was rampant discrimination in most labor markets and government offices. The Southern congressional bloc was crucial in denying rights (Katznelson, 2005; Lieberman, 1998: 51–6). Whatever the legislation, Southerners sought to exclude them from its coverage. If they failed, they ensured program administration was placed in the hands of local officials, who in the South were hostile to black applicants (Brown, 1999; Sugrue, 1996). Even antilynching bills were destroyed. As Senator Bailey of North Carolina told the president, "I give you warning that no administration can survive without us." Roosevelt agreed: "If I come out for the antilynching bill now, they will block every bill I ask Congress to pass to keep America from collapsing. I just can't take that risk." Resisting Eleanor's pressure, he offered the 1937 antilynching bill scant support. Southern Senators filibustered it, paralyzing the chamber for six weeks and preventing all legislation (Kennedy, 1999: 342–3).African Americans were not yet members of the nation.

Not only Southerners were racists. Few whites challenged race bias, and the unions were not exempt from racist practices. The CIO – except for some leftist affiliates – either ignored black workers or maintained segregated locals (Goldfield, 1997; D. Nelson, 2001). Domestic racism remained the American exception among advanced countries; even the most liberal New Dealers felt they could do little to help African Americans. Southerners' votes in Congress secured the passage of legislation that strengthened labor, set minimum wages, and gave relief and social security – for whites. The New Deal may have strengthened the race divide, as the conditions of working-class whites improved much more than those of blacks; on the other hand, it encouraged blacks to resist – and then, too, did World War II.

The New Deal created a two-tier welfare state (C. Gordon, 1994: 293; O'Connor, 2001; Mettler, 1999: 212; R. Harrison, 1997: 268), not what the New Dealers had intended. This partly resulted from racial/Southern/gendered pressures, partly from Roosevelt's fiscal caution. He would not launch the deficit financing needed for generous universal programs (Brown, 1999: 32–9, 60–1). The upper tier had a quite generous, non-stigmatized, federally administered insurance program related to prior wages. These recipients had "earned" it. The lower tier was meaner, locally administered, and means-tested "welfare" – a word which has lived on in America, carrying derogatory tones of "unearned" or "undeserved" benefit. Industrial workers, mainly white males, were overrepresented in the upper tier; women, African Americans, poor farmers, and casual workers were underrepresented in the lower tier. This was hardly surprising: the upper tier was based on insurance and employment contributions, yet women, blacks, and other minorities had more difficulty getting permanent jobs. If the two tiers endured, this would be divisive for any working-class movement.

The New Deal provided a great step forward in social welfare, but it was not a universal system. Nor was it devised to replace private benefits, which had grown up to cater for relatively privileged workers. The New Deal allowed private insurance companies and corporations to use their own welfare capitalism to supplement the benefits provided in the Social Security Act. Employers hoped that the unilateral purchase of commercial group insurance would satisfy their workers and head off both workers' need for unions and state intervention in welfare. Unions were promoting their own health and insurance schemes (Klein, 2003: chaps. 3–5). In medical provision, the insurance companies and the medical profession eliminated almost any public provision. The rich and the stably employed had private insurance, which was profitable for the insurance companies and subsidized by government; government accepted a minimal responsibility for the unprofitable poor (C. Gordon, 2003).

The housing program also operated through two tiers. The New Deal legislated public housing for low-income families and a guaranteed mortgage program for those who could afford a 20 percent deposit, mostly middle-income families. Both programs began in 1934 to revive the house-building industry, but the private program developed faster. Wagner's bill to expand public housing came in 1937, and Congress stripped it of many of its provisions. This little struggle pitched a fragile lib-lab coalition of liberal middle-class reformers and labor unions against the influential National Association of Real Estate Boards preaching financial prudence, local control, and the dangers of socialism. A two-tier program resulted, with very different conditions for renters and buyers. In practice, the FHA mortgage program also became racially biased, and public housing became segregated. African Americans found it almost impossible to get mortgages, and if they got public housing, it was usually in the worst projects.

Nonetheless, after taking note of all these qualifications, about 75 percent of ordinary Americans did benefit considerably from the New Deal. Social citizenship had was greatly extended, and the nation was rendered more cohesive. Perhaps the remaining 25 percent were not doomed to remain outside this development in social citizenship. In other countries, the welfare state expanded gradually toward universalism after usually beginning with two-tiered systems. Why could expansion in the United States not occur, too? The answer would only come in later periods.

Labor relations in the late 1930s: Ambiguous outcome

In 1936 and early 1937, most businessmen had expected the Supreme Court to strike down the Wagner Act, but the Court upheld the act, partly because of Roosevelt's election victories, partly because the NLRB economics division presented compelling statistical data. Between 1937 and 1940, the National Association of Manufacturers and the U.S. Chamber of Commerce orchestrated a propaganda campaign against both unions and the NLRB. From 1937, NLRB rulings were helping union growth. Business lobbies advocated abolishing it on the grounds it was destabilizing industry, weakening private property, and advocating socialism. So did the conservative press and a House Committee of enquiry chaired by Southern Democrat Howard Smith. He was able to open hearings, choose most of the witnesses, and then initiate legislation. Hostile hearings culminated in the House passing Smith's bill to restrict NLRB power and increase employers' powers to resist unionization. The Senate Labor Committee stalled the bill, but after the Munich crisis of 1938, Roosevelt felt that a possible war would need the support of business and the Southern Democrats. He bent before their pressure and reconstituted the NLRB, appointing new board members who would be tougher on labor. A struggle ensued inside the NLRB, conservative lawyers against more liberal economists. In the more conservative climate of the time, the lawyers won. The economics division of the NLRB closed down in 1940. Business organizations, sensing the doors of political opportunity reopening, remained on the offensive until 1941, when World War II intervened (Stryker, 1989; Gross, 1981, 1995).

As usual, experts were on all sides of these struggles. The old NLRB labor economists were liberals, the new NLRB experts emphasized control and responsibility. Union busters also had their experts. Professional strikebreakers were backed by lawyers preaching property rights and economists preaching that perfectly free markets worked perfectly. Sociologists and human relations specialists from the University of Chicago were employed by welfare capitalists to conduct surveys and experiments that would bind workers and management together, identify "troublemakers," and obviate the need for unions. Some were involved in antiunion campaigns, such as the quack Nathan W. Shefferman – labor relations consultant and mediator, putative social scientist, motivational speaker, and union buster – formerly with the American Institute of Phrenology, now trying to keep unions out of Sears. Although Jewish himself, he lambasted unions as controlled by Jews in campaigns he designed for Sears' anti-Semitic chairman, General Robert E. Wood (Jacoby, 1997: 130–40, 301). In the end, experts had to bend before the power of their employers; politicians were bending before electoral trends.

There were also struggles inside the unions. The Wagner Act allowed them to share in the regulation of industry provided they could compel employers to recognize them. Craft workers could control entry to the craft, so an employer might yield to a craft union threatening to strike. The AFL craft unions continued bargaining, often ignoring or even attacking the National Labor Relations Board (NLRB). They hoped thus to weaken the CIO, which was cooperating with the Board. Less-skilled workers in the industrial CIO unions had to rely more on the power of the strike itself to secure recognition. Because most workers were reluctant to risk their jobs by striking until the CIO union had demonstrated its power over the employer, the CIO depended heavily on its militants to get initial recognition from employers. Workers watched for signs of success: "The reinstatement of fired activists, the humiliation of a hated foreman, or the open display of union buttons had a powerful appeal to these secret sympathizers." Then they might strike, but it was dangerous for those who had only unskilled labor to sell (Zieger, 1995: 45). Few workers were attracted by socialism. The main disputes concerned how militant they should be in pressing grievances. As a result, of militants' struggles, the unions won enough recognition strikes to bring substantial membership growth, which continued through to the war.

The NLRB aided leaders more than militants, banning direct action such as the sit-down strike. In the strike wave of 1936–1937, power within the CIO unions shifted downward to the shop floor. Leaders bargaining with employers wanted to turn member militancy on and off according to the stage of negotiations. Once a deal was struck, union leaders needed to compel the members to accept it and then to "*observe their contracts*" (Zieger, 1995: 71, emphasis in the original). Once employers had to sign contracts, they tried to include no-strike pledges and the maintenance of managerial prerogatives during the lifetime of the contract. To get contracts and win material gains, union leaders often traded these powers away, confining strikes and disputes to predictable periods at the end of the contract period, but shop-floor militants did not like being handcuffed from above. Stepan-Norris and Zeitlin (2003) say that leftist unions promoted more rank-and-file participation in decisions, so could better mobilize worker support and achieve shorter contracts containing better grievance procedures, the right to strike, and fewer managerial prerogatives than more conservative, less democratic unions. Many militants were Communists, but this mattered less to workers than the concrete gains their militancy might bring.

Workers remained divided. The AFL fought more vigorously at the shop-floor level because many locals had strong traditions of shop-floor democracy, aided by a more ethnically homogenous membership of skilled workers. They could expect more solidarity than the more ethnically and occupationally diverse industrial unions. The CIO supporters of Mineworkers leader John L. Lewis urged greater independence from the NLRB and more responsiveness to the militants. Debates inside the unions were intensifying (Zieger, 1995; Lichtenstein, 1992, 2002; Aronowitz, 1973; Tomlins, 1985). In the late 1930s, McCammon (1993) says, strikes were linked less to union strength than to the rhythms of contracts, now generating a more ritualized system of conflict resolution. Nelson's (2001) analysis of when and where unionization, strikes, and NLB-mandated elections were occurring reveals three causes of growth. There was bottom-up growth generated by worker militants – especially in 1937 – but there was then a greater top-down growth encouraged by the operation of NLRB elections as laid down in the Wagner Act. These two accounted for around two-thirds of union membership growth in the 1930s, with most of the remainder coming from broader New Deal policies. Regulatory measures designed to curb competition among employers enabled them to make more profit and afford higher wages and benefits, enabling aggressive unions to achieve more gains and recruit more members. For men such as the railroad executives, collective bargaining with independent unions "was a small price to pay for price stability and steady profits," says Nelson.

Yet most businessmen did not reason thus. Although the Wagner Act gave unions the right to organize and employers the duty to bargain with duly certified unions, it did not force employers to meet union demands or even sign a union contract. Some did so, but some big corporations such as Ford and the Little Steel firms successfully resisted with lockouts, violence, and strikebreakers, usually with local police support. In Chicago, the police killed ten striking steelworkers. The administration was unhappy about such repression, and had commissioned enquiries into strikebreaking that delivered critical reports on employer tactics. However, Roosevelt and Perkins preferred to keep disputes at arm's length, and would not intervene. This was liberal voluntarism, not corporatism.

After the Fair Labor Standards Act in June 1938, the New Deal ran out of steam. Roosevelt had made three recent mistakes (Kennedy, 1999: chap. 11). After the Supreme Court had struck down over a dozen New Deal federal and state laws in an eighteen-month period, he devised court-packing proposals that departed from constitutional tradition. His proposed purge was unpopular; when he failed to ram it through, he lost more support – although the court was chastened (Burns, 2009). Second, he intervened in state Democratic primaries, hoping to defeat conservative candidates. He failed, and was denounced for infringing states' rights. Candidates in Southern primaries now all competed in segregationist rhetoric (Leuchtenburg, 1963: 266–71). Third, he inadvertently helped on a recession – damagingly known as the Roosevelt recession. The result was a loss of popularity and Democratic losses in the 1938 midterm election. During 1937 and 1938, the various conservative factions were joining together, as the Republican leaders managed to bring together the party's regional factions, united at least in their desire to take advantage of FDR's mistakes. They forged an opportunist alliance with the Southern Democrats to block liberal initiatives. The Southerners had opposed attempts by the CIO to organize the South just as they opposed New Deal liberals using farm programs to help black farm tenants and workers. They had tired of the New Deal (Weed, 1994). For the first time since 1934, there were more "anti-spenders" than "pro-spenders" in the House (Amenta, 1998: 137).

New Dealers still permeated the administration, but their congressional base was weaker. They could propose legislation, but they could not pass it. Congress was now to the right of the nation – the undemocratic Southern delegation alone ensured this. Yet public opinion was also uncomfortable with the taxes, deficits, and bureaucratic expansion involved in their projects. Of the mass movements, only the unions survived, and they had become more respectable. Brinkley (1995: 142) notes, "Nowhere on the political landscape were there vigorous movements so common in the mid-1930s." The New Dealers were deploying one-half of Keynesian macroeconomics: deficit financing and mild inflation to boost the economy, but without commitment to full employment. Yet they hoped to shift the consumption function upward to achieve a "high consumption, low saving" economy that would eventually combine a progressive tax system, redistributive transfer payments, and greater public spending on health, education, and welfare (Barber, 1996: 128–30). This lib-lab vision was comparable to the post–World War II, Keynes/Beveridge British welfare state, but the political tide was turning against them.

Conclusion

The Great Depression had shocked the United States out of the conservatism of the previous fifty years. As we saw in Chapter 3, the progressives had failed in their radical agenda and their modernizing agenda had taken a pro-business slant. Now, however, conservatives were blamed for failing to deal with Depression, so America radicalized. Although the word "socialism" remained taboo, lib-lab reform was pushed forward from 1934 to 1938. The New Deal offered varied but sweeping reforms. Some of them helped save capitalism. Finance, housing, and agricultural assistance reforms were designed to regulate capitalism more on efficiency grounds and were pushed by modernizers in general. Business receiving aid naturally always welcomed it, but other programs extended social citizenship, and for that we need an explanation essentially combining class-driven populism and imperfect pluralism. From below came mass pressures for government to provide work and relief for the unemployed and needy, for regulation to ensure economic security for all citizens, and for some redistribution of power and wealth. I distinguished, however, between actual class movements rooted in labor and unions and more diffuse electoral support including various middle class and other pressure groups (such as the elderly or feminists). Both supported most reforms, which actually passed, and this is why they passed. These social programs were opposed by most of the propertied classes, although corporate moderates and many centrist and liberal politicians realistically recognized that the pressure coming from below made some kind of reform necessary. Many were critical in passing moderate reforms, which preempted radical ones. This was a response to class conflict, but it was an indirect, top-down response we will often see in this volume.

In the next chapter, I discuss more fully the competing theories of the rise of social citizenship in the twentieth century. The New Deal example of that rise does not support the logic of industrialism theory, for this was not an inevitable direct outcome of the industrialization of America; it was a highly contingent outcome of struggles that might have had a different outcome. If Democrats had been in power during the first three years of the Depression, as was the unfortunate Hoover, the country might have swung rightward, blocking any major social programs. Had a quasi-fascist movement attained power, there might have been social programs but of a very different hue – although I do see this as a very likely outcome. The New Deal predominantly supports what political scientists rather blandly call a power resources theory, with its core being class conflicts that then spread and blurred into a broader populism – the people onstage in the theatre of power, and in speaking roles.

However, American political institutions also contributed considerably in steering reforms in certain directions – and this is the third of the theories discussed here: institutionalism. The United States was a democracy with its own historic institutions, and reforms could only be made law through these institutions, by the elected representatives of the people. In the United States, this came through an extreme separation of powers – at the federal level between the president, the two Houses of Congress, and the Supreme Court, and with state and local governments possessing considerable powers. It mattered enormously that during the New Deal, although the president and his administration initiated reforms generally supportive of popular demands, the Court opposed them, and foot-dragging by Congress increasingly slowed the pace of reform and weakened its substance. Its most preferred method was by delegating the implementation of programs to the state and local government levels. In most of the states that produced less reform than the Roosevelt administration would have wanted. It was particularly hard on women and minorities.

Politics translated into a four-way power struggle. The first group in the struggle were popular movements mobilized by the Great Depression and their minority representatives in the administration and Congress. The second group included the business class and other conservatives and their minority representatives in the administration, a larger base in Congress and state governments, and the majority of the Supreme Court. In the third group were moderates seeking compromise in the middle – Roosevelt himself and most of his inner circle as well as some corporate liberals, moderate trade unionists, and about half of Congress. Finally, was the Southern Congressional delegation, not moderates, but in the middle in the sense that they would support federal programs if administered locally as well as legislation that did not apply to Southern workers, especially African Americans. The first three factions also came with client experts and officials, although I have not granted much causality to the "experts/officials/state capacities" stressed by elite theorists, with the few exceptions noted earlier. Experts, officials, and state agencies were hired by other power actors; lawyers, economists, social workers, agronomists, and others went every way in policy debates in deference to their employers. In the debates, only one profession spoke with virtual unanimity and had sufficient professional power to prevail in its area of interest: the medical profession. Thus, the New Deal contained no health reform. Otherwise, class pressure and the institutions of American-style democracy were what mattered most in the New Deal, not experts or agencies. Volume IV will discuss whether organized class pressures are playing a comparable role in the Great Recession of 2008. Of course, it took several years for the pressure to be sufficient to gain reforms during the Depression.

That pressure from organized populist groups was so crucial meant that white working and middle-class males benefitted more than others did, and as a corollary that the benefits were mostly attached to formal labor market participation. Women gained only if they were attached to an employed male, and the rights of women as the bearers and carers of children were only recognized, rather stingily, in the case of single mothers. That was not abnormal in the interwar period, as we see in the next chapter. The class struggle largely bypassed women. African-American males benefitted a little if they were in formal industrial employment or had jobs in the Works Program Administration, but they did not benefit if in agriculture or the South, which most were. Other minority groups barely benefitted, either. The New Deal was a two-tier affair; participation in the nation was highly stratified.

Yet as the Roosevelt administration endured, in the normal way of incumbent governments in bad economies, more Americans began to blame it for not doing more to restore prosperity. This was especially marked after the 1937 recession, to which the administration itself had inadvertently contributed. Now the pressures from below became more ambiguous, and the New Deal seemed stalled – whether this was temporary or permanent was not yet clear. In these two phases – one of reform, the other of its stalling – American-style democracy worked. Both seem to have been the will of the people, at least as expressed by their elected representatives.

It was institutionally an imperfect democracy, however. The United States had been the earliest country to move toward masculine democracy, and it had been among the early countries to enfranchise women, too. However, by the mid-twentieth century it was no longer in the vanguard. Its imperfections were glaring in the case of the segregated, poll-taxing South, but subtler elsewhere through the overweighting of rural votes and politicians, top-down patronage parties, and the backstairs influence of business corporations. These all worked in the same direction, to bias the democracy against the popular will, not grotesquely so (except in relation to African Americans), but just enough to make redistribution more difficult than it should have been in a genuinely pluralist democracy. The Supreme Court and the separation of powers between federal- and state-level government added more conservatism, and popular appeals for states' rights mainly derived from the rural and Southern imperfections just noted. These involved the institutions of American representative government, although inflected with class and race. The supposed lack of state capacity in the United States cannot have been decisive, as the New Deal did successfully create state capacity of a federal nature in various areas.

Amenta (1998) also stresses imperfect democracy. He finds that support for New Deal reforms and implementation of state-level reform were strongly correlated to the degree of democracy in each state. The broader the franchise and the weaker the control exercised by the machines, the greater the support for reform. Democratic imperfections were not confined to one region; nationally, American democracy had not kept sufficient separation between political and economic power, embedding inequalities in class power inside the polity. That was partly the legacy of the Progressive Era, better at modernizing than trimming business power. The ultimate limitation of the New Deal period was that the political system supported more conservative policies than the people did. Had the popular voice translated more directly into political power, the New

Deal would have further deepened social citizenship and Roosevelt would have deployed his shrewd reelection tactics a little further to the left.

Although reforms were passed, none were as generous as their sponsors had initially hoped. Critics of the Social Security Act or the Wagner Act often suggest that their limitations prevented any further development. The Wagner Act, however, both recognized the rights of labor unions and expected them to discipline their members, which is the normal capital-labor deal of rule-governed capitalism. There was no necessary reason embedded in the Wagner Act for the AFL or the CIO to decline as they later did rather than develop into more powerful agenda-setters, such as post-war union federations in some other countries. Nor was it certain that the welfare system would continue to embody dualism, racism, or sexism. Social-citizenship rights developed incrementally in all countries. They started with imperfect, particularistic, means-tested welfare programs biased toward better-organized workers, but struggles continued over many years to achieve a creeping universalism of rights. This was usually ensured, as Baldwin (1990) emphasizes, when they could also recruit the middle classes to the welfare-state ideal. That had begun in the New Deal; why should it not continue in the United States?

True, some New Deal programs might be difficult to extend. It would be difficult for the WPA or other relief programs to continue once mass unemployment ceased because it was hated by business, which argued that creating public jobs would raise wages beyond affordable market levels. Relief programs were supposed to be temporary, until recovery kicked in or the social security system provided unemployment benefits through insurance. It would be difficult in a democracy for public relief works to continue into better economic times when far fewer voters would be unemployed. In fact, the war produced an economic boom.

Lieberman (1998) notes that where a New Deal policy involved automatic payments of benefits, a relatively autonomous federal agency, and a relatively low level of political controversy it proved easier to expand them by opening up benefits to African Americans. The consequence was that they did get covered by Social Security, rather less by unemployment insurance and Aid to Dependent Children. In general, whether the defects of New Deal programs would be permanent would depend on the balance of power in later periods, not on the New Deal itself. In the 1960s and 1970s, the New Deal was attacked by leftist critics denouncing its two tiers and its supposed capitalist control functions. Their denunciations sometimes seemed to assume that revolutionary change might have been possible. Yet as we have seen in other chapters, reform not revolution was the destiny of the Western working class. In the 1980s, feminists added a critique of patriarchal controls, but happily, reforms have continued to erode those controls.

More recent criticism has come from neoliberals denouncing the New Deal as interfering with the freedom of markets. Smiley (2002: x) says, "The 1930s economic crisis is tragic testimony to the government interference in market economies," and he continues with unrelenting criticism of New Deal programs, arguing that they harmed overall economic efficiency, especially when attempting to redistribute resources or when disrupting institutions that defined property rights. Yet his economic judgments seem biased by class consciousness. He describes every gain for workers, every rise in taxation to pay for programs, as lowering business confidence, and he adds that this depressed investment and recovery. This is contradicted by the experience of other countries, which were securing comparable or greater reforms for workers that did not hinder either investment or recovery. As we see in the next chapter, there are alternative ways to run capitalism efficiently.

Neoliberal critics are also politically naive. If the New Deal had not interfered with property rights in order to regulate capitalism and provide secure living standards for most Americans, capitalism would have seen worse recessions, lost more legitimacy, and faced more serious social crises. Most Americans in the 1930s believed free market capitalism had brought the Great Depression upon them. How would they have reacted to further worsening? America seemed a long way from socialism or fascism, yet it might have seen turbulent, incoherent populism, resulting in chaos and decline. American capitalism needed saving, not from socialism or fascism, but from itself. Higher social classes naturally objected to regulation and taxes, but the overall effect was to restore their profits. Roosevelt, the New Dealers, and corporate liberals did just that, as they said they would, and in the process they strengthened democracy by adding social to political citizenship. "We are going to make a country," Roosevelt remarked to Frances Perkins, "in which no one is left out" (Perkins, 1946: 113). This was not strictly true, but she and her colleagues did extend citizen rights for the large majority of the country. The dialectic between class and nation had continued. The nation was strengthened – and at a good moment, given the military challenges that were about to come.

This chapter has focused on America. At various times I have emphasized its peculiarities, as I would in dealing with any country. Nation-states cage their citizens into distinctive practices, but in a more general sense, the United States was not exceptional. We do not have to go back to the Founding Fathers, multiethnicity, federalism, or other American traditions to explain why America was fundamentally different because it wasn't so very different. It was exceptional in one main respect: it had racism at home, not in an empire abroad. Overall, the New Dealers had created a lib-lab welfare regime comparable to others of the period. Only after World War II did Sweden clearly lead in the provision of social welfare. Before then, Swenson (2002) says (perhaps exaggerating), New Deal Democrats were doing more to advance progressive reform than Swedish Social Democrats, who had been in power since 1932. Yet at the end of the 1930s, the New Dealers encountered heightened resistance, led by business and Southern conservatives. What would this balance of forces produce?

Had Roosevelt's recent mistakes made all the difference? The outcome was unclear. Vice President Henry Wallace declared, "We are children of the transition – we have left Egypt but we have not yet arrived at the Promised Land" (Leuchtenburg, 1963: 347). However, the United States was not left alone to find its path. Enter World War II, the third great crisis of the twentieth century, which on balance was to turn America rightward again.

9 The development of social citizenship in capitalist democracies

Introduction: The triumph of reformed capitalism

The twentieth century saw two main economic tendencies. First, capitalism triumphed globally, and the relations between capital and labor became the core economic power struggle everywhere. The main alternatives to capitalism – fascism and state socialism – which had both repressed class conflict, fell as a result of their own contradictions. Second, the outcome of struggle was that in the West, capitalism was reformed and given a human face through universal rights of civil, political, and social citizenship. I discussed the latter process in America in the last chapter. I continue here, but in a broad comparative analysis of nations. For entwining with capitalist growth was the tightening of nation-states, so that the principal terrain of class struggle was the individual nation-state and solutions to that struggle differed by country (although not only be country, as we shall see). That justifies the nationalist part of this chapter's analysis.

As we saw in Chapter 2, divergence dominated globalizing tendencies in the first half of the twentieth century, as the West and Japan underwent rapid economic development and the rest of the world did not. Under colonialism, global inequality had surged. The few "middle-class" countries, mostly in Latin America, fell backward relative to the West and Japan. After World War II, the combination of pent-up innovation and consumer demand, the end of colonial empires, and the *pax Americana* was to pull the whole world upward, and countries around the fringes of Europe and in East Asia embarked on a catch-up development. In the period covered by this volume, the world continued to be diverse, a few living in comparative luxury, the masses remaining in dire poverty. It is the luxurious few whom I discuss here.

In 1949, T. H. Marshall argued that a growth of equal citizen rights managed the tension between capitalism and classes, generating a reformed version of capitalism. He distinguished three stages of the development of citizenship. Civil citizenship – freedom and equality before the law – he said was an achievement of the eighteenth century; political citizenship – the right to equal participation in free elections – was an achievement of the nineteenth century. Fukuyama (2011) agrees that the rule of law (civil) and accountability of government (political) are two of the criteria of good government, to which he adds the provision of social order. Marshall added his own, third element – social citizenship – which he said would be the achievement of the twentieth century. Social citizenship he defined as a series of rights "from the right to a modicum of economic welfare and security to the right to share in the full in the social heritage and to live the life of a civilized being according to the standards prevailing in the society" (1963: 74). This was a somewhat broader and perhaps vaguer form of citizenship than the other two, but its core is that inequality should not reach levels that would allow the emergence of different "societies" within the same nation, and here he focuses specifically on economic and educational criteria. He was writing about class stratification – ignoring regional, ethnic, gender, and other forms of stratification – and he was also writing about Britain, where his three-stage model works well. It does not apply in this sequence to many countries, as I have noted in an earlier work (Mann, 1987). Yet Marshall correctly foresaw the diffusion of social citizenship across the West as a whole, and his model extends to cover rising citizen rights for women and minorities. I wish to distinguish four main components within his notion of social citizenship.

(1) A relatively low level of inequality in market incomes and in wealth holdings. Because wealth declined as a source of inequality through the mid-twentieth century, income inequality became more decisive. Relative income equality resulted from a combination of low-wage dispersion and full employment, partly an achievement of advanced industrial capitalism, partly pursued as deliberate state policy.
(2) A progressive tax system that, on balance, redistributed toward the poor, canceling out some of the effects of original income and wealth dispersion.
(3) A system of welfare-state transfers, benefits in cash or in kind, especially helping those not in the labor market maintain an adequate standard of living. This redistributed toward the elderly, sick, disabled, unemployed, poor, and children. At its core, this was an insurance scheme, involving pensions, unemployment, and disability insurance and health care benefits.
(4) A universal education and health system. The schools taught literacy and numeracy, lasting at least into secondary schooling, with meritocratic access to higher educational levels. As Marshall recognized, education was important in securing access not only to economic rewards but also to its level of "civilization." There was more of a common interest here, as an industrial society – especially its white-collar and service sectors – requires educated human capital. This was even truer of health, although this had a distinctive two-part rhythm of development. The first was in the public provision of clean water and sewerage and the encouragement of hygienic practices. As the urbanization of the advanced countries brought all of the classes into closer proximity to each other, this was a common interest shared by all of the classes. All advanced countries achieved these goals before or just after World War I, but the second stage of health was equal access to medical services, and this was not a common interest.

Social citizenship could be achieved through different combinations of these four components. Welfare benefits are not the only or even necessarily the main part of social citizenship. Full employment; progressive taxes;

universal, free education; and public health provision can have the same overall effect as a welfare state. Because few scholars have studied all four components together, it has been difficult to make an overall assessment of social citizenship. I attempt it here. Note that all four encourage the development of citizenship at the level of the nation-state (although public health provisions attached people more to their locality). It is the redistributive unit for welfare and taxes, full employment offers participation in a national labor market, and education promotes facility in one's national language and culture. This was the growth of *national citizenship*, the feeling of sharing in the same community as ones co-citizens. In Volume II, I noted how the first national infrastructures – of roads, rail, postal services, military service, and educational institutions – were creating a routine sense of the nation, "banal nationalism," caging people inside their national states, converting them into nation-states. This process escalated in the twentieth century as citizenship rights intensified. Thus, nationalism also intensified, although there was nothing inherently aggressive about this. Strengthening of the nation eased class conflict, part of the modern dialectic between class and nation.

Marshall did not discuss gender and family relations, but they complicate social-citizen rights. The big picture of the twentieth century is that women continued to improve their rights, achieving legal equality, voting rights, and considerable social rights. Yet their routes toward this were distinctive. Citizenship is generally considered an attribute of the individual, yet men and women differ in terms of their social roles and their biology as the bearers and (up to now) carers of children. Moreover, most men and women do not live as isolated individuals but in families, performing somewhat different roles. The benefits of citizenship might accrue to individuals in either the public or private realms, through occupations or families. At the beginning of this period, there was relative ideological and institutional uniformity outside of agriculture: men were the breadwinners in the formal economy and were the household heads; women were subordinate caregivers in the family. This was the industrial society version of patriarchy – rule by the male household head – perhaps the most enduring power relationship and ideology through much of human history.

Of course, reality in 1914 was more complex. The peasant household economy remained important in most countries. Many women did work in the public sphere, especially working-class and (increasingly) lower white-collar women, for capitalism was generating considerable demand for labor, and women in general worked in caregiving occupations such as teaching, nursing, and social work. Feminist movements had first risen to challenge patriarchy in temperance and then in suffragist movements. Indeed, women secured the vote in a handful of countries by 1914, and in rather more by the 1930s. Nonetheless, women still had much to struggle for, in terms of social as well as political rights. Those who didn't work had dual insecurities, one set arising from men's work insecurities the other from familial difficulties such as a drunken, violent husband (the object of temperance movements) or the death of the male breadwinner. Widows and other single mothers were particularly vulnerable. Those women who had formal employment received wages on average half those of men. Labor unions might help them raise this a little if they were members, but few were. In any case, most unions were dominated by the desire for men to get a "family wage" capable of maintaining the whole family, dispensing with the need for much female labor. The institutionalized ideology of patriarchy and especially of the family wage remained important throughout this period – although dents were beginning to be made in it.

Yet distinctive social and biological roles meant that women had two alternative routes toward weakening patriarchy. One was to strive to be broadly similar to men, and this took the employment route toward equality and security, seeking improvements through the labor market. Ironically, they sought to have their labor commoditized in order to then achieve the decommodification provided by social citizenship. The other route was to seek improvement of their conditions as caregivers within the family – the "maternalist" route. The most rewarding journey was to combine both routes. Women desiring liberty from patriarchy aimed on the one hand at full rights to employment at equal wages and welfare benefits normally flowing from work, such as pensions and unemployment and sick pay. On the other hand, they aimed at maternal and parental paid leave, child care, family benefits, and control over reproductive decisions. Employers and states had preferences here, either to encourage the size of the labor force or the birthrate. In explaining the rise of social citizenship, we must relate together the market, the state, and the family.

The big picture, of course, is that social citizenship and nations did advance everywhere in the north of the world. Although much of this chapter will focus on variations in social citizenship, all welfare regimes, all tax systems became more redistributive. Full employment as a goal of government policy had also appeared, although it had to wait until after World War II to be fully developed. The rights of women also improved, although always lagging and with variation between the employment and maternal routes. Ethnic and racial minorities, where relevant, also lagged – although only in the United States, Australia, and (to a lesser extent) New Zealand did this matter much. The expansion of public education has been the most uniform development of all, with relatively little variation across nations and macro-regions, and with less variation across genders and ethnicities. Overall, Marshall was right: capitalism was being socialized, nationalized, and civilized – although civil and political rights were another matter.

Current theories of welfare states

The three main current explanations of welfare-state development extend to cover all four components of social citizenship. The first theory sees the welfare state as the product of a "logic of industrialism," functional in reproducing the skilled labor force needed in an industrial and then a postindustrial economy. It also copes with other modernizing changes: longer life expectancy (generating more pensioners and concern with medical services), urbanization, the increased separation of work from the household (so that families need more public support), and the entry of women and minorities into the labor force. This reflects the decline of the household economy and separation of household and economy, so that families can no longer offer the support to cope with the hazards of life and approaching death, and the insecurities of the economic sphere. The national community is asked to step in, developing a whole range of social services administered or regulated by the state (Wilensky, 2002). So the logic of industrialism would be more accurately termed the "logic of the reaction to industrialism," the remedying of its defects.

A certain level of economic development is also necessary before a country can develop a universal tax system or afford much of a welfare state or universal education system, so that industrialization leads progressively to more welfare (although I would prefer to say that capitalist industrialization led to this). Across nations, GDP and income per capita do correlate with welfare expenditures, although there is no exact level of wealth necessary for a country to begin welfare programs, and the correlation diminishes as countries continue to get wealthier. By the time we get to postindustrialism, the correlation in advanced countries is negligible – although this is not true of education, which has continued to expand in response to a postindustrial economy. So, overall, this theory has had variable application, more useful in this volume than the next one. Note that its logic is said to apply to all political regimes, not just democracies.

The second explanation has at its core capitalism and its class struggle. Capitalist market relations add more insecurity to our economic lives, as businesses and industries rise and fall. It is not just economic failure, however. Rising productivity through substituting machinery for human labor obviously also leads to redundancies, and capitalist desire for profit leads to continuous calculation by employers of labor costs and a drive to reduce them, perhaps by lowering wages. These hazards are felt particularly among less skilled workers. Thus, they have reacted strongly against unregulated capitalism. We have already glimpsed the revolutionary response; here we examine the reformist version of class struggle: working-class pressure to bring more security through the welfare state, equal access to education, and the redistribution of some profit to wages. This depended most upon workers' ability to develop powerful collective organizations. Much research has shown that labor strength – measured by density of union membership, extent of nationally coordinated labor-relations bargaining, and years of government by center-left parties – correlated with pretax and posttax income redistribution and generosity of welfare programs throughout the twentieth century (Allan & Scruggs,

2004; Hicks, 1999, Huber & Stephens, 2001, Pontusson, 2005; Bradley et al., 2003: 198). Social citizenship here represents the triumph of reformist labor movements, and this occurs primarily in democracies. As Lipset argued, politics is the democratic translation of the class struggle.

Some Marxists still hold onto this class model. However, most social scientists have modified it in three ways. First, where states, churches, or employers perceived the rise of the working-class movement as potentially threatening, they might seek to buy workers' loyalty with social-citizen concessions. Indeed, less class struggle than the desire to head it off at the pass brought the first welfare programs in authoritarian as well as democratic regimes (Hicks, 1999). This was the indirect or top-down model of class conflict. Second, social citizenship has been achieved not just by workers but by broader class alliances of workers, farmers, and middle-class groups. Esping-Andersen (1985, 1990) observes that blue-collar workers have never been in a majority, so on their own would be unable to pass legislation implementing their demands; they need allies. We saw in the last chapter that such an alliance was responsible for the surge of social citizenship in the United States in the New Deal period. In Baldwin's (1990) account of welfare development in Scandinavia and Britain, the middle class and farmers often play a greater role than workers. Third, not just classes have lent their weight – feminist and ethnic minority movements, populist religious movements, and the elderly have, as well. Although "gray power" movements tend to have been more influential in wresting benefits from the state in the period after 1945, nonetheless, the aging of the population has correlated with rising social transfer expenditures ever since the 1880s in some countries (Lindert, 2004). The Townsend Movement during the American New Deal was an example of gray power, as we saw in the last chapter.

In all these cases, outcomes resulted from struggle – either direct (bottom-up) or indirect (top-down) – rather than from any automatic logic (as in the industrialism explanation), so this remains more of a conflict than a consensus model. It is termed "power resources theory" by political scientists. These struggles have culminated not in revolution but reform. Indeed, these broad reformist alliances then make a claim to be the people or nation, so that movements that started out as class-centered conflict lose this tenor and become the nation, amid a broad national consensus. This is good for the further development of social citizenship. Lindert argues that welfare generosity is greater where the middle class can relate to the plight of the poor and see them as essentially the same kinds of people as themselves. This was concretized as the nation – we share great similarities with our co-citizens. Events increasing popular solidarity and the salience of the nation are good for social citizenship; those that decrease it are bad. In turn, the achievement of social citizenship reinforces the cohesion of the nation-state. We have become more nationally caged by the development of social citizenship rights.

The third explanation emphasizes political institutions and focuses on political parties, bureaucrats, and policy experts; federal versus centralized states; and proportional representation (PR) versus majoritarian electoral systems. This model is used principally to explain variations between countries. In federal systems, citizen rights often vary within countries – we saw in the last chapter how important federalism was in the United States. Federalism and PR systems are often said to increase the number of veto points within the legislative process, which can stymie welfare reforms. PR is also said to favor center-left coalition government as opposed to the conservative governments favored by majoritarian systems (Iversen & Soskice, 2009; Bradley et al., 2003: 199). Although proponents of this theory are often called institutionalists, this is a very mixed bag of political power relations – not only institutions but also political parties and state elites are stressed. The first two theories see welfare developing largely inevitably through the century, although national and regional variations in levels of social citizenship are recognized by them both and are stressed in institutional theory.

These three theories all have some strength, and are also interrelated. Industrial society does not automatically create welfare states except where there are genuinely common interests in providing services, as with water and sewerage, for example. Otherwise, reforms need the pressure of collective actors such as labor unions or organizations for the elderly, and these are embedded in political movements set amid existing institutions, which add their own peculiarities. Thus, correlations of welfare generosity with the individual variables specified above are not particularly strong (although adequate quantitative data are generally only available since 1960). The strongest correlations are those with years of center-left government in democracies, followed by union strength, both of which fit class theory, although we must explain why some countries have more center-left governments and bigger unions. A full explanation must involve many causal paths – and their disruptions amid the major contingent events of the century, such as world wars and depressions whose effects I emphasized in previous chapters.

These three theories are all supposed to have general application across industrial capitalist countries. However, not only are nation-states all a little different from each other, but broader macro-regions comprising groups of states – each with certain cultural and institutional similarities – have also become important. Two main models for analyzing these macro-regions have emerged, one focusing on two or more "varieties of capitalism," the other on "welfare-state regimes." The latter is most relevant to this chapter. I leave the varieties of capitalism model until the next volume, as it has focused on the period after 1945.

Esping-Andersen (1990) distinguished three "welfare regimes": Liberal (which I term Anglo), Social Democratic (Nordic), and Conservative European (Euro). Essentially studying the period since 1960, but originally generalizing over a much longer time period, he sees liberal countries as having small, means-tested welfare systems that leave most people dependent on the market for their livelihood. Feminist movements actually sought to increase commodification when they took the employment route toward equality. The other two regimes have bigger welfare states, but the Nordic is more universalistic than the Euro. Its benefits are rights of citizenship, based on neither need nor status, and it is more redistributive. Furthermore, women achieve more rights in both the employment and maternal aspects of life. In these respects, the Nordics offer a more advanced form of Marshall's social citizenship. The Euro welfare states are not much smaller than the Nordic ones, but they are less universalistic and redistributive, being based on the insurance principle, with benefits varying by occupational and familial statuses. Higher-status occupations receive more benefits, as do families with children, but women are not encouraged to enter the labor market – a clear preference for the maternal route for women. These distinctive statuses derive from the lesser role of socialism and the greater role of socially conscious religion (usually Catholicism). Gender relations will sometimes reinforce, sometimes complicate this, as we will see. We should not reify these regimes. I shall show in particular that the Anglo and Euro models arose largely after this period.

This typology needs to confront all four aspects of social citizenship – welfare, taxes, labor markets, and education and health systems – and must be situated amid broader historical processes, for they have had distinct historical trajectories. I begin at the beginning.

Phase 1: Development up to World War I

Before the nineteenth century, states' main functions had been war and raising taxes for war. Most provided a minimum of welfare through poor laws, but this was seen as charity, not a right of citizenship. States' civil functions were increasing through the nineteenth century, as we saw in Volume II. The increase in infrastructures of communication, education, street cleaning and lighting, and clean water and sewerage all revealed the commitment of states and parties to improve the welfare of their citizens/subjects. This can be seen as the antecedent condition of modern social welfare programs. As capitalist industrialization spread, it brought the wealth necessary to finance more public programs, especially in education and health. By 1900, primary education was near universal in the most advanced countries, secondary education was quite well-established, and university expansion was beginning.

The clearest common interest lay in public health. This was the direct consequence not of capitalism but of industrialization and urbanization. The classes were now herded together in cities, and the communication of diseases amongst them was swift; germs are classless. Common interests gave more of a sense of the nation as one, but solidarity was more directly expressed at the municipal level. This was a spur to scientific and technological innovation as it related to public health. Cleaner water and sewerage systems and pasteurization and other public health regulation leapt forward. Louis Pasteur generally ranks as the most important French person ever in French polls, and they could be right. However, countless water and sewerage engineers, from Joseph Bazalgette – the mid-nineteenth century London designer of a sewerage system reducing the incidence of waterborne diseases such as cholera – to William Mulholland – who brought clean water to Los Angeles in 1913 – collectively probably made more of an impact. True, average wages in Britain and the United States also began to rise from the 1870s, with an impact on calorific intake, but real wages remained fairly stagnant in the first four decades of the twentieth century. The marked improvement in human health revealed by rising life expectancy and human height – especially visible in the 1920s and 1930s in most advanced countries – was probably due more to the many incremental improvements in environmental health over the previous period. This was in addition to continuing improvement in human diets mainly due to the inventiveness of capitalist agriculture and its attendant branches of the chemical industry (Floud et al., 2011). Mixed in together were logics of both capitalism and industrialism, which also generated rising GDP throughout the first half of the twentieth century in most countries (briefly punctuated by world wars and the Depression), meaning that more taxes of various kinds could also be extracted for public works and welfare schemes.

Collective public concern – some of it liberal or charitable, some of it generated by working-class pressure – turned toward the problem of the security of wealth and health over a person's lifetime. These various pressures and possibilities generated the first public welfare programs modifying old poor laws and supplementing private charity with public provision. At first, most were again sponsored by local rather than national government. The famous Bismarckian German federal social insurance programs of the late nineteenth century were outweighed in Germany by a plethora of programs at the local and provincial level (Steinmetz, 1993). The educational leaders during this period – the United States, Germany, and Australia – owed this mainly to local and provincial government initiatives. There seems to have been no clear leader in public health provision.

At the turn of the century, social welfare schemes were limited. Accident insurance schemes covered less than 20 percent of the employed population, there was less sickness insurance, and almost no unemployment insurance. Unions provided their own mutual societies that (rather inadequately) insured their members against poverty. These schemes were provided for men only. The main social-citizen right proclaimed (and sometimes implemented) was for the male wage earner to receive a family wage, that is, one adequate to support his family. Union movements were almost all committed to this, so it usually followed that they would seek to reduce female labor, which was lower waged and threatened the man's right to a family wage. The labor-force participation of men and women varied considerably between countries: the employment rate of married women was five times as high in France as in Britain in 1913 (Pedersen, 1993: 71). Everywhere, women's wages tended to be only about 50 percent of men's, and pro-female employment legislation tended to be "protective": women as the weaker more vulnerable sex needed protection from long hours and sweatshops, which disproportionately employed women. In Chapter 3, we saw that this was so in America in early twentieth century.

The early leaders in welfare programs were all moderately developed countries, as Hicks (1999) shows. The fact that only one less developed country, Romania, had any welfare policies supported the logic of industrialism model. Yet within the relatively developed countries, welfare programs did not correlate significantly with GDP per capita. The richest country, the United States, was a laggard in most welfare programs, although not in education and women's rights. This suggests that the logic of industrialism model might have lost its explanatory power quite early. What does correlate strongly is union density followed by extent of leftist voting – a clear vindication of class theory.

Hicks further examines what programs countries had introduced before 1913 and whether they were *consolidated*, that is, whether they were legally compulsory or nearly so for some set of persons, and whether they were extensive and fully funded through the state. He finds Bismarckian Germany was the leader with three programs satisfying these criteria – old age, disability and survivors pensions, sickness and maternity benefits, and workers compensation. Germany was followed by Austria, Australia, the Netherlands, Switzerland, and Sweden – all with two – although Sweden acquired a third in 1916. The UK had three programs, but although one satisfied both criteria, two satisfied only one. These were the leaders, and a rather diverse collection of countries drawn from all three of Esping-Andersen's welfare regimes, which suggests that his model did not apply this early. For old-age pensions, two different systems emerged. In the German Bismarckian system of contributory, status-related pensions, higher earners received higher pensions. This spread just before the First World War to France and the Netherlands. These were basically insurance schemes. In contrast, what later became known as the Beveridge system provided flat-rate, means-tested pensions for the elderly poor out of taxes. This was a citizen right, but only for the poor, who were usually subjected to intrusive surveillance of their eligibility. Denmark had initiated this in 1891, Britain followed in 1908, and Sweden in 1913. This was more redistributive than the status-reinforcing Bismarckian system (Ebbinghaus & Gronwald, 2009). As yet, however, the amounts involved were small.

In such early welfare systems, Hicks (1999: 124–5) perceives three routes, although they are not the same as Esping-Andersen's. One he calls lib-lab and comprised both the Anglos and Nordics. The second was Bismarckian, in which a semi-authoritarian state tried to co-opt skilled workers by offering unemployment insurance, sickness benefits, and pensions, as in Germany and Austria. The third route was paternalist or social Catholic, where large religious parties depended on the votes of all classes. Hicks emphasizes that all three were attempts by liberals, the state, or churches to divert working-class support away from socialism, and that they resulted from highly variable alliances of political parties in order to head off class struggle – the top-down response to class struggle. Steinmetz (1993) concurs that in Germany, the programs were not due directly to worker unrest, but rather to state officials' perceptions of such unrest.

In labor relations, the four liberal countries actually differed considerably. Britain already dealt distinctively with class conflict in the workplace. Legal rights were granted to trade unions, but the state stayed hands-off in labor relations. Voluntarism was the defining quality of this bargaining system. By World War I, Australia and New Zealand had an entrenched system of court arbitration of labor disputes; U.S. governments, both federal and state, were still repressing labor unions. Repression was declining across Europe, eventually replaced by milder corporatist structures of labor relations, bringing workers' and employers' interest groups inside the state for compulsory state mediation. However, this can be traced back to the greater presence of collective organizations such as guilds and rural cooperatives on the one hand and more interventionist, bureaucratized states on the other in this early period (Iversen & Soskice, 2009). Voluntarism and corporatism were later to have very distinct trajectories.

World War I boosted both welfare and progressive taxation in most combatant nations, although to different extents. It created its own welfare problems – more widows, orphans, and disabilities. As we saw in Chapter 5, it also brought mass mobilized, near-total war. Because the nation as a whole was sacrificing much for the war effort, there was a diffuse sense that the people should be rewarded with some redistribution. Winter & Robert's (1997) study of London, Paris, and Berlin shows that the war also changed social-citizenship rankings. Before the war, the rights embodied in Wilhelmine Germany's social insurance programs for retirement pay, unemployment benefit, and medical care were in advance of those of Britain, whose programs were in advance of France's. During the war, all three developed programs for wives, dependants, and widows of soldiers and disabled veterans, plus a minimal level of help for the unemployed. This was still dominated by the notion of the man's family wage, with the state stepping in only in the absence of a working man in the household; other women related to the nation through their men. The German system, under the economic pressures of a war waged by an old regime, intensified the Bismarckian conception of graded privileges, a combination of some national solidarity undercut by status differences. It was now overtaken by the more universal rights programs of (fairly) democratic France and Britain. The ranking of generosity at war's end was Britain in the lead followed by France, with Germany lagging (Bonzon, 1997). There was still no significant development of welfare policies in the United States. Yet no welfare benefits were very large in this era, and these shifts had not been great.

The size of government expenditures had of course rocketed during the war, and as in other periods of European history (documented in my previous volumes), it fell after the war, although not back to prewar levels. We have better data on revenue than expenditure. As a proportion of GDP, by 1920 revenues had doubled compared to 1913 in Britain, Ireland, and Germany, and had risen by more than 50 percent in the United States, the Netherlands, and Italy. Then, in the interwar period, it continued to rise, although only in Fascist Germany and Italy – spending much more on the military – and the United States during the New Deal was the rise very substantial. Due to the war, government borrowing had zoomed upward. Afterward, debt repayment continued at about the same level, and education, health, and welfare expenses also rose steadily as a proportion of GDP. By 1937, state expenditures for eleven advanced countries averaged 11.4 percent of GDP, a doubling over forty years. Two countries, Australia and Norway, had less than half this; Germany had twice this; and France 50 percent more. The others were bunched around this average, with the United States having the highest of them at 12.9 percent (Tanzi & Schuknecht, 2000: chaps. 2, 3). As GDP per capita was also rising in the interwar period, the growth of government was noticeable almost everywhere. States had acquired more civilian roles in response to demands for more social citizenship. Yet this was to be dwarfed by the growth in citizen rights that occurred in the post–World War II period. These trends were similar across the advanced countries – with the exception of the fascist countries – although of course every country was a little different.

The problem of how to pay for the war loomed large for the combatants. The main means available were loans and war bonds, treasury printing presses, and taxes. Loans and bonds had some impact on intergenerational redistribution – they were a tax on later generations who would have to pay them back, but they had little class redistributive impact. The universal policy of taxing "excess" war profits was progressive, but only during the war itself, as these taxes were abandoned afterward. Consumption taxes, the main sources of revenue in many countries, were increased during the war. They tended to be regressive, but taxes on wealth generated much less revenue during the war because most rents and stock yields declined. The income tax was progressive everywhere, as at this time it only applied to the relatively wealthy, but its incidence varied greatly.

Income taxes were highest in prewar Britain. Its income tax had helped pay for wars for over a century – long before any other country – and its level had been raised by the Boer War and the cost of Lloyd-George's insurance program of 1911. In World War I, Britain's income tax rate then grew from 6 percent at the beginning to 30 percent at the end, and the numbers of those liable tripled. The result was markedly progressive. The combination of income tax, a "super-tax" on high incomes, and inheritance taxes accounted for almost half of all British state revenues, compared to only 22 percent in France and 11 percent in Germany. In the United States, the Democrat alliance of farmers, labor, and the South and West swept state legislatures in the elections of 1910 and 1912, so the 16th Amendment to the Constitution legalizing a federal income tax was ratified – just in time for the war. The U.S. income tax rate rose rapidly from 1.5 percent to 18.3 percent as America entered the war, and it was progressive. By 1919, it contributed half of federal revenue. Although the white Dominions relied more on war loans at generous interest rates, all but Australia increased income taxes significantly during the war, and then maintained them – the New Zealand rate rose to 30 percent. So the war boosted social citizenship in the form of progressive taxes among the Anglos, including the United States. Note that the United States was particularly uneven, introducing progressive taxes but lagging in most welfare benefits until the New Deal.

A French income tax was introduced by a Socialist and Left Radical alliance just before the outbreak of war, although it applied to few and its rate was only 2 percent. In 1917, income, wealth, and inheritance taxes were combined in a progressive package, although still with low rates. France continued to rely much more than the Anglos on regressive indirect taxes. Russia did this to an even greater extent: the regime had tried to introduce income taxes in 1914, but the war and administrative backwardness prevented progress. Germany's individual states already had small prewar income taxes. Then the socialists offered support to increased military expenditure if it could be paid for with federal progressive taxes – once again showing that for the left, domestic policy was almost always more important than foreign policy. The level of direct taxes on individuals was low, however, and there was little change during the war. Austria-Hungary took slightly more from direct taxes during the war, but Italy retained a very low direct tax burden.

Neutrals sometimes had heavy fiscal burdens during the war because blockades and other disturbances disrupted their normal trade relations and produced common sacrifices for which foreigners were blamed (for they had started the war). This also spurred on populist policies. In the Netherlands, these were implemented by an alliance between socialists and religious parties, which now achieved universal proportional representation. This ensured that personal taxes rose fourfold and became more progressive. The Dutch, as the British, were shifting the burden from indirect to direct taxes. Neutral but occupied Belgium followed after the war (Strachan, 2001: 862–904; Ferguson, 1999: 118–25; Broadberry & Harrison, 2005; Morgan & Prasad, 2009; Tanzi & Schuknecht, 2000: 56–7). Now the democracies were moving toward progressive taxes, redistribution that emphasized one lived in a national community. Income taxes proved difficult to dismantle after the war because they were so popular; they were the leading edge of social citizenship across the mid-twentieth century.

I have charted the first stirrings of social citizenship. They were small, limited by the ideology that the place of men was in the labor market, earning a family wage, and women should be the caregivers in the home – unless there was no working man there, in which case some states and provincial authorities were giving the caregiver limited financial help. They were boosted by common sacrifice in war, but with the partial exception of public health, they varied both within and between nations, and they were malleable. Nothing was yet set in stone, and they did not yet fit at all neatly into the typologies distinguished earlier.

Phase 2: Interwar trajectories: (a) The Anglos

The victorious Anglos saw democracy and the welfare state gradually deepen. They were internally peaceful, saw no attempted revolutions, and strikers and suffragettes experienced little violence (except for the United States during the Palmer raids). During the entire twentieth century, the American civil rights movement and nationalist risings in Ireland provided the most turbulence among the Anglos, and neither were forms of class struggle. These countries were combatants in world wars, but as uninvaded victors. Thus, existing political institutions endured, although they were variably deepened by sacrifice in war and war-induced populism. Gradual path-dependent development of citizen rights was common. None developed large Marxist parties or unions; their main parties of the left were either liberal, as in the United States, Canada, and Ireland, or Labour parties dominated by moderate trade unions, as in Australia, New Zealand, and the United Kingdom, initially stealing the policies and votes of larger liberal parties.

Britain, the first industrial nation, had developed the first working class. The logic of industrialism plus class power pressured toward welfare and redistribution. In the 1890s, traditional craft unions had joined with the semiskilled workers of the second industrial revolution. Britain's union-membership density remained high, rivaled only by Australia, until the mid-1920s. The franchise was extended through successive male occupational strata and then to women, as each supposedly demonstrated its "responsibility." By 1900, a number of constituencies dominated by workers were electing trade unionists as their Members of Parliament (MPs). They formed the core of a Labour Party whose emergence put pressure on the major parties to offer reforms that would please working-class voters. Thus, the Liberal Party moved leftward in the 1900s, seeking to keep its working-class voters with reforms. Lloyd-George's social insurance program of 1911, coupled with a progressive income tax, resulted. In the absence of socialist or communist parties, this became the lib-lab route toward social citizenship (Hicks, 1999: 124–5).

I noted in Chapter 3 how the war reinforced American conservatism because American military intervention had come late in the war and was quickly successful. In Britain, victory in World War I tended to legitimate the regime, although the extent of national sacrifice had encouraged a slight deepening of democracy. The vote was extended to all men during the war, and there was mild reform and the enfranchisement of many women afterward. Its impact on Ireland was different, hastening on dissident nationalism and independence from Britain – anticipating a general pattern among Britain's colonies after World War II. Yet capitalism was not weakened, and feminists had to rekindle their activism, which most had yielded up for the sake of wartime unity.

Marwick (1991) sees World War I as more radical in its effects, changing forever the relationship of the British to their state, as wartime reforms became permanent. Income tax was extended from the top 5–10 percent to practically everyone, the railways were nationalized, and welfare programs were extended. The Education Act of 1918 raised compulsory education one year and handed over its control to the state. In 1919, legislation authorized building half a million new small homes, and in 1920, unemployment insurance was extended from 2 to 11 million workers. Benefits for dependents quickly followed. It was the end, says Marwick, of laissez-faire liberalism. Women had also emancipated themselves through factory work as the men went off to fight. This led, he argues, to the liberalization of feminine codes of conduct and the enfranchisement of women.

Higher income taxes and wage increases in the war did prove difficult to undo, and some redistribution continued (Steinmo, 1993: 23–5, 104–8; McKibbin, 1998: 114–8). However, Marwick exaggerates. Of his three acts, only unemployment insurance was a major extension. The prewar period had already seen school leaving-age raised twice, the epochal National Insurance Act, growing union membership, strikes, Labour voting, and an expanding suffragette movement. Plans for legislating female suffrage had been drawn up by the Liberal government before the war, but were shelved by its onset. Indeed, across much of the West the prewar period had seen much social-policy innovation (Gauthier, 1998: chap. 3).

The war helped the labor movement. A shop stewards movement consolidated the gains of a prewar strike wave, and union membership doubled between 1913 and 1920 to 45 percent of the labor force. Labor unrest shot up, as in almost all countries in the immediate postwar period, but then a decline set in until 1932, when the level of union membership was 23 percent, followed by gradual recovery up to 32 percent by 1939. Labour Party leaders had participated in the wartime coalition government, and as the Liberal leaders Asquith and Lloyd-George bickered and the party became factionalized under electoral pressure, Labour enjoyed success. In five successive elections between 1918 and 1929, it increased its share of the vote and seats in parliament. It joined a coalition government in 1924, and in 1929 it governed alone, although with

Liberal support. By then it had reached around 35 percent of the total vote, less than the Conservatives' 40–45 percent, but outdistancing the Liberals, whom Labour was now replacing. The unions pushed Labour leftward on labor issues such as unemployment insurance. Industry developed a mild corporate bias (Middlemas, 1979), allowing voluntary consultations on matters of common concern between union leaders, employers, and government, reviving institutions set up by Lloyd-George in the war. Yet the General Strike of 1926 interrupted this, and in retaliation the Conservative government restricted strikers' rights. The Mond-Turner talks between union leaders and industrialists began in 1928 but were abandoned in 1933, mainly because of opposition from employers who did not recognize unions. Britain did not develop corporatism, and macroeconomic policy remained unchanged. Keynes had as yet little influence in his homeland. This was much less change than Marwick suggested.

Although the Labour Party was the main vehicle for gradual reform, it became more centrist and respectable in order to secure middle-class votes, just as the German SPD was doing. The left of the party was marginalized by the mid-1920s. Bad timing then brought Labour into power in 1929, when internal factionalism left it in poor condition to cope with the Great Depression (Riddell, 1999; Howell, 2002; Worley, 2005). It split, with most of its leaders going into a coalition National government, increasingly dominated by the Conservatives, which lasted until World War II. Yet the National government had an impact on conservative leaders. They did not think they could win elections by rolling back reforms. Even in the United States, dominated by conservative Republican administrations during the 1920s, they could not get rid of the income tax; the most they could do was cut rates and preserve their progressive shape. British Conservative governments seeking to keep their working-class vote and make good their claim to be the national party cautiously extended welfare benefits and maintained the progressive income tax. The coverage of its pension, health, and unemployment insurance programs was broader by the mid-1930s than in any other country, and its spending on education as a proportion of GDP was also more (Tanzi & Schuknecht, 2000: 34–6).

The Conservative Party also rebuilt itself, pressured by suffrage extensions that by 1929 had given all adults the vote. Conservative women's and youth organizations appeared, and the party sponsored magazines, films, and educational centers that extolled the virtues of patriotism, industrial peace, duty, decency, and the family, a message geared to the growing middle class, women, and deferential workers (McCrillis, 1998). All this was geared toward becoming the party of the nation. Not that class or gender were irrelevant. Middle-class men joined sporting, social, and business clubs, and women made the teas. Clubs tried to overcome religious differences in the interests of solidarity. Although the existence of class was strongly denied, clubs were segregated by class. They maintained "the right atmosphere … attracting the better sort of people." Cricket developed segregation between "Gentlemen" (unpaid amateurs) and "Players" (working-class paid professionals). The Gentlemen were called "Mr.," the Players were called by their first names – even in the English national cricket team. Football had working-class players and crowds, but the clubs were run by businessmen. Class and conservatism were resurgent, reforms were preserved, but deepening democracy was resisted in the social sphere (McKibbin, 1998).

The British Broadcasting Corporation (BBC) added ideological power to this reformed conservatism. Founded in 1922 by an electro-technical industry consortium whose financial interest was only in selling radio equipment, it never had commercials or was as capitalistic as its American counterparts. It became a public corporation in 1927, financed by taxes but autonomous of political parties and government. It was rather stuffy, avoided controversy, and usually reflected the culture of the upper middle classes, providing a paternalist version of public service, seeking to uplift the tastes, morals, and language of the nation. Regional-level broadcasters exercised more independence, and they sought to make their programs relevant to the lives of working-class listeners. Later, as the nation moved leftward during and after the Second World War, BBC radio and then television became less establishment, more classless, committed to political and class-cultural balance. It remained independent and noncommercial. When competition from private commercial television was licensed in the 1950s, its advertisers were kept well away from program content. Thus, the principal ideological medium in Britain became largely independent of those who held political and economic power, an important contribution to pluralist democracy, unlike British print journalism and almost all American media.

British women found that many of their wartime gains proved fleeting. They got higher wages during the war, but still less than men. Their supervisors were men, and they were mostly laid off at war's end, as the unions had been promised. It was different in France, where unions were weaker and had not been brought into power-sharing during the war. French employers were freer to retain women workers if they saw fit, and women were cheaper. Thus, women formed almost 40 percent of the working population in France in 1921, compared to only 29 percent in Britain (Pedersen, 1993: 123). In America, all women got the vote in 1918; in Britain, only women property owners and wives of householders over the age of thirty got the vote, although all women did in 1929. Yet Vellacott (2007) believes that British and French women might have done better without the war. In both countries, many radical feminists had opposed the war and been marginalized. At war's end, British feminism was led by upper-class Londoners enfranchised in 1918 who cared little for still-excluded working-class women. It was different in defeated Germany, Austria, and (briefly) Russia, where women got the vote immediately in 1917–1918 as socialist parties with universalistic goals seized power. Military defeat was good for women's suffrage – at least in the short run. War is culturally macho, and this war was led to defeat by a patriarchal old regime, so discrediting it through defeat was good for feminism.

American women had followed the maternal route, mainly because of the weakness of the American left, although the New Deal changed feminists' prospects. As we saw in the last chapter, feminists could agitate and get some gains in both employment and family life because of Roosevelt's dependence on a broad constituency of support that included them. In Britain, where unions were much stronger, feminists made few gains. This was partly because Labour was destroyed by the Great Depression, partly because the disdain shown by leading feminists toward working-class women helped deter the party from embracing their cause. It was also partly because unions were unresponsive to feminist maternalist demands for wives' and children's allowances, seeing these as a threat to their goal of a family wage paid to the male breadwinner. When the Labor government cut unemployment benefits during the Depression, it first slashed benefits for married women workers. There was actually less interwar progress in Britain or France compared to the United States (Cohen & Hanagan, 1991).

Australia and New Zealand were not industrialized, but they substituted the radicalism of a frontier society (as did the western states of the United States). Unions grew amid a class consciousness hostile to colonial elites, and the behavior of British officers in the war seemed to typify this for Anzac soldiers. The Australian Labour Party had profited before the war from the tariff issue that divided the two main parties. Australia, Canada, and New Zealand were all Entente victors. They lost 20 percent of their soldiers in the war, but it had boosted their economies and there was no civilian sacrifice, so few promises of a better life afterward. The Australian Labour Party was actually hurt by the war, as it had split over conscription and remained out of government until 1929 – bad timing given the onset of the Great Depression. However, unions continued to grow through the 1920s – from a density of 31 percent in 1913 to 47 percent in 1927 – then the Depression hit them, too. New Zealand and Canada both had conservative governments before, during, and after the war. New Zealand women already had the vote, but the war consolidated their labor-market position. The New Zealand Liberal Party then held power with the help of its large union wing and was the main vehicle of reform until 1935, when the country got its first Labour government. Three years later, it introduced a part means-tested, part universal pension plan, plus other means-tested benefits. Canadian union membership remained at only 14–15 percent through the 1920s, although it doubled in the later 1930s. Canadian rhythms of welfare development had a slower pace until well after World War II.

Anzac social citizenship became distinctive, however. Castles (1985; cf Starke, 2008: 54–6) prefers the term "wage-earner" to "liberal" welfare states, as they had active labor-market policies protecting workers through arbitration courts, tariffs, and public works programs, all aimed at full employment. This was helped by high rates of homeownership, a youthful population, abundant raw materials, and easy access to British imperial markets. Unemployment remained below 1 percent in New Zealand and below 2 percent in Australia until the mid-1970s. Active labor-market policies flowered during World War II, as did Keynes' influence on macroeconomic policy. Australia had established judicial wage arbitration as early as 1901. Its first Chief Justice declared that wage levels would be decided not according to "the higgling of the market" but according to the social justice required for "the average employee regarded as a human being living in a civilized community," an explicitly non-market criterion. By 1920, the principle of a living family wage was the main guideline for Anzac wage arbitrations. Wages were periodically adjusted to cost-of-living increases, keeping wage levels up and wage dispersion down. The courts also often legally required employers to grant benefits such as sickness leave that in other countries were provided by the state. This was great for men, not so good for women. The institutionalization of the family wage was oriented to the male household head, with women assumed to have primarily domestic roles.

Most Australian welfare benefits were means-tested. Only a few people claimed them, for they were residual, needed by those with no labor-market connection in a country of full employment. This is why it was a "wage-earners" welfare system, resulting from the dominance of class conflict in Australian politics. Unions and workers were interested in employment, not the family, and they were helped toward a family wage by the arbitration courts. The system had a sexist bias, because far more women were outside the labor market. Women were eligible for basic pension rights, invalidity allowances, and maternity benefits before World War I, but achieved almost nothing else until World War II and after. Aborigines were excluded until after the war.

New Zealand had early welfare programs, mainly for men, although widow's allowances (1912) and family benefits (1926) were also introduced. Employment protection laws set women's wage levels at half men's, and restricted their hours of work. As in Australia and Britain, powerful labor unions privileged class over gender. The advent of a Labour government in 1938 brought a Social Security Act that provided a full range of citizen entitlement programs: a free health system, pensions for all the retired, sickness benefits for all invalids, education for all, and the extension of family allowance to all mothers regardless of need. The votes of women had brought some progress for them. Many programs remained means-tested, targeted at the poor and needy, but they were paid for entirely out of general taxation – principally income tax – as in Australia, so the system was progressive. As in Australia, if income and/or assets fell below stated levels, benefits were automatically received. The lower 70 percent of Australians got the old-age pension. By the 1930s, the poor did not have to endure the humiliation of administrative discretion, for assessments of worthiness were abolished. Means-testing predominated in the Anglo countries, but it operated quite differently in Australia and New Zealand compared to Britain and the United States. The Anzacs had a distinct path to social citizenship (Castles, 1985: chap. 1; Castles & Shirley, 1996). However, among the Anglophones, Britain was the clear leader in social citizenship in the interwar period.

The Anglos were nonetheless an ideological family speaking the same language and sharing much of the same heritage, culture, and political system (Castles & Mitchell, 1993). Policy experts and party, business, and union intellectuals read the same books and pamphlets and adapted many of each other's institutions and policies. The famous 1942 Beveridge Report on British social insurance had a sale of 600,000 right across the English-reading world. Ireland, neutral in World War II, adopted Beveridge's recommendations on family allowances during the war. Australians, New Zealanders, and Canadians implemented it afterward. The Anglos also shared common not civil law and the highest law court for the Dominions was the Privy Council in London. They had British governor-generals, and they demonstrated loyalty to King and Empire through the wartime sacrifices of their young men. Like Britain, the Dominions were majority Protestant but relatively secular countries. To the extent that Protestantism did matter, it had contradictory effects, as conservatives were sustained by Anglicanism and Labour was boosted by Methodism and other "low churches." The Anglos (apart from the United States) shared the same internal battles over tariffs with the same outcome in the 1930s of imperial preference tariffs. Thus, there were both diversity and common models in this period.

In the first half of the twentieth century, the Anglos had been pushed a little leftward by a common lib-lab ideology. They devised two responses, one centered on taxes and the welfare state, the other on labor-market interventions, with the United States developing more spasmodically. They all tended to divide welfare programs into those based on insurance derived from employment, which – although formally gender-neutral – benefited mainly men; and universal, if rather meager, means-tested assistance programs for the very poor – of whom single mothers and pensioners were among the worst off. In Britain and the United States, although less so in Australia, single mothers and pensioners also suffered from the state snooping into their lifestyles. This distinction carried on into the form of the institutionalization of class compromise. These tended to be more voluntaristic than corporatist, so that (as in liberal ideals) the parties could freely withdraw from them. Yet Australia and New Zealand also had the intermediary form: arbitration of labor relations, including wage determination, by the courts. These differences meant that there was not yet a common Anglo cast to social citizenship.

Phase 2: Interwar trajectories: (b) The Nordics

The Nordic countries industrialized in the early twentieth century, and its industries were highly concentrated and in only a few locations. In Sweden, as Stephens (1980) showed, working-class density in employment and residence helped generate a strong labor movement, but peasant farmers were also strong. They had never succumbed to serfdom, and they still enjoyed representation in an estates assembly that now became a modern parliament. Although the official Lutheran churches were fairly conservative, Protestant sects overlapping with proto-feminist temperance movements pushed radical causes. Domestic peace endured, with the same effect as among the Anglos, generating institutional persistence and competition more than conflict. Here, however, it was more highly organized at the level of the state, which had been historically more important than in the Anglophone countries. The Nordic world developed corporatist tendencies early.

Left-of-center alliances emerged in Denmark, Norway, and Sweden between workers and farmers, and the independence of farmers from the privileged classes undercut bourgeois blocs (Esping-Andersen, 1985: 73). In Denmark, small farmers flourished through cooperatives, and industry remained artisanal. Peasants and artisans were democratic- and liberal-leaning at the beginning of the century. Political alliances formed between rural Radicals and urban Liberals, with Socialists as junior partners. This secured universal suffrage and the first welfare and labor-market reforms before, during, and just after World War I.

Norway was slow to develop industry, but its fishing and forestry sectors and impoverished peasantry, coupled with the absence of a landlord class, gave a radical impetus to its politics, as did center-periphery conflict. These generated universal suffrage in 1913. Women's movements originating from missionary and other Protestant sect organizations were strong but quite conservative, preferring to go down the maternalist route for rights. In any case, there was little demand for their labor, except on the peasant farms. The first phase of the Norwegian welfare state was mainly masculine, although a cross-class bloc of women's votes, willing to trade with other interest groups, ensured some limited success. The insurance system was extended to housewives in 1915, family allowances and pensions were introduced and then extended to single mothers, and for those that did work there was paid maternity leave. In contrast, women's rights in employment lagged. However, the growth of socialism in the 1920s was to split apart women activists into socialist and nonsocialist groups and lessen women's chances of further rights (see Sainsbury, 2001, for interwar Norwegian and Swedish feminism).

In contrast, Sweden saw late and rapid economic development from 1900, based on large-scale concentrated firms in iron, timber, and electrical power. This produced class conflict between a powerful bourgeoisie and a concentrated proletariat, although with peasant farmers as a third force. These forces, aided by radical Protestant sects, achieved universal suffrage at the end of World War I. Sweden had a bureaucratic state, a product of its imperial past, and this was active in developing the infrastructures of an industrial society. Industry boomed, and the high demand for labor meant that women were encouraged to work, so feminists might choose the employment route to rights and were pressing for reforms even before the war. In fact, the 1913 Social Insurance Act, applying to all working men and women (but not to housewives) was the first universal insurance act in the world, with broader coverage than the earlier scheme of Lloyd-George in England. Most political parties emerging in all three countries were class-based or sectoral (i.e., agriculture versus industry), as there was much ethnic and linguistic homogeneity.

The Scandinavian countries remained neutral during the war, but were hurt by the British blockade of Germany, a major trading partner for them. To avert great suffering and probable riots, governments felt they had to introduce rationing and other government controls aimed at equalizing the material circumstances, and implicitly the national solidarity, of all citizens. Of course rationing generated a black market sustaining class inequalities, and this in its turn generated popular resentment. As neutrals, their regimes were neither legitimated nor delegitimated by the war, and as war gave government no increased powers to deploy, it pushed them toward more redistributive taxes and benefits and more conciliatory strategy toward labor. The nation was strengthening.

The Danish and Swedish Social Democratic vote began to rise in 1920–1921, and the Norwegian vote from 1927. In union density, Denmark and Norway both experienced a surge followed by some decline, but the decline was less than elsewhere. Sweden saw no decline at all, but continuous steady growth, from 10 percent in 1913 to 21 percent in 1918 to 54 percent in 1939. Danish union density had begun at 23 percent in 1913, saw some decline in the 1920s, and recuperation in the 1930s, all at lower density level than the Scandinavians. Thus, wartime promise was only fully realized among neutrals. Elsewhere, the unions of the First War period saw hothouse growth, and were then unable to cope well with peacetime capitalist development. The war was best for progressive reformist causes if you remained neutral. Military power relations made a difference.

In 1924, the Danish Socialists became the largest party, and remained so until 2001. Yet lacking an absolute majority they always needed coalitions to rule. During the Great Depression, they made a deal with farmers: agricultural subsidies and trade union restraint in return for an active policy to boost employment through control of prices, exports, and imports. This steered Denmark out of the Depression toward Keynesian planning. A reform act of 1933 consolidated and rationalized diverse welfare programs (Esping-Andersen, 1985: 76; Flora, 1983). Norwegian Socialists were more leftist. They formed their first government in 1927, but their radical policies produced capital flight and their quick demise. In 1930, the party shifted to reformism, and profited from the Great Depression to form a long-lasting government with agrarian support in 1935. In Sweden, the origins of welfare programs and progressive taxes lie with bureaucratic and center party elites, not with the socialists. However, World War I made a difference. Like Denmark and Norway, neutral Sweden suffered economic dislocation as the British blockaded its trade with Germany. The war increased state expenditure and the shared experience of the common people. The combination led to a surge in progressive taxation, which could not be turned back after the war (Steinmo, 1993: 62–8, 81–5). To abort growing popular discontent, the wartime conservative government set up an Unemployment Commission that sponsored work-relief programs, although the pay was well below market rates. Unemployment remained high after the war and the programs continued. The first small social insurance schemes had been introduced by agrarian and centrist parties in 1913 and then in the 1920s. The Social Democrats followed a similar path to the Norwegians, becoming permanently reformist after 1928.

The Great Depression discredited Swedish conservatives and brought in a Social Democratic-led government. It turned the work programs leftward 1932–1934 by paying wages at market rates and developing deficit-financed public spending for recovery. Key to this was a deal with the Agrarian Party that gave farmers public loans and agricultural protection. There were close links between the party's leaders – especially finance minister Ernst Wigforss – and the economists of the Stockholm School – led by Bertil Ohlin and Gunnar Myrdal. Sweden's corporatist traditions made it easier for expert government advisors to help steer government policy toward countercyclical spending as a response to recession. Wigforss was championing this before 1932, and Keynes acknowledged an intellectual debt to the earlier Swedish economist Knut Wicksell. As the Depression worsened, Ohlin rejected cuts in nominal wages and public expenditures, arguing for bolder measures of increased public works and investments plus expansionary monetary policy to fight unemployment. By 1932, he had embraced the multiplier effect, although the Swedes did not adopt Keynes' concept of aggregate demand. Stockholm economics now had great influence on the Social Democrats and the unions. The Stockholm School seemed to offer a viable third way between a capitalist and socialist economy, attaining a high level of social equality without undermining economic efficiency. In the post–World War II period, this third way came to dominate the Nordic countries as a whole.

It was in the 1930s that Swedish women achieved major rights breakthroughs: maternity benefits available to nearly all mothers; free child delivery and medical checkups; allowances for single mothers; freer access to abortion; repeal of a law banning contraceptives; and a law forbidding employers from firing women because of engagement, marriage, or pregnancy. This was taking both the employment and maternal routes at the same time – which obviously provides the most rights for women. Again, labor shortages mattered – this time the result of population decline – but in conjunction with an alliance between a united women's movement and the Social Democrats (plus the compromise with farmers), this produced a major policy innovation: the costs of reproduction in the family was paid by taxation of the whole nation. The Swedish Social Democrats said in fact that their policies were aimed at providing a "people's home," indicating their commitment to the model of a national community. The working class had transmuted into "the people." In contrast, the more conservative tenor of Norwegian women's movements, coupled with the rise of Socialism, meant that they remained split throughout the 1930s between the employment and maternalist routs, so achieved little of either.

Corporatism also developed in Sweden. The Socialist-Agrarian alliance was formalized in 1936 and acquired corporatist institutions through the Saltjoban agreement of 1938 between capital, labor, and the state. The union federations – including middle-class unions – and the farmers' organizations were brought inside state committee rooms in order to hammer out national agreements to regulate wages and bring more predictability and fewer strikes and lockouts. By the end of the 1930s, Scandinavian employers were reconciled to this system. Whether or not this redistributed between the classes, the nation was the distributive unit. Finland lagged because it only had a tiny labor movement (Korpi, 1978; Katzenstein, 1985; Esping-Andersen, 1985, Baldwin, 1990).

Until after World War II, the Nordic countries broadly resembled the Anglos, although they were more corporatist, which was to matter considerably in the long run. By 1930, Denmark had the highest proportion of social spending to GDP, followed closely by Finland, the UK, Sweden, New Zealand, Norway, and Australia (Lindert, 2004, additional tables). This was joint leadership by Nordics and Anglos, except in the field of gender relations, where Swedish women had acquired decidedly more citizen rights than any other country. The Nordic welfare states as a group did not outstrip all others until the 1960s (Hicks, 1999: 124–5).

Phase 2: Interwar trajectories: (c) The Euros

It was different for countries in continental Europe, some of whom were buffeted away from earlier paths by the world wars. As we saw in Chapter 6, defeat for the German, Austrian, and Russian Empires produced an upsurge of class struggle and rapid deepening of democracy, social welfare, and redistribution in the 1920s. In this period, the fullest form of democracy was felt to be proportional representation, so all European countries except the UK and Spain adopted it (although France was to waver repeatedly between the two systems).

France differed from the others – a victor in World War I, and less changed by it. The most reliable time series for French union membership (those registered to vote at Confédération Generale du Travail [CGT] union conferences) reveals a 33 percent increase between 1913 and 1920, followed by a decline to 1934 of about 25 percent – the interwar norm. French density rates were quite low, however, probably never rising above 15 percent of the nonagricultural labor force (Kriegel, 1969: 67; Prost, 1964: 315). Strike rates showed a similar surge followed by decline as in Britain, as employers refused to yield and disillusion set in among workers. Socialist Party membership rocketed in 1918–1919, but in 1920 came a major schism between Socialists and Communists, mainly over relations with the Russian Bolsheviks. The Socialists now became more moderate and went into electoral alliances with the centrist Radical Party, leaving the smaller Communist Party as the main bearer of an ostensibly revolutionary socialism – although often compromised by the Comintern line (Kriegel, 1969). French unions split three ways, into Socialist, Communist, and Catholic federations. As before the war, bursts of expansion on the left led to factionalism, then decline (Ansell, 2001). Governments of the right dominated most of the 1920s, and only in 1936 did the left return to power in the form of the ambitious Popular Front government. Within two years, however, internal squabbles and fierce resistance by the right led to its disintegration.

There was little redistribution between the classes and few enhanced benefits for workers in interwar France. Politics remained conservative, and the nation remained strongly divided by class. A much-needed broadening of the tax base was discussed but never implemented. Controversies over who would pay stymied social-policy initiatives (Adamthwaite, 1995; B. Martin, 1999) and inequality remained high. A sharp reduction in wage differentials immediately after the war was reversed by the deflationary policies of the 1920s. They briefly narrowed under the Popular Front, and social transfers as a proportion of GDP almost doubled, although only to 1.1 percent – half the British level. Data on income and wealth inequality between the rich and the rest show big differences from Britain. Inequality fell around World War I in both countries, but in France it rose through most of the interwar period, unlike British inequality, which fell fairly continuously after 1925 (Atkinson & Piketty, 2007: chaps. 3, 4).

Grayzel (1999: 10, 225, 245–6) says that in Britain and France, "the war's lasting influence on gender was more conservative than innovative" because war discourses saw women in terms of motherhood. French debates on issues as diverse as German atrocities in Belgium, industrial labor, uniforms, Khaki fever, rape, venereal disease, pacifism, and mourning all focused on the supposed threats they posed to motherhood –an "anchor for stabilizing gender." Women's wartime sacrifices did not make them politically equal (McMillan, 2004). Thébaud (2004: 185–99) sees the main transformations for French women coming not from the war itself but from longer-run changes in work, consumption, domesticity, and control over fertility. Middle-class women benefitted most, she says, from the expansion of education that improved access to clerical, teaching, and caregiver jobs. The war had also liberalized dress codes, as in Britain. Women had abandoned their corsets for war work, and refused to go back into them afterward (Brachet-Campseur, 2004). This must have been quite a relief.

A few French welfare improvements span off from the war. Refugee flows and labor mobility had overstrained commune-based health care and poverty relief. Larger cities took over more of these functions, also receiving assistance from the state. Provisions for the poor were increased at the city level and in the private sector, and then nationally through state subsidies to local authorities. Women's gains were not primarily the result of feminism – which was weak – or of an alliance with the working-class movement – which was also weak and oriented to the problems of male workers. France's distinctive parental model of welfare – giving welfare benefits to mothers – was primarily due to the pressure exerted by employers, Social Catholics, and especially pronatalists. During the war, 1.4 million Frenchmen were killed, lowering the birthrate. France's population was now declining; resurgent Germany's population was larger and growing. Politicians concerned about mobilization for a future war became pronatalists and supported incentives for women to marry and have children. Increased business coordination during the war had also strengthened employers' associations. Some of them developed *welfare capitalism*, providing pensions to workers and benefits to their wives and children, trying by these means to reduce labor turnover and keep down wages, union strength, and strikes. The high rate of female employment also tended to keep wages low.

French men had little chance of getting a family wage, but they could get insurance for injuries or retirement. The failure of French feminists to win the vote (because centrist deputies feared women might vote for the right, against the Republic) meant that, unlike their British and American counterparts, they could not call on a substantial voting constituency to support their demands. They had to rely on pronatalism and social Catholicism to improve women's welfare. This meant that although all feminist movements were somewhat torn between demands for improvements in women's working lives and their roles as wives and mothers, French women were pushed more down the maternal route with family and children's allowances. The gains were real, and women received benefits regardless of their employment or marital status.

Health and old-age benefits for workers took a mutualist form, as workers and employers paid contributions into private insurance schemes with less state involvement than in the Anglo countries. By 1939, 55 percent of the population was covered, and it jumped to 70 percent in 1945. France could not match the British system of unemployment insurance, but laws on family allowances and health and social insurance came in a burst between 1928 and 1932, then again in the 1939 Code de la Famille. Timothy Smith (2003: 131) says that the 1928 Health Insurance Law was "the Magna Carta of the modern

French welfare state." It redistributed more toward women and children than the working class. The 1945 decrees then consolidated and broadened the coverage of these programs into being an important part of the French welfare-state system that endures today (Pedersen, 1993: chaps. 2, 5; Dutton, 2002; Timothy Smith 2003; Dreyfus et al., 2006). Mutualism plus Social Catholicism formed a distinctive blend of French social citizenship. Overall, France was unusual in being less dominated by the male-breadwinner ideology because of the weakness of the left and the strength of pronatalists and welfare capitalists. This was the maternal route. Pedersen terms this in a gender-neutral way the *parental* route, which was "compensating adults for dependent children irrespective of earnings or need" (1993: 17–18).

The war had a bigger impact on defeated countries. With the German old regime swept away and the SPD swept into power, the Weimar Republic (1918–1933) deepened social citizenship. Austria did, too, in the years 1918–1923, when Socialists dominated. Germany saw expansion and consolidation of decentralized and piecemeal welfare programs into national ones – some organized through employers and unions, some by the state – underpinned more by notions of collective social citizenship than individual rights, although this was challenged by the political right and the churches (Hong, 1998). There was more state coordination of worker-employer conflict, and a system of unemployment insurance imposed by the state urged on by labor unions, against the objections of employers – both proto-corporatist tendencies. There were national programs for young persons, unemployment assistance and insurance (financed by employees and employers), and occupational insurance for accidents and diseases. In most of these respects, Weimar trailed only Britain in generosity (Tanzi & Schuknecht, 2000: chap. 2). There was a flowering of the notion of "scientific social work," systemic and couched in somewhat biological and naturalized rhetoric, soon to be greatly intensified by the Nazis (Steinmetz, 1993: 202). Overall, social expenditure doubled, from 19 percent of all government expenditures in 1913 to 40 percent in 1929–1930 (Flora & Heidenheimer, 1981), higher than any other country. Enzberger, the German finance minister, reformed the income tax, making it more progressive in 1919–1920, with the top rate set at 60 percent. In consequence, right-wing extremists killed him in 1921. Hyperinflation narrowed income differentials, which also fueled class conflict. The term "welfare state" was now first coined, but by conservatives deriding Weimar welfare as "softness" undermining German national pride and military prowess (Flora & Heidenheimer, 1981).

The SPD demanded the eight-hour day, compulsory industrial arbitration, and unemployment insurance. It pressed for national health insurance and redistributive taxation so that the burden of war reparations would fall on the rich. It claimed that poverty and insecurity were creations of capitalism and not individual moral failings – a major break with the views of the charities. The state had a duty to materially assist its less-fortunate citizens through a range of programs: "maternal advising, welfare programs for infants and small children, school health services, correctional education, juvenile court assistance, social housing programs, and ... monetary relief" (Hong, 1998: 159). Socialist feminists demanded and got gender reforms, too. Divorce was liberalized in the direction of no-fault divorce, mother-advice centers and kindergartens spread, wartime maternity benefits were maintained, and paid maternity leave for industrial workers was introduced (Mouton, 2007). The federal constitution enabled the SPD to comprehensively reform some *Länder* (provinces), notably Prussia, the biggest.

Yet the gulf between socialists and Christian conservatives produced unresolved policy tensions. The old regime was implacably opposed, entrenched in the judiciary, military, heavy industry, and East Elbian landowning elite, backed ideologically by the Churches. Social Christianity, which tended to support welfare policies, although of a different hue, was weakened, not to flower until after 1945. Many conservatives were opposed not just to the republic's socialist tinges but to democracy itself. The right had compromised in 1918–1919 in order to survive when revolution seemed possible. Now that revolutionary options had disappeared, they backtracked, refusing compromise, seeking to exclude the Social Democrats from government, and to downgrade parliament in favor of rule through the emergence powers provided by Article 48 of the Weimar constitution – the clause from which Hitler was later to profit. They were engaged in "class conflict from above" (Mommsen, 1996: 453, 220).

Some on the right favored the parliamentary route, but there were authoritarian nationalist alternatives, such as fascism. The war had been a positive experience for many junior officers and NCOs. The combination of nationalism, classless comradeship, and strong discipline imposed from above promised an alternative route to solving class and political conflict (as we see in the next chapter). Veterans in Germany, Italy, Austria, Romania, and Hungary made fascism into a mass movement. Postwar Germany was riddled with armed paramilitaries seeking to suppress the conflicts of Weimar democracy by force. Greater class struggle in Germany and Austria was, in the end, counterproductive, generating a stronger conservative and fascist backlash that suppressed labor movements and stalled social citizenship.

As in some other countries, union membership declined through the 1920s, from a high point of 48 percent in 1920 to 30 percent in 1931. This was still a significant force, and the Socialist/Communist vote held up at around 30–40 percent. This was as good as working-class movements could get in the interwar period, but could the class alliances of the immediate postwar years hold? That depended on the middle class, peasants, and people from all classes in small towns and villages lying outside of the socialist sphere of influence. They were tempted away from the centrist parties that had thrived immediately after the Republic was established – the Catholic Center Party, liberal and moderate conservative parties, and small special interest parties committed to democracy. Socialists were losing the battle for the center and facing a resurgent right.

Who would pay for every item of welfare was fiercely contested. Reverses were encountered, goals were jettisoned. In 1923, the eight-hour day law of 1918 was watered down, felt on the left to be a major loss (Mommsen, 1996: 220). Conflict between the socialist and communist camps did not help, but the decisive feature of late 1920s politics was the hollowing out of middle-class liberalism. Weitz (2009: 145) says Weimar "lost the middle class in the inflation," as its investments and savings become worthless. The liberals declined, the conservative parties became less committed to democracy. The old regime was determined to abandon democracy, and it had the power to sway small-town rural and middle-class Germany through the politics of deference and nationalism. Even the Catholic Center Party finally abandoned democracy. The socialists and communists remained large, but out of power. There was little chance of a worker-peasant or worker–middle-class alliance. In this context, the Nazis rose up, in a different sense embodying a rightist class alliance, for they were relatively classless, although drawing above all from the public sector and small-town Germany, tired of class conflict and believing it could be solved by violence, by "knocking their heads together." All this led first to authoritarian and then Nazi Fascist rule, as discussed in Chapter 10. It also meant that employers, far more yielding to reforms in order to maintain their power, turned to the Nazis to repress labor.

Nonetheless, in the context of the 1920s, the social citizenship of the Weimar Republic was in the forefront, with universal suffrage, a welfare state, redistributive taxation, a commitment to full employment, and full organizing rights for workers. Perhaps Germany could move further into social democracy, as its "evolutionary socialists" argued. Although powerful forces were stirring on the right, the triumph of Nazism owed much to the Great Depression. The Depression hit Japan less hard, but enough to help conservatives and the military stifle emerging liberals. In these countries, military Keynesianism remedied Depression. Too much class struggle was not good for reform, because it divided the nation, and the fascist or militarist right could generate popular support to seize power.

Under the Nazis, most Weimar family and marriage programs were maintained and even expanded, although within a eugenicist, racial framework that excluded non-Aryans. Additional benefits for women depended on thorough medical examinations to determine their "biological worth" as Aryans, and this deterred many women. No-fault divorces were now permitted in cases of unfruitful or mixed-race marriages. Propaganda exhorting women to have more children were not generally successful, and Himmler's infamous Lebensborn program encouraging men to impregnate women before going to the front was an attempt to remove illegitimacy from public view. As we see in Chapter 10, the Nazis extended social security provisions, and their tax policy was not regressive. They wanted to keep workers happy while they repressed their leaders – a violent version of top-down welfare, heading off the working-class movement at the pass. Yet two-thirds of state expenditure went to the military, a much higher proportion than in any other country except fellow-fascist Italy. Welfare benefits were outweighed by the way the military buildup was financed and then by the war itself, so that the real monetary value of the programs declined. In both Germany and Italy, the labor unions were destroyed, and welfare programs were one way the regime controlled the people – a top-down form of corporatism (Mouton, 2007; Schmitter, 1974). The fact that Nazi social security policies became institutionalized before the war meant that they survived afterward. Then, with the extreme right and left both crushed, they were extended beyond Aryans to all citizens by the long-delayed emergence of a broad compromise (not quite an alliance) between the Social Democrat center-left and the Christian Democrat center-right.

Interwar employers

Like Esping-Andersen, I have emphasized class alliances, especially between the organized working class, farmers, and sections of the middle class. Yet some have additionally seen employers as supporters of welfare states; others emphasize political institutions, especially the electoral system. I first consider employers.

Swenson (2002) analyzes Sweden and the United States in this period, and stresses not the working class but corporate liberals who became *welfare capitalists*, sponsoring welfare programs for their skilled or specialized workforces in order to tie them down with the golden chains of pensions, accident insurance, and other benefits. A second motive was to prevent workers embracing labor unions by granting them benefits normally the staple of union demands. Such employers feared that in more competitive markets, their prices might be undercut by smaller firms paying lower wages and benefits, so, Swenson says, they favored state-run programs paid out of levies raised on all employees and employers. This would have the effect, they reasoned, of driving out smaller competitors who could not afford such benefits. Swenson does not deny class conflict, but says that for welfare programs to be achieved business acquiescence is required, because in a capitalist society their power is too formidable to be ignored. Business confidence again!

Swenson notes that in Sweden, large corporations and employers' associations came to favor this route, striking a deal whereby the Social Democrats and big business together agreed policies to drive out inefficient employers and their workforces and upgrade workers' skills. This Rehn-Meidner Model saw low wages subsidizing inefficient firms. Better to drive them out and encourage efficient firms to grow using well-paid, high-skilled labor, retrained if necessary during periods of unemployment. Swenson's evidence on the United

States is poor. He relies on the three usual suspects – Gerard Swope, Walter Teagle, and Marion Folsom – and on business acceptance of the Social Security Act of 1936 after it had been implemented. As we saw, business – led by corporate liberals – was influential in drafting the act, yet this was because they saw they could no longer resist some such act, and in the drafting process they weakened it. Under pressure, American business went for a minimal welfare state – just as Bismarck and Social Catholicism had done earlier, and as Stalin was doing with the Soviet working class.

Mares (2003) adds some support to Swenson in the cases of France and Germany, where employers' associations dominated by large firms often supported private or public contributory social insurance programs. Those representing small firms usually opposed these. In all of her ten case studies, some business interests supported the schemes. Most schemes were sustained by what she calls "strategic alliances" between capital and labor. They were their second-best choices, and had resulted from the need to compromise. On the other hand, she shows that employers were rarely agenda-setters, for they almost never introduced social-policy proposals. They had also been softened up by shifts in political power that made their initial outright opposition to welfare untenable (2003: 259; cf Korpi, 2006).

Thus, once some bigger employers – generally those with bigger profit margins – recognized the growing power of labor movements in stable democracies, a tipping-point occurred as they scurried to find a compromise that would secure their long-term interests. This was an indirect, top-down effect of class conflict. Employers were not forced to change; instead, those with broader and longer-range vision sought to head off rising class conflict at the pass. By joining in the discussions to bring in basic social security programs, and so mollify the unions, they could ensure that the programs were not very radical or redistributive. It was also at this point that large corporations realized that social security contributions would fall more heavily on smaller firms employing low-wage labor, and this became a secondary motive in their conversion. They yielded more where labor was strong, as it was in Sweden, and less in the United States, where labor was weaker. Where labor had overreached and alienated most of the middle class and peasants, upper classes could turn with relief to suppression, and sometimes fascism. In some stable democracies where labor was politically better entrenched and moderate, employers – like liberals, states, and churches before them – compromised with labor to avert worse consequences. The limits imposed by business confidence can be breached if struggles from below present a specter of far worse consequences for business than just reform. This is not so very different a model after all. It is how Hicks had explained the early Bismarckian and Social Catholic routes to welfare, which were also the indirect effect of class conflict. Indeed, where labor was subsequently to lose much of its power – as in the United States and Britain from the 1970s – employers promptly abandoned compromise. They pressed home their advantage, emasculating unions and intensifying inequality.

Electoral systems

I will also only yield a little ground to those arguing for the causal power of political institutions. By the interwar period, the Anglos already had majoritarian, first-past-the-post electoral systems; almost all the Nordics and Euros had adopted proportional representation by the late 1920s. These differences were then largely "frozen," as Rokkan puts it, into enduring international differences. Because later it became clear that those countries with proportional representation also tended to have greater social-policy spending, I should try to explain the emergence of this difference.

Iversen and Soskice (2009) accept the employer-centered arguments given above, and say that employers seeking high employer-specific skills from workers were prepared not only to do deals with unions but also to support PR systems that would bring center-left coalitions into power. They would bring about reformed employment policies. They produce an ingenious "rational choice" model of employer and union reasoning they say underlies this outcome. However, they produce no actual evidence on employer or union preferences, and I remain skeptical of this rational-actor model. I prefer Lipset and Rokkan's (1967) argument that PR was adopted in countries with politically relevant social cleavages – not just between the classes but between agriculture and industry, between center and periphery, and between ethnic or religious groups. The greater the cleavages, the greater the number of distinct political parties to represent the various interests, and the greater the support for PR systems that allow smaller parties to elect deputies. In the 1920s, paranoia about the rise of socialism also made some major establishment parties dislike a majoritarian system they feared might enshrine socialist rule. Iversen & Soskice (2009) note that in Nordic countries, distinct agrarian parties emerged out of the old estate-based assemblies of the region, and in European countries distinct Catholic parties formed because of their distrust of secular conservative parties. They challenge Rokkan's main argument, however, by claiming that some majoritarian countries, such as the UK and the United States, were just as multiethnic or multireligious as many of the PR countries. Yet as Rokkan noted, British and American ethnic and religious minorities or their rural populations rarely generated their own political parties to challenge the dominant two-party system. Thus, neither main party supported a change to PR.

So why did the Anglos first develop majoritarian elections? These democracies were not like the PR countries, which were a series of separate states each making its own choice of electoral system. The Anglos formed one system, the British system, which had established majoritarian elections centuries ago. These were then exported to Britain's white colonies, including those in North

America, and adopted there in the eighteenth and nineteenth centuries as the normal way of doing political business (except for the odd Australian state) when the colonies became independent. Moreover, in Britain, Australia, and New Zealand the rise of Labour parties was swift. Had the established center party managed to hang onto more of its constituencies for longer, it might have done a deal with Labour to establish PR, but Labour had its secure working-class constituencies and quickly realized that a majoritarian system would favor them. They simply replaced the Liberals as one of the two main parties. We need not explain the Anglos' majoritarian electoral systems in terms of twentieth-century characteristics, class, ethnicity, or religion. The single Anglo system was already set; comparative analysis of states can lead us astray if the cases are not independent.

From the 1950s, PR has been associated with bigger welfare states. It is argued that PR favors center-left alliances, majoritarianism the center-right. Yet this argument does not work across mid-century, because the major reforms came in the United States from 1933, in New Zealand from 1938, from 1943 to 1950 in Australia, and in 1945 to 1950 in Britain, all coming when Labour or the Democrats had won absolute majorities in first-past-the-post elections. Federal political systems are also sometimes said to favor conservatism, as it is supposedly more difficult to effect reforms through them. Yet competition between their different state governments had contributed to America and Germany's educational leads in the first half of the century (Lindert, 2004). In Australia, New South Wales led the way in welfare, providing models for the federal government to follow. Federalism enabled reform in these cases. Thus, I conclude that neither PR versus majoritarian elections nor federal versus more centralized government had much general impact in this period.

Conclusion

A logic of industrialism helped generate the first movements toward social citizenship. It was especially strong in public health provisions throughout this period. Thereafter it continued to influence education. Public health measures and education systems across the advanced countries were less variable than the other aspects of social citizenship. By 1939, more than 90 percent of the population of all the countries considered here had basic literacy in their national language, and they had universal, compulsory schooling for children starting in the age range five to seven and continuing until the age range of fourteen to sixteen. This was the most universal force pushing toward Marshall's notion of the nation-state containing civilized beings. This did not end class and other inequalities inside elementary schools, and higher-level schools were less universal, more class reinforcing. The main cause of such universal expansion was elite consensus over the needs of a modern society, supplemented in the case of primary education with pressure coming from labor, liberal, and feminist reformers plus Protestants or anticlericals, according to the different ideological configurations in each country. Pressures for the later expansion of high schools and universities came more from the middle classes, more variably assisted by lib-labs and feminists. Education was the sphere in which females were attaining most rights, and the profession of teaching was being feminized almost everywhere. Education presented a distinctive version of Marshall's tension between class and citizenship: schools were stratified, yet they socialized children into a common national culture. This tension was beginning to be managed by a meritocratic model of education, although this did not come into full fruition until the 1950s.

Underlying the growth of all social-citizen rights was increasing recognition that the masses were onstage and had to be placated. So I have relied mostly on a power resources model to explain the extent of rights as well as differences emerging between countries, amended to note that power struggles might take either a direct or an indirect form. Direct class struggle intensified – although unevenly – during this period, but was also softened by alliances between workers, farmers, and sections of the middle class, sometimes with collaboration from social Christian movements. This propelled social citizenship onward, but the absence of a broad alliance hindered its propulsion. The indirect effects were that reforms sometimes came from authoritarian states, sometimes from socially conscious churches, and sometimes from corporate liberals, but they were all recognizing the forward march of labor and the strength of the alliances it was building, so they sought to head this off with preemptive reforms. Without strong labor movements and voting, however, these actors did not need to protect themselves through reforms, so rarely pressed for them.

I have also identified other sources of variation. I argued that World War I and the Great Depression had contingently intervened to variably assist or hinder reform. World War I had produced a great ideological ferment. It had taken Russia right out of the Western family of nations and produced the Soviets distinctive blend of advanced social citizenship, but without any genuine civil or political citizenship. World War I and the Depression had produced a similar blend in fascist countries – they had helped consolidate lib-lab and Nordic routes to social citizenship, but they had torn apart any possible common Euro variant. The Depression also destroyed incumbent governments almost everywhere, regardless of whether they were of the right, left, or center, inserting an element of randomness into international differences, especially in continental Europe but also within the Anglo nations. In Britain and Australia, it destroyed incumbent Labour governments and divided their labor movements. It had the opposite effect in the United States and New Zealand, where it unseated conservative governments and brought in lib-lab parties embarking on progressive reforms. In Britain and Australia, the setback was only temporary because of the effects of World War II, but in the United States – the country worst hit (along with Germany) by the Depression – it led to more profound change. As we saw in the last chapter, the U.S. New Deal affected a catch-up with the other Anglophones in its welfare and job-creation programs.

Women's social citizenship rights made less progress in this period. They were hindered almost everywhere by the ideological dominance of the male breadwinner/female caregiver model. France was the main exception. Under rightist pressure, France was turned around to favor women who were caregivers, although in other ways France was not more supportive of women. There were considerable international differences. Lewis (1992) shows that the UK and Ireland encouraged a strong male-breadwinner model of the household, in which women worked part-time. France developed a modified male-breadwinner model, with tax transfers to households with children. The Nordic countries had only a weak male-breadwinner model, with extensive provision of crèches, and separate taxation and maternity rights for women.

Overall, social citizenship was slowly deepening, as legislation was implemented efficiently by states over their territories in response to social struggles that had been turned inward onto those territories. This was a universal tendency of the transnational process of industrialization, but it was expressed nationally, nation by nation. The struggle over rights was implicitly nationalizing the population, increasing common rights and culture, and redistributing among them. The masses were clearly onstage, making substantial material demands, receiving rather lesser benefits. Varied political alliances appeared and reforms of very different scope were introduced. The pattern does not fit well into the three welfare regime types proposed by Esping-Andersen. The Nordic and Anglo countries had become joint leaders in social citizenship; leadership in education was provided by Protestant countries scattered across the three regimes – including the United States. The Anglos were not yet lagging. Yet the difference between Nordic corporatism and Anglo voluntarism was in place, and this came to matter considerably in later decades. As we see in Volume IV, World War II had a major effect, for the sacrifices of nations as either winners, losers, or neutrals acted upon prewar variations to begin the consolidation of social citizenship into the distinct macro-regional types still with us today.

10 The Fascist alternative, 1918–1945

Introduction

This and the next chapter discuss the two main alternatives to capitalist democracy: fascism and communism. They were also responses to the need to bring the masses onstage in the theater of power, but they attempted active mobilization of the masses through their invention of the party-state. The Communists originally saw the party as active mobilization from below, although once in power this reversed into top-down mobilization. Fascism was double-edged before the seizure of power, but equally top-down afterward.

Chapter 6 discussed leftist revolutions in central Europe after the Great War. When they failed, rightist counterrevolutions imposed stronger and more despotic states mobilizing an "organic" nation, influenced by fascism. The fascist-inflected state combined *infrastructural power* – the capacity of the state to enforce policies through infrastructures penetrating its territories – and *despotic power* – the ability of state elites to make their own arbitrary decisions. The state was militaristic, and fascism was in a way the culmination of the long tradition of European imperial militarism. The nation was supposedly without internal divisions, organic or integral, intolerant of political, ethnic, and religious diversity; this was a reaction against globalization, an erection of stronger bars around state cages. Many rightists saw mass society and parliamentary democracy as widening social divisions, deepening political conflict, and producing chaos and violence. Carl Schmitt said the parties had become like mass armies confronting each other on the battlefield. Corruption was deemed endemic in liberal politics; instead, a despotic state would impose order, unity, and morality. Fascism was the most extreme form of these authoritarian nation-statisms, as I explained in my book *Fascists* (2004). I refer the reader there for empirical and bibliographic detail on fascism. This chapter will generalize, refer to some more recent literature, and refine some of the arguments I made in the book.

Fascism presupposed a prior period of state and nation strengthening. European militarism had increased the state's fiscal and military bureaucracies; in response, the propertied classes had demanded representative government. As rulers and people increased their interactions, states acquired more civilian functions, and their infrastructures – roads, railways, postal service, education – increased the nationalization of territories and populations. Nationalism blended with democratization. Now it was believed the whole people must rule, because it shared a common heritage and culture. This undermined the three multiethnic Empires – Habsburg, Romanov, and Ottoman – where conflicts between imperial rulers and locals were transformed into conflicts between ethnic or religious communities. Local disprivileged elites mobilized their community against the imperial dynasty. Croats, Slovenes, and others contested Turkish or Serb domination, Romanians contested Hungarian; Slovaks resented local Czech dominance, and almost everyone resented the dominant Germans, Russians, and Turks who then responded with their own nationalisms. As cosmopolitans, Jews were considered antinational by all. The state's role was not to institutionalize conflict between interests, as in liberal or social democracy, for it was thought that a single party or movement could rule and represent the whole people – just as Marxists did. Class conflict and sectional interests were to be transcended.

Before 1914, nationalists had urged states to mobilize the nation and use force to defeat the corrosive forces of liberalism and socialism. Most of the ideas of fascism were already circulating, exciting some intellectuals, although not yet creating mass movements. They were held in check by old regimes that distrusted mass mobilization and hoped to control the masses through conservative, client-state parties. State functions were widening, but most conservatives saw the state as merely the preserver of order and the aggrandizer of territory. As on the left, the state was not yet the bearer of a moral project.

Had Europe remained at peace, state expansion would have slowly continued. Enfranchising workers and women would increase social welfare programs, and mildly statist late-development economics would have prospered on the semi-periphery. Some countries had already introduced restrictions of movements across borders, but starting in 1918 passports ensuring state control of international movement were an institutionalized feature of travel almost everywhere. As Torpey (2000) concludes, governments increasingly used national documents, including passports, as a legal device to "embrace" individuals under their control and to exclude aliens. Passports became a crucial way of nationalizing and caging their citizens.

The Great War intervened, militarizing the nation-state and giving it new functions. Even noncombatant states were compelled by blockades to introduce rationing and active labor-market policies. Although many wartime institutions were dismantled afterward, postwar governments were now expected to alleviate unemployment and housing shortages. Social was to be added to political citizenship. More ambitious schemes of social reconstruction and economic development circulated. On the left, socialists vanquished their anarcho-syndicalist rivals (except in Spain) and began to see revolution or reform as accomplished through state action. In Russia, war and civil war unexpectedly made the Bolsheviks ardent statists. Elsewhere, liberalism mutated into lib-lab or social democracy, and moderate statism crept forward.

The democracies won the war and enforced territorial losses on Germany and Russia; the Habsburg and Ottoman Empires disappeared. The peace treaties replaced them with new nation-states so that in late 1920 all but one of Europe's twenty-eight states had constitutions enshrining parliamentary elections, competing political parties, and guarantees for minorities. Most suffrages excluded women, some excluded many men, some executives had powers rivaling legislatures, and political practices were often at odds with constitutional norms. However, democracy seemed the coming ideal. The omens for tolerant nationalism were not so good. In practice, the treaties turned the states over to a single dominant ethnicity, and millions of refugees from ethnic or religious minority populations were fleeing to their national "homelands."

Between 1920 and 1945, democracy retreated, battered by despots of the right, in what Huntington (1991) called the first "counter-wave" against democracy. Northwestern Europe – Scandinavia, the Netherlands, Belgium, France, Britain, and Ireland – deepened their representative forms of government; yet by 1938, fifteen of Europe's twenty-seven governments were rightist dictatorships, most claiming to embody a single organic nation. In other continents, the four majority-white former British colonies – the United States, Canada, Australia, and New Zealand – had democracies for whites. South Africa and Rhodesia also had parliamentary institutions for their white minorities. The two major Asian states – Japan and China – became authoritarian; in Latin America, only Uruguay, Colombia, and Costa Rica stayed consistently democratic, with fluctuations elsewhere. So the interwar period saw two global blocs, one liberal democratic the other despotic. Both main blocs sought infrastructurally stronger states; only one also sought greater despotic powers. Among its ranks emerged fascism.

Fascists only embraced more fervently than anyone else the central political icon of our time – the nation-state – a mild form of which now dominates the world. Late development was already leading to a slightly more active role in economic development. State socialism was to take this to extremes in Russia. In an age of continuing imperialism, fascism also brought a form of late development in political and military power relations. It also brought – or intended to bring – a retreat of globalization, as it erected greater national barriers around all the sources of social power – except for ideology, for fascist ideas spread around the world, making for the same contrary tendencies contained in socialism.

Fascism defined

Fascist beliefs must not be dismissed as crazy, contradictory, or vague. Fascists offered plausible solutions to modern problems, and got mass electoral support and intense commitment from militants. Few fascists were sadists or psychopaths, or people with a "rag-bag" of half-understood dogmas and slogans flitting through their heads, as some suggest (Paxton, 2004: 16–17) – or no more so than the rest of us. Fascism was a movement of high ideals, able to persuade a substantial part of two generations of young people that it could bring about a better social order. It might appear to be a weaker form of secular salvationism than Marxism, as its theory of history was less about achieving an eventual utopia than in endorsing continuous struggle between the strong and the weak, nation and nation, race and race. This was in a sense a focus on means rather than ultimate ends, yet it was through the struggle that the "New Man" would be created, and he was the utopian ideal. Both fascists and Marxists then perpetrated great evil, not accidentally or as the resurgence of the primitive, but as willed, "modern" behavior. When confronted by difficulties, they did not compromise with their enemies but instead radicalized, engaged in a kind of continuous revolution. The difference between them was that Marxists were perverting their ideals, while massive violence was a necessary and virtuous part of the creation of the fascist New Man.

There are two main schools of interpretation of fascism. An "idealist nationalist school" focuses on fascists' nationalist beliefs. It sees fascism as a "political religion" embodying a "mythic core of national regeneration" (Gentile, 1990: Griffin, 2002). This does capture the secular salvationism I have identified, but it tends to be a descriptive approach, weak on explaining why such a mythic core should arise in the 1920s. In contrast, a "materialist school" focuses on fascism's class base, said to be petit bourgeois or bourgeois, and on fascism's role in saving capitalism from the left when in difficulties in the 1920s and early 1930s (Hobsbawm, 1994; Lipset, 1963; Poulantzas, 1974; Renton, 2000; Carsten, 1980). They do offer a clear causal explanation of the rise of fascism, but it is an overly simple one. Barrington Moore (1967) offered a more complex, class-centered-plus-the-state explanation, and others provide nuanced multifactor theories attuned to the subtle differences between the movements in different countries (Payne, 1995; Paxton, 2004). I follow them, at the same time seeking a more theoretically integrated explanation in terms of the four sources of social power – ideological, economic, military, and political – which all played important roles in the rise and fall of fascism.

I define *fascism* as the pursuit of a transcendent and cleansing nation-statism through militarism[1]. This definition contains four main elements.

(1) *Cleansing nationalism.* Ideologically, fascists favored an organic nation. Aliens within and outside subverted the unity and purity of the nation and had to be purged. Racial fascism, like Nazism, was the extreme form, applying racial conflicts hitherto used by Europeans only within their overseas empires to within Europe and even within the individual nation. Its consequence was terrible: the physical removal of other races, and indeed others with supposed genetic defects, from the nation. This was a very aggressive

[1] Note that since *Fascists* I have changed the "paramilitary" component into a "military" one in order for the category to cover both paramilitarism and aggressive war.

form of internal nationalism in which racism originally devised to explain differences between major macro-regions of the world became turned inward within Europe and Germany itself.

(2) *Statism*. Politically, fascists saw state power as "the bearer of a moral project," capable of achieving economic, social, and moral development through fascist elites and corporatism. This was the top-down side of fascism; order would be enforced from above. Because the nation is organic, its state must be despotic, with a singular, cohesive will expressed by a party elite adhering to the "leadership principle," and ultimately obeying a single leader. This was in fact a "single party state," such as Communist regimes. Scholars used to emphasize fascist totalitarianism. Today, it is generally recognized that corporatist, syndicalist, and bureaucratic elements were undercut by both fascists' wilder radicalism and the need to compromise with other powerful actors, such as churches and capitalists. So fascism was more totalitarian in its goals than in its actual rule. Fascism welded together the four power sources, creating a single party state wielding formidable infrastructural and despotic powers over the people.

(3) *Transcendence*. The combination of (1) and (2) is a nation-statism, which could transcend social conflict. Fascists rejected conservative notions that traditional social order is harmonious; they rejected liberal and social democratic notions that the conflict of interest groups is normal to society; and they rejected socialist notions that harmony could be reached by overthrowing capitalism. Fascists attacked both capital and labor. They said they would "knock both their heads together" and subordinate them to the nation. Private interests would be subordinated to national interest, planning and social welfare would be imposed from above, and interest groups would be brought inside the state in syndicalist or corporatist institutions.

Transcendence was revolutionary in intent, seeking transformation of all the sources of social power. Fascists, just like the Bolsheviks, were highly ideological, driven by value rationality, but in order to seize and hold power, fascists were opportunists, tilting toward capitalism and making deals with old regimes. Fascists ultimately lacked interest in capitalism and class. Nation and state comprised their center of gravity, not class. They tended to attack not capitalism per se but finance, foreign or Jewish capitalism. In Romania and Hungary, where these forms of capitalism dominated, fascism was anticapitalist and pro-proletarian. Nonetheless, there was always conflict within fascist movements between opportunists and radical ideologists remaining committed to transcendence. The radicals lost out on matters of class, but in the process radicalism was deflected away from class onto ethnic cleansing and the complete political subordination of the individual to the regime. "All else pales before that radical transformation in the relation of citizens to public power," says Paxton (2004: 142). In reality, fascism deflected transcendence from class to nation and state.

(4) *Militarism*. Military power dominated fascist organization. Before their seizure of power, this was expressed through "paramilitaries" welling up from below – knocking heads together, they called it. This was the bottom-up aspect of fascist mobilization, the mass party rising up to overthrow elites. It did so violently. No fascist movement was simply a political party – it was always uniformed, marching, armed, and violent. Paramilitarism caged fascists as an army does soldiers. It also won the respect of many neutrals, because fascist violence could seemingly end class conflict. Paramilitarism was not strong enough to overcome regular armies. Only when fascists subverted armies by

attracting soldiers to their cause could they seize power. Thereafter they pursued militaristic domestic and foreign policies, leading them into devastating wars that soon proved their hubris. As we have seen, imperialism had long been normal, and those seeking late empires in the twentieth century (except for the United States) did it with more nationalism and militarism than earlier empires had done. However, their highly aggressive nationalism was to prove their undoing.

The combination of these four elements made fascists revolutionaries of the right, although they were focused more on the nation-state and transforming and expanding ideological, military, and political power relations than on economic relations. Fascists sought to liberate themselves from the corrosive effect of transnational capitalism, and of globalization more generally, with policies of national economic autarchy. Yet they granted a degree of autonomy to capitalists and major churches, provided they did not contest overall command by the party state. These were the major exceptions to fascism's totalitarian aspirations. There were variations between countries, of course. Italian fascism had more interest in statism, and developed corporatist and syndicalist institutions; Nazis focused more on racist nationalism. Some think this precludes a generic definition of fascism, although I do not. I cover here the five main fascist movements in Europe – Italy, Germany, Austria, Hungary, and Romania. Yet the influence of fascism was broader. Milder authoritarian regimes stole fascist ideas and practices; during World War II, half a dozen other European nationalist movements flirted with fascism and joined the Axis Powers. Fascism also influenced countries across the Middle East, Asia, and Latin America. It erected high national barriers against globalization, but its diffusion was in fact global. Later chapters examine Chinese and Japanese fascist movements. Fascism did not long endure; in 1945, it collapsed almost everywhere. In the meantime, it had changed the world.

The rise of fascism

(1) Italy. Italian fascism emerged from conflicts over Italy's participation in World War I. An alliance between nationalists and pro-war socialists (like Mussolini himself) produced the first few hundred fascists. As the war ended, this was enlarged into a paramilitary force with an influx of military veterans. The movement preached nationalism and statism and sought paramilitary violence to end Italy's disunity. There was little ethnic sense of the nation, however, and cleansing was directed only against political not ethnic enemies. The rapid transition to full male suffrage in Italy was generating turbulent mass movements, both socialist and Catholic *popolari* (populists), and Italy's old regime was divided. The Catholic Church saw the secular state as its enemy; liberal and conservative elites lacked popular roots and could not effectively mobilize nationalism because they had maneuvered Italy into a reckless, unpopular war. Riley (2010: chap. 2) notes that in the prewar period, elites (and also the growing socialist party) were highly localized. Giolitti liberalism that survived through the war into the brief period of democracy was really only half-democratic. Giolitti ruled through northern-based parliamentary parties and southern-based clientelism. Liberal Italy was ripe for the taking.

The fascist surge into power came early, and amid postwar turbulence had a more direct class component than fascism in other countries. Some of the upper classes turned to fascists to rescue them from lower-class insurgency. This was so of Po Valley landowners assailed by socialist and popolari unions, backed by the local military and businessmen oriented to agriculture. Elsewhere, the class bias in fascist membership was toward the middle and especially the lower middle classes. Most industrialists and bankers preferred the semi-authoritarian traditional parties to protect their interests. Fascism also attracted those with stronger links to nationalism or the state, such as the military, police, and civil servants or those from northeastern "threatened" border regions, all of whom were overrepresented. Paramilitary violence appealed to the military-cum-macho values of many demobilized young men. The defection of Roman elites from democracy made the seizure of power possible. The fascist "March on Rome" in 1922 was not opposed by the state or the army, and thereafter elites came to terms with Mussolini's regime. Landowners, capitalists, the army, and the Church were incapable of developing their own conservative authoritarianism, so some were driven to dealing with the fascists – and fascists with them. This was pragmatic compromise, not continuous revolution.

All of this involved thousands not millions of people – the paramilitary striking power of thousands and the betrayal of democracy by elites. The socialists and popolari had the numbers and votes to oppose the fascists, but they did not have equal paramilitary force, national presence, or the desire to construct center-left alliances. Most Italians did not much mind the seizure of power, but they were irrelevant to it. So the three main factors in fascist triumph were war-induced paramilitarism, class struggle in which some of the possessing classes turned to fascism, and a divided state, both of whose halves – old regime and democratic – were quite fragmented.

(2) Germany. Germany was the most important country to go fascist. The Nazis were the largest fascist movement, with the largest paramilitaries and the largest vote. In 1932, adding together the large fascist vote of 37 percent and the votes of their conservative authoritarian allies yielded a majority, and the Nazis got control of the state the following year by mostly legal methods. Over the next two years, they imposed a Nazi dictatorship, and they did not significantly compromise with other power holders. Theirs was continuous revolution in pursuit of their utopian goals.

We know much about Nazism's main constituencies of support. There was no correlation between class and Nazi membership or voting – unlike Italian fascism. Although the Nazi Party underrepresented workers, the Sturmabteilung

(SA) paramilitary overrepresented them, as did the Hitler Youth. Although the Nazis did not appeal much to urban-industrial working-class communities, they were supported by workers living and working elsewhere. They were the party most able to project themselves as classless. Their spokespeople ranged from Prussian princes to railway clerks, retired generals to students and workers, speaking in varied accents – a display of classlessness epitomized by Hitler, the little corporal with an Austrian accent. As in Italy, rural classes moved from underrepresentation to overrepresentation. Many peasant farmers (although few agricultural laborers) became Nazis, and the Nazis did better in rural and small-town settings than in big cities. As in Italy, the educated nation-statist bourgeoisie was overrepresented, including professions such as civil servants, teachers, architects, foresters, and veterinarians. Public-sector manual workers were also well represented, partly because many were former soldiers. These groups were responsive to statist and *völkisch* nationalist Nazi themes. The business classes were underrepresented, but because most of them supported conservative authoritarians, they were implicated in the maneuverings that brought the Nazis to power. The influx of educated young people made party members and leaders younger than those of other parties, and they claimed to represent the new, young Germany. Before the Nazi seizure of power, Catholics were very underrepresented as members and voters. In July 1932, 38 percent of Protestants voted for the Nazis, but only 16 percent of Catholics did. This was bigger than any class differences.

Nazis were neither social marginals nor economic losers. Their careers rarely suggest failure. Socially, they were at the heart of civil society, more active in voluntary associations than the adherents of any other party. This was a strong but uncivil society. As in Italy, fascists were not drawn from the main arenas of modern class struggle – few were businessmen, classic petty bourgeoisie, private-sector managers, or urban-industrial workers. Their membership and electoral support came from people who felt themselves outsiders to class conflict, tired of seeing it rend Germany apart, responding to the Nazi claim to transcendence.

By the time of the coup in 1933, the Nazis had more than 1 million members. They were more active than members of other movements: local leaders could call out militants to march, demonstrate, pack halls, and brawl. Members left their jobs and gave generously of their time and energy. Conservative and liberal parties were dominated by notables; they did not march or demonstrate. Their meetings were polite, showing deference to the platform and the high social status of the speakers. If their meetings were disrupted by determined hecklers or pushing and punching, they could not call on their supporters for a determined collective response. They were overwhelmed by the greater enthusiasm and violence of the Nazis. Even the socialists and communists, who had invented the notion of militant comradeship, were worsted. SA troopers were young, mostly working class, often single, living together in barracks, their subsistence paid for out of party funds. Like the Italian *squadristi*, they were caged into a life of disciplined comradeship, drinking together, and enjoying intermittent violence. SA units went marching into socialist and communist stronghold areas in order to provoke attacks on them. The brawls were intended to "toughen by battle" their own members, intimidate opponents, and show that the "Marxist threat" was responsible for the violence (Merkl, 1980: 373). Nazi propaganda and a biased press then transmitted this claim to millions who had never directly witnessed the violence. They promised once in power to provide a state committed to order.

Again, the condition of the old regime was important. War defeat had unseated the monarchy and its loyal conservative parties, and it had shrunk the armed forces. The old regime could no longer rule. As democracy faltered from 1930, conservative authoritarians took over, but lacked popular support. From the early years, big business had opposed Weimar democracy, but had supported conservative authoritarians. Business saw that Nazis were ferociously anticommunist and favored the leadership principle in industry. Ultimately, the Nazis would uphold their authority rather than that of workers. Nonetheless, Hitler was helped into power not by business but by the old regime – the military, civil service, judiciary, and conservative political parties that by 1932 had embraced authoritarian rule. Lacking mass mobilization themselves, they needed the Nazis, and foolishly believed they could control them.

The Nazis thrived on the failure of the other parties who governed with little success through the Depression. The middle class was alienated by inflation, the working class by unemployment, falling wages, and longer working hours (Weitz, 2009: 145). The Nazis also made positive appeals to the voters. Nazi classlessness made claims to transcendence plausible, and as Brustein (1996) shows, its economic program brought many votes. It was detailed, plausible, mainly borrowed from German Keynesians, yet articulated in terms of simple slogans of national unity that required putting all Germans to work. The Nazis also thrived on geopolitical revisionism, restoration of the lost territories. A Great Power resenting its loss of territories, sucked into the central European tensions of Germanic, Jewish, and Slav peoples, Germany had refugees, threatened borders, and ethnic "enemies" at home and abroad. In my analysis of the backgrounds of Nazi perpetrators of genocide, I found that former refugees from the lost territories and adjacent border areas were overrepresented (Mann, 2005: 223–8). At election times, the Nazis played down their anti-Semitism, and anti-Semitism was rarely given by Nazis as a reason for having joined the party. However, a more general organic nationalism had broad appeal. This was sufficiently popular to bring the Nazis to the brink of power. Their own paramilitarism and the complicity of the old regime then enabled them to seize power. Class figures rather less as a direct cause than it did in Italy.

(3) Austria. Two distinct fascist movements emerged in the core of the former Habsburg Empire: Austro-Fascism and Austrian Nazism. Both emerged out of postwar paramilitaries, demanding the restoration of lost territories and exploiting the intensity of Austrian antipathy toward Slavs and Jews. Austro-Fascism was based more in the old regime, top-down and pro-capitalist. It strengthened amid political stalemate between the two big parties – the Social Christians and the Socialist Party. The political crisis was intensified by the Great Depression. Nazism was the more cross-class movement. The rise of Hitler next door in Germany was the tipping-point, as it undermined the appeal of both Austro-Fascism and Socialism and gave the prize to the local Nazis. Both sets of paramilitaries launched coups, and both succeeded with the help of the armies of, respectively, Austria and Germany, in the Anschluss of 1938.

(4) Hungary and Romania. These two countries had fought on opposite sides in the Great War; Hungary was a big loser, Romania a victor. The ensuing Civil War in Hungary resulted in the crushing of the left, allowing the old regime to reemerge, embittered and radicalized. Rule was by a dual state composed of the traditional executive and bureaucracy and a parliament dominated by the gentry. Yet the old regime now contained a younger generation of radical rightists, making revisionist demands for the return of lost territories and voicing racism and anti-Semitism. Romania differed; its landed gentry was dispossessed, but this and war victory gave added legitimacy to the monarch, bureaucracy, and army.

Both old regimes survived, radicalized. Large fascist movements only emerged in the mid-1930s, well after the threat from the left had subsided. Thus, fascists had no capitalist bias; indeed, they were rather proletarian in their composition, forming their own labor unions. Romanian fascism blurred over into a milder corporatism, as in the economic theorist Manoilescu's strategy for late development. The Romanian Legion was led by military veterans, students, the sons of priests, civil servants, and teachers, who led many peasants and workers. There was a strong relationship between the Legion and the Romanian Orthodox Church, and a less strong one between the Arrow Cross and the Hungarian Catholic Church. In both cases, paramilitarism was used as both an electoral mobilizing machine and a way to repress rivals. The Legion perpetrated one unsuccessful coup. An unequal dance of death ensued, in which military triumphed over paramilitary power, and radicalizing conservative authoritarians in control of the state triumphed over fascists. Only the chaos of the last war years allowed the fascists a brief, doomed victory.

So fascists were distinctive; they were not simply a vehicle for class interests. They were nobody's dupes, and their movement was more bottom-up than other authoritarians. Apart from Italy, where they came quickly into power, electioneering was also important, and fascists were pioneers in techniques of mobilizing militants and manipulating voters. Unlike conservative authoritarians, fascists could not use the power of the state to fix elections (until after they seized power). Ironically, although fascists did not believe in democracy, it was vital to their success. The masses were to be brought onstage and allowed to wreak some havoc there, but their lines were to be scripted by a fascist elite.

The first paramilitary cohort, without whom fascism would not have gotten off the ground, were mainly young military veterans. Then came two waves of young recruits, with cadets, students, athletes, and street hooligans overrepresented. Fascism's main strength was its attraction to young people of all classes, willing to give more of their time and energy than activists in any other political movement. The Nazis won the German student elections each year from 1930 onward – they won most converts among the best educated. Fascism also recruited disproportionately among refugees, threatened border regions, state employees (including armed forces), state-owned or state-protected industries, and churches that saw themselves as "the soul of the nation" or "the morality of the state" – such as Romanian Orthodoxy or German Protestantism, but not German Catholicism. It is not surprising that nation-statism should appeal most to those with a close structural relationship to the nation or state, or that its militarism should appeal most among veterans and young men.

Fascism's relationship to class varied greatly. Only in Romania did it attract the organized working class. It usually attracted those on the margins of class conflict, persons of all classes in smaller or newer industries, agriculture, and the service sector. These were looking at organized class conflict from the outside, crying "A plague on both your houses," impressed by fascist claims to transcend class. The level of threat posed by each working-class movement was not correlated with fascist strength. The threat may have seemed substantial (although it had already peaked) in Italy; it was more apparent than real in Austria and Germany, which had large but preponderantly moderate labor movements; Romania and Hungary had a tiny left by the time fascism loomed, and fascism provided their main labor movements. Class was less central to fascism than nation-statism. Fascists transmuted the values of citizen warfare into paramilitarism and aggressive nationalism, offering an alternative modernity and renewing Romanticism by emphasizing sentiments, emotions, and the unconscious. They saw that modern organizations such as crowds, mass movements, total war, and the mass media might encourage emotions as much as reason. This fusion often gave their propaganda an edge, tugging at the emotions as much as reason, but it could only work in conditions of crises where institutionalized ideologies and remedies could not work. Then people might turn to a new secular salvationism.

Fascist movements emerged from below, not through electoral majorities but through activist minorities providing popular pressure, a movement neither of elites nor of the millions, but of the thousands. We cannot explain fascism in terms of a supposed weakness of civil society or mass society vis-á-vis the state. Hagtvet (1980) showed that Weimar Germany contained a very vibrant civil society (so, too, did Austria); Koshar (1986) showed Nazis were more likely to belong to voluntary associations than the adherents of other movements. Riley

(2005, 2010) showed that the density of civil-society associations in North-Central Italy, especially in rural areas, gave organizational resources to the fascist movement. He says that the absence of such associational resources in Spain helps explain why the Franco regime there was merely a top-down corporate dictatorship, despite similarities between the two countries. All this should not be surprising. Sociologists studying new social movements today emphasize that they almost invariably use existing social networks and associations in order to grow (see McAdam et al., 1996). Let us now examine the continental context of fascist success.

The two Europes

There was a geographical basis to fascism's rise in interwar Europe. The map I gave in *Fascists (*2004: 38) revealed a clear geographic fracture: almost all the regimes of East, central, and Southern Europe went despotic; those of Northwestern Europe remained liberal democratic. There were two Europes. In the first one – except for Czechoslovakia (which in any case curtailed the rights of its German and Slovak minorities) – liberal democracy comprised a single bloc of eleven Northwestern countries: Finland, Sweden, Norway, Denmark, Iceland, Ireland, Britain, the Netherlands, Belgium, Switzerland, and France. This bloc comprised three socio-cultural zones: Nordic, Anglophone, and Low Country, linked through a sea-trading economy and political and ideological similarities. They had embraced constitutional rule well before 1900. The Anglos spoke English; the Nordic countries (except for Finland) spoke mutually intelligible dialects of the same language group. Apart from Ireland, which was in any case part of the UK until 1922, they had rather depoliticized religions. The Northwest shared a great deal.

The despotic family formed a second Europe, a geographic bloc in the center, east, and south of the continent. Apart from most of Germany, Estonia, and Latvia, they comprised most of the Catholic countries and all the Eastern Orthodox countries in Europe. They comprised all the European countries except for Ireland, which retained strong church-state links. They contained two distinct socio-cultural zones, Latin/Mediterranean and Slav/East and Central European. Their languages were more diverse, and they were not a trading bloc. The center and east also contained a large number of Jews, the most cosmopolitan people in Europe (along with gypsies), and therefore antithetical to organic nationalists. Already subjected to pogroms by Russian Slavophiles before the war, Jews suffered more in Poland after the war.

Between the two Europes lay a "frontier zone," centered on France and Germany. These two countries might have gone the other way, producing a more despotic France and a parliamentary Germany. The main prewar proto-fascist theorists (Maurras, Barrès, Sorel) were French, and in the later interwar period, French quasi-fascist movements loomed large. Had the election due in

1940 been held, the quasi-fascist Parti Social Français (PSF) might have won more than 100 parliamentary seats (Soucy, 1992). Later, the Vichy collaborating regime had much domestic support. The frontier zone also contained Spain, which saw the most evenly balanced and violent interwar struggle between democracy and despotism. Also along the frontier zone, somewhat imperfect democracies existed in Finland, Czechoslovakia, and in Austria before 1934.

Northwestern despotic movements became moderately popular in countries adjacent to the frontier, as in Czechoslovakia, Belgium, and Finland, although they were not nearly as popular as those over the border in the second Europe. Despotic and fascist movements situated further northwest received less than 2 percent of the votes in elections. The decisive factor in the first Europe was that conservatives resisted despotic rightists, social democrats resisted revolutionaries, and both compromised their conflicts through democratic institutions, which thus deepened, as we saw in Chapter 9. Nondemocratic movements in Austrian, German, and Spanish free elections got 35–40 percent of the votes; across the half-free elections of Eastern Europe they won convincingly. Had fascists been freer to organize there, they would have garnered more votes than the 20 percent or so that they did in Hungary and Romania. Despotic movements manipulated executive powers during elections, but they had much more appeal than in the Northwest. There were two Europes, one firmly liberal democratic the other attracted by more despotic visions – with an oscillating frontier zone between them.

Historical sociologists have tried to explain why two very different regimes dominated the twentieth century. Barrington Moore (1967) analyzed the conditions making for democracy or authoritarianism in the modern world, focusing on the relations between alliances linking the main social classes – aristocracy, bourgeoisie, and peasantry – and an "agrarian bureaucratic state" (the monarch, court, and royal officials). Although from time to time he brought militarism and wars into the explanation, he did not theorize them – or religious movements, either. The military shortcoming was then remedied by Tilly, Downing, and myself; Ertman, Gorsky, and others have added further refinements. Moore also overstrained his argument in purporting to explain the rise of Russian Communism, German Fascism, and Japanese militarism in terms of the same power configurations. I already noted the inadequacies of this in explaining the emergence of communism in Russia in Chapter 6. Here I make similar points in relation to fascism. Although I will argue that the existence of an authoritarian or semi-authoritarian state was a necessary condition of the rise of fascism, it was by no means the only one. As in Russia, World War I was equally responsible, and in both cases ideological power relations were a necessary part in explaining how the two sets of revolutionaries ruled, once in power. Barrington Moore strained toward timelessness in his explanation, but each phase of historical development adds its own causal paths, as we shall now see once again.

Explanation: Four crises in the two Europes

The authoritarian surge in the second Europe was a response to a cascade of economic, military, political, and ideological crises brought on by World War I, piling on top of each other, interacting with prior power structures. Prewar fascists comprised only cliques of officers and intellectuals. Without the war, there would have been no broad authoritarian surge, and fascism would have been a footnote in world history, Hitler would have lived and died in obscurity, and there would have been no Holocaust and probably no Second World War.

(1) *Economic* crisis came in recessions, which came at War's end and then again as the Great Depression struck in 1929. In between came lesser inflation crises; interwar economies were never very buoyant. As governments were now expected to wield economic policies to ameliorate hardship, weakening economies delegitimated governments and discredited existing political parties (Weitz, 2009). Then came the Nazis – with the passive support of millions of voters. Obviously, had there been a period of boom after this war comparable to the one that followed World War II, there would have been no significant fascism. These serious economic difficulties were a necessary cause of fascist success.

However, economic difficulties were not a sufficient cause. All countries suffered economically, and most did not turn to fascism. The Great Depression bit deepest in the United States and Canada, and they stayed democratic. These two were followed in suffering by despotic Austria and Poland, but then came democratic Czechoslovakia and Ireland before we get to Germany (and Australia). Overall, there was no relationship between the depth of the Depression and despotic outcomes. The Depression caused the collapse of whatever government was in power, whether of the right or left (as we saw in Chapter 8). Nor did rightist coups occur more frequently during economic crisis. They came throughout the interwar period, amid relatively good times as well as bad. Most coups occurred in the more backward countries, but probably that was because the most developed countries (except for Germany) had already generated liberal democracy before World War I. In any case, fascism was not confined to backward countries. The countries with the biggest fascist movements were at all levels of economic development – from advanced Germany, through Austria, Italy, and Hungary, to backward Romania. Economic crises weakened all governments of the period, but they cannot directly explain fascism.

Did the capitalist class call in fascists to protect its relations of economic production? Paxton (2004: 28–32, 49–52) says that the Bolsheviks had made conservative elites in Italy and Germany so fearful of Communism that anything – even Fascism – seemed preferable. Yet was there a general threat to capitalist property relations across Europe? The Bolshevik Revolution was followed by failed revolutions in Austria, Germany, Hungary, Italy, and Spain, and the Soviet Union remained isolated. The revolutionary left was defeated in Europe by 1922. In Japan, a leftist surge (liberal more than socialist) had petered out in the late 1920s; in China, General Chiang Kai-shek defeated the Communists in Shanghai in 1927. In fact, almost all rightist surges occurred after serious revolutionary threat from below had died away. Capitalism did not really need protecting from the left. It could look after itself.

True, profits were squeezed by center-left governments and the Great Depression. Perhaps capitalists used rightist coups to force labor to bear more of the costs. Yet Northwestern political elites were devising better strategies of profit maximization. Corporate liberalism in the American New Deal and Social Democratic compromise in Scandinavia protected capitalist profit and allowed more rights to labor. Liberal democracy, not authoritarian rightism, was the most rational strategy for increasing capitalist profits. Keynes was demonstrating at this time that capitalism could be saved by boosting consumption and workers rights.

So why did some upper classes reach for the despotic or fascist gun when neither property nor profits were much threatened? They had been frightened in the insurrectionary period after 1917. Why not exploit the left's present weakness to crush it altogether? It is difficult today, when capitalism has been seemingly triumphant, to appreciate that in this problematic period many feared capitalism was failing. The left might not be strong enough to affect a revolution, but it might do enough to produce disorder. The Soviet Union was industrializing and sending out Comintern agents across the world. Fear can rationally arise from a threat that is low in probability but high in damage if it ever did materialize. "Better safe than sorry," upper classes reasoned. Moreover, capitalism is based on greed. If more immediate profit can be extracted at the expense of wages, capitalists seek this route if they think they can get away with it. I argued in the last chapter that welfare capitalists needing to retain skilled or experienced workers offered the golden chains of higher wages and health and pension benefits only when unions reached a certain level of strength. When unions are weak, employers are likely to seek to crush them altogether. Any labor militant in the United States today can tell us that!

Yet most of the rich turning to the gun were not industrial capitalists but agrarian landlords, officer corps, and church hierarchies – the old regime. Land reform was being pressed across Europe, and landlords feared their ability to control states might not last much longer. Most were rentiers deriving profit from the least modern parts of the economy, and profits were declining due to global overproduction. They still controlled officer corps and ministries of the interior, so why not launch a coup? Officer corps and churches reasoned similarly. The military perceived that its caste autonomy and budgets were threatened by democratic civilian control. Churches feared secularizing liberals and socialists who were separating church and state, threatening church property, and contesting their control over education and marriage – and they could mobilize the community of the faithful, especially in rural areas.

Democracy was betrayed above all by the old regime. Paxton says fascists made a "historic compromise" with old regimes who believed they could control these rude provincials. Conservatives "normalized" fascists by inviting them to share power: "At each fork in the road, they choose the antisocialist solution," he says. In 1922, General Armando Diaz advised King Victor Emmanuel III not to deploy the army against Mussolini's March on Rome, as it might be unreliable. The king, however, went much further, making Mussolini prime minister! In 1933, the aristocrat Franz Von Papen made Hitler chancellor because he thought he could control him. Paxton continues, "No insurrectionary coup against an established state has ever so far brought fascists to power. Authoritarian dictatorships have several times crushed such attempts," and he instances Romania. So, he concludes, the behavior of upper-class accomplices is the crucial element in explaining fascists' rise to power (2004: 87–97). This is the main class part of the explanation, and again, it is a necessary although not sufficient part of the explanation.

(2) *Military* crisis. The war brought defeat and territorial losses for some and demobilization, dislocation, and unstable geopolitics for all. Neutrals and combatant countries experiencing no territorial changes experienced the least dislocation, and this included most of the countries of the Northwest. The military crisis was more severe in the second Europe, because this contained the defeated powers. It endured longer where revisionists continued to challenge the peace treaties, demanding the restoration of their lost territories. Embittered refugees and nationalists kept fighting for restoration in Austria, Germany, and Hungary. Even in victorious Italy, many denounced the "mutilated peace," whereby Italy had been denied the territories promised on joining the Entente side. The successor states of the vanquished multinational empires feared they might not survive at all. Romanians and French worried whether they could keep their territorial gains, and Serbs feared they might lose their control over Yugoslavia.

Yet timing seems a problem for military as well as economic crises. Only Italian Fascists (1922) and Bulgarian authoritarians (1923) took power soon after the war, and these countries had suffered the fewest losses. Germany had time to recover. Reparations were settled in 1930, and the allied occupation of the Rhineland was known to be temporary. Hitler's coup in 1933 was surely too late to be directly attributed to defeat in World War I. Hungarian politicians knew their revisionism was impractical; Austrians knew they could not restore the empire. War defeat did not directly produce fascism.

The war did contribute to the first postwar rightist surge, undermining the immediate prospects for democracy. More specifically, it provided the paramilitaries. Total war had mobilized millions of men to fight and many more millions of men and women to provide economic and logistical support. It increased state powers, gave a larger military component to the notion of citizenship, and brought new military values. The nation in arms proved disciplined yet comradely, elitist yet egalitarian, for officers and men had fought alongside each other, with the officers taking higher casualties. Most young males had been conscripted, and by 1918, most wanted to quit the armed forces and return home. A few leftists among them took to politics, demanding a more just and pacific society. After a spurt of workers' and soldiers' councils, they were absorbed into civilian leftism, which was usually antimilitarist. Some veterans idealized the disciplined cross-class comradeship of the front, and were disenchanted with postwar strife-torn civilian democracy. Extolling military virtues, they devised the rightist paramilitary.

Paramilitaries and veterans' leagues grew in most countries. They won a Civil War in Finland; repressed the Hungarian Marxist regime in 1919–1920; repressed leftist and foreign opponents in early postwar Germany, Austria, and Poland; and overthrew civilian government in Bulgaria in 1923. They provided the core of first-wave fascism. In Italy, they actually were the Fascist Party. Veterans' movements then trained young men attracted by the combination of demonstrating, marching, and brawling. Fascism also presupposed some of the effects of modernity on young people – the liberation of young males from family discipline, of young females from much of the burden of childbirth, the growth of organized sports, the growth of professions requiring extensive education, and especially the growth of citizen warfare. Student and cadet associations and gymnastic and other sports clubs rallied round fascist banners. During the twentieth century, age-cohort effects remained important in politics; they brought a cult of youth and distinctive youth cultures – this one leaned to the right. Some veterans were pushed by values imbibed at the front into claiming that paramilitary organization could now achieve social and political purposes in peacetime. The paramilitary "caged" young single men within the comradeship, hierarchy, and violence of the "cell," "nest," or *fascio* (a tied bundle of sticks), a symbol suggesting the union of coercion and binding ties.

Veteran paramilitarism barely appeared in democratic Britain. There was some in France, and the newly formed American Legion was used by rightists as a Red-busting organization in the 1920s. Yet compared to veteran fascism in Germany, Italy, Hungary, or Romania, these were insignificant. Victory versus defeat plus struggles over lost territories offers part of the explanation for the difference between the two Europes, through the medium of military power relations. The war converted fascism from merely a movement of intellectuals into a mass movement of a few thousand. Because they idealized violence, when it came to street battles, even with leftists who also organized paramilitaries, they usually won.

Again, this was a necessary but not a sufficient cause, for street fighting alone would in normal circumstances plunge fascists into defeat. Paramilitarism could not defeat state militarism, but because armies had been downsized by the Versailles and Trianon Treaties and some were riven by ideological disputes, state monopoly of the means of violence faltered. The Italian army stood aside during the March on Rome partly because the high command feared fascist sympathies lower down the command chain. The German army stood passively by as the Nazis consolidated their rule. Knox rightly says it would be "naïve reductionism" to believe that social class or economic interest determine political behavior. In this case, he says, "politics and war led the way, society followed" (2009: 40, 315). So let us turn to politics.

(3) *Political* crises were severe only in the second Europe. By the 1880s, all the Northwestern countries had competitive party systems, free elections, and little executive interference. Even in colonies in Europe, in Ireland and Norway locals had sent elected representatives to the colonial power's parliament. Even the two marginal cases, Finland and Czechoslovakia, had been allowed representative provincial government within the Russian and Austrian Empires. When the suffrage was extended to lower classes and women, their organizations took their cues from entrenched institutions (Luebbert, 1991). The first Europe's states were unitary, not dual, dominated by parliamentary institutions used to handling conflict between classes, religious communities, and regions. In the last chapter, we saw Nordic and Anglo countries dealing with conflicts by advancing democratic social citizenship (cf Schmitt, 1988). Fascist parties were latecomers, and as party competition already dominated these states, there was little space left for fascists (Linz, 1976: 4–8). Whatever World War I or the Great Depression might throw at the Northwest, it coped through constitutional changes of government. Governments weakened by crises were voted out of office, and other parties replaced them. Democracy pioneered the electoral technique of coping with crisis through self-renewal. That is its greatest strength.

In contrast, across the second Europe more fragile states experienced war-induced political dislocation. Vanquished regimes lost legitimacy, and some were pressured by refugees. Italy had only a little dislocation, over Trieste and the South Tyrol. Two victors, Romania and Serbia, had to cope with a different problem: how to incorporate new territories that had transformed the country. Serbs had to institutionalize politics that would ensure their own dominance yet leave other Yugoslav ethnic groups not too unhappy. Romanians now had a larger and overwhelmingly rural country. This was no longer the oppressed "proletarian nation" of the region. The brand-new successor states had to build from scratch.

In the second Europe, parliaments had either barely existed before 1914 (as in the Russian or Ottoman Empires) or had shared political power with a monarch, generals, or a ministerial regime commanding substantial office patronage (as in Germany, Austria, Hungary, Bulgaria, Romania, Serbia, and Italy). These were "dual states," with parliamentary and executive institutions each enjoying partial sovereignty. The armed forces and police were controlled by an executive that could manipulate elections and parliaments by office patronage and selective repression, declaring martial law, banning parties, and so forth. Then starting in 1918, the peace treaties and a triumphant center-left demanded a move toward democratic parliaments. At a stroke, Germany and Austria got parliamentary sovereignty and full adult suffrage, as Spain did in 1931. Italy had a major suffrage extension in 1918. These shifts were not accompanied by comparable changes in control over the armed forces or police and legal institutions that remained dominated by the old regime. Nor had parties internalized the rules of the democratic game. In reality, most liberal and conservative parties were rather illiberal and socialist movements were insufficiently pragmatic. There was little chance of broad parliamentary alliances to preserve and extend democratic institutions.

The new states were simultaneously transformed into nation-states amid movements mobilizing national identities. There were established imperial nations (Russian, German, Magyar, Ottoman), proletarian nations (Ukrainian, Romanian), newer sub-imperial nations (Serb, Czech), and minorities of all these in other states. Where nationalities differed in their religions, this reinforced their mutual unease. Complex claims were being made on these states, without established institutions for coping. Safer perhaps for those who controlled the executive part of the state to repress if faced with crisis.

Eugene Weber said, "Twentieth-century fascism is a byproduct of disintegrating liberal democracy" (1964: 139). This is not correct, however. Liberal democratic states rode out the crises. Rather, authoritarianism and fascism emerged from crises of the dual state, an old regime moving toward democracy and the nation-state just as they were beset by the economic and military crises mentioned above. This produced a coup by the old regime, executive half of the state against the democratic half of the state. The ability of Northwestern conservatives to move from notable to mass parties ensured constitutional survival. Elsewhere, it was the failure of conservatives to effect this transition that produced authoritarianism. Where they were disunited or lacked mobilizing powers, this opened the door to fascism. Although the political crisis owed much to long-term processes of economic and geopolitical development, and something to short-term economic and military crises, it also had specifically political causes.

Political power relations can also explain why fascists were only strong in a few of the despotic countries. Where the old regime remained stronger, it subordinated fascism. In Spain in the 1930s, only the monarchy was gone. The army and the Church remained intact, determined to preserve the old order. General Franco could defeat a strong left and subordinate what became a large fascist movement within his regime. In Romania, King Carol and Marshal Antonescu wielded enough political and military power to repress a large fascist movement until the latter stages of the war. In Germany, the monarchy was gone, the army was much reduced, and a vibrant democracy curtailed but did not eliminate old regime powers. The Nazis emerged through that democracy, wielding too much mass mobilization for the old regime. In Italy, the old regime retained more power, but its party system was weak, unable to counter fascist mobilizing abilities. A deal was struck, and Mussolini's political skills gradually gave him the upper hand. All the countries differed, but through the variations, we can perceive a general trend. In this second Europe, the strength and unity of the old regime was inversely related to fascist power. Where stronger and more united, it generated despotic rightism; where weaker and disunited, fascists were given their opportunity. So the three different outcomes – fascism, conservative despotism, and democracy – are best explained by political power relations determining responses to economic and military crises.

(4) *Ideological* crisis. The near-simultaneity of the economic, military, and political crises brought a sense of a general civilizational crisis, and a search for new ideologies. However, non-fascist authoritarians did not live much at the ideological level; they pragmatically stole as much fascist clothing as was needed to stay in power, seeking to defuse fascism's radical, bottom-up thrust. Fascism was a more transcendent intellectual movement, although its intellectuals were second-rate men such as Maurras, Barrès, and race theorists such as Chamberlain and Gobineau, plus a host of middlebrow journalists, popularizers, and pamphleteers – down to the infamous anti-Semitic forgery *Protocols of the Elders of Zion*. In the interwar period, fascism attracted major intellectuals in Italy and Romania, but elsewhere it remained a movement of the lesser intelligentsia, indeed of propagandists.

Yet fascism resonated among the well-educated – students in high schools and universities, seminary and military academy students, and the most highly educated middle-class professional strata. Salvatorelli (1923) described this constituency as the "humanistic bourgeoisie." Between 1900 and 1930, student numbers increased fourfold across the developed world, the highest rate of expansion in the twentieth century. It was even higher in the second Europe; this threatened old regime controls over educational institutions. In the 1960s, the surge caused a leftward explosion in student politics; in the 1920s it went to the right. D'Annunzio was the first nationalist to exploit theatrical publicity and glorify youth, and Mussolini quickly imitated him. Fascism was youthful, therefore it was modern, the society of the future – so fascists proclaimed. Fascism was not just for thugs.

Fascists claimed to "resacralize" a society grown materialistic and decadent (Gentile, 1990; Griffin, 2002), mobilizing values, norms, and rituals. They claimed a civilizational crisis encompassed government, morality, science, social science, and the arts. Socialists were denounced as "Asiatic barbarians," liberals were "decadent" and "corrupt," science was "materialistic" and "degenerate," "elderly" culture needing rejuvenating. Militarism was justified by national myths about internal and external enemies, and the legitimacy of aggressive expansion (Knox, 2009: 315). Fascists promoted their own rituals, art, architecture, science, and social science, their own youth movements, and a cult of the new man, appealing to the emotions as well as reason. This was truly a secular salvationism. They exploited the emotional power of music, marching, rhetoric, painting, graphic design, sculpture, and architecture. Paxton says "emotions ... carefully-managed ceremonies, and intensely charged rhetoric ... immediate sensual experience" were more important than truth in Nazi ideology (2004: 16–17).

Ideologies cannot be validated scientifically. To be successful, new ideologies require not truth but plausibility and emotional appeal, a seeming ability to make sense of the world at a time when established ideologies flounder. In the interwar period, traditional ideologies struggled with contemporary crises across one-half of Europe. Conservatism distrusted the masses that were now on stage; liberalism seemed corrupt and insufficiently nationalist. Socialism distrusted the nation and brought more class conflict, but not seemingly its solution. The impact of economic difficulties – and especially of the Depression – was mainly indirect: conservatives, liberals, and socialists all had their chance to solve them. Where they failed, fascists might be given their chance, as happened in Germany.

Economic, military, and political crises had generated an ideology with an alternative modernity and salvation focused on nation, state, and war. Capitalism was not at the center of its interest, and fascism was not the center of interest for capitalists. Across the second Europe, conservative despots seized power, stealing fascist clothes and repressing the fascists. They saw modernity as desirable but dangerous, liberalism as corrupt, socialism as chaotic, and secularism as immoral. A few embraced the notion of an elite vanguard mobilizing the masses to state-led economic development and cultivation of order and hierarchy – fascism. Across Northwestern Europe, democracy remained intact, self-sustaining, faced with very small fascist or conservative despotic movements. The problem for Marxist theories is that the depth of the recession and the strength of labor movements were not correlated with the rise of fascism. Northwestern countries suffered as badly in the Depression as others, and they had as powerful labor movements. In the Northwest, however, democracy was established before the Great War and was now institutionalized. There fascists remained small minorities, socialists withstood communists, conservatives withstood organic nationalists, and both subscribed to an instrumental political rationality of swing voters and the middle ground. The first Europe responded to crisis by moving into the political center, to widen the suffrage and deepen liberal into social or lib-lab democracy, as we saw in the last chapter.

A few second-rate intellectuals and agitators had found thousands of militants among demobilized soldiers, especially in defeated armies. Amid difficult economic and geopolitical times, their greater commitment to violence could take on and perhaps overcome the militants of the left. As economic difficulties intensified – but only in countries where democracy was not thoroughly institutionalized – political parties were discredited and millions of people found fascist ideology plausible. The millions were not ultimately decisive; instead, old regime elites (probably only in the hundreds) mounted coups where they had the strength to do so, and where they did not they supported fascist coups – their core decision being not to call in the army instead. All four sources of social power must be invoked to explain the rise of fascism. They each provided distinct but necessary roles.

Fascists in power

Because only two fascist regimes exercised power for any length of time, I will here discuss only Italy and Germany. Once in power, their fascists did not continue to mobilize the people against elites. Instead, they imposed single-party dictatorship and came to terms with the capitalist class. As long as capitalists produced what the fascists wanted, and did not engage in politics, fascists would rid them of independent unions and militant workers. As most fascists cared little about religion, they signed concordats with churches; thus, both capitalists and churches had a measure of local autonomy from the regime. This was not true of the armed forces. Hitler purged the high command and subordinated it to his aggressive projects, also protecting himself with party militias, first the SA then the Schutzstaffel (SS). After the seizure of power, the SS and the Gestapo became rather like a praetorian guard for this despotism.

Creating a more militarized, sacred nation-state and exaggerating the "threat" posed by domestic and foreign enemies had consequences. Fascist regimes couldn't easily settle down into enjoying power. They had their radicals to satisfy and they needed the image of a permanent revolution (Mann, 1996; Paxton, 2004: 148). Ideological power mattered once they had seized power – as it did among the Communist regimes – as it continuously drove them forward toward their utopian goals. Once in power, Fascist paramilitarism was for a while deployed at home against racial or political enemies, but then it was deflected abroad into aggressive war. As we will see in Chapter 12, its militarism was recklessly utopian, leading to ultimate defeat that destroyed the entire family of authoritarian rightists. The manner of their downfall proved without doubt that fascists were not mere reactionaries or stooges of capitalism or anyone else. They willed ideologically both their successes and their ultimate failure.

Italian Fascism was somewhat less ideological than German. It was a coalition of socialists, syndicalists, conservative nationalists, radical squadristi, and agrarian reactionaries. Mussolini himself favored a socialist-flavored fascism, but his opportunistic antennae led him to play off the various factions against each other. The result was both a corporatist state and a dispersal of state sovereignty among various institutions: a monarchy, traditional bureaucracy, the Fascist Grand Council, the Ministry of Corporations, the Syndicates, the Party, and the Duce himself. This was not a totalitarian state, although Mussolini proudly proclaimed that it was. The Fascist Party was able to appropriate much of the local associational density of Italian society and to become self-sustaining, alongside the state. Radicals and syndicalists were bought off with monopoly control over the unions and bargaining, just as the employers' associations were given similar powers on the other side of the bargaining table (Riley, 2010: 61–8). Elsewhere, the regime pragmatically conceded some powers to non-fascist elites. In the countryside, landowners took over fascist organization during 1922. It took longer in the towns, where radical *fasci* continued to generate turbulence through the 1920s. The fascist unions became more middle class, dominating the lower and middle ranks of the civil service and local government. After the coup, the Partito Nazionale Fascista (PNF) contained a declining worker and peasant presence, as middle-class and civil servant opportunists joined.

Despite its narrowing base, the regime became quite popular. The elections of 1924 were not entirely free, but the large fascist majority was mostly genuine. There was relief that order had been restored. The fascists had killed somewhere between 700 and 1,700 leftists and populari in their early struggles. Once firmly in power, after about 1926, they needed little further violence and the regime achieved a broad if not very intense popularity. The introduction of special courts and secret police did not lead to terror; 80 percent of those tried of political offences were acquitted, and most of those convicted were sentenced to less than three years' imprisonment. From 1927 to the end, there were only thirty-one political executions. In World War II, only 92 Italian soldiers were condemned to death, compared to the 4,000 death sentences handed out by its "liberal" predecessor in World War I – and to the 35,000 death sentences of the German Wehrmacht. There was not much disaffection aside from discontented local party bosses.

De Felice (1974: chap. 2) argued that the regime had the active consent of Italians. The regime coped quite well with the Great Depression. Government expenditure grew substantially, with some modest improvements in education and welfare programs. Italian fascism was moderately efficient at economic management. Fascist trade unions and women's, youth, and leisure movements provided genuine services for their many members. Berezin (1997) emphasizes the importance of fascist rituals in penetrating the practices of everyday life, appropriating and intensifying ordinary patriotism, harnessing Catholicism and the village priest to its projects. World War II brought unpopularity, however. Police reports indicate that from 1943, many Italians regarded the food shortages and bombing as the consequences of a stupid war, forced on a weak regime by the more powerful Germans (Abse, 1996). This was the second time a reckless participation in world war had been inflicted on Italy, and again it severely weakened the state. It became deeply split, and many rose up against fascism. Yet before then, a few thousand old fascist fighters and more numerous opportunists seem to have ruled Italy without undue strain. They could have ruled a lot longer without war.

The fatal weakness was militarism. Through war, Mussolini deflected transcendence and satisfied his radicals. He believed in it, anyway. Military expenditure trebled under fascist rule, and by 1937 absorbed 10 percent of GNP, higher than in any other country. Mussolini intervened on Franco's side in the Spanish Civil War. He declared, "War is to men as maternity is to women." Unfortunately for him, this was not accurate for Italian men, who were more sensible when war was inflicted on them. Italy could cope with its invasion of Ethiopia, where it was only copying other powers' imperialism, atrocities and all – Britain was also using mustard gas on natives in the interwar period – but Italy's entry into World War II, stimulated by the Wehrmacht's extraordinary success in 1940, proved its undoing. Italy was militarily not of the first rank, so everything depended on Germany. This subordinated Mussolini to Hitler, however. Under Hitler's pressure, the Italian radicals were given freer rein, and Mussolini committed his greatest crime, yielding up Italy's Jews for slaughter. Then, as Hitler's military power waned, Mussolini's Italian allies – king, court, and generals – deposed him.

If Mussolini represented fascism at its (not very good) best, Hitler stood for the worst. Through the 1930s, his regime "radicalized," a euphemism for more dictatorship, racism, aggressive war, and mass murder of civilians. Every aspect of life was to be penetrated. Robert Ley, who ran the Nazi Labor Office, remarked that the only private individual in Nazi Germany was someone asleep. Nazi militarism was also turned abroad. Class conflict was not transcended, but suppressed, and capitalists were allowed to continue reaping profit, although they had to produce for a war that would be a racial war. "Dominating everything," says R. Evans (2006: xv), "was the drive to war, a war that Hitler and the Nazis saw from the very beginning as leading to the German racial reordering of Central and Eastern Europe and the re-emergence of Germany as the dominant power on the European Continent and beyond that, the world." Hitler wanted much more than the restoration of the lost territories; he wanted global domination through war, an utterly utopian goal.

Because his main goal was a cleansed empire, and his main means to achieve it military power, Hitler was prepared to sacrifice the German economy to the buildup to war. The military crystallization of the state triumphed over the economic. Publicized civilian innovations such as the Autobahn and the Volkswagen involved negligible expenditures compared to rearmament. Military expenditures were just less than 10 percent of GNP in 1937, slightly lower than Italy's, almost double the percentage in Britain and France. Yet military Keynesianism did generate full employment and even rising wages. Aly (2007) stresses that the Nazis were anxious to head off worker discontent, so helped them with many social security programs, even doubling holiday entitlements, and landlords' ability to raise rents or eject tenants was reduced.

The onset of war in 1939 increased the desire to keep workers happy. In 1940, the Nazi state stopped taxing overtime pay, and in 1941 it introduced a national health insurance scheme for all. Obviously, only Aryans qualified for any of this, and even for them this was not the whole story, however. Limited consumption goods and rationing helped cancel out rising prosperity. Germans, with few desirable goods in the shops, banked their savings. The banks, with no other investment opportunities available to them, put the savings into government debt, which did not pay them back. Germans – especially middle-class Germans with savings – were bled dry without coercion, often without their knowledge, to pay for this "silent system" of war finance. However, the effect of these two trends may have been seen as class leveling, seeming to add some credence to the Nazi claim to the transcendence of class differences. This was to bolster German patriotism during the war, as we see in Chapter 14.

Most importantly, in 1937 and 1938 the Nazi regime doubled the share of national output going to the military to 20 percent, an increase probably unprecedented by any state in peacetime. It caused an economic crisis, which Hitler simply ignored. Instead, he called for more military spending (Tooze, 2006: 138–43, 253–9, 354–5, 659; R. Evans, 2006). There was also an economic logic behind this. It was driven forward by the quest for autarchy, which turned inevitably into military expansion in order to territorially control the resources needed by the German economy, such as the Romanian oil fields or Ukrainian cornfields. This was the most militaristic contemporary state, by far, and of course, as Hitler's wars proceeded, most Germans suffered tremendously. Aly's claim that the war continued to bring them economic benefits is absurd. True, German soldiers and administrators could loot the resources of conquered countries and send them home, but the shortages of food and devastation of bombing in Germany overwhelmed any such benefits, except for the Nazi elite. The Nazi regime did not have the virtues of most ideological regimes of the left or of some moderate nationalist regimes of being relatively honest and committed to the provision of public goods. Its corruption was indeed a core part of the regime, as each party leader skimmed resources off the top to increase their personal wealth. Though Hitler did introduce more public goods, they were overwhelmed by the sufferings his wars inflicted on Germans.

Nazi radicalization proceeded until Germany provoked World War II, and committed genocide against Jews and gypsies, mass murder committed against the mentally disabled and homosexuals, and politicide committed against Polish and other foreign elites. Hitler sought to cleanse the German lands of inferior races and genetically unworthy Germans. Genocide of the Jews was probably not his original intention; he expected that discrimination and violence would force them to flee, yielding up much of their wealth as they fled. It was when they did not leave, and when his conquests netted him vast numbers of additional Jews as well as gypsies that the idea of killing them all became policy.[2] Eastern conquests meant there were simply too many Slavs to be eliminated, despite their racial inferiority. Only their leaders would be murdered (in a politicide), and the rest would be the "helots" of their German masters. Conquests in the West would be milder, as these were not inferior races. Only Jews and those who opposed him there would be killed. War and genocide, especially of Jews, were Hitler's terrible legacies.

I deal with the war in Chapter 14, and I have already written a book on genocide, *The Darkside of Democracy* (2005). Here, I briefly narrate the process of racial radicalization. *Social Darwinism*, the notion that humans were divided biologically into superior and inferior groups, was widespread in the advanced world at the beginning of the twentieth century. It was applied to races and classes alike: the white race was considered (by whites) superior to the decadent yellow race and the savage black race; the upper class saw the lower classes as its biological inferiors. Eugenics theory seemed to scientifically confirm this. To preserve white superiority, it was important to restrict racial interbreeding; to preserve the strength of the nation, the upper classes should breed faster than the lower classes; and the mentally disabled and criminals should not be allowed to breed at all. These were widely held beliefs in all advanced countries, some of which went as far as sterilizing criminals, pregnant unmarried teenagers, and the mentally disabled. Only the Nazis went in for killing them, however.

Before World War I, Germany had not exhibited more racism or anti-Semitism than other countries. France may have been more anti-Semitic, and Poland and Russia certainly were. German colonists were no more racist than British or French colonists, although the German military was more ruthless toward rebel natives than most European colonial armies by now (Hull, 2005; cf Mann, 2005: 100–7), but Germans were used to ruling over Poles, and they regarded them and other Slavs as racial inferiors. In World War I, Germans had conquered vast swathes of eastern territory that they saw as a vast space (*Raum*), barely cultivated yet capable of being settled. The soldiers had been shocked as they dug their trenches to find the artifacts of prehistoric peoples lying just below the surface. They took this as archaeological evidence of how primitive the region still was. General Ludendorff had set up an eastern administration, Ober Ost, which governed and extracted resources ruthlessly, also maintaining a sense of a cultural mission to civilize the primitive peoples of the region. As local resistance to German rule increased, so did German negative stereotypes of the locals. In the doomed postwar struggle to recapture the lost territories in the east, the German paramilitary Freikorps saw Slavs as embodying a "terrible ferocity," to which they responded in kind. To the Germans, "the

[2] This is a controversial issue that has generated no absolutely decisive answers. My own views can be found in *Darkside*, (2005: chap. 7). See also Christopher Browning's (2004) authoritative review of the evidence.

East appeared as an area of races and spaces, which could not be manipulated, but only cleared and cleaned" (Liulevicius, 2000: 152–3).

The idea of the need for *Lebensraum*, room for life, spread during the Weimar Republic. It was widely believed that too many Germans were crowded into too small a country, and overseas settler colonies were blocked by the British navy. Plenty of land for settlers could be seized across the eastern borders in a *Mitteleuropa* empire. The collapse of the Austrian Empire intensified the lure of *Anschluss*, union with Austria. Austria was much more anti-Semitic, Hitler was an Austrian, and his first clique of supporters came predominantly from an anti-Semitic Vienna-Munich axis. Among the early Nazis, general ideas about racial biology were given two distinct European applications: the creation of settler colonies in the east of the continent, and the attribution of inferiority to the Slav and Jewish races.

Killing started in Germany itself. The seizure of power in 1933 led to the incarceration of thousands of communists and socialists in concentration camps, where many were killed. Then criminals, homosexuals, gypsies, Jews, and the mentally handicapped were given steadily worsening treatment. In 1938, the Nazis moved beyond sterilization of mentally disabled people to exterminating them, a decisive moment, for the regime had shifted from being merely highly repressive to mass murder, and was training large numbers of people in murder. Nazi anti-Semitic policy was not yet so terrible as this, although legislation expelled Jews from the civil service, armed forces, teaching, the arts, then from the professions, backed from a flood of local bans against Jews in public halls, arenas, and swimming pools. The Nuremberg Laws defined in detail who was Jewish and proscribed intermarriage (Friedlaender, 1997: 141–51).

Between 1933 and 1938, Hitler subjugated non-Nazi elites. Political parties, civil servants, the high command, and to a lesser extent capitalists and churches were subordinated to Nazi goals. It harnessed despotic and infrastructural power capable of penetrating deep into civil society to implement its directives. It was totalitarian in theory but in practice, this single party state was not quite that. Despotic states always have less infrastructural power than they want. They believe that enemies within are working tirelessly to destroy their power, but when the dictator discovers he cannot enforce everything, he reacts in ways that typically reduce the top-down bureaucratic chain of command at the heart of the totalitarian model. Hitler cultivated two main strategies. One was to supervise the state part of the party state with paramilitary security forces, especially the SS and the Gestapo. The other was to divide-and-rule among the party elite, allowing the various "chieftains" to control their own area of administration, but encouraging rivalry amongst them and having them report directly to himself or his trusted inner circle rather than to any collective body of either the party or the state. This created a factionalized despotism, which one scholar has gone so far as to call "polycratic" (Broszat, 1981). In this case, despotic power would seem to somewhat undermine infrastructural power, which is not a possibility I earlier envisaged (Mann, 1988a; 2008).

Hitler's acquisition of more powers also shifted the balance of power inside the Nazi movement. Because compromise with conservative elites had ended, the influence of conservative Nazis waned. Schacht fell when he opposed subordinating the economy to the war machine. Göring, initially a conservative Nazi, radicalized to retain his power. Radicals were aided by the "leadership principle" and especially by the practice termed by Kershaw (1997, 1998: chap. 13) "working towards the Fuhrer," acting to anticipate his intent, which was almost universally assumed to be radical. Whether consciously intended or not, this was actually a way to reduce factionalism, increase the cohesion of policies the various factions chose, and maintain a high level of infrastructural power through common purpose rather than bureaucratic institutions. It also depended on what Weber called charismatic authority, under which officials are chosen and rewarded not according to their technical competence but to their devotion to the leader and fervor in adopting his vision. Few Nazis were contemplating mass murder, but few opposed it because this would oppose the Fuhrer, which was almost impossible to contemplate – it would also kill one's career. Nazis who "could get things done," as the radical euphemism went, were applauded, and this put pressure on more cautious colleagues and superiors.

I attempted to explain why anti-Semitism so overwhelmed Nazism in my book, *The Darkside of Democracy* (2005), and will not repeat it here. The Anschluss in 1938 brought in the more virulent Austrian strain of anti-Semitism, however, sparking off a pogrom more violent than anything yet seen in Germany. Thousands of Jews fled abroad, others were dumped over borders, the rich were ransomed for emigration. Hitler was now going beyond what I called in *The Darkside* his "Plan A" – pressuring Jews to leave – into his "Plan B" of "wild deportations," emigration assisted by violence. In November 1938, the Nazi leadership tried to spread violence into Germany with a pogrom, *Kristallnacht*. Hitler said privately, "The Jews should for once get to feel the anger of the people" (I. Kershaw, 2000: 138–9). More than 100 Jews were killed, and 80,000 fled the country, but this violence shocked many Nazis. Some *Gauleiter* refused to transmit the pogrom orders. Müller-Claudius noted in conversations with forty-one elite Nazis in 1938 that twenty-eight (63 percent) expressed strong disapproval of Kristallnacht. Only two (5 percent) clearly approved. Göring was upset about the potential damage to the economy, and even Hitler worried about looting getting out of hand. The regime pulled back. It compensated by intensifying "euthanasia," the mass murder of mentally disabled persons.

Hitler also enjoyed success in risky foreign-policy ventures opposed by conservative Nazis. German troops occupied the Rhineland in 1936 and took over Austria in the Anschluss in 1938. The Sudetenland followed, then all of

Czechoslovakia. All came without firing a shot, increasing Hitler's popularity and his power within the country and the Nazi movement. It also increased the attractions of Eastern Lebensraum, the political influence of "ethnic Germans" (Germans from outside the Weimar territories), and the sense of a threat posed by supposed "Judeo-Bolsheviks." Expansion into Poland drew Nazi Germany into war with the Western Powers in 1939, but the Wehrmacht brought swift victory in Poland, the Low Countries, and France. Denmark and Norway followed. The Soviet Union was attacked in mid-1941.

Although Hitler had now bitten off more than he could chew, in December he declared war against the United States. Many Germans, including most generals, now knew defeat was probable, but wartime patriotism plus the Gestapo made it impossible to oppose Hitler or his radicalizing goals. Thus, the leadership as a whole – Reichsleiter, Gauleiter, SS leaders, civilian governors and generals – came to endorse "elimination" of all inferior races. Euphemistic code words indicated a loosening of moral bounds. "Fanaticism" was good. Militants would be "toughened," "steeled," "hardened," made "ice-cold" for "ruthless," "severe," "special projects." Enemies were dehumanized: Jews, gypsies, Bolsheviks, Slavs, and Asiatics were "enzymes of decomposition," "international maggots and bedbugs."

All of Hitler's inner circle conspired in this. Himmler told his top SS men in 1938 that the next decade would see an "ideological struggle of the entire Jewry, freemasonry, Marxism, and churches of the world. These forces – of which I presume the Jews to be the driving spirit, the origin of all the negatives – are clear that if Germany and Italy are not annihilated, they will be annihilated ... we will drive them out with an unprecedented ruthlessness" (I. Kershaw, 2000: 130). In 1941, Göring, Himmler, and Heydrich together formulated the "Final Solution." Göring declared, "This is not the Second World War, this is the Great Racial War." Goebbels' diary describes "a life and death struggle between the Aryan race and the Jewish bacillus." He declared Germans must rule "brutally" over Eastern nations (Kersten, 1956: 120; S. Gordon, 1984: 100; Goebbels, 1948: 126, 148, 185, 225, 246). These leaders were aware how their mass murder would be judged in the rest of the world, but believed their actions were historically necessary. In the future, they said, they would be thanked for their "toughness" in overcoming conventional morality. Had they won the war, they might have been – which is perhaps just as frightening a thought as genocide itself. The winners rewrite history. The Nazi willed genocide and murderous ethnic cleansing, and these had none of the ambiguities of catastrophic policy mistakes cohabiting Stalin's atrocities. The Hitler regime was probably the worst the world has ever seen.

Top-down radicalization was aided by Hitler's destruction of German opposition, the diffusion of the Leadership Principle, and geopolitical successes. Had German elites shown more resilience in the first years of the new regime, they might have strengthened Nazi conservatives and generated a less murderous version of fascism. Their complicity in the seizure of power made them powerless to stop this terrible displacement of Nazi radicalism onto genocide amid aggressive war. It intensified through the war right up to the moment of Germany's total defeat.

The extent of complicity by ordinary Germans in the Holocaust has evoked much debate. I showed in *The Dark Side of Democracy* (2005: chaps. 8, 9) that a sample of perpetrators consisted disproportionately of committed Nazi and SS members, and that the core NCOs and lower officers were already inured to atrocities through experience in the euthanasia project or the Polish massacres beginning in 1939. That ensured the presence of experienced radicals in most German units asked to commit mass murder later. Then the normal social pressures of hierarchy (obeying orders), careerism (if one hesitated, no promotion), and comradeship (if one shot deliberately high, comrades had to kill more) kicked in to secure compliance among ordinary Germans and collaborators. The total number of perpetrators may have been as high as 300,000, although this was only 3 percent of Germans at the time. Obviously, a much higher proportion knew at some level what was going on, but we know from our own experience of the human ability to turn our faces away from horror.

Genocide is not specifically German, as mass murder has been perpetrated by people of many nationalities around the world. Nor was Nazi genocide "banal" in Hannah Arendt's (1968) use of the word. The actual killers could not escape the blood, guts, and terrible stenches of death. The desk killers such as Eichmann (for whom she coined the label), who did not kill, did not experience such unpleasantness, but they were fanatic Nazis zealous for extermination, not banal bureaucrats. The Holocaust was certainly "modern," although not as in the celebrated usage of Bauman (1989). Each group that accomplished genocide used the most modern techniques available to them, and for the Germans this included poison gases already used on rats and factory-like extermination camps, as Bauman says. Yet Hutu perpetrators of genocide in Rwanda at the end of the century were not so modern. They did have some Kalashnikovs, but most of the killing was by machetes. Turkish perpetrators against Armenians at the beginning of the century also had some guns, but the main weapons were knives, ropes (for strangling), and starvation. They all shared in a quite different face of modernity: they were extreme nationalists asserting that rule by the people (the demos of democracy) meant rule by their ethnic group (the ethnos), with other ethnicities being violently cleansed. Their modernity was essentially ideological and political.

Hitler's overriding goal became genocide. He refused to exploit live Jews as slave-laborers, preferring them dead. As we see in Chapter 14, his response to bad wartime odds was to make them worse by aggression against even stronger enemies. So the simple explanation of fascism's demise is that Hitler killed it. The other Nazis would probably have compromised with other German elites and been more cautious about war. In contrast to my complex explanation of the rise of fascism in terms of all the sources of social power, I have given a single-factor – indeed, ultimately a single-person – explanation of its fall. For the only time in this book, I attribute enormous causal power to an individual. This is not a routine feature of societies, but it certainly figured large here.

Hitler is also generally credited with charisma. Many party leaders, generals, and others say they went into Hitler's presence geared up to argue with him over policy, yet they left reassured that he knew best. As for the rank and file of the party, films of the Nuremberg rallies reveal that he held them in the palm of his hands. Max Weber defined *charisma* as:

> a certain quality of an individual personality, by virtue of which he is set apart from ordinary men and treated as endowed with supernatural, superhuman, or at least specifically exceptional powers or qualities. These are such as are not accessible to the ordinary person, but are regarded as of divine origin or as exemplary, and on the basis of them the individual concerned is treated as a leader (M. Weber, 1978 edition: I, 241).

This clearly applies to Hitler. Yet three qualifications seem in order. First, it seems too much of a coincidence that not only Hitler but at least two other fascist leaders – Mussolini in Italy and Codreanu in Romania – were also credited with charismatic authority. It seems that Weber can be criticized for emphasizing the qualities of the leader rather than the followers' need to believe in the leader. Charisma is not just a quality of an individual but a relationship between leader and follower, and in crisis situations in which more routinized forms of authority no longer seem to offer solutions (Weber accepted this point). Second, the ideology of fascism actually embodied the leadership principle. The leader was supposed to be extraordinary. The need to believe in the leader was stronger than in any other movement save a religious one in which leaders are credited with divine authority. Third, the charismatic relationship between Hitler and the Nazis was of enormous significance for the world – as that between Codreanu and his Legionaries was not – because Germany was a Great Power capable of committing genocide and fighting a devastating world war for five years against great odds. Thus, fascism's doctrines and power structure plus Germany's military power made possible Hitler's charismatic impact on the world – which was, unfortunately, considerable.

Was fascism much of an alternative?

The answer turned out to be no. Firstly, its merging of all four power sources was inherently despotic, greatly curtailing human freedoms. Secondly, the most powerful fascist regime proved suicidal. Fascism's enemies did not win because they were more virtuous, or because civilization inevitably defeats barbarism, but because there were more of them, and they were better armed. Without Hitler's Germany, fascism would have lasted much longer, and so would other European and Asian rightist despots. Fascism made a deal with capitalists, steering the overall economy and allowing capitalists to make profits. This proved quite good at economic development, until subordinated to aggressive war. There was a family resemblance between its top-down corporatism and the bottom-up corporatism of the Nordic countries, which was also good for economic development. Fascism was also good at instilling national pride; German fascism was distinctively good at mass mobilization warfare. The Wehrmacht proved this, fighting hard to the bitter end, long after defeat was inevitable (Italian soldiers were more sensible). Fascism was an ideology generating viable if appalling policies. Mussolini would have lasted much longer without Hitler, and so would German Nazism itself. I have emphasized that militarism was a necessary part of fascism, but it need not have been so reckless. Racism was also a persistent tendency of fascism, brought to culmination by the Nazis, and racism was once again suicidal, as it now was in the overseas empires. The treatment of Jews and especially of Slavs made for implacable enemies who thought that no compromise was possible with the Nazis, only their utter destruction. The death of fascism was self-willed, an enormous example of human irrationality, fatal in Europe for its allies. Of Europe's rightist despots, only Franco in Spain and Salazar in Portugal had remained sensibly neutral (and non-racist) in the war, so they survived longer, although isolated.

Fascism ultimately strengthened its enemies. It helped deepen social and liberal democracy in the West and strengthened state socialism in the East. We should not regard its failure or either of those expansions as inevitable, as indicating a broad evolutionary process. Without Hitler, the Soviet Union would have remained isolated, the Japanese, British, and French empires would have lasted longer, and the United States would not have become the world Superpower able to impose a more universal globalization across the world. Without him, there would have been longer-enduring, milder forms of fascism and corporatism in the world, and less convergence across it. Fascism proved to be a rearguard action against globalization that failed.

Fascism seems today like a period piece, offering solutions to crises arising only in the aftermath of World War I, when borders remained disputed, military veterans formed paramilitaries, and class conflict rose – and then the Great Depression struck. World War II had opposite effects – few disputed borders, no paramilitaries, revolution only in Asia, and in the West reformed capitalism and liberal and social democracy, both with secure parliamentary means of self-renewal. This spread gradually to much of East and South Asia; seemingly stable state socialism arose in the Soviet Bloc and China; and elsewhere came decolonization and mild "Third World" versions of socialism and nationalism. Fascism's defeat brought a new world order, making fascist solutions appear irrelevant. Its elimination meant the expansion of more universal globalizations.

11 The Soviet alternative, 1918–1945

Securing the revolution

State socialism provided the second major alternative to democratic capitalism. As we saw in Chapter 6, the Russian Revolution was caused by uneven economic development, repressive but vacillating state intervention in class relations, and – above all – defeat in total war. The Bolsheviks, armed with a revolutionary ideology, seized the state, killed the ruling family, sidelined religion, abolished capitalism, introduced one-party rule, and pushed through many other changes – truly a revolution. The Soviet system is generally called "Communism," and although that term is inaccurate (for Marx, communism was a future society and Soviet leaders considered communism to be their eventual goal rather than their present), I will retain that conventional term.

The Soviet Union presented a viable alternative to democratic capitalism, a radically different way of bringing the masses onstage in industrial society. It claimed to provide a global future, and this diffused across the world, but when it shifted from the project of world revolution to socialism in one country, it erected barriers against globalization. It developed an industrial economy, if at enormous human cost, to the point whereby in World War II it could outproduce Germany in all spheres of armaments. In the postwar period, the country then became one of the world's two Superpowers. Against this, the Soviets abandoned their initial democratic ideals. Weber had predicted this, arguing that if economic and political bureaucracies were conjoined under the same state power, personal freedoms would die, unlike countries in which capitalism and the state are separated. A person living under state socialism would have no more power than the ordinary fellahin in ancient Egypt, said Weber. He was right. Weber further argued that it was a more rational bureaucracy than that in ancient Egypt, so was less breakable (1978: 1402–3, 1453–4). This proved only half-right. The communists held onto power for more than half a century, seemingly invulnerable, but they finally collapsed in the 1980s. Throughout the century, the Soviet Union represented the main example of revolutionary change, the main alternative to capitalism and liberal and social democracy, admired or hated throughout the world.

The Soviets came to shape events elsewhere – first encouraging revolution abroad, then unintentionally depressing its chances. Labor movements across the world were at first greatly encouraged. Although labor leaders were often hostile to the Bolsheviks, rank-and-file militants responded with an enthusiasm based less on Marxist ideology than a perception that capitalist exploitation could be overthrown by people similar to themselves. There was additionally a strong body of support for socialism and communism among intellectuals across the world. Although liberal democratic and then social democratic capitalism provided the dominant model of advanced societies, their advance was pragmatic, one reform at a time, less ideological, hardly offering salvation. The Bolsheviks were also anti-imperialist, which increased their popularity across much of the world.

So a strike wave rippled across the world after the Bolshevik Revolution, but this also strengthened the resolve of the capitalist and imperialist powers to keep Bolshevism at bay. They intervened in the Russian Civil War hoping to crush the Revolution, although war weariness and the immensity of the country ensured their failure. So instead, they isolated the Soviets and sought to undermine their own labor radicals by tarring them by association with a communism increasingly unpopular in the West, although not yet in the colonies and developing countries.

By the early 1920s, the Bolshevik Revolution had been revealed in all its ambiguity. A revolution had been made by a few thousand Bolsheviks seizing unexpected opportunities presented by war, mobilizing a small industrial working class in an overwhelmingly agrarian country. They had bought the temporary support of peasants by ratifying their land seizures, creating a mass of family farms far from their socialist ideals. Committed in principle to socialist democracy, they could not have won any election, but they were Russia's best chance for the restoration of order. Driven onward by a utopian salvation ideology, they aspired to the total transformation of society, but in the here and now, they were confronted by postrevolutionary chaos and a four-year Civil War fought against conservative forces determined to keep their privileges by all necessary means, aided by ten foreign expeditionary forces.

Amid all this, it would be utopian to expect them to have held elections, recognize the legitimacy of their enemies' parties, and establish a pluralist democracy. However, it might have been possible to rule through what they themselves called proletarian democracy, allowing for freedom of expression and pluralism within the single Communist Party and retaining democratic soviets in the factories and neighborhoods. This would have allowed the main initial allies – the Left Socialist Revolutionaries and Mensheviks – plus proliferating small groups such as the Democratic Centralists, Workers' Opposition, Workers' Truth, and Workers' Group to voice alternative policies. Factory studies show that workers wanted and expected these freedoms, but through the 1920s, all these groups were suppressed in order to give the Bolshevik leadership untrammeled power. One-man management and bourgeois specialists also came back. Workers went on strike, denouncing "commissarocracy," but were suppressed. All this corroded worker support. By the late 1920s, workers would probably have preferred to cast off rule by the Bolshevik Party (Pirani, 2008; K. Murphy, 2005).

The despotic route was chosen because the Bolsheviks maintained their transformational ideology amid very unfavorable conditions. Theirs was not an ordinary dictatorship with limited goals; the Bolsheviks pursued total transformation. They claimed their despotic rule was only temporary, because they expected revolution to quickly spread elsewhere. All they were doing, they said, was hanging on until that happened. When they set up their international organization, the Comintern, they made its official language German, not Russian; Berlin was expected to be the headquarters of world revolution. However, in 1918, Berlin failed them. Then unfavorable conditions multiplied: they were beset by civil war until 1921, bringing devastation, famines, forced population movements, factory closures, forcible requisition of peasant produce, concentration camps, and reprisals on those suspected of collaboration with the enemy. One hundred and fifty thousand armed Red Guards, mainly from city factories, were deployed to seize peasants' grain by force. Holquist (2002) observes that much of this represented continuity with World War I rather than Bolsheviks innovations, although Trotsky's civil war policies were more ruthless than any Russia had seen before. His methods succeeded in winning the Civil War and bringing peace and order.

The Civil War is sometimes represented as excusing Bolshevik despotism. Military power was certainly needed to preserve the revolution. Of course, military power had been necessary to achieve revolution in the first place, but now the Bolsheviks proclaimed "war communism" and Red Terror, which trapped them, as military power is inherently despotic. Yet Red Terror also welled up from class discontent below. It was a "plebian war on privilege" (Figes, 1997: 520–36). White Terror was worse, especially for workers, peasants, and Jews. A White victory would have been a worse disaster, given that its leaders were reactionaries lacking a social base other than armed Cossacks (Suny, 1998: 88–94, Holquist, 2002; Raleigh, 2003). If we factor in the political drift rightward elsewhere in the East of Europe in the 1920s, the Whites were more likely to generate a fascist than a liberal regime. The Civil War discredited the White alternative to the Bolsheviks, and its polarization helped destroy more moderate movements from liberals to the Socialist Revolutionaries to Green peasant movements. Those who pose a happier counterfactual than Bolshevism in the form of a tsarist regime that might have liberalized and produced a half-democratic, half-decent form of capitalism forget the harsh realities of war and civil war and the ideological strength of the divine right of kings when compared to the frailty of Russian liberalism. Had Russia managed to stay out of the world war, such a counterfactual might have been possible, but because of wars, by 1920 Russia would be White or Red, and the latter seemed to more people to be the better of the two.

The Reds won, but the Civil War left a country in ruins; food shortages; a communist state permeated with militarism, terror, and prison camps; and a highly statist economy of war communism, incurring peasant enmity, with a working class shredded by wars from 4 million to just more than 1 million. To avoid chaos, there now needed to be some relaxation of rule, and indeed this moment occasioned their one great pragmatic act, the New Economic Policy (NEP), introduced in 1922, which permitted independent proprietors to produce goods for the market, good news for peasant family farms and small producers and traders. They were compromising on economic power, but on that alone. Despite the return of famine in 1924–1925, the NEP helped alleviate popular discontent and allowed the Soviet economy to return in the late 1920s to the level of 1913. Factories and worker organizations revived. In the big factory studied by Murphy, workers expressed their grievances, went on strike, held rowdy meetings, and criticized regime policy up until about 1926. This was only temporary pluralism. From about 1926, the union was subordinated to management and "the factory committee that had been created during the revolution to defend workers was transformed into an institution to lengthen work hours, increase productivity, and drive down wages." Given such institutional control, workers were unable to organize, and it was not necessary to arrest many people to secure compliance. Even during the first Five Year Plan period, when workers' real wages were halved, Stalinist loyalists kept control of the factories. The Bolsheviks kept some worker support within the party, and this assisted rule not by but over the proletariat (K. Murphy, 2005: 227, 207).

This period did not prove very good for women, either, although it was proclaimed they had been liberated from patriarchy. Many were expelled from factories when men returned from war or migrated from the countryside. The Bolshevik regime became more culturally conservative and patriarchal through the 1920s and 1930s, despite the high level of participation by women in the labor force (E. Wood, 1997; Fitzpatrick, 1999). Formal employment emancipation without any changes in the family increased women's "double burden" in the labor market and the household, so that women's lives were more onerous under communism than capitalism. Revolution had brought the masses onstage, but in nonspeaking roles.

The Stalinist single party state

The Bolsheviks were on their own in a hostile world. Yet they emerged from the Civil War and the NEP with belief still intact in their ability to effect a total transformation. This, they believed, would then serve as a beacon to the world. Capitalism would be replaced by socialism, which in Russia meant collective control of the means of production initially by a single party-state elite acting as the representative of the proletariat. This would lead Russia at breakneck speed to modernization through forced industrialization ending in economic growth and plenty, and in equality between all classes and between men and women. This could be done with minimal compromise with existing institutional realities. Perhaps never before in the history of humanity had such an ideological vision of salvation been accompanied by a supposed blueprint of how to achieve it. True, between 1928 and 1930, there were fractious debates within the party over how best to organize the economy. Industries organized into "syndicates" or "trusts" enjoyed some autonomy from the central authorities, and were supported by some of the party. Yet the centralizers allied with Stalin won out. Socialism could only be achieved, so most of the party believed, by an all-embracing autarchic plan directed from above, independent of the world economy. This was "socialism in one country," to be achieved before any world revolution. Eventually there would be a world revolution, but for the moment, there would be one giant caged segment fighting against capitalist globalization.

So emerged the socialist version of the single party state. In this case, as in Nazism, the party and the state were not merged but kept partially separate, with the party dominant, watching over the state at every level of its operation, ensuring that most of the radical policies of the leadership were implemented throughout the mass party, giving it a degree of infrastructural power rare in developing countries. Indeed, this is often called *totalitarian* – the ultimate combination of despotic and infrastructural power. There are both virtues and limitations in applying that term. Certainly, the Bolsheviks and especially Stalin sought to establish totalitarian rule, and they had the mass party to help them implement it. Yet implementation was imperfect. In any case, totalitarianism suggests a bureaucratic and static system that was not the case with Soviet rule. I prefer to add Trotsky's notion of a "permanent revolution" in a "single party-state," indicating that radicalization of structures by the party elite continued up to the postwar period of Soviet stagnation and decline (see Mann, 1996).

Brown (2009: 105–14) identifies six key features of the communist party state. Two were political: the monopoly of power (the "leading role") of the Communist Party, and "democratic centralism," whereby there could be supposedly open discussion within the party of policy issues, but after a decision was reached, it would be implemented unswervingly and in disciplined fashion throughout the party and society. Two were economic: noncapitalist ownership of the means of production and a command rather than market economy – which was also substantially autarchic. The last two were ideological: legitimacy rested on building a Communist society, and this would be at the global level, built by an international Communist movement. I would add, as does Fitzpatrick (1999: 3–4), that Marxism-Leninism was a totalizing ideology involving passionate hatred of "class enemies" and a commitment to achieve utopian goals, a secular salvation. I would replace Brown's "democratic centralism" (which played almost no rule after 1930) with "militarized socialism." There was always civilian control of the military, but the model of socialism came partly from military organization and discipline, although not as much as in fascism. P. Gregory's (2004: chap. 3) list of Stalin's "principles of government" is congruent with this: a command system based on collective farms and forced industrialization; the suppression of views that diverged from the party line; the partial merging of the Communist Party with the state administration; the banning of political factions; the subordination of interest groups to the encompassing interests of the party state; and Stalin sitting atop it all as a dictator settling all disputes among the leaders. The economic system operated through the regime extracting output from producers and returning part of this output to them as a wage. The rest was retained by the party state as "rent" from which it could pay its own costs, reinvest, and pay for the military.

This was a totalitarian design, welding together ideological, economic, military, and political power under the control of the party-state elite and its dictator, mobilizing considerable despotic and infrastructural power. Stalin was not charismatic: the revolutionary ideology not the leader drew the commitment of party members. Human freedoms were in extremely short supply, as in fascism. In practice, however, the regime could not be totalitarian. Instead, it was polycratic, sometimes verging on chaos. This was partly because although dissent in the party could not be openly expressed, there were still major disagreements resulting in foot-dragging or even contrary policies implemented at the local level. It was also due to a backward yet rapidly industrializing and urbanizing society, lacking stable infrastructures for implementing policy. Surveillance was not easy. Amid a highly mobile population, party members could move around rapidly, reacting to a reprimand or even a death sentence in one province by moving to a party position in another. There were innumerable "dead souls," persons flourishing the party membership cards of dead relatives and friends. Nearly half the Leningrad party cards checked in 1935 were false or invalid. As cards carried privileges denied to kulaks, former tsarist officials, and many others, they had a high black market price. Moscow had almost no sight of local party records. "The party in the thirties," says Getty (1985: 37), "was neither monolithic nor disciplined. Its upper ranks were divided, and its lower organizations were disorganized, chaotic, and undisciplined." Monitoring costs were too high to allow what was dictated at the top to actually be done at the bottom. That would have needed a massive supervisory structure or incentives so producers could see that working harder was worth it, but the regime was committed to lowering inequality not increasing it with differential incentives, and it did not have enough loyal cadres to supervise the whole.

Moreover, the position of peasants, workers, the intelligentsia, and administrative workers all differed. Class differences remained, despite the elimination of the former ruling class, a narrowing of economic inequalities, and the fact that residual conflict among the classes was now indirect, being mediated by the state. The party and the state never fully merged. State officials would develop some autonomy, and then the party would cut them down before the process recurred.

With the failure of revolutionary socialism in Europe and Asia in the 1920s, the Bolsheviks felt isolated and insecure. They thought they could not afford the geopolitical weakness brought by the slower-paced industrialization of the NEP, so they pressed for centralized "forced industrialization," with defense industries at its core. They made massive defense investments, and the armed forces briefly became part of the Stalinist coalition against other Bolshevik factions, perhaps its sole direct venture into political power relations (Shearer, 1996; Samuelson, 2000; Stone, 2000). This made more urgent a project shared by most Bolsheviks, as it was shared by almost all Marxists coming into power in the twentieth century: agriculture had to yield up its surpluses to feed the towns and subsidize industrialization, yet this required coercive policies against the peasantry (P. Gregory, 2004: chap. 2). Compulsory purchases of farm produce began in 1928, in response to another famine, and the fateful decision to collectivize agriculture was implemented between 1930 and 1936. This was Barrington Moore's conception of "labor repressive agriculture" in spades.

The attack on the peasants, more than the first consolidation of Bolshevik rule and the Civil War, was the most decisive step in the perversion of socialist ideals. It was the most systematic domestic use of military power so far. The central problem was that by 1919, 97 percent of the land was in the hands of peasants, and 85 percent of them held medium-sized plots. This new property-owning peasant class was strongly opposed to collectivization, and constituted the vast majority of the Soviet population. Either the regime had to ease off its attempt at forced industrialization and settle for a more gradual route toward socialism or it would have to use the utmost military violence against these peasants to achieve it.

Stalin and most of the party leaders chose the cruder latter option; they thought they had seen too much reformism going nowhere in the West. Russian Marxism was in any case a drive for industrialization. Once that was achieved, the West could be matched and the USSR defended. Then relaxation into genuine socialism could occur – so the theory went. After the exile of Trotsky, resistance within the party was led by Bukharin, who wished to continue the NEP, compromise with the peasants, and simultaneously develop agriculture and industry. However, he was frustrated by lack of peasant cooperation, and outmaneuvered by Stalin, who attracted most of the leadership to his position. Bukharin was then dismissed from the Central Committee (Service, 1997: 169–70). So ended open disagreement among the party leaders. Peasant resistance was more resilient and violent, escalating in some places to assassinations of Communist Party officials. This led to virtually another civil war, peasants against the party and its urban-industrial core constituencies. By 1930, the regime was deploying large contingents of security police and paramilitary "worker brigades" to expropriate the land. Stalin claimed it was only an attack on a "kulak" class of substantial peasant landowners, but in reality, virtually all peasants opposed the policy. The regime forcibly deported peasants from their land to far-off places. By the end of 1931, more than 1.8 million had been deported to mainly desolate areas. About a third died in the process through disease and starvation (Viola, 1996). Their former plots were then reorganized into *sovkhozy* (state farms) and *kolkhozy* (collective farms). By the end of 1931, more than 60 percent of the remaining peasants were inside these farms, having relinquished their animals and most of their tools. In the kolkhozy, the peasants could work part-time on their own strips of land, just as in classic medieval feudalism. As Lewin (1985: 183–4) says, Russia was going through a second serfdom, although with a single lord – the party state.

The end did not justify the terrible means. Because of the coercive methods used, the state and collective farms were never successful, and they proved a drain on the economy. The best guess is that agricultural production fell 25–30 percent from its pre-collectivization peak (Federico, 2005: 207). Agriculture could not subsidize industry, as was intended. Instead, consumption was sacrificed to subsidize industry – especially the defense industries – which by 1933 were exacting a disproportionate share of scarce resources (Stone, 2000). Hunter (1988) and R. Allen (2004), using very different methods of calculation, both suggest that had the NEP continued, by 1939 agricultural productivity would have been 15–20 percent higher. Cooperatives combined with private cultivation could also have done much better.

Hobsbawm (1994: 383) claims this terrible collectivization "reflected the social and political conditions of Soviet Russia, rather than the inherent nature of the Bolshevik project." It was actually both. Not only in Russia, but also in different conditions in China, Vietnam, and Cambodia communist parties chose forced collectivization as their inherent project, in spite of the Soviet example. So, after World War II, did most of the communist parties of Eastern Europe – although all but Romania and Albania later softened their policy. In fact, collectivization was not only a socialist ideal and way to achieve the desired industrialization; it was also seen as the way to control the peasantry and smash traditional village hierarchies believed (probably correctly) to nurture class enemies. In acquiring power, the Communists had often been pragmatists, but once in power, just as the Nazis, they were more often ideologues relying additionally on military power, believing against all sociological intelligence in their ability to totally and rapidly transform society through forced industrialization.

Although Stalin himself made things worse, we cannot attribute the entire agrarian disaster to the regime. There had already been two famines in the 1920s, and harvests failed again in 1931 and 1932. The 1932–1933 famine that resulted came partly from natural conditions such as weakened plants, pest infestations, and the cumulative effect of declining food and seed stocks forcing yields down below subsistence levels. Someone was going to starve; Stalin's contribution to the famine was forced requisitions to ensure this would not be the urban population. Tauger has suggested that not only subsequent historians but also Stalin himself neglected natural causes and blamed human agency – the historians blaming Stalin, Stalin blaming counterrevolutionary peasants. The Great Famine of 1932–1933 resulted in the deaths of 4–6 million mostly rural people. It was not genocide confined to or aimed at the Ukraine, as Ukrainian nationalists or the recent misleading account of T. Snyder (2010) have suggested. The famine did kill lots of people, but was more widespread than just the Ukraine, and it resulted from a combination of bad harvests, policy mistakes, local resistance, and callous indifference once the famine had started (Tauger, 2001; Viola, 1996: 158–60; Service, 1997: 202; Davies & Wheatcroft, 2004). Some relief came from the 1933 harvest onward, as the regime lessened coercion, lowered production quotas to achievable levels, and gave peasants incentives to produce more. There was further relaxation after World War II, when agriculture settled down into less coercive mild growth, mostly achieved by expanding into marginal lands without improving productivity, which also left environmental disaster in its wake. Soviet agriculture was always a mess.

There was an ironic benefit of forced collectivization. Peasants driven off their farms were forced to migrate to the cities, where they provided a labor force for industrial expansion. Peasants were converted into masons and machinists (R. Allen, 2003: chap. 5, 186). Population losses through collectivization and then because of World War II also combined with successful Soviet policies in the education of women, in health, and in industrial development to effect an early demographic transition to lower fertility. This prevented the normal population explosion in developing countries that tended to wipe out economic gains there (Allen, 2003: chap. 6). We do not normally think of the Soviet Union as belonging with the developing countries – it was the "Second" not the Third World – but this was itself a Soviet achievement.

The military model of coercive centralization was also applied to industry. One-man management backed up by party unions ensured substantial control over labor. The regime provided full employment, which was unique in the world at that time, and the unions distributed welfare benefits and housing, which were unique in a developing economy. Workers were told constantly that this was their state, and they did benefit more than peasants. Limited labor productivity could be achieved through a blend of ideological exhortation and coercion. "Planning" conjures up images of bureaucracy, stability, and perhaps lethargy, but such tendencies were constantly undermined, "revolutionized," by massive mobilization campaigns, as workers were directed into "hero projects," gigantic construction, mining, or industrial projects in far-off regions, in which conditions were often extremely harsh. The hero projects also committed the worst environmental destruction of modern times (discussed in Volume IV). This was a hyperactive regime, capable of mobilizing collective commitment through a blend of ideological and military power, exercised not through the regular army but through extensive NKVD security troops. The armed forces were kept at arm's length from the state, but the security forces – a kind of praetorian guard – kept watch over the party state. Their head was normally Stalin's right-hand man.

The main material incentives (such as housing) were only achieved through hard work and loyalty. Occasionally, workers could mount collective resistance, especially in provincial areas dominated by single industries, but they had to be careful not to go beyond petitioning or demonstrations lest retribution descend on them. More usually, relief might be sourced surreptitiously, as workers and local management entered into informal alliances against the state and its plans. Labor hoarding was one covert way that management could achieve its quotas and workers could enjoy full local employment. P. Gregory (2004: 268–72) says the command economy rested on a "nested dictatorship," a hierarchy of dictators stretching down from Stalin, the Politburo, and Gosplan (the main planning agency) through thousands of petty dictators to the bosses of factories and farms. If workers labored hard and kept their noses clean, nothing terrible was likely to happen to them.

Intellectuals did better, provided they did not step out of line. Stalin destroyed the committed Marxist intellectuals and cultural avant-garde who had flourished in early postrevolutionary years. They were too independent and their ideas too subversive, but intellectuals were important in Russia, and Stalin wished to preserve them as regime ornaments and to use to encourage science, technology, and literacy. By giving them good salaries, high status, and some autonomy in prestigious scientific and cultural institutions, he ensured compliance provided they prefaced their work with paeans of rather nonspecific praise to socialism. Intellectuals remained materially privileged and largely nonpolitical through Soviet times.

For technical and administrative workers conditions were different again. Actual planning of all industrial sectors in a country the size of Russia would have involved an enormous bureaucratic apparatus well beyond the available resources. In practice, economic planning merely handed down aggregate targets and quotas, and even these were subject to perennial bargaining between ministries, local prefects, and factory directors, who all then sought to fulfill the plans as best they could. P. Gregory says that real planning meant "virtually all economic instructions were based upon the principle that this year's activity would be last year's plus a minor adjustment." The lower levels of the system were inherently resistant to initiative (2004: 271). Nonetheless, the universal commitment to "minor adjustments" gave the system a capacity for slow but steady growth. Those with technical skills also had a degree of autonomy because the party hierarchy lacked the expertise to supervise them closely.

After Stalin began introducing rationing and distinctive privileges for valued persons, the famous *blat* system of corruption emerged. Ledeneva (1998: 37) defines this as "an exchange of 'favors of access' in conditions of shortages and a state system of privileges." Things got done by perpetual exchange of favors through informal networks cutting right across formal hierarchies.

Favors were usually requested not for oneself but for someone else in one's circle of friends and relations. Then at some later date the favor would be reciprocated. It was indirect exchange of services (not money), so it built up large informal cliques of cooperation. It was especially useful in the 1930s among officials as a way of getting quotas and targets met by informal methods (after Stalin's death it became more a way of getting scarce consumer goods). The regime's Five-Year Plans were mostly propaganda, the economy really running on less formal understandings, which until 1937 was implicitly accepted by the regime (Fitzpatrick, 1999: 4; Easter, 2000; P. Gregory, 2004: chaps. 5, 6; Davies, 1996). This was not a totalitarian system – some say it was chaos (Davies, 1989: chap. 9; Getty, 1985: 198), although this is an exaggeration. As Easter (2000) says, we should not view informal networks as completely subverting the system; rather, they helped the system work. It is important to note that this was not simply corruption in which material resources raked off the top are simply a deduction from productivity. As other regimes with a highly ideological component – I shall instance both socialist and nationalist regimes in this volume and the next – Soviet leaders stole less and provided more public goods than have most of the leaders of developing countries. In fiscal terms, they were fairly honest.

For a would-be totalitarian such as Stalin, the blat system remained a source of continuing frustration that he did not in reality control the entire party state. When things were not working out as intended, he could either offer more incentives or increase coercion. He chose the latter, and it turned into arbitrary terror, highly destructive for the party state.

Stalin's atrocities

Stalin and the Politburo were frustrated by the inadequacies of the totalitarian model. It did not work as it was supposed to. Stalin himself was morbidly insecure, paranoid, but the leading Bolsheviks generally had a radical view when the party state failed. They blamed political opposition and sabotage for all the difficulties. Even low work effort was called "wrecking" by enemies of the people. Rooting out enemies became the goal in the 1930s. Because Stalin distrusted the military (as became clear in his purges), he relied on security police – especially the massive NKVD – for this. It became his praetorian guard, protecting him from dissidents, the army, and even the party itself, a mixed form of military and political power. Its role was another reason this state was not actually totalitarian; this was divide-and-rule with overall order provided by terror.

One method of coercive control was to extend the scope of forced labor. By 1936, more than 800,000 people were in prison work camps where criminals and managers and workers who had failed to meet quotas were worked half to death on infrastructural projects. Many thousands died. The most notorious camps were those engaged in the massive construction works for a canal linking the White and Baltic Seas. However, this slave-labor system was never profitable; it took healthy workers and turned them into invalids. It was motivated less by profit, more by the desire to repress "anti-Soviet elements" thought to be subverting socialism. A dose of radical treatment might encourage the others to work harder (Khlevniuk, 2004, 200, 332).

Then Stalin and the Moscow *nomenklatura* elite turned on wreckers and class enemies inside the party – "enemies with party cards" (as Mao was also to do). This was distinctive to leftist party states and not fascist regimes, which were much more comradely. Terror was first turned against former oppositionists and anyone who could conceivably be labeled Trotskyist. Terror seemed to zig-zag, without any discernibly consistent policy thrust. People were arrested, then released, then arrested again. It was first used at middling levels of the party state; no Central Committee member was arrested until mid-1937. The elite then lost its unity, and Stalin's paranoia had freer reign, escalating into the Great Terror – fratricide within the party state aimed against its upper levels, including in 1938 members of the Politburo itself. It was now "centrally organized chaos," say Getty and Naumov (1999: 583), spreading out uncontrollably at lower levels across more of the country (cf. Easter, 2000; Lupher, 1996). The party was torn apart by denunciations of conspiracy and sabotage, with an incredible 1.5 million arrests and 700,000 executions, including virtually all of the Old Bolsheviks who had made the revolution, plus many younger committed socialists. In a loosely organized party, the purge was erratic, with a large element of luck involved in whether those below top levels survived. It wreaked havoc in the officer corps of the armed forces and the Party Central Committee, from both of which about 70 percent of members were purged. The nomenklatura – the higher officials of the party state – numbered 32,899 members at the beginning of 1939, but 14,585 of them had been appointed since 1937, an indication of the scope of the purges, and to Stalin a sign that radicalization and the NKVD had finally secured a loyal elite (Service, 1997: 236). The military was subordinated to the party, and more particularly to its security agencies.

These three great atrocities – the deportations and famine, the prison camps, and the Great Terror – were initially in stark contrast with what had been the general Soviet treatment of national minorities. The Bolsheviks had opposed tsarist imperialism, and were aware that Great-Russian chauvinism, domination by ethnic Russians, remained a threat to the development of a relatively classless society. During the revolutionary and Civil War period, the Bolsheviks had formed alliances with numerous popular resistance movements among national and linguistic minorities, of whom there were more than 100. Such collaboration had developed into a distinctive nationality policy. Decisions were made in Moscow on major issues facing the whole Soviet Union, and provincial security apparatuses were also kept firmly under centralized control to prevent national separatism appearing. Yet other local and regional power was wielded by party cadres drawn from non-Russian nationalities, and nationalities were given their own regional territories and governments. Their distinctive cultures and languages were also supported. This generous policy had been reinforced in the late 1920s with a cultural revolution aimed at suppressing Russian ethnic culture.

The Bolsheviks believed that nationalism was a veiled form of class-based grievance induced by the colonial nature of the tsarist state. They assumed that nationalism was a developmental phase all peoples went through before they could reach internationalism, so they expected nationalism in the USSR to gradually wither away. They were so unconcerned that they introduced what have been called "affirmative action" programs on behalf of ethnic minorities, allowing them to control republics and districts in which they were the majority. Stalin himself had been associated with this policy when he was nationalities commissar. Yet this policy actually encouraged national identities, and this was eventually a factor in the collapse of the Soviet Union. In the context of the 1920s and early 1930s, this tolerant anti-imperialist policy stood in marked contrast to the racism still dominating the British Empire and French empire, a contrast noted by Third World nationalists.

However, things changed in the 1930s when Soviet leaders began to fear the nationalism of Ukrainians, the largest minority. Then, as the threat of Hitler and the Japanese loomed larger, so did fear of border nationalisms. Instead of Soviet ethnic Germans being a way of carrying pro-Soviet sentiments into Germany, the reverse might happen: they could become Hitler's fifth column in the Soviet Union. Stalin reacted to the German threat and the failure of the West to respond to his overtures for an alliance by concluding his Non-Aggression Pact with Hitler (see Chapter 14). This allowed the Soviets to swallow up the Baltic states and half of Poland as buffers against Hitler, but it had imperial consequences. Because there were very few Polish or Baltic communists, these newly acquired republics were ruled by ethnic Russians, which as the Bolsheviks themselves knew would foment nationalism among the subordinated populations.

As the geopolitical threats mounted, Stalin had in any case concluded that he could not afford to alienate Russians by privileging minorities. So he reversed policy and used Russian nationalism to bolster his defenses, committing atrocities against minorities who might conceivably be ethnically linked to Russia's enemies abroad. The first two bursts of deportations of counterrevolutionary nationalities such as Germans, Poles, Belarussians, and Koreans came in 1935 and 1937. There were more deportations, mainly against Caucasian people such as the Chechens, during World War II. Indeed, some Caucasian groups did collaborate with the Germans, but the deportation of border people was part of a major shift of the Stalinist regime, away from Soviet internationalism toward Great-Russian nationalism (I. Martin, 2001; J. Smith, 1999). At its core were a number of atrocities against national minorities, Stalin's fourth type of atrocity.

All four atrocities came in a wave that then tended to ease off. Surviving kulak deportees were given citizen rights, convicts were treated better, the Politburo halted the Terror, and the supposedly dangerous minorities were dispersed. Stalin appeared to learn from his mistakes, and he was always sensitive to signs of resistance among workers. The secret police kept him informed about worker morale, and he would head off local resistance either by increasing local welfare provision or reducing national reinvestment and instead increasing consumption, as in 1934 and 1937 (P. Gregory, 2004: chap. 4). Yet the cumulative effects of all these forms of coercion were enormous. By 1941, around 4 million were inmates of the Gulag camp system, with another 2 million doing corrective labor (Mann, 2005: 323–30; Khlevniuk, 2004; Getty & Naumov, 1999: appendix 1).

Then the war interrupted these policies, except for the maltreatment of nationalities. Fear of Caucasian people collaborating with the Germans led to further deportations that continued even after the Soviet Union was winning the war. Under the cover of war, Stalin was now seeking to rid Russia of troublesome border people. After the war, arrests and incarcerations resumed, although with a declining number of deaths. The liberation in 1945 of Eastern Europe by the Red Army and its subsequent domination by Russians intensified Soviet imperialism. The Baltic Republics were forcibly incorporated into the Soviet Union, and signs of nationalist discontent in the Ukraine and Belarussia were ferociously suppressed. There were now two distinct Western imperial rings: the Western parts of the Soviet Union itself were directly ruled and kept docile by recognition that dissent would be ruthlessly suppressed; East-Central Europe formed an outer ring of indirect empire, ruled by the Soviet authorities through notionally sovereign states whose elites exercised some limited autonomy. Socialist internationalism disappeared as the Soviet Union belatedly became, in its Western zones, an empire.

The early estimates of Stalin's atrocities given by Conquest, Rummel, and others put total deaths upwards of 30 million. Recent scholarly estimates are much lower, in the 8–10 million range (bad enough, one might think). Most of Stalin's atrocities contained mixtures of intention, bungling, callousness, and unintended consequences, preventing the term "totalitarian" being very useful in this context. As Service (1997: 241–53) observes, Stalin was committed to totalitarian goals, spurred on by his own paranoia – and his hand was everywhere at the higher levels of policy-making. Yet although policy was centrally instigated, it was implemented outside of his range of vision. Service concludes, "The goal was so ambitious that even its half-completion was a dreadful achievement." With the violence, the center deported and imprisoned masses of people without thought of what the machinery might be to handle them at their destination. Then local officials – "little Stalins" – and popular forces took matters into their own hands, and got the dirty business done.

Had the terror worked? It is difficult to tell. Stalin and his clique had used intense despotic power that had initially subverted the infrastructural power of the single party state. The regime almost fell apart, but it did not. Surviving party officials toed Stalin's line, as did state administrators. Productivity resumed its upward drift and the military recovered sufficiently to defeat Hitler five years later. This was a regime staffed at all levels by administrators who had to find covert means to fulfill plans and targets, and who were often pursuing their own private interests and vendettas. Stalin's paranoia was partly a product of the structure he had erected. Because almost everyone had something to hide, their behavior was often suspicious. Regional and local officials were seizing the opportunity to liquidate their rivals and enemies, peasants were opposing forced industrialization and hoarding or eating their crops and animals, some minority nationalities sympathized with the Germans or Japanese, and there was some opposition within the Party, even including contacts with exiles such as Trotsky (Thurston, 1996: 25, 34, 50–3). All of this gave the Terror a dynamic of its own, independently of Stalin. The loyal police hierarchy was pressed hard to fulfill large quotas of supposed counterrevolutionaries. They had difficulty finding enough of them, but still believed that a real conspiracy must be buried deep down there somewhere. As one policeman said, "To find a gram of gold, it's necessary to sift tons of sand" (quoted by Thurston, 1996: 83). There was also popular sympathy for some atrocities. Most of the established urban population believed the peasants were hoarding their produce, and many workers assisted in their repression. Moreover, workers continued to show a residual support for a regime that ruled in their name.

It is difficult to gauge the level of popular support for the regime, for there were no elections, opinion polls, or open demonstrations of sentiments. There was some popular support for the Terror, manifested in widespread denunciation of officials as counterrevolutionaries. Soviet citizens experienced a fundamental contradiction: they were being constantly promised a better future, yet right now they experienced oppression. Thus, a polarized quasi-class consciousness developed between "us" the people and "them" the new Communist elite. Ordinary people were happy to denounce the elite – and whomever else they disliked. Peasants were especially delighted to get revenge on the officials who had exploited them, and even when they themselves were denounced and arrested, many only rather pathetically claimed that a mistake must have been made in their case. Some Communists signed false confessions, apparently believing that this was for the good of the revolution. Others signed because they felt guilty for doubting Stalin's policies or for engaging in devious personal stratagems.

There was a whole range of possible stances between absolute loyalty and out-and-out dissent, and most people occupied it, ambivalent and often confused. There remained a widely shared belief in the ideals of the revolution, coupled with disillusionment with the present regime. There was not yet a more generalized cynicism. The ideology still exercised its power in obtaining compliance (Thurston, 1996; R. Davies, 1997; Kotkin, 1995; Fitzpatrick, 1999; and various essays in Fitzpatrick, 2000). Among exploited textile workers, for example, officials were denounced in terms of Marxist class categories, and as long as workers used this language in petitions and demonstrations and did not start sacking local party headquarters, they might get concessions from the regime (Rossman, 2005).

How much of this was a product of Stalin himself? Had Lenin survived or Trotsky become party secretary, would things have been very different? Most scholars say Lenin would not have countenanced the Terror within the party nor the mass deportations, and it may be that the sheer level of atrocities owed much to Stalin and his circle. The regime would have been a party dictatorship whoever led it, and one-party rule is inherently uncongenial to pluralism. If we look around at the Communist regimes that sought forced industrialization of a fundamentally agrarian society, we find only single parties with very little pluralism within them. We do find variations in atrocity levels. We find a leadership worse than Stalin in Cambodia; another in China committed a single greater atrocity (in numbers of the dead) – Mao's Great Leap Forward – plus a major confused party purge, the Cultural Revolution and its suppression. We find a third leadership in Vietnam committing somewhat fewer atrocities. A fourth in North Korea seems very harsh and deeply unsuccessful. Easily the mildest regime in the Communist family has been Cuba, but Castro's regime did not attempt forced industrialization.

The economic balance sheet

The fundamental problem with Communism was that it came to power in agrarian societies but its unwavering ideological goal was rapid industrialization. This could only be secured by taking more of the surplus from peasants, always the vast majority of the population, and then by depressing wage levels, for only out of agriculture and wages could investment capital be found for industry. There was no way that rapid industrialization could avoid being extremely coercive, a perversion of socialist ideals of democracy. The economic ideal overrode the political ideal, as one might expect in regimes embodying Marxist materialism. It was only a question of how many atrocities would accompany this coercion, and these did vary. As with fascism, although to a lesser extent (as socialism did not in theory venerate leadership), the leader in despotic systems also mattered. Mao's saving grace was that he was capable of learning from his big mistakes. Castro was positively benign compared to his peers. However, although Lenin might have been nicer than Stalin, and Stalin's paranoia was particularly bad news, Lenin (and Trotsky) would likely have been corralled by his ideals into forced industrialization, despotism, and at least some atrocities.

We should put this in context. During the interwar period, democracy was in retreat everywhere except the rich countries. The main alternative ideal in the east of Europe was not democracy but despotism of the right. The Russian people had overthrown the tsarist version of that and few wanted it back. Communism, even Stalinism, was the best political system many (perhaps most) thought they could get. As in most forms of regime (including democracy), most people got on with their lives, used trusted networks of kin and friendship to make things informally a little better, and avoided politics. If they did so, then they might get accorded some of the privileges the regime handed down.

Perhaps the main reason the regime won support was that it was successful in two of its major goals: industrialization and defense of the homeland. In a state-planned economy that did not actually function according to the plan, it is easy to spot turf wars, shortages, bottlenecks, and other botches. Yet this supposedly ramshackle version of forced industrialization brought economic growth. Just how much is hotly debated, but the interwar period was not one of great success in the West. The capitalist economies were fairly stagnant, and most experienced decline during the Great Depression period. The Soviet Union insulated itself from that. The gap also continued to widen between the few rich economies and the bulk of the world mired in poverty.

Seen in comparative terms and measured in aggregate statistics between 1928 and 1970, the Soviet economy probably did well, although we cannot be certain because of often inadequate and dishonest official statistics. Its average growth factor of around 4 percent exceeded that of any other country in the world at that time except for Japan and its colonies. Even if we exercise skepticism about Soviet figures and reduce its growth to, say, between 2.5 percent and 3 percent, it would still be better. It is also reinforced by statistics of life expectancy from birth. This doubled between 1900 and 1950, from 32 years to 65 years – a rate of increase greater than that of any other country (Maddison, 2001: table 1–5A). As we saw in Chapter 4, Japan had not been a democratic society either, still less its colonies.

There was a reason for the Soviet and Japanese success rates: state planning is effective in late-developing countries at least in the industrializing phase. If the elite can identify from other countries' experience the institutions necessary for industrialization, central planning may be more effective than market competition, especially if the state is relatively incorrupt and not skimming much off the top. With the rise of the corporation, the West was in any case experiencing more planning within larger economic units. It is unlikely that had the tsarist regime continued, it could have achieved this level of growth, as Paul Gregory asserts (1994: 136–7). For as R. Allen (2003: 33–46) notes, tsarist growth had depended heavily on the high price of wheat, and wheat and other primary commodity prices collapsed after World War I. It was also unlikely that either agricultural productivity could have risen or industry expanded much, given the likely collapse of agriculture. Allen (2003: 9–10) also thinks we should compare like with like – the Soviet republics to their non-Soviet neighbors. Soviet Central Asia and the North Caucasus Republics were the poorest regions of the Soviet Union, but they all had per capita GDP well above their non-Soviet neighbors Turkey, Iran, and Pakistan. Agriculture remained the great Soviet weakness, but heavy industry was its strength – especially in the 1930s, which saw a 12 percent annual industrial growth rate. In 1932, the Soviets had to import 78 percent of their machine tools; five years later, less than 10 percent were imported.

Most of this growth was transferred into reinvestment in heavy industry – especially the defense industries, which expanded greatly in the 1930s as threats from Germany, Japan, and Britain (in Stalin's eyes) grew. Only in the 1960s was much of the surplus channeled into consumer goods. Yet there was also improvement in urban per capita consumption between 1928 and 1937 – which Allen (2003: chap. 7) argues carried over into national consumption levels as a whole. Yet Mark Harrison (1994) argues the reverse. It seems that men's real wages fell and women's employment expanded greatly, but at lower wage levels. Although average individual wages fell, this was offset in two wages. First, the combination of men's and women's wages produced slightly higher household incomes; second, the Soviet Union had slashed unemployment rates to near zero (which Western economists believe led to inefficient overemployment). Rationing ended and skilled workers could live comfortably, but the main benefit – perhaps the main achievement of Communist regimes – was education. Soviet citizens became highly educated and literate, more so than comparable developing capitalist countries. There was also adequate healthcare. Starting in 1937, a big public housing program also started. All of these were designed to avoid mass discontent. Anthropometric indicators of health status reveal improvement, and such data, unlike GDP measures, are not easily manipulated. There was continuing decline in mortality, continuing growth in average physical stature, and earlier physical maturation among children, all indicators of greater health in absolute terms and relative to the contemporary experience of most other countries (Davies & Wheatcroft, 2004). It was a long way from the promised utopia – which kept getting put off – but it was distinct material improvement (Suny, 1998: 240–50).

The Soviet Union achieved the opposite of Marshall's three stages of citizenship. The population got some social citizenship (for Marshall, the last stage) without enjoying either political or civil citizenship. It had two positive qualities of most highly ideological party states of the left: it was relatively honest and genuinely committed to economic development. These virtues were revealed not merely at the top but throughout the mass party. Little of the surplus was skimmed off in corruption, and more of it went into reinvestment and public goods than in most developing countries of the world. As we saw, this had not been so of ideological parties of the fascist right. However, in my fourth volume, we will see that such virtues were later also revealed in much milder nationalist regimes of the left, center, and right alike.

Aggregate statistics conceal unevenness. Although the regime managed to keep inequalities quite low, the worst off was the rural population; skilled workers, newly employed women, and migrants from the countryside to the towns were all relatively well-off. Industrialization and urbanization brought upward mobility for millions, and because the housing, welfare benefits, and employment were provided by the state, the regime got much of the credit. The ironies continued, however. As we saw, many of these migrants made their move as a result of Stalin's dreadful forced collectivization policies. The unemployment rate lowered, but partly because of the deaths caused by the regime. Industrial growth also owed something to large imports of advanced technology from Britain and the United States – paid for by exporting grain and timber that were sorely needed by the Soviet people. Moreover, as Wheatcroft observes, most people's experience was probably not of steady improvement, as development was interspersed with famines, shortages of goods caused by planning failures, mass atrocities, and finally war. The overall balance sheet may have been favorable, but real life was varied and full of terrible ironies. The most privileged of all were party members, yet they were the most vulnerable to the Great Terror. None of this should lead to the terrible conclusion that Stalinism was necessary for growth, however. Forced collectivization was economically harmful as well as intrinsically horrendous. Its one good outcome – labor mobility – could have been secured by nicer means. The other atrocities had no positive economic role. Stalin could have done a lot better.

Allen (2003: chap. 8) gives the most convincing overall explanation of Soviet growth. He sees two main causes. First, investment went mainly to heavy industry and was heavily protected inside what was largely an autarchic economy. In this phase of the world economy, protectionism worked, as Japan also showed. Second, the imposition of high output targets combined with soft budgetary constraints meant that because output and not profit was primary, the state provided bank credits to keep firms solvent and producing. No depression was possible in this system. State planning overrode market considerations, and it specifically overrode the normal development strategy of this era – exporting primary products and importing machinery. The statist version of socialism worked, just as the statist version of imperialism was working in the Japanese Empire of the period.

Stalinism was a qualified economic success (except in agriculture), but a political and ideological nightmare – a worse version of the unequal power achievements made by the Japanese Empire, revealed in Chapter 4. Socialism as an economic project was quickly discovered to be an unachievable utopia in an enormous, backward country such as the Soviet Union if the goal was modernization through forced industrialization, which was how Marx was interpreted in the twentieth century. The regime, cleaving to its salvation ideology, reacted to this contradiction with terrible violence against the peasants and an ad hoc array of nasty practices elsewhere. All this had very little relationship to socialism, but it was a recognizably socialist nightmare, a perversion of socialist ideals, a party-state dictatorship not of but over the proletariat (and everyone else, too). In narrowly economic terms, the results (if you were not one of the dead or deported) were quite good. In a backward economy, the ratio of eating to starving was excellent, and so was the level of health and literacy. So in this period, the most transparent failure of the Bolsheviks was not in economic but political and ideological power. They had half-intentionally created a monstrous dictatorship, an absolute inversion of socialist ideals, at its worst committing mass atrocities on a scale unprecedented in prior history. It is difficult to defend this in terms of its economic success, even in the interwar period (in the postwar period, capitalism was to do much better than communism). Is human happiness that dependent on material success? Yes, if you are starving, as many across the world still were. Many Soviet citizens and sympathetic outsiders held out hope throughout this period that with greater economic success would flow civil and political liberalization. Defeating scarcity would produce regime relaxation. They still believed that the future might be red. For them, the jury was still out on state socialism.

In any case, this was not the worst regime in the world during the interwar period. In 1941, many Ukrainians – weary of Stalinist exploitation – welcomed the Wehrmacht into their land. Under Hitler, however, they discovered a deeper level of exploitation and even worse atrocities. By 1944, they were warmly welcoming the Red Army back again. The greatest achievement of Stalinist Russia proved to be that very diversion of resources from consumption into military production that kept living standards down and subsidized massive armed forces, which then at great self-sacrifice successfully defended Soviet citizens – including Jews and gypsies – from Hitler. The Soviet Union owed its existence to World War I, and it was then very good at World War II, as we will see in Chapter 14.

The impact of communism abroad

Because industry not agriculture was the symbol of modernity across the world, the Soviet Union's apparent industrial success was widely admired. Ideologies of state socialism diffused globally. To revolutionaries in agrarian societies, the Soviet (and later the Chinese) route seemed a shortcut to freedom from material want, giving them great confidence that history was on their side. Because millions of peasants across the world were suffering gross exploitation, revolutionary ideologies were resonant among them. After World War II, the Bolshevik and Maoist routes were admired and frequently emulated across the poorer countries of the world. Indeed, throughout the world late development was being better achieved by infrastructurally powerful states than by free markets – provided the state elite was genuinely committed to development more than lining its own pockets (Kohli, 2004). The most positive thing to be said about Communist leaders is that their ideology was genuine. They were sincerely committed to developing their economies, almost whatever the cost. Although there was corruption, it was much less than in most developing countries.

As real socialism was sacrificed and atrocities grew through the 1920s and 1930s, this had a negative overall effect, especially on the West. Most Western socialists were harmed by the ability of the Bolsheviks to hold onto power repressively and maintain a seemingly threatening degree of global power. The one case of "actually existing socialism" could not win many converts in the West, outside those leftists disillusioned with just how pusillanimous socialist parties might be to get into power. Foreign communist parties did expand somewhat as a result of this disillusion, glorifying in Russian economic growth statistics, boosted by selective tours of Soviet Potemkin villages (show villages). However, they were rarely a major force in the West, and the Bolshevik card, the Red Peril, was played with success by bourgeois parties and employers abroad from the early 1920s onward. Communist parties and unions were its easiest targets, but all parties of labor experienced difficulties during Red Peril scares. Had the Soviet regime been a desirable form of socialism, such propaganda would have had the opposite effect.

The Bolsheviks also intervened more directly abroad. In March 1920, they replaced the ineffectual Second International with a Third International, to defend the Revolution in Russia and to serve "as a preliminary step of the International Republic of Soviets towards the world-wide victory of Communism." Revolution was believed to be a global affair. The crunch came in August 1920, as the second Congress of the International, renamed the Comintern, adopted Lenin's 21 Conditions as its charter. These included the provisions that all affiliated parties were to adopt the structure of the Russian Communist Party, defend the Soviet Union, struggle against reformist Social Democracy (now a term of abuse for Moscow), and subordinate themselves to a permanent central committee centered in Moscow.

Few foreign parties and unions would accept control from abroad or denunciation of reformism. Some parties split as a result. Kriegel (1969) says that the French Socialist Party was not reformist, so did not understand the Moscow line. After what she regards as the largely "accidental" result of an abstract debate at the decisive Congress of Tours, most party members transformed themselves into the Communist Party; the dissidents left to form an initially smaller Socialist Party. In Norway, Italy, and Czechoslovakia the labor movement continued to maintain rather uneasy links with the Comintern. Elsewhere, it was generally the smaller dissident groups (often drawn from newer industrializing areas) who left socialist parties to form communist parties. Through the 1920s, the Communists became the left because they lay outside the institutions of reformist compromise, and bourgeois parties would rarely cooperate with them. So reform-versus-revolution was switched to conflict between socialists and communists. Communist parties claimed more commitment to revolution (and did indeed launch unsuccessful insurrections in several countries), but they were also usually more centralized and less democratic, favoring organization not movement. Socialist parties became more diverse, including ultraleft advocates of movement as well as those of mutualist and reformist persuasion. As revolutionary movements became more fractured, social democracy revived after flagging in the mid-1920s.

There was one positive aspect of the fracture between reform and revolution. Although it might be said that it weakened the working class, the presence of a competitor on its left meant that Socialists and Communists competed electorally and for union members. This probably stiffened up the reformism of the socialist parties. Socialists managed to combine reforms and government coalitions with bourgeois parties; Communists offered a sense of participating in a disciplined, global movement to achieve a utopia. Control of communist parties by Moscow was a decided negative, however. The strategy of foreign Communist parties had to be cleared first with Moscow. Moscow's general line was that global revolutionary needs, coordinated by the Comintern, must come before the needs of a single country's labor movement. In contrast, socialist parties viewed politics as national. In decades that saw greater national economic protectionism and the faltering of the League of Nations, the national argument seemed more powerful. Cooperation between the two types of party became more difficult, and Communists were seen as unreliable allies.

The Moscow leadership of the Comintern was in practice subservient to the leadership of the Communist Party of the Soviet Union. This was built into the constitution of the International from the start, with its commitment to defend the Soviet government. It was quickly given organizational force, as Moscow began to send out secret emissaries to watch and if necessary subvert foreign Communist leaderships. The prestige of the Bolsheviks was such that foreign loyalists could always be found to do their bidding; and as long as the Comintern endured, they could be rewarded with control of the local Party – purging could be institutionalized. All this was profoundly undemocratic. It also produced policies insensitive to local conditions. Because Moscow was often ignorant of these, it tended to substitute the lessons of its own experience in Russia. The Bolsheviks had successfully split the Social Revolutionaries in Russia, persuading the left wing to cooperate, isolating the right wing for suppression (followed later by the left wing, too). Splitting tactics were used abroad, but when none of these factions were participating in government, their splits could not be resolved and factionalism between them endured, weakening them all. This proved particularly damaging to the Italian movement, faced with the rise of Fascism, where loyal Communists were ordered to provoke a split in 1921. Moscow also imposed its Russian Civil War experience on the West. In 1923, Red Army experts were sent to Germany to organize an insurrection for which there was little support. The Communist enclaves perished bloodily.

These policies revealed the Comintern systematically subordinating the needs of foreign parties, not to the global needs of revolution but to the needs of the Soviet regime. For much of the 1920s, Comintern policy was ambiguous or contradictory. Sudden exhortations to insurrection alternated with United Fronts – cooperating either with the rank and file or leadership of other workers' parties and unions. Then in 1928 came a switch to a more consistent line of revolutionary purity and class against class – rigid noncooperation with all other parties and unions. This had been partly precipitated by the Chinese disaster of 1927, when the Shanghai Communists were annihilated by their supposed allies – Chiang Kai-shek's troops – the alliance having been urged on the local Communists by Comintern agents. However, the rhythm of the policy switch was more closely related to the power struggle among the Bolsheviks and the emergence of Stalin as supreme leader. Foreign purges became a spin-off of Stalin's domestic purges. There was one consistency in the Comintern line: any foreign leader showing consistent commitment to any political line – that is, showing independence from Moscow – was purged.

To treat foreign Communist parties as pawns in other games was not conducive to their health. One big party – the Norwegian – left the Comintern in disgust, leaving behind only a small splinter group. Those who stayed in the Comintern lost either members or lives. We have already seen the disasters that befell the German KPD as a result of premature insurrection and attacks on social fascism. The two most important remaining parties – the French and the Czech – were reduced from 131,000 and 350,000 members in 1921 to 28,000 and 35,000 in 1932 (Drachkovitch & Lazitch, 1966: 186–7). Most labor militants in the West were repelled by attacks on non-Communist comrades and the purging of Communist leaders. Hitler forced further changes of direction because the Soviet Union was now faced by an aggressive power with designs on central Europe. At first, the shift benefitted foreign communists. Starting in 1935, popular fronts of all workers' parties, aimed against fascism, were back in favor. These had immediate results in France and Spain, enabling Communists to take part in government, fight in their defense, and profit from disillusionment at their fall. They revealed the consistent role that Communist parties should have taken: encourage reformism leftward, and if it fails, claim a sellout. This was a brief golden age for the Comintern (Suny, 1998: 297–306). In August 1939, however, Stalin entered a Non-Aggression Pact with Hitler, forcing Communist parties to end their anti-Fascist fronts. In 1941 when Hitler attacked the Soviet Union, the line was again reversed. Western Communists, hitherto neutral in the war and often interned, were suddenly asked to help defend the world against Fascism. Communists were bemused, especially working-class members who were not initiates into the worldwide needs of labor. The British and American parties were virtually destroyed in the process (not that they mattered much, anyway). In this phase, Comintern logic was primarily geopolitical. Of course, as we see in the next chapter, the Soviet Union was not the real villain of the piece. After being rebuffed in his attempt to form an alliance with the West, Stalin had to switch to a Non-Aggression Pact with Hitler to buy neutrality and time. When attacked by Hitler, he had to ally with the West.

The development of the Soviet Union under Stalin accelerated its harmful effects on Western labor movements. The outcome of World War II then left the Soviets the masters of Eastern Europe, and the most anti-Communist state, the United States, was hegemonic over Western Europe and most of the rest of the world. The multiple global segments of the imperial period were simplified into two, one of them autarchic the other more open-ended. Two extreme countries came to pattern the globe, each a negative reference point for the other. Soviet dictatorship in Eastern Europe and Soviet global militarism became unacceptable from most Western standpoints, from capitalists to most Marxists. All Western labor movements were weakened by the argument of their opponents that socialism was already established in the USSR and Eastern Europe – as totalitarianism and imperialism. Stalin was putting the final nail in the coffin of revolutionary socialism in the West, after it had been destroyed in the Soviet Union. The Union itself would survive somewhat longer, and its popularity would last longer in poorer countries of the world. That the foundations might be rotten was not yet clear, but now came the war, whose result would destroy the Fascist alternative yet seemingly strengthen the Communist one, just as it strengthened Western democratic capitalism. One alternative was gone, the other still seemed viable, and this was also true in Asia.

12 Japanese imperialism, 1930–1945

The biggest geopolitical shift of the twentieth century was the resurgence of Asia, over two or three centuries a fairly stagnant continent whose development had failed to match that of Europe and America. By the twenty-first century, three Asian countries – China, India, and Japan – were thrusting back to become Great Power rivals to Europe and America, but their thrusts had different rhythms. India remained a part of the British Empire until 1945. Its resurgence came later than the others, and its forms were the closest to European postwar models, combining democracy, capitalism, and avoidance of imperialism. China remained deeply divided by civil war until 1947, and then it became Communist, although also broadly non-imperial. Japan was the earliest Asian developer. The forms of its development were adapted from earlier Western models, including a form of representative government, capitalism, and imperialism, all given a distinctive Japanese coloration. By the end of the 1930s, Japan had a fairly advanced state-coordinated capitalist economy and had acquired a substantial empire in Asia through exercising formidable military power, becoming a full partner in the imperialism that by then covered most of the world. Its representative government had withered, however. Why did it take the imperial and quasi-despotic path? That is the central question of this chapter.

Ratcheting up militarism

With hindsight, the escalation of Japanese military imperialism through the 1930s seems inexorable, but it was not. In four incidents in China, Japanese soldiers took foreign policy into their own hands to ratchet up aggression. Only a fifth ratchet, the 1941 attack on Pearl Harbor, was a collective decision made at the highest government level. The first incident was in 1928, when Japanese soldiers killed the Chinese warlord ruler of Manchuria, thus extending Japanese influence there. This was seen in Japan as a mistake, and it led to the demise of the conservative government that had failed to stop it. More important were the incidents of 1931, 1935, and 1937, which coincided with rightward movement in Japan itself. Underlying these incidents and reinforced by them was the autonomy of military power in Japan, noted in Chapter 4, which now took a turn toward fascism. Japan in this period represented the triumph of military over economic and political power. My underlying quest in this chapter is to discover how this happened and why it eventually shifted

Japan onto a suicidal path, entering into two wars, in China and against the United States, which it was unlikely to win. How and why did reason fail? To answer that, I must retrace the path taken.

We saw in Chapter 4 that in the mid-1920s political power was finely balanced between conservatives and liberals. The Great Depression then tilted this against the liberals. With exquisitely bad timing, the liberal Minseito Party government returned Japan to the gold standard in 1930, just as the Depression hit. Furthermore, the government had begun deflating the economy in 1929 in order to return to the standard. Doing this in the teeth of a Depression slashing demand and investment worsened the recession and a run on the yen. The Smoot-Hawley tariffs introduced by the United States in 1929 had undermined pro-American Japanese liberals, and in 1931, British withdrawal from the gold standard was seen as the fall of the international liberal order. Japanese bankers realized the yen would soon be under pressure, and began selling their yen for dollars, appearing to confirm nationalist accusations that finance capitalists were traitors. The Minseito government raised interest rates, and its domestic reform package – including votes for women and concessions to unions and tenant farmers – was abandoned. This checked the forward momentum of liberalism, but the government fell in December, the normal fate of governments engulfed by the Depression. In Japan, liberals were destroyed, but conservatives and militarists were boosted. Without the Depression, would Japan have avoided aggressive militarism? It is hard to say, but it is possible. The Japanese trajectory was the opposite scenario to the American, but resembled in some ways the German. Nation-states were proving their diversity.

There was falling demand, production cartels, cutbacks, wage cuts, and layoffs. Industry declined, although not as much as in the West, and agriculture suffered as silk exports and rice prices fell. Welfare capitalism declined, as few employers could now afford it. Liberals and the Home Ministry Social Bureau sometimes favored workers rights, but were hostile to socialism or strikes. Now former liberals joined with conservatives to support repression, and this proved effective against the sectionalized, segmented labor movement described in Chapter 4. Neither socialism nor a lib-lab alliance emerged from the Depression in Japan.

The Home Ministry did sponsor paternalistic reform measures in health insurance, factory conditions, and other social arenas, but discouraged sector-wide unions and repressed strikes. Most grievances were settled by compulsory mediation, and by 1936, 62 percent of strikes were settled by the police – "sabre mediation" (Garon, 1987: 206–7) – which made workers understandably cautious in pressing dissent (Taira, 1988: 637–40; A. Gordon, 1985: 250–1). Strikes remained few until after World War II, and unions did not rise above 8 percent of the workforce and generally confined their activities to the plant or company level.

These shifts in political power outweighed the rise of labor in mass production. By 1940, 66 percent of manufacturing employment was in factories. In other circumstances, this might have led to a more powerful working-class movement; here it did not. The government bureaucracy also expanded. By 1928, there were 1.3 million civil servants – four times the size of the armed forces – and they performed many responsibilities that in Western countries were handled by private agencies. Capitalism was becoming more state-coordinated. Like the armed forces, they imbibed an ideology of public service on behalf of the emperor and the nation and were mostly a conservative force. Many of them railed against the pursuit of private interests by parties, business, and unions, and urged "reform" in a despotic statist direction. Reform became a slogan of the right. Faced with such hostility, the unions split and in the late 1930s were absorbed into corporatist "patriotic societies" (Garon, 1987: 198–218; Taira, 1988: 640–6; Odaka, 1999: 150–7; A. Gordon, 1991: 287–92). Socialism became more a doctrine of intellectuals than of workers. The Japanese were apparently moving back from being citizens to subjects once again.

Indeed, street demonstrations after the Depression were dominated not by workers and unions but ultranationalists led by young officers and former colonial settlers. These were violent, often accompanied by murders. Minseito Prime Minister Hamaguchi was the first prominent victim in December 1931, beginning a sequence of assassinations and coup attempts through the 1930s that intimidated moderates. One of their leaders later reminisced that Hamaguchi's assassination lit "the fuse of the military and civilian reform movement's attack on the upper and privileged classes." He described Finance Minister Inoue as "the running dog of the zaibatsu, or even as the mortal enemy of the national masses." He sent Inoue a sword, inviting him to commit hara-kiri. Inoue resisted the offer, but was soon killed by an officer of the Blood Pledge Corps. Other politicians and zaibatsu chiefs followed him to their deaths. Junior officers were now intervening violently in politics, probably with minority support within the high command. Without restraint from the ministries or the court, paramilitarism was no longer tameable.

The economic policies of the new Seiyukai Party conservative government proved effective. Takahashi, its brilliant finance minister, promptly took Japan off gold, lowered interest rates, introduced deficit financing, and boosted countercyclical government spending by 20 percent via the direct creation of money. His intuitive Keynesianism ensured that Japanese industry revived, exporting its way out of depression by mid-1932 (Nakamura, 1988: 464–8). Against his advice, the increased government spending went mostly to the military. In 1935, he did push through a reduction in military spending but that earned him an assassin's bullet the following year (Metzler, 2006: 199–256). Military spending continued increasing under a government dominated not by politicians but by rightist reform bureaucrats. Allied to nationalists, they introduced greater controls on industry, ending market allocation by the price mechanism in iron, steel, and chemicals where government investment also increased. This was going beyond mere state-coordination to state domination of capitalism. The suppression of labor involved forcibly lowering wages, which helped aggregate recovery. The economy remained fairly buoyant for most of the 1930s, although workers and peasants saw little reward. It was a quicker economic recovery than the liberal capitalist economies managed, resembling the Nazi recovery (Cha, 2000). As in Germany, the economic and military successes of the despotic regime made it popular. There was no quick way back, even to the half-citizen, half-subject Taisho-era democracy (Berger, 1977: 105–17, 346; A. Gordon, 1985: chaps. 9, 10; Nakamura, 1988).

Comparative and historical sociologists have shown that the growth of democracy is generally correlated positively with the strength of the working-class movement and negatively with the power of the landlord class (Rueschemeyer et al., 1992). Japan broadly fits this thesis because working-class weakness and landlord strength kept genuine democracy at bay, although the timing of the Great Depression and successful imperialism greatly assisted antidemocratic forces. Liberal political factions began to shift rightward, and by the mid-1930s there were almost no real liberals left. The small leftist Social Masses Party garnered 5 percent of the vote in the 1936 diet elections and 9 percent in 1937. To avoid assassination, its leaders abandoned their anti-imperialism and embraced popular imperialism (A. Gordon, 1991: 302–15). Japan had become a country in which almost everyone favored imperialism. This boded ill for the peace of East Asia

The Depression also impacted Japanese imperial choices. Market-oriented expansion presupposed low-tariff international trade, important for Japan for it needed to import raw materials and machinery for its heavy industries. Advanced equipment came mostly from the United States, raw materials came mostly from the British Empire, and oil came from the United States and the Dutch East Indies. Japan paid for these by exporting labor-intensive textile goods. The Depression hit this exchange hard, as did the wave of protectionism that then swept the international economy. Add the Soviet Union and Nazi Germany, and the world seemed to be dividing into autarchic empires. Japanese fears grew of an "ABCD encirclement" by America, Britain, China, and the Dutch. Takahashi's export boom was going more to Manchuria and North China rather than the United States or the British Empire. All this boosted the case of those arguing for a direct colonial imperialism aimed at an enlarged economic autarchy. The "resource imperialism" of Taiwan and Korea might be extended into Manchuria and North China, now seen as lifelines for Japan to avoid "strangulation" by the liberal empires. Minerals could be secured by occupying the territories in which they lay as colonies. Territories not markets, or rather, markets would be secured by acquiring further territories. Those who wanted aggression for economic purposes and the total-war faction discussed in Chapter 4 united on this strategy (Lockwood, 1954: 117; Iriye, 1974; Duus, 1996: xv–xviii; Sugihara, 2004).

So for both domestic and foreign reasons, the shift toward liberalism and informal imperialism in the 1920s was reversed in the 1930s. Reform bureaucrats and the military gained power at the expense of political parties intimidated by assassins egged on by populist nationalists, with half-open support from some higher military officials (Iriye, 1997: 62–72; Nish, 2002: 180–2; Benson & Matsumura, 2001: 30–42). Two main shifts were occurring with the state: the bureaucracy was growing in numbers and power, and it was being increasingly colonized by the military. What had started in the Meiji reforms as merely a state-coordinated capitalism had temporarily become a little more liberal, before becoming more despotic and militarized. The sources of social power were being fused somewhat uneasily together as elites rejected pluralist democracy. There was a leading spirit in the fusion, however, for the military was beginning to lead both the state and capitalism by the nose.

The Army Ministry and the Foreign Office had been fighting a turf war over Manchuria since 1906, but the army became really troublesome when Chiang Kai-shek began to revive Kuomintang fortunes in China after 1926. Chiang was being egged on by his own nationalists to restore Chinese authority over Manchuria and North China. Japanese settlers and businessmen there felt threatened by this nationalist revival, and urged Japanese imperialism be stiffened. The Japanese foreign service resisted this pressure, and was denounced as sympathizing more with the Chinese nationalists than with its own fellow citizens. Mutual provocations from Japanese and Chinese nationalists tended to destabilize both governments (Brooks, 2000: chap. 5).

This fused with destabilization underway in the military itself. During the 1920s, the Kwantung Field Army – which protected the Japanese railroads in Chinese Manchuria – had attracted ambitious and political young Japanese officers who felt this was where the imperial action would be. In September 1931, a number of them conspired to fake a sabotage of the main railroad line and persuade the army (against the wishes of the government and their own commander) to attack the larger armies of the local Chinese warlords. Manchuria was now overrun by the Japanese. Ishiwara was the senior staff officer involved, although some senior military and court figures were probably complicit. Ishiwara saw the Manchurian invasion as a short, decisive war useful to build up resources for a later total war. He judged that other powers would not intervene: the Soviet Union was in the middle of a Five Year Plan, the West was preoccupied with the Depression; a year later, things might be different. Now was the time to strike (Peattie, 1975: 114–33).

When the invasion happened, some in Tokyo were angry, including Emperor Hirohito. Minseito government ministers briefly tried to stop it, but with little support they felt forced to acquiesce. After all, the action had been successful and had created new facts on the ground. This began a sequence of failures to stand up to the armed forces that would cost civilians dearly over the next ten years (Bix, 2001: 228–41). This government fell anyway, and after a wave of assassinations by shadowy officer groups, the last government staffed by party politicians fell in May 1932. Reform bureaucrats formally replaced them, but gradually lost power to the military. Shidehara's liberal policy had depended on cooperation between the powers, and this lessened through the Great Depression and Manchurian venture (Akami, 2002). The policy of informal empire in China had depended on negotiating deals with local Chinese warlords and capitalists (Matsusaka, 2001: 354). Although some across Japanese-occupied areas of Manchuria and China did cooperate (Barrett & Shyu, 2001), others did not wish to alienate Chinese national sentiment and were playing the Japanese and Chinese governments against each other. Lacking sufficiently reliable allies, the Japanese attempted more direct colonial rule, setting up the puppet state of Manchukuo in Manchuria. The Japanese government announced that it had liberated the "Manchus" from domination by China, a typically fraudulent colonialist claim.

Manchukuo alienated the Western imperial powers, the League of Nations, and world opinion. However, as Ishiwara had predicted, it was only words. Japan quit the League and the fuss subsided – but backlash came from China. Japanese rhetoric to the contrary, most inhabitants of Manchuria considered themselves Chinese, and were considered as such by other Chinese. Whatever anti-Manchu sentiments lingered in Chinese republicanism were now swamped by anti-Japanese sentiments. Liberating Manchuria from the Japanese became the insistent demand of Chinese nationalists (Mitter, 2000), and their boycotts of Japanese goods finished off any chances of a Shidehara diplomacy.

Manchukuo seemed worth colonizing because it had substantial economic resources. Its new government – a partnership of Japanese military officers and capitalists – provided more order, and borrowing from German World War I and Soviet models, the regime pioneered a mixed public-private–ownership economy running under five-year plans. Manufacturing production rose five-fold and GDP rose by 4 percent annually between 1924 and 1941 – the normal rate across Japan's early empire (Maddison, 2004: 25). With order restored and the economy vibrant, Japan moved toward less direct rule through Manchurian elites. The puppet ruler – the resurrected Qin Emperor Pu yi – had little autonomy, and multicultural Manchu nationalism was mainly propaganda, yet locally rule was through elites and existing institutions. Manchukuo was described as a "brother country," a "branch house" of the Japanese family. Resistance was murderously repressed, but most resistance came from peasants whose lands had been expropriated and given to Japanese and Korean settlers. Back in Japan, the public followed sanitized accounts of progress with pride.

The million Japanese settlers coming into Manchukuo in the 1930s were important symbols of upward mobility for poor Japanese peasants aspiring to their own farms. "Manchurian colonization was a social movement before it became a state initiative," says L. Young (1998: 307; cf Nish, 2002: 177–82). Manchukuo reality differed from the propaganda, however. Only about 10 percent of the incoming settlers became farmers; most became bureaucrats in the occupation authority or white-collar workers in industries. Some settlers were pressed into part-time soldiering to defend the occupied areas from local "bandits" (dispossessed peasants). Given their ignorance of local conditions, the settler-farmers were less competent as farmers than the locals they had displaced. For most of them, this proved to be a long way from the paradise proclaimed by the Japanese media. Settler-adventurers who failed and returned to Japan tended to turn their discontent against those refusing to pour more resources into the colonies. There they affected a murderous juncture with the militarists in far-right organizations.

After the initial media war frenzy subsided, some noticed that Manchukuo's contribution to the Japanese economy was less than promised. Support for a more informal empire began to revive in the home ministry and foreign office, and army budgets were attacked in the diet 1933–1935 (Wilson, 2002). Even militarists realized that Manchukuo could not alone provide the autarchic economy they sought, so they schemed for North China, as well. Because power in Japan was shifting rightward, the solution to inadequate colonies was seen as more colonies. Yet the ensuing war with China was to starve Manchukuo of investment funds, preventing fulfillment of its second five-year plan (Mitter, 2000: 94–129; Duus, Myers, and Peattie, 1996; Nish, 2002: 178–82; L. Young, 1998: 41–3; Barnhart, 1987: 39). As Japan drifted toward nationalism, corporatism, and militarism, the army acquired more power, first through sympathetic civilian politicians, then through its own rule (L. Young, 1998: 119–29). A purge of "dangerous thought," initially launched against communists, then embraced socialists, liberals, and internationalists. In 1936, an old rule was reinstated that only serving officers could be military ministers, giving the high command a veto within the cabinet and more access to the emperor. In the same year, the extremists overreached themselves in a failed coup attempt, but that persuaded them to seek to achieve their goals more subtly, within the state. Aided by the inability of Japanese diplomats to defend Japanese residents in China and Manchuria against local nationalists, they secured the destruction of the Foreign Office. Its diplomats had been walking a tightrope between instructions from Tokyo, the need to work with the local Chinese, and conforming to the international norms of the treaty ports. As Tokyo shifted rightward, the diplomats' advice was ignored, and in 1937–1938 the diplomatic corps was disbanded, its responsibilities handed over to a new military-dominated authority (Brooks, 2000: 200–7; Nish, 2002: 180).

The military was now in control but divided on strategy. The navy tended to favour a southern advance of influence across the Pacific, recognizing that this carried a risk of war with Britain and the United States. Some higher officers wanted to avoid this at all costs; others did not. The navy was divided, although they agreed on a holding operation in the North to contain the Soviets and Chinese. A few army officers supported this, but most focussed on expansion in North China, but they in turn were divided between total war, Imperial Way, and control factions.

Total-war advocates such as Ishiwara sought a National Defense State to build up Asian resources to challenge the capitalist West. This involved securing dominance over China, although they hoped to do this without major war. This was obviously imperialist and ideological, but it was also gradualist. The control faction was more pragmatic; it sought a deal with the Soviets and developing economic planning and military technology and building up Manchurian defenses. This view was especially prevalent among general staff planners who believed that Japan did not have the resources to take on another Great Power as well as China.

In contrast, the Imperial Way was more ideological than the other two. It centered on rabid anti-Communism, urging war against the Soviet Union. It downplayed the contribution to victory of material factors such as productive capacity or population size. Such economistic calculations were seen as the stock-in-trade of liberal and Marxist enemies. Imperial Way favored decisive battles won by offensive élan deriving from Japan's superior spiritual values. This was a kind of secular salvationism, although it came wrapped up in technocratic and tactical terms. Japan had long known that it would be inferior to its opponents in numbers and perhaps technology, but Japanese *seishin* or "spiritual mobilization" could substitute for material inferiority, said Prime Minister Konoe. A study group analyzing two defeats by Soviet forces in 1939–1940 concluded that the Japanese were only about 80 percent as effective in technology and organization as Soviet troops, and that "the only method of making up for the missing 20% is to draw upon spiritual strength" (Tarling, 2001: 42).This was similar to Nazi militarism in its almost mystical worship of the national spirit. So was the combination of harsh discipline and ferocious fighting spirit that treated enemy soldiers and civilians brutally. Whereas the Nazis cultivated a high degree of egalitarian comradeship between officers and men, differences of rank were profound in Japan and discipline was brutal. Persistent through Japan's rising militarism was a belief in German-style *Blitzkrieg*, the sudden, overwhelming, decisive offensive. This had supposedly worked in 1894, 1905, and 1931, just as it worked for the Nazis between 1936 and 1940.

The arguments between these three army factions were more about means and priorities than ultimate ends, as all favored imperial expansion. There was no resolution of their debates, however. Instead, policy documents typically contained references to all three strategies but were vague about the resources needed for them – which were mostly beyond Japan's capacity, anyway. All the factions wanted war and expansion in Asia, however, and they all wanted more military control of the state. Official policy documents endorsed aggression, if in somewhat contrary directions (Peattie, 1975: 186–90; Hane, 1992: chap. 12; Bix, 2001: 308–13).

Once again, army action on the ground decided the direction. In 1935, Japanese army units acting without orders from above created two new puppet regimes in North China and one in Mongolia. Military facts on the ground put an end to negotiations then underway between Japan and the Kuomintang (KMT). A much bigger escalation then occurred after an incident in 1937 at the Marco Polo Bridge near Beijing. Although fighting between Chinese and Japanese units stationed there probably began accidentally, Japanese army and naval units quickly arrived to escalate it, this time supported after the fact by Prime Minister Prince Konoe, his cabinet and the emperor. The control faction on the general staff, favoring saving resources for a war against the Soviets, was overruled (Bix, 2001: 317–23).

These military escalations precipitated a full-scale war with China that then merged into the Pacific War, to last up to Japan's total defeat in 1945. Things seemed promising for Japan in 1937. The KMT government still lacked the infrastructural power to rule large parts of the country, and had to retreat. Konoe and influential army planners banked on the Imperial Way, hoping that one swift blow would knock China out of the war. Hirihito urged Konoe to engineer a decisive battle, and Konoe replied that he would "annihilate" the nationalist regime. Henceforth, he said, his government would deal with Chiang Kai-shek only on the battlefield and at the surrender table. He saw Chiang's regime as the only obstacle to Chinese acquiescence in a Japanese-led Asian revival, liberating itself from Anglo-American capitalism and Soviet Communism. The Japanese did not yet rate the Chinese Communists as significant opponents.

Ishiwara and total-war advocates opposed this war. They warned against the consequences of too ideological an aggression, and they now realized the mobilizing power of Chinese nationalism. The invasion, Ishiwara warned, "will be what Spain was for Napoleon, an endless bog" (Barnhart, 1987: 89). He saw China as eating up resources needed for Japan's future, and indeed, the war did drain manpower and undermine the Japanese economy. Ishiwara's criticisms resulted in his removal from the general staff. In any case, he did not have a solution, either. Like others, he had hoped for Chinese acquiescence in a Japanese leadership of Asia against the Westerners, but he had been misled by Chiang's strategy of seeking a deal with Japan until he finished off the Communists. Although Chiang showed class solidarity with the Japanese – they both wanted to extirpate Communism from Asia – there could be no geopolitical solidarity between them. Most Chinese now saw the main imperial enemy not as the West but Japan, and the United States was now increasing its loans to China. China was frustrating Japan's chances of achieving self-sufficiency even before the war with the West began (Barnhart, 1987: 90, 104–14).

By now, Japan had a centrally directed economy in hock to the military's short-term needs. The sources of social power had been imperfectly fused, with the military providing the key direction of policy. The remaining political choice was between military rule and a quasi-fascist corporatist state, but neither could quite triumph. Elements of both, together with conservative civilian politicians (whose parties had been dissolved) and zaibatsu businessmen continued to bicker and strike deals as Japan went into a world war. This was imperfect, conflict-ridden fusion. The initial draft of the 1938 National General Mobilization Law would have introduced a corporatist state, but the final draft allowed all the main factions too much institutional autonomy for that (Berger, 1988: 121–53, 160–1). In good times, the Japanese system could rely on the common interests, culture, and modernizing intent of oligarchs, bureaucrats, capitalists, and the educated upper middle class to generate agreed policies of development. However, different parts of the state were vulnerable to covert takeover by ruthless, well-connected factions, especially of the armed forces. Many favored the anti-parliamentary corporatism sweeping other states of the period. As elsewhere, they claimed they possessed more technocratic expertise and a greater concern with the national interest than selfish and disputatious parties (Berger, 1977: 67–74). A few of these were fascists.

Was Japan fascist?

There were fascist influences on Japan, and there were also some fascists. In the 1920s and 1930s, across large swathes of the world fascism was seen as the most modern political movement, attracting disproportionately young people. Young officers proved its main carriers in Japan (Nakamura & Tobe, 1988). They endorsed violence and assassination as a tool for accomplishing political change against "the enemy within." They saw this as "principled," not "wild" violence (the German SS made the same distinction). Their victims included two prime ministers, a foreign minister, and numerous generals, admirals, and zaibatsu bosses. The police and popular reaction to these assassinations was often ambivalent, for many sympathized not with the victims but with the perpetrators (Berger, 1988: 107). However, this violence was not exercised from below by populist groups, as was Nazi paramilitarism. It came from within the armed forces, led by its middling against its senior levels, although always with the support of some general officers. As we have seen, their provocations at home and abroad were extremely important in influencing Japanese choices, but this came not from any great political mobilizing power but from their command in practice of parts of the Japanese military machine.

There were also blackshirts, national socialists, and other small fascist and fascist-leaning societies and intellectuals who were sympathetic to Germanic corporatist ideas such as those of Othmar Spann. They were much less influential than the officers, however, and they were adapting European fascism into a distinctively Japanese form: the statist element was monarchist, but their style of nationalism privileged the armed forces as the true embodiment of the nation. There was also a nativist far-right movement, "Japanism," which rejected all foreign imports – parliaments, capitalism, socialism, and fascism alike – and this also had some resonance among the officer corps (Berger, 1977: 163–4, 171). All these groups pressed for a militaristic form of imperialism. L. Young (1998: 11–13) sees an "imperialized nationalism," encompassing "cultural, military, political and economic" spheres alike (my four sources of social power) sweeping across Japan.

So did Japan become fascist? Most Western scholars say no (e.g., Duus & Okimoto, 1979), although some say yes (Bix, 1982; A. Gordon, 1991: 333–9; Barrington Moore, 1967), as do some Japanese scholars whose work I cannot read. The debate has turned on whether there was at this point a radical break from previous Japanese history, but it is also important whether the break was from top-down to bottom-up politics. Fascism elsewhere was a mass movement mobilizing from below. There were Japanese fascist groups, mainly among the military and discontented former colonial settlers. Such people were generally overrepresented in fascist movements across the world; in Japan, they lacked mass support among workers, peasants, or the middle classes, whose rightists generally favored harmonious visions of the tennosei, the emperor cult. Nor did the numerous small groups coalesce into a single movement, as they aimed at influencing elites either from within or by terrorist assassinations. Fascists could not penetrate to the heart of the emperor state or the military because their views could not be reconciled with the tennosei. Hirohito declared that he would not accept in cabinet or court posts "any person holding fascistic ideas" (Bix, 2001: 254). The major political shifts in interwar Japan involved relations among elites, they did not mobilize the masses, and they did not break with the Meiji Constitution.

Chapter 10 defined fascism as "the pursuit of a transcendent and cleansing nation-statism through militarism"; that is, a fascist movement mobilizing the masses to create a more powerful state and a more unified nation by means of violent suppression of class, ethnic, and other conflicts. Yet Japan lacked a major bottom-up mobilizing force. In some other respects, especially its paramilitarism, it fits quite well, so some call it a top-down fascism. The Japanese regime of the period 1938–1945, however, was closer to the Metaxas regime in Greece, the King Carol-General Antonescu regimes in Romania, or to Franco in Spain than to the Hitler or Mussolini regimes. I termed such regimes "authoritarian corporatist," developing a mass movement from above, organized by the regime itself (Mann, 2004: 46–8). This was not the Japanese case. Plans to develop a mass-mobilizing single party came to nothing amid bickering between conservative politicians, bureaucrats, big business, and military officers. As these elites shared militarism, the label of military fascism fits Japan best, the adjective qualifying the noun.

First Chinese dragon reviving: The Kuomintang

Two Chinese dragons were stirring – one nationalist, one communist. Opinions are still divided about Chiang Kai-shek and his nationalist Kuomintang. Some consider it hopelessly corrupt: whatever liberal sentiments the regime nurtured were swamped by authoritarianism. Reform schemes and anticapitalist sentiment were rhetorical, in practice undermined by favors to the warlords, landlords, and capitalists financing the regime. Although in the coastal regions regulation and public investment was increased, this was undercut by lack of resources and corruption, with funds going mostly to the regime's friends (Eastman, 1984, 1990: especially 9–30; Wright, 1991; Foran, 2005: 49–51). The regime was corrupt and dominated by the upper classes – although Chiang, perpetually short of funds, could also be ruthless in extracting taxes from them.

The regime stifled liberals and their reforms. The inner circle of the KMT aspired to create a corporatist authoritarian not a liberal state, but it wasn't fascist (Barrington Moore, 1967, 187–201). Eastman (1984: chap. 2) thought the KMT "Blue Shirt" movement fascist, but all his sources were Japanese attempting to discredit the KMT. Chiang, the Blue Shirts, and the New Life Movement were endorsing the kind of authoritarian modernization practiced widely across the world – from Attaturk's Turkey to Meiji Japan – and they remained largely faithful to Sun yat-Sen's ideals (M. Chang, 1979). The KMT said dictatorship was needed during the stage of tutelage of the people. Mao did not claim the KMT was fascist, but a traditional Asian dictatorship.

The KMT did attempt statist reforms in the provinces of eastern China under its direct control. It attempted to improve infrastructures (especially railroads) and public health. Standard Mandarin was encouraged and education expanded. A part of the military was modernized, its elite divisions officered by graduates of the new Whampoa Military Academy. Household registration began to spread the burden of taxation and military conscription more evenly. The regime tried to stabilize prices, amortize debts, and reform banking, and the currency reform of 1935 did lessen the regime's dependence on the grain tax and on the army to extract it.

Strauss (1998) says that the KMT focused on the same core tasks that concerned earlier European states: building an effective military, a taxation system to finance it, and a foreign service to cultivate alliances. For these purposes, the KMT promoted an independent civil service. Foreign service officers became more technically and linguistically competent, they held office longer than their political bosses, and they achieved some autonomy. The KMT lessened the inequalities of the treaty ports and tried, although without success, to bring British and American pressure against Japanese encroachments. The Finance Ministry borrowed from the fiscal practices of the treaty port authorities and did increase revenue. The government recognized the unevenness of its territorial control and often looked the other way where policy could not be implemented. However, Strauss concludes, "The Nationalist government was, at least in the critical sectors of tax and foreign affairs, capable of building strong and proactive institutions under exceptionally difficult circumstances" (1998: 191). P. Huang (2001) has a similar view of the Republic's legal system. New laws protected individual ownership, capital, and investment, and individual replaced patriarchal principles in family law. Yet there was less change in the cases brought before the courts, as judges compromised between the law and community practices.

Zanasi (2006) sees a rise of corporativists, led by Wang Jingwei and influenced by Keynesianism, the New Deal, socialism, and fascism. Able to pursue late development, they could use national planning agencies to coordinate the state and private-sector bankers and industrialists of the coastal regions. Chiang Kai-shek himself envisaged an authoritarian-utopian developmental regime influenced by fascism, with a state-controlled military-industrial complex. He nationalized the leading banks and managed to subordinate finance capital to his goals (Coble, 1986). However, this provoked Wang to desert and collaborate with the Japanese, who he felt might better preserve the autonomy of Chinese capitalism. Chiang's modernization projects, armies, and bribes to warlords had to be paid for and he succeeded in raising loans and taxes from industry. For a time, he managed to raise taxes in the lower Yangzi region, as well. Yet this provoked the landlords, the main taxpayers, to thwart the government's land-reform program that sought to reduce peasants' rents (Bernhardt, 1992: 178–88). Whatever the KMT pronounced in the capital, it remained in the provinces dependent on landlords and warlords who usually ensured that reform remained only on paper. Some warlords ran their own ministates. Chiang Kai-shek made too many pragmatic compromises with his allies to make his nationalist rhetoric into a genuine ideology.

Relations with peasant taxpayers became strained. As the tax burden increased, local leaders – heads of local lineages or religious cults – sought to evade their tax-collecting duties, and in many places the tax yield went down. The state responded with tax-farming, allowing groups of entrepreneurs, clerks, and bullies to exact the taxes and take a cut themselves (Duara, 1988: 43). This growth in indirect rule was politically dangerous, weakening the links between the state and local power brokers. The KMT actually furthered this by seeking to counter landlord power at the province and county levels by bringing in outside KMT party members to staff local offices. Many proved rapacious carpetbaggers, lacking local legitimacy, alienating the local notables whom they were displacing in office (Benton, 1999: 177–8). Van de Ven concludes, "The contradictions between the various constituencies of the Nationalists – Overseas Chinese, commercial elites, workers, peasants, some militarists and even some landlords – proved too difficult to reconcile and bring together into a cohesive political order" (2003: 93; Geisert, 2001). It was only would-be despotic rule, although the Chinese remained largely subjects not citizens.

This raises a counterfactual question. Could Nationalist China have developed into a modern semi-authoritarian state with effective rule and some development of citizen rights over its territories? It eventually achieved this in Taiwan after 1945, moving into democracy in the 1990s. On the mainland, however, its internal contradictions were severer. It remained narrowly based, facing interregional strife and almost no peasant support, unwilling to mobilize peasants because this might encourage communist infiltration of the KMT. Without some combination of elite solidarity and mass mobilization, which both Meiji Japan and Communist China possessed, such a large country could not be propelled into substantial economic development and political order. It is difficult to see how these could have been achieved by the KMT, but we do know the answer to this question: because the regime was not given the time. It was shredded by a devastating war against the Japanese.

In 1937 and 1938, Japanese forces attacked and made deep advances along main communication lines, capturing city after city in the East. Most of the KMT elite divisions and their Whampoa-trained officers were destroyed, and the regime lost the richest parts of the country. Yet Chinese guerillas lurking in the rural rear cut the rail lines so that more Japanese troops were required to defend them. In 1937, the Japanese had assumed that three divisions would suffice to force the KMT to sue for peace. Two years later, they had twenty-four divisions in China (total Japanese army strength was only thirty-four divisions). They had bitten off more than they could chew.

Military historians differ on the quality of the KMT military (D. Gordon, 2006). A good half of its paper strength consisted of the half-trained levies of semiautonomous warlords, and even some of the KMT's own armies were of dubious worth. There was incompetence, corruption, and lack of coordination, but probably more significant was the sheer backwardness of China, especially as the KMT had just been deprived of the most advanced areas. It was particularly hard for the KMT to keep on raising and training troops to replace the terrible losses suffered in the initial Japanese onslaught, and then to continue conducting a war of attrition. First orderly conscription, then disorderly press-ganging of soldiers resulted. "China was an agrarian society that could not cope with the demands imposed by modern warfare," concludes van de Ven (2003: 295; cf Dreyer, 1995: 181). Military power shredded Chiang's regime. Yet aided by the size of the country and rising Chinese nationalism, it did continue fighting so that Japanese forces became bogged down.

Chiang Kai-shek himself was a reluctant fighter against the Japanese. He preferred to compromise with the Japanese as he finished off the warlords and Communists – he called this policy "first unite within, then resist the enemy without." "The Japanese," he said, "are a disease of the skin; the Communists are a disease of the heart" (Dreyer, 1995: 172). He was unable to carry through this policy, however. In the Xian Incident in 1936, his own troops took him prisoner to force him into fighting the Japanese rather than the Communists. He was released with the help of Stalin, who still believed only Chiang could spearhead Chinese resistance against Japan. Nationalist pressures now forced Chiang into a united front with Communist and other anti-Japanese forces. In fact, for the next three years he had to lavish large subsidies on the Communist base areas, the large majority of Communist revenue. For the moment, the politics of national resistance overwhelmed those of class struggle.

In its three occupied Eastern provinces, Japan also ruled through warlords. Some collaborated because they saw no realistic alternative, some out of personal rivalry with Chiang, some because they believed the Japanese could best restore order, and a few were ideological collaborationists – identifying with the invaders' cause, seeing Japanese tutelage as the way to modernize (Barrett & Shyu, 2001). Obstinate Chinese resistance elsewhere combined with overstretched Japanese lines of communication to produce stalemate. Japanese army orders were to take no prisoners (the Chinese often also killed their prisoners), and sometimes to make no distinction between soldiers and civilians. Inadequately supplied, the army had to live off the land. Japanese commanders declared that the international laws of war could not apply in China. All of this produced atrocities.

Tominaga Shozo remembers China vividly. He reported for duty as a junior officer in China in July 1941, along with twenty-one others. He noted that the experienced soldiers they met had "evil eyes." He underwent several days of officer training, at the end of which each trainee had to behead a bound Chinese prisoner with his sword. Tominaga worried about how well he would accomplish this, and was relieved when he was successful. He remembers, "At that moment, I felt something change inside me. I don't know how to put it, but I gained strength somewhere in my gut." He says he later realized he himself had acquired evil eyes. Tominaga says that the ordinary soldiers had a different final task – they had to bayonet a bound captive. He comments:

> After that, a man could do anything easily. The army created men capable of combat.... Human beings were turned into murdering demons. Everyone became a demon within three months. Men were able to fight courageously only when their human characteristics were suppressed. So we believed. It was a natural extension of our training back in Japan. This was the Emperor's Army" (Cook & Cook, 1992: 41–3).

In 1937, this was the Imperial Way on Chinese ground.

The Chinese called them an "army of locusts" (Hata, 1988: 302). The 1937 Rape of Nanking was probably the worst atrocity, in which anywhere between 35,000 and 200,000 unarmed Chinese were killed, and thousands raped. The numbers remain controversial and important in international politics today, yet the popular circulation of much higher death figures is not well-grounded (Askew, 2002; Bix, 2001: 332–6). Japanese journalists witnessed the atrocities, horrified. One asked Lieutenant-Colonel Tanaka Ryukichi to justify the killings. He replied, "Frankly speaking, you and I have diametrically different views of the Chinese. You may be dealing with them as human beings, but I regard them as swine. We can do anything with such creatures" (Ferguson, 2006: 477). Japan used poison gas in China; a germ warfare program may have killed up to half a million. Chinese children were given buns laced with cholera, and planes dropped plague-carrying fleas and anthrax-laden feathers. Victims were cut apart to check the progress of the diseases (Barenblatt, 2003). These programs were comparable to dreadful Nazi experiments on Jewish prisoners. The Japanese anti-Communist campaign of 1941 was also ferocious. The order was the "Three Alls": kill all, take all, burn all. They devastated several Communist base areas. The Japanese Empire could be benign if unthreatened, but resistance brought on terrible atrocities.

Japanese militarism was by now unfortunately distinctive, as it had not been earlier. It regarded prisoners of war as "military supplies" to be expended and then eliminated if no longer of use. The death rate among Anglo-American prisoners of the Japanese was seven times higher than among those held by the Germans and Italians. Japanese soldiers lacked much conception of basic human rights, but this was also evident in the harsh treatment of Japanese soldiers themselves. Officers would habitually strike their soldiers, and this was justified as "the iron fist" or "the whip of love." Old Japanese virtues of bushido loyalty, when wedded to the Imperial Way, were corrupted and deprived of moral sense. This was not a traditional Japanese vice; in 1905, against the Russians, there seem to have been no such atrocities. Something had changed in the Japanese military. Perhaps contempt for enemies grew with military success; perhaps atrocities were due to a growing class gulf between educated officers and men recruited from poor rural areas. Violence was felt to be necessary to keep them disciplined and courageous. Japanese soldiers were repeatedly told they would be killed by the enemy if captured, and so they did to POWs what they thought would be done to them had the positions been reversed. This strengthened the no-surrender ethos: as death was inevitable, make it meaningful through "glorious self-annihilation" (Tanaka, 1996: 71, 195–6, 197–215). None of this could endear them to the populations over whom they ruled.

The Japanese remained bogged down in China. In 1938, Japan had 600,000 troops in China, and had so far suffered 62,000 killed. Between 1938 and 1944, the battle lines changed little, although the Communists gradually increased the scope of their base areas. The Japanese controlled the cities and communications routes of the East and through warlords controlled some other regions. Guerillas harassed them in most rural areas, however, and they lacked the resources to press further forward. Yet neither the KMT nor the Communist forces could win set-piece battles with the Japanese. It was stalemate.

Japanese civilians were kept away from China decision making, and the Cabinet dealt almost entirely with domestic policy. Foreign policy was run by Liaison and Imperial Conferences dominated by military men, the Privy Council president, and the emperor. The army refused to negotiate with Chiang, and when negotiations did loom, the Japanese expected Chiang to make concessions. Yet Chinese nationalism was too aroused by Japanese atrocities, and Chiang himself was not likely to yield at the negotiating table what the Japanese army could not win on the battlefield (Berger, 1977: 236). He was pressured to demand a restoration of Chinese borders as they had existed before the Marco Polo Bridge incident and the restoration of Manchurian autonomy, yet any Japanese government that agreed to such terms would be overthrown. Tokyo was now controlled by the military men who had initiated the aggression. If they lost power, they would not be able to protect their interests within Japan. Some within the Army Planning Board saw that even if Japan occupied all of China, it would still need trade with the British and Americans. Yet few wanted to ask favors of the Anglo-Saxons, widely seen as depriving Japan of its rightful place in the world. Prince Konoe, prime minister from 1937, repeatedly declared that latecomers to imperialism such as Germany, Italy, and Japan would have to fight their way to justice. Peace, he said, was in the interest of status quo powers (I. Kershaw, 2007: 106–8). That was true; if empires were still in demand, wars would result. European wars had now become world wars.

Japan had initially been lured into China by military insubordination, and was now trapped there by the militarism pervading Tokyo. Collective military rule was backed by extreme lower officers and nationalist pressure groups willing to kill those who disagreed. There was little opposition voiced from below. It is difficult to know the extent of popular support for the war, lacking any equivalent of the Gestapo reports on the popular mood. Because the Japanese media were tightly controlled, however, most Japanese thought the war was going quite well. Even when real news began to seep back, basic patriotism kept up support. Kumagaya Tokuichi, a machinist, remembers, "I imagined that a single shot from our army would just blow the Chinks away." In any case, he remarked, "war means jobs for machinists." Nogi Harumuchi recalls the enormous crowds who came to meetings addressed by nationalists. He remembers being overwhelmed by nationalist feelings: "I wanted to build Greater East Asia." Fukushima Yoshie went to teach kindergarten in Manchuoko, as, "We have to take care of the children of Manchuria because Manchuria has been taking care of Japan" (Cook & Cook, 1992: 47, 51–4, 57). They believed they were doing good, a common delusion of imperialism. As in Germany, military Keynesianism boosted the regime's popularity. The military budget rocketed in 1938 from 15 percent to 24 percent of GDP and then leveled off until 1940 (when it rose again). At the same time, GDP itself grew about 30 percent between 1937 and 1941, during the China war (Hara, 1998: 226–7, 257). It certainly seemed that war was good for the economy, although reality was probably otherwise.

J. Snyder (1991: 120) concludes that Japanese imperialism was by the end of the 1930s irrational, even in the residual goal that was now dominant: protecting the power of the military-rightist alliance. It was now embarked on policies that would almost inevitably destroy it. Chinese nationalist ideology was now too powerful for Chiang to pragmatically accept any terms Tokyo might offer (Eastman, 1984; Nish, 2002; Tarling, 2001; Akami, 2002; Huang & Yang, 2001: 73–5, 137; Barnhart, 1987: 49, 91–104). The war would in any case have run on for a few more years – until realists on both sides admitted complete exhaustion and cut a deal – but then came Pearl Harbor and the Americans, and that changed Chinese calculations. Although much of the Japanese elite underestimated American power and will, neither Chiang nor Mao did so. They saw that Japan would eventually be defeated. So their strategy became neither to attack nor negotiate, but to essentially wait until the United States defeated Japan. They had to defend themselves, but their main strategy was to build up their forces for a future civil war against each other.

The KMT armies and the Communist and other guerilla forces did contribute to the Allied victory by tying down 1 million Japanese soldiers throughout the Pacific War. True, these Japanese were mostly raw recruits rather than experienced troops, and Japan needed more planes and ships and the skilled men to operate them in the Pacific, not more infantry. Yet Japanese casualties in China mounted alarmingly, and Japan's recovery after the Depression was weakened by the military expenditures incurred in China. This boosted inflation, drained Japan's foreign exchange, and starved investment. Although the Chinese could not win the war, they could prevent the Japanese from winning it. From 1937 to about 1942, that was more the achievement of the KMT than the Communists; after that date, the achievement was shared more equally. I deal with the rise of the second Communist dragon in the next chapter.

Empires of the Sun and of the Eagle

In Southeast Asia, Japan had pursued a more market-oriented strategy in the early and mid-1930s, with some informal empire in Vietnam and a purely market diplomacy in relation to the vital oil of Java and Sumatra. After receiving a bloody nose at Nomonhan in 1939, Japan signed a neutrality pact with the Soviets. Now the navy's strategy of expanding southward began to be viewed more favorably in Tokyo. When Hitler overran France and the Netherlands, their colonial possessions in Vietnam and the East Indies beckoned. "Seize this golden opportunity! Don't let anything stand in the way," urged Army Minister Hata Shunroku in June 1940 (I. Kershaw, 2007: 91). Because Japanese leaders did not expect Britain to last long against Hitler, its Asian colonies might also be acquired. The lure of an alliance with Germany and a strike southward grew. This was pushed by much of the navy, whose budget it would greatly benefit, although not by its head – Admiral Yamamoto – who still believed Japan could not wage a successful war against the United States. The army was also coming around to the notion that defense in the North and offense in the South would be the best strategy. As the Americans had broken Japanese codes, they knew about these shifts in strategy. They continued to be well-informed until the Pacific War began.

Japan still depended crucially on foreign imports, especially oil. Although its resource imperialism in Manchuria, North China, Korea, and Taiwan now provided about 20 percent of the mainland Japanese GDP, it had not yielded returns across all economic sectors. As Barnhart says, "From the very beginning, the original total war officers had stressed the importance of not antagonizing the West until self-sufficiency was achieved. They failed spectacularly, and their failure was not due to any Western actions" (1987: 267). The temptation to strike out for the oil of the Dutch East Indies seemed a way to extend resource imperialism. In 1938, the United States had begun shipping military supplies and credits to Nationalist China, and the British were planning a railroad from Burma to ship more supplies to the Nationalists. This contributed to stalemate in the China War and increased Japanese hostility to the Anglophone Powers.

In August 1940, Japan founded the Greater Asian Co-Prosperity Sphere, the euphemism for what in reality would be a direct empire. Next month, it occupied Northern Indochina (Vietnam) and joined the Axis alliance. It put on hold a planned offensive against the USSR in the summer of 1941. It looked as if Japan was considering more southward imperialism in the Pacific. From the U.S. perspective, the three powers still attempting direct empire – Germany, Italy, and Japan – were opposing the more democratic, free-trading powers (i.e., informal empires). The United States hoped to detach Japan from its alliance with Germany, and some Japanese also wanted this, but they lost influence as Japanese elites began to believe through 1940 and 1941 that Germany would win the war in Europe. The initial success of Operation Barbarossa in Russia pushed Japan over the edge. Banking on a German victory, the regime reasoned that Japan must seize its opportunity across the Pacific. The war was about to become global.

There were some dangerous mutual misunderstandings, as is normal in the run-up to wars. Japan and the United States embodied very different forms of imperialism, and they both failed to understand the threat each posed to the other. Hence, the different key metaphors of threat: where the United States feared brutal totalitarianism the Japanese saw strangulation by global economic tentacles, the liberal monster. Both were only exaggerations of the kind of empire the other represented. Japanese imperialism did have brutal and totalitarian tendencies, and the U.S. power was stretching right across the Pacific and Asia with its supposedly Open Door policies and a navy powerful enough to enforce oil embargos.

The main issue in dispute between the United States and Japan remained China. In 1932, the Stimson Doctrine had declared American hostility to Japan's use of force in China and the founding of Manchukuo. The Doctrine remained in force, although it was largely rhetorical. It was buttressed by sending military supplies to Chiang Kai-shek, but these were far outweighed by continuing trade with Japan, which received 80 percent of its oil from the United States. The problem, said one U.S. diplomat to Roosevelt, was that, "We have large emotional interests in China, small economic interests, and no vital interests" (Kennedy, 1999: 501–2). Yet the United States continued to demand that Japan return to the status quo existing before 1931, and the Japanese continued to ignore it. Japanese leaders, hawks and doves alike, refused, believing that the date of 1931 would include abandoning Manchukuo and its 170,000 Japanese settlers. This, they thought, would have disastrous consequences for Japan's economy and particularly for any government that agreed to it (Tsonuda, 1994; Toland, 1970: 144–5).

Because the United States lacked military strength in the region to deter Japan, it flexed economic muscles instead. Its response to signs of a coming southward advance was not to come to terms, as the Japanese had hoped, but "to advance from a patchwork of export restrictions to full-blooded financial warfare against Japan." In May 1941, the administration moved toward embargoing almost all exports from the United States or British Empire. Oil was the crucial resource; Japanese companies had already secured approval for licenses for gasoline from the United States for another nine months, and ordinary crude oil for thirty-two months. The only thing that would stop this was to freeze Japanese assets in the United States, as then Japan would not be able to pay for the oil. Roosevelt approved this measure, perhaps without realizing the consequences for Japan, although Assistant Secretary of State Acheson knew exactly what he was doing. Roosevelt's position remains unclear, although he had appointed the hawkish Acheson as someone who would escalate the pressure on Japan. The official story is that Roosevelt only discovered in September that Japan had received no oil since July (Miller, 2007: 108, 123, 167, 175, 203–4; cf Barnhart, 1987).

The effect of the embargoes and freeze was the opposite of that intended. Liberals could not understand militarists. These offensive economic moves did not bring Japan to the negotiating table. In the eyes of Japan's military fascism, they were "an assault on the nation's very existence" (Miller, 2007: 242). This precipitated a last desperate fling. Japanese planners variously estimated that the navy could last without oil supplies for six months up to two years. They also saw that the United States was expanding its Pacific fleet. They reasoned as Hitler did: as Japan could not win a long war, "blitz warfare" (the Japanese translation from the German) was necessary in the form of a short but devastating blow struck against American (and British) power. Admiral Yamamoto still argued against war, but when he failed to persuade the emperor yet wished to remain in his position, he proposed an attack on Pearl Harbor as the best strategy in May 1941. This was tested in war games in September and adopted as military policy in mid-October.

At the same time, negotiations continued. Some Japanese, including Prime Minister Konoe and the emperor, opposed war with the United States. Konoe was authorized to negotiate but not allowed to make significant concessions. The understanding in Tokyo was that if he could not negotiate a peace, Japan would attack. Both sides toyed with the possibility of compromise in late 1941, but that foundered as before on China. The issue of Manchuoko could have been detached from the rest of China, allowing Japan to remain in Manchuoko but quit China. It was curious (from a realist point of view) that the higher priority than war with each other was for Japan the war against China, and for the United States the war against Hitler. So why did Japan continue to antagonize the United States by its southward moves? Why didn't Roosevelt let Japan alone in China (for the moment) and pour more resources into what he saw as the more crucial struggle against Hitler? This would also give the United States time to build up its military resources so that at a later date it could more convincingly deter Japan from aggression. Kennedy (1999: 513–4) asks these questions but cannot answer them. The confrontation was between the power of Japanese militarism and rising American consciousness of its own imperial potential. Neither easily allowed the two regimes the more sensible option of backing off, but what remains difficult to explain is why Japanese militarism had passed beyond the bounds of reason. Only inordinate slices of luck could have brought a good war for Japan, and many of the Japanese elite recognized that. Irrationality is by definition difficult to explain. It is usually the residual in our explanations, but here it brought on war across the Pacific.

In October, Konoe, having failed to negotiate a compromise, was forced out of office and replaced by General Hideki Tojo, a hardliner. Tojo did initially continue negotiations, although neither side would offer significant concessions. On November 25, White House officials concluded that war seemed inevitable. Secretary of War Stimson recorded in his diary, "The question was how could we maneuver them into the position of firing the first shot without allowing too much danger to ourselves" (Kennedy, 1999: 515). Next day, Cordell Hull explicitly returned to the position of insisting that Japanese forces be withdrawn from the whole of China, including Manchuria, as a precondition for normalization of United States-Japanese relations. The Japanese found this an unacceptable ultimatum and ended the negotiations. On December 1, the emperor approved the plan for an attack on Pearl Harbor. On the 8th (Hawaiian time), the attack began. Japan would conquer an empire or go down fighting. Tojo managed both.

Few in the United States had expected such a reaction. The United States' ability to read Japanese codes warned them an attack was coming, but they didn't know where. The day before the attack, they knew when, but still not where. They expected landings in Asia or the Philippines, not an aerial attack on American territory. Pearl Harbor was taken by surprise, and all its battleships there were destroyed. American leaders could not believe that Japan, a country manifestly economically inferior to the United States, with perhaps 5 percent of its heavy industrial capacity, would attack its sovereign territory (Iriye, 1987: 149–50; 1997). Indeed, it is not easy for anyone to understand why Japan would take on the United States when already fully engaged in China. The American economic warfare reinforced by a hardline on China strengthened the Tokyo militarists and brought the navy into the aggressive strategy to secure its oil (Evans & Peattie, 1997: 447, 471–82). Tojo repeatedly declared that the embargoes would strangle Japan, the navy would run out of oil in two years, and the United States would only grow stronger. The chances of success in war were not great, he conceded, but the alternative was that America would reduce Japan to "a third-class nation after two or three years if we just sit tight." Peace under American domination or war against all odds but with honor – that was the choice (Tarling, 2001: 76–8; I. Kershaw, 2007: 365). The military fascist regime preferred the latter.

The Japanese could have backed down, and the Americans had reasoned that they would, but it would have been rather like Britain backing down in either 1914 or 1940 – a repudiation of imperial ambitions, a humiliation. Such behavior is not unheard of; Gorbachev did it in the 1980s – but it is uncommon. We only need to add that Japan was a militarist regime dominated by a half-fascist ideology, influenced by its own prior experiences and Hitler's success, to explain why its response was such an aggressive Blitzkrieg. No one inside either Japan or the United States had been killed in any previous international war, so few had any real understanding of the horrors of total war. The Japanese decision in 1905 was repeated: make a preemptive strike. Japan would pulverize the American fleet; seize British, Dutch, and American colonial possessions across the Pacific; and establish a defensive perimeter across the Pacific to secure the oil of Borneo and Sumatra. Secure in its Asian fortress, Japan could then negotiate secure access to all these markets from a position of strength, helped by Germany's supposedly irresistible force in Europe. They did not expect to win a war with the United States, but merely to reach a position from which they could negotiate from strength, with the help of Hitler. They were proved mostly correct; most of this did come to pass except for the final stage – the negotiated end to the war.

Japanese leaders were somewhere between confident and hopeful of victory in a short offensive war, pessimistic about a longer war, but hopeful that negotiations would prevent that happening. They believed the United States would sue for peace after the first devastating blows and then there could be compromise. Admiral Sadatoshi later conceded, "Such optimistic predictions … were not really based on reliable calculations." One problem was that – as Hitler – Japanese militarists despised the softness of liberal democracies. Their ideologies had a strong emotional component of pride plus contempt for the liberal West. They took American mouthing of Wilsonian rhetoric at face value. Had they appreciated the reality of American imperialism and not gone for the rhetoric, they would have realized that the United States had never been averse to using its military in "wars of choice," as for example in World War I. Yamamoto was right on both counts: Pearl Harbor was the best strategy, but it still wouldn't work.

There is a conspiracy school saying Roosevelt actually wanted the Japanese to attack, so that he could get America into World War II and achieve American global domination afterward. Although solid evidence for this is lacking, the Americans did not try hard to negotiate, but there is no evidence that they lured the Japanese into Pearl Harbor. Even after the unexpected destruction of a quarter of the American Pacific fleet in its home port (luckily no aircraft carriers were in port at the time), and the invasion of a dozen countries across the American perimeter of economic interest, the result was not negotiation but all-out war. The Senate voted unanimously for war, the House voted for it by 388 votes to 1. The eagle felt humiliated and was enraged. Emotions took over on both sides. The United States rejected compromise not only because it would not repudiate its imperialism but also because it had no need to. Japan was incapable of hurting the U.S. mainland – and that made the Pearl Harbor attack stupid. America could fight a war with no danger to the homeland; Japan could not.

The Japanese got a conflagration across the Pacific and their own utter destruction; the Americans got a global empire. It seemed appropriate that the last great battle was fought by the Kwantung Field Army, the cause of so much trouble. In August 1945, the Red Army, recently joining the war in the East, rapidly overpowered its inadequately equipped divisions, killing 80,000 Japanese. Nearly 3 million Japanese died in the Pacific War, although Chinese casualties were four times that. Even if some of the big battles had gone better for the Japanese, it is difficult to see any other final outcome. The great naval battle of Midway in June 1942 is often seen as decisive. It narrowly went against Japan – ten accurate bombs in ten minutes out of thousands dropped on the Japanese fleet made all the difference. Even if Japan had won this battle, however, and gone on to seize Australia, the United States would have regrouped, built more carriers and planes, and come back again. Between 1941 and 1945, the Japanese produced 70,000 planes, no mean feat, but at the cost of great civilian suffering. The United States produced 300,000 (Ford's Willow Run assembly lines produced a B-24 bomber every 63 minutes) and got an economic boom. It also got the atom bomb. When its principal initiator, Robert Oppenheimer, witnessed the first full test of the bomb, he declared, "I am become death, the destroyer of worlds." He had certainly become the final destroyer of the Japanese world. The United States had acquired the economic and military power and the ideological will to become the greatest power in the world. From now on, it acted accordingly, not like the Wilsonian charitable association it sometimes pretended to be.

The success of the Japanese preemptive strike of 1941 did shatter European colonialism across East and Southeast Asia. Japan now had the only empire in the region. It contained 350 million people, second in numbers only to the British Empire. Yet Japanese military occupation was thinly spread, increasingly harsh, and short-lived. Except for French Indochina, where the Japanese struck a deal that left the colonial administration in place, they entered everywhere posing as liberators of the Asian peoples from the white colonial yoke. This earned them a cautious welcome from local nationalists. They promised independence to Burma, the Philippines, and Indonesia in 1942 or 1943 and to Indochina in 1945. However, liberation was a facade (Goto, 2003: 291), a slogan, a response to the question asked in Tokyo: "Don't we have a slogan like the Americans' democracy?" (Tarling: 2001: 127). Japan really wanted the economic and human resources of the region to fulfill its war aims (Peattie, 1996; Goto, 2003). In wartime, it was much too stretched to adopt the developmental and assimilationist policies of its first-wave colonies further north. The Pacific War now raged, and all colonial policy was subjected to the needs of the military. Resources were spread thinly over an enormous area at some distance from Japan. The million Japanese in China would have come in handy for civilian colonial tasks.

The first Japanese Empire had been of the neighborhood; the second one was further across the seas, but without settlers and with few civilian administrators. There was no money to spare to build the infrastructures or the public-private enterprises of the first wave. Instead, the Japanese simply took over the mines, plantations, oilfields, and factories of the European colonizers and handed them over to Japanese corporations. As in occupied China, the cities and areas of valuable resources were controlled, but not the hinterlands. The occupied peoples, including even Taiwanese and Koreans, were subordinated to the needs of the Japanese military, which became ever harsher once the tides of war turned against Japan. Unlike the other empires, the colonized peoples were not invited to fight in its armed forces. As early as November 1941, Japanese forces were ordered to live off the land, which meant they either simply seized what they needed or they paid fixed prices whose value then dropped. Shortages of money and materials meant that forced labor became the norm, involving much abuse and callous neglect. The infamous Burma railway cost the lives of perhaps 100,000 laborers. To avoid mass raping of local women, the Japanese military authorities set up organizations whereby thousands of women were forced into prostitution, "comfort stations," servicing Japanese soldiers. The Japanese occupiers also demonstrated much more racism in Southeast Asia than they had in the North, which made them callous toward local suffering.

The economic hardship of war worsened things. Most regional exports of sugar, tea, coffee, and rubber had previously gone to Europe and America. Because Japan needed much less of these products, they went unsold. Most producers had lived at just above subsistence level, now the consequences were dire. "As a consequence of Japanese misrule numerous people suffered and died in their villages, at their workplaces, or on road sides; many without ever seeing a Japanese" (Sato, 1994: 199–200; cf Duus, 1996; Tarling, 2001: chaps. 4–6). Such atrocities result less from deliberate intent than from a callous regime under pressure. In this respect, the second Japanese Empire can be compared to the Irish or Indian famines or Mao's Great Leap Forward.

Nonetheless, indigenous civil servants and white-collar workers were willing to serve their new masters, as they served their old ones, although they could now do business in their own language rather than English, French, or Dutch. Thailand was a client state, formally independent and indeed enjoying some autonomy. Its fascist-leaning oligarchy became an inactive ally of Japan. Everywhere collaboration was a necessity for survival (which is why there were so few reprisals against collaborators after the war). Yet the Japanese soon alienated local nationalists, who began guerilla resistance in the hinterlands. Forced labor and Japanese reprisal raids brought mass support to the nationalists, who emerged strengthened by the war (Goto, 1996, 2003). As the victorious Americans did not want colonies and the British and Dutch could not reassert theirs, much of the region moved quickly to establish political independence. The Japanese had indeed liberated Asia, although not as they had intended.

Conclusion

In the conclusion of Chapter 3, I listed the conditions favoring American informal imperialism. In contrast, five conditions favored a more direct Japanese imperialism.

(1) Its lack of indigenous natural resources pushed Japan into expansion, unlike the Americans. In this case, expansion was not just by Japanese business interests abroad, as was mainly the case with the United States. Additionally, the Japanese homeland had been threatened by other empires, at least until 1905. Popular nationalist movements could be mobilized around an imperialism that integrated homeland and colonies for ostensibly defensive purposes.

(2) The Japanese military was well-suited to direct imperialism in the neighborhood. The first-wave colonies were within logistical reach of its army, supplied by its navy, and the growing effectiveness and ferocity of the army was suited to conquest and ruthless pacification – until it began overreaching in China.

(3) There was support from both above and below for social imperialism. Conservative oligarchs, fearing liberal democracy, sought to cling onto power by mobilizing peasant support for imperialism. Peasants formed the rank and file of the armed forces and many aspired to upward mobility through colonial settlement. This boosted a populist nationalism exploiting a diffuse sense of both threat to and opportunity for the Japanese people. No large mass movement opposed it. The organized working class got weaker, and conservatives and reform (i.e., rightist) bureaucrats intimidated middle-class liberals and pushed them rightward into accepting a nondemocratic form of government.

(4) The Constitution mattered, as in the United States, but this one had not devised clear rules for assigning or dividing political power. It encouraged power groupings to struggle over access to the emperor, who was vital for approving policy. The army's initial successes in conquest and pacification increased its power in Tokyo, and allowed military violence within Japan to help decide the domestic struggle with the backing of the populist nationalists. An expansionist military regime finally secured the person and authority of the emperor. Because he symbolized the nation, it, too, became embroiled in the imperial project.
(5) These interests devised imperial mission statements justifying direct rule over other Asian peoples considered kin who could be uplifted and civilized by empire. What was unusual about the first wave of Japanese direct empire was that it really did produce economic and educational growth and greater longevity of life, its success reinforcing the lure of further imperialism.

Neither the rise nor the demise of the Japanese direct empire, nor indeed its domestic military quasi-fascism was predetermined, however. There were four Rubicons, which might not have been crossed: Korea in 1910, Manchuria in 1931, China in 1937, and Pearl Harbor in 1941. The Great Depression added another great contingency aiding the drift rightward. Until Korea in 1910, real national security fears had been coupled with effective military force in a power vacuum created by the collapse of imperial China. This enabled the capture of a profitable indirect empire. If powers can expand, they normally will do so. After 1910, Japan was objectively much less insecure, yet the annexation of Korea was a normal imperial escalation from indirect imperialism with unreliable clients to direct imperialism. This required an enhanced military capacity for repression plus cultural assimilation policies. The 1931 Rubicon in Manchuria was different: an autonomous escalation by the military, although reflecting changes in the balance of power within Japan, especially the state. It reinforced the gradual liberation of the military from any control from above. In turn, when boosted by the third Rubicon, the full-scale invasion of China in 1937, this turned into a military fascism able to act autonomously and create constraining facts on the ground. Although Manchuria was economically valuable and could be pacified and ruled, escalation in China revealed that by now the Japanese military was more than simply a responsive instrument calibrated to security fears and economic profit. It was the dominant power actor with its own interests and martial values. The final Rubicon at Pearl Harbor revealed that this had become suicidal.

This represented the perversion of the Meiji Restoration, the triumph of strong military over wealthy country, of military over economic and political power. Its state only returned to the largely despotic state of the Restoration after a period of liberalism. The end result was not merely the culmination of long-term structural tendencies but also of fluctuating balances of power at home and abroad, and the accidents of war that became more important as Japan militarized. Japanese militarism was distinctive. It over-relied on Blitzkrieg and repressive pacification; and its quasi-fascist ideology prevented recognition of the strength of the counter-nationalisms roused in China and the United States, which it saw as being less martial nations. Had political power struggles in Tokyo had a different outcome, a different East Asian Co-Prosperity Sphere might have appeared, centered on a Japanese indirect and informal empire dominating East and Southeast Asia, but with an increasing role within this framework for a reviving China. Just as interimperial rivalry proved the eventual Achilles Heel of European imperialism, however, so Japan's failed imperialism in China delayed the coming Asian resurgence. Japanese imperialism had overreached and collapsed, and both Japan and China were left devastated by their wars, leaving the United States temporarily dominant over this continent. Even deprived of military power, postwar Japan was able to revive and surpass its previous economic power, and to develop after a short period of American rule a new version of Taisho half-democracy – this time free elections producing single-party rule from 1955 to 2009. Japanese ideologies shifted substantially as a consequence of the absence of militarism, much reduced emperor worship, and a capitalism reverting to mere state coordination of enterprises. World War II had an immense impact on Japan.

American was preferable to Japanese imperialism because informal imperialism is more benign and more open than direct imperialism. Informal empire is calibrated more to global economic advantage, uses less violence, and is less malign than an empire that subordinates economic interest to military and nationalist concerns. Unlike Sombart, I prefer traders to heroes. In China, however, the victorious "heroes" were also materialists.

13 Explaining the Chinese revolution

In Chapter 6, I discussed the first Marxist revolutionary wave inspired by the Bolshevik Revolution in Russia. Apart from Russia itself, this wave was a failure, only provoking a more severe counterrevolutionary wave installing fascist and other rightist despotisms. The second wave was more successful. Again, it swept outward from a single revolution, of the Chinese Communist Party (the CCP). In 1949, after an epic thirty-year struggle punctuated by many defeats and much suffering, the CCP conquered the whole of mainland China and established itself over the most populous nation on earth. That government still endures today. I seek to explain this, the most significant revolution of the twentieth century, which was to provide the most successful alternative to Western capitalist democracy. I begin with narrative and end revisiting theories of revolution. I repeat my definition given in Chapter 6: a revolution is a popular insurgent movement transforming radically and violently at least three of the four sources of social power. The struggle and the achievements of the CCP easily meet these criteria.

Early trials and tribulations

The CCP had begun in the most modern part of China, around Shanghai and Guangzhou, as a normal Marxist party with an intellectual leadership provided by students and teachers and a rank and file of urban workers – especially skilled workers; the left wing of the KMT did better among the unskilled. Through the 1920s, the CCP remained small but committed to Marxist-Leninist conceptions of class and anti-imperialism, convinced by the success of the Bolsheviks that history was on their side. They too were salvationists. Soviet Comintern agents advised them. They had to adapt to the local situation, because China was very different from Russia. Shanghai workers retained their ties to their rural birthplaces, clan, ethnic and linguistic groups, guilds, and the pervasive secret societies of China. The Communists recruited through these diverse networks (Perry, 1993; S. Smith, 2000; Dirlik, 2003).

They discovered in 1927 that all their ideology and organization would count for nothing if they could not defend themselves. Chiang Kai-shek's army launched a surprise attack in Shanghai, killing 5,000 of them. The survivors fled south to remote rural areas of Kiangsi province. The days of Marxist innocence were over. This would now be militarized socialism or death. A revolutionary war must be fought from the countryside. Mao's war strategy emerged: envelop the cities from the countryside. Only at the final stages would the cities be attacked. This was the first of Mao's many theoretical innovations.

Although the insurrections of Russian peasants had been a necessary condition for the Bolshevik Revolution, the Bolsheviks had not organized many peasants and peasant grievances were not central to their ideology. Chinese Communism differed. It was a peasant revolution; obviously, no revolution in a more than 90 percent agrarian country could succeed without peasant participation, and CCP leaders had always known that. They now knew that their very survival would depend on peasants. To develop a revolutionary program, they had to produce an analysis of rural-class exploitation. This was the second major innovation. They distinguished four main classes. The unit of analysis was not the individual but the household.

Because the old gentry-scholar-bureaucrat class had faded, the highest class was considered to be *landlords*. These did not perform labor, except incidentally, and their principal source of revenue was either rent from tenants or profit from the labor of poor peasants. They could also exploit the perquisites of local office, various dues (for example, paid for them to organize temples and other community associations), local businesses (inns, distilleries), and they were also moneylenders. They were viewed as exploiters by the Communists.

Rich peasant households did labor, but they gained much or most of their income from the labor of those poorer than themselves. They might have lesser forms of the additional perquisites just listed. They were predominantly exploiters.

Middle-peasant households generally owned the land they tilled, and they owned their tools and perhaps some animals, but they were neither exploited nor did they significantly exploit the labor of others.

Poor-peasant households owned little or no land, animals, or tools. They mostly rented their land or worked as laborers, the "poor and hired." They perpetually struggled to pay their land rent and were endemically indebted across much of China. They were mostly close to subsistence and were clearly exploited.

The CCP allowed for regional variations. The commercialized east had more tenants, exploited mainly through rents paid to landlords and rich peasants. Tenants paid no taxes. The west and north contained more peasant proprietors, paying taxes to the state but not rents. However, all were exploited through landlords' or rich peasants' additional roles as usurers, officials, and community organizers. Inequalities of landholding were large: 10 percent of the Chinese population owned 70 percent of the land, the overwhelming source of subsistence. Adverse economic conditions could push poor and many middle peasants into debt to landlords or rich peasants and then toward malnutrition and death. This was exploitation, however one defines it. The Communists continued to argue about the relative weight of the urban-industrial versus the rural and of the middle versus the poor peasants in the coming revolution. Yet they knew that to succeed they had to achieve two things. First, they must redistribute the lands and wealth of the exploiters to the exploited. Yet, second, this could only be done if the CCP could create its own protected base areas, supported by local peasants organized into revolutionary militias. Only when safely ensconced militarily in an area with political support from peasants could the CCP begin to tackle exploitation. Then they could gradually expand their soviets, conquer the cities from the countryside, and achieve the socialist revolution. Their revolutionary theory when applied on the ground concerned military as much as economic power. These were decidedly unorthodox Marxists! How many Western Marxists have even analyzed military balances of power, let alone placed them at the center of their analyses?

Kiangsi was supposed to be the seedbed soviet. At its peak it contained 3 million people, rural and moderately remote, so defensible, but not particularly poor. During 1931 and 1932, the Communists built up their base areas. They began radically, their 1931 Land Law confiscating the land of landlords without compensation, giving them to poor and middle-peasant households to hold in private ownership. Rich peasants' lands were redistributed, but they could keep land if they worked it themselves. Tenancy was in principle eliminated, and the dues and perquisites of office were abolished and taxes made more equitable. There would be elections for local governments and a commitment to education. In 1933, a land investigation concluded that redistribution must speed up, with resistance crushed by force (Wei, 1989: 48). Yet politics also entered into Communist calculations. Those of all classes might be temporarily part of the masses if they supported the revolution, those who opposed it were feudal, and waverers were part of the bourgeois revolution with which temporary alliances might be struck. There were perennial arguments about the loyalty of middle peasants, although they were usually treated as allies of the revolution. In this phase, the CCP was radical, influenced by Stalin's anti-kulak policy (Goodman, 2000: 24–7).

Mao came to believe that this radical policy was counterproductive, alienating not only landlords and rich peasants but also some middle peasants. Too much struggle also harmed production levels, harming Communist ability to finance a war. Mao wanted to pick on the landlords and conciliate richer peasants, so favored gradual tax, rent, and interest-rate reduction policies over land redistribution. This was to be his third major innovation – but not yet, because the Returned Student faction closer to Moscow was in charge of the party and believed radical reform would mobilize enough poor peasants as volunteers for the red armies. Many peasants did help implement the policies, and they provided supplies, recruits, and intelligence. Party veterans later recalled that never again in their peregrinations around China were they to receive such a warm welcome. The CCP was less corrupt than KMT or warlord regimes, and more united – once policy had been decided. These were ideologues committed to the cause, tightly knit in a Leninist party. They were not raking off the top and they usually did what they promised. Commissars disciplined the militias, enforcing rules on the treatment of civilians. The CCP seemed to have a lot going for it (Waller, 1972: 34, 44–6; Lotveit, 1979: chap. 6; Shum, 1988: 9–11; Dreyer, 1995: 165–7, 189–94).

Yet radical policies so antagonized landlords and rich peasants that most went over to the KMT, mobilizing their many poorer clients to provide militia and labor forces to aid KMT armies. In return, the KMT promised to cede them political control of their own localities (Wei, 1989). The alienation of local elites and their clients left the Communists little margin for military error. Chiang's forces were slowly and methodically advancing by fortifying villages set amid encircling blockhouses to separate the Communist guerrillas from their base areas. This forced the Communists into set-piece battles to which they were ill-suited. They evaded the first four attempts at encirclement, but in the fifth one, the positional warfare adopted by the Returned Student leadership led them to defeat. The Communists were forced to flee Kiangsi to begin the epic Long March to Yenan in the far northwest. Only 5 percent of those starting the Long March actually arrived there. The Communists were in poor shape, and Yenan was remote and dirt-poor. Chiang pressed the local warlords to finish them off, but as Japanese pressure increased, he was forced (by his own soldiers) to turn and form the First United Front with the Communists. The Japanese focused their attack on Chiang, their strongest Chinese opponent, so the Communists had breathing space to build up new base areas, from which they eventually emerged to conquer China (Dreyer, 1995: 173–4, 182–200; Benton, 1992: 468–9). A necessary cause of the Chinese Revolution was the Japanese invasion. As in Russia in 1917, this revealed the importance of war in weakening the power of a regime that would otherwise have repressed revolution.

With Mao now its leader, the CCP concluded that in Kiangsi leftist excesses and positional warfare had led to defeat. The party now became more guerrilla-centric and politically pragmatic, seeking to win over intermediate elements among rich peasants, small landlords, and their urban counterparts. Even enlightened gentry might be included in the progressive alliance (Shum, 1988: 14–15). The CCP hoped to seduce bourgeois reformists and enlightened gentry inside the United Front. However, these were seen as pragmatic, temporary means to achieve the goal of socialist salvation.

The peasant problem

Mass support would have to center on poor and middle peasants, but Chinese peasants seemed poor revolutionary material. Bianco (2001, 2005) analyzes about 3,500 cases of violent peasant conflict occurring between 1900 and 1949. This might seem a lot, but Bianco says their actions were not revolutionary:

> [They were] a fundamentally defensive response to a *specific* and *local* aggravation of the peasants' condition. The peasants did not rebel against an exploitative established order,

> but against some new development posing a threat to that order. Had the status quo not been altered by the arrival of soldiers, bandits, locusts, the imposition of a new tax, or whatever, the peasants would not have rebelled (2001: 3–4, emphasis in the original).

Thus, Communists arriving in a locality were greeted with suspicion, seen less as saviors than as yet more outsiders potentially destabilizing their lives. Moreover, 68 percent of the conflicts were directed against the state, mostly protests against unfair county taxes or military conscription the KMT had raised. A further 14 percent of conflicts were with other peasants, family lineages, or villages, and these were generally the most violent and long-lasting. That left only 8 percent directed against landlords or moneylenders on whom a Communist class line might focus (2001: 63–4, 19). This does not suggest that peasants would find a class analysis of their exploitation plausible.

Much ritual was involved in these jacqueries. The peasants might damage property or beat-up disliked lower officials and landlords' agents. In what was called a " great feast," the peasants feasted in the estates of the local gentry (Mao noted this with delight in his report on peasant uprisings in Hunan). There were also strikes in which peasants left their tools in front of the local administration offices, signaling a refusal to work (Bianco, 2005: chap. 4; cf Chen, 1986: 134–43). These were ways of signaling discontent before the police or soldiers arrived, which might persuade higher officials to investigate their grievances before turning to repression. If the authorities did repress, the peasants rarely fought back. The ringleaders might flee to become bandits, the others might submit and hope for leniency.

In the commercialized agriculture of the Lower Yangzi, tenancy dominated and resistance focused more on rents than taxes. Peasants launched rent strikes and sometimes rioted and damaged property. In about one-third of cases, the authorities stepped in to settle on terms partially favorable to the peasants, so they had found reformist methods of insurgency. They showed little interest in Communism: their anti-landlord protests targeted abuses of the system, not the system itself; they had little class consciousness, and were keen to conserve community values. They practiced ritual violence but did not want a revolution (Bernhardt, 1992: chap. 6; Chen, 1986: 173–8). Perry calls resistance movements in North China "protective," because they defended the local community (as did the Red Spear militias and secret societies) or "predatory," as in banditry. Most grievances were economic, but protest formed more along communal than class lines and varied according to local ecologies (1980: 3–5, 248–58). Communists would have difficulty with such peasants, for their class line seemed irrelevant.

The main reason for their conservatism was that landlords were too powerful to be frontally challenged. They were "quadrilateral beings": rent collectors, merchants, usurers, and officials (Wolf, 1969: 132). This overwhelming local power gave peasants two possible motives for compliance. First, because this was the only order they knew, they might have been genuinely attached to

Confucian values of duty, patriarchy, and harmony and have feared the disruption and chaos that might lie outside of it. So landlord power might have been considered legitimate, especially if it showed some humanity at difficult times. This fits James Scott's (1976) notion of reciprocal justice, which he considers dominated Asian peasant communities: if landlords performed their traditional community functions, peasants reciprocated. Second, peasants might have been afraid of landlord power. In practice, it is often difficult to distinguish legitimacy from fear. If one has no alternative to compliance, landlord power may have been accepted as normal, a word that in English (and French) blends together the senses of the usual and the moral. Commitment to Confucian order and deference to landlords and the state could be an adaptation to unequal power relations. If these could be changed, peasants might be more receptive to revolution.

That is how the Communists reasoned: they could not win by simply urging peasants to overcome the class enemy. They had to first undermine landlords' and officials' coercive power. If they succeeded, deference would be revealed as dependent on conditions that no longer existed. This had been the leftist strategy in Kiangsi, and it had not worked for long enough. So the Communists developed alternative strategies.

Communist organizational strategies

The CCP postponed forcible land redistribution so as not to alienate the entire propertied class. Instead, it substituted either a tax reduction policy for poor-peasant owners – called "equitable burden" – or reductions in rents, interest rates, and "unfair" dues. Sometimes it relied on moral community pressure placed on the rich to ease the burden of debt on the poor. Village "struggle meetings" pressured the rich; so did forcible "food- and seed-borrowing struggles" (Goodman, 2000: 62–3; Chen, 1986: 144–50). Across much of North China in 1937, KMT forces fled before the Japanese, and the Communists crept into mountainous border areas between the Japanese lines of communications, setting up small base areas in defensible locales. In the one studied by Hartford (1989), they introduced progressive taxes, participatory village government, and defense militias. The Communists faced repeated attacks from the Japanese and landlord militias. Yet the landlords became vulnerable once the Communists had introduced village meetings at which peasants could speak out. As this base area consolidated, rent and tax reductions brought more poor-peasant support. The Communists survived better than the local Nationalists or warlords who alienated the peasantry by dragging their heels on reform and prioritizing provisioning militias over peasant well-being. However, not many peasants volunteered to fight outside of their own base area (Hartford, 1989; Paulson, 1989).

In other northern regions, tenancy and rent was rare and tax issues were more important. Tax reform could be implemented noisily through village meetings dominated by emboldened poor peasants, or more quietly by administrative fiat without causing massive class conflict. Where the Communists could gradually increase their power, landlords found themselves squeezed by higher taxes. They might react by trying to join the party or offering their daughters in marriage to Communists, but as the taxes got more progressive, they had to sell some of their land, and the inflation helped the poor pay their debts and buy land. Redistribution often occurred more through economic mechanisms than political fiat (Van Slyke, 1986: 700; Selden 1995: 22–3).

Short-term needs required a divide-and-rule strategy to undermine the unity of the "quadrilateral being." The CCP allied with some local elites against others, reducing the unity of the landlord-official class; then peasants could see landlords might be further challenged. This strategy was used in the central and eastern base areas run by the New Fourth Army, and in the bigger northern base areas founded by the Long Marchers and secured by the CCP main fighting force, the Eighth Route Army.

Some local elites did not oppose a seemingly reformist CCP. Communist cadres often quoted Sun Yat-sen, and many were educated and from privileged backgrounds. Local elites favoring some reform often despaired of the corruption of the KMT. In 1940, Han Guojun led part of the provincial gentry into an alliance with Chen Yi, commander of the Communist New Fourth Army. He wrote to a friend, "I have heard that the Jaingnan New Fourth Army is not like the Guominfang [the KMT], that it's not corrupt, and that it wins battles. The Nationalists want me to go to Chongqing [the new Nationalist capital], but I won't. They can only lose battles. How can we continue to support them? The New Fourth Army offers hope." The United Front helped the cadres draw some patriots into the Communist ranks. Local elites also hated KMT carpetbaggers coming in to usurp their own administrative powers. These tensions weakened the links between central state and locally dominant classes. Under KMT rule, warlords continued taking their cut, whereas the Communist forces usually adhered to the party's "three major disciplines and eight-point rules" of conduct. Even some KMT officers were won over, providing intelligence to the Communists. The KMT found it more difficult to woo Communist officers and cadres (Benton, 1999: 155–8, 177–8, 191; Shum, 1988: 231).

Recruitment policies varied according to the radicalism and sense of security of the local party. The remnants of the Kiangsi soviets who did not embark on the Long March were very insecure. At first, they comprised mainly the wounded, women, and the elderly who had retreated into the local mountains, with no strategy except self-preservation. They sought help wherever they could, from groups as unrevolutionary as bandits, "spirit soldiers," and ethnic minorities. They initially controlled only mountain villages, from which they sporadically descended to attack traffic, kill known reactionaries, and collect "contributions." In the villages, they downplayed land redistribution in favor of rent and interest-rate reductions. If they pursued the radical class line, they lost; leftists ended up dead. This was a Darwinian process, the survival of the fittest played over many local terrains. The survivors still kept faith with Marxism-Leninism and party discipline, but they were preserving them for better times through pragmatic, manipulative, "red heart, white skin" policies. Effective base areas also resisted central party interference, as local knowledge and tactical flexibility enabled survival. After three difficult years, they began to flourish and were invited by the CCP to form the nucleus of the United Front's New Fourth Army, not far from Shanghai (Benton, 1992: 479–500).

Their new eastern bases lay near the Yangzi and Huai Rivers in a relatively prosperous area. The Japanese had put the regional KMT armies to flight but then settled into defensive positions, leaving the rural areas alone. Strong KMT forces remained only along the Yangzi. The Communists had time to regroup in upland areas. The two main partners in the "United" Front now focused on undermining each other rather than attacking the Japanese. Both were trying to swallow up other militias active in the region. In 1939, Chen Yi, commander of the Communist New Fourth Army, distinguished ten militias active in his sphere of operations. Some were simply bandits, yet Chen Yi sought to ally with them in order to isolate Han Deqin, the KMT governor. He provoked the governor to attack him, which alienated those who favored the United Front, including some of Han Deqin's own officers. Thus, the Communists managed to dominate this part of the region. In Wannan, the second main base area, the KMT governor launched a surprise attack in 1941 and destroyed the local Communists (Benton, 1999: 325–6, 523–4; Dreyer, 1995: 256). Communism depended ultimately on its militias.

The class line varied according to the balance of power. Similar to the Bolsheviks, the CCP combined commitment to secular Salvationism with pragmatic, opportunistic means. If weak, the cadres practiced "the enemy of my enemy is my friend." When first entering a region or where they felt weak, they compromised, concealing ultimate goals, entrenching themselves within the community. They appealed to local elites and their networks of kinship and native places, although they knew that in the short run this undercut the chances of land redistribution (Benton, 1999: 168–75; Goodman, 2000; Hartford, 1989; Perry, 1984: 445; C. Chang, 2003: 87–9). They downplayed other policies, too. They were committed to building the "new democratic family" to replace Confucian patriarchy with free marriage choice, monogamy, and equal rights for women, but this was in tension with basing economic policies on the household not the individual. Usually, the senior male dominated the household and expected to get the land. The CCP tried to give women household members equal rights to land, but if faced with strong cultural resistance did not press it. Land redistributed to poor households usually went to the senior male. Only divorced or widowed women heading households got ownership rights. Stacey (1983) calls this "democratic patriarchy": reform gave the masses rights to independent family farming, but "patriarchy was made more democratically available to masses of peasant men."

The recruitment of elites was often devious. When Chen Yi arrived in a county, he would research the backgrounds, accomplishments, and networks of dissatisfied gentry, and then use his cultural and social capital, his kin and educational networks, his good manners and his scholarship to woo them. He would stress (or invent) common connections, exchange poems, and create local artistic and literary societies. He would flatter the gentry by asking them to preside over official meetings, keeping them in the dark about real decisions. Gentry support came through exploiting common origins or schools, religious communities, secret societies, or fictive kinship acquired through blood brotherhood rituals. *Guanxi* – connections – enabled Marxism to be sinicized (Benton, 1999: 173–4, 185–6).

This led into "revolutionary dualism," combining "unity" and "struggle," the carrot and stick of Communist strategy. Once the party had established a local toehold, unity policies were accompanied by struggle meetings, encouraging peasants to air grievances about abuses, "speak bitterness," and denounce the abusers to their faces in public meetings. The official slogan was "Win the support of the progressives, neutralize the middle-of-the-roaders, and focus attacks on the reactionaries." Because such terms were not familiar to landlords or peasants, most of them did not know who was a reactionary or feudalist. All kinds of personal grudges were settled under cover of such terms, which led to the party instructing members to denounce only the most notorious landlords and rich peasants, plus their "dogs legs," their bully boys. Instead of "Down with the bastions of feudalism," lower cadres were urged to shout, "Down with Wang who seized and occupied the land." An orchestrated village denunciation of a notorious abuser, during which party cadres stayed in the background, might force a confession and offer of compensation. If instead Wang fled, his land or property might be redistributed to the poor – or to the most politically supportive among the poor. Cadres were instructed not to let the peasants go over the top, into violence. The party kept debating the correct balance between unity and struggle and between conciliation of elites and stirring up the masses (Chen, 1986, esp. 181–201).

Where Communist militias ruled, a landlord had the options of fleeing (perhaps losing his property) or appearing to cooperate. If the Communists were well-entrenched, better join them. If the KMT eventually returned, a landlord would probably be spared retribution. If the return of the KMT seemed imminent, landowners might reveal their true sentiments. One told a Communist, "Heh! Still pressing us to pay grain tax! Fuck you!... The Guomindang armies will be here in a minute. Gonna cut your little prick off!" (Esherick, 1998: 362–3)

It was often an uphill struggle. When the cadres entered the "feudal fortress" of Yangjiagou, an isolated mountain village in Shaanxi province, they were appalled that the peasants appeared to accept their exploitation. The villagers lived in dirt caves on the gloomy side of the valley; the landlords lived in fine villas on the sunny side, surrounded by monuments lauding their ancestors. The villagers were day laborers, sharecroppers, and tenants, all without economic security, living in fear of being fired by the landlord and so losing all access to subsistence. The Communists said the peasants acted as "obedient slaves" accepting that "the master is exalted and the servant base" and that "wealth and poverty come from Heaven." They seemed such unpromising revolutionary material that the Communists initially abandoned class struggle and recruited anyone, promising "no army service, light tax burden, and victory in all your lawsuits." Not many politicians could match that offer! (Esherick, 1998: 347) Once such "impure" class materials could be welded into militias capable of defending a base area, the real class goals might be gradually revealed. Eventually it worked here, and this village became Mao's headquarters. A similar slow sequence was evident in Long Bow Village, also in Shaanxi. Even after the Communists had secured control here in 1947, the peasants were still ultracautious. If the Communists were forced out again, reprisals against collaborators would be terrible. Communist militiamen took a donkey and cart from rich landlords and led it around the village for several days, offering them to poor peasants but failing to find a taker (Hinton, 1966: 124).

Above all, the CCP had to convince peasants they could defend them. If they could demonstrate that, they could begin to implement reforms, and then perhaps revolution. They started with the advantage that landless peasants often volunteered for the Communist militias. A soldier's pay provided subsistence, and their families were generally looked after by the CCP when they were away. As poor and lower middle peasants would benefit most from reform and redistribution, this was also a motive to join the militia. Once a base area was established, military recruitment – alongside tax collection – became the responsibility of the village, and the village authorities would coerce villagers to fulfill their recruiting quota. Revolutionary militias were built from within the community. This added to their effectiveness in defense, although they might be reluctant to fight elsewhere (Goodman, 2000: 7, 260; Perry, 1980: 58; Chen, 1986: 383–401).

Revolution was difficult in the prosperous Yangzi delta. The CCP could extract taxes from trade at marketplaces and withhold as taxes a portion of the rents paid to absentee landlords – but this would not mobilize and reorganize rural communities. As prosperous peasants did not seek the meager pay of a Communist soldier, the party could not build up its armed forces to impose revolution. The peasants did not volunteer for the militias and they fought poorly if coerced, so the Communists brought in unemployed workers from Shanghai to be their soldiers. They proved good soldiers, but not very useful for revolution within the community because they were strangers (Liu, 2003:23–8).

Mao's policy of *yila yila* involved zigzagging, courting, and manipulating a social group, followed by an attack on it. In regions where nationalist or Japanese forces became more active, landlords were accused of collaborating with them. Some were imprisoned, others fled. If this produced a backlash, the cadres eased off reforms and allowed enlightened gentry and progressive landlords into the movement. The landlords and rich peasants had to shoulder the tax burden but did not have to join the militias, dominated by poorer peasants. So the peasants and not the upper classes gained control of military power relations – under the ultimate control of the party. This was building up future infrastructures of power, mobilizing the peasants and interposing the party between them and the traditional elite.

The CCP built up networks of village assemblies, agricultural mutual help groups, educational associations, women's groups, and village defense militias, all mobilizing the locals. In one poor northern base area, the incoming Communist cadres tried to ally with the Red Spear militias and even with bandits. This was not initially successful, but when Japanese forces threatened the area, the militias fought alongside the Communists. When security returned, the Communists started labor-intensive economic projects yielding more surplus from the harsh local ecology than could normal cultivation practices. Reconstruction involving mass labor mobilization and the revival of local artisanal trades were important to Communist success across the northern bases (Perry, 1980; Goodman, 2000: 63; Esherick, 1995).

The administration was layered. The outer, most visible layer consisted of the United Front anti-Japanese associations, whose membership was open to all. The Communists rarely purged this layer – even former village heads were kept on. The government structure was normally composed of equal numbers of Communists, non-Communist leftists, and middle of the roaders, the 3:3:3 system first introduced in Yenan (Van Slyke, 1967: 142–53). The next layer comprised peasants' and workers' associations, with membership according to economic position. Finally, at the core was the party branch, staffed with carefully selected people, either intellectuals or reliable poor or middle peasants. The poor were generally considered worthier but poorer quality activists; the middle peasants were the reverse. The elite, confined to the outer level, was sidelined. Peasant participation, under CCP control, had gradually taken the village and the militia out from under the feet of the gentry (Chen, 1986: part II; Goodman, 2000: 28). Through village, educational, and militia institutions, the CCP was mobilizing the peasantry toward implementing tax, rent, and interest-rate reductions, limited land redistribution, and struggle meetings, defended by peasant militias.

A "moderate" phase lasted from the formation of the Second United Front in 1937 to late 1939, although in most areas only in 1940 was land redistribution much pursued (Goodman, 2000: 8, 57). Then a more radical phase was coupled with the Hundred Regiments northern offensive against the Japanese in 1940. When this offensive failed, policies were moderated once again. Future premier Deng Xiaoping, then political commissar of the Red Army's 129th Division, counseled restraint in March 1941: "The Public Security Bureau is not a terrorist organisation and should be part of the democratic system. It has a duty to protect any anti-Japanese organisations and individuals. Those landlords who are not anti-government enjoy rights and freedom of speech, as well as religion and thought, just the same as workers and peasants" (Goodman, 2000: 57). The reverse also led to party purges in the "rectification campaign" of 1942–1944. The leadership unified around Mao to eliminate the pro-Soviet faction. Those who opposed Mao were allowed back in the party if they engaged in self-criticism – "cure the illness and save the patient." It resulted in a more disciplined party. Where control was established during the late war phase, mass mobilization campaigns were launched for economic cooperation, elections, and conscription into the permanent Red armies (Esherick, 1995: 67–8). In some base areas, land redistribution now began again (Goodman, 2000: 21–3).

The Vanguard Communist Party

The cohesion of the party was crucial to success. Communist base areas were separated from each other in an archipelago of ministates that might have fragmented. The party ideology provided unity of goal, and its discipline gave it a vanguard of party cadres – ideological, ascetic, fairly uncorrupt – hotly debating the party line but then implementing it collectively. Most leaders had come from the cities, although often the sons and daughters of peasants (such as Mao). The closing of the universities in the war against Japan provided successive waves of returned students. In the Taihang base area, intellectuals provided about three-quarters of county-level officials, although much less at subcounty level (Goodman, 2000: 67–8). From Shanghai came young people fleeing from the Japanese occupation, alongside former KMT political prisoners freed under the United Front. Many went back to their areas of origin to provide the nucleus of a local base area (van Slyke, 1986: 631). The cadres were young but diverse, including industrial workers, students, teachers, and other intellectuals, and even overseas Chinese. Women were employed as teachers, nurses, administrators, accountants, and propagandists. The New Fourth Army was at first well-educated and cosmopolitan, although as it grew it recruited more peasants. In the north, the Eighth Route Army was mainly peasant apart from higher officers and commissars (Bianco, 2001: 30; Benton, 1999: 54–73).

New recruits rarely arrived as convinced Communists. They were young people versed in city politics, vaguely leftist, anti-Japanese, and disillusioned with the KMT. The eventual leader of the Taihang base area was from a gentry family, graduate of Shanxi University, already active in Beijing unions. He confessed, "We were city boys. What did we know?… Here I was supposedly to be developing base areas and I had no idea what they were, let alone how to set one up." Most were required to attend a "university" or "high school," unwittingly financed by the KMT, as the subsidy it provided to the Red armies to fight the Japanese was partially diverted there. About 10,000 students a year graduated from "Resistance University" in Yunan, and about 8,000 from its high school, having received a heavy dose of Communist doctrine reinforced by collective singing, discussion groups, and physical labor. Political commissars supervised education, welfare, and loyalty and political deviations were countered by "rectification campaigns." There was no equivalent to this in the KMT. Through discipline, propaganda, and struggle sessions, weaker or more ambivalent recruits were weeded out; the remainder were firmed up as Communists. There were month-long meetings for low-level cadres as well as village meetings to criticize cadres – in the middle of war and civil war. There was more control over the cadres than over the peasants. A formidable ideological power organization maintained the discipline of the CCP (Li, 1994: chap. 10; Esherick, 1995: 49, 59–61; Goodman, 2000: 9–11, quote from 11; Chen, 1986: chap. 6).

Most cadres sent into newly captured communities were trained students or teachers. They targeted local teachers for recruitment, seeing them as open to modernizing ideals, and they were respected by the peasants for their knowledge of the world. Most teachers had been educated in the cities but could not find employment there, given the war and Japanese occupation (Benton, 1999: 89–99; Bianco, 2005). Local teachers also had the advantage of speaking the local dialect. In North China, says Goodman (2000: 269) a "peasant or farmer … would probably have found it difficult to differentiate between a soldier speaking Japanese and a soldier speaking Fujianese" (which many cadres spoke). Little concealment of ultimate party goals was necessary with the teachers, a part of the vanguard along with poor and middle peasants. There would have been no revolution without this political elite, armed with an ideology that they represented modernity and progress – and realizing that once they passed a point of no return, they had to continue fighting. The peasant revolution was their construction. They articulated genuine peasant discontent, but this was not a spontaneous uprising (Bianco, 2005: 439; Chen, 1986).

Civil War and victory

Their tactics eventually worked. From the Long March to the formation of the protected base camps to militarized mass mobilization projects, a model of militarized socialism developed that both protected and fed the peasants, then lowered rents and taxes, and finally redistributed land. In Taihang base area in Shanxi Province, big class changes occurred. In 1936 when the base area started, landlords held 26 percent and rich peasants held 23 percent of the land.

These proportions steadily declined through to 1944, when they held respectively 5 percent and 13 percent of the land. Poor peasants also declined in numbers because redistribution made many of them into middle peasants, whose landholding increased from 31 percent in 1936 to 65 percent in 1944. Political control over both county- and village-level politics also passed from landlords and rich peasants to intellectuals and middle-peasant village cadres. This was a major redistribution of wealth and political power, as was the virtual elimination of tenancy in the base areas (Goodman, 2000: 29–33, 258–65).

Past a point of no return, peasants had more to fear from the return of the KMT or the Japanese than from the Communists. During the war, both launched predatory raids involving killings on a scale the Communists tried to avoid. After the war against Japan ended, the KMT forces at first believed they were triumphing and launched White Terror against collaborators with the Communists. By now, peasants would usually defend the revolution, because they were also defending themselves. Without their support, the party cadres would have been massacred. By now, the cadres were energetically redistributing land. When Communist officials allowed or could not stop it, poor and middle peasants, believing victory was in sight, exacted terrible vengeance against the wealthy, revealing that deference to the "quadrilateral being" had rested more on power than on ideological consensus (Bianco, 2005: 453). It had needed a prolonged war and civil war to bring them to this point. Now land and tax redistribution was an advantage to the Communists. This was ultimately a Marxian class revolution, although achieved through escalating reformism and military struggle. The three-way war (to say nothing of warlords and bandits) had so disrupted rural China that order was no longer real enough to be restored. That cut away the most powerful force that had hitherto produced peasant compliance with the class society both the KMT and Japanese represented.

In 1945, as the Japanese laid down their arms, the CCP and the KMT both expanded rapidly across the areas formerly under Japanese control. The KMT had much bigger forces and could occupy most of the cities and the more prosperous agricultural areas. The last Japanese offensive, the Ishigo offensive of 1944, had shredded the elite KMT divisions – the last of the Japanese contributions to the Chinese Revolution. Now the Civil War pitted half-trained infantry armies against each other. Maybe if one or two closely fought battles in 1948 had gone the other way, the Communists would not have won (Westad, 2003: chap. 6). Wars add such contingencies. Yet the old KMT weaknesses remained; factionalized, their generals failed to combine as effectively as the more party-disciplined Communists. They had also failed to mesh their anti-Japanese campaign with political ideals in a genuinely popular cause. Indeed, after 1945 they collaborated with former Japanese quislings. When the KMT took over cities, they used Japanese soldiers to staff urban police forces that did them no good among the Chinese. Nor did corrupt carpetbagging KMT officials, "the new nobility," descending on the cities; nor did rampant inflation. The KMT could not deliver much-needed reform, and as a result, there were labor strikes, student riots, and repeated calls for reform in the areas under its control. Although it had shown reforming tendencies in the 1920s and early 1930s, its growing dependence on landlords and businessmen stymied its reformist wing. In contrast, the Communist underground resurfacing in the cities promised reforms that they had already introduced in the areas they had occupied. In this respect, they could be believed (Westad, 2003: 70–6, 143; Pepper, 1999: 10–94, 132–94).

In rural zones newly acquired by the KMT, the elite simply changed allegiance from Japan to the KMT, and there was no reform. In areas newly acquired by the Communists, those who had collaborated with the Japanese were deposed. No longer requiring their cooperation, the CCP intensified rent and interest-rate reductions and progressive taxes and encouraged the peasants to press forward. In May 1946, the CCP intensified struggle, and ordered a new commitment to land redistribution, once each base area had been secured. Some peasants were slow to commit themselves, not quite believing the tide had finally turned; others could hardly be restrained from seizing land and goods and beating and killing their former masters. This encouraged others not to miss out on the opportunity, and the cadres' main role soon became to restrain the violence and make redistribution a more orderly process. For party leaders, land redistribution was not principally an object in itself but the main means of overturning traditional power relations in the village and forming militias that could press home the attack elsewhere. It would help "adjust heaven" (Pepper, 1999: 243–330; Westad, 2003: 128–37).

Success had its problems. In "old" areas conquered and already revolutionized before the Japanese surrender, the rent, rate, and tax programs had often already slashed the landholdings of the landlords and rich peasants and introduced broad equality. This tended to demobilize the peasants. They had achieved what they had desired, now they could sit back and enjoy it. As Li (2008) puts it, ironically, the CCP was faced with "a serious shortage of landlords." Nothing daunted, it invented new enemies such as "masked landlords," "landlords in decline," "buried landlords" (who had buried their wealth), "landlords within the party," "bad cadres," and "cadres with landlord origins." So struggles were launched to unmask the traitors and dig up wealth and family roots. The peasants must continue *fanshen* ("to turn the body") and *fanxin* ("to turn the heart/mind"), the twin material and ideological requirements to create a genuine revolutionary. In areas conquered more recently, the CCP might reverse the policy, inventing new class categories to blunt peasant radicalism – new rich peasants (enriched by CCP rent rate, and tax policies) were said to differ fundamentally from old rich peasants, who remained class enemies. Because the goals were multiple – ideological, economic, military, and political – they often contradicted each other. Too much economic revolution blunted political and military mobilization. Too much political mobilization threatened economic production levels – on which military victory also depended. Mobilization was good for party democracy, which the leaders liked – until they realized it reduced their own controls. There was no rest for the revolutionaries, whose policies zigzagged across the sources of social power.

Manchuria was the acid test during the final stages of the Civil War. Whoever controlled its industrial resources would probably win. Under Japanese occupation since 1934, neither side was already implanted there. The Communist Eighth Route Army poured in by land, resupplied with Japanese arms handed over to them by Soviet forces (who had taken the Japanese surrender there). Half a million KMT troops were armed and transported to Manchuria by the United States. The Communists got there first and occupied the cities. For the first time they had to defend cities, not attack them. The city elites had either fled before the Japanese invasion or were discredited by collaboration. Their local control had been broken (Levine, 1987: 244–6). Manchuria had more land inequality and landless laborers, but was also more prosperous, so that exploitation was not experienced so catastrophically. The Communists went through their usual repertoire of reforms. With elites broken and no immediate retribution coming, Manchurian peasants responded. The party intensified struggle meetings and land redistributions, and peasants enlisted in the thousands in the Communist armies. Levine (1987: 10) says, "Revolution was a means – the most important means – of fighting the war." The Communists now had military power edges: more unity of command and volunteer troops, better supplied by civilian villages; and women's associations, fired up by land reform and the political changes accompanying it.

Military success became self-reinforcing as peasants and townspeople realized the Communists would win. Now Communism was welcomed as relief from civil war. At last, China could have a single government that could keep order (Westad, 2003: 114, 121–8). If the Communists had possessed any boats, they would have taken Taiwan, too. By late 1948, the United States realized the KMT was losing and ceased its arms supplies. Stalin and Truman had reached an implicit understanding to stay out of the civil war. They were war-weary.

When the Communists finally entered the cities of the coastal zone, they came not as conquerors but national liberators. They declared they were willing to compromise with those with useful skills, whether workers, professionals, or managers. They confronted few capitalists because under the KMT two-thirds of industry was nationalized and most capitalists who had collaborated with the Japanese had fled to Hong Kong. The Communists maintained a broad front for the first two years of their rule, and left Hong Kong well alone, content to offer inducements to capitalists there to return (Pepper, 1999: chap. 9; cf Westad, 2003: chap. 8). Once again, their policy was to consolidate their hold on their base area, now the whole of China, and only then commence the revolution. As we will see in Volume IV, this is exactly what they did.

China and theories of revolution

This was an agrarian revolution, a harbinger of most revolutions attempted in the post–World War II period. Two main explanations of its success have been advanced by historians of China: one stressing nationalism; the other class conflict. Chalmers Johnson gave the clearest nationalist explanation. He argued that the Kiangsi experience taught the Communists that land reform and Marxist-Leninist ideology could not politicize the peasant masses. Instead, the war against Japan and KMT misrule gave them the opportunity to mobilize Chinese nationalism. He says they "eschewed their old slogans of class warfare and violent redistribution of property in their post-1937 propaganda and concentrated solely on national salvation." "Peasant nationalism" was part of the "mass nationalism" sweeping the world in the first half of the twentieth century. It differed from KMT nationalism, which appealed mainly to intellectuals and urban folk but had little appeal among the peasant masses. The Communists provided social mobilization and a national myth, and their base-area governments "served as instruments for helping the rural masses attain a political understanding of the war to serve as a gloss on their personal experience." The war "broke the hold of parochialism on the Chinese peasant … and sensitized [peasants] to a new spectrum of possible associations, identities and purposes. Foremost among the new political concepts were those of "China" and "Chinese nationality." The war, suitably exploited, generated national identity and nationalism" (1962: 3–5). Johnson said that China provided the first anticolonial social revolution.

The war with Japan did have nationalizing effects. The terrible behavior of Japanese armies forced national identity on the locals, giving them a sense of belonging to a broader collective identity, in opposition to the Japanese. Yet this cannot explain very much. Most Communist base areas lay outside the areas of Japanese advance, and they were not formed for the purpose of resistance to them. By the time the Japanese did threaten Communist base areas, most were already well-established (van Slyke, 1986: 631). Nor were peasants as hostile to the Japanese as Johnson suggests. Rather, they tried to figure out who would win the war in their area: the Japanese, the KMT, the CCP, or warlords. They submitted to those they thought would win, as submission to the victors would avoid retaliation. Even the Japanese became bearable as rulers if one submitted, and the Japanese could maintain order. There is little evidence that peasants' choice of rule was greatly swayed by anti-Japanese sentiments (Chen, 1986: 513–4). In fact, where Japanese repression became atrocious, it tended to be effective, driving out the Communists and crushing peasant desire to resist (Hartford, 1989: 94). Japanese and Communist forces had little contact with each other until 1941. “Everywhere, during the first four years of the China war,” says Bix (2001: 347), “the Japanese area armies slighted Communist troops controlled by Mao Tse-Tung, regarding them as mere “bandits,” and directing virtually all their main blows against the “Nationalist” forces of Chiang kai-Shek.” The Japanese air force focused on bombing KMT strongholds.

Actually, both Chiang and the Communists were reluctant to take on the Japanese. The Communists did set up guerilla forces behind Japanese lines, thus acquiring some nationalist credentials. Yet this also enabled them to avoid committing the major military resources that serious battles would have required. There was a temporary change in CCP strategy in 1940. The Hundred Regiments offensive was an attempt to break out of their northwestern strongholds, but the Japanese counterattacked and drove the Communists back, making big gains. Chastened, they returned to guerilla warfare mainly against pro-Japanese warlords, easier targets. The CCP and the KMT both became intent on preserving their forces for a later confrontation against each other. In some regions, they were more likely to attack each other than the Japanese. In central and Eastern China, the main struggle was between the Communist New Fourth Army and KMT forces (Dreyer, 1995: 234–44, 252–4; Benton, 1999).

As Johnson says, the formation of the United Front against the Japanese, which lasted nominally to the end of the Pacific War, benefited the Communists more than the KMT. It gave them new legitimation among nationalists, showed they could subordinate class to national interests, and made their class enemies a little less likely to betray them to the Japanese (Shum, 1988). However, as Kataoka (1974) suggested, the Front was for the Communists primarily an opportunity to move forward on their domestic agenda. The nationalist myth became very important after the defeat of the Japanese, when Mao and the CCP declared themselves the national saviors – which is why in China today Mao is still remembered positively. Although an important factor in their eventual success, nationalism was not the main one.

The alternative class model is associated especially with Mark Selden (1971). He argued that peasants would fight for the Communists because they addressed the root problems of rural society: gross inequalities of landholding, wealth, and power. In 1935, the KMT government undertook a massive study of more than 1 million households occupying one-fifth of the country’s land. Although the average size of farms had been declining over many decades because of increasing population pressure, inequality of landholding between households was very large: 60 percent of all farming households possessed only 18 percent of the land; 20 percent held 60 percent of the land. The Gini coefficient calculated on size of holdings showed a concentration ratio of 57 percent, indicating high overall inequality. In normal times, Chinese peasants could subsist despite this, but warlordism and civil wars pushed many under during this period (Myers, 1969).

The Communists redressed this with land redistribution, reductions of rent, interest payments, and taxes. Selden emphasized poor- and middle-peasant participation in Communist organizations and the care the CCP took in its rectification campaigns to rule justly and equitably and purge corrupt officials. This was Mao's mass line, the Yenan Way, "the discovery of concrete methods for linking popular participation in the guerilla struggle with a wide ranging community attack on rural problems." My own account has tended to endorse Selden's arguments, but – as Johnson notes – Selden ultimately fails to explain how peasant fears were overcome, and his praise of Communist virtues is often naive, exaggerating peasant enthusiasm for revolution (1971: 77, 120, 177, 208–10, 276; his 1995 essay restates his arguments without this naivety).

Johnson, Selden, and most others say little about the overall health of the Chinese economy or the relations of production in each area of Communist success or failure. Are these omissions justified? The 1930s was the crucial decade for the growth of Chinese Communism. It was also the decade of the Great Depression. We might expect the two to be related. Foran (2005: 22) names recessions and depressions as the first of five elements in his explanation of modern revolutions. Because population growth had already eaten away at the cushion required by an agrarian society living near subsistence level, a depression could make the difference between life and death. The Depression's impact on China was delayed because China was not on the gold but the silver standard, which depreciated as a result of the global Depression. For a time, this was good for exports and local agricultural prices. The Depression then did hit hard in 1933. Agriculture was affected the worst. As prices fell, landlords' profits were squeezed, and in turn they squeezed the peasants, increasing their debts and sometimes forcing them off the land. Commercial fortunes varied; the Depression affected the commercialized lower Yangzi much more than distant Yenan. Across most of China, the Depression was experienced more as "distant thunder," occurring somewhere else, ominous perhaps, but not hurting us here (Wright, 2000). Shanghai was integrated into the international economy and experienced difficulties, yet even there few complained about a depression. Overall, there was probably economic growth in some regions and stagnation or slight decline in others. Peasants were suffering most (Myers, 1989; Rothermund, 1996: 110–15). Communist success did not correlate to economic depression. The CCP did well in both prosperous Manchuria and in backward areas, and it had begun well in prosperous Eastern China before being militarily defeated there.

The impact of the Depression was less than that of war or environmental disasters such as floods, droughts, locusts, and bubonic plague. Foran (2005: 46–57) acknowledges this in his detailed discussion of China, if not in his general conclusion. Famine in spring remained a perennial threat across much of China. In parts of Yenan, famine lasted intermittently from 1928 to 1933. Even in the lower Yangzi there were crop failures and famine in 1935. From 1931 in Manchuria, from 1934 in parts of North China, and from 1937 in Northern, Eastern and central China, wars caused greater devastation and hardship for the peasants than the troubles of world capitalism. Dikes were deliberately burst, villages destroyed, peasants killed, taxes raised, and millions of soldiers were like locusts, feeding off the fields and storehouses. Wars especially harmed the KMT. It had to exact higher taxes to finance its large armies, especially after it lost the more economically advanced regions to the Japanese. Taxes were not legitimated by any discernible ability to throw out the Japanese. Where they were in control, the Communists fought less costly guerilla warfare and exacted much less taxation. KMT military strategy was also less peasant-friendly. When in 1938 it blew the dikes of the Yellow River to block the Japanese advance, the flooding killed almost 1 million peasants. It repeated dike-blowing tactics in 1945 when attacking Communist bases. Communist armies seemed lesser locusts.

Different relations of production are said to make some peasants more revolutionary than others. Some argue that the impact of global capitalism revolutionized those peasants disrupted by the entry of commercialized agriculture into a country. Peasants hitherto producing for their own and local markets were displaced by large-scale commercial, export-oriented agriculture. Under this pressure, peasants lost their land and became laborers or tenants of large estates or plantations – or they moved out of agriculture to become laborers in construction, manufacturing, or mining. There they were likelier recruits to revolutionary movements. This is what Foran calls "dependent development" (cf Barrington Moore, 1967; Wolf, 1969; Migdal, 1974; Paige, 1975).

Paige says export agriculture sectors set amid a more traditional subsistence economy are most likely to produce peasant revolutions, especially if dominated by sharecroppers and migrant laborers. More limited rebellions and reform movements are generated by commercial haciendas, plantations and smallholders. However, his statistical analysis of countries has been criticized, and the relationship is probably rather slight (Somers & Goldfrank, 1990). Wickham-Crowley (2001) shows that squatters and migrant laborers were more likely to support revolution in Latin America; in China, peasant revolution was not related to newly commercialized agriculture. Some regions had been commercialized for centuries, others were still not commercialized, and in parts of the North China plain it was bringing not capitalism but what P. Huang (1985) calls "involution," whereby the marginal product of a family plot fell below the average wage for labor. Greater output was necessary to keep the family alive, but it had to result from everyone working harder, not from greater productivity. These "proletarianized" peasant households remained vulnerable to the slightest of economic or environmental downturns, but, heads bent down to their work, they were not receptive to Communism. Commercialized agriculture did not generate more Communism, however. Kiangsi, the first rural soviet established, had contained some commercial sectors, but the main base areas in Yenan and Shensi in the Northwest did not. The Communists generally established their base areas in defensible mountainous areas, so they recruited more peasant support from the least commercialized areas, although this was for military not economic reasons. They found recruits in varied economic conditions. Neither terrible poverty nor *J-curve* conditions (where rising prosperity then gave way to recession) nor commercialization or dependent development nor types of tenancy could predict Communist success. It was less the condition of local agriculture that mattered than the entry and subsequent power of Communist militias. Where they did not enter, there was no revolution, whatever the relations of production. Where they did enter, they attuned their policies to local realities, including the relations of production.

Wolf says commercialization generated the key peasant grievances (1969: 130–1), but adds that the middle peasants were the core revolutionaries in the twentieth century. China is his principal case. He says poor peasants and landless laborers were too dependent on landlords for their subsistence, so had insufficient tactical power to launch or sustain a revolution. Rich peasants, on the other hand, had little incentive to revolt and too much to lose. The middle peasants, in contrast, had both resources and motivation. Wolf also identifies peasants in peripheral areas as a second revolution-prone group: "The only component of the peasantry which does have some internal leverage is either landowning 'middle peasantry' or a peasantry located in a peripheral area outside the domains of landlord control." The key, he says, is that these two groups are "tactically mobile … it is the middle and poor but 'free' peasant, not constrained by any power domain, which constitute the pivotal groupings for peasant uprisings." The Yenan and Shensi peasants' isolation gave them more political freedom, and nearby mountain fastnesses allowed military retreat, if necessary. Almost all Communist bases were either on the northern mountain periphery of China or in upland border areas between provinces, where the military weakness of the state gave Communists breathing space to win peasant support and build up their defenses (Wolf, 1969: 291–3; cf Esherick, 1995: 56; Kataoka, 1974: 294–5).

Wolf's explanation is in terms of political and military power capacities, not economic exploitation. He then adds an ideological power element. He recognizes that peasants could not start a revolution unaided, and followed the leadership of the "intelligentsia in arms." He adds an ideological irony, saying of the middle and peripheral peasants, "This is also the peasantry in whom anthropologists and rural sociologists have tended to see the main bearers of peasant tradition" (1969: 292) – cultural conservatives make peasant revolutions! His explanation includes all four power sources.

Yet the middle peasants were not so revolutionary. Although the CCP believed middle peasants did make better militants, they were less easy to recruit than poor peasants. The recruitment of middle versus poor peasants mostly depended on local CCP policy. Where its policy was moderate, more middle peasants were recruited; where policy was radical, more poor peasants were. Overall, the party recruited more poor peasants, although as a result of Communist redistribution many ended up as middle peasants – social mobility through Communism!

A much simpler economic exploitation model applies to China. Different relations of production, different types of exploitation, as specified by Paige or Wolf, mattered relatively little. Under the KMT and warlords, China had varied ecologies and economies but one broad system of rural-class exploitation, based according to region on either rents or taxes, but everywhere reinforced by landlords' extractions through usury, privileges, fees for running local associations, corrupt control of local administrations, and the political and military power to exact arbitrary levels of all these. Overwhelming the many local differences across China was this brute exploitation, which – as the CCP argued – broadly pitted landlords, rich peasants, moneylenders, and officials against middle and poor peasants. This was sometimes exploitation by taxes, sometimes by rent, but it was always buttressed by the quadrilateral being – rent collectors, merchants, usurers, and officials – stressed by Wolf himself. That was the economic-power part of the explanation.

Although peasants knew they were exploited, they had thought this was the permanent lot of humanity. Once the Communists were able to demonstrate that they could remove the quadrilateral being's coercive power and redistribute land, wealth, and power to them, enough middle and poor peasants in areas of different relations of production rallied behind them to spread the belief that it was possible to overthrow this exploitative order and replace it with a more just one. This was a long, slow, and uneven process set amid war and civil war. The military power of Communism enabled a class revolution by forming peasant militias defending each base area against the dominant classes. The best explanation of this revolution was offered by Mao and his cadres, who designed strategies to exploit guerilla warfare flexibly but to the full.

Foran (2005) has advanced the most elaborate theory of Third World revolutions. He argues that in all the successful social revolutions of the twentieth century – Mexico, 1910–1920; Cuba, 1953–1959; Iran, 1977–1979; Nicaragua, 1977–1979; and China (he excludes Russia) – five conditions are always found: dependent economic development; an economic downturn; a repressive, exclusionary and personalist state; a strong political culture of opposition; and a "world-systemic opening." In contrast, in less successful or failed revolutions (which he also analyzes), these were less pronounced. However, we have already seen that his first two conditions, dependent development and economic downturn, do not work very well in China. Nor did they in Russia, as we saw in Chapter 6.

Foran's third variable is a repressive, exclusionary, and personalist state, repressive and excluding almost everyone from a share in rule, even important elites. The ruler depends on personal loyalties, a fragile basis of rule. Most scholars today see this as the most vulnerable kind of state, which is the most important precondition of revolution (Goldstone, 2004, 2009). However, I noted in Chapter 6 two kinds of vulnerability – factionalism and narrowness or a lack of state infrastructural power. Wickham-Crowley (2001) adds military power. Personalist regimes develop praetorian guards, good at protecting the ruler and repressing normal dissidence, but poor at fighting wars or civil wars. They resist military professionalization and can be beaten by armed insurgents. Goodwin (2001) says such states have low military and policing capabilities. He gives what he calls a "state-centered paradigm" with the state as "the most important factor" explaining revolution.

Was the KMT regime personalist, exclusionary, and highly repressive, or did it have weak infrastructures? Chiang Kai-shek was the undisputed leader of this party state, and it was fractious. However, his regime was not exclusionary. He had done deals with many warlords, and there were also distinct leftist and rightist factions; anyone could join. Its weakness did not lie in excluding elites or the urban intelligentsia or bourgeoisie from participation in rule. Quite the reverse: Chiang sought desperately to integrate them into the state. This might seem to have been a weak state in other ways, however. Chiang lacked sufficient infrastructures to make his writ run in many provinces, and local elites often obstructed his reform efforts. On the other hand, the Communists were much weaker until near the end. Chiang had crushed them first in Shanghai then in Kiangsi, and was on the point of crushing them for good in Yenan. His fiscal and military infrastructures were certainly up to the task of destroying them for a third time, but then the Japanese intervened. No Asian state could cope with the Japanese, although the KMT regime did succeed in holding them at bay. Unlike Russian armies in World War I, Nationalist soldiers did not refuse to fight, despite heavy losses. The Chinese state seems stronger than the sociologists' model suggests, but its infrastructures had been shredded by the Japanese. This state was not as infrastructurally strong or as cohesive as the two states with which it was at war, Japan and, from 1945, the Communist party state. State weakness was only exposed by war against two unusually strong states. This is not the same thing at all. The Chinese revolution does not fit the sociological theories well – and it was the most important modern revolution!

Foran's fourth variable is the strength of oppositional political culture. Scholars argue that revolutionary leadership emerges out of urban dissident intellectuals and that successful revolutionary movements expand from their peasant or worker base to draw in a broad, urban, multiclass opposition (Goodwin, 2001: 27; Wickham-Crowley, 2001; Goldstone, 2009). In China, the cities and universities did provide a stream of young men and women to the CCP. After the abortive 1911 revolution, the cities bred many reformers. Alienated from warlord and KMT rule, many then shifted toward Communism to become the ideological power elite I described above, committed to the cause, convinced that history was on their side, morally driven away from corruption – secular salvationists. Yet the second half of this model does not apply because the cities remained Nationalist up to near the end of the Civil War. As Mao had predicted, the cities would have to be encircled from the countryside before being seized by military force. China again differs from the sociological model.

Foran's final variable is an opening of the world system, although his world system is more geopolitical than capitalist. In the Chinese case, he rightly stresses the Japanese invasion, although he doesn't understand how this affected the party's core political and military practices. Early military defeats, followed by war and civil war, forced the Communists into becoming a highly militarized party, exercising military discipline over its members and peasants in the base areas. The revolution came from battlefields pitting Japan against China and the Chinese against each other – a decidedly military opening of the world system!

Sociologists focus on economic and political variables, although with a dose of ideology thrown in. All three were necessary conditions of revolution. Most peasants had major economic grievances; the Communists found out how to implement a more popular economic structure on the ground. The KMT regime combined political fractiousness (although not exclusion) with weakening infrastructural power. The CCP cadres were wholly committed to salvation, for which they repeatedly risked their lives. Yet they could also vary their means of getting there according to local material conditions, balances of power, and changing threats and opportunities. Without any of these conditions, they would not have achieved revolution.

Previous theories fail to sufficiently stress the one thing that in China persistently stares us in the face. War obviously does enter into grounded empirical narratives (for example, Foran's) but not sufficiently into the theories. Skocpol (1979) sees war as a necessary background condition of revolution. Wickham-Crowley (2001), analyzing Latin American cases, understands that revolutionaries always need military power to survive and perhaps to win. This he sees as one of three main causes of insurgent strength, alongside strong peasant support and cross-class, multi-institutional support for the guerillas in the towns. Even this would not do justice to the military activities of the Chinese Communists, however. Once they left Shanghai for Kiangsi, their revolution was a war, lasting twenty years. To survive, the party militarized, and its struggles were first and foremost military. One cannot analyze this revolution without giving a central place to military power relations – more central even than in the Russian Revolution. The social organization of coercion mattered above all else for the Communists, in their armed struggles against the KNT and the Japanese, for their ability to discipline and coerce the peasants in their zones of control, and for their policies once they had seized power.

Without their military power, all of the Communists' economic, political, and ideological acumen would still have led them to defeat. Two military interventions allowed the possibility of Communist triumph across China. They can be seen as the influence of the world system, although they were not economic and war is not very systemic. The Japanese invasion allowed the Communists to survive and build up their strength in distant base areas while the Nationalist forces bore the brunt of the war. As Skocpol (1979:147–50, 240–2) notes, a key impact of this invasion was to weaken the solidarity between local elites and the state, a process that had been underway from the nineteenth century as Chinese elites had withdrawn from the Qing regime and then failed to agree on its successor. The Japanese invasions put almost unbearable pressure on them. Second, the Pacific War between Japan and the United States prevented either Japanese domination of China or rule shared between Japan and the Nationalists. Either of these outcomes would probably have left them strong enough to destroy the Communists in a final civil war. When the Americans destroyed Japanese power, the Communists could win the Civil War, impose their version of autarchy over a large part of Asia, and so block universal globalization with a second Communist segment. Their militarized socialism, allied to the class appeal of Communism identified by Selden and Esherick, gave them more support among peasants, and that proved decisive in a low-tech civil war. The supreme irony was that Japan and the United States, two fiercely anti-Communist powers, unintentionally helped Communism triumph in the most populous nation on earth. Such is the power of unintended consequences. State weakening is a necessary cause of modern revolutions. Here in the most important revolution of them all, war weakened the state, but in a peculiar way. Others would shortly try to emulate this path to revolution. I discuss them and move onto a more general theory of revolution in Volume IV.

14 The last interimperial war, 1939–1945

World War II was the third Great Dislocation of the twentieth century. It was the most global, and (hopefully) both the last interimperial war and the last war to engulf Europe. It would in fact first fracture and then destroy European power. I will ask the same questions of it that I asked of World War in Chapter 5: what caused it, what determined its outcome, and what were its aftereffects? The second question must be answered mostly in terms of military power relations, and at critical moments, I will give a blow-by-blow account of the war. The other two questions require broader explanations.

Europeans date the onset of the war to September 1939, when Hitler invaded Poland; they, together with Americans, place its end at mid-1945, when Germany and then Japan surrendered. Yet this was only the central phase of a longer series of wars. Japan had attacked China in 1931 and again in 1937. Millions of Chinese were dead before either Poland or Pearl Harbor were attacked. Italy invaded Abyssinia in 1935, and with Nazi Germany helped Franco win the Spanish Civil War between 1936 and 1939. Italy invaded Albania in April 1939. Between 1936 and 1939, Hitler had managed to swallow up the Rhineland, Austria, and Czechoslovakia through aggression, but without having to fight. The war in Asia did not end until 1949, when Chinese communists defeated the KMT. The interconnections of these wars made them far more than half-global. They were started by the Axis Powers seeking to found "late" empires through military aggression believing they were establishing rights already secured by other empires. The Allies were defending their own empires. These were interimperial wars, the culmination and hubris of European traditions of militarism and imperialism, now exported to others. This was the first near-global war, for only Latin America escaped it. I dealt with the war in Asia in Chapter 12. Here I focus on the war against Germany.

Causes

There seems such a clear link between the outbreak of World War II in the West and the settlement terms of World War I that it is tempting to see the one as rising from the other. This was only partially so. Certainly, the peace settlements made at Versailles and Trianon had not solved all the geopolitical problems that had caused the first war, and they had created new problems, too. Austria-Hungary, the initial aggressor, had been destroyed, and the Trianon Treaties had replaced it with a number of small states who would be unable to stand up to either Germany or Russia if attacked. Hitler cut his aggressive teeth on Czechoslovakia and Poland in the lead-up to the war. Nor could Germans in central Europe any longer divide their loyalties between Vienna and Berlin. If Germans in Austria, Czechoslovak Sudetenland, Poland, and other areas now wished to be part of a major German power, it could only be a *grossdeutsch* empire led from Berlin. After 1933, this meant it would be led by Hitler.

German power had not been destroyed in 1918 because German leaders had sued for peace before the country could be occupied. The Entente powers could not influence the sovereign postwar regime that developed there, and they were divided over the peace terms. Only France, fearful of Germany and seeking compensation for its greater sufferings, consistently sought to crush German power. The British were a little more conciliatory, having suffered less and wishing to preserve a continental balance of power with Germany as a counterweight to France and the Soviet Union. The Americans were even more conciliatory, because they had barely suffered at all and wanted Europe kept a multistate system rather than an Anglo-French preserve. All three worried about Bolshevism and looked to Weimar Germany as a European bulwark against its export. These were mixed and often divisive motives.

The Versailles Treaty appeared vindictive. Article 231 stated, "The Allied and associated governments declare, and Germany accepts the responsibility for, all the loss and damage suffered by the Allied and associated governments as a consequence of the war imposed upon them by the aggression of Germany and her allies." German border territories were handed over to adjacent states; German colonies were handed over to the new League of Nations, which then handed them over "in trust" to the victorious empires. Reparations were to be paid for war damage, mainly to France. The German army was restricted to 100,000 men without a General Staff. Three Rhineland zones were to be occupied for five, ten, and fifteen years, pending fulfillment of the terms. The blame was clear, the penalty harsh. Keynes appreciated the folly of this:

> If we aim deliberately at the impoverishment of Central Europe, vengeance, I dare predict, will not limp. Nothing can then delay for very long that final civil war between the forces of Reaction and the despairing convulsions of Revolution, before which the horrors of the late German war will fade into nothing, and which will destroy, whoever is victor, the civilization and the progress of our generation (1919: 251).

He was correct, although he did not see the role of fascists, revolutionaries of the right, in the future horrors.

In theory, the terms of the peace treaties were enforced by the League of Nations and the Great Powers. However, the League was allowed little autonomy by powers who were themselves divided. Economic problems surfaced, as we saw in Chapter 7. Germany's parlous state weakened the international economy, and the size of its reparations payments destabilized international finances. British capital and the pound sterling could not maintain their prewar hegemony. The United States and its dollar might be able to take over, but Americans would not yet accept this.

The war had exhausted France and weakened Britain. Yet Britain had more imperial possessions than ever, its military forces were larger, and its statesmen still saw the world as their oyster. The United States had very little empire and not much of an army – although after 1922 its navy was equal to Britain's – nor politicians much interested in the world. In World War I, 50,000 Americans had lost their lives in the wars of others. Better to stay away from this martial continent, said most Americans. FDR repeatedly promised to keep the United States out of war and out of Europe, although American influence in East Asia was growing greater than Britain's. So up to the mid-1930s, Britain and the United States were about of equal weight in global geopolitics (Edgerton, 2005; McKercher, 1999). The old diplomatic game had been destabilized; Japan strengthened; France weakened; Germany broken militarily, blamed exclusively for the war, and placed under partial foreign domination. America was an isolate, the Soviet Union a pariah.

Germany remained the West's flash point, just as Japan was the East's. Yet a second war did not seem inevitable. Reparations were compromised, and then ended. The Rhineland would have been fully restored to Germany without war, and probably the Sudetenland, too. Nor were Britain or the United States hostile to Germany. British governments still saw France as the greater continental power until around 1935, and Britain and the United States had assisted German economic recovery and pressured France to make concessions to Germany.

There were tensions in these relations. Yet most Europeans hoped they were done with war and aggressive nationalism. It needed Nazism and Hitler to convert the tensions into war in Europe. This was explained mainly by the legacy of Versailles, German domestic politics, and the Great Depression, although the Nazis emerged as part of a broader fascist-leaning movement through much of Europe, as we saw in Chapter 10. This nationalism believed in the cleansing virtues of violence and war. Fascists were now urging the military seizure of whatever territory seemed ripe for the picking, exaggerating the capacity of the New (fascist) Man to overcome material war odds. German Nazism and especially Hitler himself were fascist to excess.

From the beginning, Hitler intended to make war to found a great empire. He did not see war merely as an instrumental means of attaining a material goal. The mix of metaphysics and biology in his ideology saw "eternal laws of life on this earth, which are and will remain those of a ceaseless struggle for existence ...[a]... struggle for life." The "aristocratic principle of Nature" was "the right of the stronger" (Wette, 1998: 18–20). This was social Darwinism, with the nation substituted for Darwin's species – a total ideology of salvation through struggle between nations and races, and therefore with a certain degree of power among its believers. To attain his German Reich, four stages were necessary. First, he would rebuild Germany and strengthen its state and nation. The state would be despotic, free from enervating political conflict. The nation would be cleansed of both class conflict and "unfit" races and groups, especially Jews, Slavs, and the disabled and criminal. Within a few months of taking power, seventy concentration camps were built for trade union leaders, Communists, Social Democrats, and anyone else preaching class politics before any Jews were arrested, and mass killing started with the disabled, not Jews. Germans would emerge as the master race, remilitarized materially and spiritually, ready for great warrior endeavors.

Second, Hitler would recover all the lost territories of the peace treaties. Most German politicians said they wanted this, but he was serious about it. Third, he wanted an empire to the east enclosing the many ethnic German communities that had settled there over the centuries. He would reinforce rule with millions of new German colonists, settling a land racially cleansed of Jews and Slavs. He recognized that this would involve destroying Russian power. Fourth, to protect this eastern-tilting empire, he must also expand westward and northward to subjugate the edges of the continent, creating client states there. He was uncertain about the fate of Britain. Because he did not want overseas colonies, he seemed content to let the British Empire survive, provided it accepted his dominance. In the late 1930s, however, he became more hostile to the British, seeing them as obstructive. On the other hand, he realized that the fall of the British Empire around the world would benefit Germany less than the United States, Japan, and the Soviet Union. Thus, he thought it might be better to prop it up. He did not want either a global war or a global empire. He would have been content with German expansion all around the periphery of Europe, in the East, the Middle East, and North Africa, similar to Napoleon's peak ambitions, although ruled far more directly and severely. He did not want an end to fractured imperialism; he just wanted to found the dominant empire.

The world remained in ignorance of his plans until they were substantially accomplished. He was able to get away with expansion because he accomplished it in stages. The first stage of strengthening Germany itself was even admired abroad. Some were worried by the anti-Semitism, although the West also harbored this, and not even the violence of Kristallnacht in 1938 or the Viennese pogrom in 1938 seemed greater than pogroms occurring further east in the continent. This was not yet a genocidal regime, and it seemed milder than Stalin's. There was more alarm on the European left, appalled by Hitler's suppression of Socialists, Communists, and labor unions. Together with the Spanish Civil War and Italy's destruction of Abyssinia, Hitler dented the left's prior affinity for pacifism. By the late 1930s, most British and French leftists were urging standing up to Hitler. Conversely, much of the right approved of the treatment of the German left, and privately wished they could do the same to their own left.

The second stage involved the recovery of the lost territories. Again, there was some sympathy abroad. The principle of self-determination was well-established within Europe (if not in the overseas empires), and most of the inhabitants of the Rhineland, Austria, the Sudetenland, and other predominantly Germanic territories wanted unification with Germany. France could have sent troops in and retaken the Rhineland in 1936, as Hitler privately conceded, but few French favored such aggression. Italy might have tried to stop the Austrian Anschluss in 1938, but it was never likely to. Hitler's domestic popularity grew as he recovered lost territories without war. At the same time, he was rearming, building up Germany's strength in case he was opposed.

The third stage did cause alarm abroad. Although Hitler got away with annexing Czechoslovakia without war, his invasion of Poland precipitated a war with France and Britain he had not expected. He was shocked when Britain declared war, forcing him to fight in the West before he could launch an attack on the Soviet Union. Yet he saw war as the inevitable outcome of racial struggle, and his quick success on the Western Front persuaded him to repeat Blitzkrieg on the Soviets. His thousand-year Reich seemed within reach. He had reached that point through fascist militarism and despotism – especially through the Fuhrer Principle, which induced the working toward the Fuhrer described in Chapter 10. His political power had overridden the limits to militarism that in a democracy ordinary Germans would probably have opposed. They were now apprehensive. Gestapo and other police reports say that every time war seemed to loom on the horizon they became fearful; every time Hitler managed to achieve his goals without war, they cheered. The people were irrelevant, however. Hitler had destroyed all organized opposition, and an army of informers reported on individual dissent. Hitler had welded together all four sources of power, and Germans were atomized and powerless. The vast majority did not want war, but they could not stop it (Wette, 1998: 11–12, 120–4, 151–5). Absent Hitler, and there probably would have been no World War II – and this war changed the world even more than the first one.

So the immediate cause of World War II, focusing the general drift of European military and political power onto aggressive warfare, was Adolf Hitler. This was not World War I, in which miscalculations all round had produced a war of unintended consequences, if set within a broader culture of militarism. Although there were miscalculations and unintended consequences, one man and his powerful country started the second war, wielding a salvationist ideology of aggressive nationalism. Decisions were again set amidst general ideological predispositions, including the new dread of Communism, but in 1939 most Europeans, scarred by the Great War, were less militaristic than they had been in 1914. That sentence contains the two further tragic European causes of war, however.

The first tragedy was the unevenness of contemporary militarism and nationalism. Europe had fractured into two, as we saw in Chapter 10. Fascist and fascist-tinged regimes in center, East, and South Europe were taking nationalist militarism to new heights, but governments and peoples in the Northwest were in retreat from militarism, embracing nicer, cuddlier versions of nationalism. Britain and France had been burned by the first war. British leaders saw their country as a "satiated" power, aware that their control over a fourth of the world's land surface was getting precarious. Imperial interests lay in peace and collective security to preserve what Britain already had. France was much more insecure on account of the German threat to metropolitan France and badly needed peace. Stalin did not want war, either. He was busy transforming his economy and weakening his party and military with his fratricide. The United States was even more pacific than the other democracies, and obsessed by domestic issues. Mussolini was keen on war, but only against Africans. Europeans scurried around to avoid war, which only reinforced the contempt and appetite of fascists. When they did face up to the possibility of war, each country hoped others would do the fighting. The shared foreign policy was to spill the blood of others: Britain hoped to spill French blood; both hoped that East European or Russian blood would turn back Hitler; Stalin might have spilled Russian blood if others would spill theirs, too. This suited Hitler's plan to divide his enemies so that he could defeat them one by one (Carley, 1999: 31). Only Hitler was fully prepared to spill as much German blood as was necessary. Because he recognized the difference, it emboldened him. The Europeans were incapable of rattling their swords to deter Hitler.

In the end, British and French leaders were prepared to fight. They talked about defending democracy, although they cared not a fig for Czech or Polish democracy, and outside of Europe they themselves had despotic empires. Chamberlain and Churchill, Blum and Daladier were united in defending empire abroad as well as democracy at home. As late as December 1944, Churchill was thundering, "'Hands off the British Empire' is our maxim, and it must not be weakened or smirched to please sob-stuff merchants at home or foreigners of any hue" (B. Porter, 2006: 80). German, Italian, and Japanese demands for their own empires produced the war, but their enemies were vigorously defending theirs (Overy, 1999: xi–xii, 104, 297–302). It was a collision between imperialists, the old regime seeing peace and collective security as the better way to preserve empire; the arrivistes believing they would have to fight to get one. This was the culmination of European militarism, and also its ruin.

If Hitler did mean war, France would be in the firing line because it held the disputed territory of Alsace-Lorraine and had been the hard-liner on reparations. French politicians knew France's power had declined, and that Germany's had increased. This was evident in demography, for the difference in birth rates was increasingly favoring German power. French politics remained fractious for most of the interwar period, so there was little domestic modernization. Because French government and industry remained rightist, there was little corporatism, although government intervention and cooperation between capital and labor would have been useful for military modernization, as Britain was showing. The British national governments of the 1930s were mainly Conservative, but the Tory Party shared in the post–World War I and post-Depression consensus, and the governments of Baldwin and Chamberlain extended social welfare benefits and trade union rights. Thus, when major military expansion finally took off in both countries in 1938, Britain benefitted from more class cooperation than France.

French leaders became ever more conscious of the need for allies. They needed them in Eastern Europe, but the crucial ally was Britain. France could not even move its 750,000 colonial troops to metropolitan France without help from the Royal Navy. To their disgust, French leaders found themselves supporting British projects to rebuild German power up to the mid-1930s in order to keep the British happy, although German revival might threaten them! In turn, Britain depended on the French army to hold Germany away from the Channel. The recent rise of air power seemed to make the threat worse, especially as the British and French overestimated the size of the Luftwaffe. The British expected the immediate destruction of much of London if war broke out. If Britain was threatened at home, then the rebellious Irish, Egyptians, Indians, and white South Africans could cause more trouble. It could be the end of the British Empire. British leaders should have been more worried by French weakness than they seemed to be.

Yet British power seemed at its height, and military neglect in the 1920s was being remedied in the 1930s. Armed with Liddell Hart's theory of air power and Baldwin's dictum "the bomber will always get through," Conservative governments under Baldwin and Chamberlain strengthened the Royal Air Force and Royal Navy. Britain's military budget and armaments production levels were now higher than Germany's. Seven British aircraft carriers were launched; the Germans and Italians had not launched any. Britain's armed forces were technologically advanced, and between half and two-thirds of all national scientific research was for war (Edgerton, 2005). The army was the weak link, as leaders were more concerned with protecting the empire than Europe, and the Indian army remained the main land instrument for that. Economic policy was also about protecting the empire through tariffs. In November 1931, the Foreign Office warned, "A high protective tariff, combined with empire preference, implies a measure of dissociation from Europe, a corresponding diminution of our influence over European affairs.... World recovery (the aim of our policy) depends on European recovery; European recovery on German recovery; German recovery on France's consent; France's consent on security (for all time) from attack" (Steiner, 2005: 668, 775). This was acute. Unfortunately, French security was declining just as Hitler's power was rising.

The British commitment to Europe was a supposed ability to help fight a long war in France, backed as in the first war by a naval blockade of Germany. Chamberlain was also committed to airpower, and his notion of deterrence from the air anticipated post-1945 defense theories. However, given treasury economic orthodoxy, to which Chamberlain deferred, military expansion had to be modest, and it came at the expense of a field army capable of intervening in France. The Inskip Report, approved by the Cabinet in December 1937, set out a cap on military spending over the next five years of £1.5 billion, and it enumerated four defense priorities. The highest was the defense of Britain, followed by maritime communications and imperial defense. Last came continental commitments (Imlay, 2003: 78).

Although British airpower might be able to hurt Germany and deter an attack on Britain, it could hardly prevent an attack on France. Britain remained dependent on France's short-war ability to hold up any German attack, for it was not offering the French much short-term help. In World War I, by 1916, Britain had fielded almost sixty divisions in France. In 1937, there were only two underequipped divisions ready with two more projected. "Two, and two more later," Stalin sarcastically remarked. Chamberlain had an eventual goal of five to be ready by 1942, the date, he reckoned, when the German economy would be ready for war. He did not understand that Germany no longer had an autonomous capitalist economy, but one subordinated to the war-making goals of its dictator. Hitler was ready by 1940, but even after frenetic British activity during the "phony war" period from September 1939 to May 1940, there were still only nine British divisions in France when Hitler attacked – not enough to support the French army. Yet all – empire as well – might be lost if the French collapsed. It very nearly was lost.

Appeasement

The lack of war readiness of Britain and France played a major role in the Czechoslovak crisis of 1938. Chamberlain and Daladier hoped that Hitler could be talked away from war. Chamberlain saw the Munich agreement with Hitler of September 29, 1938, as a victory for peace because Hitler had been threatening to seize all of Czechoslovakia by force. Yet Hitler got the Sudetenland and most of the Czech defensive fortifications without a fight, and he could soon get the rest if he broke the agreement, as he fully intended to do. Daladier doubted whether Hitler could be stopped, but in the negotiations, he deferred to Chamberlain in order to keep the British onside. Chamberlain was backed by French Foreign Minister Bonnet, who fought tirelessly to keep France out of a war (Imlay, 2002: 34; du Réau, 1993). As Chamberlain did, Daladier saw the Munich agreement as buying time for rearmament, which expanded apace in both countries in 1939. That was the rational part of appeasement. From now on, Daladier, his General Staff, and even Bonnet recognized they would soon be at war with Germany. They differed in their view of the chances of success, but they felt they had no choice. A corner had been turned, and French *redressement* or recovery was underway (Imlay, 2002: 38–42, 136–7).

The United States had played no part in this diplomacy; the American administration was bound into virtual inactivity by the Neutrality Acts of the late 1930s. Roosevelt, says Kennedy (1999: 419), was "a powerless spectator at Munich, a weak and resourceless leader of an unarmed, economically wounded, and diplomatically isolated country. He, and America, had counted for nothing in the scales of diplomacy." However, Roosevelt did draw the same lessons as the others, and American rearmament also began.

Chamberlain himself coined the term "appeasement." He saw it as double-sided. He would conciliate Hitler, finding peaceful ways to help him expand in central Europe (for which Chamberlain cared nothing), buying time for limited rearmament – not enough to be provocative or to breach treasury orthodoxy, but enough to build up British strength, including a bigger British army in France (Imlay, 2002: 81–93). As Ferguson (2006: 325–30) points out, the treasury was wrong. Britain might have rearmed with a vengeance without much harm to the economy; after all, this had pulled Germany and Japan out of the Depression, and it was to shortly pull the United States out, too. Chamberlain and Halifax, his Foreign Secretary, were prepared to go further in conciliating Germany. German expansion into the Balkans, Chamberlain remarked, would be "a lesser evil than war with Germany" (Carley, 1999: 39). He even suggested Germany be given some African colonies, at the expense of Portugal or Belgium. Chamberlain wanted to appease Hitler with the territories as well as the blood of others.

The foolish part of appeasement was Chamberlain's own, for he believed Hitler would honor his guarantees. Chamberlain was a decent man who believed in peace, compromise, economic progress, and anti-Communism. He assumed that other statesmen did likewise, including Hitler. Chamberlain's weakness was his vanity, especially of his own diplomatic skills and judgment of men. These combined into the belief that because Hitler had given his word to him, he would keep it. In contrast, Churchill, although initially quite favorable to Hitler as a bulwark against Communism, had by 1937 radically switched, and thereafter regarded Hitler as simply evil. Perhaps it took a thug to know a thug, but Churchill Mark II was right. Hitler said of the appeasers, "Our enemies are little worms. I saw them at Munich," and he believed throughout the Polish crisis of 1939 that Britain "was only bluffing."

Chamberlain still had a big parliamentary majority and much popular support. Britain and France were not betrayed by a handful of appeasers, for public opinion did not want war, and the two parliaments faithfully reflected that, imposing limits on militarism. This was not the same as World War I, when elites alone had decided whether it would be war or peace. That was true in Germany, Italy, Japan, and the Soviet Union but not in Britain or France – or in the United States – where democracy was working, but for peace. By the time of Munich, some change had occurred. An opinion poll showed British opinion evenly divided over whether to aid the Czechs, but when Chamberlain returned from Munich waving his infamous bit of paper, declaring "peace in our time," there was a surge of relief and he was greeted as a hero who had averted war. In Britain, his policy resonated among very different groups: pacifists who hated war; those seeing Britain as a satiated power, with everything to gain from peace and everything to lose from war; those seeing Britain and France as still too weak to confront Hitler; and those seeing realistically that there was little Britain could do to help the Czechs. Chamberlain's social basis of support came from the establishment, from industrialists and financiers doing business with Germany, and from old regime and Conservative Party grandees who feared class revolution. The main opposition came from Churchill-led Tories and the Labour Party, who saw Munich as a disaster and war as now inevitable. As in France, the left had shifted during the 1930s from being antimilitarist to being antifascist. After Munich, Labour was even willing to put more weapons of war in the hands of Tory imperialists. Yet the Churchill Tories hesitated to attack their own government, whereas Labour saw political advantage in it, so the warmongers lacked a common strategy (Imlay, 2002: 194–206; Worley, 2005: 213–5).

The British government was slowly gearing up to fight a long, defensive war, similar to World War I, but this couldn't help Czechoslovakia. That would have required a short-war potential, with France aiding the Czechs by invading Germany, opening a second front against Hitler. As the Czech army and its defenses were quite strong, and the German military was not yet as strong as the French and British believed (as Hitler and his high command privately recognized), there was a good chance of deterring Hitler with the threat of a two-front war. If war did come, there was a chance of overcoming Germany in early 1938. The initial stages of such a policy would have depended on Daladier and the French, not the British. Yet after the fall of the Popular Front in April 1938, the rightist French government needed parliamentary votes from deputies who were soft on fascism. French parties were less unified than British ones, and party chieftains such as Bonnet had more autonomy. In France as in Britain, by now, much of the left wanted tougher action, but the left did not speak coherently and the conservative government was unlikely to listen. The French military was preparing for a long war in defense of France, and opposed invasion of Germany – as indeed did most French people. So the French could not deter Hitler in 1938 by threatening a two-front war, and they realized that their projected alliance with several East European states was impracticable. Indeed, they were not even reliable allies. Far from helping Czechoslovakia against Hitler, Polish leaders were claiming some Czech territory and asking Hitler to help them get it.

The chance to confront Germany in 1938 went by. Over the next twelve months German military strength rose from being inferior to combined French, British, and Czech strength to being about equal to Anglo-French forces (Ferguson, 2006: 361–8). Hitler now had his eyes firmly set on the conquest of

Poland, and for this he felt he first had to acquire the remaining "rump" Czech state. In March 1939, he invaded and swallowed it without serious Czech opposition, allowing Poland to seize its desired piece of Czech territory (foolishly supping with the devil). This ended appeasement. The Cabinet overruled Chamberlain and insisted he give guaranteed support to Poland. Churchill was no longer a strident voice in the wilderness, but the leader of a cross-party alliance comprising Conservative backbenchers and almost all Liberal and Labour MPs. A similar alliance was forming in France, also with growing public support, but the nationalism that was mobilized was seen as defensive. It is not true that nationalism in general was responsible for the war, but German fascist-inflected nationalism was.

Although the Polish government was not viewed sympathetically, being anti-Semitic and greedy, Britain and France did now guarantee Polish sovereignty. Yet what could they do if Hitler invaded Poland? They might declare war, but they could not get aid to Poland in time to prevent its conquest. Hitler did not believe they would actually declare war, so he invaded Poland, but they did – and so the world war started in the West.

There was also an ideological cause of the failure to prevent war, and this was the second European tragedy. Some British and French leaders had argued for an alliance with the Soviet Union, which was also threatened by Nazi aggression. The Soviets could have sent troops to help Czechoslovakia, provided either the Polish or Romanian government would give passage across their country to the Red Army. Romania seemed willing, provided France and Britain would protect them; Poland might have been pressured. We do not know if such an alliance would have deterred Hitler from war. Maybe it would, but if he had nonetheless gone to war, this alliance might have quickly defeated him, saving millions of lives, including those of most Jews and gypsies. Why didn't Britain and France ally with the Soviet Union, as they were to do four years later?

Stalin's purges made some doubt Russia's usefulness as an ally, for he had eliminated 3 of the 5 Soviet marshals, 15 out of 16 army commanders, 60 of the 67 corps commanders, and 136 of the 199 divisional commanders. Altogether, 40,000 officers were purged from the army and navy, leaving only 7 percent of the 1941 army officer corps with higher military education. Nonetheless, in July 1939, the purged Red Army demonstrated its usefulness in the Far East, mauling Japanese forces at Nomohan, and German armed forces were still not near their strength of 1940. Surely, the British and French could not doubt they would be better off with the Soviets than without them.

The biggest stumbling block to the alliance was the fracture of the continent into Communism and anti-Communism. Political leaders in Britain and France hated the Soviet Union, fearing that any Russian movement westward could foment revolution. In 1918, Churchill himself had attempted from his position as secretary of state for war to get a full-scale British military expedition into

Russia to defeat the Bolsheviks (Lloyd-George had restrained him and then sent him off to the colonial office where he could do less harm). Churchill had swallowed his ideological distaste on realist geopolitical grounds. It had been British policy for centuries to support a balance of power in continental Europe. When Napoleon had managed to dominate Europe, Britain had allied with Russia in order to attack him from both sides; likewise in World War I, allying with Russia against Germany. Exactly the same logic was called for now. Churchill was fiercely anti-Communist, yet believed this was the only way to save the empire. There are revisionist historians today who believe the opposite: that in fighting rather than in coming to terms with Hitler, Churchill was bankrupting and destroying the empire (Charmley, 1993). Yet that is with the benefit of hindsight, with knowledge of the unexpected but complete collapse of France and Stalin's own turn to appeasing Hitler, which was the consequence of Western appeasement. It was this combination that left Britain alone and on the path to bankruptcy.

In 1938 Churchill believed, together with some senior civil servants and generals, Tory backbenchers, and non-pacifist Liberal and Labour MPs that the only way to deter or destroy Hitler was through an Anglo-French alliance with the Soviet Union. Churchill and Robert Vansittart, chief official at the Foreign Office, worked hand in glove with Soviet Foreign Minister Maxim Litvinov and Soviet Ambassador in London Ivan Maisky. Churchill told Maisky that Britain and Russia should "arm to the teeth," for the "common enemy is at the gate." A less powerful cross-party group, headed by former ministers Reynaud, Paul-Boncour, and Mandel, formed in France. Roosevelt, on the sidelines, still did nothing to help.

Yet Chamberlain and the appeasers would not accept the alliance, and they clung onto power until after war was declared – in fact, until after the disastrous British campaign in Norway in 1940. Chamberlain dismissed Eden and sidelined Vansittart when they pressed for the alliance. After Hitler tore up the Munich agreement, Chamberlain's position has been seen, in Carley's words (1999: 181), as "illogical .... incomprehensible," except in terms of "ideologically motivated" anti-Communism, rooted in the fear that war might bring revolution. In September 1938, Daladier tried to persuade the German ambassador to Paris that war would only benefit the Soviets, for "revolution, irrespective of victors or vanquished, was as certain in France as in Germany and Italy. Soviet Russia would not let the opportunity pass of bringing world revolution to our lands." He told the U.S. ambassador, "Cossacks will rule Europe." Even in September 1939, Bonnet remained "absolutely convinced that Stalin's aim is still to bring about world revolution" (Carley, 1999: 43, 47–8). Their position and that of many on the British and French right continued to be that Western security could be achieved by making concessions to Hitler, and giving him a free hand in the East to overcome Communism. As former Prime Minister Baldwin said, if there was fighting in Europe, better "to see the

Bolshies and Nazis doing it" – the blood of others again. An alliance with the Soviets against Hitler might produce a war that benefitted Communism. The Bolshevik Revolution had been the product of the first war; other revolutions might result from a second one. Despite the evils of Nazism, they feared revolution more than they feared Hitler. Chatfield, the British First Sea Lord, and Cabinet Secretary Hankey argued in 1937 that making concessions to Nazi Germany and Fascist Italy was a logical reaction to Soviet Communism and French "unreliability." British Conservatives declared that with the Popular Front, France had gone "half-red," sunk into "socialistic ruin" (Carley, 1999: 257; Parker, 1993: 69; Post, 1993: 214–15, 260–1). These arguments were paralleled on the French right. "Rather Hitler than Blum [the French Socialist leader]" said many (Berstein & Becker, 1987: 371–88; Jackson, 2001, 2003: 112–6; R. Young, 1996: 67–8). In February 1937, Stalin had offered a military alliance with France, but the French general staff rejected it. The reason, says Alexander (1992: 291–8), was "ideological prejudice." Anti-Communism was a powerful emotion in this period, clouding instrumental reasoning.

Hitler's continuing aggression did force serious negotiations in Moscow between April and August 1939. British public opinion polls of May and June showed more than 80 percent of respondents supporting an immediate Soviet alliance. Chamberlain was hounded in the House of Commons by MPs shouting, "What about Russia?" His deputy chiefs of staff stated in August that without early, effective Russian assistance, the Poles "cannot hope to stand up to a German attack." They also presciently warned that if an alliance was not made with Russia, Stalin would make a pact with Hitler in order to swallow up part of Poland.

Chamberlain remained obdurate. He said, "I confess to being deeply suspicious of [Russia]. I cannot believe that she has the same aims and objects that we have or any sympathy with democracy as such" (Carley, 1999: 133). That was true but irrelevant. He also bizarrely claimed the British position would not "be greatly worsened if we had to do without them" (Parker, 1993: 236). Quite apart from any Soviet military help, even the economic blockade of Germany would have gaping holes in it if the Soviets were not allies. A French proposal at the conference asked that the Soviets intervene to save Poland, if necessary. When the Soviets responded, asking for reciprocal guarantees in case Hitler attacked them, France and Britain refused. Stalin concluded correctly that they wanted Russians to do their fighting for them. Anglo-French proposals for mutual assistance remained vague, whereas Molotov (who had replaced Litvinov as Soviet foreign minister) wanted "ironclad guarantees." The talks finally broke down when Britain and France failed to get the Polish government to guarantee the passage of Soviet troops through Poland if Germany attacked. Poland remained suicidal to the end, but Daladier had privately instructed his chief negotiator not to concede Russian passage and the French military attaché defended Polish objections (R. Young, 1996, Carley,

1999: 195). The Bolshevik nightmare still terrified much of the West, forcing them into ideologically driven geopolitics. Although Hitler was clearly the aggressor, the British and French governments bear some responsibility for the outbreak of World War II. Their perception of class interests became more emotionally entrenched than were national interests – and this helped bring on war.

In the end, the Soviets could not sign. They did not believe that Chamberlain, Daladier, or Bonnet would keep their word (Carley, 1999: 142–3, 149–59). Stalin now turned to his alternative defense policy, a nonaggression pact with Hitler – the worst outcome for the West. The first contacts were made in May 1939, but the Soviets stood off until the end of July or the beginning of August, when the Germans told them an invasion of Poland was imminent. There was no collective security pact available with the West, so the best security guarantee for the Soviets was to grab half of Poland, the Baltic States, Finland, and Bessarabia. Hitler was agreeable, provided he got the rest. Similar to Churchill, Stalin was willing to sup with the devil to defend his empire. Chamberlain, Daladier, and the appeasers had not been willing. These conservatives proved themselves more ideological in geopolitics than Fascist or Communist regimes (Parker, 1993: 347, 364–5). Churchill the imperial realist differed. As he was to say when Hitler invaded the Soviet Union, "If Hitler invaded Hell, I would at least have made a favourable reference to the Devil in the House of Commons" (Colville, 1985: 480).

War: The fall of France

Most expected World War II in the West to follow the same stalemated pattern as World War I, but it did not. France fell precipitously. Its long-war preparations collapsed, and those of Britain almost did, too. Why France failed, in such contrast to World War I, has provoked much agonized debate in France. For many years, historians sought profound reasons for such a profound defeat: French society was decadent, divided, decaying (for a recent restatement, see Ferguson, 2006), but revisionism has surfaced and different views now predominate. We must distinguish the initial French military defeat from the political collapse that followed.

France looked militarily strong by 1940. It had embarked on modernization and expansion from 1937. Its army was large and quite well-trained, and the French rate of tank and aircraft production in 1939 exceeded Germany's. France had more troops and heavier tanks and artillery; British tanks also had heavier armor than German Panzers. French solidarity also improved in the final year of peace. No French general expected to lose, and no German general expected easy victory. In May 1940, French troops fought well when they were well-led, and the number of French dead was somewhere between 50,000 and 90,000, a sizeable figure for a two-week war (May, 2000: 7; Jackson,

2003: 12–17, 161–73,179–82). The Wehrmacht had not actually planned a Blitzkrieg or "lightning war," although they needed one because they were not yet equipped for a long war. Only Guderian and Rommel saw that tanks could achieve a Blitzkrieg – although only after an initial infantry breakthrough, for tanks cannot easily break well-prepared defenses.

The campaign was actually decided in five days, May 10–14, when five German Panzer divisions traversed the supposedly impenetrable, lightly guarded Ardennes hills and forests, taking the French by surprise. That surprise was the basic cause of victory, and it was achieved with the aid of luck. A German invasion had initially been planned for late autumn 1939 and then postponed. In January 1940, the plans for the invasion were found in a crashed German plane in Belgium and passed to the French. They revealed a Wehrmacht attack through Belgium into the plains of the most northern part of France. This was what the French had anticipated, and also where they were preparing their own possible push into Belgium and Germany. So the French sent their best forces and most of the reserves up there. The elite forces of both armies would then have clashed head-on. Supported by British, Belgian, and perhaps Dutch forces, the French believed they had a good chance of success. So did most German generals, who did not want to fight this campaign at all. When the German high command realized there had been a breach of security, they changed the line of attack further southeast, to the Ardennes. They also attacked in the north through Holland and Belgium, but these were feints.

In the Ardennes, elite Wehrmacht divisions faced mediocre French forces, General Corap's Ninth Army, backed by almost no reserves. Corap had complained over the "slovenly" state of his troops for some months, but for the high command his sector was a low priority (Jackson, 2003: 160). These French forces were outnumbered in tanks, which was not the case elsewhere. The French general in charge of the next sector further east could have sent support but failed to do so, as he had been deceived by Goebbels' bluff about an attack through Switzerland. There was a striking failure to process intelligence by the French high command, which ignored reports of a German buildup of forces in the region. Intelligence failure was then compounded, as the French and British continued to believe that the Ardennes attack was a feint to draw troops down from Belgium. Only after four days, as the Germans crucially broke through over the River Meuse at Sedan, did they realize with horror that this was the real line of attack.

At the Meuse, the Germans also had two strokes of luck. The first crossing was made at night over a sluice and island complex whose ecology produced blind spots in the French ability to spot attacks. The crossing resulted from the resourcefulness of a single infantry unit attached to a Panzer division. The second and main crossing was by the tanks over two pontoon bridges, which consistently inaccurate Allied bombing failed to touch. Both were part accidental, part incompetence turning points of the kind that occur frequently in the heat and fog of war. The watching General Guderian commented, "The success of our attack struck me as almost a miracle." A fierce decisive battle at Sedan then pitted elite German troops against Corap's ragged corps on May 13–14. Some French units fled; others did fight well, but unavailingly. This was, as in 1870, "the disaster at Sedan" (May, 2000: part V, quote from p. 414; Jackson, 2003: 161–73).

On May 15, Prime Minister Reynaud told Churchill simply, "We are beaten." On the same day, Guderian ordered his Panzers to race west to the sea. They faced few allied troops, and they cut off the main French armies to the north. A prompt Anglo-French counterattack southward to cut the Panzers' own lines of communication would have been a good response. Some allied officers urged this, and a British tank division started south and won a victory at Arras before stopping, Allied decision making was slow and ponderous, however (the Germans had counted on this in their Ardennes plan), and the response was hindered by the replacement of General Gamelin as supreme commander. His successor, General Weygand, needed a few days to settle in, and by then it was too late.

The biggest problem for Guderian and Rommel was now to convince Hitler that speed was all. Twice they were halted on the way to the sea by his caution, but by May 20, they had reached it. The Battle of France was essentially over, ten days after it started. French and British forces were cut off in the North, and retreated toward the northern French coast. General Gort first considered evacuating British troops on the 19th. Helped by Hitler's delays, Goering's mistaken assurance that the Luftwaffe would finish off the British Expeditionary Force, and fierce French resistance at Lille, the evacuation was accomplished from May 28 onward. Four-fifths of the BEF – 224,000 men – plus 111,000 French and Belgian troops were evacuated from Dunkirk to England on a flotilla of small boats, a remarkable achievement. They would live to fight another day. Belgian forces surrendered on May 28; Paris was occupied on 14 June; and France capitulated on June 25.

This was a battlefield victory, based narrowly on military power relations. It was not the victory of one whole society over another; it was first achieved by a surprise attack helped by a massive French intelligence blunder and two strokes of luck. However, it was exploited by distinctive German field superiorities. Guderian and Rommel shone out above other commanders, but structurally, German commanders in the field could modify orders from above and make their own decisions according to the situation on the ground. This happened even down to the squad level – as at the vital sluice on the Meuse. This greatly helped the dynamism of the German advance and made more costly the ponderous command structure of the Allies. Poor coordination between French, British, and Belgian forces did not help their cause. The French blunder must also be situated amid weakness in intelligence and communications. General Gamelin later confessed, "We had no advance knowledge of where and how the Germans would attack" (May, 2000; Jackson, 2003: 39–46; Frieser, 2005).

Any general weaknesses of French society or politics were largely irrelevant to the days of May 1940. Counterfactuals might be proliferated. Had surprise not been achieved, would there have been stalemate long enough for the British to achieve air superiority and swing the fortunes of war back again? Would the Japanese not have attacked Pearl Harbor? Or would Stalin have independently launched an opportunistic attack on Germany from the east to get a cut of the spoils? Who knows? The fortunes of war are the most contingent part of world development, and here they had favored Hitler. The consequence was to encourage him to attack again in Russia, to encourage Mussolini to attack Greece, and to encourage the Japanese to obliterate Pearl Harbor. The notion that Fascist and near-Fascist regimes could substitute martial valor for material resources in Blitzkrieg warfare was now firmly entrenched. As a result, the war in the West became a world war that transformed that world.

However, deeper French class and political weaknesses were exposed in June in the surrender and its aftermath. The French government could have retreated abroad, taking the fleet, air force, and many thousands of soldiers with it, using the resources of the colonies to continue fighting alongside the British in other theaters. Hitler feared this and offered lenient armistice terms. A few French forces did flee abroad, but not the government or the high command of either army or navy. They lacked the will to fight on, as did most elites (Jackson, 2003: chap. 3). The naval command was peculiarly self-destructive, refusing Churchill's increasingly desperate requests to move their ships to British or French colonial ports. Instead, they gave him vague promises that they would ultimately scuttle their ships. Churchill could not take the risk that all French captains would do so; if French ships were added to German ships, the ensuing navy would be more powerful than the Royal Navy – and that would be the end of British power. So only days before the Germans seized control of the home ports of the French Mediterranean fleet, he ordered an attack on it in Mers el Kébir harbor. Several French capital ships were sunk, with the tragic loss of more than 1,000 French sailors, killed by their ally! This ruthlessness appalled the French but impressed Roosevelt – he now knew the British would fight on and be a useful ally. Ironically, the rest of this French fleet was later scuttled by its commanders.

France's ideological divisions now surfaced fully, and this must create doubt as to whether the French could have sustained a long war if the debacle of May had not happened. As Imlay (2003) says, the development of corporatist class compromise in Britain had made the country capable of a long collective struggle, but this had not happened in France. Although most French supported the war effort in 1940, there was no *Union Sacrée*, as in the first war. How could there be, when as recently as November 1938 Daladier had rescinded the labor laws passed in 1936 by the Popular Front and outlawed the large Communist Party? Anti-Socialism, anti-Communism and proto-Fascism were rampant among conservatives, in the general staff, and among industrialists – who also opposed government planning of armaments production. On May 16, even before his defeat was clear, General Gamelin tried to deflect blame by falsely claiming that Communist penetration had sabotaged army morale. Others falsely denounced the munitions workers for sabotaging French war production. Gamelin's successor, Weygand, was as concerned in the last days of the war with the specter of a nonexistent Communist uprising in Paris (shades of the Paris commune!) as with the German advance (Berstein & Becker, 1987: 371–88; Alexander, 1992: chaps. 4, 5; Jackson, 2001: 114–18).

French conservative leaders now made a virtue out of not "deserting," not leaving France. When the revered Marshal Pétain joined in the chorus, this argument won out. Weygand refused to allow the army to flee abroad, and became minister of defense in the Vichy collaborationist regime of Pétain and Laval, to which most conservatives (and many others) now swore allegiance. Pleas from colonial governors and generals to allow them to continue fighting abroad were denied (Jackson, 2001: 121–29). When the British heard this, they moved ruthlessly to sink the French Mediterranean fleet with much loss of French lives, to avoid the Germans seizing it. As the reality of French defeat sunk in, participation in Vichy and collaboration with the Germans broadened beyond the right (it included the young Francois Mitterand). Most French learned to live with the Germans, and many actively collaborated. The initial establishment of Vichy was by those who saw a chance to regenerate a France shorn of the ideals of 1789 – more reactionaries unable to understand that Hitler was something completely different. Ironically, it was de Gaulle, as Churchill a man of the right, who realized the need for national unity across class lines and who offered an informal Union Sacrée to the Socialists and Communists, embodied in the Free French forces and the Resistance.

British survival

This was the moment of the passing of French power and empire. There was no single moment of the passing of British power, for that was a process lasting several years, but this was the first and greatest blow. Britain had always relied on a balance of power on the continent of Europe. For all its naval power, its great empire, its leading-edge economy (its standard of living remained a third higher than Germany's in the 1930s), its ability to draw on the global resources of the Anglophone world, the security of the British Isles still depended on that balance of power. Yet in 1939, the Soviets made their pact with Hitler, and in 1940, Germany seized France and occupied the Channel ports. The British were alone, in mortal danger for the first time. The empire and an independent Britain might be no more.

Churchill overcame those in the War Cabinet who suggested offering terms to Hitler, although he himself briefly considered it. This is the point at which revisionist historians are at their most plausible, for Hitler was more focused on aggression in the east and he might have left Britain and its empire alone ... at least for a while. I doubt Hitler would feel safe with a rearming naval and imperial power on his western border, however. The only outcome of the looming war in the east that would have benefitted Britain would be a continuing stalemate weakening both the German Reich and the Soviet Union.

Britain did just hold out; it was still a Great Power. The two air forces were quite evenly matched, and British fighter planes narrowly won the Battle of Britain in the summer and autumn of 1940, helped by the German blunder of switching from targeting airfields to cities. This victory thwarted any German invasion; defeat would have ensured invasion, and the British army was not good enough to resist for long. But after the Battle of Britain, German landing craft crossing the Channel would now be easy targets for the RAF, and the Japanese were to demonstrate at Pearl Harbor and off Singapore what enormous damage planes could do to warships lacking planes to cover them. For Hitler, his invasion preparations had been mainly intended to bring the British to terms. Britain was not his major target for the present. Unexpectedly, the British would not come to terms, and the Battle of Britain was the first defeat he had suffered. British armed forces then rallied after early defeats in Greece and North Africa to secure the Middle East and achieve a fluctuating stalemate in North Africa – with American assistance. The Battle of the Atlantic was also close-run – the U-boats almost strangled Britain's main supply routes. This battle did not go the Allies' way until May 1943, well after the United States had joined in. This might have gone much worse for Britain: had the United States stayed neutral, Britain's blockade strategy would have blown back in its face, for the U-boats had the capacity to cut off Britain's lifelines from the rest of the Anglophone world. Britain itself would have been blockaded.

Britain had advantages. Apart from submarines, its navy was superior, its planes were better deployed, it could continue drawing on the resources of the empire (recruiting 2.5 million Indians into its armies), its advanced technology included the invention and development of radar, and it demonstrated intelligence ingenuity in cracking the German Enigma military codes yet managing to keep this secret. Added to these resources was high British morale, although there was criticism that "the old gang" politicians conducting the war had been ambivalent and slow to mobilize. They became happier when Churchill subordinated his imperialism to populist defense of the nation. Most people admired Churchill's defiant rhetoric and felt he expressed their own sentiments. Despite intermittent grumbles, they were prepared to sacrifice for ultimate victory – which few seemed to doubt. It was democracy against fascism, they believed, although usually expressed less abstractly. The Mass-Observation diarists (the best insight into contemporary opinion) said that what Britain meant to them was prosaic, even clichéd – the countryside, the villages, the sense of gentle order, and the "easy tolerance and good humour" of the people, evidence that a sense of commonality pervaded the people. These aspects of "banal nationalism" were worth defending. They did not preclude going on strike, for the strike rate held up. Nor did they preclude feminist objections to discrimination – including the frustration of women servicing antiaircraft batteries that they were not allowed to fire the guns. There was much less fear of voicing discontent, and much less high-flown nationalist rhetoric or flag-waving patriotism, than in Germany and Italy (Mackay, 2002: 253; Addison, 1975). The recently published reports of the new Home Intelligence Department, which sent out agents to listen to what people were saying, reveal that people distrusted the "propaganda" of the BBC, delivered in "plummy" upper-class accents reminiscent of the old-gang elites who had led us into this mess. The reports also reveal that working-class people were more committed to the sacrifices of war than were the middle classes, and that class resentment was building up over this. When exhorted by propaganda to brace themselves with more effort, they said they were already braced, "Fault lies in high places, not with us working people" and, "We're not jittery; I suppose they are" (Addison & Crang, 2010). Patriotism went hand in hand with incipient socialism and feminism. Morale was different in America because the continent was never attacked. I deal with this in Volume IV.

Churchill, experienced in World War I and fully aware of Britain's desperate situation, recognized the need for a populist war strategy, the mobilization of women's labor, and the bringing of the Labour Party and trade union leaders into government. Labour then made clear that the price for popular sacrifice must be progressive reform intensifying social citizenship rights. Ernest Bevin, union leader and Britain's new foreign secretary, inserted into Churchill and Roosevelt's 1941 Placentia Bay statement of war aims a clause securing, "for all, improved labour standards, economic advancement and social security." Labour ministers were put in charge of most domestic policy (which Churchill considered less important), and this ensured that reforms would actually happen. They commissioned William Beveridge to produce his famous report on welfare. In December 1942, Beveridge proposed that in return for a flat-rate weekly contribution, benefits would be provided to all as a universal right of citizenship for sickness and injury, unemployment, old age, maternity, orphans, and widows – what he called a comprehensive "cradle-to-grave" welfare state. The report was immensely popular. A Gallup poll revealed 86 percent of respondents saying it should be implemented. The Labour Party as well as a progressive Tory group endorsed it. Churchill did not, but was then chastened into voicing vague expressions of support. A Ministry of Reconstruction was set up, and official White Papers endorsed Beveridge's social insurance proposals; it remained vaguer on the National Health Service and full employment. By 1943, polls showed that most men and women expected eventual victory in the war would be followed by major improvements in their lives (Mackay, 2002: chap. 6). Social citizenship was Britain's secular version of a Union Sacrée.

The United States had begun rearmament in 1939 and speeded it up after the German breakthrough at Sedan. With the British victory in the Battle of Britain, Roosevelt and his advisors recognized that Britain was worth assisting, at a price short of declaring war. As Britain was paying for everything it received from the United States, its dollar and gold reserves were running dangerously low. The British Ambassador to Washington, Lord Lothian, met reporters in New York with the cheery greeting, "Well boys, Britain's broke; it's your money we want." The Neutrality Act, still supported by a majority in Congress and public opinion, prevented direct American aid to warring foreign states, but trade and lease agreements might side-step this. The trade of old American destroyers for U.S. access to British bases in the Caribbean came in October 1940. The British gained little materially from the deal, but they had secured a precedent that quietly abandoned U.S. neutrality. It was followed by the lend-lease program of March 1941, Roosevelt's own idea and a defeat for the isolationist lobby. Roosevelt justified it in a radio "fireside chat" to the nation by saying, "If Great Britain goes down, the Axis powers will control the continents of Europe, Asia, Africa, Australasia, and the high seas – and they will be in a position to bring enormous military and naval resources against this hemisphere." He again denied any intention of sending armies to Europe, but concluded with, "We must be the arsenal of democracy." Sixty percent of his listeners said they agreed. The administration hawks, Stimson, Knox, Admiral Stark, and Morgenthau, favored entering the war on Britain's side, but Roosevelt knew that neither Congress nor public opinion would agree, yet.

Increasing trade with Britain led to an increasing U.S. military presence in the Atlantic in defense of its shipping. There was a series of incidents as German U-boats sank American merchant ships. As Roosevelt became convinced it would be necessary to join in the war, he used the sinkings to push public opinion toward war. American marines occupied Iceland in July 1941. Public opinion supported this move just as it supported sending aid to Britain, but it continued to oppose sending American soldiers into war. Roosevelt would still not risk taking on Congress, although he privately told Churchill "he would wage war, but not declare it, and that he would become more and more provocative. He would look for an incident which would justify him in opening hostilities." Delay suited the U.S., however, as long as Britain did not collapse, as American military might was building (I. Kershaw, 2007: chaps. 5, 7). The United States would eventually have entered the war, but in December, Roosevelt got more than an incident to help him. He got Pearl Harbor.

The folly of Hitler and the Japanese brought Britain the powerful allies it needed: Russia, invaded by Hitler in June 1941; and the United States, attacked at Pearl Harbor in December. Britain's role could then be seen to have been a holding operation, maintaining itself undefeated until the Russians and Americans arrived. Then Britain became the assistant in bombing Germany and in the North African and Italian campaigns, and the base from which the invasion of France could be launched and the second front opened. The United States would have been hard-pressed to invade Europe without Britain, but Britain had survived only by mortgaging its economic assets to the United States. As South African Prime Minister Jan Smuts remarked of the Empire in 1945, "the till is empty." The empire was finished, despite victory. Nonetheless, its war effort made Britain a more civilized place, as we will see in Volume IV.

The decisive Eastern Front

The most important battles lay elsewhere. Hitler had long been bent on the conquest of "Judeo-Bolshevism." On July 31, 1940, Hitler had told his shocked generals that he wanted an invasion of the Soviet Union the following spring. He abandoned his invasion plan for Britain and focused eastward. He was initially seeking oil and the removal of the British from the Mediterranean and Middle East. The Italians proved ineffective allies, so German troops were sent into Greece and Mediterranean islands with great success. Rommel was at first successful in North Africa, although his surge was not maintained, and the British held on there and in the Middle East. Yet Hitler regarded all of these campaigns as a diversion; he was really looking due east.

Increasing German pressure in the Balkans and on Romania and Bulgaria had brought tensions with the Soviets. Stalin's foreign policy was not world revolution, but continuity with tsarist goals: to secure more access to the Baltic and Black Seas. At this point, Soviet policy meant getting Britain to recognize the Soviet occupation of the three small Baltic States (acquired from his Non-Aggression Pact with Hitler) and securing friendly regimes in Bulgaria and Romania. Stalin worried over Britain's refusal to grant Baltic recognition and its courtship of Turkey, which might thwart Russian dominance in the Black Sea. He also had to worry about Hitler's expansionism (Gorodetsky, 1999: 316).

Thus, Stalin was thinking realist geopolitics and assumed Hitler and Churchill were doing the same. Churchill certainly was, but neither Stalin nor Churchill dreamed that Hitler would open a two-front war by invading the Soviet Union before he had finished off Britain. In fact, Churchill assumed Hitler and Stalin were negotiating to strengthen their mutual relationship, and he first perceived Hitler's buildup in the east as pressure on Stalin to come to a deal. For his part, Stalin believed Britain was just as hostile to him as Germany, and was feeding him intelligence about Hitler's aggressive intentions to provoke him into a war with Germany (he was right, but so was the British intelligence). Stalin became cautious. Aware of the clash of interests with Hitler over Romania and the Balkans, he tried hard not to provoke him. He signaled Russian intention to defend its interests by sending troops to the Romanian border, which infuriated Hitler, who expected neighbors to adopt a supine position. Stalin was happy that Germany and Britain were fighting each other and did not intend to get involved.

He did not understand Hitler, however, a far more ideological and emotional man and a believer in short wars. Hitler had been shocked in 1939 when Britain and France had declared war on him, but stunning success in France had restored his confidence. He was now a convinced exponent of Blitzkrieg. He perceived that Germany was near the limits of its military production capacity, but Britain, Russia, and America – which he believed would eventually join the war – were all still expanding. The economic inferiority of Germany could only worsen through time. His pressure for intensified rearmament created bottlenecks that could be resolved by raw materials and foodstuffs extracted from more conquered countries (Evans, 2006: 370). Because he also wanted Lebensraum for German colonists, he would risk a major war against the Soviet Union; better to fight it now than later. He despised Slavs and Communists, and believed the Wehrmacht could smash through Soviet defenses and destroy a ramshackle, unpopular regime. It is curious that he made no effort to get the Japanese to attack the Soviet Union from the east. True, Japan's leaders had been offended by Hitler's 1939 pact with Stalin, and since then had been moving southward into the Pacific rather than northward to threaten the Soviet Union, but Hitler was never a good ally, and that was a weakness, for the Axis was never as cohesive an alliance as was that of its enemies. Moreover, to Hitler the Soviets oddly seemed an easier target than Britain. Better to finish off Russia, and then use the resources of all greater Europe to attack Britain. It was his decision alone. The last meeting of the Reich Cabinet had been in early 1938, and from then on the major decisions were Hitler's. Any influence had to be wielded on him personally, but his generals, despite voicing misgivings, did not seriously oppose him (Tooze, 2006: 460; I. Kershaw, 2007: chap. 2). Barbarossa was his biggest mistake.

Not only Germans doubted the resilience of the Soviets. The U.S. War Department advised the president that Hitler would conquer the Soviet Union in one to three months; British military chiefs said six to eight weeks (Kershaw, 2007: 298–9). Stalin's purges seemed to indicate that his regime was held together only by terror, and the typical officer in 1941 commanded at two ranks higher than his experience would normally warrant. It was a massive self-inflicted wound (Glantz, 1998: 27–31). It encouraged Hitler, who believed he mobilized great ideological power: the fighting spirit of the *Herrenvolk* would triumph over the Bolshevized Slav *Untermenschen* in a final showdown with the "Jewish-Bolshevik conspiracy" (Overy, 1999: 206; Megargee, 2006). Impatient, overconfident, he resolved on all-out attack – Operation Barbarossa.

In November, Hitler decided to go ahead with Barbarossa when it seemed clear Stalin would not lie supine in the Balkans in the face of German expansion. Because the invasion must be massive, preparations took more than six months, until June 22, 1941, and were on such a scale that they became evident to all intelligence services, and to the ordinary Poles of Warsaw who watched German tanks and trucks rumbling through their streets for ten whole days. Soviet intelligence had accurate knowledge of the preparations and correctly deduced Hitler's intentions. However, what was finally reported to Stalin was an equivocal version. No one wanted to be the one to tell Stalin he was absolutely wrong (Gorodetsky, 1999: 130, 187; D. Murphy, 2006: 215, 250); Stalin sometimes killed those who disagreed with him. He explained away the troop movements as a likely German thrust southward into the Balkans. Ten days before the invasion, he reprimanded Marshal Zhukov, his chief of staff, who had already risked three recommendations of a pre-emptive strike, saying, "Hitler is not such an idiot" as to open "a second front by attacking the Soviet Union" (Gorodetsky, 1999: 279; Glantz, 1998). Hitler was an idiot, and so was Stalin. One does not usually associate Stalin with naive trust, but he had almost destroyed his regime and his country, and he certainly destroyed hundreds of thousands of lives. With the entry of the Japanese, it was Fascist and near-Fascist despotism against an unholy but pragmatic alliance of capitalist democracy and Communist despotism.

Hitler almost got away with his Blitzkrieg. Had he managed to overturn the Communist regime, he would have had vast Russian resources to exploit. Then the Americans might have come to a deal with him, sacrificing the British. As the initial success of Operation Barbarossa had encouraged the Japanese to attack Pearl Harbor, the Americans had to defend themselves in the Pacific. The result there would have been the same, the defeat of Japan and an American empire across the Pacific. After Pearl Harbor, Hitler declared war on the United States, because he wanted to unleash his U-boats on Atlantic shipping without any restraints – another attempt at a short-war Blitzkrieg. Had the entry of the United States into the war against Germany been delayed, the result might have been the same, if accomplished by atomic bombs dropped on Germany. Alternatively, a global stalemate between Germany and the United States might have developed, had Hitler acquired atomic weapons himself. These are very speculative counterfactuals, but had Barbarossa succeeded, the world would have been different.

Hitler's attack was not a surprise to the Soviet general staff, but they had been prevented by Stalin from deploying against it and were only halfway through a major reorganization. The Wehrmacht, operating across a wider front than most military strategists considered sensible, smashed through the first two Russian defensive lines, taking Minsk and Kiev in July and causing immense Russian losses. After two weeks, Hitler and General Halder believed the campaign was won. The Russians had lost the equivalent of 229 divisions, most of their sapper battalions, and most of their planes and tanks. The Germans destroyed in 1941 what their intelligence had believed was the entire Soviet military strength – but it was not. The Russians had a further two defensive lines, and they resisted or retreated in good order once Stalin rescinded his order that no one retreat. Although Stalin did make an enormous mistake in 1941, he had earlier built up his country's military strength. Feeling isolated and embattled by world capitalism, he had expanded his defense investment from the mid-1930s as the threat from Germany, Japan, and Britain seemed to mount. His mistake throughout was to cultivate so much secrecy. By preventing his enemies from realizing how formidable his military machine was, he lacked the power of deterrence (Samuelson, 2000).

The German Army Group Center might have pushed more determinedly for Moscow in mid-October 1941, rather than veering off to Kiev, just when Stalin was considering suing for terms or retreating further eastward. However, the Germans were stopped before Moscow, and Stalin's resolve hardened. In the summer, the Wehrmacht veered south aiming for Caucasus oil fields and to block the Volga at Stalingrad. The Soviets were learning fast and had instituted reforms, including reducing political controls over the troops. Stalin left war more to the generals, and withdrew most of his party commissars from the military. Above all, the Soviet industrial miracle made good the losses in an incredibly short space of time (Glantz, 1998: 127, 141, 165, 188; Overy, 1996: 4; Tooze, 2006: 588–9).

Soviet state socialism proved itself highly effective at war. It got more military output from given economic inputs than the Nazis. With less iron and coal, it produced more armaments. The territory under Soviet control was turned into what Stalin called "a single armed camp," and the command economy proved better at channeling resources into a single goal of military expansion than the capitalist economies. The United States achieved its phenomenal military expansion from the much greater inputs of a more technologically advanced economy. Both developed mass production systems for producing large runs of relatively few weapons. By contrast, Germany stuck with high-quality skilled workmanship and technological complexity, generating very good but expensive weapons. The result was that mass overpowered batch production; quantity overpowered quality (Overy, 1996: 182–207). Germany, despite the totalitarian appearance, uneasily combined Fascism with capitalism, and Hitler's strategy placed impossible demands on them. Counting on a short war in Russia, he had not focused rearmament on Operation Barbarossa, but was also building up resources for the war against Britain – and for what he saw as the next imminent campaign, against the United States. Thus, he did not have enough military resources to throw eastward during 1942, given the resilience of the Soviets. By 1943, German military production was rivaling the Soviet, but by that time it was facing relentless Anglo-American bombing. German armaments production became more efficient, but less sufficient for waging the intensifying two-front campaign Hitler had unleashed against himself (Tooze, 2006; Kroener, 2003: 1).

Nazi Germany was not helped by the racist savagery of the Wehrmacht and the SS against Soviet civilians, especially the non-Russian minorities who might have become his allies. Once again, making friends was not Hitler's strong point. Once again, an empire was undermined by its racism. The atrocities committed against Poles in 1939 had been a stage in the escalation. There were murmurings against this within the army, not yet thoroughly permeated with Nazi ideology. In this campaign, Jews were only a secondary target, after Polish elites (Rossino, 2003). Then, up to the end of 1941, the Holocaust against the Jews and the genocide of the gypsies were committed by the SS and German police units, whose officers and NCOs were often either SS or Nazi Party members, and whose "organizational culture" had become genocidal (Westermann, 2005; cf Mann, 2005: chaps. 8–9). Yet starting in 1942, the Wehrmacht fully cooperated and often participated in the racial-cleansing mission among Jews and Slavs.

By now, this was from top to bottom Hitler's own army. Hitler had sidelined senior officers who he thought were unreliable. The officers were now almost twice as likely to be Nazi Party members as were the civilian German middle class. Soldiers' diaries reveal a profound racism, an unthinking division between the master race and the Untermenschen – Jews, gypsies, and Slavs. Biological and biomedical models predominated. Slavs were said to be "infected" with Bolshevism. German policy was that soldiers should live off the land, which meant extracting food by force. Most German soldiers' diaries reveal belief in Lebensraum, involving clearing away indigenous populations so that Germans could settle and colonize it. The administrators of occupied Ukraine saw themselves as legitimately linked to Europe's history of conquest and rule, often comparing their rule abroad to British rule in India. There could be no "civilizing mission" among the Untermenschen Slavs, of course, but they noted that this had also been so in white settler colonies (Lower, 2005: 3–21). Imperial models still lived.

German planners needed the east to supply food to Germany. Slav helots would produce it, and more than half a million slave laborers were taken back to Germany. The remaining Slavs were to be eliminated to make room for German settlers. There was a deliberate starvation policy in the Ukraine through a food-chain hierarchy with German combat troops at the top, then rear troops, then German civilians, then foreign laborers, and finally, if anything remained, Soviet citizens. The Germans starved most of their Soviet POWs to death – 2 million of them – as well as starving "superfluous" Ukrainian cities, banning incoming food supplies, closing markets, and shooting "hoarders." The population of Kiev fell from 840,000 in July 1941 to 220,000 by December 1943. The round-ups of slave-laborers for Germany were harsh and arbitrary (Berkhoff, 2004: 186, 317). The Soviets were not much better with their POWs, and when Soviet troops and partisan guerillas responded with their own atrocities, enraged German soldiers killed entire local populations assumed to be partisans. This was the only way in which under-trained, undermanned rear units felt they could control the captured regions, buttressed by almost unthinking racism and a war planned from the top as one of annihilation (Bartov, 1985; Fritz, 1995; Kay, 2006; Megargee, 2006; Umbreit, 2003; T. Snyder, 2010).

That such ferocious racism was self-defeating was the only bright spot in an appalling campaign in which the two greatest ills of modern times – murderous ethnic cleansing and a war of annihilation – were conjoined. Ukrainians, having initially welcomed the Wehrmacht as liberating them from Stalinism, engaged in partisan warfare against the Germans, and then welcomed back the Red Army, which they saw as representing (said the young Krushchev, who served there) "our people" (Berkhoff, 2004: 304). Whatever they thought of Stalin, Soviet citizens knew Hitler was worse, and so they defended themselves, the nation, and the Soviet regime. They sacrificed in the factories, working twelve to sixteen hours a day (it was the only way to get food). Unlike Germany, women bore equal burdens. More than half of the labor force and substantial numbers of soldiers were female by the end of the war. Soviet soldiers accepted enormous losses, at the same time maintaining the patriotic morale and fanatical hatred of the enemy necessary for victory. Mawdsley (2005: 399) concludes, "Both nationalism and socialism were vital to the stability and survival of the Stalinist system." Yet the United States and Britain supplied much of the food and raw materials for the Soviet war effort, perhaps another necessary ingredient for Soviet resilience.

When the Russians counterattacked and encircled the Wehrmacht at Stalingrad in January 1943, the German advance stopped. The German Army Group South might have exploited its strengths and fought a war of maneuver rather than being trapped into the attrition at Stalingrad. Russian generals had learned how to take advantage of superior numbers of men and machines by means of "combined arms doctrine" to effect encirclement and deep battle. This was revealed at Kursk over nine days in July 1943, the biggest land battle ever, fought over the possession of a rail junction town 500 miles south of Moscow. Both sides committed vast forces, including most of their tanks. The Germans transferred forces from France for their attack, and Zhukov established eight lines of defensive emplacement within the bulge he occupied. This was "deep battle." In an area 118 miles wide and 75 miles deep, the Soviets had rushed in 1.3 million men and 3,444 tanks; the Germans had 900,000 men and 2,700 tanks. It was a terrifying experience for the soldiers. Under an immense Soviet bombardment, wrote one German infantryman, "The German troops were frozen with fear, unable to move or even scream at times and at other times driven to howling like animals while desperately trying to bury themselves deeper to escape the terror, while clutching one another like children.

Those who peered out were thrown back into the shelter in pieces" (W. Dunn, 1997: 190). Nevertheless, the Germans advanced with their latest Tiger tanks and Ferdinand assault guns. The Russians countered by using their multiple lines of emplacements to get in behind the advancing Tigers where their armor was thinnest. Inferior Soviet T-34 medium tanks were sent on suicide missions, crashing into the Tigers, blowing up both tanks and their crews. By July 13, the Germans had made only small gains and Hitler knew he did not have the resources to continue on this scale. He began transferring men to Italy to deal with the Anglo-American invasion of Italy. The follow-up battles at Kharkov and Belgorod then killed even more Germans. The Soviet advance was now slow but inexorable, although the Germans never broke.

The Eastern Front was where Wehrmacht invincibility was shattered and the German inferiority in overall resources was exposed – over 80 percent of total German losses were incurred there. The Western allies were responsible for about 20 percent of the 3.5 million German military fatalities, the Soviets for 80 percent. In 1944, there were still more than 100 German divisions fighting in the East, compared with only 15 German divisions in France (fighting a similar number of allied troops). Soviet forces destroyed or disabled in total around 600 Axis divisions between 1941 and 1945, and the Germans could not easily replace their losses. During 1943, for example, the Soviet production of tanks totaled 27,300. After we deduct their enormous losses that year, this was a net gain of almost 5,000. In contrast, Germany could produce only 10,747 tanks, a net gain of less than 2,000. Germany had banked on short wars and had taken longer to gear up for a long and total war. Only in 1944 was the entire economy put on a war footing, as 12 million foreign – virtually slave – laborers were imported. German production of war materiel now greatly increased, but by then it faced fully geared Soviet and American war economies producing more armaments in every category than the Germans could muster. German losses in tanks, planes, artillery, and other weaponry mounted so that there was no net increase (Mueller, 2003; Overy, 1996: 63–100, 321). Losses in manpower also mounted, and there was no centralized control; the generals had to battle for manpower against Albert Speer, in charge of war production. The use of slave labor helped but it needed extensive supervision. Hitler and other Nazi ideologues resisted mobilizing German women, a unique German disadvantage, and the Wehrmacht had to dig deeper for recruits among older men and boys (Kroener, 2003). However, Communism suffered greatly in saving not only itself but also capitalism.

Victory

As with all major wars, this one consisted of thousands of engagements between military units in which bravery or luck might tilt the theater balance in different ways. Yet the law of averages tilted more and more toward the

Allies. In a war of combined arms, victory required a combination of land, air, and sea power, and on more than one front. To explain the causes of Germany's defeat, we might begin with the explanation given by Hitler's foreign minister Ribbentrop: the unexpected power of resistance of the Red Army; the vast supply of American armaments; and the success of Allied air power. The GDP of the British Empire was higher than that of Germany and Italy combined, and Japan was overweighted in the East by the United States. If we add the massive resources of the United States and the USSR, the allies had the ability to wage a war of attrition that ground the Axis down. Of course, over and above the materiel disparities lay fascism's aggression, counting on its own resources and new men for victory, neglecting the importance of allies, favoring militarism over diplomacy. It was suicidal because it meant that it would be greatly outnumbered. The greatest weakness of fascism was its inability to generate many allies, which was the product of its own aggressive nationalism. It was only because the Allies were so numerous that their material resources were overwhelming. Germany, Italy, and Japan ultimately lacked geopolitical power, and that destroyed them.

The Germans would be overextended if the Allies fought a ruthless war of attrition. Stalin and Zhukov were ruthless – with their own troops as well, repeatedly sending them directly across minefields, clearing the way with their deaths for following waves of attack (W. Dunn, 1997). Ruthlessness was also evident in the British sinking of the French fleet and Allied area bombings of Germany and Japan, increasingly through incendiary bombs. This devastated whole cities, killing hundreds of thousands of civilians. The firebombing of Dresden, Tokyo, and many smaller cities, and the atomic bombing of Hiroshima and Nagasaki, were war crimes as conventionally defined, because they were deliberately aimed at civilian districts and made no distinction between factories and houses. All were consumed by fire or fallout. A German corporal raged in a letter home at "the vile terror attack" on Düsseldorf, in which "innocent German men, women and children were killed in the most barbarous manner." He concluded, "Now we actually know only too well what Churchill and his infamous clique of British … war criminals mean by the concept of 'civilization'" (Fritz, 1995: 85–6). Fritzsche (2008: 260) remarks, "When it came to the Jews, many Germans let themselves be bombed into a clear conscience" – but the reasoning could also be applied to the Allies who could bomb with a clear conscience because of Nazi atrocities.

The Americans committed so many resources to bombing in order to save the lives of their own troops on the ground. As with the British in Iraq in 1920, this was early "risk-transfer militarism." The British now added the harsh motive of revenge for their sufferings under bombardment, which continued through the V-2 rockets until war's end. Both were led toward area bombing and firebombing by the inaccuracy of so-called precision bombing. Relentless bombing, backed by the Allied blockade, decimated, starved, and disoriented civilian populations. Their labor productivity went down, but they did not cease their war effort. The bombing campaign did suck in the Luftwaffe to total destruction, and it disrupted war industries and transportation. It was important in driving Italy out of the war, and it took a steady toll of German industry and its workers. Speer's team estimated in early 1945 that Allied bombing had led to about a third less production of tanks, trucks, and aircraft for the year 1944. The atomic bombs shortened the war and saved American lives by making invasion of the Japanese main islands unnecessary. In Europe, the loss rate among Allied aircrews was also high (Overy, 1996: chap. 4). Eisenhower and Montgomery were also ready to practice a grinding war on the ground, which killed many of their own soldiers. Their troop losses in France were comparable with the trenches of World War I, but the Americans could keep on replacing them. It did not help the coordination of the Allied landings that Eisenhower and Montgomery were at such loggerheads, but they and the Red Army ultimately possessed the resources to keep going longer than the Germans.

As in the Great War, Germany had the better soldiers, although not the better sailors. It always took more Allied troops to defeat a given number of Germans, as the German infantrymen consistently inflicted about 50 percent higher casualties than their British or American counterparts. As in the first war, the Germans also had a more mission-oriented command system, giving more combat autonomy to officers and NCOs so that they could move more flexibly and rapidly than their opponents. They also remained leaner, more fighting-focused, with a higher proportion of combat to support and service troops (Dupuy, 1977: 234–5; van Creveld, 1982). There had also been improvements since World War I. As a result of Nazism, German armies were now more classless than other armies. Higher class or education did not get you promoted, authority and courage did. Second, at a time of lagging militarism elsewhere, young German men had already been under military discipline in the 1930s, both in the Hitler Youth and the paramilitary National Labor Service. Millions had been enrolled as volunteers in collective mobilizations, the *Volksgemeinschaft* (national community) in practice (Fritzsche, 2008: 51). The *Wehrmacht* had then added a more rigorous and harsher operational training than that practiced in any other army, and a harsher punishment system for military officers. The combination, as Fritz (1995) notes, generated a collective elitism, a sense of superiority won through greater commitment and sacrifice, a sense of a *Frontgemeinschaft* (front community) which was the cutting edge of the Volksgemeinschaft.

The soldiers were disproportionately Nazi members, idolizing Hitler, loyal almost to the end. This was especially true of SS regiments that had transmuted from mere party praetorian militia to a highly disciplined and ideologically committed fighting force, protecting the faith as well as the regime. Although German soldiers were experiencing defeat and the Americans were experiencing victory, the American desertion rate was several times higher than the German until the last six months (van Creveld, 1982: 116). German infantrymen embraced the dreadful sufferings of the Eastern Front with nihilist bravado, boasting of their sufferings, lack of equipment, and the probability of death. Their diaries and letters echoed Hitler's own boast after the seizure of Crete, "The German soldier can do anything." However, infantryman Martin Pöppel expressed the growing bitterness of the soldiers after his capture in late 1944: "We drove past kilometer after kilometer of Allied artillery positions, thousands of guns. With us it was always 'Sweat Saves Blood,' but with them it was 'Equipment Saves Men.' Not with us. We didn't need the equipment, did we? After all, we were heroes" (Fritz, 1995: 61).

From around the time of Kursk or Stalingrad, equipment and numbers would almost inevitably overpower heroes (M. Harrison, 1998: 1–2; Tooze, 2006). The turning point in the Pacific had come in June 1942 with the American naval victory at Midway, in which a third of the Japanese carrier-based aviators lost their lives and could not be replaced. Yet this resulted from ten bombs out of thousands dropped hitting Japanese carriers. It might have been otherwise. In the first half of the war, battles were close-run, their result depending on complex military factors that might have easily gone otherwise. The last turning point was in the battle of the Atlantic, where a cumulative buildup of Allied resources, technology, and tactics produced a tipping-point in April and May 1943. Radar, improved convoy techniques, code breaking, and longer-range aircraft equipped with powerful searchlights produced a reversal in kill ratios: U-boats, not Allied merchantmen, were now being sunk (Overy, 1996: chap. 2). Ribbentrop lamented these tipping-points, saying, "Germany could have won." Yet the second half of the war saw the steady grinding down of the Axis Powers by larger economies focused tightly on military purposes. The first half was far from inevitable, in contrast to the second half. It was indeed lucky for Germany that its grinding down resulted in a collapse that obviated any need for the atom bomb.

From 1943, Hitler seems to have realized he could not win, but hoped divisions between the Soviets and the West would lead to a negotiated peace. He was wrong: those divisions erupted only after his defeat. In June 1944, the Normandy beachhead was established, the Soviets advanced westward across their border, the British Indian Army advanced across Burma, and the Americans advanced across the Philippine Sea. They worried about counterattacks, and sometimes their advances stalled, but it was now unlikely the tide could be turned. German and Japanese resources were running down.

Positive ideological morale was not decisive. Until the last months when no one could doubt what the endgame would be, all sides had high morale, except the Italians. Overy (1996: chap. 9) makes much of the discontent and plotting of senior German officers and postwar retrospective surveys in which Germans said they had been staring defeat in the face since 1943. Yet Germany and Japan kept on fighting right to the bitter end. The German army took half its losses in the last year of war, when the cause was already lost. As I. Kershaw (2011) says, this is relatively unusual in war, and in many ways this is the war's most interesting feature. When generals and leaders realize they are losing, they generally seek for terms. When soldiers and civilians realize the war is lost, they express discontent and the workers go on strike. They did in World War I, as we saw in Chapters 5 and 6. Why did World War II differ?

Compliance came from mixed motives. Some of them were similar to those that had kept soldiers and civilians compliant for almost all of World War I (discussed in Chapter 5). Desertion was risky in highly organized wars. How could a soldier get food and shelter outside of the army? Civilians had very little autonomous power and tried to keep their heads down. In this case, Goebbels' propaganda machine also made German soldiers and civilians believe that their enemies did not take prisoners. The Japanese believed this too. Indeed, it was often true, especially on the Eastern Front where the Red Army – seeking revenge for atrocities inflicted by Germans on them – now burned, murdered, and raped Germans on a horrifying scale. For example, more than 1 million German women were raped. So soldiers felt safer within the army than outside of it. Inside, however, there were distinctive constraints for the Japanese and German armies. They practiced unusually harsh discipline, as they had not in the past. Far more of their soldiers were executed after courts-martial: an astonishing 20,000 in the Wehrmacht, compared to the British 40, French 103, and American 146 – and compared to 48 in the German army in World War I. So terror was a factor, but more important in the German army (says Kershaw) was the way Nazi values of leadership and will reinforced the strong traditions of duty and loyalty of German militaries. General Reichardt, commanding Army Group Centre on the Eastern Front, aware of the devastation all around him, of the losses his men were suffering, and of the defeat looming, said in his letters to his wife that he sometimes did wrestle with his conscience. What kept him going was

> the machine of duty, the will and the unquestioned "must" application of the last ounce of strength work automatically within us. Only seldom do you think about the big "what now." For most of the war, this was also personalized into loyalty to the charismatic Hitler, but this did not survive right to the end, for an endless succession of defeats in the last two years of war destroyed his charisma. By the end of March 1945, only 21 percent of a sample of soldiers captured by the Western Allies still had faith in Hitler, whereas in January 62 percent had (Kershaw, 2011: 197, 220, 260).

Nonetheless, the feeling was widespread that Hitler had brought a classless society, and this increased the sense of national solidarity, as it did in Britain. Nationalism was by now a much more important factor than in World War I. A sense of shared citizenship was real even in despotic regimes.

Stauffenberg's plot to kill Hitler in 1944 failed when the bomb only lightly wounded him. Yet the plotters had found little support within the military. The main response was outrage against their treason, although mixed in with fear of Hitler's reprisals against anyone who might be accused of plotting or merely expressing dissent. Loyal generals also benefitted from corruption in the form of tax-free gifts of land and cash. Terror, commitment, and material interest went hand in hand. The German generals in Italy had delayed surrender until the last minute for fear not only of Hitler but also of the reaction from their own soldiers; they might be strung up.

The civilian hierarchy was also transformed after the plot, and the state administration was thoroughly subordinated to the party. More power was given to Himmler, Goebbels, Bormann, and Speer. Himmler's SS brought the savagery it had already practiced in the east into Germany itself. Goebbels was put in charge of total war, and continued his barrage of propaganda, persuading Germans that miracle weapons were on the point of appearing. Bormann made sure that local administrations were run by veteran Nazis, "the men of the first hour," and Speer kept production going by intensifying slave labor (Kershaw, 2011: 35–53). Nor did the civilian population flinch before the aerial devastation (nor did they in Japan), and the party-dominated state administration carried on quite efficiently under the terrible bombing. It responded promptly – power was quickly restored, water carts appeared on the streets, and factories were shifted underground. Wages were paid, the post was delivered, and "defeatists" were executed. A routinized, terroristic control system, unlike anything seen in World War I, induced the realistic fatalism that there was nothing one could do except ensure personal survival until the end came. Kershaw (2011: 149, 400) comments, "There was no collapse of discipline either in the workplace or in the army. People carried out to the best of their ability what they took to be their duty," ultimately because they were trapped by "the structures of rules and mentalities underlying them." Charismatic authority remained in place, he says, even when Hitler's own charisma was disappearing, a form perhaps of Weber's "routinization of charisma." The perennial paradox of military power – the coupling of hierarchy and comradeship – was intensified and generalized to most of the German population as well as the Japanese. These were ferociously militarized, highly caged national societies, but it is depressing that – with the exception of the more sensible Italians – almost no one rejected such dreadful militarism.

The war had been precipitated by one man – Hitler – and his fascism, although the recent aversion of the liberal democracies to war, deterrence, and Communism had encouraged him. It killed around 70 million people – a staggering figure – 60 percent of them civilians. The biggest carnage had occurred on the Eastern Front, followed by the Sino-Japanese war. The most casualties, at least 25 million, were Soviet citizens. The highest proportion of the national population killed, almost 20 percent, was of Poles, although Jews were the ethnic group suffering most – perhaps 70 percent of European Jewry died, somewhere around 6 million in all. The war, whose immediate cause was fascism, destroyed fascism. The ferocity and racism of its late imperialism was suicidal.

Fascism collapsed, and the German Werewolf organization supposed to carry on guerilla war after defeat lasted only weeks, as did resistance in Japan. Their populations welcomed the release from bombing and the peace brought by their conquerors, and they were soon embracing the democratic and capitalist forms they had already tasted before fascism or military fascism had seized possession of them.

The two world wars obviously changed much, but were they a necessary cause of great transformations of power relations or did they merely hasten on transformations already underway that would have occurred anyway, without war? I leave more general discussion of this to Volume IV, after assessing more thoroughly the changes brought by the Second World War. However, we can already see that this war – itself a bloody fracturing of the world – hastened on the end of the fracturing of rival empires, and led to the development of world-destroying weapons as well as a more universal triumph of Western market capitalism, the nation-state system, and the American global empire than would otherwise have occurred. This entrenched the tripartite globalizations of capitalism, the nation-state, and American empire under which we still live. This was only justice, because European imperialism, imitated by the Japanese, had been the deeper cause of the war. The war also cemented the power of the Soviet Union, made the United States the dominant world power, led to a dangerous Cold War between them, and reduced racism around the world. American-imposed order intensified globalization, which even before the fall of the Soviet Union was beginning to make inroads into both the Comecon countries of the Soviet Bloc and into China. It finished off France and Britain as leading powers and made Japan and Germany – and indeed the whole of Europe – into economic but not military powers. It helped produce a Golden Age of capitalism and social citizenship, especially among men. It gave Communism a new lease on life in the Soviet Bloc and it handed China over to Communism. In the Middle East, it was to cause deep instability. The first truly global war did indeed change the world, but that story is reserved for Volume IV.

15 Conclusion

I leave theoretical conclusions to my fourth volume, although it is already obvious that to understand the development of modern societies we must give broadly equal attention to the causal power and interrelations of all four sources of social power: ideological, economic, military, and political. This was very evident in this period, with its intensifying ideological struggles between democratic capitalism, communism, and fascism, and its self-destructive racism; its capitalism whose powers of both creation and destruction had never been higher; its two devastating near-global wars and the global threat of the atom bomb; and its intensifying nation-states and global empires. It is unlikely any one of these could be primary.

In a varied world, generalizations are hazardous. Each macro-region, each country, each region within countries, was different in one way or another, and this obviously reduced the homogenizing effect of globalizations. All countries are exceptional in the sense often used by Americans to refer to their own country. The myth of a unique American exceptionalism is deeply entrenched in American nationalism and politician's rhetoric – but it is false. The United States' principle exception in this period was that it suffered from serious white racism at home, whereas other Western countries had racism in their colonies. The United States was not unique in having almost no socialism, as the other Anglo countries did not either. Although the United States initially lagged in some aspects of social citizenship (but not in educational rights or progressive taxation), it caught up in the New Deal. I have noted country differences where these had important consequences, as American racism did, but for the most part, national peculiarities have served to reduce what might otherwise be seen as universal causes and effects into mere tendencies.

My early chapters charted the rise of the European multipower-actor civilization to global dominance. Its capitalism, cohesive yet squabbling states, and especially its militarism interacted dynamically to enable the acquisition of empires, and this was then emulated by Japan. Most of the world became subsumed under empires, obviously a globalizing trend, although fractured. Each empire erected fences around itself and intermittently fought against the others. Imperial tariffs restricted transnational trade, natives fought for "their own" mother country, often against their own neighbors. Colonies erected state boundaries where none had previously existed, and native colonial elites spoke and wrote in the language of the mother country – English or French or Spanish or Portuguese or (briefly) Japanese. There was not a single imperialism, but twelve of them. This was a veritable multipower-actor civilization, extraordinarily dynamic because of the degree of competition it involved. Yet it was a self-destructive dynamic.

Other chapters charted domestic developments in the imperial homelands. The dynamism of capitalism and the entry of the masses onstage in the theater of power led to class struggle, revolution, and reform and the achievement of popular national citizenship. However, they also charted terrible hubris, as the self-destructive racism and militarism of Europe culminated in two world wars, devastating the continent, bringing two waves of revolution, murderous regimes, the destruction of the European empires, and the rise of the two imperial successors – the United States and the Soviet Union – the marcher lords of the European periphery. In this half-century, military power changed the world, bloodily fracturing it until the conditions of postwar peace allowed some recovery.

The half-century also saw much ideological fracturing. Militarism remained an important ideology, figuring large in diplomacy between states, intensifying noninstrumental, value-driven, and emotional concerns with its distinctive pursuit of glory, honor, and status. There was also ideological conflict between market-oriented and state-oriented schemes of how the economy should work. Polanyi characterized this as the "double-movement" of capitalism, and he identified this period as first enshrining free market principles, which was then countered by more statist ideologies, boosted by the three Great Dislocations of this period – two world wars and the Great Depression. Arguments over market versus state resulted mostly in institutionalized compromised ideology, more instrumental than transcendent, driven only a little by ultimate values or emotions. The two models offered alternative political economies, but choices between them were usually made pragmatically and dispassionately. It is true that they were also tinged with distinct conceptions of human freedom – freedom from others versus freedom through others – but both these were also institutionalized in Western values. Their conflict was not extra-systemic and it was not too difficult to find pragmatic compromises between them.

Far more serious were the conflicts between, on the one hand, the rising ideologies of communism and fascism – both of which promised salvation on this earth through the wholesale reorganization of society – and on the other hand the institutionalized ideologies of democratic or monarchical capitalism (which also had mutual conflicts). The resolution of these conflicts was violent, accomplished through revolutions and world wars. In the end fascism was destroyed, capitalist democracy became hegemonic in the West, and Communism ruled a large sliver of the East. In the colonies, racial ideological conflict was also rising.

In this period Europe, Russia, and China experienced a great surge in ideological power. My second volume charted a decline of religious ideologies in nineteenth century Europe; the first half of the twentieth century saw two and a half secular equivalents of salvation religions – Communism and Fascism, with Japanese militarism providing the half. Virulent anti-Communism also rose in capitalist countries, often blocking instrumentally rational decisions such as acting collectively to deter Hitler or devising mutually beneficial policies of economic development in the American informal empire. These transcendent value-driven and emotion-driven ideologies rebounded to harm the interests of those who wielded them. In terms of political power relations, "vanguard" parties – in Japan a vanguard military – were the main organizations mobilizing ideological power, and where these were successful half-totalitarian party states resulted. Enlightenment values did not rule the West, let alone the Rest of the world. "Rational choice" models are often inapplicable. This was a half-century of extraordinary ideological power.

The most general tendency in the West was the dual triumph of reformed capitalism and national citizenship. The dynamism of capitalism had been evident for hundreds of years, although its irregular cycles meant that economic development was always somewhat jagged. The dominant tendency was economic growth, through a process labeled by Schumpeter as capitalism's capacity for creative destruction (1957: 82–5). The growth of movements of resistance against capitalism was also rather jagged, spearheaded in this period by socialist and lib-lab political parties and labor unions, but the conflict was usually compromised into reformed capitalism. Only when near-total war devastated countries, delegitimizing states and intensifying class struggle, did successful revolutions occur. In the West, social citizenship and welfare states grew through the period, although more for men than women. Feminists were still stuck disputing the merits of two different routes to gender equality, through their labor-market employment or through maternal work in the household. In the West, male subjects became citizens; females were citizens mainly through their menfolk.

In the West and Japan, despite the devastation wrought by world wars and depression, the economic trajectory was upward. All classes got substantially healthier, better fed, longer lived, better educated, and richer. Fifteen percent of the world's population had done incredibly well, despite their internecine wars. Their overall GDP and GDP per capita were persistently rising, and as of yet, few saw the downside of this. Nature was still an apparently bottomless pit from which resources could be extracted and into which waste could be deposited. Insofar as anyone worried about pollution, they were satisfied that "cleaner" oil seemed poised to replace dirtier coal as the principal fuel of industrialization. Other indices of Western well-being also pointed upward. Improvement in nutrition and greater calorific intake among the masses became physically visible. An increase in human height can be seen as indicators of better health and general well-being. As evidenced mostly through records kept on soldiers, prisoners, and schoolchildren, the average height of males in eight investigated developed countries (Australia, France, Germany,

Great Britain, Japan, Netherlands, Sweden, and the United States) rose by 2.3 centimeters (1 inch) between 1850 and 1900, but then between 1900 and 1950 it rose by no less than 5.8 centimeters (2.3 inches). Less is known about women's height, although increases were also found among the few records on girls. The period from 1900 to 1950 actually saw the biggest increases in longevity and dietary standards, although it was after 1950 that GDP per capita and real wages were to see their biggest increases. Floud et al. (2011) document all this at great length. They argue that this can be seen as a speeding up of a process comparable to Darwin's evolutionary biology, and they credit it to improved public health regimes, better housing conditions, and better diets – the joint products of reformed capitalism and bigger government, especially at the local level. The dramatic first half of the twentieth century, with its terrible wars and its Great Depression, had paradoxically brought good news for the mass of the population.

I identified four main reasons for the triumph of a capitalism reformed and regulated by government.

(1) Because capitalism had provided the first breakthrough to an industrial society, it became institutionalized in the most advanced economies; communism triumphed in relatively backward countries. This gave capitalism an "unearned" economic advantage. It did not give great military advantage to capitalism – both fascism and communism were effective in war – but the global economic struggle between capitalism and state socialism was always unequal, although it was not fully revealed until the 1950s, which I discuss in Volume IV.

(2) Entrepreneurialism within an environment of market competition was better than its rivals at generating growth at the leading edges of technology. It was especially good at shifting gears, developing new industries as old ones concentrated and stagnated – the core of Schumpeter's creative destruction. We saw this proceeding in Chapter 7, even in the depths of the Great Depression. Market capitalism was not superior to either state socialism or Japanese state-coordinated capitalism in achieving late development catch-up. Indeed, a substantial degree of planning was probably superior to markets in this endeavor, as we saw in the cases of Japan and the Soviet Union. However, market capitalism was superior at innovation. A good example of this was the second industrial revolution at the beginning of the century, driven by corporate capitalism and a patent system that delivered scientific and technological innovation into profitable private ownership. This was an advantage that capitalism had earned.

(3) Reformed capitalism triumphed because although capitalists vigorously defended their property rights, determined opposition from below usually forced them into making compromises, the process being aided by centrists and pragmatists (including corporate liberals) seeking compromise and the institutionalization of class conflict through legislative intervention. Their main motive was the desire to head off class conflict at the pass, before it got really serious. Where compromise failed to happen, as in Russia and Germany, this helped spur on communist and fascist revolutions, the effect of which was to forcibly suppress class conflict. Elsewhere, class compromise and the granting of more and more citizen rights predominated.

Marx believed that capitalists were incapable of collective organization because they were divided by market rivalry. Only the collective laborer, the working class, he believed, was capable of much collective action. This half-century proved him wrong on capitalists and half-wrong on workers. Capitalists initially tried to repress labor movements, but this usually failed. So across the mid-twentieth century, aided by the outcomes of wars, they grudgingly and collectively accepted state intervention to smooth over the dysfunctional tendencies of capitalism as well as accepting redistributive deals with organized workers, as long as these left their own ownership and control rights intact. On the other side of the barricades, workers achieved a measure of class solidarity, but this was undercut by sectionalism, segmentalism, and nationalism, which aided class compromise. Strikes and labor agitation rose significantly from just before World War I to World War II (Silver, 2003: 82, 126–7), but these were as often instruments of sectional or segmental worker power as of class power.

Socialism thus proved less of a threat than many capitalists had feared as it mutated into milder social democratic or lib-lab reformism. The foundations of reformed capitalism – welfare states, universal public health and education, progressive taxes, legitimate collective bargaining, and Keynesian macroeconomic policies – were laid down before 1945, although (apart from public health) their consolidation came later. They all involved bigger government, more citizenship, and intensifying nation-states. The reforms were also beneficial for collective economic power, and not only for the lower classes. Class conflict, once institutionalized into collective bargaining, produced more stable labor relations, and stability is a virtue much prized by capitalists operating within unpredictable markets. There were no revolutions or even much social turbulence where this route was followed. Representative government also enabled crises to be surmounted much more easily and peaceably than despotic rule: regimes failing to cope with the crisis were voted out of office and the opposition party routinely replaced it, whereas despotic regimes faced more succession crises. The welfare reforms and Keynesian macroeconomic planning also kept up mass demand, and this too was good for capitalism, although the full emergence of a high-productivity, high-demand economy only occurred in the decade after World War II.

(4) There was also an edge in political power relations. Market capitalist countries mostly converged politically on a liberal or social form of representative government, which was more attractive to the citizenry than the party-state despotism into which communism and fascism degenerated. This degeneration served as an important negative reference point for most people in the West, steering them away from socialism and fascism. Yet whereas social citizen rights in this period advanced across the whole of the West, the development of political and civil rights, of democratization, was more uneven. Huntington (1991) notes that this period saw a short-lived wave of democratization immediately after World War I, but this was followed by a counter-wave lasting through the 1920s and 1930s, during which half of Europe moved toward despotic government (see Chapter 10). The fall of fascism and other despotic regimes in World War II would obviously assist democratization in the West, and it was hoped that the process of decolonization just beginning then would also favor democracy. As of yet, however, the advantages of democracy were not as evident as they seemed after the second war. Communism, and for a short time fascism, had considerable influence across substantial parts of the world, especially outside of the West.

Before 1945, all of these developments were underway among the white race (and some of them in Japan also), but not elsewhere. A Great Divergence had widened between the 15 percent West, successfully industrializing, democratizing, nationalizing, and reforming and the 85 percent Rest where economic and political power relations had stagnated under colonialism. Gains in GDP and representative government in the colonies and in the few independent poorer countries (other than Japanese colonies) remained negligible in this period. The West developed; the Rest did not – the single greatest fracture of the world in this period. The West mostly moved toward democracy and more citizen rights in nation-states; the colonies remained under imperial despotism as subjects. This was conceptualized at the time by much of the West as being largely due to its own racial superiority (although this confidence was not to last much longer). I concluded that imperialism did generally hold back the economic development of the colonies, although the main source of rising inequality was not direct exploitation (although there was plenty of this) but more simply that the mother countries industrialized and the colonies did not. Perhaps the combination might be seen as a single exploitative capitalist world system. Colonial elites and their client natives profited greatly from exploitation of the mass of the natives. Yet the fact that most empires did not turn a profit for the mother country reduces the systemic character of this. This can be seen as the racial phase of globalizations, although with the twist in the tail that because the white race dominated capitalism, it also took the brunt of the Great Depression, which tempted me to rename it the Great White Depression.

White domination also grew in a more physical sense. Among the Rest, the average height of males, in contrast to the West, remained static or grew only very slightly in this period, although it was to rise greatly in the post-1950 period. The same was true of life expectancy and literacy. In the West and Japan in 1950, the average literacy rate was 93 percent – almost everyone could read and write. In Latin America and China, literacy reached around 50 percent, but in other less-developed countries it was only around half that. Massive improvements there came only after 1950. Fertility rates tell the same story. The average number of children born to each woman in the West declined most in the first half of the century, good news for the health of mothers and children. Among the Rest, the decline occurred largely in the second half of the century (Steckel and Floud, 1997: 424; Easterlin, 2000). The Rest still had almost no social citizenship or welfare states for either men or women (nor did they in the first decades following this period). The West plus Japan and the Rest were almost living on different planets. Yet as the twentieth century progressed, the imperial authorities sought to get more profit from their colonies and began to introduce some limited development projects that somewhat improved education, industry, and state infrastructures, although this was not sufficient to begin a process of global convergence. Instead, it had an unexpected outcome:

against imperial expectations, the newly educated natives were not grateful; they were bent on resisting and overthrowing colonialism.

I have tried to separate long-term structural tendencies from more contingent events. Many tendencies were long-term. The rise of capitalism, nation-states, and empires and of nationalism, imperialism, and racism had been long-term processes; underneath, anti-imperialism was stirring through this half-century. Citizen rights had been increasing since at least the eighteenth century. States had been increasing their revenues and expenditures, and they were increasingly mobilizing mass armies through conscription and reservist systems, which also furthered notions of citizenship. In this period, we have seen both warfare and welfare tightening the caging of citizens by the nation-states, at the same time bringing them onstage. Material resources were distributed and redistributed within national boundaries and education in the national language also furthered notions that a population formed a single people or nation.

As in Volume II, class and nation were not opposites. They grew together, entwined, each encouraging the development of the other. As the grip of state and capitalist bureaucracies tightened on the people, they reacted with insurgent movements. As men from the lower classes, minorities, and women achieved more rights as citizens, this in turn strengthened the nation-state and capitalism. Mass-mobilization warfare contained varied dynamics of class and nation. Both wars increased nationalism, enhancing perceptions of national identity and more aggressive nationalism. Yet as the first war dragged on, perceptions that unequal sacrifices were being made increased class consciousness. For nations whose war experience went well, reformist class consciousness was boosted. This was also so for neutral nations badly affected by the war who also had to sacrifice. Reformers did best where they could form broad alliances between workers, peasants, and middle-class elements. Then they could plausibly claim to lead the people, as Swedish Social Democrats did most strikingly. Thus, class transmuted into nation, shifting the nation a little leftward, but for nations whose war went badly, hostility to the ruling regime increased, as did an aggressive class consciousness. This led to revolutionary explosions, after which the Bolsheviks claimed that the working class was the nation. When the other revolutions failed, reformism flourished for a time. However, it did not last, for these reformers failed to transform class into nation. Indeed, much of the people and the dominant classes alike tired of continuing class conflict and invited fascists and other despots in to end it. In the process, they got a much more aggressive nationalism than they had bargained on. Thus, the dialectic between class and nation continued through this period. We will see in Volume IV that World War II introduced its own versions of this dialectic.

How inexorable were such developments? The answer must involve posing counterfactuals, asking what-if questions. What if particular events, especially the three Great Dislocations, had not occurred? These crises had important effects, but they might have simply hastened on outcomes that would have happened anyway rather than being their necessary cause. For example, colonialism was greatly weakened by world wars, especially the second one. Even without the impact of war, the colonies would probably have self-destructed more slowly, as white racism combined with developmental projects were intensifying anti-imperialist sentiments among the natives. Yet the fact that decolonization would then have come later meant it would happen at a different historical and social juncture, amid influences that might have pushed it down different tracks of development. This involves proliferating the counterfactuals to a point where pure speculation takes over. We can cope with one counterfactual, changing one variable, but not with many.

I feel more confident in saying that without the world wars and their outcomes, there would have been no successful communist revolutions, no fascism, and no American global dominance. I have explained why in previous chapters, but we must then ask whether those wars and their outcomes were themselves contingent events or whether they were the consequences of deep-rooted structures and causes. The answer is a bit of both, although mainly the latter, and mainly those lying with military and geopolitical power relations. I have emphasized the historical longevity of European militarism and imperialism. Imperialism within Europe had changed seamlessly into imperialism across the globe; in Europe war had for many centuries been the default mode of diplomacy resorted to when negotiations were viewed (quite early) as failing. Japan then imitated Europe, partly because it felt that its own autonomous survival depended on imperialism, although I argued that making Japanese imperialism more militaristic owed much to more contingent events and processes. I also emphasized that because European expansion contained an ideological thrust to spread civilization, enlightenment, or the word of God across the world, each state's aggression was seen as defensive, backed by unique civilizational or national values. As in previous centuries, statesmen also sought status and honor, both personal and that of their country, which made it difficult for them to back down once diplomacy was in difficulty. These were all fairly structural tendencies. I absolved capitalism from much blame for these wars. Its secular tendencies were not warlike, although of course capitalists as individuals were as nationalist as others. They were content to profit from either swords or ploughshares, and they could find more profit in swords once war was declared.

I found similar processes of causation in all three Great Dislocations of the period – the two world wars and the Great Depression. All of them had multiple causes, which piled up on top of each other as a growing crisis found out weaknesses in contemporary social structure that otherwise might never have become seriously threatening. The lack of mutual understandings between British and German leaders in the run-up to the first war; the counterproductive anti-communism of British and French leaders in the run-up to the second war; and the liquidationist ideology of American leaders in the Depression were all weaknesses that were only exposed when piled on top of other antecedent conditions. Each condition tended to be the product of a causal chain distinct from the others. Although structural processes were embedded in all four sources of social power, they entwined in complex and often contingent ways, and this means that we cannot identify a single, underlying structural cause nor can we model power development in terms of a singular social system.

There were thus many contextual particularities – mistakes and misunderstandings, especially among those possessing more power. In the run-up to World War I, liberalism prevented British leaders from deterring German aggression, and the German high command's secret military mobilization plans, unbeknownst to most German civilian leaders, involved seizing Belgian territory, a move that was almost bound to bring France and Britain into the war. Russian leaders discovered that the army could not technically be mobilized merely against Austria-Hungary, so they mobilized against Germany, too. Probably the biggest mistake came when the Archduke Franz Ferdinand's open automobile made the worst possible wrong turn one day in Sarajevo. Such particularities are necessary to explain why Great Dislocations happened, but so, too, are more structured processes. Japanese mistakes were all in the same direction toward increasing militarism. Hitler emerged on the back of traditional militarism, German nationalism fueled by the settlement of World War I – the general allure of fascism at this time – and a more general failure of capitalism. That we find both structure and contingency within and between all four sources of social power makes singular conclusions about overall meaning or ultimate primacy in this period impossible. It depended where you stood and whom you were, and it depended on a whole array of processes and contingencies.

The end of the second war in 1945 concluded my present period. It brought a decisive victory, but it was not clear how much this would change power relations. Fascism had been killed, although many feared that it might soon be reborn. Civil war was raging in China with an uncertain outcome, and Soviet Communism had been strengthened by the war. The European empires had been weakened, although it was unclear how much life they still had in them. There was uncertainty over whether the United States would back off from a global role as it had after World War I. In most capitalist countries, economic elites were divided between Keynesian and classical economics, but most assumed that postwar demobilization and dislocation – both domestic and international – would weaken economies and possibly lead to crises such as those of the 1920s or 1930s. They also feared that this might lead to the flowering of new or old extremist ideologies. To contemporaries, late 1945 brought enormous relief (even to Germans and Japanese), but also enormous uncertainty. What we are inclined today to regard as the underlying structural trends of the period seemed largely unclear at the time.

Their fears were not realized. Within five or six years, a better world was emerging, and not just among whites. Fascism was dead and buried and communism was thriving but only in a compact bloc of countries, as the Chinese Communists joined the Bolsheviks in successful revolution. Geopolitics were simplifying as the European empires declined and their militarism, and that of Japan, rapidly weakened. This left only the United States and the USSR as major military powers, although their confrontation was only just beginning to be stabilized by joint possession of nuclear weapons. There was an apparent settlement of the problems of the international economy as the Bretton Woods system was implemented, and Keynesian and classical economics were being blended together inside the advanced capitalist countries. Growing welfare states, progressive taxes, and the pursuit of full employment meant a further rise in social citizenship, increasingly among women, too. Postwar economic growth spread for a time right across the world, and a combination of capitalist growth and state infrastructural improvements in the less-developed countries was raising the height, life expectancy, and literacy of human beings there. We know that all this happened, generating a brief "Golden Age," but the peoples of 1945 did not.

The biggest picture of all has been the rise and then the fall of European dominance in the world. European civilization had expanded its ideological, economic, military, and political powers – each with a distinctive rhythm of development. The overall dynamism this involved generated a historically unprecedented multipower-actor imperialism. Europeans had been fortunate in that when they became capable of expanding overseas, the power of major civilizations elsewhere was stagnant or declining. The British were even more fortunate, emerging as a naval power and a very cohesive state in the moment when it could exploit the European balance of power to achieve the biggest empire of all. Both expansions, European and British, were made finally inevitable by their industrialization. The globe was now fractured in a new way, between the rich, white West plus Japan and the poor, nonwhite Rest. It was then further fractured by national and imperial rivalries. Then quite quickly came the self-inflicted destruction of European civilization through its own militarism, racism, and nationalism. It was succeeded by only two global empires, and then only one, accompanied by the accelerated global growth of capitalism, the decline of racism, the decline of interstate war, and the universal spread of the nation-state ideal across the world. They combined into a process of universal but still multiple globalizations, the subtitle of my fourth volume.

Bibliography

Abramowitz, Moses 1979 "Rapid growth potential and its realization: the experience of capitalist economies," in Edmund Malinvaid (ed.), *Economic Growth and Resources*. New York: St. Martin's Press, Vol. I, pp. 1–30.

Abramowitz, Moses & Paul David 2001 "Two Centuries of American Macroeconomic Growth. From Exploitation of Resource Abundance to Knowledge-Driven Development," *SIEPR Discussion Papers*, 01–05.

Abse, Tobias 1996 "Italian Workers and Italian Fascism," in Richard Bessel (ed.), *Fascist Italy and Nazi Germany*. Cambridge: Cambridge University Press.

Adamthwaite, Anthony 1995 *Grandeur and Misery: France's Bid for Power in Europe, 1914–1940*. London: St. Martins Press.

Addison, Paul 1975 *The Road to 1945*. London: Jonathan Cape.

Addison, Paul & Jeremy Crang (eds.) 2010 *Listening to Britain: Home Intelligence Reports on Britain's Finest Hour May-September 1940*. London: Bodley Head.

Akami, Tomoko 2002 *Internationalizing the Pacific*. London: Routledge.

Al-Sayyid, Afaf 1968 *Egypt and Cromer*. New York: Praeger.

Aldcroft, David 2001 *The European Economy 1914–2000*. London: Routledge, 4th edition.

2002 "Currency Stabilisation in the 1920s: Success or Failure?" *Economic Issues*, Vol. 7, Part 2.

Alexander, Martin 1992 *The Republic in Danger: General Maurice Gamelin and the Politics of French Defence, 1933–1940*. New York: Cambridge University Press.

Allen, Keith 2003 "Food on the German Home Front: Evidence from Berlin" in Gail Braybon (ed.), *Evidence, History and the Great War: Historians and the Impact of 1914–1918*. Oxford: Berghahn Books.

Allen, Robert 2004 *Farm to Factory. A Reinterpretation of the Soviet Industrial Revolution*. Princeton, NJ: Princeton University Press.

Allen, Theodore 1997 *The Invention of the White Race, 2 vols.: I – Racial Oppression and Social Control; II – The Origin of Racial Oppression in Anglo-America*. New York: Verso.

Aly, Goetz 2007 *Hitler's Beneficiaries: How the Nazis Bought the German People*. London: Verso.

Amenta, Edwin et al. 1994 "Stolen Thunder? Huey Long's 'Share Our Wealth,' Political Mediation, and the Second New Deal," *American Sociological Review*. **59**: 678–702.

1998 *Bold Relief: Institutional Politics and the Origins of Modern American Social Policy*. Princeton, NJ: Princeton University Press.

Amenta, Edwin & D. Halfmann 2000 "Wage wars: institutional politics, the WPA, and the struggle for U.S. social policy." *American Sociological Review*. **64**: 506–28.

Amenta, Edwin & Theda Skocpol 1988 "Redefining the New Deal: World War II and the development of Social provision in the United States" in Margaret Weir et al. (eds.), *The Politics of Social Policy in the United States*. Princeton, NJ: Princeton University Press.

Amsden, Alice 2001 *The Rise of "the Rest": Challenges to the West from Late-Industrilaizing Economies*. New York: Oxford University Press.

Anderson, Benedict 1988 "Cacique Democracy in the Philippines: Origins and Dreams." *New Left Review*, No. 169.

Anderson, Benjamin M. 1979 *Economics and the Public Welfare: A Financial and Economic History of the United States, 1914–1946.* Indianapolis: Liberty Press.

Anderson, David 2004 *Histories of the Hanged: Britain's Dirty War in Kenya and the End of Empire*. London: Weidenfeld.

Anderson, Perry 2010 "Two Revolutions," *New Left Review*, Jan–Feb, pp. 59–96.

Andornino, Giovanni 2006 "The nature and linkages of China's tributary system under the Ming and Qing dynasties," *Working Papers of the Global Economic History Network*, London School of Economics, No. 21/06.

Ansell, Christopher 2001 *Schism and Solidarity in Social Movements: The Politics of Labor in the French Third Republic*. Cambridge: Cambridge University Press.

Anweiler, Oskar 1974 *The Soviets: The Russian Workers, Peasants, and Soldiers Councils, 1905–1921.* New York: Pantheon Books.

Appleby, John 2001 "War, politics, and colonization, 1558–1625" in Nicholas Canny (ed.), *The Oxford History of the British Empire, Vol. I, The Origins of Empire*. Oxford: Oxford University Press.

Archer, Robin 2007 *Why Is There No Labor Party in the United States?* Princeton, NJ: Princeton University Press.

Arendt, Hannah 1968 *Eichmann in Jerusalem: A Report on the Banality of Evil*. New York: Viking.

Armitage, David 2000 *The Ideological Origins of the British Empire.* Cambridge: Cambridge University Press.

Arnold, David 1993 *Colonizing the Body: State, Medicine and Epidemic Disease in Nineteenth-Century India*. Berkeley & Los Angeles: University of California Press.

2000 *Science, Technology and Medicine in Colonial India*. Cambridge: Cambridge University Press.

Aronowitz, Stanley 1973 *False Promises: The Shaping of American Working Class Consciousness*. New York: McGraw Hill.

Arrighi, Giovanni 1994 *The Long Twentieth Century*. London: Verso.

2007 Adam Smith in Beijing. Lineages of the 21st Century. London: Verso.

Arrighi, Giovanni & Beverly Silver 1999 *Chaos and Governance in the Modern World System.* Minneapolis: University of Minnesota Press.

Atkinson, Anthony & Thomas Piketty 2007 *Top Incomes over the Twentieth Century*. Oxford: Oxford University Press.

Atkinson, Anthony et al. 2009 "Top Incomes in the Long Run of History," *NBER Working Paper*, No. 15408.

Auchincloss, Louis 2001 *Theodore Roosevelt*. New York: Henry Holt.

Audoin-Rouzeau, Stephane & Annette Becker 2002 *14–18: Understanding the Great War.* New York: Hill and Wang.

Auerbach, Alan & Yuriy Gorodnichenko 2011 "Fiscal multipliers in recession and expansion," *National Bureau of Economic Research*, Working Paper No. 17447.

Auslin, Michael 2004 *Negotiating with Imperialism: the Unequal Treaties and the Culture of Japanese Diplomacy*. Cambridge, MA: Harvard University Press.

Ayala, Cesar 1999 *Sugar Kingdom: The Plantation Economy of the Spanish Caribbean, 1898–1934*. Chapel Hill, NC: University of North Carolina Press.
Bairoch, Paul 1982 "International industrialization levels from 1750 to 1980," *Journal of European Economic History*, **11**: 269–334.
Balderston, Theo 2002 *Economics and Politics in the Weimar Republic*. Cambridge: Cambridge University Press.
Baldwin, Peter 1990 *The Politics of Social Solidarity*. Cambridge: Cambridge University Press.
Barber, William 1985 *From New Era to New Deal: Herbert Hoover, the Economists, and American Economic Policy, 1921–1933*. New York: Cambridge University Press.
1996 *Designs Within Disorder: Franklin D. Roosevelt, the Economists, and the Shaping of American Economic Policy, 1933–1945*. New York: Cambridge University Press.
Barnhart, Michael 1987 *Japan Prepares for Total War: The Search for Economic Security, 1919–1941*. Ithaca, NY: Cornell University Press.
Bartlett, Robert 1994 *The Making of Europe. Conquest, Colonization and Cultural Change, 950–1350*. Princeton, NJ: Princeton University Press.
Bartov, Omer 1985 *The Eastern Front, 1941–1945, German Troops and the Babarisation of Warfare*. London: Macmillan.
Bauman, Zygmunt 1989 *Modernity and The Holocaust*. Ithaca, N.Y.: Cornell University Press.
Bayly, Christopher 1996 *Empire and Information: Intelligence Gathering and Social Communication in India, 1780–1870*. Cambridge: Cambridge University Press.
2004 *The Birth of the Modern World 1780–1914*. Oxford: Blackwell.
Beaudreau, Bernard 1996 *Mass Production, the Stock Market Crash, and the Great Depression*. Westport, CT: Greenwood Press.
Becker, Jean-Jacques 1977 *1914: Comment les français sont entrés dans la guerre*. Paris: Presses de la Fondation nationale des sciences politiques.
1985 *The Great War and the French People*. Leamington Spa: Berg.
Bellamy, Paul 1997 *A History of Workmen's Compensation, 1898–1915: From Courtroom to Boardroom* New York: Garland Publishing.
Bensel, Richard 2000 *The Political Economy of American Industrialization, 1877–1900*. New York: Cambridge University Press.
Benson, John & Takao Matsumura 2001 *Japan 1868–1945: From Isolation to Occupation*. London: Longman Publishing.
Benton, Gregor 1992 *Mountain Fires: The Red Army's Three-Way War in South China 1934–1938*. Berkeley & Los Angeles: University of California Press.
1999 *New Fourth Army: Communist Resistance along the Yangtze and the Huai, 1938–1941*. Berkeley & Los Angeles: University of California Press.
Berezin, Mabel 1997 *Making the Fascist Self*. Ithaca, NY: Cornell University Press.
Berger, Gordon 1977 *Parties Out of Power in Japan, 1931–1941*. Princeton: Princeton University Press.
1988 "Politics and mobilization in Japan, 1931–1945" in Peter Duus (ed.), *The Cambridge History of Japan, Vol 6: The Twentieth Century*. Cambridge: Cambridge University Press.
Bergère, Marie-Claire 1989 *The Golden Age of the Chinese Bourgeoisie, 1911–1937*. Cambridge: Cambridge University Press.
Berkhoff, Karel 2004 *Harvest of Despair: Life and Death in Ukraine under Nazi Rule*. Cambridge, MA: Harvard University Press.
Berkowitz E & K. McQuaid 1992 *Creating the Welfare State: The Political Economy of 20th Century Reform*. Lawrence, KS: University Presses of Kansas.

Bernanke, Ben 2000 *Essays on the Great Depression*. Princeton, NJ: Princeton University Press.

Bernanke, Ben & Harold James 1991 "The Gold Standard, Deflation, and Financial Crisis in the Great Depression: An International Comparison" in Glenn Hubbard (ed.), *Financial Markets and Financial Crises*. Chicago: University of Chicago Press.

Bernhardt, Kathryn 1992 *Rents, Taxes and Peasant Resistance: the Lower Yangzi Region, 1840–1950*. Stanford, CA: Stanford University Press.

Bernstein, Michael 1987 *The Great Depression. Delayed Recovery and Economic Change in America, 1929–1939*. Cambridge: Cambridge University Press.

2002 *A Perilous Progress: Economists and Public Purpose in Twentieth-Century America*. Princeton, NJ: Princeton University Press.

Berstein, Serge & Jean-Jacques Becker 1987 *Histoire de l'anticommunisme en France, 1917–1940*. Paris: Olivier Orban.

Bertrand, C. L. 1977 *Revolutionary Situations in Europe*, 1917–1922. Montreal: Concordia University Press.

Beschloss, Michael 2002 *The Conqueror: Roosevelt, Truman and the Destruction of Hitler's Germany, 1941–1945*. New York: Simon & Schuster.

Betts, Raymond 1961 *Assimilation and Association in French Colonial Theory, 1890–1914*. New York: Columbia University Press.

Bianco, Lucien 2001 *Peasants Without the Party. Grass-Roots Movements in Twentieth-Century China*. New York: M. E. Sharpe.

2005 *Jacqueries et révolution dans la Chine du XXe siècle*. Paris: Editions de la Martinière.

Billig, Michael 1995 *Banal Nationalism*. London: Sage Publications.

Bin Laden, Osama 2005 *Messages to the World: The Statements of Osama Bin Laden*, ed., Bruce Lawrence. London: Verso.

Bix, Herbert 1982 "Rethinking 'Emperor-System Fascism': Ruptures and Continuities in Modern Japanese History," *Bulletin of Concerned Asian Scholars*, Vol. **14**: 13–22.

2001 *Hirohito and the Making of Modern Japan*. New York: Harper-Collins.

Blackburn, Robin 1997 *The Making of New World Slavery: from the Baroque to the Modern, 1492–1800*. London: Verso.

Blee, Kathleen 1991 *Women of the Klan. Racism and Gender in the 1920s*. Berkeley & Los Angeles: University of California Press.

Blum, Edward 2005 *Reforging the White Republic: Race, Religion and American Nationalism, 1865–1898*. Baton Rouge: Louisiana State Press.

Blustein, Paul 2001 *The Chastening: Inside the Crisis That Rocked the Global Financial System and Humbled the IMF*. New York: Public Affairs.

Bond, Brian 2002 *The Unquiet Western Front: Britain's Role in Literature and History*. New York: Cambridge University Press.

Bonnell, Victoria 1983 *Roots of Rebellion*. Berkeley & Los Angeles: University of California Press.

Bonzon, Thierry 1997 "Transfer payments and social policy" in Jay Winter & Jean-Louis Robert (eds.), *Capital Cities at War, 1914–1919*, pp. 305–341. Cambridge: Cambridge University Press.

Bonzon, Thierry & Belinda Davis 1997 "Feeding the cities," in Jay Winter & Jean-Louis Robert (eds.), *Capital Cities at War, 1914–1919*. Cambridge: Cambridge University Press.

Boot, Max 2002 *The Savage Wars of Peace: Small Wars and the Rise of American Power*. New York: Basic Books.

Bordo, Michael & Hugh Rockoff 1996 "The Gold Standard as a 'Good Housekeeping Seal of Approval'," *Journal of Economic History*, Vol. **56**: 389–428.
Bordo, Michael et al. 1999 "Was Expansionary Monetary Policy Feasible During the Great Contraction? An Examination of the Gold Standard Constraint," *NBER Working Paper*, No. 7125.
Bordo, Michael et al. (eds.) 1998 "Editor's Introduction" to their *The Defining Moment: The Great Depression and the American Economy in the Twentieth Century*. Chicago: University of Chicago Press.
Bosch, Aurora 1997 "Why is There No Labor Party in the United States? A Comparative New World Case Study: Australia and the U.S., 1783–1914," *Radical History Review*, **67**: 35–78.
Boudreau, Vince 2003 "Methods of Domination and Modes of Resistance: The U.S. Colonial State and Philippine Mobilization in Comparative Perspective" in Julian Go & Anne Foster (eds.), *The American Colonial State in the Philippines: Global Perspectives*, pp. 256–90. Durham, NC: Duke University Press.
Bourke, Joanna 1999 *An Intimate History of Killing: Face-to-Face Killing in Twentieth-Century Warfare*. New York: Basic Books.
Brachet-Campseur, Florence 2004 "De l'odalisque de Poiret à la femme nouvelle de Chanel: une victoire de la femme?" in Evelyne Morin-Rotureau (ed.), *1914–1918: combats de femmes*. Paris: Autrement.
Brandt, Loren 1989 *Commercialization and Agricultural Development in East-Central China, 1870–1937*. Cambridge: Cambridge University Press.
Breitman, Richard 1981 *German Socialism and Weimar Democracy*. Chapel Hill: University of North Carolina Press.
Brennan, Lance et al. 1997 "Towards an Anthropometric History of Indians under British Rule," *Research in Economic History*, Vol. **17**: 185–246.
Brenner, Robert 2006 "What is, and what is not, imperialism," *Historical Materialism*, **14**: 79–105.
Brinkley, Alan 1996 *The End of Reform*. New York: Random House.
Broadberry, Stephen & Mark Harrison 2005 "The economics of World War I: an overview" in S. Broadberry & M. Harrison (eds.), *The Economics of World War I*, pp. 3–40. Cambridge: Cambridge University Press.
Broadberry, Stephen & Peter Howlett, 2005 "The United Kingdom during World War I: business as usual" in S. Broadberry & M. Harrison (eds.), *The Economics of World War I.*, pp. 206–234. Cambridge: Cambridge University Press.
Brooks, Barbara 2000 *Japan's Imperial Diplomacy: Consuls, Treaty Ports, and War in China 1895–1938*. Honolulu: University of Hawai'i Press.
Broszat, Martin 1981 *The Hitler State. The Foundation and Development of the Internal Structure of the Third Reich*. London: Longman.
Broue, Pierre 2005 *The German Revolution, 1917–1923*. Leiden: Brill.
Brown, Archibald 2009 *The Rise and Fall of Communism*, 2009. New York: HarperCollins.
Browning, Christopher 2004 *The Origins of the Final Solution: The Evolution of Nazi Jewish Policy, September 1939-March 1942*. With contributions by Juergen Matthaeus. Lincoln: University of Nebraska Press.
Brunner, Karl 1981 "Epilogue: Understanding the Great Depression" in K. Brunner (ed.), *The Great Depression Revisited*, pp. 316–58. Boston: Mattinus Nijhoff.
Brustein, William 1996 *The Logic of Evil: The Social Origins of the Nazi Party, 1925–1933*. New Haven, CT: Yale University Press.
Bry, Gerhard 1960 *Wages in Germany, 1871–1945*, Princeton, NJ: Princeton University Press.

Bryant, Joseph 2008 "A New Sociology for a New History? Further Critical Thoughts on the Eurasian Similarity and Great Divergence Theses," *Canadian Journal of Sociology*, Vol. **33**: 149–67.

Bucheli, Marcelo 2005 *Bananas and Business: The United Fruit Company in Colombia, 1899–2000.* New York: New York University Press.

Buettner, Elizabeth 2004 *Empire Families: Britons and Late Imperial India*. Oxford: Oxford University Press.

Bulmer-Thomas, Victor 1994 *The Economic History of Latin America Since Independence*. Cambridge: Cambridge University Press.

Burk, Kathleen 1982 *War and the States: The Transformation of British Government, 1914–1919.* London: Allen & Unwin.

Burroughs, Peter 2001 "Imperial Institutions and the Government of Empire" in Andrew Porter (ed.), *The Oxford History of the British Empire, Vol. III: The Nineteenth Century*, pp. 170–197. Oxford: Oxford University Press.

Cain P. J. & A. G. Hopkins 1986 "Gentlemanly Capitalism and British Overseas Expansion – Part I 1688–1850," *Economic History Review*, **39**: 501–25.

2002 *British Imperialism, 1688–2000.* Harlow: Pearson.

Calata, Alexander 2002 "The role of education in Americanizing Filipinos" in Hazel M. McFerson (ed.), *Mixed Blessing: The Impact of the American Colonial Experience on Politics and Society in the Philippines*, pp. 89–97. Westport, CT: Greenwood Press.

Calder, Lendol 1999 *Financing the American Dream: A Cultural History of Consumer Credit*. Princeton, NJ: Princeton University Press.

Callwell, Colonel C. E. 1906 *Small Wars: Their Principles and Practice*. London: His Majesty's Stationery Office, 3rd edition.

Campbell, Ballard 1995 *The Growth of American Government: Governance from the Cleveland Era to the Present.* Bloomington, IN: Indiana University Press.

Cannadine, David 2001 *Ornamentalism: How the British Saw their Empire*. London, Allen Lane/Penguin.

Canny, Nicholas 2001 "Introduction" in N. Canny (ed.), *The Oxford History of the British Empire, Vol. I: The Origins of Empire*. Oxford: Oxford University Press.

Carley, Michael Jabara 1999 *1939: The Alliance That Never Was and the Coming of World War II.* Chicago: Ivan R. Dee.

Carsten, F. L. 1972 *Revolution in Central Europe, 1918–1919*. Berkeley & Los Angeles: University of California Press.

1980 *The Rise of Fascism*. Berkeley & Los Angeles: University of California Press.

Carsten, Francis 1977 *Fascist movements in Austria: From Schoenerer to Hitler.* London: Sage.

Cecchetti, Stephen & Georgios Karras 1994 "Sources of Output Fluctuations During the Interwar Period: Further Evidence on the Causes of the Great Depression," *Review of Economics and Statistics*, **76**: 80–102.

Cell, John 2001 "Colonial Rule" in Andrew Porter (ed.), *The Oxford History of the British Empire, Vol. III: The Nineteenth Century*. Oxford: Oxford University Press.

Centeno, Miguel 2002 *Blood and Debt: War and the Nation-State in Latin America*. College Park, PA: Penn State University Press.

Cha, Myung Soon 2000 "The colonial origins of Korea's market economy" in A. Latham & Heita Kawakatsu (eds.), *Asia-Pacific Dynamism, 1550–2000*, pp. 86–103. London: Routledge.

Chan, Gordon 2003 "The Communists in Rural Guangdong, 1928–1936," *Journal of the Royal Asiatic Society*, **3**/13: 77–97.

Chandler, Alfred 1977 *The Visible Hand: The Managerial Revolution in American Business*. Cambridge, MA: Belknap Press.
Chang, John 1969 *Industrial Development in Pre-Communist China*. Chicago: Aldine.
Chang, Maria Hsia 1979 "Fascism and Modern China," *The China Quarterly*, **79**, 553–67.
Charmley, John 1993 *Churchill: The End of Glory*. London: Hodder and Stroughton.
Chase, Kenneth 2003 *Firearms: A Global History to 1700*. New York: Cambridge University Press.
Chatterjee, Partha 1993 *The Nation and Its Fragments: Colonial and Postcolonial Histories*. Princeton: Princeton University Press.
Chen, Yung-fa 1986 *Making Revolution: The Communist Movement in eastern and Central China, 1937–1945*. Berkeley & Los Angeles: University of California Press.
Childers, Thomas 1983 *The Nazi Voter: The Social Foundations of Fascism in Germany, 1919–1933*. Chapel Hill: University of North Carolina Press.
Chou, Wan-yao 1996 "The Kominka movement in Taiwan and Korea" in Peter Duus et al. (eds.), *The Japanese Wartime Empire, 1931–1945*, pp. 40–68. Princeton, NJ: Princeton University Press.
Clark, Daniel 1997 *Like Night and Day: Unionization in a Southern Mill Town*. Chapel Hill: University of North Carolina Press.
Clavin, Patricia 2000 *The Great Depression in Europe, 1929–1939*. New York: St. Martins Press.
Clemens, Elizabeth 1997 *The People's Lobby: Organizational Innovation and the Rise of Interest Group Politics in the United States, 1890–1925*. Chicago: University of Chicago Press.
Clemens, Michael & Jeffrey Williamson 2004 "Wealth bias in the first global capital market boom, 1870–1913," *The Economic Journal*, **114**: 304–37.
Cline, William 2004 *Trade Policy and Global Poverty*.Washington, DC: Institute for International Economics.
Coatsworth, John 1994 *Central America and the United States: The Clients and the Colossus*. New York: Twayne.
Coble, Parks 1986 *The Shanghai Capitalists and the Nationalist Government, 1927–1937*. Cambridge, MA: Harvard University Press.
Cohen, Lizabeth 1990 *Making a New Deal: Industrial Workers in Chicago, 1919–1939*. Cambridge: Cambridge University Press.
2003 *A Consumers' Republic: The Politics of Mass Consumption in Postwar America*. New York: Knopf.
Cohen, Nancy 2002 *The Reconstruction of American Liberalism, 1865–1914*. Durham, NC: University of North Carolina Press.
Cohen, Stephen 2001 *Failed Crusade: America and the Tragedy of Post-Communist Russia*. New York: Norton.
Cohen, Warren 2005 *America's Failing Empire: US Foreign Relations Since the Cold War*. Oxford: Blackwell.
Cole, Harold et al. 2005 "Deflation and the International Great Depression: A Productivity Puzzle," *NBER Working Paper*, No. 11237.
Collingham, E. M. 2001 *Imperial Bodies: The Physical Experience of the Raj, c. 1800–1947*. Cambridge: Polity.
Collins, Randall 1994 "Why the Social Sciences won't become high-consensus, rapid-discovery science," *Sociological Forum*, **9**(2): 155–77.
2008 *Violence: A Micro-Sociological Theory*. Princeton: Princeton University Press.
Colville, Sir John 1985 The Fringes of Power: 10 Downing Street Diaries, 1939–1955. London: Hodder & Stoughton.

Conklin, Alice 1998 *A Mission to Civilize: The Republican Idea of Empire in France and West Africa 1895–1930*. Stanford: Stanford University Press.
Connor, Walter 1991 *The Accidental Proletariat: Workers, Politics, and Crisis in Gorbachev's Russia*. Princeton: Princeton University Press.
Cook, Haruko & Theodore Cook 1992 *Japan at War: An Oral History*. New York: The New Press.
Costa, Dora 2000 "American Living Standards, 1888–1994: Evidence From Consumer Expenditures," *NBER Working Paper*, No. 7650.
Cott, Nancy 1987 *The Grounding of Modern Feminism*. New Haven: Yale University Press.
Couch, Jim & William Shughart 1998 *The Political Economy of the New Deal*. Cheltenham, Glos.: Edward Elgar.
Cox, Ronald 1994 *Power and Profits: US Policy in Central America*. Lexington, KY: University of Kentucky Press.
Coyne, Christopher 2007 *After War: The Political Economy of Exporting Democracy*. Stanford, CA: Stanford University Press.
Craig, Douglas 1992 *After Wilson: The Struggle for the Democratic Part, 1920–1934*. Chapel Hill, NC: University of North Carolina Press.
Crawcour, Sidney 1997a "Economic change in the nineteenth century," in Kozo Yamamura (ed.), *The Economic Emergence of Modern Japan*. Cambridge: Cambridge University Press.
1997b "Industrialization and technological change, 1885–1920," in Kozo Yamamura (ed.), *The Economic Emergence of Modern Japan*. Cambridge: Cambridge University Press.
1998 "Industrialization and technological change, 1885–1920," in Duus (ed.), *The Cambridge History of Japan, Vol 6: The Twentieth Century*. Cambridge: Cambridge University Press.
Cronin, James & Carmen Sirianni (eds.) 1983 *Work, Community & Power: The Experience of Labor in Europe and America, 1900–1925*. Philadelphia: Temple University Press.
Crosby, Alfred 1993 *Ecological Imperialism*. Cambridge: Cambridge University Press.
Crowder, Michael 1968 *West Africa Under Colonial Rule*. Evanston, IL: Northwestern University Press.
Cumings, Bruce 1990 *The Origins of the Korean War, Vol. 1, Liberation and the Emergence of Separate Regimes, 1945–1947. Vol. 2, The Roaring of the Cataract, 1947–1950*. Princeton, NJ: Princeton University Press.
2004 *North Korea: Another Country*. New York: New Press.
Dalrymple, William 2002 *White Mughals: Love and Betrayal in Eighteenth-Century India*. London : HarperCollins.
Daniel, Ute 1997 *The War From Within: German Working-Class Women in the First World War*. Oxford & New York: Berg.
Darwin, John 2009 *The Empire Project. The Rise and Fall of the British World-System, 1830–1970*. Cambridge: Cambridge University Press.
David, Paul & Gavin Wright 1999 "Early Twentieth Century Growth Dynamics," *SIEPR Discussion Papers in Economic and Social History*, No. 98–3.
Davies, Gareth & Martha Derthick 1997 "Race and social welfare policy: the Social Security Act of 1935," *Political Science Quarterly*, **112**: 217–36.
Davies, R. W. 1989 *The Soviet Economy in Turmoil, 1929–1930*. Cambridge: Cambridge University Press.
1996 *The Industrialisation of Soviet Russia, vol. 4, Crisis and Progress in the Soviet Economy, 1931–1933*. Basingstoke, Hants: Macmillan Press.

Davies, R. W. & Stephen G. Wheatcroft 2004 *The Industrialisation of Soviet Russia, Vol 5: The Years of Hunger: Soviet Agriculture, 1931–1933*. New York: Palgrave Macmillan.
Davis, Belinda 2000 *Home Fires Burning: Food, Politics, and Everyday Life in World War I Berlin*. Chapel Hill: University of North Carolina Press.
Davis, Colin 1997 *Power At Odds: The 1922 National Railroad Shopmen's Strike*. Urbana, IL: University of Illinois Press.
Davis, Lance & Robert Huttenback 1987 *Mammon and the Pursuit of Empire*. Cambridge: Cambridge University Press.
Davis, Mike 2000 *Late Victorian Holocausts. El Niño Famines and the Making of the Third World*. New York: Verso.
Dawley, Alan 1991 *Struggles for Justice: Social Responsibility and the Liberal State*. Cambridge, MA: Harvard University Press.
De Felice, Renzo 1974 *Mussolini il Duce*. Turin: Einaudi.
DeLong, Bradford 1990 "Liquidation Cycles: Old Fashioned Real Business Cycle Theory and the Great Depression," *NBER Working Paper*, No. 3546.
DeLong, Bradford & Andre Shleifer 1991 "The Stock Market Bubble of 1929: Evidence from Closed-end Mutual Funds," *The Journal of Economic History*, **51**: 675–700.
Dickinson, Frederick 1999 *War and National Reinvention: Japan in the Great War, 1914–1919*. Cambridge, MA: Harvard University Press.
Digby, William 1901 *Prosperous British India: A Revelation from the Official Records*. Ann Arbor: University of Michigan Press.
Dilks, David 1969 *Curzon in India, Vol 1: Achievement*. New York: Taplinger.
Dirlik, Arif 2003 "Beyond Chesnaux: workers, class and the socialist revolution in modern China," *International Review of Social History*, **48**: 79–99.
Dodge, Toby 2003 *Inventing Iraq: The Failure of Nation-Building and a History Denied*. New York: Columbia University Press.
Domhoff, William 1990 *The Power Elite and the State. How Policy is Made in America*. New York: Aldine De Gruyter.
1996 *State Autonomy or Class Dominance? Case Studies in Policy Making in America*. New York: Aldine de Gruyter.
Domhoff, William & Michael Webber 2011 *Class and Power in the New Deal: Corporate Moderates, Southern Democrats, and The Liberal-Labor Coalition*. Stanford, CA: Stanford University Press.
Dosal, Paul 1993 *Doing Business with the Dictators: A Political History of United Fruit in Guatemala, 1899–1944*. Wilmington, DE: Scholarly Resources.
Doyle, Michael 1986 *Empires*. Ithaca, NY: Cornell University Press.
Drabble, John 2000 *An Economic History of Malaysia, c.1800–1990: The Transition to Modern Economic Growth*. London: Macmillan.
Drachkovitch, Milorad & Branko Lazitch 1966 "The Communist International" in M. Drachkovitch (ed.), *The Revolutionary Internationals, 1864–1943*, pp. 159–202. Stanford, CA: Stanford University Press.
Drake, Paul 1991 "From Good Men to Neighbors: 1912–1932" in Richard Lowenthal (ed.), *Exporting Democracy*, pp. 3–40. Baltimore: Johns Hopkins University Press.
Drayton, Richard 2000 *Nature's Government: Science, Imperial Britain, and the 'Improvement' of the World*. New Haven, CT: Yale University Press.
2001 "Knowledge and Empire" in Peter Marshall (ed.), *The Oxford History of the British Empire, Volume II: The Eighteenth Century*, pp. 231–252. Oxford: Oxford University Press.

Drescher, Seymour 2002 *The Mighty Experiment: Free Labor versus Slavery in British Emancipation*. New York: Oxford University Press.

Dreyer, Edward 1995 *China at War, 1901–1949*. London: Longman.

Dreyfus, Michel et al. 2006 *Se protéger, être protégé. Une histoire des Assurances sociales en France*. Rennes: Presses universitaires de Rennes.

Drukker, J. W. 2006 *The Revolution that Bit its Own Tail: How Economic History Changed our Ideas on Economic Growth*. Amsterdam: Aksant.

Duara, Prasenjit 1988 *Culture, Power, and the State: Rural North China, 1900–1942*. Stanford: Stanford University Press.

Duménil, Gérard & Dominique Lévy 1995 "The Great Depression: A Paradoxical Event?" *CEPREMAP*, paper no. 9510, Paris.

Dunn, John 1972 *Modern Revolutions*. Cambridge: Cambridge University Press.

Dunn, Walter 1997 *Kursk: Hitler's Gamble, 1943*. New York: Praeger.

Dupuy, Trevor 1977 *A Genius For War: the German Army and the General Staff, 1807–1945*. Englewood Cliffs, NJ: Prentice-Hall.

Dutton, Paul 2002 *Origins of the French Welfare State: The Struggle for Social Reform in France 1914–1947*. Cambridge: Cambridge University Press.

Duus, Peter 1995 *The Abacus and the Sword: The Japanese Penetration of Korea, 1895–1910*. Berkeley and Los Angeles: University of California Press.

1996 "Introduction" in Duus et al. (eds.) 1996 *The Japanese Wartime Empire, 1931–1945*. Princeton: Princeton University Press.

Duus, Peter & Daniel Okimoto 1979 "Fascism and the History of Prewar Japan: The Failure of a Concept," *Journal of Asian Studies*, **39**: 65–76.

Easter, Gerald 2000 *Reconstructing the State: Personal Networks and Elite Identity in Soviet Russia*. New York: Cambridge University Press.

Easterlin, Richard 2000 "The Worldwide Standard of Living since 1800," *Journal of Economic Perspectives*, **14**: 17–26.

Eastman, Lloyd 1984 *Seeds of Destruction: Nationalist China in War and Revolution, 1937–1949*. Stanford: Stanford University Press.

1990 *The Abortive Revolution. China under Nationalist Rule, 1927–1937*. Cambridge, MA: Harvard University Press.

Eckelt, Frank 1971 "Internal Policies of the Hungarian Soviet Republic" in Ivan Volgyes (ed.), *Hungary in Revolution, 1918–1919*. Lincoln: University of Nebraska Press.

Eckert, Carter 1996 "Total war, industrialization and social change in late colonial Korea" in Peter Duus et al. (eds.), *The Japanese Wartime Empire, 1931–1945*. Princeton, NJ: Princeton University Press.

Eckes, Alfred 1995 *Opening America's Market: U.S. Foreign Trade Policy since 1776*. Chapel Hill: University of North Carolina Press.

Edgerton, David 2005 *Warfare State: Britain, 1920–1970*. Cambridge: Cambridge University Press.

Eichengreen, Barry 1992 *Golden Fetters: The Gold Standard and the Great Depression, 1919–1939*. New York: Oxford University Press.

1996 *Globalizing Capital: A History of the International Monetary System* Princeton, NJ: Princeton University Press.

Eichengreen, Barry & Peter Temin 1997 "The Gold Standard and the Great Depression," *NBER Working Paper*, No. W6060.

Eiji, Oguma 2002 *The Genealogy of 'Japanese' Self-Images*. Melbourne: Trans Pacific Press.

Elkins, Caroline 2005 *Britain's Gulag: The Brutal End of Empire in Kenya*. London: Cape.

Eltis, David 2000 *The Rise of African Slavery in the Americas*, Cambridge: Cambridge University Press.
Elvin, Mark 1996 *Another History. Essays on China from a European Perspective*. Sydney: Wild Peony Press.
Epstein, Philip et al. 2000 "Distribution Dynamics: Stratification, Polarization and Convergence Among OECD Economies, 1870–1992," *London School of Economics, Department of Economic History Working Papers*, No. 58/00.
Esherick, Joseph 1995 "Ten theses on the Chinese revolution," *Modern China*, **21**, 45–76.
1998 "Revolution in a feudal fortress," *Modern China*, **24**, 339–77.
Esping-Andersen, Gosta 1985 *Politics against Markets*. Princeton: Princeton University Press.
1990 *The Three Worlds of Welfare Capitalism*. Cambridge: Cambridge University Press.
Etemad, Bouta 2005 *De l'utilité des empires*. Paris: Armand Colin.
2007 *Possessing the World: Taking the Measurements of Colonisation from the 18th to the 20th Century*. New York: Berghahn Books.
Evans, David & Mark Peattie 1997 *Kaigun: Strategy, Tactics and Technology in the Imperial Japanese Navy, 1887–1941*. Annapolis, MD: Naval Institute Press.
Evans, Richard 2006 *The Third Reich in Power*. London: Penguin.
Ewell, Judith 1996 *Venezuela and the United States: From Monroe's Hemisphere to Petroleum's Empire*. Athens, GA: University of Georgia Press.
Fackler, James 1998 "Propagation of the Depression: Theories and Evidence," in Mark Wheeler (ed.), *The Economics of the Great Depression*, pp. 95–126. Kalamazoo, MI: W.E. Upjohn Institute for Employment Research.
Fairbank, John (ed.) 1968 *The Chinese World Order. Traditional China's Foreign Relations*. Cambridge: Cambridge University Press.
Federico, Giovanni 2005 *Feeding the World: An Economic History of Agriculture, 1800–2000*. Princeton, NJ: Princeton University Press.
Feldman, Gerard 1966 *Army, Industry, and Labor in Germany, 1914–1918*. Princeton: Princeton University Press.
1977 *Iron and Steel in the German Inflation, 1916–1923*. Princeton, NJ: Princeton University Press.
Ferguson, Niall 1999 *The Pity of War: Explaining World War I*. New York: Basic Books.
2002 *Empire: How Britain Made the Modern World*. New York: Basic Books.
2004 *Colossus. The Price of America's Empire*. London: Penguin.
2006 *The War of the World*. London: Penguin.
Ferro, Marc 1972 *The Russian Revolution of February 1917*. New York: Prentice-Hall International.
Field, Alexander 2006 "Technological Change and U.S. Productivity Growth in the Interwar Years," *The Journal of Economic History*, **66**: 203–36.
2011 *A Great Leap Forward.1930s Depression and US Economic Growth*. New Haven, CT: Yale University Press.
Fieldhouse, David 1973 *Economics and Empire 1830–1914*. London: Weidenfeld & Nicolson.
1999 *The West and the Third World: Trade, Colonialism, Dependence, and Development*. Oxford: Blackwell.
Figes, Orlando 1997 *A People's Tragedy: A History of the Russian Revolution*. New York: Viking Books.
Finegold, Kenneth & Theda Skocpol 1984 "State, Party and Industry: From Business Recovery to the Wagner Act in America's New Deal" in C. Bright &

S. Harding (eds.), *Statemaking and Social Movements*, pp. 159– 92. Ann Arbor, MI : University of Michigan Press.

1995 *State and Party in America's New Deal*. Madison: University of Wisconsin Press.

Fink, Leon 1997 *Progressive Intellectuals and the Dilemmas of Democratic Commitment*. Cambridge, MA: Harvard University Press.

Fischer, Claude & Michael Hout 2006 *Century of Difference: How America Changed in the Last One Hundred Years*. New York: Russell Sage Foundation.

Fitzpatrick, Sheila 1999 *Everyday Stalinism. Ordinary Life in Extraordinary Times: Soviet Russia in the 1930s*. Oxford: Oxford University Press.

Flora, Peter 1983 State, Economy, and Society in Western Europe 1815–1975: A Data Handbook. Volume I: *The Growth of Mass Democracies and Welfare States*. London: Macmillan.

Flora, Peter & Arnold Heidenheimer 1981 *The Development of Welfare States in Europe and America*. New Brunswick: Transaction Books.

Floud, Roderick et al. 2011 *The Changing Body. Health, Nutrition and Human Development in the Western World since 1700*. Cambridge: Cambridge University Press.

Foran, John 2005 *Taking Power: On the origins of Third World Revolutions*. Cambridge: Cambridge University Press.

Fowkes, Ben 1984 *Communism in Germany under the Weimar Republic*. London: Palgrave Macmillan.

Fraser, Steve 1989. "The Labor Question" in S. Fraser & Gary Gerstle (eds.), *The Rise and Fall of the New Deal Order*, pp. 55–84. Princeton, NJ: Princeton University Press.

Friedlaender, Saul 1997 *Nazi Germany and the Jews. Vol I: The Years of Persecution, 1933–1939*. New York: HarperCollins.

Friedman, Edward 1991 *Chinese Village, Socialist State*. New Haven: Yale University Press.

Friedman, Milton & Anna Schwartz 1963 *A Monetary History of the United States, 1867–1960*. Chicago: University of Chicago Press.

Frieser, Karl-Heinz 2005 *The Blitzkrieg Legend: The 1940 Campaign in the West*. Annapolis: Naval Institute Press.

Fritz, Stephen 1995 *Frontsoldaten. The German Soldier in World War II*. Lexington, KY: University Press of Kentucky.

Fritzsche, Peter 2008 *Life and Death in the Third Reich*. Cambridge, MA: Belknap Press.

Fukuyama, Francis 2011 *The Origins of Political Order*. New York: Farrar, Straus & Giroux.

Galassi, Francesco & Mark Harrison, 2005 "Italy at War, 1915–1918" in Broadberry & Harrison (eds.), *The Economics of World War I*, pp. 276–309. Cambridge: Cambridge University Press.

Galbraith, John 1963 *Reluctant Empire: British Policy on the South African Frontier, 1834–1854*. Berkeley: University of California Press.

Gallagher, J. A. & R. E. Robinson 1953 "The Imperialism of Free Trade," *Economic History Review*, Vol. **6**, 1–15.

Gallie, Duncan 1983 *Social Inequality and Class Radicalism in France and Britain*. London, UK: Cambridge University Press.

Garon, Sheldon 1987 *The State and Labor in modern Japan*. Berkeley & Los Angeles: University of California Press.

Gatrell, Peter 2005 *Russia's First World War. A Social and Economic History*. Harlow: Pearson.

Gauthier, Anne Helene 1998 *The State and the Family*. Oxford: Clarendon Press.

Geary, Dick 1981 *European Labour Protest, 1848–1939*. New York: St. Martin's Press.
Geisert, Bradley 2001 Radicalism and Its Demise: *The Chinese Nationalist Party, Factionalism and Elites in Jiangsu Province, 1924–1931*. Ann Arbor, MI: University of Michigan Press.
Gelber, Harry 2001 *Nations Out of Empires: European Nationalism and the Transformation of Asia*. New York: Palgrave.
Gellman, Irwin 1979 *Good Neighbor Diplomacy: United States Policies in Latin America, 1933–1945*. Baltimore: Johns Hopkins University Press.
1995 *Secret Affairs. Franklin Roosevelt, Cordell Hull and Sumner Welles*. Baltimore: Johns Hopkins Press.
Gentile, Emilio 1990 "Fascism as political religion," *Journal of Contemporary History*, **25**: 229–52.
Gerstle, Gary 1989 *Working-Class Americanism: The Politics of Labor in a Textile City, 1914–1960*. Princeton, NJ: Princeton University Press.
Getty, J. Arch 1985 *Origins of the Great Purges: The Soviet Communist Party Reconsidered, 1933–1938*. New York, Cambridge University Press.
Getty, J. Arch & Oleg Naumov 1999 *The Road to Terror. Stalin and the Self-Destruction of the Bolsheviks, 1932–1939*. New Haven: Yale University Press.
Gill, Graeme 1979 *Peasants and Government in the Russian Revolution*. New York: Barnes & Noble Books.
Glantz, David 1998 *Stumbling Colossus: The Red Army on the Eve of World War*. Lawrence: University of Kansas Press.
Gleditsch, Kristian 2004 "A revised list of wars between and within independent states, 1816–2002," *International Interactions*, **30**: 231–62.
Gluck, Carol 1985 *Japan's Modern Myths: Ideology in the Late Meiji Period*. Princeton, NJ: Princeton University Press.
Go, Julian 2003 "The Chains of Empire: State Building and 'Political Education' in Puerto Rico and the Philippines" in J. Go & A. Foster (eds.), *The American Colonial State in the Philippines: Global Perspectives, pp.* 182–216. Durham, NC: Duke University Press.
2004 "America's Colonial Empire: the Limits of Power," *Items & Issues* (Quarterly of the Social Science Research Council), Vol. 4.
2008 *American Empire and the Politics of Meaning: Elite Political Cultures in the Philippines and Puerto Rico during U.S. Colonialism*. Durham: Duke University Press.
2011 *Patterns of Empire. The British and American Empires, 1688 to the Present*. New York: Cambridge University Press.
Godfrey, John 1987 *Capitalism at War: Industrial Policy and Bureaucracy in France, 1914–1918*. Leamington Spa: Berg.
Goebbels, Josef 1948 *The Goebbels Diaries, 1942–1943*. Garden City, NY: Doubleday.
Goebel, Thomas 2002 *A Government by the People: Direct Democracy in America, 1890–1940*. Durham, NC: University of North Carolina Press.
Goldfield, Michael 1989 "Worker insurgency, radical organization, and New Deal labor legislation," *American Political Science Review*, **83**: 1257–82.
1997 *The Color of Politics: Race and the Mainsprings of American Politics*. New York: The New Press.
Goldfrank, Walter 1979 "Theories of revolution and revolution without theory," *Theory and Society*, **7**: 135–65.
Goldin, Claudia & Lawrence Katz 1999 "The Shaping Of Higher Education: The Formative Years in the United States, 1890–1940," *Journal of Economic Perspectives*, **13**: 37–62.

2003 "The 'Virtues' of the Past: Education in the First Hundred Years of the New Republic," *NBER Working Paper,* No. 9958.

Goldin, Claudia & Robert Margo 1992 "The Great Compression: Wage Structure in the United States at Mid-Century," *Quarterly Journal of Economics*, **107**: 1–34.

Goldstone, Jack 2001 "Toward a fourth generation of revolutionary theory," *Annual Review of Political Science*, **4**: 139–87.

2004 "Its all about state structure: new findings on revolutionary origins from global data," *Homo Oeconomicus*, **21**: 429–55.

2009 "Revolutions," in Todd Landman & Neil Robinson (eds.), *The Sage Handbook of Comparative Politics*, pp. 319–347. Los Angeles: Sage.

Goodman, David 2000 *Social and Political Change in Revolutionary China: The Taihang Base Area in the War of Resistance to Japan, 1937–1945.* New York: Rowman & Littlefield.

Goodwin, Jeff 2001 *No Other Way Out: States and Revolutionary Movements, 1945–1991.* New York: Cambridge University Press.

Gordon, Andrew 1985 *The Evolution of Labor Relations in Japan: Heavy Industry, 1853–1955.* Cambridge, MA: Harvard University Press.

1991 *Labor and Imperial Democracy in Prewar Japan.* Berkeley & Los Angeles: University of California Press.

2003 *A Modern History of Japan from Tokugawa Times to the Present.* New York: Oxford University Press.

Gordon, Colin 1994 *New Deals: Business, Labor and Politics in America, 1920–1935.* New York: Cambridge University Press.

2003 *Dead on Arrival: The Politics of Health Care in Twentieth-Century America.* Princeton, NJ: Princeton University Press.

Gordon, David 2006 "Historiographical Essay: The China-Japan War, 1931–1945," *Journal of Military History*, **70**, 137–82.

Gordon, Robert 2005 "The 1920s and 1990s in mutual reflection," *NBER Working Paper,* No. 11778.

Gordon, Robert & James Wilcox 1981 "Monetarist Interpretations of the. Great Depression: An Evaluation and Critique" in Brunner (ed.), *The Great Depression Revisited*, pp. 49–107. Boston: Mattinus Nijhoff.

Gordon, Robert & John Veitch 1986 "Fixed investment in the American business cycle, 1919–1983" in R. Gordon (ed.), *The American Business Cycle: Continuity and Change*, pp. 267–335. Chicago: University of Chicago Press.

Gordon, Sarah 1984 *Hitler, Germans and the "Jewsish Question."* Princeton, NJ: Princeton University Press.

Gorodetsky, Gabriel 1999 *Grand Delusion: Stalin and the German Invasion of Russia.* New Haven: Yale University Press.

Gorski, Philip 2003 *The Disciplinary Revolution – Calvinism and the Rise of the State in Early Modern Europe*. Chicago: The University of Chicago Press.

Goto, Ken'ichi 1996 "Cooperation, submission and resistance of indigenous elites of southeast Asia in the wartime empire" in Duus (ed.), *The Cambridge History of Japan, Vol 6: The Twentieth Century*, pp. 274–304. Cambridge: Cambridge University Press.

2003 *Tensions of Empire: Japan and Southeast Asia in the Colonial and Postcolonial World.* Athens, Ohio: Ohio University Press.

Grayzel, Susan 1999 *Women's Identities at War: Gender, Motherhood, and Politics in Britain and France during the First World War.* Chapel Hill: University of North Carolina Press.

Gregory, Adrian 2003 "British War Enthusiasm: A reassessment," in Gail Braybon (ed.),*Women's Identities at War: Gender, Motherhood, and Politics in Britain and France during the First World War.* Chapel Hill: University of North Carolina Press.

Gregory, Paul 2004 *The Political Economy of Stalinism: Evidence from the Soviet Secret Archives*. Cambridge: Cambridge University Press.

Griffin, Roger 2002 "The primacy of culture: the current growth (or manufacture) of consensus within fascist studies," *Journal of Contemporary History*, **37**: 21–43.

Guerin-Gonzales, Camille 1994 *Mexican Workers and American Dreams: Immigration, Repatriation, and California Farm Labor, 1900–1939*. New Brunswick, NJ: Rutgers University Press.

Gulick, L. H. 1948 *Administrative Reflections from WWII*. Tuscaloosa: University of Alabama Press.

Hacker, Jacob & Paul Pierson 2002 "Business Power and Social Policy: Employers and the Formation of the American Welfare State," *Politics & Society*, **30**: 277–325.

Hagtvet, Bernt 1980 "The Theory of Mass Society and Weimar" in Stein Larsen et al. (eds.), *Who Were the Fascists?: Social Roots of European Fascism*. Oslo: Universitetsforlaget.

Haimson, Leopold 1964–1965 "The Problem of Social Stability in Urban Russia, 1905–1917," *Slavic Review*, **23**: 619–42; 24: 1–22.

Hamilton, James 1987 "Monetary Factors in the Great Depression," *Journal of Monetary Economics*, **19**: 145–69.

1988 "The Role of the International Gold Standard in Propagating the Great Depression," *Contemporary Policy Issues*, **6**: 67–89.

Hane, Mikiso 1992 *Modern Japan: A Historical Survey*. Boulder: Westview Press.

Hannah, Leslie "Logistics, market size and giant plants in the early 20th century – a global view," unpublished paper, University of Tokyo, Faculty of Economics.

Hara, Akira 1998 "Japan: Guns Before Rice" in Mark Harrison (ed.), *The Economics of World War II: Six Great Powers in International Comparison*. Cambridge: Cambridge University Press.

Harrison, Mark (ed.) 1998 *The Economics of World War II*. Cambridge: Cambridge University Press.

Harrison, Robert 1997 *State and Society in Twentieth Century America*. London: Longman.

2004 *Progressive Reform and the New American State*. Cambridge: Cambridge University Press.

Harsch, Donna 1993 *German Social Democracy and the Rise of Nazism*. Chapel Hill: University North Carolina Press.

Hartford, Kathleen 1989 "Repression and communist success: the case of Jin-Cha-Ji, 1938–1943" in Hartford & Steven Goldstein (eds.), *Single Sparks: China's Rural Revolutions*, pp. 92–127. Armonk, NY: M. E. Sharpe.

Harvey, David 2003 *The New Imperialism*. Oxford: Oxford University Press.

Hasegawa, Tsyuyoshi 1981 *The February Revolution*. Seattle: University of Washington Press.

Hata, Ikuhiko 1988 "Continental Expansion, 1905–1941" in Duus (ed.), *The Cambridge History of Japan, Vol 6: The Twentieth Century*, pp. 271–304. Cambridge: Cambridge University Press.

Hautcoeur, Pierre-Cyrille 2005 "Was the Great War a watershed? The economics of World War I in France" in Broadberry & Harrison (eds.), *The Economics of World War I*, pp. 169–205. Cambridge: Cambridge University Press.

Hawks, Francis (ed.) 2005 *Commodore Perry and the Opening of Japan. The Official Report of the Expedition to Japan*. Stroud, Glos: Nonesuch.

Haydu, Jeffrey 1997 *Making American Industry Safe for Democracy: Comparative Perspectives on the State and Employee Representation in the Era of World War II*. Champaign: University of Illinois Press.

Hayes, Jack Jr. 2001 *South Carolina and the New Deal*. Columbia: University of South Carolina Press.

Headrick, Daniel 1981 *The Tools of Empire*. Oxford: Oxford University Press.

Healy, David 1963 *The United States in Cuba, 1898–1902: Generals, Politicians and the Search for Policy*. Madison, WI: University of Wisconsin Press.

Healy, Maureen 2004 *Vienna and the Fall of the Habsburg Empire*. Cambridge: Cambridge University Press.

Hewitson, Mark 2004 *Germany and the Causes of the First World War*. Oxford & New York: Berg.

Hicks, Alexander et al. 1995 "The programmatic emergence of the social security state," *American Sociological Review*, **60**: 329–49.

1999 *Social Democracy and Welfare Capitalism: A Century of Income Security Politics*. Ithaca, NY: Cornell University Press.

Hidalgo, Julio 2002 "Cacique democracy and future politics in the Philippines" in Mcferson (ed.), *Mixed Blessing: The Impact of the American Colonial Experience on Politics and Society in the Philippines*, pp. 209–240. Westport, CT: Greenwood Press.

Higgs, Robert 1989 *Crisis and Leviathan: Critical Episodes in the Growth of American Government*. New York: Oxford University Press.

Hinton, James 1973 *The First Shop Stewards' Movement*. London: George Allen & Unwin.

Hinton, William 1966 *Fanshen: A Documentary of Revolution in a Chinese Village*. New York: Monthly Review Press.

Hirsch, Susan 2003 *After the Strike: A Century of Labor Struggle at Pullman*. Urbana, IL: University of Illinois Press.

Ho, Samuel Pao-San 1984 "Colonialism and Development: Korea, Taiwan and Kwantung" in Ramon Myers & Mark Peattie (eds.), *The Japanese Colonial Empire, 1895–1945*. Princeton: Princeton University Press.

Hobsbawm, Eric 1994 *The Age of Extremes: The Short Twentieth Century, 1914–1991*. London: Michael Joseph.

Hobson, John A. 1902 *Imperialism, A Study*. New York: James Pott and Co.

Hogan, Heather 1993 *Forging Revolution: Metalworkers, Managers, and the State in St. Petersburg, 1890–1914*. Bloomington, IN: Indiana University Press.

Holden, Robert 2004 *Armies Without Nations: Public Violence and State Formation in Central America 1821–1960*. Oxford: Oxford University Press.

Holquist, Peter 2002 *Making War, Forging Revolution: Russia's Continuum of Crisis 1914–1921*. Cambridge: Harvard University Press.

Honey, Michael 1993 *Southern Labor and Black Civil Rights' Organizing Memphis Workers*. Urbana: University of Illinois Press.

Hong, Young-Sun 1998 *Welfare, Modernity and the Weimar State: 1919–1933*. Princeton, NJ: Princeton University Press.

Hough, Jerry 1997 *Democratization and Revolution in the USSR, 1985–1991*. Washington, DC: Brookings Institute.

Howell, David 2002 *MacDonald's Party: Labour Identities and Crisis, 1922–1931*. Oxford: Oxford University Press.

Huang, Jing 2000 *Factionalism in Chinese Communist Politics*. Cambridge: Cambridge University Press.

Huang, Meizhen & Hanqing Yang 2001 "Nationalist China: Negotiating Positions During the Stalemate, 1938–1945" in David Barrett & Larry Shyu (eds.), *Chinese Collaboration with Japan, 1932–1945*. Stanford: Stanford University Press.

Huang, Philip 1985 *The Peasant Economy and Social Change in North China*. Stanford, CA: Stanford University Press.
1990 *The Peasant Family and Rural Development in the Yangtzi Delta, 1350–1988*. Stanford, CA: Stanford University Press.
2001 *Code, Custom and Legal Practice in China*. The Qing and the Republic Compared. Stanford, CA: Stanford University Press.
Huggins, Martha 1998 *Political Policing: The United States and Latin America*. Durham, NC: Duke University Press.
Hull, Isabel 2005 *Absolute Destruction: Military Culture and the Practices of War in Imperial Germany*. Ithaca: Cornell University Press.
Hunt, Richard 1970 *German Social Democracy, 1918–1933*. New Haven: Yale University Press.
Hunter, Holland 1988 "Soviet agriculture with and without collectivization, 1928–1940," *Slavic Review*, **47**: 203–16.
Huntington, Samuel 1991 *The Third Wave*. Norman, OK: University of Oklahoma Press.
Hyam, Ronald 2001 "Trusteeship, Anti-Slavery and Humanitarianism" in Andrew Porter (ed.), *The Third Wave*. Norman, OK: University of Oklahoma Press.
Ikegami, Eiko 1997 *The Taming of the Samurai Honorific Individualism and the Making of Modern Japan*. Cambridge, MA: Harvard University Press.
2004 *Bonds of Civility: Aesthetic Networks and the Political Origins of Japanese Culture*. Cambridge: Cambridge University Press.
Imlay, Talbot 2003 *Facing the Second World War: Strategy, Politics, and Economics in Britain and France 1938–1940*. New York: Oxford University Press.
Ingham, Geoffrey 1984 *Capitalism Divided?* London: Macmillan.
2009 *Capitalism*. Cambridge: Polity Press.
Inikori, Joseph 2002 *Africans and the Industrial Revolution in England: A Study in International Trade and Economic Development*. Cambridge: Cambridge University Press.
International Labor Office 1938 *Industrial Labor in India*. Geneva: ILO.
Iriye, Akira 1974 "The failure of economic expansionism, 1918–1931" in Bernard Silberman & Harry Harootunian (eds.), *Japan in Crisis*, pp. 237–269. Princeton, NJ: Princeton University Press.
1987 *The Origins of the Second World War in Asia and the Pacific*. London: Longman.
1997 *Japan and the Wider World: From the Mid-Nineteenth Century to the Present*. New York: Longman.
Irons, Janet 2000 *Testing the New Deal: The General Textile Strike of 1934 in the American South*. Urbana: University of Illinois Press.
Iyer, Lakshmi 2004 "The Long-term Impact of Colonial Rule: Evidence from India," unpublished paper: http://www.people.hbs.edu/liyer/iyer_colonial_oct2004.pdf
Jackson, Julian 2001 *France: The Dark Years, 1940–44*. New York: Oxford University Press.
2003 *The Fall of France: The Nazi Invasion of 1940*. New York: Oxford University Press.
Jacoby, Sanford 1997 *Modern Manors. Welfare Capitalism Since the New Deal*. Princeton, NJ: Princeton University Press.
2004 "Economic ideas and the labor market: origins of the Anglo-American Model and prospects for global diffusion," Department of Sociology, UCLA, Theory and Research in Comparative Social Analysis, Paper No. 22.

Jahn, Hubertus 1995 *Patriotic Culture in Russia during World War I*. Ithaca, NY: Cornell University Press.

James, Harold 2001 *The End of Globalization: Lessons From The Great Depression*. Cambridge, MA: Harvard University Press.

2006 *The Roman Predicament: How the Rules of International Order Create The Politics of Empire*. Princeton, NJ: Princeton University Press.

James, J. & M. Thomas 2000 "Industrialization and wage inequality in nineteenth-century urban America," *Journal of Income Distribution*, **8**: 39–64.

Janos, Andrew & William Slottman (eds.) 1971 *Revolution in perspective : essays on the Hungarian Soviet Republic of 1919*. Berkeley: University of California Press.

Jenkins, Craig & Barbara Brents 1989 "Social Protest, Hegemonic Competition, and Social Reform: A Political Struggle Interpretation of the Origins of the American Welfare State," *American Sociological Review*, **54**: 891–909.

John, Richard 1997 "Government institutions as agents of change: rethinking American political development in the early Republic, 1787–1835," *Studies in American Political Development*, **11**: 347–80.

Johnson, Chalmers 1962 *Peasant Nationalism and Communist Power; The Emergence of Revolutionary China 1937–1945*. Stanford: Stanford University Press.

Jorda, Oscar et al. 2010 "Financial Crises, Credit Booms, and External Imbalances: 140 Years of Lessons," *NBER Working Paper*, No. 16567.

Jordan, Donald 1987 "The place of Chinese disunity in Japanese army strategy during 1931," *China Quarterly*, **109**: 42–63.

Kataoka, Tetsuya 1974 *Resistance and Revolution in China: The Communists and the Second United Front*. Berkeley & Los Angeles: University of California Press.

Katz, Michael B. 2001 *The Price of Citizenship: Redefining the American Welfare State*. New York: Metropolitan Books.

Katznelson, Ira 2005 *When Affirmative Action Was White: An Untold History of Racial Inequality in Twentieth-Century America*. New York: Norton.

et al. 1993 "Limiting Liberalism: The Southern Veto in Congress, 1933–1950," *Political Science Quarterly*, **108**: 283–306.

Kaufman, Bruce 2003 "John R. Commons and the Wisconsin School on Industrial Relations Strategy and Policy," *Industrial and Labor Relations Review*, **57**: 3–30.

2006 "Industrial Relations and Labor Institutionalism: A Century of Boom and Bust," *Labor History*, **47**: 295–318.

Kay, Alex 2006 *Exploitation, Resettlement, Mass Murder: Political and Economic Planning for German Occupation Policy in the Soviet Union, 1940–1941*. New York: Berghahn Books.

Keegan, John 1978 *The Face of Battle*. Harmondsworth: Penguin.

Keene, Jennifer 2001 *Doughboys, the Great War, and the Remaking of America*. Baltimore: Johns Hopkins Press.

Keller, Morton 1994 *Regulating a New Society: Public Policy and Social Change in America, 1900–1933*. Cambridge, MA: Harvard University Press.

Kenez, Peter 2006 *The History of the Soviet Union from the Beginning to the End*. Cambridge: Cambridge University Press.

Kennedy, David 1999 *Freedom From Fear: The American People in Depression and War, 1929–1945*. New York: Oxford University Press.

Kerbo, Harold R. & Richard A. Shaffer 1986 "Unemployment and Protest in the United States, 1890–1940: A Methodological Critique and Research Note," *Social Forces* **64**: 1046–56.

Kershaw, Greet 1997 *Mau Mau from Below*. Athens: Ohio University Press.
Kershaw, Ian 1998 *Hitler, 1889–1936: Hubris*. New York: Norton.
2000 *Hitler, 1936–1945: Nemesis*. London: Allen Lane.
2007 *Fateful Choices. Ten Decisions that Changed the World 1940–1941*. London: Penguin Books.
2011 *The End, The Defiance and Destruction of Hitler's Germany, 1944–45*. London: Penguin Press.
Kersten, Felix, 1956 *The Kersten Memoirs, 1940–1945*. London: Hutchinson.
Kessler-Harris, Alice 2001 *In Pursuit of Equity: Women, Men, and the Quest for Economic Citizenship in 20th-Century America*. New York: Oxford University Press.
Keynes, John Maynard 1919 *The Economic Consequences of the Peace*. London: Macmillan.
1937 "The General Theory of Employment," *Quarterly Journal of Economics*, **51**: 209–23.
1973 *The General Theory of Employment Interest and Money*. London: Macmillan.
Khlevniuk, Oleg 2004 *The History of the Gulag: From Collectivization to the Great Terror.* New Haven, CT: Yale University Press.
Kiernan, Kathleen et al. 1998 *Lone Motherhood in Twentieth Century Britain*. Oxford: Clarendon Press.
Kim, Duol & Ki-Joo Park 2005 "Colonialism and Industrialization: Manufacturing Productivity of Colonial Korea, 1913 – 1937," working paper.
2008 "Colonialism and Industrialisation: Factory Labour Productivity of Colonial Korea, 1913–37," *Australian Economic History Review*, **48**: 26–46.
Kindleberger, Charles 1986 *The World in Depression, 1929–1939*. Berkeley & Los Angeles: University of California Press.
Kirk-Greene, Anthony 2000 *Britain's Imperial Administrators, 1858–1966*. Basingstoke: Macmillan; New York: St. Martin's Press.
Kleppner, Paul 1982 *Who Voted? The Dynamics of Electoral Turnout, 1870–1980*. New York: Praeger.
Knox, MacGregor 2009 *To the Threshold of Power, 1922/33: Origins and Dynamics of the Fascist and National Socialist Dictatorships*, Volume 1. New York: Cambridge University Press.
Kocka, Juergen 1984 *Facing Total War: German Society 1914–1918*. Leamington Spa: Berg.
Kohli, Atul 2004 *State-Directed Development: Political Power and Industrialization in the Global Periphery*. Cambridge: Cambridge University Press.
Koistinen, Paul 1967 "The Industrial-Military Complex in Historical. Perspective: World War I," *Business History Review*, **41**: 378–403.
Kolko, Gabriel 1963 *The Triumph of Conservatism; A Re-Interpretation of American History, 1900–1916*. New York: Free Press of Glencoe.
Kornhauser, Arthur 1940 "Analysis of 'Class Structure' of Contemporary American Society" in George Hartman & Theodore Newcomb (eds.), *Industrial Conflict: A Psychological Interpretation*. New York: Cordon.
1952 *Detroit as the People See It: A Survey of Attitudes in an Industrial City*. Detroit: Wayne University Press.
Korstad, Robert 2003 *Civil Rights Unionism: Tobacco Workers and the Struggle for Democracy in the Mid-Twentieth-Century South*. Chapel Hill: University of North Carolina Press.
Koshar, Rudy 1986 *Social Life, Local Politics and Nazism: Marburg, 1880–1935*. Chapel Hill: University of North Carolina Press.

Kriegel, Annie 1969 *Aux origines du communisme francais, 1914–1920.* Paris: Flammarian.

Kroener, Bernard 2003 "Management of human resources, deployment of the population and manning the armed forces in the second half of the war, 1942–144" in Kroener et al. (eds.), *Organization and Mobilization of the German Sphere of Power, Part 2: Wartime Administration, Economy and Manpower Resources, 1942–144/45*, pp. 787–1140. Oxford: Clarendon Press.

LaFeber, Walter 1984 *Inevitable Revolutions: The United States in Central America.* New York: Norton.

1993 *The New Empire: An Interpretation of American Expansion, 1860–1898.* Ithaca, NY: Cornell University Press.

1994 *The American Age: United States Foreign Policy at Home and Abroad since 1750.* New York: Norton.

Lal, Deepak 2004 *In Praise of Empires. Globalization and Order*. New York: Palgrave MacMillan.

Langley, Lester D. 1980 *The United States and the Caribbean: 1900–1970.* Athens, GA: University of Georgia Press.

Lemke, Douglas 2002 *Regions of War and Peace*. Cambridge: Cambridge University Press.

Lenin, Vladimir I. 1939 *Imperialism, the Highest Stage of Capitalism: A Popular Outline*. New York: International Publishers.

1947 "Left-Wing Communism, an Infantile Disorder," his *Selected Works*. Moscow: Progress Publishers.

Lenman, Bruce 2001a *England's Colonial Wars 1550–1688*. London: Longman.

2001b *Britain's Colonial Wars 1688–1783*. London: Longman.

Leonard, Thomas 1991 *Central America and the United States: The Search for Stability*. Athens, GA: University of Georgia Press.

Leuchtenberg, William 1963 *Franklin D. Roosevelt and the New Deal, 1932–1940.* New York: Harper & Row.

Leuchtenburg, William E. 1963 *Franklin D. Roosevelt and the New Deal.* New York: Harper Perennial.

Levine, Steven 1987 *Anvil of Victory: The Communist Revolution in Manchuria, 1945–1948*. New York: Columbia University Press.

Levinson, Jerome & Juan de Onis 1970 *The Alliance That Lost Its Way*. Chicago: Quadrangle Books.

Levy, J. S. 1983 *War in the Modern Great Power System, 1495–1975*. Lexington, KY: University of Kentucky Press.

Levy, Jonah 2005 "Redeploying the State: Liberalization and Social Policy in France" in Wolfgang Streeck & Kathleen Thelen (eds.), *Beyond Continuity: Institutional Change in Advanced Political Economies*, pp. 103–126. New York: Oxford University Press.

Lewin, Moshe 1985 *The Making of the Soviet System*. London: Methuen.

Lewis, George 2006 *Massive Resistance: The White Response to the Civil Rights Movement*. New York: Oxford University Press.

Lewis, Jane 1992 "Gender and the Development of Welfare Regimes," *Journal of European Social Policy*, **2**: 159–73.

Lewis, Jill 1983 "Red Vienna: Socialism in One City, 1918–27," *European History Quarterly*, **13**: 335–54.

Lewis, Joanna 2000 *Empire State-Building. War and Welfare in Kenya, 1925–52*. Athens, OH: Ohio University Press.

Li, Lincoln 1994 *Student Nationalism in China, 1924–1949*. Albany, NY: State University of New York Press.

Lichtenstein, Nelson 1992 *Labor's War at Home: The CIO in World War II*. Cambridge: Cambridge University Press.
2002 *State of the Union: A Century of American Labor*. Princeton, NJ: Princeton University Press.
2003 *Labor's War at Home: The CIO in World War II*. Philadelphia: Temple University Press.
Lieberman, Robert C. 1998 *Shifting the Color Line: Race and the American Welfare State*. Cambridge, MA: Harvard University Press.
Lieuwen, Edwin 1961 *Arms and Politics in Latin America*. New York: Praeger.
Lim, Taekyoon 2010 "The neoliberalisation of the Korean state: double-faced neoliberal reforms in the post-1997 economic crisis era," unpublished paper, UCLA Dept. of Sociology.
Lin, Justin Yifu & Peilin Liu 2008 "Development Strategies and Regional Income Disparities in China" in Guanghua Wan (ed.), *Inequality and Growth in Modern China*, pp. 56–78. Oxford: Oxford University Press.
Lin, Yi-Min 2001 *Between Politics and Market Firms, Competition and Institutional Change in Post-Mao China*. New York: Cambridge University Press.
Lindbom, Anders 2008 "The Swedish Conservative Party and the Welfare State: Institutional Change and Adapting Preferences," *Government and Opposition*, **43**: 539–60.
Lindert, Peter 1998 "Three centuries of inequality in Britain and America," Department of Economics, University of California at Davis, Working Paper Series No. 97–09.
2004 *Growing Public. Social Spending and Economic Growth since the Eighteenth Century*. Cambridge: Cambridge University Press.
Linz, Juan 1976 "Some Notes Toward a Comparative Study of Fascism in Sociological Historical Perspective" in Walter Laquer (ed.), *Fascism. A Reader's Guide*, pp. 3–121. Berkeley & Los Angeles: University of California Press.
Lipset, Seymour Martin 1960 *Political Man*. New York: Doubleday.
1963 *Political Man*. London: Heinemann.
Lipset, Seymour Martin & Gary Marks 2000 *It Didn't Happen Here. Why Socialism Failed in the United States*. New York: Norton.
Lipset, Seymour & Stein Rokkan 1967 "Cleavage Structures, Party Systems, and Voter Alignments: an Introduction" in their *Party systems and voter alignments: Cross-national perspectives*. Glencoe, IL: The Free Press.
Little, Douglas 2002 *American Orientalism: The United States and the Middle East Since 1945*. Chapel Hill: University of North Carolina Press.
Liu, Chang 2003 "Making revolution in Jiangnan. Communists and the Yangzi Delta countryside, 1927–1945," *Modern China*, **29**: 3–37.
Liulevicius, Vejas 2000 *War Land on the Eastern Front*. Cambridge: Cambridge University Press.
Lockwood, William 1954 *Economic Development of Japan*. Princeton, NJ: Princeton University Press.
Logevall, Frederik 1999 *Choosing War: The Lost Chance for Peace and the Escalation of War in Vietnam*. Berkeley: University of California Press.
Lone, Stewart 2000 *Army, Empire and Politics in Meiji Japan. The Three Careers of General Katsura Tar*. New York: St. Martin's Press.
Long, Ngo Vinh 1998 "South Vietnam" in P. Lowe (ed.), *The Korean War*. Basingstoke: Macmillan.
López-Calva, Luis & Nora Lustig (eds.) 2010 *Declining Inequality in Latin America A Decade of Progress?* Washington: Brookings Institution Press and United Nations Development Programme.

López de Silanes, Florencio & Alberto Chong 2004 "Privatization in Latin America: What Does the Evidence Say?" *Economia*, **4**: 37–111.

Lotveit, Trygve 1979 *Chinese Communism 1931–1934. Experience in Civil Government*. London: Curzon.

Lowe, Peter 2000 *The Korean War*. Basingstoke: Macmillan.

Lowenthal, Abraham 1995 *The Dominican Intervention*. Baltimore, MD: Johns Hopkins University Press.

Lower, Wendy 2005 *Nazi Empire-Building and the Holocaust in Ukraine*. Chapel Hill, NC: University of North Carolina Press.

Luebbert, Gregory 1991 "Social Foundations of Political Order in Interwar Europe," *World Politics*, **39**: 449–78.

Lundestad, Geir 1998 *"Empire" by Invitation: The United States and European Integration, 1945–1997*. New York: Oxford University Press.

Lupher, Mark 1996 *Power Restructuring in China and Russia*. Boulder, CO: Westview Press.

Lynd, Michael 1999 *Vietnam: The Necessary War: A Reinterpretation of America's Most Disastrous Military Conflict*. New York: The Free Press.

Lynn, John 1997 *Giant of the Grand Siècle: The French Army, 1610–1715*. Cambridge: Cambridge University Press.

Lynn, Martin 2001 "British Trade Policy and Informal Empire in the Mid-Nineteenth Century" in Andrew Porter (ed.), *The Oxford History of the British Empire, Vol. III: The Nineteenth Century*. Oxford: Oxford University Press.

Lyttleton, Adrian 1977 "Revolution and Counter-Revolution in Italy, 918–1922" in Charles L. Bertrand (ed.), *Revolutionary Situations in Europe, 1917–1922: Germany, Italy, Austria-Hungary*, pp. 63–81. Montréal: Centre interuniversitaire d'études europeénnes.

Ma, Debin 2006 "Shanghai-based industrialization in the early 20th century: a quantitative and institutional analysis," *Working Papers of the Global Economic History Network*, London School of Economics, No. 18/06.

Ma, Xiaoying & Leonard Ortolano 2000 *Environmental Regulation in China: Institutions, Enforcement, and Compliance*. Lanham, MD: Rowman & Littlefield.

MacFarquhar, Roderick 1983 *The Origins of the Cultural Revolution. Vol II: The Great Leap, 1958–60*. New York: Columbia University Press.

Mackay, Robert 2002 *Half the Battle. Civilian Morale in Britain during the Second World War*. Manchester: Manchester University Press.

Maddison, Angus 1982 *Phases of Capitalist Development*. Oxford: Oxford University Press.

1998 *Chinese Economic Performance in the Long Run*. Paris: OECD Development Centre.

2001 *The World Economy: A Millennial Perspective*. Paris: OECD.

2007 *Contours of the World Economy, 1–2030 AD*. Oxford: Oxford University Press.

Mäher, Neu 2008 *Nature's New Deal: The Civilian Conservation Corps and the Roots of the American Environmental Movement*. New York: Oxford University Press.

Mahler, Vincent & David Jesuit 2006 "Fiscal redistribution in the developed countries: new insights from the Luxembourg Income Study," *Socio-Economic Review*, **4**: 483–511.

Mahoney, James 2001 *The Legacies of Liberalism: Path Dependence and Political Regimes in Central America*. Baltimore: Johns Hopkins University Press.

Maier, Charles 1987 "The two postwar eras and the conditions for stability in twentieth-century Western Europe" in his *In Search of Stability*. Cambridge: Cambridge University Press.

Malesevic, Sinisa 2010 *The Sociology of War and Violence*. Cambridge: Cambridge University Press.

Mamdani, Mahmood 1996 *Citizen and Subject: Contemporary Africa and the Legacy of Late Colonialism.* Princeton: Princeton University Press.

Mandel, David 1983 *The Petrograd Workers and the Fall of the Old Regime: From the February Revolution to the July Days, 1917.* London: MacMillan.

Mann, Michael 1993 *The Sources of Social Power*, Vols. I & II. Cambridge: Cambridge University Press.

1988 "The autonomous power of the state: Its origins, mechanisms and results" in M. Mann (ed.), *States, War and Capitalism*. Oxford: Basil Blackwell.

1996 "The contradictions of continuous revolution" in Ian Kershaw & Moshe Lewin (eds.), *Stalinism and Nazism: Dictatorships in Comparison*, pp. 135–157. Cambridge: Cambridge University Press.

2004 *Fascists*. Cambridge: Cambridge University Press.

2005 The Dark Side of Democracy: Explaining Ethnic Cleansing. New York: Cambridge University Press.

2006 "The sources of social power revisited: a response to criticism" in John Hall & Ralph Schroeder (eds.), *An Anatomy of Power. The Social Theory of Michael Mann*, pp. 343–396. Cambridge: Cambridge University Press.

2008 "Infrastructural power revisited," *Studies in Comparative International Development*, **43**: 355–65.

Manning, Jonathan 1997 "Wages and purchasing power" in Winter & Robert, (eds.), *Capital Cities at War, 1914–1919*, pp. 255–285. Cambridge: Cambridge University Press.

Manza, Jeff 2000 "Political sociological models of the U.S. New Deal," *Annual Review of Sociology*, **26**: 297–322.

Mares, David 2001 *Violent Peace: Militarized Interstate Bargaining in Latin America*. New York: Columbia University Press.

Marshall, Peter 2001 "Introduction," in P.J. Marshall (ed.),*The Oxford History of the British Empire, Vol. II: The Eighteenth Century*. Oxford: Oxford University Press.

Marshall, T. H. 1963 "Citizenship and social class" in his *Sociology at the Crossroads*. London: Heinemann.

Martin, Benjamin 1999 *France and the Après Guerre 1918–1924: Illusions and Disillusionment*. Baton Rouge: Louisiana State University Press.

Martin, Terry 2001 *The Affirmative Action Empire. Nations and Nationalism in the Soviet Union, 1923–1939*. Ithaca, NY: Cornell University Press.

Marwick, Arthur 1991 *The Deluge: British Society and the First World War*. London: Macmillan.

Marx, Karl 1959 *Capital*, Vol. III. New York: International Publishers.

Marx, Sally 2002 *The Ebbing of European Ascendency: An International History of the World, 1914–1945*. Oxford: Oxford University Press.

Matsusaka, Yoshihisa 2001 *The Making of Japanese Manchuria, 1904–1932*. Cambridge, MA: Harvard University Press.

Maurin, Jules 1982 *Armée – Guerre – Societé: Soldats Languedociens, 1899–1919*. Paris: Sorbonne.

Mawdsley, Evan 1978 *The Russian Revolution and the Baltic Fleet: War and Politics, February 1917–April 1918*. London: Macmillan.

2005 *Thunder in the East: The Nazi-Soviet War, 1941–1945*. London: Hodder Arnold.

May, Ernest 2000 *Strange Victory: Hitler's Conquest of France*. New York: Hill and Wang.

Mayer, Joseph 1977 "Internal Crisis and War since 1870" in Charles L. Bertrand (ed.), *Revolutionary Situations in Europe, 1917–22*. Montreal: Concordia University Press.

McAuley, Mary 1991 *Bread and Justice: State and Society in Petrograd, 1917–1922*. Oxford: Clarendon Press.

McBeth, Brian 2001 *Gunboats, Corruption, and Claims: Foreign Intervention in Venezuela, 1899–1908*. Westport, Connecticut, and London: Greenwood Press.

McCammon, Holly 1993 "From Repressive Intervention to Integrative Prevention: The U.S. State's Legal Management of Labor Militancy, 1881–1978," *Social Forces*,**71**: 569–601.

McCrillis, Neal 1998 *The British Conservative Party in the Age of Universal Suffrage: Popular Conservatism, 1918–1929*. Columbus, OH: Ohio State University.

McKean, Robert 1990 *St. Petersburg Between the Revolutions: Workers and Revolutionaries, June 1907–February 1917*. New Haven, CT: Yale University Press.

McKercher, Brian 1999 *Transition of Power: Britain's Loss of Global Pre-eminence to the United States, 1930–1945*. Cambridge: Cambridge University Press.

McKibbin, Ross 1984 "Why was there no Marxism in Great Britain?" *English Historical Review*, **49**: 297–331.

1998 *Classes and Cultures: England 1918–51*. Oxford: Oxford University Press.

McLean, David 1995 *War, Diplomacy and Informal Empire: Britain, France and Latin America, 1836–1852*. London: Tauris.

McLean, Iain 1983 *The Legend of Red Clydeside*. Edinburgh: John Donald Publishers.

McMillan, James 2004 "The Great War and Gender Relations the Case of French Women and the First World War Revisited" in Gail Braybon (ed.), *Evidence, History and the Great War: Historians and the Impact of 1914–1918*, pp. 135–153. Oxford: Berghahn Books.

Mead, Walter Russell 2001 *Special Providence: American Foreign Policy and How It Changed the World*. New York: Century Foundation/Knopf.

Meaker, Gerald 1974 *The Revolutionary Left in Spain 1914–1923*. Stanford: Stanford University Press.

Megargee, Geoffrey 2006 *War of Annihilation: Combat and Genocide on the Eastern Front, 1941*. Lanham: Rowan & Littlefield.

Melancon, Michael 1997 "The Left Socialist Revolutionaries and the Bolshevik Uprising" in Vladimir Brovkin (ed.), *The Bolsheviks in Russian Society: The Revolution and the Civil Wars*. New Haven: Yale University Press.

Merkl, Peter 1980 *The Making of a Stormtrooper*. Princeton, NJ: Princeton University Press.

Mettler, Suzanne 1999 *Dividing Citizens: Gender and Federalism in New Deal Public Policy*. Ithaca, NY: Cornell University Press.

Metzler, Mark 2006 *Lever of Empire: The International Gold Standard and the Crisis of Liberalism in Prewar Japan*. Berkeley & Los Angeles: University of California Press.

Meyer, John et al. 1997 "World society and the nation-state," *American Journal of Sociology*, **103**: 144–81.

Middlebrook, Martin 1972 *The First Day on the Somme, 1 July 1916*. New York: Norton.

Middlemas, Keith 1979 *Politics in Industrial Society, The Experience of the British System Since 1911*. London, Andre Deutsch.

Migdal, Joel 1974 *Peasants Politics, and Revolution*. Princeton, NJ: Princeton University Press.
Milanovic, Branko, Peter Lindert, & Jeffrey Williamson 2011 "Measuring Ancient Inequality," *National Bureau of Economic Research*, Working Paper No. 13550.
Miller, Edward 2007 *Bankrupting the Enemy: The US Financial Siege of Japan Before Pearl Harbor*. Annapolis, MD: Naval Institute Press.
Minami, Ryoshin 1994 *The Economic Development of Japan: A Quantitative Study*. Basingstoke, Hants: Macmillan.
Mink, Gwendolyn 1995 *The Wages of Motherhood: Inequality in the Welfare State, 1917–1942*. Ithaca, NY: Cornell University Press.
Misra, Maria 2003 "Lessons of Empire: Britain and India," *SAIS Review*, **23**: 133–53.
Mitchener, Kris & Marc Weidenmier 2008 "Trade and Empire," *Economic Journal*, **118**: 1805–34.
Mitter, Rana 2000 *The Manchurian Myth: Nationalism, Resistance, and Collaboration in Modern China*. Berkeley & Los Angeles: University of California Press.
Moeller, Robert 1986 *German Peasants and Agrarian Politics, 1914–1924: The Rhineland and Westphalia*. Chapel Hill: University of North Carolina Press.
Mommsen, Hans 1996 *The Rise and Fall of Weimar Democracy*. Chapel Hill, NC: University of North Carolina Press.
Moore, Barrington 1967 *Origins of Dictatorship and Democracy*. Boston: Beacon Press.
1978 *Injustice: The Social Bases of Obedience and Revolt*. White Plains, NY: M. E. Sharpe.
Moore, Robin 2001 "Imperial India, 1858–1914" in *The Oxford History of the British Empire, Vol. III: The Nineteenth Century*. Oxford: Oxford University Press.
Morgan, David 1975 *The Socialist Left and the German Revolution: A History of the German Independent Social Democratic Party, 1917–1922*. Ithaca, NY: Cornell University Press.
Morgan, Stephen & Shiyung Liu 2007 "Was Japanese Colonialism Good for the Welfare of Taiwanese? Stature and the Standard of Living," *China Quarterly*, **192**: 990–1013.
Mosk, Carl 2001 *Japanese Industrial History: Urbanization, and Economic Growth*. London: M. E. Sharpe.
Moulton, Harold 1935 *The Formation of Capital*. Washington, DC: The Brookings Institution.
Moure, Kenneth 2002 *The Gold Standard Illusion: France, the Bank of France, and the International Gold Standard, 1914–1939*. New York: Oxford University Press.
Mouton, Michelle 2007 *From Nurturing the Nation to Purifying the Volk: Weimar and Nazi Family Policy, 1918–1945*. Cambridge: Cambridge University Press.
Mueller, Rolf-Dieter 2003 "Speer and Armaments Policy in Total war" in Kroener et al. (eds.), *Organization and Mobilization of the German Sphere of Power, Part 2: Wartime Administration, Economy and Manpower Resources, 1942–144/45*, pp. 293–892 (sic). Oxford: Clarendon Press.
Murphy, David 2006 *What Stalin Knew: The Enigma of Barbarossa*. New Haven: Yale University Press.
Murphy, Kevin 2005 *Revolution and Counterrevolution: Class Struggle in a Moscow Metal Factory*. Oxford: Berghahn Books.
Myers, Ramon 1989 "The world depression and the Chinese economy 1930–1936" in Ian Brown (ed.), *The Economies of Africa and Asia in the Inter-war Depression*. London: Routledge.

Nakamura, Takafusa 1988 "Depression, recovery, and war, 1920–1945" in Duus (ed.), *The Cambridge History of Japan, Vol 6: The Twentieth Century*, pp. 171–188. Cambridge: Cambridge University Press.

Nakamura, Yoshihisa & Ryoichi Tobe 1988 "The Imperial Japanese Army and Politics," *Armed Forces and Society*, **14**: 511–25.

Naoroji, Dadabhai 1887 *Essays, Speeches, Addresses and Writings*. Bombay: Caxton Printing Works.

Neiberg, Michael 2005 *Fighting the Great War: A Global History*. Cambridge, MA: Harvard University Press.

Nelson, Bruce 2003 *Divided We Stand: American Workers and the Struggle for Black Equity*. Princeton, NJ: Princeton University Press.

Nelson, Daniel 1969 *Unemployment Insurance: The American Experience, 1915–1935*. Madison: University of Wisconsin Press.

2001 "The Other New Deal and Labor: The Regulatory State and the Unions, 1933–1940," *Journal of Policy History*, **13**: 367–90.

Ninkovich, Frank 1999 *The Wilsonian Century: U.S Foreign Policy since 1900*. Chicago: University of Chicago Press.

2001 *The United States and Imperialism*. New York: John Wiley.

Nish, Ian (ed.) 1998 *The Iwakura Mission in America and Europe: A New Assessment*. Richmond, Surrey: Curzon Press.

2002 *Japanese Foreign Policy in the Interwar Period*. Westport, CT: Praeger.

Nolan, Michael 2005 *The Inverted Mirror: Mythologizing the Enemy in France and Germany.* New York: Berghahn Books.

Novak, William J. 2008 "The Myth of the 'Weak' American State," *American Historical Review*, **113**: 752–72.

Novkov, Julie 2001 *Constituting Workers, Protecting Women: Gender, Law and Labor in the Progressive Era and New Deal Years*. Ann Arbor: University of Michigan Press.

Nye, Joseph 2004 *Soft Power: The Means to Success in World Politics*. New York: PublicAffairs.

O'Brien, Patrick 2004 "Colonies in a Globalizing Economy 1815–1948," LSE Department of Economic History, *Working Papers of the Global Economic History Network*, No. 08/04.

O'Brien, Patrick & Leandro Prados de la Escosura (eds.) 1998 "The Costs and Benefits for Europeans from their Empires Overseas," special issue of *Revista de Historia Economica*, i: 29–92.

O'Brien, Ruth 1998 *Workers' Paradox: The Republican Origins of New Deal Labor Policy, 1886–1935*. Chapel Hill, NC: University of North Carolina Press.

O'Connor, Alice 2001 *Poverty Knowledge: Social Science, Social Policy and the Poor in Twentieth-Century U.S. History*. Princeton, NJ: Princeton University Press.

O'Rourke, Kevin & Jeffrey G. Williamson 2002 "After Columbus: Explaining Europe's Overseas Trade Boom, 1500–1800," *Journal of Economic History*, **62**: 417–56.

Obstfeld, Maurice & Alan Taylor 2004 *Global Capital Markets: Integration, Crisis and Growth*. New York: Cambridge University Press.

Odaka, Konosuke 1999 "'Japanese-Style' Labour Relations" in Tetsuji Okazaki & Masahiro Okuno-Fujiwara (eds.), *The Japanese Economic System and its Historical Origins*. Oxford: Oxford University Press.

Offe, Claus & V. Ronge 1974 "Theses on the theory of the state" in Anthony Giddens & David Held (eds.), *Classes, Power and Conflict*. Berkeley & Los Angeles: University of California Press.

Offer, Avner 1989 *The First World War: An Agrarian Interpretation*. Oxford: Clarendon Press.
1995 "Going to War in 1914: A Matter of Honor?" *Politics & Society*, **23**: 213–41.
Offner, John 1992 *An Unwanted War: The Diplomacy of the United States and Spain over Cuba, 1895–1898*. Chapel Hill, NC: University of North Carolina Press.
Ohlmeyer, Jane 2001 "Civilizinge of Those Rude Partes: Colonisation within Britain and Ireland, 1580–1640" in *The Oxford History of the British Empire, Vol. I: The Origins of Empire*. Oxford: Oxford University Press.
Olds, Kelly 2003 "The Biological Standard of Living in Taiwan under Japanese Occupation," *Economics and Human Biology*, **1**: 187–206.
Olson, James 1988 *Saving Capitalism: The Reconstruction Finance Corporation and the New Deal, 1933–1940*. Princeton, NJ: Princeton University Press.
Orren, Karen 1993 *Belated Feudalism: Labor, the Law, and Liberal Development in the United States*. New York: Cambridge University Press.
Overy, Richard 1999 *The Road to War*. London: MacMillan.
Paige, Jeffrey 1997 *Coffee and Power: Revolution and the Rise of Democracy in Central America*. Cambridge, MA: Harvard University Press.
Pakenham, Thomas 1991 *The Scramble for Africa*. New York: Random House.
Pamuk, Sevket 2005 "The Ottoman economy in World War I" in Broadberry & Harrison (eds.), *The Economics of World War I*, pp. 112–136. Cambridge: Cambridge University Press.
Park, James 1995 *Latin American Underdevelopment: A History of Perspectives in the United States, 1870–1965*. Baton Rouge: Louisiana State University Press.
Parker, Robert 1993 *Chamberlain and Appeasement: British Policy and the Coming of the Second World War*. London, Macmillian.
Parthasarathi, Prasannan 2001 *The Transition to a Colonial Economy: Weavers, Merchants and Kings in South India, 1720–1800*. Cambridge: Cambridge University Press.
Patterson, James 1967 *Congressional Conservatism and the New Deal*. Lexington: University of Kentucky Press.
Paulson, David 1989 "Nationalist guerillas in the Sino-Japanese War: the 'die-hards' of Shandong Province" in Hartford & Goldstein (eds.), *Single Sparks: China's Rural Revolutions*, pp. 128–150. Armonk, NY: M. E. Sharpe.
Paxton, Robert 2004 *The Anatomy of Fascism*. London: Penguin.
Peattie, Mark 1975 *Ishiwara Kanji and Japan's Confrontation with the West*. Princeton, NJ: Princeton University Press.
1988 "The Japanese colonial empire, 1895–1945" in Duus (ed.), *The Cambridge History of Japan, Vol 6: The Twentieth Century*, pp. 217–270. Cambridge: Cambridge University Press.
1996 "Nanshin: the Southward Advance, 1931–1941" in Duus (ed.), *The Cambridge History of Japan, Vol 6: The Twentieth Century*, pp. 189–242. Cambridge: Cambridge University Press.
Pedersen, Susan 1993 *Family, Dependence and the Origins of the Welfare State: Britain and France, 1914–1945*. Cambridge: Cambridge University Press.
Pedroncini, Guy 1967 *Les mutineries de 1917*. Paris: Presses Universitaires de France.
Pepper, Suzanne 1999 *Civil War in China. The Political Struggle, 1945–1949*. Berkeley & Los Angeles: University of California Press.
Perez, Louis Jr. 1983 *Cuba Between Empires, 1878–1902*. Pittsburgh: Pittsburgh University Press.
1990 *Cuba and the United States: Ties of Singular Intimacy*. Athens, GA: University of Georgia Press.

1998 *The War of 1898: The United States and Cuba in History and Historiography*. Chapel Hill, NC: University of North Carolina Press.

Perkins, Dwight 1975 "Growth and changing structure of China's twentieth-century economy" in D. Perkins (ed.), *China's Modern Economy in Historical Perspective*. Stanford, CA: Stanford University Press.

Perkins, Frances 1946 *The Roosevelt I Knew*. New York: Harper.

Perry, Elizabeth 1980 *Rebels and Revolutionaries in North China, 1845–1945*. Stanford, CA: Stanford University Press.

1984 "Collective violence in China, 1880–1980," *Theory and Society*, **13**: 427–54.

1993 *Shanghai on Strike: The Politics of Chinese Labor*. Stanford, CA: Stanford University Press.

Piketty, Thomas & Emmanuel Saez 2003 "Income Inequality in the United States, 1913–1998," *Quarterly Journal of Economics*, **118**: 1–39.

Pipes, Richard 1990 *The Russian Revolution*. New York: Knopf.

Pirani, Simon 2008 *The Russian Revolution in Retreat, 1920–24: Soviet Workers and the New Communist Elite*. New York: Routledge.

Pletcher, David 1998 *Diplomacy of Trade and Investment: American Economic Expansion in the Hemisphere, 1865–1900*. Columbia: University of Missouri Press.

Plotke, David 1996 *Building a Democratic Political Order: Reshaping American Liberalism in the 1930s and 1940s*. New York: Cambridge University Press.

Polanyi, Karl 1957 *The Great Transformation: The Political and Economic Origins of Our Time*. Boston: Beacon Press.

Pomeroy, William 1974 "The Philippines: a Case History of Neocolonialism" in Mark Selden (ed.), *Remaking Asia. Essays on the Use of American Power*. New York: Pantheon.

Porter, Andrew 2001 "Introduction," in Andrew Porter (ed.), *The Oxford History of the British Empire, Vol. III: The Nineteenth Century*. Oxford: Oxford University Press.

Porter, Bernard 2004 *The Lion's Share. A Short History of British Imperialism, 1850–2004*. Harlow: Longman.

2005 *The Absent-Minded Imperialists: What the British Really Thought About Empire*. Oxford: Oxford University Press.

2006 *Empire and Superempire: Britain, America and the World*. New Haven, CT: Yale University Press.

Post, Gaines Jr. 1993 *Dilemmas of Appeasement: British Deterrence and Defense, 1934–1937*. Ithaca, NY: Cornell University Press.

Poulantzas, Nikos 1974 *Fascisme et dictature*. Paris: Seuil/Maspero.

Pratt, Edward 1999 *Japan's Proto-Industrial Elite: The Economic Foundations of the Gono*. Cambridge, MA: Harvard University Asia Center.

Procida, Mary 2002 *Married to the Empire: Gender, Politics and Imperialism in India, 1883–1947*. Manchester: Manchester University Press.

Prost, Antoine 1964 *La C.G.T., 1914–1939*. Paris: Colin.

Quadagno, Jill 1984 "Welfare capitalism and the Social Security Act of 1935," *American Sociological Review*, **49**: 632–47.

1994 *The Color of Welfare*. New York: Oxford University Press.

Rabinbach, Anson 1985 *The Austrian Socialist Experiment: Social Democracy and Austromarxism, 1918–1934*. Boulder, CO: Westview Press.

Rabinowitch, Alexander 2004 *The Bolsheviks Come to Power*. Chicago: Haymarket Books.

Raleigh, Donald 2003 *Experiencing Russia's Civil War: Politics, Society and Revolutionary Culture in Saratov 1917–1922*. Princeton, NJ: Princeton University Press.

Rappoport, Peter & Eugene White 1993 "Was There a Bubble in the 1929 Stock Market?" *The Journal of Economic History*, **53**: 549–74.
1994 "Was the Crash of 1929 Expected?" *American Economic Review*, **84**: 271–81.
Rawski, Thomas 1989 *Economic Growth in Prewar China*. Berkeley & Los Angeles: University of California Press.
Ray, Rajat Kanta 2001 "Indian Society and the Establishment of British Supremacy, 1765–1818" in P.J. Marshall (ed.), *The Oxford History of the British Empire, Vol. II: The Eighteenth Century*. Oxford: Oxford University Press.
2003 *The Felt Community: Commonality and Mentality before the Emergence of Indian Nationalism*. New York: Oxford University Press.
du Réau, Elisabeth 1993 *Edouard Daladier, 1884–1970*. Paris: Fayard.
Reid, Richard 2007 *War in Pre-Colonial Eastern Africa*. London & Nairobi: The British Institute.
Renton, David 2000 *Fascism: Theory and Practice*. London: Pluto.
Reynolds, Lloyd 1985 *Economic Growth in the Third World*. New Haven, CT: Yale University Press.
Richardson, David 2001 "The British Empire and the Atlantic Slave Trade 1660–1807" in P.J. Marshall (ed.), *The Oxford History of the British Empire, Vol. II: The Eighteenth Century*. Oxford: Oxford University Press.
Richardson, Philip 1999 *Economic Change in China, c. 1800–1950*. Cambridge: Cambridge University Press.
Riddell, Neil 1999 *Labour in Crisis: The Second Labour Government, 1929–1931*. Manchester: Manchester University Press.
Riga, Liliana 2009 "The ethnic roots of class universalism: rethinking the 'Russian' revolutionary elite," *American Journal of Sociology*, **115**: 649–705.
Riley, Dylan 2005 "Civic Associations and Authoritarian Regimes in Interwar Europe: Italy and Spain in Comparative Perspective," *American Sociological Review*, **70**: 288–310.
2010 *The Civic Foundations Of Fascism In Europe: Italy, Spain, And Romania, 1870–1945*. Baltimore: Johns Hopkins University Press.
Ritschl, Albrecht 2005 "The pity of peace: Germany's economy at war, 1914–1918 and beyond" in Broadberry & Harrison (eds.), *The Economics of World War I*, pp. 41–76. Cambridge: Cambridge University Press.
Robertson, David 2000 *Capital, Labor, and State: The Battle for American Labor Markets from the Civil War to the New Deal*. Lanham, MD: Rowman & Littlefield.
Robinson, David 2000 *Paths of Accommodation: Muslim Societies and French Colonial Authorities in Senegal and Mauritania, 1880–1920*. Athens: Ohio University Press.
Robinson, Robert 1984 "Imperial Theory and the Question of Imperialism after Empire" in Robert F. Holland & Gowher Rizvi (eds.), *Perspectives on Imperialism and Decolonization*. London: Frank Cass.
Roces, Mina 2002 "Women in Philippine Politics and Society" in Mcferson (ed.), *Mixed Blessing: The Impact of the American Colonial Experience on Politics and Society in the Philippines*, pp. 159–189. Westport, CT: Greenwood Press.
Rockoff, Hugh 1998 "The United States: from ploughshares to swords" in Mark Harrison (ed.), *The Economics of World War II: Six Great Powers in International Comparison*, pp. 310–343. Cambridge: Cambridge University Press.
2005 "Until it's over, over there: the US economy in World War I" in Broadberry & Harrison (eds.), *The Economics of World War I*, pp. 310–343. Cambridge: Cambridge University Press.

Rodgers, Daniel 1998 *Atlantic Crossings: Social Politics in a Progressive Age*. Cambridge, MA: Harvard University Press.

Romer, Christina 1990 "The great crash and the onset of the Great Depression," *Quarterly Journal of Economics*, **105**: 597–624.

1992 "What Ended the Great Depression?" *Journal of Economic History*, **52**: 757–84.

1993 "The nation in depression," *Journal of Economic Perspectives*, **7**: 19–39.

Roorda, Eric 1998 *The Dictator Next Door: The Good Neighbor Policy and the Trujillo Regime in the Dominican Republic, 1930–1945*. Durham, NC: Duke University Press.

Rosen, Nir 2010 *Aftermath*. New York: Perseus.

Rosenberg, Emily 1982 *Spreading the American Dream: American Economic and Cultural Expansion 1890–1945*. London: Macmillan.

1999 *Financial Missionaries to the World: The Politics and Culture of Dollar Diplomacy, 1900–1930*. Cambridge, MA: Harvard University Press.

Rossino, Alexander 2003 *Hitler Strikes Poland: Blitzkrieg, Ideology and Atrocity*. Lawrence: University Press of Kansas.

Rossman, Jeffrey 2005 *Worker Resistance under Stalin: Class and Revolution on the Shop Floor*. Cambridge, MA: Harvard University Press.

Rothenberg, Gunther 1977 "The Habsburg Army in the First World War: 1914–1918" in Robert Kann et al. (eds.), *The Habsburg Empire in World War I*, pp. 73–86. Boulder, CO: East European Quarterly.

Rothermund, Dietmar 1996 *The Global Impact of the Great Depression*. London: Routledge.

Routh, Guy 1980 *Occupation and Pay in Great Britain 1906–1979*. Basingstoke, Hants: Macmillan.

Roy, Tirthankar 1999 *Traditional Industry in the Economy of Colonial India*. Cambridge: Cambridge University Press.

2000 *The Economic History of India 1857–1947*. Delhi: Oxford University Press.

Roy, William 1997 *Socializing Capital: The Rise of the Large Industrial Corporation in America*. Princeton, NJ: Princeton University Press.

Roy, William & Rachel Parker-Gwin 1999 "How Many Logics of Collective Action?" *Theory and Society*, **28**: 203–37.

Rutherford, Malcolm 2006 "Wisconsin Institutionalism: John R. Commons and His Students," *Labor History*, **47**: 161–88.

Ryder, A. J. 1967 *The German Revolution of 1918: A Study of German Socialism in War and Revolt*. Cambridge: Cambridge University Press.

Salvatorelli, Luigi 1923 *Nazional-fascismo*. Turin: Gobetti.

Samuelson, Lennart 2000 *Plans for Stalin's War Machine: Tukhachevskii and Military-Economic Planning, 1925–1941*. Basingstoke, Hants: Macmillan.

Sanders, Elizabeth 1999 *Roots of Reform: Farmers, Workers and the American State, 1877–1917*. Chicago: University of Chicago Press.

Sarti, Roland 1971 *Fascism and the Industrial Leadership in Italy, 1919–1940: A Study in the Expansion of Private Power under Fascism*. Berkeley & Los Angeles: University of California Press.

Sato, Shigeru 1994 *War, Nationalism and Peasants*. London: M. E. Sharpe.

Saul, Norman E. 1978 *Sailors in Revolt: The Russian Baltic fleet in 1917*. Lawrence: Regents Press of Kansas.

Saul, S. B. 1960 *Studies in British Overseas Trade, 1870–1914*. Liverpool: Liverpool University Press.

Schlabach, Theron 1969 *Edwin Witte: Cautious Reformer*. Madison, WI: State Historical Society of Wisconsin.

Schlesinger, Arthur Jr. 1960 *The Age of Roosevelt: The Politics of Upheaval*. Vol. III. Boston: Houghton Mifflin.
Schmidt, Hans 1998 *Maverick Marine: General Smedley D. Butler and the Contradictions of American Military History*. Lexington: University Press of Kentucky.
Schmitt, Hans 1988 *Neutral Europe between War and Revolution, 1917–23*. Charlottesville: University Press of Virginia.
Schmitter, Philippe 1974 "Still the Century of Corporatism?" *Review of Politics*, **36**: 85–131.
Schoonover, Thomas 1991 *The United States in Central America, 1860–1911*. Durham, NC: Duke University Press.
2003 *Uncle Sam's War of 1898 and the Origins of Globalization*. Lexington: University Press of Kentucky.
Schoultz, Lars 1998 *Beneath the United States: A History of U.S. Policy Toward Latin America*. Cambridge, MA: Harvard University Press.
Schroeder, Ralph 2007 *Rethinking Science, Technology and Social Change*. Stanford: Stanford University Press.
2011 *An Age of Limits: Social Theory for the 21st Century*, unpublished ms.
Schultze, Max-Stephan 2005 "Austria-Hungary's economy in World War I" in Broadberry & Harrison (eds.), *The Economics of World War I*, pp. 77–111. Cambridge: Cambridge University Press.
Schumpeter, Joseph 1957 *Capitalism, Socialism and Democracy*. New York: Harper.
1961 *The Theory of Economic Development*, New York: Oxford University Press.
1982 *Business Cycles*, 2 vols. Philadelphia: Porcupine Press.
Schwartz, Stuart (ed.) 2004 *Tropical Babylons: Sugar and the Making of the Atlantic World, 1450–1680*. Chapel Hill: University of North Carolina Press.
Schwarz, Jordan 1993 *The New Dealers*. New York: Knopf.
Selden, Mark 1971 *The Yenan Way in Revolutionary China*. Cambridge, MA: Harvard University Press.
1995 "Yan'an communism reconsidered," *Modern China*, **21**: 8–44.
Sen, Sudipta 2002 *Distant Sovereignty: National Imperialism and the Origins of British India*. New York: Routledge.
Service, Robert 1997 *A History of Twentieth-Century Russia*. London: Allen Lane, Penguin.
Shanin, Theodor (ed.) 1971 *Peasants and Peasant Societies*. Harmondsworth, Middlesex: Penguin.
Sharkey, Heather 2003 *Living with Colonialism: Nationalism and Culture in the Anglo-Egyptian Sudan*. Berkeley & Los Angeles: University of California Press.
Shearer, David 1996 *Industry, State, and Society in Stalin's Russia, 1926–1934*. Ithaca, NY: Cornell University Press.
Shefter, Martin 1994 *Political Parties and the State: The American Historical Experience*. Princeton, NJ: Princeton University Press.
Shils, Edward & Morris Janowitz 1948 "Cohesion and Disintegration in the Wehrmacht in World War II," *Public Opinion Quarterly*, **12**: 280–315.
Shimazu, Naoko 2009 *Japanese Society At War: Death, Memory and the Russo-Japanese War*. Cambridge: Cambridge University Press.
Shin, Gi-Wook et al. (eds.) 2006 *Rethinking Historical Injustice and Reconciliation in Northeast Asia: Korean Experience*. London: Routledge.
Shlaes, Amity 2008 *The Forgotten Man: A New History of the Great Depression*. New York: HarperCollins.
Shum, Kui-Kwong 1988 *The Chinese Communists' Road to Power: The Anti-Japanese National United Front, 1935–1945*. Oxford: Oxford University Press.

Siegelbaum, Lewis H. 1983 *The Politics of Industrial Mobilization in Russia, 1914–1917: A Study of the War-Industries Committees*. New York: St. Martin's Press.
Silbey, David 2005 *The British Working Class and Enthusiasm for War, 1914–1916.* London: Frank Cass.
Silver, Beverly 2003 *Forces of Labor: Workers' Movements and Globalization since 1870.* Cambridge: Cambridge University Press.
Simon, Matthew 1968 "The pattern of new British portfolio investment, 1865–1914" in A. R. Hall (ed.), *The Export of Capital from Britain 1870–1914*, pp. 15–44. London: Methuen.
Sinha, Mrinalini 1995 *Colonial Masculinity: The "Manly Englishman" and the "Effeminate Bengali" in the Late Nineteenth Century*. Manchester: Manchester University Press.
Sirianni, Carmen 1980 "Workers' Control in the Era of World War I: A Comparative Analysis of the European Experience," *Theory and Society*, **9**: 29–88.
Skidelsky, Robert 1983 *John Maynard Keynes: Hopes Betrayed*. London: Macmillan.
Sklar, Martin 1988 *The Corporate Reconstruction of American Capitalism, 1890–1916.* Cambridge: Cambridge University Press.
Skocpol, Theda 1979 *States and Social Revolutions*. Cambridge: Cambridge University Press.
1980 "Political Response to Capitalist Crisis: Neo-Marxist Theories of the State and the Case of the New Deal," *Politics & Society*, **10**: 155–202.
1992 *Protecting Soldiers and Mothers: The Political Origins of Social Policy in the United States*. Cambridge, MA: Harvard University Press.
Skocpol, Theda & Edward Amenta 1985 "Did Capitalists Shape Social Security?" *American Sociological Review*, **50**: 572–75.
Skocpol, Theda & John Ikenberry 1983 "The Political Formation of the American Welfare State in Historical and Comparative Perspective," *Comparative Social Research*, **6**: 84–147.
Smil, Vaclav 2005 *Creating the Twentieth Century: Technical Innovations of 1867–1914 and their Lasting Impact*. Oxford: Oxford University Press.
Smiley, Gene 2000 "A Note on New Estimates of the Distribution of Income in the 1920s," *The Journal of Economic History*, **60**: 1120–8.
2002 *Rethinking the Great Depression*. Chicago: Ivan Dee.
Smith, Jason 2006 *Building New Deal Liberalism: The Political Economy of Public Works, 1933–1956.* New York: Cambridge University Press.
Smith, Jeffrey 2007 *A People's War: Germany's Political Revolution, 1913–1918.* Lanham, MD: University Press of America.
Smith, Jeremy 1999 *The Bolsheviks and the National Question, 1917–23.* New York: St. Martin's.
Smith, Robert 1989 *Warfare and Diplomacy in Pre-Colonial West Africa*. London: James Currey.
Smith, Steve 1983 *Red Petrograd: Revolution in the Factories, 1917–18.* Cambridge: Cambridge University Press.
Smith, Thomas 1988 *Native Sources of Japanese Industrialization, 1750–1920.* Berkeley & Los Angeles: University of California Press.
Smith, Timothy 2003 *Creating the Welfare State in France, 1880–1940.* Montreal and Kingston: McGill-Queen's University Press.
Snyder, Jack 1991 *Myths of Empire*. Ithaca, NY: Cornell University Press.
Snyder, Timothy 2010 *Bloodlands: Europe between Hitler and Stalin*. New York: Basic Books.
Sombart, Werner 1976 *Why is There No Socialism in America?* New York: Sharpe.

Soucy, Robert 1992 *Le Fascisme français, 1924–1933*. Paris : Presses Universitaires de France.
St. Antoine, Theodore 1998 "How the Wagner Act came to be. A prospectus," *Michigan Law Review*, **96**: 2201–21.
Stacey, Judith 1983 *Patriarchy and Socialist Revolution in China*. Berkeley & Los Angeles: University of California Press.
Steckel, Richard 2002 "A History of the Standard of Living in the United States," *EH. Net Encyclopedia*, http://eh.net/encyclopedia/article/steckel.standard.living.us
Steinberg, Mark 2001 *Voices of Revolution, 1917*. New Haven, CT: Yale University Press.
Steindl, Frank 2005 "Economic Recovery in the Great Depression," *EH.Net Encyclopedia*, http://eh.net/encyclopedia/article/Steindl
Steiner, Zara 2005 *The Lights That Failed: European International History, 1919–1933*. Oxford: Oxford University Press.
Stepan-Norris, Judy & Maurice Zeitlin 2003 *Left Out: Reds and America's Industrial Unions*. New York: Cambridge University Press.
Stephens, John 1980 *The Transition From Capitalism to Socialism*. London: Macmillan.
Stoler, Anne 2002 *Carnal Knowledge and Imperial Power: Race and the Intimate in Colonial Rule*. Berkeley & Los Angeles: University of California Press.
Stone, David 2000 *Hammer and Rifle: The Militarization of the Soviet Union, 1926–1933*. Lawrence, KS: University Press of Kansas.
Stone, Norman 1975 *The Eastern Front, 1914–1918*. New York: Scribner.
Stouffer, Samuel et al. 1949 *The American Soldier: Studies in Social Psychology in World War II. Vol II: Combat and Its Aftermath*. Princeton, NJ: Princeton University Press.
Strachan, Hew 2001 *The First World War: To Arms*. New York: Oxford University Press.
Strauss, Julia 1998 *Strong Institutions in Weak Polities: State Building in Republican China, 1927–1940*. Oxford: Clarendon Press.
Stryker, Robin 1989 "Limits on the Technocratization of the Law: The Elimination of the National Labor Relations Board's Division of Economic Research," *American Sociological Review*, **54**: 341–58.
Subrahmanyam, Gita 2004 "Schizophrenic governance and fostering global inequalities in the British Empire: the UK domestic state versus the Indian and African colonies, 1890–1960," unpublished paper.
Sugihara, Kaoru 2000 "The East Asian Path of Economic Development: A Long-term Perspective," Discussion Papers in Economics and Business, 00–17, Graduate School of Economics, Osaka University.
2004 "Japanese imperialism in global resource history," *LSE Working Papers of the Global Economic History Network*, No. 07/04.
Sullivan, Patricia 1996 *Days of Hope: Race and Democracy in the New Deal Era*. Chapel Hill, NC: University of North Carolina Press.
Sumner, William Graham 1899 "The Conquest of the United States by Spain," *Yale Law Journal*, January.
Summers, Lawrence 1986 "Some skeptical observations on real business cycle theory," *Federal Reserve Bank of Minnesota Quarterly Review*, No. 1043.
Suny, Ronald 1998 *The Soviet Experiment*. Oxford: Oxford University Press.
Swenson, Peter 2002 *Capitalists against Markets: The Making of Labor Markets and Welfare States in the United States and Sweden*. New York: Oxford University Press.

Szostak, Rick 1995 *Technological Innovation and the Great Depression*. Boulder, CO: Westview Press.

Taira, Koji 1988 "Economic development, labor markets, and industrial relations in Japan, 1905–1955" in Duus (ed.), *The Cambridge History of Japan, Vol 6: The Twentieth Century*, pp. 606–653. Cambridge: Cambridge University Press.

Tampke, Jürgen 1978 *The Ruhr and Revolution*. Canberra, ACT: Australian National University.

Tanaka, Yuki 1996 *Hidden Horrors: Japanese War Crimes in World War II*. Boulder, CO: Westview Press.

Tanzi, Vito 1969 *The Individual Income Tax and Economic Growth*. Baltimore: Johns Hopkins University Press.

Tanzi, Vito & Ludger Schuknecht 2000 *Public Spending in the 20th Century*. Cambridge: Cambridge University Press.

Tarling, Nicholas 2001 *A Sudden Rampage: The Japanese Occupation of Southeast Asia, 1941–1945*. Honolulu: University of Hawai'i Press.

Tauger, Mark 2001 *Natural Disaster and Human Action in the Soviet Famine of 1931–1933*. Pittsburgh: University of Pittsburgh, CREES, Carl Beck Papers.

Temin, Peter 1976 *Did Monetary Forces Cause the Great Depression?* New York: Norton.

1981 "Notes on the causes of the great depression" in Brunner (ed.), *The Great Depression Revisited*, pp. 108–124. Boston: Mattinus Nijhoff.

1989 *Lessons from the Great Depression*. Cambridge, MA: MIT Press.

1997 "Two Views of the British Industrial Revolution," *Journal of Economic History*, **57**: 63–82.

Thébaud, Françoise 2004 "La Guerre et après?" in Evelyne Morin-Rotureau (ed.), *1914–1918: combats de femmes*. Paris: Autrement.

Thomas Leonard *The Search for Order, 1877–1920*. New York: Hill & Wang.

Thurston, Robert 1996 *Life and Terror in Stalin's Russia, 1934–1941*. New Haven, CT: Yale University Press.

Tilly, Charles 1990 *Coercion, Capital, and European States, AD 900–1990*. Oxford: Blackwell.

1993 *European Revolutions 1492–1992*. Oxford: Blackwell.

Tokes, Rudolf 1967 *Bela Kun and the Hungarian Soviet Republic*. New York: Praeger.

Toland, John 1970 *The Rising Sun: The Decline and Fall of the Japanese Empire, 1936–1945*. New York: Random House.

Tomlins, Christopher 1985 *The State and the Unions: Labor Relations, Law, and the Organized Labor Movement in America, 1880–1960*. New York: Cambridge University Press.

Tomlinson, B. R. 1993 *The Economy of Modern India, 1860–1970*. Cambridge: Cambridge University Press.

1999 "Economics and empire: the periphery and the imperial economy" in Andrew Porter (ed.), *The Oxford History of the British Empire, Vol III: The Nineteenth Century*. Oxford: Oxford University Press.

Tooze, Adam 2006 *The Wages of Destruction: The Making and the Breaking of the Nazi Economy*. London: Allen Lane.

Topik Steven & Allen Wells 1998 *The Second Conquest of Latin America: Coffee, Henequen and Oil during the Export Boom, 1850–1930*. Austin: University of Texas Press.

Torpey, John 2000 *The Invention of the Passport: Surveillance, Citizenship and the State*. New York: Cambridge University Press.

Trotsky, Leon 1957 edition *History of the Russian Revolution*. Ann Arbor: University of Michigan Press.
Trubowitz, Peter 1998 *Defining the National Interest: Conflict and Change in American Foreign Policy*. Chicago, IL: University of Chicago Press.
Tsonuda, Jun 1994 "The final confrontation: Japan's negotiations with the United States, 1941" in James Morley (ed.), *Japan's Road to the Pacific War*, pp. 1–105. New York: Columbia University Press.
Tsutsui, William 1998 *Manufacturing Ideology*. Princeton, NJ: Princeton University Press.
Umbreit, Hans 2003 "German Rule in the Occupied Territories, 1942–1945" in Kroener et al. (eds.), *Organization and Mobilization of the German Sphere of Power, Part 2: Wartime Administration, Economy and Manpower Resources, 1942–144/45*, pp. 833–1070. Oxford: Clarendon Press.
Valocchi, Sreve 1990 "The Unemployed Workers Movement of the 1930s: A Reexamination of the Piven and Cloward Thesis," *Social Problems* **37**: 191–205.
van Creveld, Martin 1982 *Fighting Power: German and US Army performance, 1939–1945*. Westport, CT: Greenwood Press.
van de Ven, Hans 2003 *War and Nationalism in China, 1925–1945*. London: Routledge/Curzon.
Van Slyke, Lyman 1967 *Enemies and Friends, the United Front in Chinese Communist History*. Stanford, CA: Stanford University Press.
1986 "The Chinese communist movement during the Sino-Japanese war 1937–1945" in John Fairbank & Albert Feuerwerker (eds.), *The Cambridge History of China, Vol 13: Republican China 1912–1949*, Part 2. Cambridge: Cambridge University Press.
van Zanden et al. 2011 "The changing shape of global inequality 1820–2000: exploring a new data-set," *Universiteit Utrecht, CGEH Working Paper Series*, No. 1.
Vandervort, Bruce 1998 *Wars of Imperial Conquest in Africa, 1830–1914*. Bloomington, IN: Indiana University Press.
Veeser, Cyrus 2002 *A World Safe for Capitalism: Dollar Diplomacy and America's Rise to Global Power*. New York: Columbia University Press.
Vellacott, Jo 2007 *Pacifists, Patriots and the Vote: The Erosion of Democratic Suffragism in Britain During the First World War*. Basingstoke: Palgrave Macmillan.
Verhey, Jeffrey 2000 *The Spirit of 1914: Militarism, Myth, and Mobilization in Germany*. New York: Cambridge University Press.
Vermes, Gabor 1971, "The October Revolution in Hungary: From Károlyi to Kun" in Volgyes (ed.), *Hungary in Revolution, 1918–1919*, pp. 31–60. Lincoln: University of Nebraska Press.
Villacorte, Wilfriedo 2002 "The American influences on Philippine Political and Constitional Tradition" in Mcferson (ed.), *Mixed Blessing: The Impact of the American Colonial Experience on Politics and Society in the Philippines*, pp. 135–154. Westport, CT: Greenwood Press.
Viola, L. 1996 *Peasant Rebels Under Stalin*. New York: Oxford University Press.
Voss, Kim 1994 *The Making of American Exceptionalism: The Knights of Labor and Class Formation in the Nineteenth Century*. Ithaca: Cornell University Press.
Wade, Rex 1984 *Red Guards and Workers' Militias in the Russian Revolution*. Stanford, CA: Stanford University Press.
2000 *The Russian Revolution*. Cambridge: Cambridge University Press.
Walford, Cornelius 1878–1879 "The Famines of the World, Past and Present," Parts I and II, *Journal of the Statistical Society of London*, **41** & 42.

Walker, Samuel 1997 *Prompt and Utter Destruction: Truman and the Use of Atomic Bombs Against Japan*. Chapel Hill, NC: University of North Carolina Press.

Wallace, Michael et al. 1988 "American labor law: its impact on working-class militancy, 1901–1980," *Social Science History*, **12**: 1–29.

Waller, Derek 1972 *The Kiangsi Soviet Republic: Mao and the National Congresses of 1931 and 1934*. University of California Berkeley, Center for Chinese Studies: China Research Monographs.

Wallerstein, Immanuel 1974 *The Modern World-System*. New York: Cambridge University Press.

Wallis, John & Wallace Oates 1998 "The Impact of the New Deal on American Federalism" in Bordo et al. (eds.), *The Defining Moment: The Great Depression and the American Economy in the Twentieth Century*, pp. 155–180. Chicago: University of Chicago Press.

Ward, John Manning 1976 *Colonial Self-Government: The British Experience, 1759–1856*. London: Macmillan.

Washbrook, D. A. 2001 "India 1818–1860: The Two Faces of Colonialism" in Andrew Porter (ed.), *The Oxford History of the British Empire, Vol. III: The Nineteenth Century*. Oxford: Oxford University Press.

Webber, Michael 2000 *New Deal Fat Cats: Business, Labor, and Campaign Finance in the 1936 Presidential Election*. New York: Fordham University Press.

Weber, Eugene 1964 *Varieties of Fascism*. Princeton, NJ: Van Nostrand.

Weber, Max 1978 edition *Economy and Society*, 2 vols., ed., Gunther Roth & Claus Wittich. Berkeley & Los Angeles: University of California Press.

1995 edition *The Russian Revolutions*. Ithaca, NY: Cornell University Press.

2002 edition *The Protestant Ethic and "The Spirit of Capitalism."* Los Angeles: Roxbury Publishing Company.

Weed, Clyde 1994 *The Nemesis of Reform: The Republican Party During the New Deal*. New York: Columbia University Press.

Wei, William 1989 "Law and order: the role of Guominfang security forces in the suppression of the communist bases during the soviet period" in Hartford & Goldstein (eds.), *Single Sparks: China's Rural Revolutions*, pp. 34–61. Armonk, NY: M. E. Sharpe.

Weinstein, James 1968 *The Corporate Ideal in the Liberal State, 1900–1918*. Boston: Beacon Press.

Weitz, Eric 2009 *Weimar Germany: Promise and Tragedy*. Princeton, NJ: Princeton University Press.

Welch, Richard Jr. 1985 *Response to Revolution*. Chapel Hill: The University of North Carolina Press.

Wesseling, H. L. 1989 "Colonial wars: an Introduction" in J. A. de Moor & Wesseling (eds.), *Imperialism and War*: Essays on Colonial *Wars* in Asia and Africa. Leiden.

2005 "Imperialism and the roots of the Great War," *Daedalus*, **135**, Spring.

Westermann, Edward 2005 *Hitler's Police Battalions: Enforcing Racial War in the East*. Lawrence: University Press of Kansas.

Wette, Wolfram 1998 "Militarist and pacifist ideologies in the last phase of the Weimar Republic" in Wilhelm Deist et al. (eds.), *Germany and the Second World War. Vol I: The Build-Up of German Aggression*, pp. 9–81. Oxford: Clarendon Press.

Wheare, J. 1950 *The Nigerian Legislative Council*. London: Faber & Faber.

Wheatcroft, Stephen & R. W. Davies 2004 *The Years of Hunger: Soviet Agriculture, 1931–1933* London: Palgrave.

White, Eugene 1990 "The Stock Market Boom and Crash of 1929 Revisited," *The Journal of Economic Perspectives*, **4**: 67–83.

Whitney, Robert 2001 *State and Revolution in Cuba: Mass Mobilization and Political Change, 1920–1940*. Chapel Hill, NC: University of North Carolina Press.

Wiarda, Howard 1995 *Democracy and Its Discontents. Development, Interdependence and US Policy in Latin America*. Lanham, MD: Rowman & Littlefield.

1999 "Introduction" and "Central America: The Search for Economic Development" in Leonard (ed.), *Central America and the United States: The Search for Stability*. Athens, GA: University of Georgia Press.

Wildman, Allan 1980 *The End of the Russian Imperial Army*. Princeton, NJ: Princeton University Press.

Wilensky, Harold 2002 *Rich Democracies: Political Economy, Public Policy, and Performance*. Berkeley & Los Angeles: University of California Press.

Williams, Gwyn 1975 *Proletarian Order: Antonio Gramsci, Factory Councils and the Origins of Italian Communism, 1911–1921*. London: Pluto Press.

Williamson, Jeffrey 2006 *Globalization and the Poor Periphery Before 1950*. Cambridge, MA: MIT Press.

Williamson, Samuel Jr. & Ernest May 2007 "An Identity of Opinion: Historians and July 1914," *The Journal of Modern History*, **79**: 335–87.

Wilson, Sandra 1995 "The 'New Paradise': Japanese Emigration to Manchuria in the 1930s and 1940s," *The International History Review*, **17**: 249–86.

2002 *The Manchurian Crisis and Japanese Society, 1931–33*. London: Routledge.

Wimmer, Andreas & Yuval Feinstein 2010 "The rise of the nation-state across the world, 1816 to 2001," *American Sociological Review*, **75**: 764–90.

Winter, Jay 1986 *The Great War and the British People*. Cambridge, MA: Harvard University Press.

1997 "Surviving the War: Life Expectation, Illness and Mortality Rates in Paris, London, and Berlin, 1914–1919" in Winter & Jean-Louis Robert (eds.), *Capital Cities at War: Paris, London, Berlin, 1914–1919*, pp. 487–524. New York: Cambridge University Press.

Witte, Edwin 1962 *The Development of the Social Security Act*. Madison: University of Wisconsin Press.

Wolf, Eric 1969 *Peasant Wars of the Twentieth Century*. New York: Harper & Row.

Wolff, E. N. & M. Marley 1989 "Long-term trends in US wealth inequality: methodological issues and results" in R. Lipsey & H. S. Tice (eds.),*The Measurement of Saving, Investment and Wealth*, pp. 765–844. Chicago: University of Chicago Press.

Wong, Joseph 2004 *Healthy Democracies: Welfare Politics in Taiwan and South Korea*. Ithaca, NY: Cornell University Press.

Wood, Bryce 1961 *The Making of the Good Neighbor Policy*. New York: Columbia University.

Wood, Elizabeth 1997 *The Baba and the Comrade: Gender and Politics in Revolutionary Russia*. Bloomington: Indiana University Press.

Woodiwiss, Anthony 1992 *Law, Labour, and Society in Japan: From Repression to Reluctant Recognition*. London: Routledge.

Worley, Matthew 2005 *Labour Inside the Gate: A History of the British Labour Party Between the Wars*. London: Tauris.

Wright, Tim 1991 "Coping with the world depression: the Nationalist government's relations with Chinese industry and commerce, 1932–1936," *Modern Asian Studies*, **25**: 649–74.

2000 "Distant thunder: the regional economies of Southwest China and the impact of the great depression," *Modern Asian Studies*, **34**: 679–738.

Young, Crawford 1994 *The African Colonial State in Comparative Perspective*. New Haven, CT: Yale University Press.

Young, G. M. 1957 *Macaulay, Prose and Poetry*. Cambridge, MA: Harvard University Press.

Young, Louise 1998 *Japan's Total Empire. Manchuria and the Culture of Wartime Imperialism*. Berkeley & Los Angeles: University of California Press.

Young, Robert 1996 *France and the Origins of the Second World War*. London: Macmillan.

Zanasi, Margherita 2006 *Saving the Nation: Economic Modernity in Republican China*. Chicago: University of Chicago Press.

Zanetti, Oscar & Alejandro Garcia 1998 *Sugar and Railroads: A Cuban History, 1837–1959*. Chapel Hill, NC: University of North Carolina Press.

Zeitlin, Maurice 1980 "On Classes, Class Conflict and the State: an Introductory Note" in M. Zetlin (ed.), *Classes, Class Conflict and the State*. Cambridge, MA: Winthrop.

Zeman, Zbynek 1961 *The Break-Up of the Habsburg Empire, 1914–1918: A Study in National and Social Revolution*. London: Oxford University Press.

Zieger, Robert 1995 *The CIO, 1935–1955*. Chapel Hill: University of North Carolina Press.

Ziemann, Benjamin 2007 *War Experiences in Rural Germany, 1914–1923*. New York: Berg.

Zuber, Terence 2002 *Inventing the Schlieffen Plan: German War Planning, 1871–1914*. New York: Oxford University Press.

Zuckerman, Larry 2004 *The Rape of Belgium: The Untold Story of World War I*. New York: New York University Press.

Index